British Battleships of World War Two

The development and technical history of the Royal Navy's battleships and battlecruisers from 1911 to 1946: by Alan Raven and John Roberts

ROYSTERER

British Battleships of World War Two

The development and technical history of the Royal Navy's battleships and battlecruisers from 1911 to 1946: by Alan Raven and John Roberts

Naval Institute Press

To Vanessa and Gina

Published in the United States by
The United States Naval Institute
Annapolis, Maryland.

Second impression 1978; third impression 1981.

Library of Congress Catalog No.
76–22915
ISBN 0–87021–817–4

Acknowledgments. The authors wish to extend their thanks to the following persons and organisations, for their invaluable assistance in the compilation of this book. In particular, we should like to mention David Brown, for not pulling his punches; Peter Hodges, for his unstinting help with information about naval weapons; David Lyon and George Osbon of the National Maritime Museum; Antony Preston; Miss V. Riley, of the Admiralty Library; Frank Mantle; Morris Northcott; P. H. Stokes; David Weldon; Norman Friedman, and the staff of the Naval Historical Branch.

Photographs are reproduced by courtesy of: Imperial War Museum, National Maritime Museum, Ministry of Defence, P. H. Stokes, U.S. Archives, Wright & Logan.

Overleaf: *Hood* and *Barham* at Malta in 1938.

Edited by Michael Boxall.
Designed by David Gibbons.
Printed by T. & A. Constable Limited, Edinburgh, Scotland.
Bound by Hunter & Foulis Limited, Edinburgh, Scotland.

Introduction

The greater part of the material in this book is drawn from official sources which, in many instances, have only recently been made available to the public. Much care has been exercised in interpreting and, where possible, checking the facts and figures obtained: where discrepancies exist—as they inevitably do in a subject so complicated as this — they have been noted.

Although the book cannot lay claim to perfection (for even official documents are occasionally in error), it is emphasised that the information presented herein is the most accurate available at the time of writing. In the past, authors have been severely limited by the fifty-year and, more recently, the thirty-year restrictions applied to official documents. Now, however, there is little excuse for perpetuating the errors of the past. For today's writer, there can be no substitute for original research, if he is to attain any degree of accuracy, and we have sought to take the advantages offered, for the first time, of access to the official contemporary records.

The drawings accompanying the text have been prepared after close study of official references, including the 'as fitted' general-arrangement plans and gun manuals. Where desirable, modifications have been made to these, based on the evidence of photographs and written information, to depict ships at times for which no official drawings exist.

Complementing the drawings, the photographs have been chosen in order to illustrate the many changes carried out during the lifetime of the ships described, and preference has been given to good quality and to hitherto unpublished views. Reference has also been made to many other photographs in the process of researching the subject, for confirmation of alterations and additions.

Although concerned primarily with the Second World War, the book embraces the full technical history of the relevant battleships from 1911 to 1946. This was considered desirable, because it would be difficult for the reader to fully appreciate the vessels under consideration without a fairly detailed description of their origins and of the events that affected them during their lengthy peacetime careers. The First World War provided much of the technical experience from which the battle fleet of 1939 was evolved, and this could not be ignored without leaving a large gap in the overall sequence of events. Similarly, the period from 1919 to 1939 had many serious and far-reaching effects on the quality of the British fleet in the Second World War.

The book begins with a description of the origins and early life of the *Queen Elizabeth* class, and ends after the close of the Second World War, having dealt with the intervening events more or less chronologically. In order to maintain the descriptions of the ships and their subsequent careers in an easily comprehensible sequence, references to most of the older vessels are to be found in several chapters. *Hood*, for example, is described as originally built; then, in separate chapters, subsequent alterations and additions are described – firstly to 1930, and later to 1941. It is hoped that this system will obviate the mental acrobatics required in reading, say, the history of the *Queen Elizabeth* class from 1911 to 1946 and then having to turn back to 1912 to begin the story of the *Royal Sovereign* class. Moreover, it enables the background of the various periods to be contained within convenient chapters between the detailed descriptions of the ships themselves.

In compiling this volume, our aim has been to provide a balanced book that will be both of interest to the general reader and of real worth to the expert requiring a high degree of technical detail. It is hoped that we have achieved a reference work of value to all who are interested in the capital ships that once commanded the oceans of the world.

Alan Raven and John Roberts, 1976

Malaya as completed.

Contents

LIST OF LINE DRAWINGS

LIST OF SHIPS' PARTICULARS

Explanatory Notes

Design Procedure

The Naval Staff of the Admiralty initiated a new design by preparing a specification for the type of warship required. The Controller (Third Sea Lord), who had overall responsibility for the production of naval material, passed this specification – known as "Staff Requirements" – to the Director of Naval Construction (DNC). The DNC's department prepared outline designs based on experience gained from previous ships and information obtained from experiments with models, and armour and bomb trials. The DNC suggested modifications if the complete Staff Requirements were difficult to meet, especially where treaty limitations necessitated strict control of the displacement figure. Sketch designs were then prepared from the most promising outline designs, other departments having been consulted concerning equipment for which the DNC was not directly responsible. For example, the Engineer-in-Chief (E in C) provided an estimate of the weight of and space required for machinery capable for producing the shaft horse-power estimated by the DNC, and the Director of Naval Ordnance (DNO) provided estimated weights and particulars of the armament.

Usually, more than one sketch design was prepared, in order to show variations to the principal characteristics desired. These designs had to be worked out in some detail, so as to ensure that the particulars could be realised in the completed ship. The sketch designs, together with a descriptive legend and an estimate of cost, were then submitted for Board approval.

The hull form of a new ship was decided by the DNC, having regard to the speed required and other important considerations, and the design work would then proceed along the following lines:

1. Detailed calculation of the weights, buoyancy, draught, trim, stability, effect of damage, strength of hull, structure, etc.
2. Preparation of large-scale building drawings of the hull form, scantlings of the main structures, watertight sub-division and the purpose for which every compartment in the ship was to be used.
3. Preparation of drawings showing the arrangement of main and auxiliary machinery.
4. Preparation of specifications describing in detail all parts of the ship's hull, fittings, machinery, electrical equipment and armament; the quality and composition of the materials to be used, method of construction and standards of workmanship.

As the work progressed, all departments would be continually consulted by the DNC to ensure that the design was coordinated and that all requirements were being met. In the case of a capital ship, about nine months were required, from the receipt of Board approval of the sketch design, to bring the design to a stage where tenders could be invited from shipbuilders or full details could be sent to a royal dockyard. The detailed design was usually re-submitted for final Board approval before tenders were invited. (For the battleships of the 1936–40 programmes, shipbuilders were selected contrary to the normal tendering procedure, and design information was passed to them as it became available.). Separate contracts were placed for hull, hull fittings and electrical equipment; propelling and auxiliary machinery; armour; armament; and minor equipment (capstans, pumps, cranes, etc.).

The expeditious completion of a ship depended largely on the punctual installation of the main armament turrets during the fitting-out stage. In peacetime, it was estimated that twelve months were required to complete a capital ship after the installation of the last turret – in anticipation of which, heavy guns and mountings were usually ordered in advance. A similar procedure was adopted for the armour for the battleships of the 1936 and later programmes. At that time, the armour manufacturing capabilities were limited but the building programme was large. Contracts for a substantial part of the armour were therefore placed well in advance, so that its manufacture was spread over a long period, thus ensuring that the desired rate of manufacture would not exceed the capacity of the armour firms. Four years were allowed for the production of the armour for ships of the 1936 programme.

Displacement

The weight of a ship is equal to the amount of water it displaces. A displacement figure, therefore, represents the exact weight of a ship. In this book, all displacement figures and weights are expressed in English tons (1,016 kilogrammes).

Tons per inch (tpi)

Immersion. This is an expression of the weight required to increase the draught of a ship by one inch. The figure varies according to the water-plane area (the horizontal area of a ship at its waterline). In this book, all such weights should be read as referring to a ship in its legend condition, floating on an even keel.

Dimensions

Length:
Length (oa) is the overall length of a ship from stem to stern. Its main use is with regard to docking limitations. Length (pp) is the length between the perpendiculars – the forward perpendicular being the intersection of the load waterline and the stem, and the after perpendicular being the axis of the rudder(s). It is used extensively in calculations, and it controls such things as manoeuvrability.

Beam:
The beam of a ship is the width of the hull at any given point. Throughout this book the beam given is the maximum, i.e. the width of the hull at its widest. The beam, in relation to length, controls the hull form; but the main factors that determined the beam of battleships were the restrictions imposed by the Panama and Suez canals, and by docking facilities. The beam also affects stability and rolling characteristics: the greater the beam the higher the initial stability and the quicker the roll. A wide beam, however, has a detrimental effect on damage control, for if an outboard compartment be flooded, the resultant heel is greater than would be the case in a ship with a narrow beam.

Draught:
The draught of a ship is the depth of water from the keel to the waterline. The draught of a ship is restricted by docking facilities and by harbour and canal passage considerations. Even if this were not so, a very deep draught is undesirable because water pressure increases with depth and the penetration of a deep hull would result in more rapid flooding than in a vessel with a shallow draught.

Armament (see also Appendices 1 and 2)

Calibre (cal):
The calibre of a gun is the diameter of its bore. The length of the bore is usually measured in calibres. A 15-inch 42-calibre gun has a calibre of 15 inches and a bore length of 42 x 15 inches, = 630 inches.

Calibre radius head (crh):
The pointed head of a projectile is described in multiples of the shell's calibre. Thus a 6 crh shell is more pointed and streamlined than a 4 crh shell.

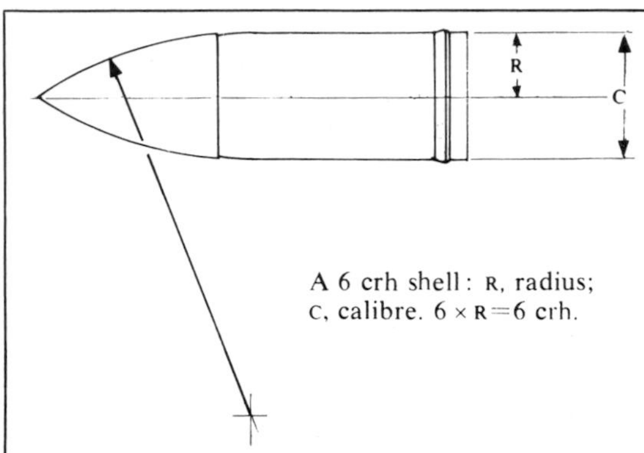

A 6 crh shell: R, radius; C, calibre. 6 × R = 6 crh.

Creep:
The slow training and elevating speeds of gun-mountings are known as creep speeds. They must be steady if the gun is to be laid accurately on to a target.

Effective full charge (efc):
The life of a gun barrel is measured by the number of full charges that can be fired before the barrel needs relining. So a gun with a life of 300 efc can fire 300 projectiles with a full charge before relining is necessary.

Muzzle energy (m.e.):
The muzzle energy of a gun is a measure of the kinetic energy contained in a projectile when it leaves the muzzle of a gun. It is the product of a projectile's weight and velocity. In this book, it is expressed in foot-tons (f-t). Very simply, it may be said that a muzzle energy of 10,000 foot-tons is sufficient, theoretically, to move an object weighing 1 ton, a distance of 10,000 feet.

Muzzle velocity (mv):
The speed of a projectile as it leaves the muzzle. In this book it is expressed in feet per second (fps). A speed of 2,450 feet per second is equal to about 1,670 miles per hour.

Range:
The horizontal distance between a gun and its target. Unless otherwise stated, all ranges given in this book are the maximum that could be achieved.

Rate:
When firing at a moving target, the range of the target is constantly changing. The rate at which this change takes place is known as "rate of change of range" or "range rate" or simply "rate".

Ready-use ammunition:
Ammunition stored close to a gun instead of in a magazine. For weather-deck open mountings, it was stored in bullet-proof steel lockers or racks.

Protection

There were two basic types of steel protection employed in British dreadnoughts: armour (cemented and non-cemented) and protective plating.

Cemented armour:
The last major development of armour was the Krupp process of the 1890s, known as KC (Krupp Cemented). Other equivalent methods of armour production were subsequently developed, but no great improvement was made in the quality of the armour until the period between the wars. During this period, the production of improved qualities of steel alloy and the introduction of new methods of manufacture led to an increase in the power of armour to resist penetration. The basic principles, however, were much the same as those of the Krupp process.

The basic steel alloy used, was of high tensile strength and contained small amounts of nickel, chromium and manganese. Later, other alloying elements were introduced, including vanadium (before the First World War), molybdenum and possibly, tungsten. First, the percentage of carbon in the face of the steel plate was increased by cementing. This process was originally carried out by placing charcoal on the face of the plate and heating it in a furnace for about three weeks, during which, the carbon in the charcoal would be absorbed into the face of the plate. Later processes were more sophisticated but achieved the same result. The depth to which the carbon penetrated depended on the length of time the plate remained in the furnace and the process that was employed.

After being allowed to cool, the plate was machined or bent, as required. It was then heated slowly to a fixed temperature, after which the face of the plate was rapidly cooled – originally, with cold water. This rapid cooling made the high-carbon steel on the face of the plate very hard. The back of the plate remained comparatively soft.

Non-Cemented armour:
This was produced in the same way as cemented armour except that the cementation process was omitted.

Protective plating:
The main difference between armour and protective plating is that armour has a hard face and a soft back, whereas protective plating, although heat-treated, is of uniform strength and hardness. High-tensile steel was originally used for protective plating, but after the First World War it was superseded by an improved high-tensile steel (known as 'D' steel) and non-cemented armour.

Armour gratings:
The openings, where ventilator trunks, funnel uptakes, etc., passed through armoured or protective decks, represented weak points in the protection of ships. They could not be completely blocked, but armour grills or gratings formed from deep girders, were fitted to prevent missiles from passing through.

Stability

The standard comparative measure of a ship's stability is its initial transverse metacentric height (GM) which is established from the following.

Centre of gravity (G):
The sum of the weights of all the parts of a ship can be said to exert a single total downward force through a central point known as the centre of gravity. The movement of the ship in

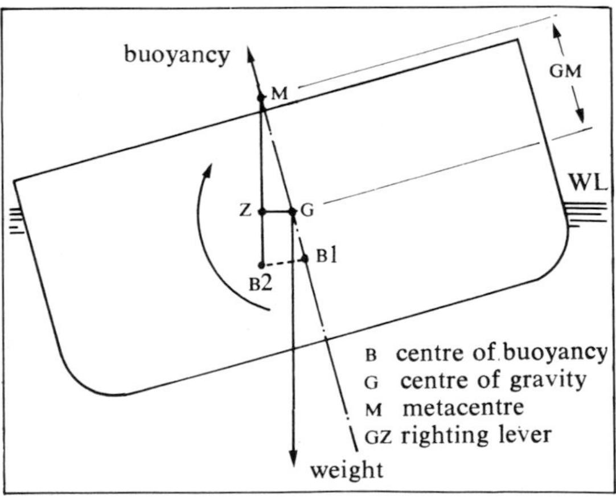

any direction will not alter the position of its centre of gravity but the moving, addition, or subtraction of weight, will.

Centre of buoyancy (B):
The forces exerted on the underwater hull of a vessel, by the water in which she is floating,

can be resolved into a single force that acts through a central point known as the "centre of buoyancy". This force is equal and opposite to the weight of the ship acting through G. The centre of buoyancy occupies the same position as the centre of gravity of the water displaced by the ship's hull. The position of B is controlled by the underwater shape of the hull, and moves as the underwater shape alters – because of increases or reductions in draught, rolling, pitching, trim or heel.

Metacentre (M):
When a ship is at rest on an even keel, G and B are on the middle-line. If the ship inclines, B will move to the low side of the ship, describing an approximate arc about a point (M) where the vertically upward line of action of B passes through the middle-line. The distance between G and M is the metacentric height.

Righting lever (GZ):
The horizontal distance between G and the line of action of BM is known as the righting lever. The greater this distance, the greater the tendency to return to the upright. Hence, when the GM is high the stability is high and when the GM is low the stability is low. If M is below G or if, as a result of flooding, G moves sufficiently off-centre to make the GZ negative, the ship will become unstable and will capsize. It might be assumed, therefore, that the higher the GM, the better; but, in fact, this is not the case. A high GM gives a ship a short, quick roll, which – although the ship is very stable – makes a poor platform in a seaway. A ship with a low GM will roll long and slow (indeed, if the GM is too low, she will tend to hang for a few seconds at the end of her outward roll before returning to the upright) ;thus providing a good gun platform, allowing gun-sights and range-finders to be kept on target with comparative ease, and enabling remote power-control and stabilising gear to keep up with the speed of roll. Clearly, in the design of warships, a compromise must be achieved between the conflicting demands of stability and gunnery.

The stability of a ship in damaged and undamaged conditions is affected by a number of variables, the more important of which are described below.

Angle of stability:
The angle of maximum stability is that at which GZ is at its greatest and the tendency to return to the upright is at a maximum. The range of stability is the angle at which GM becomes zero, up to which point, a ship will return to the upright.

Freeboard:
This is the height of a ship's hull from the waterline to the weather-deck edge. As a ship lists or heels, the GZ tends to increase steadily as the freeboard is submerged until the deck edge is reached. As the deck becomes submerged, the GZ decreases. It follows, therefore, that the higher the intact freeboard, the better the range of stability.

Free surface:
If a fuel-oil or water tank is not completely filled, the surface of the liquid moves to the low side when the ship rolls. This alters the position of the centre of gravity of the liquid and, consequently, the centre of gravity of the ship itself. As G moves to the low side of the ship, it reduces the GZ and, therefore, the level of stability. Baffles were usually fitted in tanks to reduce the free surface effect. A similar effect is produced by any addition in the ship of free surface liquid due to weather or action-damage or fire-fighting, and dwarf walls and sills were fitted to restrict the flow of such liquid.

Top-weight:
Additional weight above G is known as top-weight. It will raise the position of G and therefore reduce the GM and will have an adverse effect on stability. Conversely, the addition of weight below G will lower the position of G and increase the level of stability.

Reserve of buoyancy:
The watertight volume of a ship's hull is known as the buoyant volume – the percentage below the waterline being the buoyancy and that above the waterline, the reserve of buoyancy. A vessel flooded by a volume of water equal to, or greater than, the volume of the reserve of buoyancy, will sink. It follows, therefore, that the greater the volume of buoyancy, the higher the chances of survival when flooding occurs.

Effect of flooding:
Flooding can cause the loss of a ship by reducing the reserve of buoyancy, causing her to sink, or by reducing her stability, causing her to capsize. Floodwater can affect stability by adding to the weight of a ship and moving the position of G and/or by its free-surface effect. (It could also be considered that a compartment in direct communication with the sea is no longer part of the buoyant volume and that the position of B has moved).

(Note: there is also a longitudinal GM that is employed in the calculation of trim. Unless otherwise stated, all GMs referred to in this book are transverse and relate to initial stability in an undamaged ship. The GM figure tends to stay constant up to an angle of heel of about 10°, after which it reduces.)

Miscellaneous specialist terms

Armour shelf:
Lower edge of the recess in a ship's side, designed to accommodate the armour belt.

Board Margin:
A weight margin added to the design weight calculations, to allow for additions during construction and for minor variations from the design.

Casemate:
Armoured enclosure, usually containing a gun mounting.

Citadel:
In this context it is a general term for the armoured box enclosing the machinery and magazine spaces. It was formed by the armoured deck, belt and bulkheads.

De-gaussing coil:
Electric cable run round the hull of a ship and connected to a generator, in order to demagnetise the ship as a defence against magnetic mines.

'Fearnought' curtain:
Trade name for a type of fireproof asbestos screen.

Glacis plate:
Sloping armour, protecting the lower perimeter of an armoured position.

Inclining experiment:
Deliberately heeling a ship to establish its exact level of stability. This was achieved by noting the amount of weight required to heel the ship to a particular angle, together with a detailed appraisal of the ship's condition.

MD cordite:
Modified cordite – like the original Mark I

but with the percentages of the ingredients altered.

Panting:
In-and-out movement of a ship's hull plating, caused by the action of the sea.

Paravane:
Torpedo shaped device towed by a hawser from each side of a ship from the bow in order to cut the mooring wires of mines which might be in the path of the ship.

Protective deck:
A deck constructed of protective plating.

SC cordite:
An improved form of cordite introduced in the late 1920's to give superior ballistic regularity.

Sighting-port:
Aperture for a gun-sight in the front of the gun-house.

Sighting-hood:
Armoured cover protecting the gun-sights protruding through the roofs of gun-houses.

Starfish:
Spurs projecting from the top of the lower mast, to which the standing rigging of the topmast was fixed.

Trim:
The fore-and-aft level of a ship.

TSR aircraft:
Torpedo-spotter-reconnaissance aircraft.

Walking pipes:
The pipes that carried hydraulic pressure from the fixed to the revolving structure of a gun turret. They had rotating joints which allowed them to 'walk' round with the turret as it trained.

Weakening of cordite cases:
Cordite stowage cases were deliberately weakened so that, if the cordite were ignited, it would blow out the weakened section and burn. If it were tightly enclosed it would explode.

'Wooded' and 'wooding':
When a gun, or gun-sight, is trained in a direction where its line of fire, or sight, is blocked by the ship's structure. This comes from the days when ships were built of wood.

List of Abbreviations

AA	anti-aircraft
ABU	auto barrage unit
AC	alternating current
ACNS	Assistant Chief of Naval Staff
ADO	Air Defence Officer (or Organisation)
AFCC	Admiralty fire-control clock
AFCT	Admiralty fire-control table
AIC	action information centre
ALO	air look-out
AP	armour-piercing
APC	armour-piercing capped
BD	between-decks
BL	breech-loading
BM	breech mechanism
C in C	Commander-in-Chief
CID	Committee of Imperial Defence
CP	centre-pivot
CPBC	common pointed ballistic cap
CPC	common pointed capped
CRAA	close-range anti-aircraft
CRBF	close-range barrage-fire
crh	calibre radius head
CT	conning-tower
DAM	Director of Air Material
DC	direct current
DCHQ	damage-control headquarters
DCNS	Deputy Chief of Naval Staff
DCT	director-control tower
DEMS	defensively-equipped merchant ship
DF	direction-finder
DNC	Director of Naval Construction
DNI	Director of Naval Intelligence
DNO	Director of Naval Ordnance
D of P	Director of Plans
DTSD	Director of Training and Staff Duties
dwl	deep waterline
efc	effective full charge
E in C	Engineer-in-Chief
EOC	Elswick Ordnance Company
fps	feet per second
f-t	foot-tons
GM	metacentric height
GRU	gyro rate unit
HA	high-angle
HACP	high-angle control-position high-angle calculating-position
HACS	high-angle control-system
HA/LA	high-angle/low-angle
HE	high explosive
HFDF	high-frequency direction-finder
HP	high-pressure
HT	high-tensile
HV	high-velocity
IFF	identification friend or foe
KC	Krupp cemented
KNC	Krupp non-cemented
kw	kilowatt
LA	low-angle
LP	low-pressure
LRAA	long-range anti-aircraft
lwl	load waterline
me	muzzle energy
MFDF	medium-frequency direction-finder
MG	machine-gun
MRS	medium-range system
mv	muzzle velocity
NC	non-cemented
oa	overall
PAC	parachute and cable
pp	between perpendiculars
PPI	plan position-indicator
psi	pounds per square inch
QF	quick-firing
RADAR	radio detection and ranging
RDF	radio direction-finding
RFW	reserve feed-water
RPC	remote power-control
rpg	rounds per gun
rpm	revolutions per minute rounds per minute
RT	radio-telegraphy
RU	ready-use
SAP	semi-armour-piercing
SHP	shaft horse-power
STAAG	stabilised tachymetric anti-aircraft gun
TBS	talk between ships
tpi	tons per inch
TS	transmitting-station
UD	upper-deck
UP	unrotated-projectile (rocket)
VFDF	variable-frequency direction-finder
VHFDF	very high-frequency direction-finder
wt	watertight
WT	wireless-transmitter

1. The Queen Elizabeth Class, 1912 to 1919

By the end of the nineteenth century, the battleship had evolved into a standard type of about 15,000 tons displacement. Propelled by steam reciprocating engines at a speed of around 18 knots, they carried a mixed calibre armament of 12-inch, 6-inch, 12-pdr and 3-pdr guns. The rapidly improving performance of heavy guns and their associate fire-control equipment was, however, leading towards increased battle ranges at which the smaller weapons could not be brought to action. Moreover, long range necessitated the use of salvo firing if any success were to be achieved, and this form of fire control required a uniform armament of at least eight heavy guns, whereas the standard battleship carried only four 12 inch weapons.

British resistance to a radically new type of battleship was strong because of the large capital investment that had been made in existing types, and because the then largest battle fleet in the world would be reduced to premature obsolescence. Nevertheless, the revolution came about, influenced by Admiral Sir John Fisher, who, rather than allow a foreign power to take the lead, pushed through – in record time – the design and construction of HMS *Dreadnought*. This ship, launched on 10th February 1906, provided the basis on which all future battleships, collectively known as Dreadnoughts, were to be designed. Of 18,000 tons displacement, she was propelled by steam turbines at a speed of 21 knots and carried a uniform armament of ten 12-inch guns. A number of 12-pdr guns were also carried, to provide protection against close-range torpedo-boat attacks.

For such a revolutionary design, *Dreadnought* proved highly successful, and to maintain the supremacy of the British fleet, a programme of Dreadnoughts, was rapidly put in hand. The *Bellerophon* class (*Bellerophon*, *Temeraire* and *Superb*) under the 1906 Estimates, and the *St. Vincent* class (*Collingwood*, *St. Vincent* and *Vanguard*) under the 1907 Estimates, were generally similar to *Dreadnought* except that they carried an anti-torpedo boat armament of 4-inch guns, and the latter class also carried the 12-inch 50-cal Mk XI instead of the earlier 12-inch 45-cal Mk X gun. *Neptune* (1908 Estimates), and *Colossus* and *Hercules* (1909 Estimates), introduced the super-firing turret aft, and the *Orion* class (*Conqueror*, *Monarch*, *Orion* and *Thunderer*) of the 1909 Estimates produced the first major departure from the *Dreadnought* design. With a displacement of 22,200 tons, these ships abandoned the wing gun-turrets of the earlier designs in favour of an all centre-line armament of ten 13.5-inch guns with super-firing turrets, forward and aft. They were followed by the generally similar *King George V* class (*Ajax*, *Audacious*, *Centurion* and *King George V*) of the 1910 Estimates and the *Iron Duke* class (*Iron Duke*, *Marlborough*, *Benbow* and *Emperor of India*) of the 1911 Estimates. To deal with the larger types of torpedo craft, which had been introduced since the completion of *Dreadnought*, the latter class were armed with a 6-inch gun secondary battery.

The *Iron Duke* class were followed by the *Queen Elizabeth* class which were the oldest of our capital ships to serve actively during the Second World War. They form the natural beginning to our narrative and, conveniently, a natural break between the *Dreadnought* of 1906 and the *Vanguard* of 1946. Although the design was basically similar to that of the *Iron Duke* class of the previous year's programme, it incorporated a number of innovations of major importance and the class can be regarded as a transition point in British battleship design.

It was originally intended that the capital ships of the 1912 programme – three battleships and one battlecruiser – should follow standard design practice and carry the usual 13.5-inch gun armament. Early in 1912, the legends and sketch designs for these ships were virtually complete, awaiting Board approval only, before being presented to the Cabinet in February. Some concern, however, was felt about their value, because it was known that both the USA and Japan were building ships to carry a 14-inch gun armament, and it had also been reported – incorrectly – that the German *König* class were to mount guns of this calibre. A solution was found by the new First Lord of the Admiralty, Winston Churchill. Appreciating the great advance that had already been made with the introduction of the 13.5-inch gun, he suggested a further increase in gun calibre to 15 inches. This presented problems, because although designs had been prepared for a 15-inch gun, no such weapon had yet been manufactured.

Because of the time required for the production of heavy guns and mountings, it was necessary to order them before ordering the ship in which they were to be installed. Furthermore, guns were not ordered in any quantity until an experimental weapon had been built, successfully proof-fired and accepted for service. In the case of the 15-inch gun, this process would have resulted in an unacceptable delay in the laying down of the ships of the 1912 programme. It had to be decided, therefore, whether to lay down ships designed to mount totally untried weapons, or ships whose armament was considered inadequate to counter the contemporaneous ships of other navies. The Director of Naval Ordnance, Rear-Admiral Moore, was confident of the success of the new gun and was "ready to stake his professional existence upon it".[1] And so, with some misgivings, the full outfit of guns was ordered. One gun was to be hurried to completion, four months in advance of the rest, in order to carry out proof firing for range and accuracy, and for the production of range tables and other details. This decision involved considerable risk, but in the event, proved justified.

Having decided on the calibre of the main armament, it was necessary to produce sketch designs for the ships that were to carry it. The initial design was along standard lines, specifying ten guns in five turrets, two forward, two aft and one amidships; a speed of 21 knots and an armoured belt of 13 inches thickness. It was quickly realised, however, that the great weight of the 15-inch shell would allow a reduction in the number of guns to

[1] Churchill, *The World Crisis*, Butterworth, 1923–31.

Right: *Barham* fitting out and as completed, 1916.

eight while maintaining superiority in the weight of broadside. Ten 13.5-inch Mark V guns, firing the heavy 13.5-inch shell, produced a broadside of 14,000 pounds, whereas eight 15-inch guns provided a broadside of over 15,000 pounds. The space and weight made available by the omission of the fifth turret could be utilised for additional boilers to provide higher speed. The War College estimated that a speed of 25 knots, or more, would be required for an effective fast wing for the battle fleet, capable of out-manoeuvring the German Fleet, as it would be constituted in 1914–15.

From the basic requirements for an armament of eight 15-inch guns, sixteen 6-inch guns and a speed of 25 knots, three sketch designs were prepared. The details of these designs together with those for *Iron Duke* are given in Table 1.

Table 1: Comparison of *Iron Duke* with new battleship sketch designs

	Iron Duke	*R3*	*R3**	*R4*
Displacement	25000 tons	27000 tons	27000 tons	27000 tons
Length (pp)	580 feet	600 feet	600 feet	615 feet
Beam	90 feet	90½ feet	90½ feet	90 feet
Draught	28 feet	28½ feet	28½ feet	28½ feet
Armament	Ten 13.5 in Twelve 6 in	Eight 15 in Sixteen 6 in	Eight 15 in Sixteen 6 in	Eight 15 in Sixteen 6 in
Armour:				
Belt at wl	12 inch	13 inch	12 inch and 13 inch	13 inch
Upper belt	8 inch and 6 inch	8 inch and 6 inch	6 inch	8 inch and 6 inch
Conning-tower	11 inch	12 inch	11 inch	12 inch
Barbette (max)	10 inch	11 inch	10 inch	11 inch
Turret wall	11 inch	12 inch	11 inch	12 inch
Turret roof	4 inch and 3 inch	5 inch	5 inch	5 inch
Torpedo bulkhead	1½ inch and 1 inch	1½ inch and 1 inch	2 inch and 1½ inch	1½ inch and 1 inch

In designs R3 and R4, the armour protection was generally similar to that in *Iron Duke* except for an increase of 1 inch in the thickness of the belt at waterline, conning-tower, barbettes and turret walls and roofs. Thick, longitudinal bulkheads afforded underwater protection abreast the magazines and engine rooms; the boiler rooms were protected by the coal bunkers. In design R3*, torpedo protection bulkheads were added, extending the full length of the magazine and machinery spaces. These bulkheads were 2 inches thick, abreast the magazines and engine rooms and 1½ inches thick, abreast the boilers where they had coal outside them. To compensate the additional weight of these bulkheads, the belt at the waterline was kept to a thickness of 12 inches as in *Iron Duke*, except abreast the engine room, where it was increased to 13 inches. The upper belt was reduced to a uniform thickness of 6 inches and the remaining armour was of the same thickness as that in *Iron Duke*.

In R3 and R3*, the main armament was disposed as in *Iron Duke*, but with 'Q' turret omitted. In design R4, the third turret was placed amidships, at upper-deck level, and was unable to fire directly aft. The estimated cost for a dockyard-built ship to R3 design was £2,100,000; R3* was £30,000 less and R4, £30,000 more.

One more innovation remained to be included in the new design – completely oil-fired boilers. The 25-knot speed was an essential requirement and considerable advantages could be obtained by the adoption of oil fuel. Oil was more efficient than coal, could give equal endurance for less weight and it made refuelling a simple and clean procedure. Coal, however, could not be rejected without careful consideration. Oil came from the Middle East and presented a vulnerable line of supply whereas coal was readily available in Britain. Furthermore, coal bunkers provided protection from shells and torpedoes. It was thought that oil could give no such protection, and also, that it constituted a fire risk. The decision to carry oil fuel only, was not made, therefore, until after design R3* had been approved by the Board, in June 1912. The adoption of oil meant a saving in weight, which enabled the thickness of the belt to be increased to a uniform 13 inches, and the torpedo bulkheads, to a uniform 2 inches, thus providing some compensation for the loss of the protective effect of the coal.

Table 2: Legend particulars of Design R3*, July 1912

Load displacement	27,500 tons
Deep displacement	31,300 tons
Length (pp)	600 feet
Length (oa)	644 feet 3 inches (including stern-walk)
Beam (max)	90 feet 6 inches
Draught at lwl	28 feet 9 inches
Draught at dwl	32 feet
tpi	98 tons
SHP	75000
Speed at load draught	25 knots
Fuel at load draught	650 tons
Oil fuel capacity	3,500 tons
Coal capacity	100 tons
Complement as a private ship	831
Armament:	Eight 15 in 42-cal BL Sixteen 6 in 45-cal BL Four 21 in torpedo tubes (submerged)
Armour:	
Belt (amidships)	13 inch, 6 inch
Belt (forward and aft)	6 inch, 4 inch
Bulkheads (forward and aft)	6 inch, 4 inch
Barbettes	10 inch to 4 inch
Gun-houses	11 in sides, 13 in faces, 5 in roof
Conning-tower	11 in sides, 4 in roof
Conning-tower tube	6 inch
Torpedo-director tower	6 inch
Torpedo-director tower tube	4 inch
Funnel-uptakes	1½ inch
Torpedo bulkheads	2 inch
Backing behind side armour	2 inch (min)
6 inch battery	6 inch
Forecastle-deck (over 6 in battery	1 inch
Upper-deck (amidships)	2 inch, 1¼ inch
Main-deck (forward and aft)	1¼ inch
Main-deck (amidships)	1 inch
Middle-deck (amidships)	1 inch
Lower-deck (forward)	3 inch, 1 inch
Lower-deck (aft)	3 inch, 2½ inch
Weights (tons):	
General equipment	750
Armament	4,550
Machinery	3,950
Oil fuel	650
Armour & protective plating	8,600
Hull	8,900
Board margin	100
Total:	27,500

Left: *Queen Elizabeth* at Mudros in 1915.

Below left: *Barham* with the Grand Fleet at Scapa Flow in 1917.

Having developed a design for a fast battleship, it was decided that no battlecruiser should be included in the 1912–13 Estimates. After approval by the Board, four battleships to design R3* were ordered during the latter half of 1912. The Federated Malay States offered to pay for an additional ship and in honour of this generous gift, the fifth ship was named *Malaya.* A sixth vessel – *Agincourt* – was ordered under the 1914–15 Estimates, but was cancelled in August 1914.

Table 3*:* **Construction of the *Queen Elizabeth* class**

	Laid down	Launched	Completed	Built
Barham	24th February 1913	31st December 1914	October 1915	John Brown
Malaya	20th October 1913	18th March 1915	February 1916	Armstrong
Queen Elizabeth	21st October 1912	16th October 1913	January 1915	Portsmouth
Valiant	31st January 1913	4th November 1914	February 1915	Fairfield
Warspite	31st October 1912	26th November 1913	March 1915	Devonport

Armament

In the *Dreadnought* and *Bellerophon* classes, the main armament consisted of ten 12-inch 45-cal Mark X guns. Increasing battle ranges made it desirable to increase the power of future heavy guns and to achieve this, a new high-velocity 12-inch gun – the Mk XI – had been designed for the next generation of *Dreadnought* battleships. The higher muzzle velocity was effected by increasing the weight of the propellant charge and this necessitated a corresponding increase in the length of the gun to 50 calibres. Unfortunately, the new weapon proved inaccurate. The heavy charge ". . . did not always become fully combusted (as distinct from ignited) before the projectile left the muzzle; and as the degree of combustion varied from round to round, the performance of the gun was irregular."[1]

The failure of the 12-inch Mk XI. led to a re-consideration of the problem of increasing the power of heavy guns. Instead of raising the velocity, it was decided to increase the weight of shell by introducing a gun of 13.5-inch calibre. Its greater momentum meant that the 1,250-pound 13.5-inch shell did not lose its velocity as quickly as the 850-pound 12-inch shell. So, although the 13.5-inch Mk V gun had a muzzle velocity equal to that of the 12-inch Mk X and lower than that of the 12-inch Mk XI, its striking velocity and penetrating power at long range were much greater. The gun was very reliable and accurate, and was further improved by increasing the shell weight to 1,400 pounds.

The 15-inch Mk I gun was designed on the same principle, with a low velocity/heavy shell combination. It was even more successful than the 13.5-inch gun and was probably the most efficient heavy gun ever produced for the Royal Navy. For security reasons, while under development, it was always referred to as the "14-inch experimental".

Although the 15-inch Mk I twin mounting was basically similar to the 13.5-inch mounting, careful attention to detail was required in the design stage so as to allow for the higher recoil effect and the increase of the revolving weight to 750 tons. Special care was necessary in the design of the supports for the latter.

Cross-section of 15-inch Mk I gun on twin Mk I(N) mounting

The guns could be loaded at all angles of training and elevation and the maximum elevation was 20°, giving a range of 24,300 yards. The maximum rate of fire was two rounds per gun per minute. For the first time, turret training was effected by a hydraulic swashplate engine, which provided a more satisfactory 'creep' than previous training-mechanisms, with the result that turrets could be trained more smoothly, and small alterations in turret bearing were easier to achieve.

The original design was for sixteen 6-inch 45-cal Mk XII guns on P IX mountings

Table 4: Particulars of British main armaments

Calibre	12-inch	12-inch	13.5-inch	13.5-inch	15-inch
Mark	X	XI	V	V	I
Length of Bore	45-cal	50-cal	45-cal	45-cal	42-cal
Wt of gun without BM	56 tons 16 cwt	65 tons 13 cwt	74 tons 18 cwt	74 tons 18 cwt	97 tons 3 cwt
Wt of shell	850 lb	850 lb	1,250 lb	1,400 lb	1,920 lb
Wt of charge	258 lb	307 lb	293 lb	297 lb	428 lb
Muzzle energy	47,875 f-t	53,046 f-t	63,190 f-t	60,675 f-t	79,910 f-t
Muzzle velocity	2,850 fps	3,010 fps	2,700 fps	2,500 fps	2,450 fps
Penetration of KC plate at muzzle uncapped AP projectile	16 inches	16.8 inches	17.3 inches	17.3 inches	18 inches
Striking energy at 10,000 yds	21,270 f-t	23,570 f-t	31,280 f-t	33,215 f-t	45,550 f-t
Striking velocity at 10,000 yds	1,900 fps	2,000 fps	1,900 fps	1,850 fps	1,850 fps
Penetration of KC plate at 10,000 yds uncapped AP projectile	10.6 inches	11.2 inches	12.2 inches	12.5 inches	14 inches

The above penetration figures are for an uncapped AP projectile striking a plate at the normal, i.e. with the axis of the shell at 90° to the face of the plate. If the plate were inclined the penetration would naturally be reduced and for a 15-in uncapped shell at 10,000 yards range this would be approximately 13.2 inches at 20° inclination and 12.2 inches at 30° inclination. A capped shell would give about 10% to 20% improvement at low velocities and 30% to 50% at high velocities.

[1] Bacon, *From 1900 Onward* . . . . Hutchinson, 1940.

The four 15-inch turrets of *Queen Elizabeth* in 1915: **right**, 'X' and 'Y'; **below**, the forward turrets.

twelve in the main battery on the upper-deck, and four on the main-deck, aft. Early in the First World War, however, defects in this system were revealed by the *Iron Duke* class, whose secondary armament was similarly arranged. The guns in this class were very close to the waterline, and well forward, and the gun-ports were constantly being washed away by the sea. The ports, therefore, were unshipped but, as the revolving shields of the 6-inch guns were not watertight, water could gain free entry to the battery and mess-decks. This was overcome by fitting rubber seals between the gun-shields and the ship's side, and dwarf walls were added at the rear of the 6-inch guns, to restrict the movement of any water that had entered the battery. It was also found necessary to remove the 6-inch guns on the main-deck aft, as these were too close to the water to be operated when at sea. Similar alterations were made in the *Queen Elizabeth* class. Dwarf walls, about three feet high, were fitted at the rear of the 6-inch guns and the shields were made watertight. *Queen Elizabeth* was completed with the after 6-inch guns but these were removed between 1915 and 1916, and the remainder of the class was completed without them. Two 6-inch guns were fitted abreast the boats on the forecastle-deck to compensate the loss of the after battery. These two guns were removed in 1916, despite the fact that they were said to be worth the entire 6-inch battery on the upper-deck.

The three foremost 6-inch guns on each beam, could fire from 1° across the bow to 29° abaft the beam. The remainder could fire from 13° off the bow to 45° abaft the beam, which meant that after 1916, the 6-inch guns had a blind arc of fire of 90° across the stern. The gun-bays were separated by 1½-inch screens but were open on the inboard side to a passage extending the full length of the battery. During construction, port and starboard batteries – forward and aft – were divided by 2-inch centre-line bulkheads. Shell was supplied to the forward end of each battery by a dredger-hoist, and cordite – from the main-deck – through Miller's hatches by means of whips worked by single overhead drums. Stowage was provided for 30 rounds of ready-use ammunition per gun, and ready-use L-hooks were fitted in the vicinity of the whips on the main-deck. This system of ammunition supply was strongly criticised by the Captain of *Excellent*. He pointed out that pre-dreadnought experience of supplying 6-inch ammunition by whips through Miller's hatches, had proved, demonstrably, unsatisfactory. This, he said, was why the *King Edward VII* class had been fitted with dredger-hoists for all 6-inch ammunition – greatly improving its supply to the guns. His criticism was rejected on the grounds that the 6-inch guns of the pre-dreadnoughts formed an important part of the main armament. In the dreadnoughts, however, they were intended to repel torpedo-boat attacks; in this role, they would be required for short spells only, without need of a constant supply of ammunition. It was also considered important to retain a system that provided a break in the cordite supply, between magazine and battery. These arguments were not without foundation, but the retention of the slow system resulted in a large number of ready-use cartridges being stowed in the batteries. During the Battle of Jutland, *Malaya*'s forecastle-deck was penetrated by a 12-inch shell which detonated in the starboard 6-inch battery, destroying 'S3' gun and starting a cordite fire. The fire caused more than a hundred casualties, put the entire battery out of action and almost resulted in the loss of the ship. As a result of this experience, the whips and Miller's hatches were replaced by dredger-hoists, which reduced the chain of cordite between the guns and the 6-inch magazine. In addition, the tops of the cordite-hoists were enclosed by small, flash-tight handing rooms with 1-inch thick walls to prevent a cordite fire in the battery being transmitted to the magazine by way of the hoist. It was suggested that the rear of each gun-bay be enclosed by a screen, but this was rejected because it would have presented obstacles to the command of the batteries.

Anti-aircraft defence was provided by two 3-inch guns, mounted abreast the funnels on the forecastle-deck. During the war it was proposed that these be replaced by two 4-inch high-angle guns, sited in the positions occupied by the two forecastle 6-inch guns. This modification, however, was not carried out, and all the ships of the class retained their two 3-inch guns until well after the war. When *Queen Elizabeth* was completed in January 1915, 3-inch high-angle guns and mountings were in short supply and for a brief period, she carried one 3-inch and one 3-pounder instead of two 3-inch guns.

In 1912, it had been suggested that the 15-inch guns could be fitted in triple mountings but this idea does not appear to have received serious consideration. There was also a proposal to fit a number of 12-pounder guns to strengthen the anti-torpedo-boat armament but this was rejected as it was considered that the 12-pounder would add little to the existing 6-inch firepower and it was undesirable to have three different calibres in a ship.

Fire-control equipment

The design specified a main armament-control position in an armoured tower overlooking the conning-tower, with an armoured, revolving hood containing a 15-foot range-finder above it. In January 1915, it was decided to fit all new capital ships with main armament-directors and all the ships of the class were equipped with two, tripod-type director-sights, before completion – one in the existing revolving hood and one in a director-tower on the fore-top. Each turret was also equipped with a 15-foot range-finder and an open director-sight for local control. In late 1914, it was decided to fit the latter, the order for *Valiant* and *Barham* being placed in December 1914 and for the remainder of the class, in March 1915. All the ships of the class were so equipped on completion. The entire main armament could also be controlled from 'B' turret (see pages 22 and 24).

The original 6-inch gun-control positions were abreast the conning-tower and behind its

Left: the bridge and funnels of *Warspite* in 1917.

armour. Secondary armament-directors were ordered in December 1914, but lack of productive capacity delayed their delivery. *Queen Elizabeth* was fitted with a temporary 6-inch director installation in November/December 1916 and this was replaced by the full equipment in March 1917. *Malaya* and *Valiant* were fitted in April 1917, and *Warspite* and *Barham*, in July 1917. A secondary director-tower was fitted on each side of the compass-platform.

Protection

The disposition of armour was similar to that of the *Iron Duke* class, but with some improvements and some retrograde changes. In general, the protection – particularly of the decks – was inadequate; but considering the limited displacement available, it is doubtful if any great improvements could have been made without the benefit of hindsight. The main belt extended from 'A' to 'Y' barbettes (see page 22) and was approximately 13 feet deep. The plates from which it was formed were 13 feet deep and 15 feet wide. The depth of the belt at its maximum thickness (13 inches) was six feet. The upper four feet of the belt tapered to a thickness of 6 inches, and the lower three feet, to a thickness of 8 inches. This was an improvement upon the *Iron Duke* class in which the main belt was in three tiers of 8-inch, 12-inch and 9-inch plates. But the upper belt in *Queen Elizabeth* was only 6 inches thick, compared to 8 inches in *Iron Duke*. The ideal fighting draught was considered to be half-way between the extreme deep and light draughts – about 31 feet 5 inches. This placed the lower edge of the belt about 6 feet 8 inches below the ship's waterline.

The remainder of the vertical protection was equal to or better than that of the *Iron Duke* class, but deck protection was generally reduced in thickness and was widely spread over four decks. This was completely inadequate against long-range gunfire and – after Jutland – additional 1-inch high-tensile steel plating was fitted on the middle-deck, over the magazines.

Barham

1918: profiles and sections

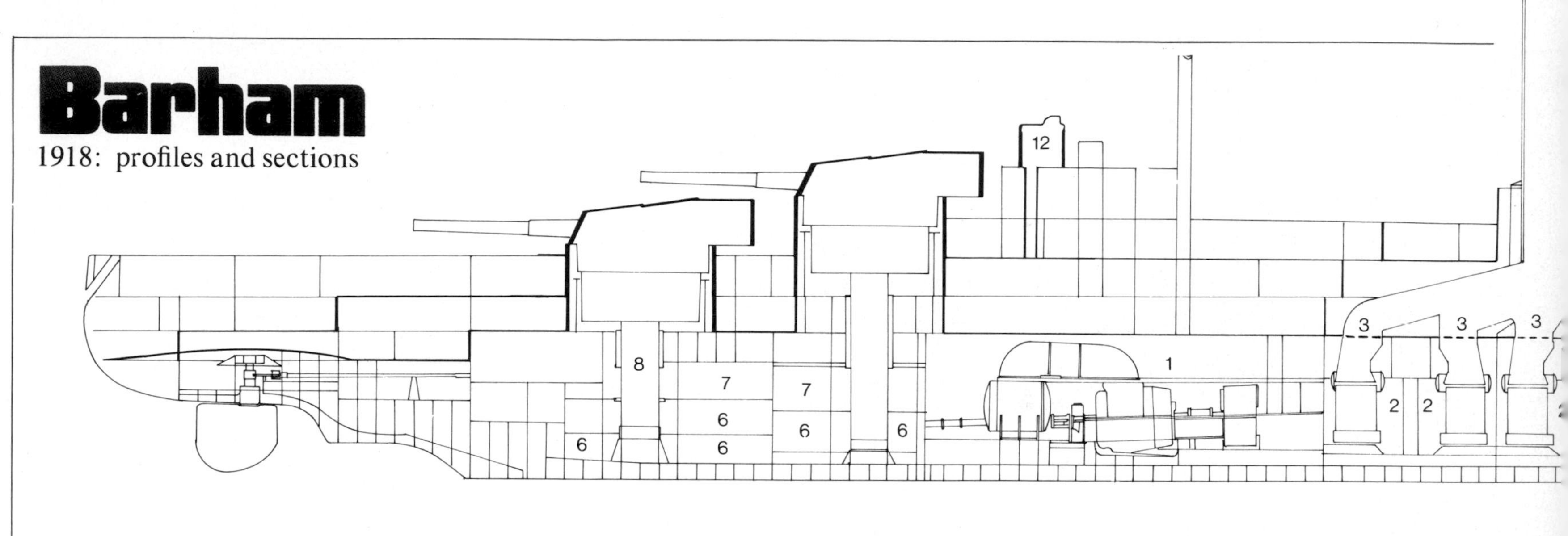

Inboard profile▲

1 Engine room
2 Boiler room
3 Boiler room uptakes
4 Torpedo room
5 Torpedo-head magazine
6 15-inch Shell room
7 15-inch Magazine
8 Handing room
9 6-inch Shell room
10 6-inch Magazine
11 Conning-position
12 Torpedo-control tower

Sections▶

A at frame 64 looking forward
B at frame 78 looking forward
C at frame 108 looking forward
D at frame 158 looking aft

Outboard profile▼

D

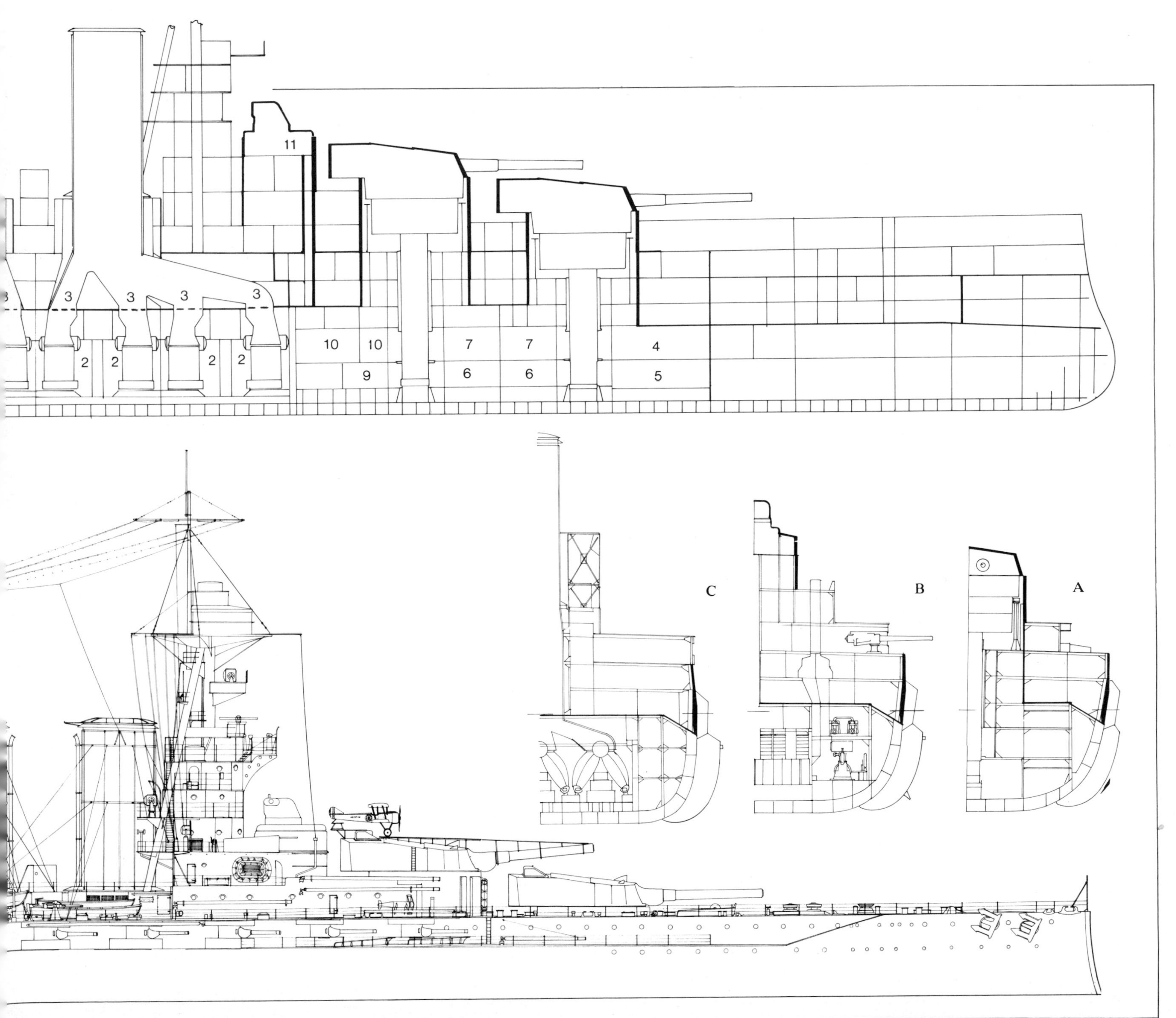
11
3
3
3
3
10
10
7
7
4
2
2
2
2
9
6
6
5
C
B
A

Barham

1918: deck plans

It has proved impossible to interpret the official plans of *Barham* for this period, as a result of the many overdrawn alterations on the drawings. Internal compartments have therefore been omitted from this reproduction.

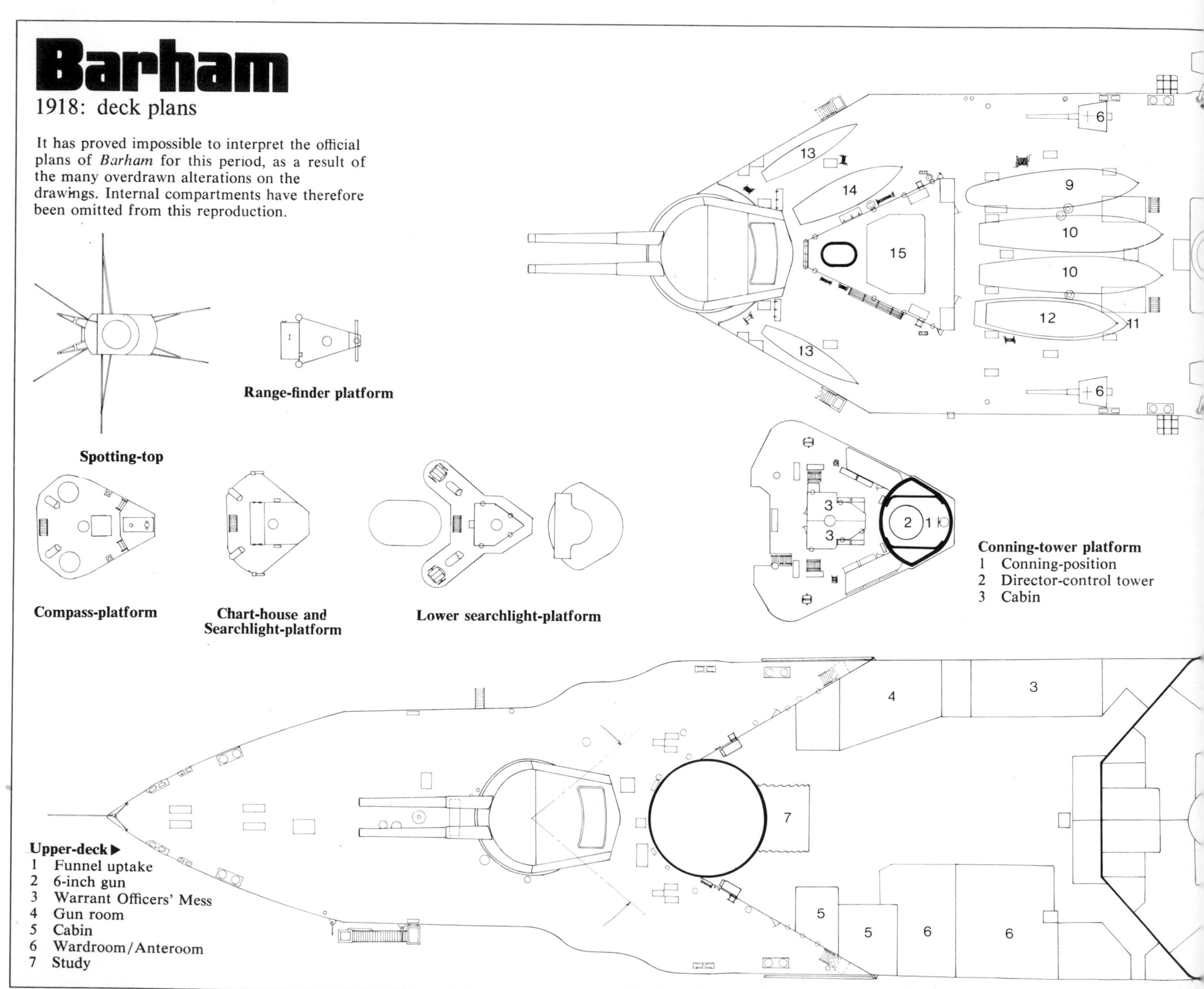

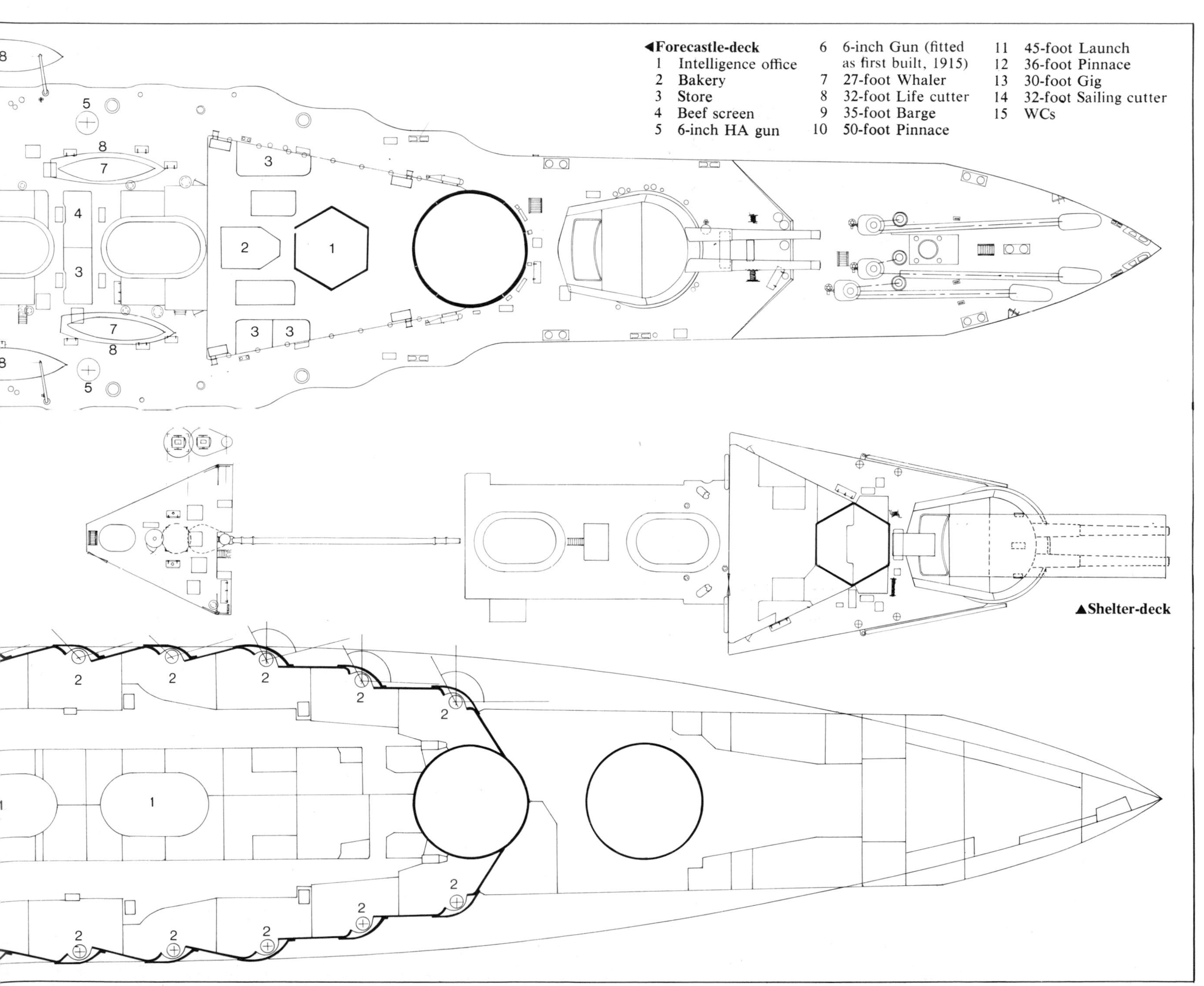
◀Forecastle-deck
1 Intelligence office
2 Bakery
3 Store
4 Beef screen
5 6-inch HA gun
6 6-inch Gun (fitted as first built, 1915)
7 27-foot Whaler
8 32-foot Life cutter
9 35-foot Barge
10 50-foot Pinnace
11 45-foot Launch
12 36-foot Pinnace
13 30-foot Gig
14 32-foot Sailing cutter
15 WCs
▲Shelter-deck

PARTICULARS OF THE *QUEEN ELIZABETH* CLASS, 1915 to 1919

Displacement
Load displacement (approx): 29,200 tons as completed; 29,400 to 30,200 tons in 1917.

Deep displacement:	As completed	1917
Barham	32,910 tons	33,590 tons
Malaya	33,220 tons	33,530 tons
Queen Elizabeth	33,020 tons	34,050 tons
Valiant	33,280 tons	33,910 tons
Warspite	33,410 tons	33,670 tons
Tons per inch:	98 tons	

Dimensions

Length:	oa:	oa, including stern-walk:	pp:
Barham	639 ft $9\frac{1}{4}$ in	644 ft	600 ft $0\frac{1}{4}$ in
Malaya	640 ft 1 in		600 ft 2 in
Queen Elizabeth	640 ft $10\frac{1}{2}$ in	646 ft 1 in	601 ft $4\frac{1}{2}$ in
Valiant	639 ft 3 in		600 ft
Warspite	639 ft 5 in	644 ft 7 in	600 ft

Beam: 90 feet 6 inches.

Draught: 30 feet 6 inches to 30 feet $11\frac{1}{2}$ inches (mean); 33 feet 10 inches to 34 feet $2\frac{1}{2}$ inches (mean deep).

Armament
Eight 15-inch breech-loading Mk I : twin mounting Mk I.
Twelve 6-inch breech-loading Mk XII : single P IX mounting.
Two 3-inch high-angle.
Four 3-pounder saluting guns (carried in peacetime only).
Five Maxim machine-guns.
Four 21-inch submerged torpedo tubes.

Ammunition stowage (1919)
15-inch : 100 rounds per gun.
6-inch : 130 rounds per gun; 100 star shell for ship.
3-pounder : 64 rounds per gun.
20 torpedoes.

Armour
Belt: 13 inch tapering to 6 inch and 4 inch forward and aft.
Upper belt: 6 inch.
Bulkheads: 6 inch and 4 inch forward, 6 inch and 4 inch aft.
Turrets: 11 inch sides, 13 inch face, $4\frac{1}{4}$ inch roof.
Barbettes: 10 inch to 7 inch above belt, 6 inch to 4 inch below.
6-inch battery: 6 inch.
Conning-tower: 11 inch sides, 3 inch roof, 4 inch revolving hood.
Conning-tower tube: 6 inch to upper-deck, 4 inch below.
Torpedo conning-tower: 6 inch.
Torpedo conning-tower tube: 4 inch to upper-deck.

Protective plating
Vertical: Torpedo bulkheads, 2 inch (1 inch + 1 inch).
Magazine end-bulkheads, 2 inch (1 inch + 1 inch); increased to 3 inch (1 inch + 1 inch + 1 inch) after Jutland.
Funnel-uptakes, $1\frac{1}{2}$ inch.

Horizontal: Forecastle-deck, 1 inch over 6-inch battery.
Upper-deck, 2 inch to $1\frac{1}{4}$ inch from 'A' to 'Y' barbettes.
Main-deck, $1\frac{1}{4}$ inch at forward and after ends.
Middle-deck, 1 inch, increased to 2 inch over magazines, after Jutland.
Lower-deck, 3 inch at extreme ends, $2\frac{1}{2}$ inch over steering gear, 1 inch forward.

Machinery
The machinery for *Queen Elizabeth* and *Malaya* was manufactured by Wallsend Slipway, that for *Warspite* by Hawthorn Leslie, and for the remaining ships of the class, by the builders.
Parsons (*Malaya*, *Queen Elizabeth* and *Warspite*) and Brown Curtis (*Barham* and *Valiant*) direct-drive turbines, four shafts.
75,000 SHP = 24 knots at 300 rpm.
Maximum sea-going speed, 67,500 SHP = 23.25 knots.
24 large-tube boilers, maximum working pressure 285 pounds per square inch.

Fuel and endurance
3,300 tons oil fuel (normal maximum stowage).
100 tons coal.

Fuel consumption:	SHP	Speed	Tons per hour
Full power	75,000	25 knots	40.5
4/5 power	60,000	24 knots	31.4
3/5 power	45,000	22.5 knots	25.2
2/5 power	30,000	20.5 knots	18

Radius of action:
8,600 nautical miles at 12.5 knots.
3,900 nautical miles at 21 knots.

Building Costs
Barham £2,408,000; *Queen Elizabeth* £3,014,103; *Malaya* £2,945,709; *Valiant* £2,537,037; *Warspite* £2,524,148.

Underwater protection

The original designs included anti-torpedo nets, but in July 1912, their use was seriously re-considered. Arguments for their retention were few, but those against were many. They were easily damaged by gunfire and so could cause obstruction to guns and propellers. The fixing of the heels for the net-booms weakened the side armour. They were very heavy (120 tons) and the occasions when they could be used were infrequent.

These points were debated during a conference on board HMS *Enchantress*, at Torbay in July 1912, and – with only one dissentient – a vote was passed favouring the abolition of net defence for the ships of the 1912 programme.

The weight saved, by abolishing the nets, was used to improve internal protection against torpedoes and mines. This protection consisted of longitudinal bulkheads, 2 inches thick, extending from the forward to the after submerged torpedo rooms, and from the middle-deck to the ship's bottom. The ends were closed by transverse bulkheads, also 2 inches thick and these – after Jutland – were strengthened by the addition of 1-inch plating.

For the greater part of their length, these longitudinal bulkheads traversed the fuel-tanks in which oil was stored at a considerable head of pressure. This necessitated careful attention to detail in the design of the tanks and special care was necessary to ensure oil-tightness while maintaining their full structural strength. The system was tested by installing a similar structural arrangement in the old battleship *Hood*, and experimenting to determine its efficiency against mine and torpedo explosions. Modifications based on these experiments were embodied in the final design.

Machinery

The turbines were arranged in two sets, each set consisting of one low-pressure ahead and one low-pressure astern – in the same casing – on the inner shaft, and one high-pressure ahead and one high-pressure astern on the

Below: *Valiant* on exercises in late 1918. The main-topmast has been replaced and flying-off platforms have been fitted on 'B' and 'X' turrets.

wing shaft. The engine space was divided longitudinally into three compartments, the low-pressure turbines being in the centre engine room and the high-pressure turbines in the wing engine rooms. Reaction-type geared cruising turbines were fitted at the forward end of each high-pressure turbine in *Queen Elizabeth*, *Warspite* and *Malaya* only, these ships having Parsons turbines, whereas *Barham* and *Valiant* were equipped with Brown Curtis turbines. Twenty-four boilers in four rooms, supplied steam to the turbines at a pressure of 175 pounds per square inch. Yarrow boilers were fitted in *Warspite* and *Barham*, and the rest of the class carried Babcock and Wilcox boilers.

The machinery was designed to provide a speed of 23 knots at full power with 56,000 shaft horse-power, and 25 knots at overload power with 75,000 shaft horse-power. With few exceptions, the machinery realised design expectations; but as the designed displacement of the class was greatly exceeded, much of the value of the high power was lost. Most of the class could make 25 knots under good conditions, but there was very little margin for adverse circumstances such as running at deep displacement or with a foul bottom. War conditions prevented a normal programme of machinery trials being carried out; and the records of the trials that were conducted are incomplete and, in some cases, must be considered unreliable. The following results were obtained from trials carried out during the First World War.

Warspite:
Two contractor's trials off the west coast of Ireland on 11th April 1915 produced the following results:
1½-hour full-power trial: 56,580 SHP, 274 rpm, 24.1 knots, oil consumption 45.7 tons.
2-hour overload-power trial: 75,510 SHP, 24.65 knots.
The ship had last been undocked on 22nd March 1915.

Valiant:
During a two-hour full-power contractors' trial in the Firth of Clyde on 27th February 1916, the ship developed 275 rpm with 57,315 SHP. The speed and oil consumption were not recorded. At overload power she developed 71,112 SHP. The ship had not been in dock since she was launched in November 1914.

Malaya
The records of *Malaya*'s contractors' trials are the most comprehensive for the class. They were carried out in the North Sea on 17th February 1916. The ship had been undocked on the 14th January 1916 and had a clean bottom. Displacement at the commencement of the trial was 32,976 tons and mean draught was 33 feet 5½ inches.
Two-hour full-power trial: 57,332 SHP, 280 rpm, 23.5 knots, oil consumption 66 tons.
Two-hour overload-power trial: 76,074 SHP, 304.7 rpm, 25 knots, oil consumption 90 tons.
Two-hour overload-power trial: 76,200 SHP, 307 rpm, 25 knots, oil consumption 90 tons.
The average steam pressure during the trials was found to be 220 pounds per square inch at the boilers and 181 pounds per square inch at the engines.

Barham:
During a two-hour full-power contractors' trial in the Firth of Clyde on 27th August 1915, the ship produced 285 rpm with 60,950 SHP. Her draught at the commencement of the trial was 30 feet 4 inches corresponding to a displacement of 29,410 tons. She had last been undocked on 31st December 1914. At overload power she produced 76,575 SHP.

Queen Elizabeth:
On a contractors' full-power trial the ship produced 57,130 SHP. No other details are known.

None of the above-mentioned trials was run on a measured-mile course and therefore the speeds given cannot be regarded as accurate. Measured-mile trials were, however, run by Barham at Bute Sound on 6th July 1916, and gave the following results:

Type of trial: overload full power.
Draught at commencement of trial: 32 feet 6 inches (forward), 33 feet (aft).
Displacement at commencement of trial: 32,252 tons.
State of sea: 0.
SHP: 70,788.
rpm: 293.25.
Speed: 23.91 knots.

The speed obtained was only 0.1 knots below that expected at the displacement, although the SHP and vacuum in the condensers was well below that obtained during the contractors' trials. Some doubt was felt, therefore, about the accuracy of these figures, and as the SHP given for the outer shafts was obviously too low, the power developed was probably much higher.

The trials showed that the ships fitted with Parsons turbines could obtain higher revolutions than those with Brown Curtis turbines. In the two ships fitted with the latter – *Barham* and *Valiant* – the obtainable power appeared to be limited by the capacity of the condensers to take the steam from the engines, although in *Valiant* it was considered doubtful if the boilers could have provided sufficient steam for more power than that actually obtained. This ship was known to be the slowest vessel in the squadron; the nozzles of her high-pressure turbines were slightly different from those of *Barham* and the vacuum band generally less than in the other ships of the class.

The results obtained by *Malaya* were considered very satisfactory. She made 306 rpm without difficulty and her fuel consumption, especially at low speeds, was much lower than had been estimated.

Admiral Jellicoe, commenting on *Barham*'s measured-mile trial at Bute Sound, considered that, as *Valiant* was slower than *Barham*, the speed of the 5th Battle Squadron as a whole could not be regarded as much more than 23 knots. He pointed out that the trial was run under ideal conditions and that the ship's displacement, at the time, was what might be expected when going into action. He concluded that this speed was only slightly in excess of that of the Battle Fleet and it was questionable whether they could get to the head of the line on deployment without blanketing the battleline. Jellicoe also pointed out that the 5th Battle Squadron possessed very little margin in speed over the 3rd Battle Squadron of the High Seas Fleet. Their value as the fast wing of the Grand Fleet was therefore somewhat limited.

It was remarked that, under deep load conditions, the turbines were unable to attain their maximum revolutions. It was proposed, that the propellers be modified so as to achieve higher power, thereby increasing the speed of the ship. Such modification, however, would result in a loss of speed at lower powers. The proposal was rejected but it was decided to alter the jets in *Valiant*'s turbines at the earliest opportunity. It is not known if this was actually done, but *Valiant* remained the slowest ship of her class until fitted with new machinery during her second reconstruction, in the late Thirties.

In order to obtain more reliable information concerning the performance of the machinery, it was decided in February 1919 that *Barham*, *Warspite*, *Valiant* and *Malaya* should carry out full-power trials. *Barham* was to undergo her trial while on passage from Scapa to Invergordon for refit; the remaining three

Queen Elizabeth in 1922.

ships, on passage south from Scapa. These trials produced results shown in Table 5.

The use of oil fuel instead of coal, required the provision of bunkers approximately thirty feet deep. The designers had no previous experience of these, so experimental tanks were built, in which the structural arrangements of a ship were represented. Knowledge gained from these experiments was later incorporated in the detailed design. Only the lower bunkers were used, thus releasing a large amount of space in the middle-deck which would have been occupied by coal. This space was unsuitable for general messing because of the difficulty of providing efficient ventilation and the necessity of maintaining efficient watertight sub-division in the vicinity of the waterline. The space was therefore employed for bathrooms and other improvements recommended by various committees. These modifications greatly improved the habitability of the class compared to previous ships.

Full oil fuel stowage was provided for 3,500 tons but as the tanks were normally kept at 95 per cent capacity, the actual maximum stowage was 3,325 tons. The maximum amount of oil carried was usually restricted to 2,800 tons because the ships were well over their designed displacement. Stowage was also provided for 100 tons of coal for domestic purposes. Four main condensers were fitted in the centre engine room and one auxiliary condenser in each of the wing engine rooms.

Auxiliary machinery

In the original design, two oil-driven, 450-kilowatt dynamos and two turbine-driven, 200-kilowatt dynamos supplied electricty, at 220 volts direct current, into a common ring main. To meet extra demands for power, a fifth, 200-kilowatt dynamo, driven by a reciprocating engine, was fitted in *Queen Elizabeth* and *Valiant* towards the end of the war, and in the other ships of the class after the war.

The distilling machinery consisted of two evaporators and one distilling condenser in each wing engine room, the two groups having a combined capacity of 650 tons per day.

Hydraulic power for operating the main armament was provided by four steam-driven, hydraulic engines, one for each turret.

Stability

In British, pre-dreadnought battleships – mainly because of the predominance of the gunnery branch – the metacentric height (GM) had been kept comparatively low, in order to provide a steady gun platform. This naturally reduced a ship's capacity to absorb damage. From *Dreadnought* onwards, the GM was gradually increased in successive designs until in the *Queen Elizabeth* class, it was higher than any previously provided in a British dreadnought. Although displacement figures were considerably exceeded in completed ships, the GM varied little from the design figure. Nevertheless, the increase in draught, produced a reduction in the reserve of buoyancy and freeboard, to the detriment of the ship's stability. The designed GM was 5.8 feet at a light displacement of 26,788 tons, 6 feet at a legend displacement of 27,700 tons and 7.79 feet at a deep displacement of 31,534 tons.

The stability calculations were based on the following legend weights.

Hull	9,034 tons
Armour	8,750 tons
Armament	4,546 tons
Machinery and engineer's stores	3,950 tons
Oil fuel	650 tons
Equipment	670 tons
Board Margin	100 tons
Total Legend displacement	27,700 tons

The weights differ slightly from those in the original legend as a result of the early modifications to the design. The actual stability figures for the completed ships were approximately as follows.

Load displacement: 29,200 tons, fully equipped with reserve feed-tanks empty and 650 tons oil on board.
Draught: 30 feet 2 inches.
GM: 5.9 feet.
Angle of maximum stability: 38°.
Range of stability: 69°.

Deep load displacement: 33,100 tons, fully equipped with fresh water and reserve feed-water tanks full and 3,400 tons of oil on board.
Draught: 33 feet 5 inches.
GM: 7.8 feet.
Angle of maximum stability: 39°.
Range of stability: 79°.

Light displacement: 28,250 tons.
Draught: 29 feet 4½ inches.
GM: 5.6 feet.
Angle of maximum stability: 38°.
Range of stability: 68°.

Alterations and additions

Apart from those already mentioned, the following modifications were made to the

Table 5: Full-power trials, *Valiant*, *Warspite*, *Barham* and *Malaya*, 1919

	Trial	Date	Place	Mean rpm	SHP	Mean speed	Oil fuel consumption	When last undocked
*Valiant**	1 hour full power	11th March 1919	On passage to Plymouth	275.2	57,703	23 knots	33 tons	9th March 1918
*Warspite***	2 hour overload	11th March 1919	NW coast of Scotland	296	75,800	23.5 knots	—	25th March 1918
*Barham****	1 hour overload	21st February 1919	On passage to Invergordon	289.9	72,872	23.8 knots	—	—
Malaya	1 hour overload	11th March 1919	On passage to Portsmouth	305.85	76,740	24.9 knots	45 tons	—

* *Valiant* also carried out four other trials on passage to Plymouth over extended periods (18 hours, 16 hours, etc.). The highest speed obtained during these trials was 23.5 knots with 66,570 SHP.
** *Warspite*'s draught at the commencement of this trial was 32 feet 10 inches (forward) 33 feet (aft) corresponding to an approximate displacement of 32,500 tons.
*** *Barham*'s draught at the commencement of this trial was 31 feet 1 inch (forward) 31 feet 7 inches (aft) corresponding to an approximate displacement of 30,500 tons.

Below: *Warspite* "dressed-up" in 1921, after her 1920 refit when she received an enlarged fore-top. Note that the aircraft platform on 'X' turret is shorter than that on 'B' turret. Only single-seater aircraft could be flown from the short type, while the heavier two-seater scouting aircraft needed the longer platform for take-off. Alongside *Warspite* in this picture is the 'K' class submarine K9.

class during and shortly after the First World War.

1. In the battleships *Hercules*, *Colossus*, *Neptune*, and, to a lesser extent, in the *Orion* class, it was found that the framing below the lower-deck, for about fifty feet from the stem, was unable to withstand the panting set up by heavy pitching. In subsequent designs, the framing was gradually increased, but in 1914, exceptionally heavy weather revealed further weaknesses in *Hercules.* It was decided, therefore, to improve the fore-part stiffening of ships in the *Iron Duke*, *Queen Elizabeth* and *Royal Sovereign* classes by adding intermediate frames between the lower-deck and the platform-deck, and between the platform-deck and the keel. Despite these modifications, however, panting was experienced during the trials of *Queen Elizabeth* in 1915, necessitating the addition of still more stiffening behind the forward side-plating. After the gun trials, additional girders were fitted under the forecastle-deck, in way of the blast from the forward 15-inch guns.

2. Early war experience demonstrated the need for improvements in watertight integrity and damage control. Large numbers of valves were fitted to the ventilation system and fittings were added, for the correction of heel by the transference of oil fuel, and for the flooding of certain watertight compartments.

3. After Jutland, anti-flash arrangements were fitted to main and secondary magazines.

4. In 1918, aircraft flying-off platforms were fitted on 'B' and 'X' turrets, in all ships of the class. Between them, the five ships carried three reconnaissance aircraft and seven fighters.

5. Between 1917 and 1918, training scales were painted on the turrets and range-clocks were fitted – one or two on the foremast and two or four on the after side of the searchlight-towers on the after funnel. After the war, two additional range-clocks were fitted on the roof of 'X' turret.

6. Searchlight-control positions were added, searchlight-towers were fitted to the after funnel and searchlight-platforms were fitted on the after superstructure and mainmast between 1916 and 1918. *Barham* also carried a seachlight-platform on the foremast. By the end of the war, each ship carried eight 36-inch searchlights – two on the bridge, four on the after funnel, one on the mainmast and one on the after superstructure. The last-mentioned was removed from all ships between 1921 and 1923.

7. Carley rafts were added between 1916 and 1917.

8. The rigs were modified several times during the war. By 1918, all ships carried a fore-topmast but only *Queen Elizabeth* carried a main-topmast. In 1919, the fore-topmast was removed from all except *Queen Elizabeth* and the main-topmast was re-fitted. The fore-topmast was removed from *Queen Elizabeth* in 1922. Main-topgallant-masts were fitted in *Warspite* in 1920, *Malaya* and *Valiant* in 1921 and *Queen Elizabeth* in 1922. The fore-topmast was replaced in *Barham* in 1921 and in *Valiant* in 1924. Various other minor alterations were made to the rig during the post-war period.

9. The fore-top was enlarged in *Queen Elizabeth* in 1919 and in *Warspite* in 1920.

10. Only *Queen Elizabeth* was completed with a stern-walk but it was removed in 1916. It had been re-fitted by 1926. Stern-walks were also fitted in *Barham*, in 1919 and in *Warspite* in 1920.

11. In all the ships of the class, the 15-foot range-finders in 'B' and 'X' turrets were replaced by 30-foot range-finders between 1919 and 1922.

12. Paravane equipment was fitted.

2. The Royal Sovereign Class, 1913 to 1919

The design for the 1913 programme hearkened back to the pre-*Queen Elizabeth* type of battleship. It had been intended that the same armament be carried as in the *Queen Elizabeth* class, but the machinery was to have been similar to that in the *Iron Duke* class, giving a speed of 21.5 knots. The new ships were to revert to combined coal and oil fuel. The reduction in speed would allow the displacement to be reduced from that of the *Queen Elizabeth* class. This, while having some economic advantage would leave little reserve for the later design additions. The estimated cost per ship was £2,150,000.

Table 6: Legend of particulars of Design T1

Load displacement	25,500 tons
Deep displacement	28,750 tons
Length (pp)	580 feet
Beam	88 feet 6 inches
Draught at lwl	28 feet 6 inches
Draught at dwl	32 feet 6 inches
tpi	91
SHP	31,000
Speed at load draught	21.5 knots
Coal at load draught	900 tons
Coal capacity	3,000 tons
Oil fuel capacity	1,500 tons
Armament:	Eight 15 in 42-cal BL 80 rounds per gun Sixteen 6 in 45-cal BL 150 rounds per gun Four 3 in HA 200 rounds per gun Four 21 in submerged torpedo tubes, 20 torpedoes
Armour:	
Belt (amidships)	13 inch
Belt (forward and aft)	6 inch and 4 inch
Upper belt	6 inch
Bulkheads (forward and aft)	6 inch and 4 inch
Barbettes	10 inch to 4 inch
Gun-houses	11 inch
Conning-tower	11 inch
Conning-tower tube	6 inch and 4 inch
Torpedo-director tower	6 inch
Torpedo-director tower tube	4 inch
Vertical protective plating:	
Funnel-uptakes	$1\frac{1}{2}$ inch and 1 inch
Torpedo bulkheads	$1\frac{1}{2}$ inch and 1 inch
Horizontal protective plating:	
Forecastle-deck	1 inch (over 6 in battery).
Upper-deck	$1\frac{1}{4}$ inch to $1\frac{1}{2}$ inch (from 'A' to 'Y' barbettes)
Main-deck (flat)	1 inch, $1\frac{1}{2}$ inch and 2 inch
Main-deck (slope)	2 inch
Lower-deck (forward)	$2\frac{1}{2}$ inch and 1 inch
Lower-deck (aft)	$2\frac{1}{2}$ inch and 4 inch to 3 inch
Weights:	
General equipment	750 tons
Armament	4,550 tons
Machinery	2,500 tons
Coal	900 tons
Armour and protective plating	8,100 tons
Hull	8,600 tons
Board margin	100 tons
Total:	25,500 tons

Early modifications to the design resulted in an increase in the displacement from 25,500 tons to 25,750 tons and a corresponding reduction in the speed from 21.5 knots to 21 knots. The 1913 programme provided for five ships to be built to this design.

In January 1915, approval was given to convert the class from combined coal and oil to oil fuel only. It was estimated that with some slight adjustments to the engines, 40,000 SHP would be developed against 31,000 SHP in the original design, thereby increasing the speed from 21 knots with 300 rpm, to 23 knots with 320 rpm. Stowage was provided for 3,400 tons of oil compared to 3,000 tons of coal and 1,500 tons of oil. Despite this great reduction in fuel weight, the radius of action remained practically unaltered. The saving in weight was offset by an increase in the ammunition stowage for the main armament from 80 rounds per gun to 100 rpg, and a number of other additions resulting in a load displacement of 25,800 tons in the modified design. The use of oil meant that seventy-five fewer stokers were needed.

Armament

In the original design, the sixteen 6-inch guns were disposed in the same manner as those in the *Queen Elizabeth* class, but in consequence of the experience in the *Iron Duke* class, this arrangement was abandoned. The main battery was moved farther aft, reducing the size of the embrasures forward, and although the battery was still too close to the waterline to be unaffected in a seaway, it proved much drier than in the earlier classes. Only mountings 'S1' and 'P1' could train directly ahead; but the two aftermost guns on each side could fire directly aft, giving a better all-round command. The four guns aft on the main-deck were replaced by two 6-inch mountings with open splinter shields, on the forecastle-deck, abreast the funnel. The 6-inch ammunition supply system was generally similar to that in *Queen Elizabeth* and, as in that class, after Jutland, the tops of the cordite-hoists were enclosed by flash-tight handing rooms.

Port and starboard 6-inch batteries were separated by the funnel-uptakes and by 2-inch bulkheads, and individual guns were separated by $1\frac{1}{2}$-inch screens. Again, the gun-bays were open at the rear, except for dwarf walls, three feet high.

Fire-control equipment

The design provided for main and secondary armament-control positions in the conning-tower, as in the *Queen Elizabeth* class.

Approval was given to fit main and secondary armament-directors while the ships were

Table 7: Construction of the *Royal Sovereign* class

	Laid down	Launched	Completed	Builder	Machinery
Royal Sovereign	15th January 1914	29th April 1915	May 1916	Portsmouth Dockyard	Parsons
Royal Oak	15th January 1914	17th November 1914	May 1916	Devonport Dockyard	Hawthorn Leslie
Ramillies	12th November 1913	12th September 1916	October 1917	Beardmore	Beardmore
Revenge	22nd December 1913	29th May 1915	March 1916	Vickers	Vickers
Resolution	29th November 1913	14th January 1915	December 1916	Palmers	Palmers

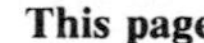

Opposite page
Top: *Royal Sovereign* on exercises with the Grand Fleet in 1916. Note the searchlight on the fore-top roof and the training scale on 'Y' turret. The two ships of the *Royal Sovereign* class in the background, each show a different arrangement of rig.
Below: two views of *Royal Oak* during trials in May 1916.

This page
Left: the forward turrets of *Revenge* – a photograph taken at Scapa Flow in 1917.
Right: cleaning out one of the 15-inch guns on *Royal Oak*.

under construction. The two main armament-directors were fitted before the ships were completed; one, in the armoured revolving hood overlooking the conning-tower and the other in a director-tower on a platform under the fore-top. The two secondary directors, positioned on the compass-platform abreast the foremast, were fitted in *Resolution* in April 1917, in *Ramillies* in June 1918 and in the remaining ships of the class in March 1917. Each turret was equipped with an open director-sight and a 15-foot range-finder for local control. The entire main armament could also be controlled from 'X' turret.

Protection

In the *Royal Sovereign* class, the tapered belt armour of earlier ships was replaced by a belt with a uniform thickness of 13 inches. A single tier, 12 feet 9 inches deep, it extended from the main-deck to 5 feet below the load waterline (compared to 4 feet in earlier ships). In the extreme deep condition, at least 4 feet of the belt would be above water. This was considered an important feature, allowing a greater degree of roll without exposing the unprotected hull below the belt. The use of un-tapered armour reduced the cost by £20 per ton. The belt was continued fore and aft by 6-inch and 4-inch armour, and closed at the ends by 4-inch transverse bulkheads, between the lower-deck and the main-deck. The 6-inch upper belt extended from 'A' to 'X' barbettes and was closed at the ends by 6-inch transverse bulkheads.

Compared with previous designs, the protective deck was moved up one level to the main-deck, its slope being angled sharply down to the base of the belt. Thus, instead of being on or below the waterline, the main protective deck was about eight feet above the load waterline, greatly decreasing the loss of armoured reserve of buoyancy, should the side armour be pierced. It also reduced the number of thick decks and, in the original design, greatly simplified the handling, embarkation and trimming of coal.

Underwater protection

Longitudinal torpedo bulkheads were fitted over the full length of the magazine, machinery and torpedo-tube compartments. Although similar in arrangement to those designed for *Queen Elizabeth*, these bulkheads in the *Royal Sovereign* class were only 1½ inches thick, reducing to 1 inch behind the side armour and in the double bottom. This, presumably, was because the original design for the *Royal Sovereign* class specified the fitting of coal bunkers, but when the ships were converted to oil fuel only, they lost the additional protection afforded by the coal. Oil also affords protection, however, so the extent of the loss is debatable. Nevertheless, in view of the

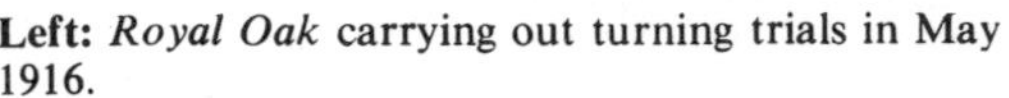

Left: *Royal Oak* carrying out turning trials in May 1916.

narrower beam of the *Royal Sovereign* class, the underwater protection was well below the standard set by the *Queen Elizabeth* class.

In March 1915, however, permission was given to fit bulges to *Ramillies* while she was still on the stocks. The detailed arrangement of these structures was based on the results of experiments being carried out on the Chatham Float, to establish the best form of underwater protection against torpedoes and mines. (Chatham Float was the name given to a series of reproductions of midship sections of warship hulls, used to test the effects of underwater explosions on a ship's hull structure and torpedo protection system. The experiments usually progressed through quarter-, half- and full-size models, before any particular system of underwater protection was considered satisfactory.) Each bulge was divided into upper and lower compartments, the lower compartments being further divided longitudinally into two sections. The inner compartment in the lower bulges were filled with 9-inch diameter, sealed, steel tubes, that were intended to disperse the force of an underwater explosion and prevent penetration of the protective bulkhead by reducing the momentum of splinters and débris. The tubes occupied a space 4 feet wide, outboard of which was air space whose width was governed by launching conditions. The bulges extended from the forward to the after submerged torpedo rooms and protruded 7 feet from the ship's sides, increasing the beam to 102 feet 6 inches and reducing the draught by about 1 foot. The bulges increased the weight by 2,500 tons including 773 tons of tubes and 194 tons of wood.

In October 1917, it was decided to fit bulges to the other four ships of the class, but in their case the prime requirement was to improve stability rather than underwater protection and the bulges were of a different design. They are described in the following section.

Stability

The raising of the protective deck increased the armoured reserve of buoyancy to an extent where the stability of the ship, even if riddled by shellfire, would be very much greater than in earlier designs. It was decided, therefore – complaints having been received about uneasy rolling in earlier ships – to lower the initial GM by reducing the beam, which would give an easier roll and a longer period, thereby providing a better gun platform. This change, however, did not prove entirely beneficial as it led to excessive heel when turning. Moreover, in action, the earlier ships proved to be not bad gun platforms and the efficiency of their gunnery was unimpaired by rolling.

The bulges fitted to *Ramillies* before her completion, effectively reversed the designed stability requirements, by increasing the beam and raising the GM. It was decided, therefore, to fit bulges to the remainder of the class in order to attain greater initial stability and improve the trim. *Revenge* was fitted with bulges between October 1917 and February 1918, and *Resolution*, between late 1917 and May 1918. The lower bulges in these vessels consisted of single watertight chambers without tube compartments, and the upper bulges were filled with a composition of cement and wood offal. This reduced the draught by about 16 inches and increased the displacement by 1,526 tons, of which 640 tons was cement and 186 tons, wood offal. The beam was increased to 101 feet 5 inches in *Revenge* and 101 feet 4 inches in *Resolution*. *Royal Sovereign* was not taken in hand until December 1920, by which time it had been decided to further increase the initial stability, by enlarging the upper bulges and increasing the waterline area. Steel tubes were fitted, replacing the wood and cement of the earlier design. The work on *Royal Sovereign* was completed in October 1924. The bulges increased her displacement by 1,474 tons, of which, 763 tons were tubes and cement.

Reports of excessive rolling having been received from the ships fitted with bulges, various experiments were carried out at Haslar to determine the best form of bulge for *Royal Oak* that – together with improved bilge keels – would eliminate this problem. The new type of bulge was fitted to *Royal Oak* during 1922 to 1924 (see page 139) and the remaining ships of the class received new bilge keels.

The following tables give the GM and range of stability at various times. The legend displacement was considerably exceeded in the completed ships, as it had been in the *Queen Elizabeth* class, but the addition of bulges fully compensated this extra weight.

Table 8: *Royal Sovereign* class, GM and range of stability as finally designed

Condition	Displacement	GM	Range
Extreme deep with 3400 tons of oil fuel (95% capacity)	29,050 tons	5 ft	69°
Legend with 900 tons of oil fuel	25,800 tons	2.67 ft	58½°
Light	24,650 tons	2.42 ft	58°

As established from an inclining experiment on *Royal Sovereign*:

Condition	Displacement	GM	Range
Extreme deep with 3400 tons of oil fuel (95% capacity)	31,160 tons	4.94 ft	67°
Sea-going with 2890 tons of oil fuel	30,650 tons	4.12 ft	59°
Legend with 900 tons oil fuel	27,970 tons	2.79 ft	57°
Light	26,770 tons	2.35 ft	56°

As established from an inclining experiment on *Revenge* after bulging:

Condition	Draught	Displacement	GM	Range
Extreme deep with 3400 tons of oil fuel (95% capacity)	32 ft 3 in	32,820 tons	5.16 ft	68.3°
Deep with 3040 tons of oil fuel (85% capacity)	31 ft 10 in	32,460 tons	5.1 ft	67.2°
Legend with 900 tons of oil fuel	29 ft 3½ in	29,590 tons	5.24 ft	62.3°
Light	28 ft 4 in	28,410 tons	5.25 ft	59.3°

Machinery

The turbines were arranged in two sets, as in the *Queen Elizabeth* class, steam being supplied by eighteen Yarrow boilers in three boiler rooms. Two funnels were provided in the original sketch design, but this was later modified and the uptakes were combined to form one large funnel.

PARTICULARS OF THE *ROYAL SOVEREIGN* CLASS, 1916 to 1919

Displacement

Load Displacement:

Royal Sovereign as completed	27,970 tons
Royal Sovereign as bulged	29,500 tons*
Revenge as completed	28,000 tons*
Revenge as bulged	29,590 tons
Ramillies as completed with bulge	30,300 tons*

Deep displacement:

Royal Sovereign as completed	31,160 tons
Royal Sovereign as bulged	32,700 tons*
Revenge as completed	31,250 tons
Revenge as bulged	32,820 tons
Ramillies as completed with bulge	33,540 tons

*approximate.

Tons per inch: as designed, 91 tons.

Dimensions

580 feet (pp) × 88 feet 6 inches, as designed.

	Length (oa):	Beam over bulges
Ramillies	620 feet 7 inches	102 feet
Resolution	620 feet 2 inches	101 feet 4 inches
Revenge	625 feet 10 inches (including stern-walk)	101 feet 5 inches
Royal Oak	620 feet 6 inches	102 feet 1 inch
Royal Sovereign	620 feet 8 inches	101 feet 6 inches

Draught:
Royal Sovereign as completed, 30 feet 9 inches*.
Ramillies as completed with bulge, 29 feet 8 inches*.
Revenge with bulge, 29 feet 3½ inches*. *mean.

Armament

Eight 15-inch breech-loading Mk I : twin mounting Mk I.
Fourteen 6-inch breech-loading Mk XII : single P IX mounting.
Two 3-inch high-angle.
Four 3-pounder saluting guns (peacetime only).
Five Maxim machine-guns.
Four 21-inch submerged torpedo tubes.

Ammunition stowage

15-inch : 100 rounds per gun.
6-inch : 130 rounds per gun; 100 star shell per ship.
3-pounder : 64 rounds per gun.
20 torpedoes.

Armour

Belt: 13 inch amidships, 6 inch and 4 inch forward and aft.
Upper belt: 6 inch.
Bulkheads: 6 inch and 4 inch forward and aft.
Turrets: 11 inch sides, 13 inch face, 4¼ inch roof.
Barbettes: 10 inch to 4 inch.
6-inch battery: 6 inch sides, 4 inch bulkheads forward and aft.
Conning-tower: 11 inch.
Conning-tower tube: 6 inch and 4 inch.
Torpedo conning-tower: 6 inch.
Torpedo conning-tower tube: 4 inch.

Protective plating

Vertical:
Torpedo bulkheads, 1½ inch and 1 inch.
Funnel-uptakes, 1½ inch between forecastle-deck and shelter-deck, 1 inch between upper-deck and forecastle deck.

Horizontal:
Forecastle-deck, 1 inch over 6-inch battery.
Upper-deck, 1 inch, 1¼ inch and 1½ inch between 'A' and 'Y' barbettes.
Main-deck (flat), 1 inch and 2 inch over magazine and machinery spaces, and 1 inch continued forward and aft.
Main-deck (slope), 2 inch.
Middle-deck, 1 inch over 'Y' magazines and torpedo rooms aft, 2 inch, 3 inch and 4 inch over steering gear. (After Jutland, the plating over 'X' and 'Y' magazines was increased to a total of 2 inches.)
Lower-deck, 1 inch to 2½ inch forward of 'A' barbette.

Machinery

Parsons direct-drive turbines, four shafts.
40,000 SHP = 23 knots at 320 rpm.
Maximum sea-going speed 36,000 SHP = 20.75 knots.

Fuel

3,400 tons oil fuel (normal maximum stowage).
160 tons coal.

Building Costs

Royal Sovereign £2,570,929; *Royal Oak* £2,488,269; *Revenge* £2,406,500; *Resolution* £2,449,680; *Ramillies* £3,295,800.

Complement 920

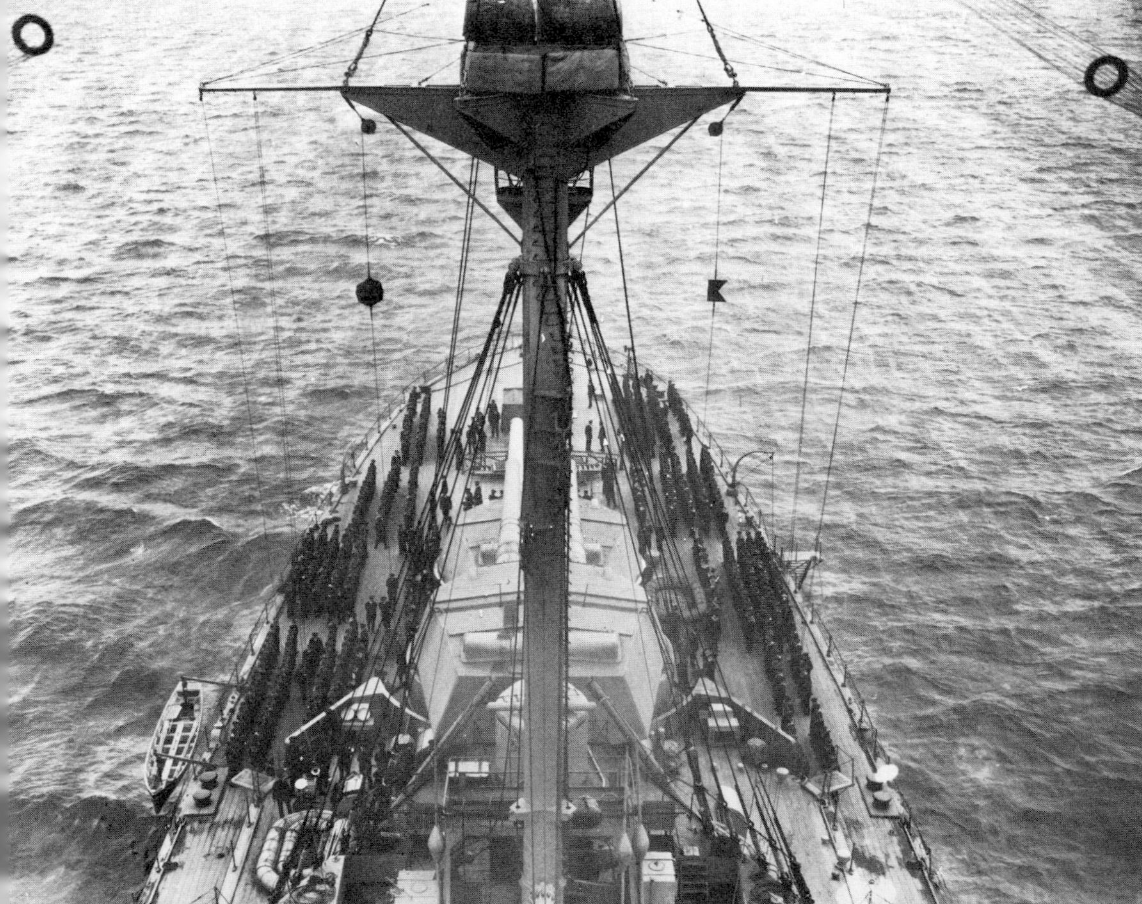

Left: looking over the bows of *Royal Oak* in 1917.

Below: the after superstructure and quarter-deck of *Royal Oak* in 1918. Splinter mattresses can be seen fitted around the starfish-platform on the mainmast.

At first, there was some concern that the fitting of bulges might result in a loss of speed, but later, it was found that the ships with bulges offered far less resistance to the sea. Again, war conditions prevented a comprehensive programme of trials, but the following results were obtained on the Skelmorlie measured mile.

Table 9: Effect of addition of bulges

	Revenge (without bulges)	*Ramillies* (with bulges)
Date	24th March 1916	30th September 1917
Draught	33 feet 1½ inches	32 feet 1¼ inches
Displacement	30,750 tons	33,000 tons
SHP	42,650	42,383
Speed	21.9 knots	21.5 knots
rpm	330	326

On trial, all the ships exceeded the designed SHP, the official figures being:

Royal Sovereign 41,115 SHP
Revenge 41,938 SHP *Ramillies* 42,356 SHP
Resolution 41,406 SHP *Royal Oak* 40,306 SHP

These figures were probably taken at the contractors' trials; where and when is not known.

Auxiliary machinery
Electricity was supplied into a common ring main at 240 volts DC by two oil-driven 125-kilowatt dynamos and two turbine-driven 200-kilowatt dynamos. In August 1917, approval was given to fit an additional 200-kilowatt dynamo driven by a reciprocating engine.

The distilling machinery was similar to that in the *Queen Elizabeth* class but of less capacity. The normal output of the evaporators was 188 tons per day, and the extreme output, 225 tons per day.

General features
All earlier British dreadnoughts were equipped with twin, balanced rudders whose steering qualities were superior to the single type; but in the design of the *Royal Sovereign* class, a single large rudder was supplemented by a small, auxilary rudder forward of it – both of them being on the centre-line. There were three main reasons for this change:

Bottom of page:
Left: *Royal Sovereign* in 1919 or 1920, before the addition of bulges.
Right: *Royal Oak* in 1919. Note the addition, by this date, of a fore-topmast, aircraft flying-off platforms, searchlight-towers and the enlarged fore-top.

Royal Sovereign class

with bulge: inboard profile

1 Engine room
2 Boiler room
3 15-inch Shell room
4 15-inch Magazine
5 15-inch Director-control tower
6 Conning-position
7 Boiler room uptakes
8 Boiler room vents
9 After Director-control tower

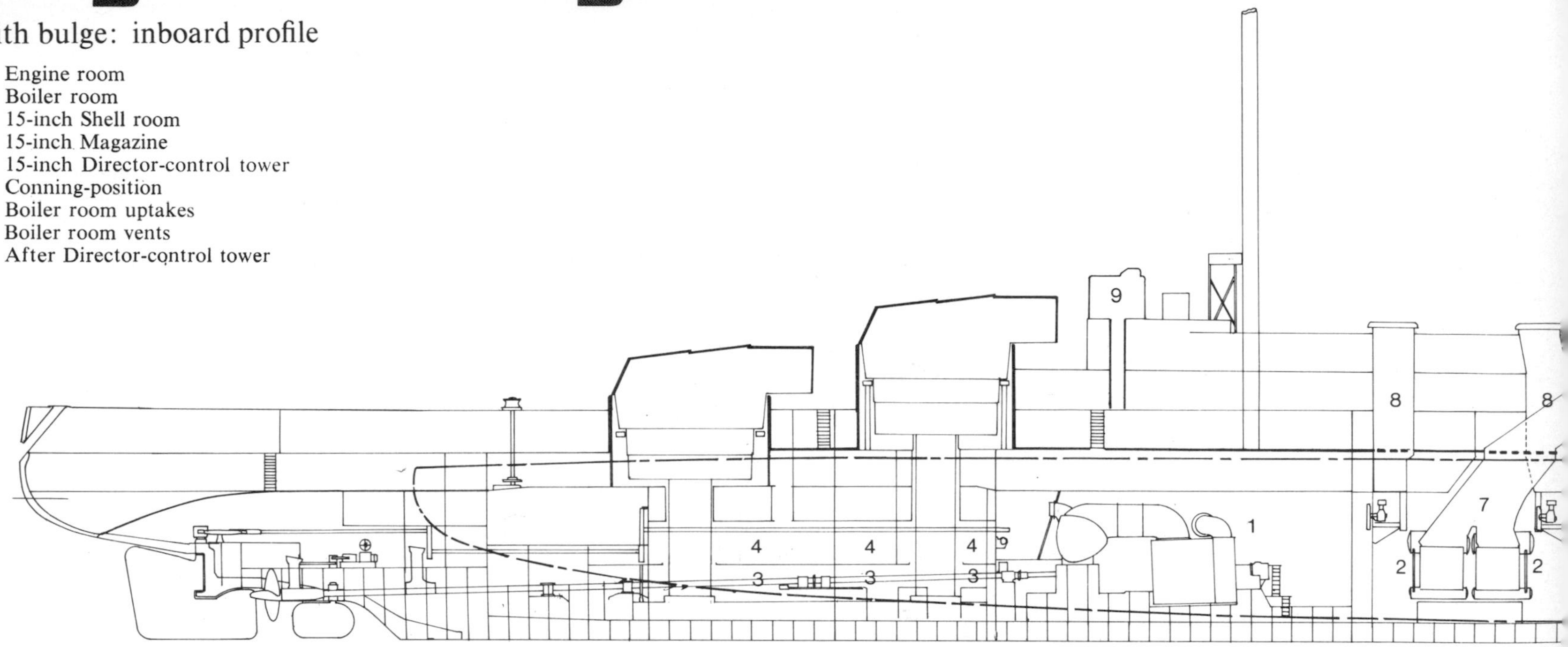

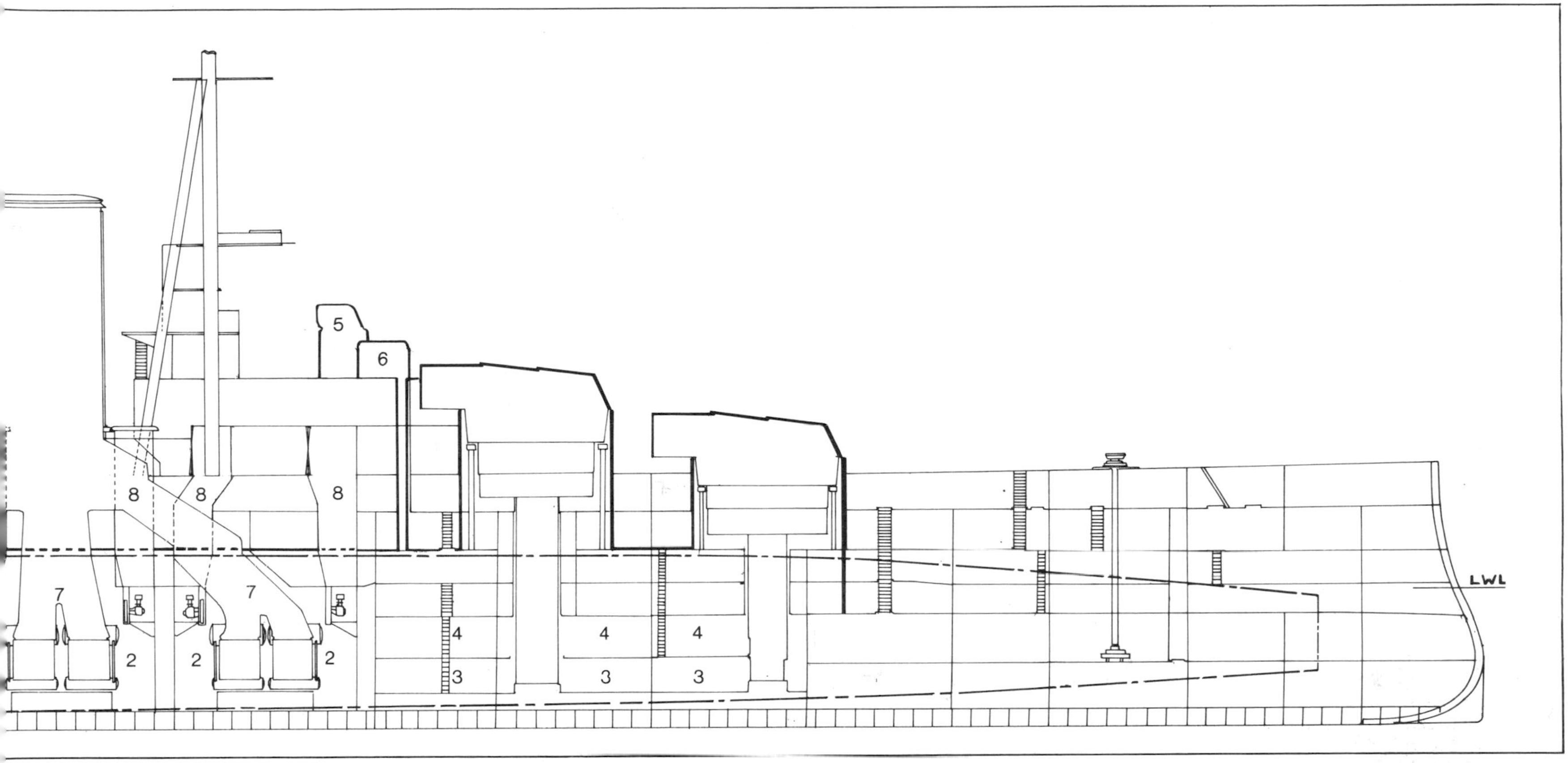

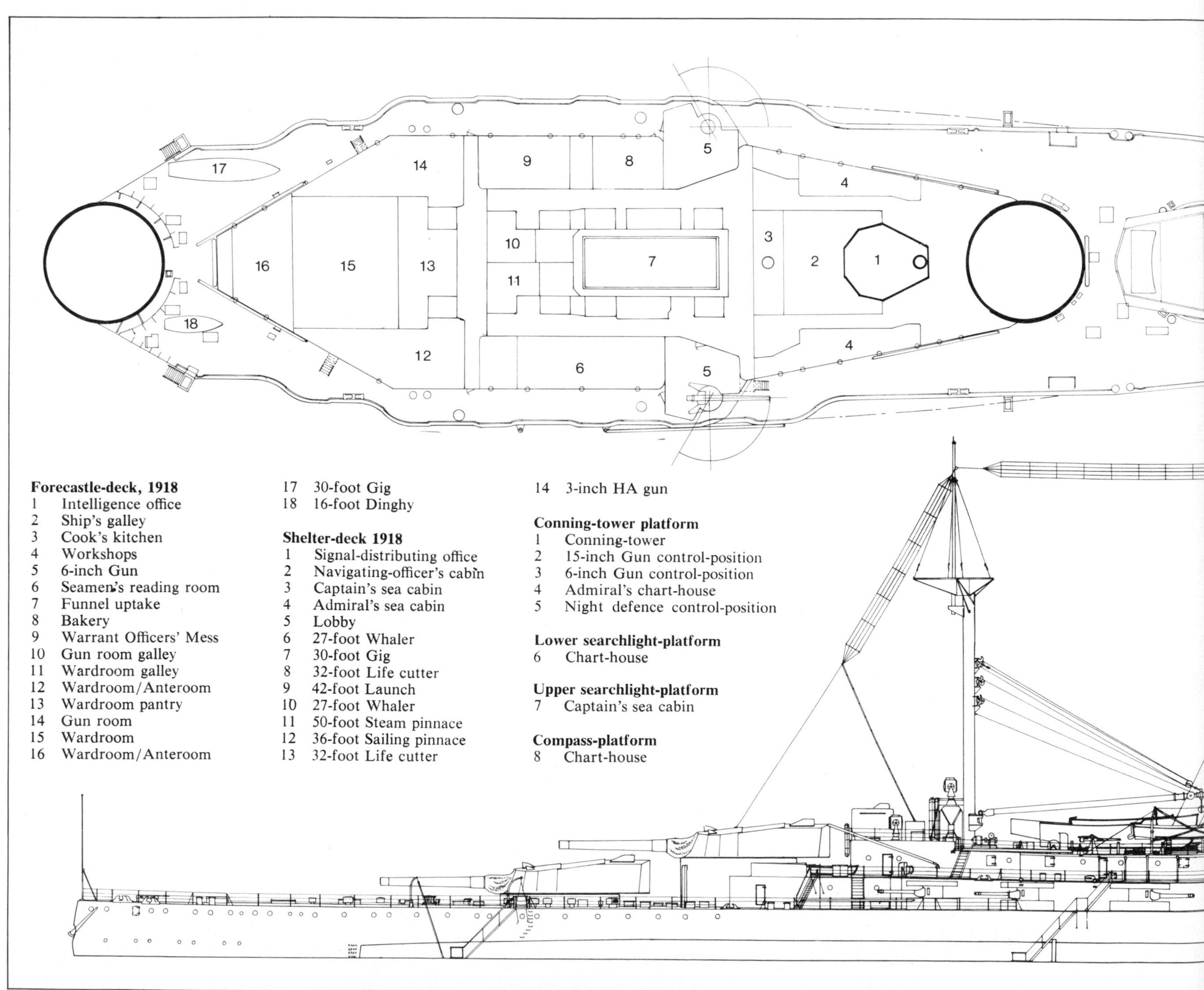
Forecastle-deck, 1918
1 Intelligence office
2 Ship's galley
3 Cook's kitchen
4 Workshops
5 6-inch Gun
6 Seamen's reading room
7 Funnel uptake
8 Bakery
9 Warrant Officers' Mess
10 Gun room galley
11 Wardroom galley
12 Wardroom/Anteroom
13 Wardroom pantry
14 Gun room
15 Wardroom
16 Wardroom/Anteroom
17 30-foot Gig
18 16-foot Dinghy
Shelter-deck 1918
1 Signal-distributing office
2 Navigating-officer's cabin
3 Captain's sea cabin
4 Admiral's sea cabin
5 Lobby
6 27-foot Whaler
7 30-foot Gig
8 32-foot Life cutter
9 42-foot Launch
10 27-foot Whaler
11 50-foot Steam pinnace
12 36-foot Sailing pinnace
13 32-foot Life cutter
14 3-inch HA gun
Conning-tower platform
1 Conning-tower
2 15-inch Gun control-position
3 6-inch Gun control-position
4 Admiral's chart-house
5 Night defence control-position
Lower searchlight-platform
6 Chart-house
Upper searchlight-platform
7 Captain's sea cabin
Compass-platform
8 Chart-house

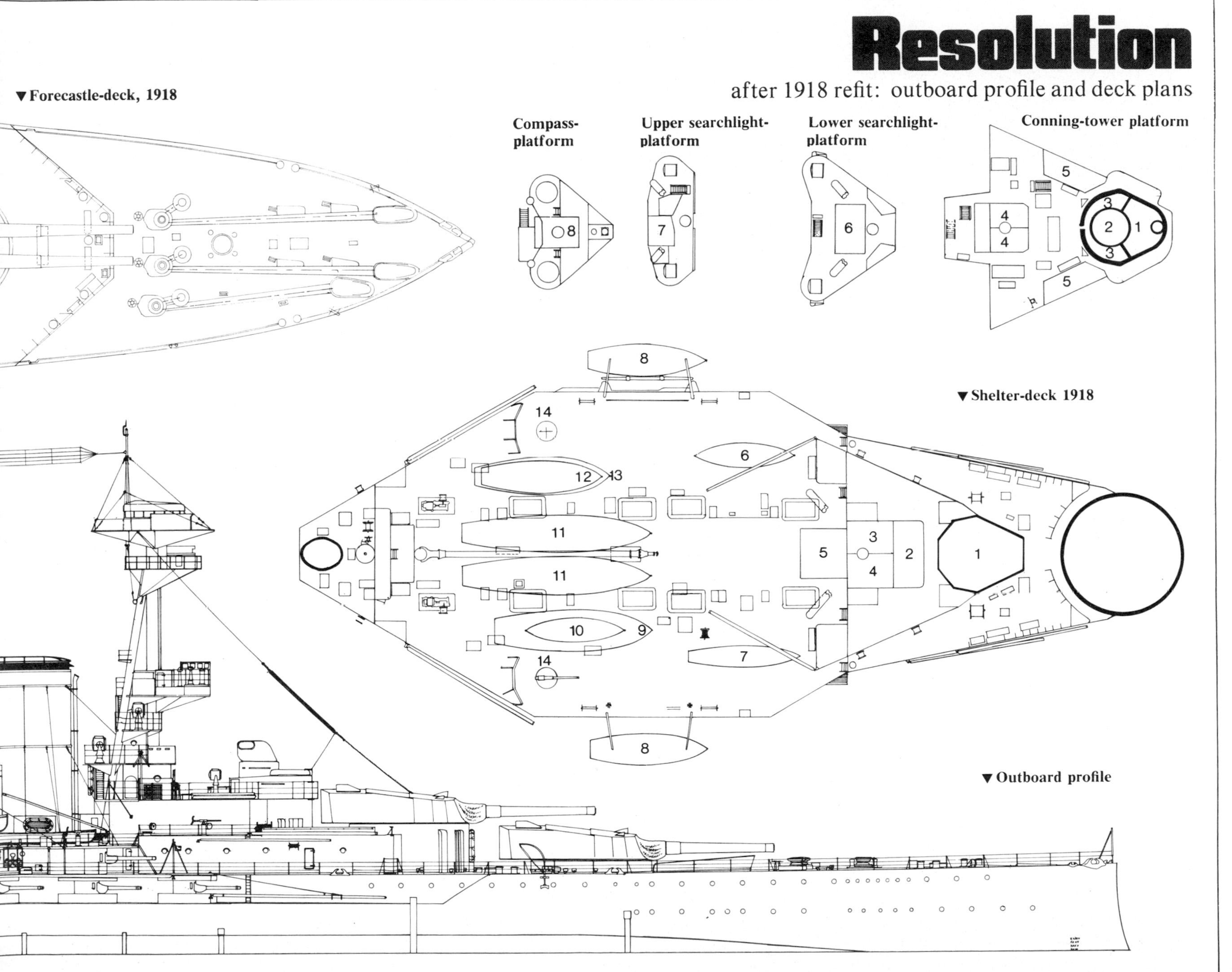
Resolution
after 1918 refit: outboard profile and deck plans
Forecastle-deck, 1918
Compass-platform
Upper searchlight-platform
Lower searchlight-platform
Conning-tower platform
Shelter-deck 1918
Outboard profile

Opposite page
Top: *Resolution* running trials on May 1918, after having been fitted with bulges. Apart from her rig, she has not otherwise been substantially altered, and retains her original fore-top and searchlight arrangements.
Centre: *Ramillies* in 1921. The searchlights have been removed from the tower at the base of the mainmast. *Ramillies* was completed with a searchlight-tower at the base of the mainmast, whilst the other ships of the class had towers of different shape added after their completion.
Below: *Royal Oak* in 1921.

This page: the forecastle deck of *Royal Sovereign* in 1919.

1. The rudders being father apart, there would be less likelihood of them being damaged simultaneously.
2. They offered less resistance to propulsion (with twin rudders this was estimated to be 3 per cent of the ship's total resistance).
3. In some of the ships with twin rudders, great difficulty was experienced in steering with the hand-gear when putting the helm over and bringing it back amidships. In the new design, the hand-gear was connected to the small rudder only, which was easier to manipulate.

The auxiliary rudder was designed to work with the main rudder or independently, in which case, it could be operated by hand, or by electric motor with Hele-Shaw or Williams-Janney steering gear. In service, however, the small rudder proved of little use independently, or in conjunction with the main rudder, and it was later removed.

The improvements to the accommodation in the *Queen Elizabeth* class were repeated in the *Royal Sovereign* class and enhanced by the addition of a large block on the forecastle-deck amidships, accommodating the wardroom and galley and other compartments. A large recreation room was also provided on the forecastle-deck.

Alterations and additions

In addition to those already mentioned, the following modifications were made to the class during and shortly after the First World War:
1. As in the *Queen Elizabeth* class, the forward part of the hull was stiffened by the fitting of intermediate frames and strengthening pieces.
2. To improve watertight sub-division, additional valves were fitted in the ventilation system and fire main, and provision was made for correcting heel by the transference of oil fuel and the flooding of certain watertight compartments. Watertight shutters were fitted under the engine room vents.
3. Additional fresh-water tanks and fresh-water pumps were fitted.
4. Wing engine room lifts were omitted.

Below: *Ramillies* about 1922–3. Just perceptible in this photograph is the range-clock at the after end of the fore-top roof.

Bottom of page: the quarter deck of *Ramillies* in late 1918. Note the range-clock above 'X' turret.

5. After Jutland, additional 1-inch high-tensile plating was fitted on the main-deck over the magazines and on the transverse torpedo bulkheads. Flash-tight scuttles were fitted to the 15-inch magazines and flash-tight handing rooms were provided for the 6-inch magazines.
6. Additional WT arrangements were fitted.
7. Aircraft flying-off platforms were fitted on 'B' and 'X' turrets in all the ships of the class in 1918. Between them, the five ships carried two reconnaissance aircraft and eight fighters.
8. Training scales were painted on 'B' and 'X' turrets ('A' and 'Y' turrets in *Royal Oak* and *Royal Sovereign*) and range-clocks were fitted on the fore-top and on the after side of the mainmast searchlight-tower. The scales were painted out after the war and the range-clocks had been removed by 1925.
9. Searchlight-towers were added to the funnel and mainmast between 1916 and 1918, and searchlight-control was fitted. *Ramillies* was completed with these towers, but the one on her funnel was shorter than those in the other ships of the class. The two searchlights on the mainmast-tower were removed from all the ships in 1921, and the tower itself was removed from *Royal Sovereign* in 1922 and from the remaining ships of the class, between 1923 and 1928.
10. Carley rafts were added, 1916 - 1917.
11. The fore-tops were modified and enlarged between 1917 and 1919, to include a searchlight-control position and a range-finder hood.
12. By 1919, all ships carried short fore- and main-topmasts, but only *Revenge* carried a fore-topgallant-mast; she also carried an additional yard on her foremast. A flagstaff was fitted to *Resolution*'s fore-topmast in 1919, but was removed in 1920.
13. *Revenge* was fitted with a stern-walk in 1919.
14. The 15-foot range-finders in 'B' and 'X' turrets were replaced by 30-foot range-finders in all ships of the class, between 1919 and 1922.
15. Paravane equipment was fitted.
16. Kite-balloon winches were fitted in *Ramillies*, *Revenge*, and *Resolution*, but were removed shortly after the war.

3. Renown and Repulse, 1914 to 1919

The 1914 programme provided for the building of three vessels of the *Royal Sovereign* class – *Renown*, *Repulse* and *Resistance* – and one repeat of the *Queen Elizabeth* class, *Agincourt*.

The *Royal Sovereign* class ships were to be identical with those of the 1913 programme, as modified up to that time, but were to have some small improvements, including torpedo bulkheads of a uniform thickness of 1½ inches. The legend for the new ships was approved by the Board on 13th May 1914.

By June 1914, it had been decided that *Agincourt* was to be built by Portsmouth dockyard and *Resistance* by Devonport dockyard. The remaining two ships were to be put out to tender. The order for *Repulse* was later placed with Palmers, and that for *Renown*, with Fairfields.

Work on all four ships was suspended with the outbreak of war and on 26th August 1914, the two dockyard ships were cancelled as it was then believed that they would not be completed in time to take part in the war.

In October 1914, on Churchill's recommendation, Admiral Fisher returned to the Admiralty as First Sea Lord, replacing the unfairly ousted Admiral, Prince Louis of Battenberg. Churchill wrote in *The World Crisis*: "Lord Fisher hurled himself into the business of new construction with explosive energy. He summoned around him all the naval constructors and shipbuilding firms in Britain, and, in four or five glorious days, every minute of which was pure delight to him, he presented me with schemes for a far greater construction of submarines, destroyers and small craft than I or any of my advisers had ever deemed possible." There can be no doubt that this work contributed considerably to the war effort, but unfortunately Fisher also turned his attention to larger ships and soon revived his campaign for lightly-armoured, heavily-armed battlecruisers. With the introduction of the fast battleships of the *Queen Elizabeth* class, it would seem that the battlecruiser concept was obsolete, but this was not the case. Although the *Queen Elizabeth* class were not intended to replace battlecruisers and, moreover, were not fast enough to provide an effective fast wing to the Battle Fleet, the principle upon which they were built was the correct one, and a similar design with increased speed, would have made the battlecruiser immediately obsolete.

Fisher was reinforced in his arguments by the actions in the Heligoland Bight on 28th August 1914, and the battle of the Falkland Islands, on 8th December 1914, which demonstrated the advantages of gun power combined with high speed, and seemingly vindicated his earlier battlecruiser policy. After the Falklands battle he asked Churchill to obtain Cabinet sanction for the construction of more battlecruisers. The First Lord refused, on the grounds that it would interfere with the construction of more important ships, and that new battlecruisers could not, in any case, be completed before the war ended. Fisher insisted that he could get the ships completed in record time, as he had done with *Dreadnought*, eight years before. He also pointed out that no British capital ship, built or building, possessed sufficient speed to overtake *Lützow*, whose speed was said to be 28 knots. Churchill eventually gave in to pressure – instigated by Fisher – from several sides, and gained Cabinet sanction for the construction of two battlecruisers.

Fisher first approached the Director of Naval Construction (DNC) about the new battlecruisers on 19th December 1914. The design was to be virtually an enlarged version of *Invincible* with speed as the prime requirement, the need of the heaviest possible armament, and armour being relegated to a very poor third place. Fisher wanted ships capable of 32 knots, with a 15-inch armament, and protection on the same scale as the early battlecruisers. He also asked for a shallow draught so that they could be used in his 'Baltic' project (amphibious assault on Germany); a plan that disappeared from the Admiralty as quickly as Fisher himself.

Only six 15-inch mountings could be made available for the new ships and the design was, of necessity, cast around these. The necessary dimensions for the required armament and speed were calculated on 21st December and, on 24th December, Fisher inspected a model of the proposed ships and asked for some modifications to be made before showing it to the Board. The model was completed two days later. On 28th December, the model was approved and the DNC was requested to proceed with the detailed design. The contractors were interviewed by Fisher on the following day. It had been decided to use the contracts for the two suspended *Royal Sovereign* class ships, *Renown* and *Repulse*, but as Palmer's did not possess a slip of sufficient length for the new vessels, their contract was transferred to John Brown. Fisher wanted the ships completed in the record time of fifteen months and had emphasised the point by saying "we must 'scrap' everyone who gets in the way." It was agreed that the fifteen months' building time could be written into the contracts, and the orders were placed immediately. The great speed with which these events progressed, outstripped the normal Admiralty procedures so that the official directive to begin the design was not given until 30th December 1914, and modified contracts were not completed until March 1915.

During the following week, the DNC's department examined the material ordered and received by Fairfield and Palmer's for the two *Royal Sovereign* ships and decided which parts could be employed in the new design, Palmer's material being diverted to Clydebank. By 21st January 1915, the builders had sufficient information to enable them to begin work, and both ships were laid down on 25th January, a little over a month after the design work had begun.

Table 10: Construction of *Renown* and *Repulse*

	Laid down	Launched	Completed	Builder	Machinery
Renown	25th January 1915	4th March 1916	20th September 1916	Fairfield	Fairfield
Repulse	25th January 1915	8th January 1916	18th August 1916	J. Brown	J. Brown

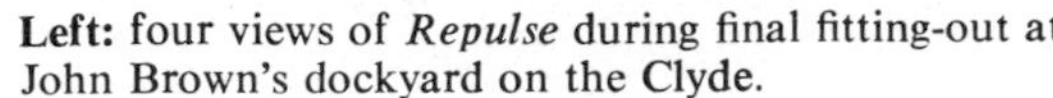

Left: four views of *Repulse* during final fitting-out at John Brown's dockyard on the Clyde.

By 12th April 1915, all the usual drawings, specifications and calculations were complete, and on 22nd April, the design received formal Board approval. No proper legend was produced but Table 11 shows the particulars of *Renown* and *Repulse* as originally designed.

Armament

Since eight guns were regarded as the minimum for efficient 'spotting' with salvo firing, the main armament of six guns – dictated by circumstances – was far from ideal. Protection of the turrets and barbettes was much less than in the 15-inch gun battleships. The turret roofs were of the same thickness but the front plates were 9-inch compared to 13-inch, and the sides were 7-inch compared to 11-inch. The barbette armour showed little improvement upon *Invincible*, having a maximum thickness of 7 inches compared to 10 inches in the *Queen Elizabeth* and *Royal Sovereign* classes.

Fisher had always objected to heavy secondary batteries in the dreadnoughts, so, despite the greater size and power of destroyers at this time, a return was made to the 4-inch gun for the secondary armament. To obtain the greatest possible concentration of firepower, the guns were to be fitted on triple mountings. Initially, the 4-inch quick-firing Mk V gun was to have been installed, but – though an excellent weapon – it was difficult to arrange for director firing. It was suggested that Evershed bearing indicators be substituted, but the First Sea Lord wanted director firing. An alternative would have been to fit the 4-inch breech-loading Mk VIII gun. This was much easier to operate in conjunction with director firing but was not so reliable as the 4-inch Mk V and lacked the latter's "immense volume of fire". The First Sea Lord would have accepted the Mk VIII, but the Director of Naval Ordnance suggested the provision of a new design of breech-loader, combining the quick-firing Mk V body with the Mk VIII breech mechanism. This was approved in April 1915, and the triple mountings carried the 4-inch breech-loading Mk IX guns.

Table 11: Particulars of *Renown* and *Repulse* as originally designed

Load displacement	26,500 tons
Deep displacement	30,835 tons
Length (pp)	750 feet
Length (oa)	794 feet
Beam (max)	90 feet
Draught at lwl	25 feet (forward) 26 feet (aft)
Draught at dwl	29 feet 3 inches (mean)
tpi	103 tons
SHP	112000
Speed at load draught	31.5 knots
Fuel at load draught	1,000 tons
Oil fuel capacity	4,000 tons
Coal capacity	100 tons
Complement	953 (967 as flagship)
Armament:	Six 15 in 42-cal BL Seventeen 4 in 50-cal QF Mk V Two 3 in HA Five Maxim MGs
Armour (all KC or equal quality):	
Belt	6 inch (amidships) 4 inch (forward) and 3 inch (aft)
Bulkheads	4 inch and 3 inch (forward) 4 inch and 3 inch (aft)
Barbettes	7 inch, 5 inch and 4 inch
Turrets	9 inch front, 7 inch sides, 11 inch back, 4¼ inch roof
Conning-tower	10 inch
Conning-tower tube	3 inch and 2 inch
Torpedo conning-tower	3 inch
Vertical protective plating:	
Funnel-uptakes	1½ inch HT side plating, 1½ inch, 1 inch HT above forecastle-deck
Horizontal protective plating:	
Forecastle-deck	¾ inch to 1⅛ inch HT
Main-deck	1 inch HT on flat, 2 inch HT on slope
Lower-deck	2½ inch HT forward and aft of citadel
Weights (tons):	
General equipment	685
Armament	3,335
Machinery	5,660
Engineers stores	120
Oil fuel	1,000
Hull	10,800
Armour and protective plating	4,770
Board margin	130
Total:	26,500

The triple TI Mk I mounting provided each gun with independent elevation up to 30°. Unfortunately, it was not a success since it required a very large crew – thirty-two men – and was generally rather cumbersome.

In January 1915, Fisher issued instructions for the new ships to carry twenty-five Vickers Type 20 automatic mines. Serious difficulties were anticipated in the carrying of these weapons, for which, rails were to have been fitted on the quarter-deck. In July 1915 – after Fisher had left the Admiralty – it was decided not to fit them.

The two 3-inch anti-aircraft guns were positioned on the shelter-deck, abreast the after funnel, and a 2-metre high-angle range-finder was fitted on the 4-inch gun director-platform, on the mainmast.

Fire-control equipment

Two tripod-type directors were provided for the main armament; one, in the armoured revolving hood over the main control-position in the conning-tower, and one in a director-tower on a platform under the fore-top. The two 4-inch director-towers were positioned on platforms; one, on the foremast, under the main director-platform and the other, on the mainmast. A 15-foot range-finder and an open director-sight were provided in each turret, for local control.

Protection

In the original design, the protection was very light – generally on cruiser scale. The main belt was 6 inches thick, 9 feet deep and 462 feet long. It extended from 'A' to 'Y' barbettes, and was continued forward by a 4-inch strake, and aft, by a 3-inch strake. The ends were enclosed by 4-inch and 3-inch bulkheads, those forward being taken up to the upper-deck. The lower edge of the belt was only 1 foot 6 inches below the designed load water-line and 4 feet 3 inches below the deep water-line. From the main-deck to the upper-deck, 1½-inch high-tensile side plating, liberally pierced by side scuttles, provided limited splinter protection to the funnel-uptakes. Above the forecastle-deck, the funnel casings were protected by high-tensile plating, 1½ inches thick on the sides, and 1 inch thick at the ends. Surprisingly, the conning-tower was quite heavily protected by 10-inch armour.

As Fisher was never very clear about the purpose of these ships, it is rather difficult to criticise the scale of protection. The very high speed for which *Renown* and *Repulse* were designed, would have enabled them to accept or decline action, at will. At the time of their construction, they could quite easily have engaged and destroyed light elements of an enemy fleet, and could have easily withdrawn in the face of a more heavily armed adversary.

If we consider that they were unlikely to engage ships of an armament greater than 9.4-inch – which, in any case, they could outrange – then their cruiser-scale protection can be considered adequate. But then it would be necessary to assume: (a) that an enemy would not have built cruisers of even greater speed; (b) that *Renown* and *Repulse* would not have attempted to use their 15-inch guns against enemy battleships and battlecruisers; (c) that an enemy would not have built ships of equal qualities, making the outcome of an action largely a matter of luck; and (d) that an enemy ship would not be built of greater size, greater speed and better protection, rendering *Renown* and *Repulse* obsolete. (The latter situation was actually brought about by the British, themselves, with *Hood,* which combined battlecruiser speed with battleship armour.)

In summary, it can be said that for use against cruisers and light elements, *Renown* and *Repulse* can hardly be faulted except on the grounds of cost, but in the long term their value, as designed, was somewhat limited. Moreover, it seems unlikely that they would not have been employed with the battlecruiser force, engaging enemy battlecruisers, when their light armour would have rendered them extremely vulnerable.

Deck protection was completely inadequate and, after Jutland, the main-deck over the double bottom was curved back into the slope inches on the flat, by the fitting of additional 1-inch plating. This modification was completed before the ships were delivered. When they joined the Grand Fleet, where the loss of the three battlecruisers at Jutland was still a fresh and bitter memory, *Renown* and *Repulse* soon became the subject of considerable criticism because of their lack of armour, and were generally regarded as white elephants. On 20th October 1916, the Commander-in-Chief of the Grand Fleet proposed that additional protection be fitted to the main-deck and lower-deck and to the vertical bulkheads around the lower conning-tower. He further suggested that because the main-decks were being increased in thickness, the thickness of the armour gratings, in trunks passing through the main-deck, also be increased. The Director of Naval Construction suggested that this improvement be extended to the lower-deck. These modifications were approved, and the work was carried out by the builders at Rosyth, in late 1916. The following additions were made:

1. Additional 2-inch high-tensile plating over the engine room on the flat of the main-deck and for 5 feet down the slope on each side.
2. Additional 1-inch high-tensile plating on the lower-deck over the steering gear aft.
3. Additional 2-inch high-tensile plating on the lower-deck over the crowns of the magazines.
4. Additional 2-inch high-tensile plating on the vertical bulkheads of the lower conning-tower space, between stations '98' and '102'.
5. Thickness of lower-deck plating immediately forward of 'A', and abaft 'Y' barbette, increased to a total thickness of 2½ inches.
6. Armour gratings in trunks on main-deck and lower-deck increased in strength.

These modifications increased the weight by 550 tons which was compensated by the fuel stowage being reduced by a similar weight.

Underwater protection

This was similar to that employed in the *Royal Sovereign* and *Queen Elizabeth* classes, but with two important differences. First, the

magazines was increased in thickness to 2 of the armoured deck, as far inboard as the longitudinal bulkhead, forming a kind of internal bulge. Experiments had established the natural tendency of underwater explosions to vent upwards and this internal bulge, extending outboard beyond the side armour, allowed such an explosion greater freedom to do so. Second, the protective longitudinal bulkheads of the type used in earlier ships, were replaced by thin longitudinal bulkheads extending the length of the machinery spaces – those abreast the boilers being doubled to form an air space. During the early stages of construction, the First Sea Lord asked for these bulkheads to be thickened to provide additional protection. Plans were accordingly made to increase the thickness of the lower section to 2 inches and the upper section to 1½ inches, which would have increased the weight by 700 tons and the draught by about 7 inches. Fairfield and John Brown pointed out, that this modification would delay completion of the ships by at least two months and it was decided to revert to the original thickness.

Machinery

Originally, it had been intended to use new light-weight machinery to produce 110,000 shaft horse-power. This was to have been achieved by turbines of a new design, a reduced amount of condensing plant and by higher boiler pressures. The new machinery would have required less space; the weights given to the Director of Naval Construction being:

Engine room	2,360 tons
Boiler room	2,390 tons
Auxiliary machinery	100 tons
Propellers	250 tons
Total	5,100 tons

But a considerable amount of time would have been needed to work out the details and, rather than risk delaying completion of the ships, it was decided to repeat the machinery of the battlecruiser *Tiger*, for which patterns were readily available. The machinery spaces, therefore, were a repeat of those in that ship, except for one additional boiler room, housing three extra boilers, to provide slightly more than the required power for the designed speed.

The Brown Curtis turbines were arranged in two engine rooms which were separated by a centre-line bulkhead. In each engine room were two high-pressure turbines – one ahead and one astern – on the wing shaft – and two low-pressure turbines – one ahead and one astern – (in the same casing) on the inner shaft. Abaft the engine rooms were the condenser rooms (also separated by a centre-line bulkhead) each containing two main condensers and one auxiliary condenser.

There were forty-two Babcock and Wilcox large-tube boilers with a maximum working

Below: broadside view of *Repulse* in the Clyde, on completion in August 1916. Note the equal height of the funnels, in comparison with the photograph on page 51.

pressure of 235 pounds per square inch. They were arranged in six boiler rooms, with three boilers in 'A' boiler room, seven in 'B' and eight in each of the remainder. The total heating surface was 157,206 square feet.

Repulse carried out her contractors' steam trials on 15th August 1916, en route to Portsmouth, and developed approximately 125,000 shaft horse-power. Proper progressive measured-mile trials were carried out on the new course at Arran on 15th September 1916, while she was on her way to join the Grand Fleet. At the time of those trials she was complete with ammunition, stores and two-thirds of her oil fuel. The wind varied from Force 5 to 6 at the start of the trial, to Force 8 at the end.

Table 12: Measured mile trials of *Repulse* off Arran, 15 September 1916

Speed	SHP	rpm	Displacement	Draught
31.725 knots	119025	275.1	29900 tons	28 ft 2½ in

Renown also carried out her steam trials on the Arran course with the results shown in Table 13.

Table 13: Trials of *Renown* off Arran, 20 September 1916

Trial	Speed	SHP	rpm	Displacement	Draught (forward)	Draught (aft)
Measured mile	32.58 knots	126300	281.6	27900 tons	26 feet	27 feet 3 inches
4 hours full power	32.284 knots	123850	279	—	—	—

In 1919, while at sea, *Renown* recorded a speed of 29.85 knots at a displacement of 31,870 tons.

Auxiliary machinery

Electricity was supplied at 220 volts DC into a common ring main by two reciprocating steam-driven 200-kilowatt dynamos, one oil-driven 150-kilowatt dynamo and one turbine-driven 200-kilowatt dynamo. The distilling machinery consisted of six evaporators and two distilling condensers, giving a combined normal output of 490 tons of fresh water per day. This machinery was arranged in two sets, one in each condenser room. Three steam-driven hydraulic pumping-engines were installed, to supply power for working the turrets.

Stability

Table 14 shows the displacement of *Repulse* as completed, and that of *Renown* in 1917, after her horizontal protection had been improved.

Table 14: Displacements of *Renown* and *Repulse* (tons)

	Renown 1917	*Repulse* 1916	Calculated
Armament	3,391	3,420	3,335
Machinery	6,068	6,009	5,660
Engineers stores	87	87	120
Equipment	685	685	685
Hull, armour and protective plating	16,189	15,653	15,570
Board margin	0	0	0
Oil fuel	1,000	1,000	1,000
Totals:	27,420	26,854	26,500

After her protection had been improved, the legend displacement of *Repulse* increased to 27,333 tons; and by June 1917, the displacement of *Renown* had further increased to 27,947 tons.

Despite the weak protection, the GM was comparatively low. The figures given in Table 15 were established by inclining experiments.

Table 15: Stability particulars of *Repulse* and *Renown*

	Repulse 1916			*Renown* 1917		
Condition	Legend	Deep	Light	Legend	Deep	Light
Draught (forward)	25 ft	29 ft 9 in	23 ft 6 in	25 ft 5½ in	30 ft 2 in	24 ft 1 in
Draught (aft)	26 ft 7 in	29 ft 7 in	25 ft 10½ in	27 feet	30 ft 1 in	26 ft 3½ in
Displacement	26,548 tons	31,592 tons	25,579 tons	24,420 tons	32,220 tons	26,145 tons
GM	3.45 ft	6.1 ft	2.8 ft	3.5 ft	6.2 ft	2.95 ft

General features

Because of the panting experienced in *Queen Elizabeth* during trials, *Renown* and *Repulse* received a considerable amount of stiffening to the forward section of the hull, in May 1915. This modification was made on the principle of 'better safe than sorry', for the structural arrangements in this area were already slightly better than those in *Tiger*, about which no adverse reports had been received.

During trials in the Atlantic, *Repulse* behaved well in a considerable sea, and had a steady, even motion. The large flare forward prevented the sea breaking over the forecastle, but did not stop the wind from blowing spray over the superstructure. The only structural weakness revealed, was a slight sinking of the forecastle-deck right forward, between the hawse-pipes. Additional pillars were later fitted under the forecastle-deck in both ships, but their construction was too light, and further weaknesses were soon revealed, first during the gun-trials and later, while in service. Both ships spent frequent periods in dockyards, having decks and bulkheads stiffened and additional pillars fitted.

In earlier ships, it had been found that funnels were too low (generally, the tops were level with the navigating-platforms) and a great deal of trouble had been caused by smoke getting into the bridge-platforms. In June 1915, the Director of Naval Construction was requested to examine the possibility of increasing funnel heights in the latest designs. He pointed out that in *Renown*, the funnels were much farther away from the compass-platform than in earlier ships and that, in any case, the bridge – for navigating purposes – was outside the conning-tower, as in the *Royal Sovereign* class. (This was to accustom officers, in peacetime, to navigate from the conning-tower platform. As most officers disdained the use of the armoured conning-tower, preferring the unprotected but higher compass-platform, it seems unlikely that the arrangement had much value.) So it was decided to make no alterations until experience had been gained from the ships of the *Royal Sovereign*

Above: the quarter-deck of *Repulse* in October 1917, showing the aircraft arrangements on 'Y' turret roof.

Below: *Repulse* in 1918, with fore-funnel raised by six feet, the addition of searchlight-towers, the main-topmast removed and with aircraft flying-off platforms on 'B' and 'Y' turrets. She is wearing an anti-rangefinder camouflage scheme, of dark- and light-grey.

class. But trouble occurred during trials, and in both ships, the height of the fore funnel was increased by about six feet.

To save weight and building time, no wood decks were fitted, and to compensate the loss of the insulating qualities of deck planking, lagging was fitted under the weather-decks, in living spaces.

The greater part of the accommodation for officers was sited in the usual area, on the main-deck aft, but the senior officers were quartered on the upper-deck, near the ward-room. Cabins for an admiral and his staff, were installed in the after end of the super-structure on the forecastle-deck.

In September 1915, large numbers of iron-workers were transferred from work on *Ramillies* at Dalmuir, to *Repulse* at Fairfields. Neither ship was completed in the specified fifteen months, but – for big ships – their building times were remarkably short.

Alterations and additions

1. *Repulse* was the first capital ship to be equipped with an aircraft flying-off platform. In the autumn of 1917, an experimental platform was erected on 'B' turret, from which, on 1st October, Squadron Leader Rutland, took off successfully in a Sopwith Pup. A second platform was erected on 'Y' turret and, on 8th October, Rutland again successfully flew his aircraft off, this time over the back of the turret. Early in 1918, *Renown* was fitted with similar platforms on 'B' and 'Y' turrets. Between them, the two ships carried two reconnaissance aircraft and two fighters.

2. Anti-flash arrangements were fitted to the magazines after Jutland.

3. Training scales were painted on 'A' and 'Y' turrets and range-clocks were fitted on the fore-top and mainmast. The training scales were painted out after the war.

4. As completed, each ship carried eight 36-inch searchlights; two on the bridge, two on the fore funnel and four on the after funnel. In *Repulse*, the searchlight-platforms on the after funnel were staggered, one searchlight being higher than the rest. Those in *Renown*

Above left: *Renown* in 1920.

Below left and above right: during her 1919/20 refit.

Below right: *Renown* after her 1920/21 refit, with the aftermost 4-inch triple mounting removed, an additional deck-house between the funnels and 30-foot range-finders added to the conning-tower hood and 'Y' turret.

were all at the same level, joined by a gangway. In 1917, the searchlight-platforms on the after funnel were replaced by four searchlight-towers. The searchlight-platforms on the fore funnel were removed and the two searchlights were re-positioned on new platforms on the mainmast. The two searchlights on the compass-platform were replaced by 9-foot range-finders and were moved down to new positions on the admiral's platform.

5. Carley rafts were added during 1917.

6. Fore-tops were modified and a 12-foot range-finder tower was fitted on the roof.

7. In 1919, *Renown* was fitted with fore- and main-topgallant-masts.

8. The bridgework was slightly modified.

Renown refit, 1919 to 1920

Renown underwent a short refit to make her suitable for the tour of H.R.H. the Prince of Wales to the United States of America and Australasia in 1920–21. The following modifications and repairs were made:

1. No. 5 4-inch triple-mounting and support were removed and the deck of No. 4 4-inch mounting was extended aft to form a roof over No. 5 gun-deck.

2. The quarter-deck, forecastle-deck, boat-deck and superstructure from the mainmast aft were fitted with wood deck planking.

3. The 15-foot range-finder in 'Y' turret was replaced by a 30-foot range-finder and a second 20-foot range-finder was fitted on the back of the revolving conning-tower hood, in addition to the 15-foot range-finder already positioned there.

4. Additional structure was built around the base of the second funnel on the shelter-deck.

5. Repairs were made to the boiler brickwork and to leaky reserve feed-water, fuel and lubricating-oil tanks.

6. General refit of auxiliary machinery.

7. Aircraft flying-off platforms were removed.

Repulse refit, 1918 to 1921

By 1917, *Renown* and *Repulse* were seen as very weak links in the battlecruiser force, and suggestions were being made for drastic

Left: *Repulse* after her 1918/21 refit with a deepened armour belt, which served to distinguish her from *Renown*.

improvements to their protection. The Director of Naval Construction proposed that the ship's sides – from the bottom of the 6-inch belt up to the forecastle-deck – be covered by armour gratings clad with ½-inch covering plates. He further proposed that the engine rooms be protected by bulges. These would extend well forward so as to avoid trim by the bow or, alternatively, they would extend the length of the engine and condenser rooms only, but would be filled with crushing-tubes to increase their weight. The C in C, Grand Fleet agreed to these proposals, in general, and suggested that additional protection be provided for the turret redoubts and front plates, and that the bulges with tubes be extended well forward to include the forward boiler rooms, in order to give a more uniform protection.

Later, it was suggested that the 6-inch belt in one of the ships be replaced by the 9-inch armour of the *Almirante Cochrane* with the thickness of the ship's side, above the belt, being increased to 4 inches of high-tensile plating. (The battleships *Almirante Latorre* and *Almirante Cochrane* were under construction at Elswick for the Chilean government. Work was suspended in August 1914, and later, the ships were purchased by the British government. *Latorre* was completed as HMS *Canada* and *Cochrane* was converted to an aircraft carrier, later becoming HMS *Eagle*.)

The other vessel could have either a new 9-inch belt, or the special gratings over the existing belt, as had been suggested by the DNC. The latter alternative would depend on the success of firing trials, but it is not known if these were ever held. By July 1918, it had been decided to take both ships in hand at Portsmouth, where *Repulse* was to be fitted with *Almirante Cochrane*'s armour. The work on *Renown* was not undertaken until 1923, but *Repulse* went into dock in December 1918 and the following modifications were made:

1. Bulges were fitted from station '31' to station '292'. The lower bulges were divided longitudinally into two compartments from station '142' to station '248', the inner lower and upper bulges being filled with crushing tubes. The bulges covered the submerged torpedo room, magazine and machinery spaces and increased the beam to 101 feet. It was necessary to lengthen the main derrick by 4 feet to allow for the increased beam. The bulges were strengthened in three places on each side, and catamaran fenders were supplied to prevent damage by the ship's boats.

2. A 9-inch armour belt was fitted from the armour shelf to the main-deck, replacing the original 6-inch armour which was then fitted between the main-deck and the upper-deck.

3. An additional 4-inch armour bulkhead was fitted between the main-deck and the upper-deck at station '286', across the after end of 'Y' barbette.

4. Additional high-tensile plating, 1-inch on the flat and 2-inch on the slopes of the main-deck over the magazines, increased the thickness to 3 inches on the flat and 4 inches on the slopes.

5. Additional 1-inch high-tensile plating was fitted on the lower-deck over the magazines, increasing the thickness to 3 inches.

6. Suitable stiffening was provided to the frames between the main-deck and the upper-deck in way of the re-positioned 6-inch belt

7. Eight above-water torpedo tubes were fitted in pairs on the upper-deck, one pair on each beam just abaft the funnel, and one pair on each beam just before the break of the forecastle.

8. An additional turbo-driven dynamo was fitted.

9. An additional set of magazine-cooling machinery was fitted.

10. Three 30-foot range-finders were fitted. One was sited behind 'A' turret (in addition to the existing 15-foot range-finder), one behind the conning-tower hood (in addition to the existing 15-foot range-finder) and one replaced the 15-foot range-finder inside 'Y' turret.

11. All magazines were lagged internally.

12. The quarter-deck and forecastle-deck were fitted with wood planking as far forward as the cable holders.

13. A main-topgallant-mast was fitted.

14. An additional wireless transmitting office was fitted between the funnels.

Repulse

1916, as after trials: outboard profile

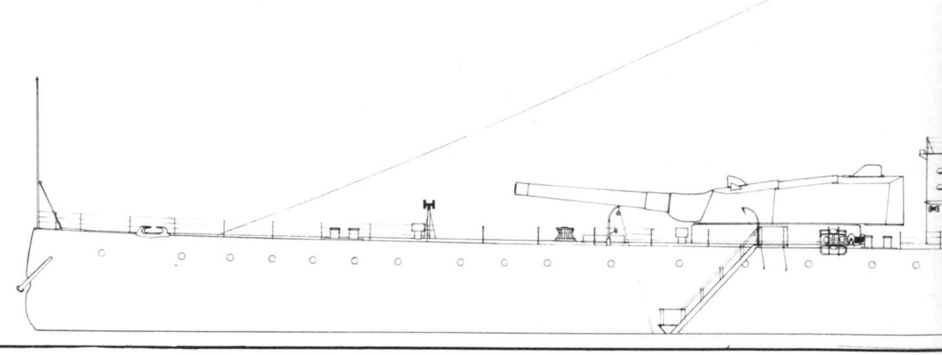

15. The admiral's platform was extended aft on each side of the fore funnel to provide a flag-deck.

It had been intended to fit protective gratings to the barbettes and gun-shields but this was not done. Photographs of *Repulse* indicate that reinforcing plates were added to the gun-shields but later, these plates were removed.

The refit, completed in January 1921, added over 4,500 tons to the displacement, but because of the additional buoyancy provided by the bulges, the increase in the draught was only 1 foot. The following figures were established from an inclining experiment conducted in December 1920.

Legend condition:
Ship fully-equipped, with reserve feed-tanks empty, 1,000 tons of oil fuel and 80 rounds per gun for the 15-inch armament.
Displacement: 32,740 tons.
Mean draught: 27 feet 11 inches.
GM: 4.9 feet.

Ordinary deep condition:
Ship fully-equipped with 104 tons of coal and 3,830 tons of oil fuel.
Displacement: 36,920 tons.
Mean draught: 31 feet 1 inch.
GM: 6.4 feet.

Extreme deep condition:
As in ordinary deep condition but with full oil-fuel stowage of 4,243 tons.
Displacement: 37,490 tons.
Mean draught: 31 feet 6 inches.
GM: 6.5 feet.

Light displacement: 31,450 tons.

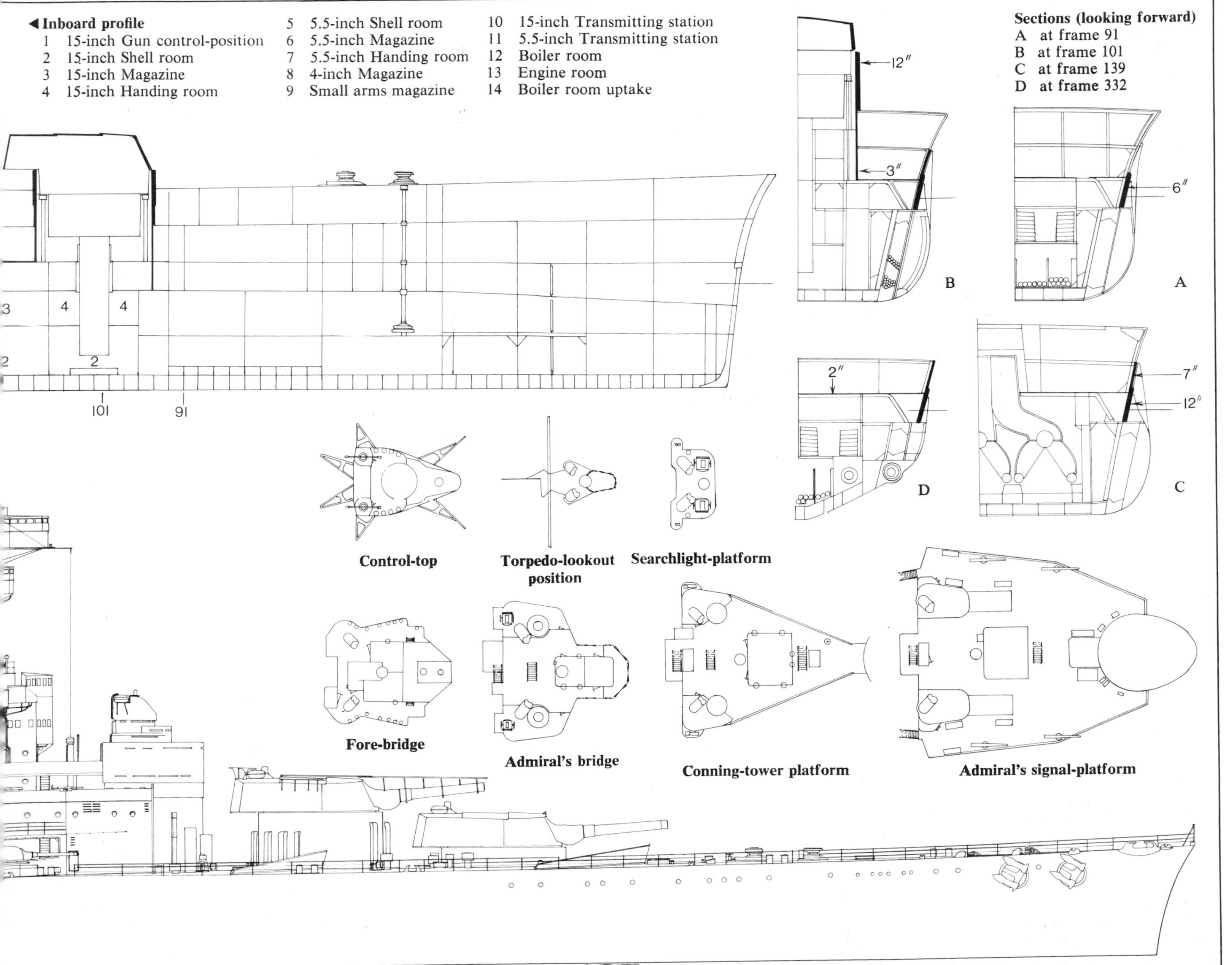
◀Inboard profile
1 15-inch Gun control-position
2 15-inch Shell room
3 15-inch Magazine
4 15-inch Handing room
5 5.5-inch Shell room
6 5.5-inch Magazine
7 5.5-inch Handing room
8 4-inch Magazine
9 Small arms magazine
10 15-inch Transmitting station
11 5.5-inch Transmitting station
12 Boiler room
13 Engine room
14 Boiler room uptake
Sections (looking forward)
A at frame 91
B at frame 101
C at frame 139
D at frame 332
12″
3″
6″
2″
7″
12″
A
B
C
D
3
4
4
2
2
101
91
Control-top
Torpedo-lookout position
Searchlight-platform
Fore-bridge
Admiral's bridge
Conning-tower platform
Admiral's signal-platform

4. Hood, 1915 to 1920

In November 1915, the Board of Admiralty approved and the Treasury sanctioned a proposal to construct an experimental battleship, the design of which was to be evolved from war experience. During the previous month, the Third Sea Lord, Admiral Sir F. C. Tudor, had given the following instructions, in a memorandum dated 4th December 1915, to the Director of Naval Construction, regarding this design: ". . . take the armament, armour and engine power of the '*Queen Elizabeth*' as the standard and build round them a hull which should draw as little water as was (*sic*) considered practicable and safe, and which should embody all the latest proposed protection and improvements against underwater attack".

The shallow draught was requested as the result of a critical examination of the *Iron Duke* and *Queen Elizabeth* designs in conjunction with a study of the effects of mine and torpedo damage. It was considered that the main faults in these designs were excessive draught and insufficient freeboard, both of which were accentuated by the large amount of fuel carried under war conditions for which insufficient allowance had been made at the design stage. In addition it was realised that the positioning of the non-watertight secondary batteries on the upper-deck effectively reduced the apparent freeboard and the angle to which the ships could heel without danger. These faults gave rise to the following conditions.

1. Because water pressure increases with depth, internal bulkheads had to withstand greater pressures than those of a shallow draught vessel.

2. The ratio of reserve of buoyancy to displacement was low.

3. The embrasures of the 6-inch guns tended to make the ships bad seaboats. They were extremely wet in heavy weather and the guns were very difficult to operate in any sort of sea.

The preliminary sketch design and legend for the new battleship were completed on 29th November, and they were submitted to the Board on the following day. By increasing the length to 810 feet(oa) and the beam to 104 feet(maximum), the DNC had reduced the draught to 26 feet 3 inches – a 22 per cent improvement upon *Queen Elizabeth*. (A 50 per cent reduction had been asked for, but this was found to be impracticable.) The form thus produced, provided an estimated speed in excess of 26.5 knots with the same shaft horse-power as in the *Queen Elizabeth* class. The secondary armament was to consist of twelve 5-inch guns, of new design, all sited on or above the forecastle-deck. The ship's side, therefore, was intact up to the forecastle-deck and this, together with the shallow draught, provided a much greater ratio of reserve of buoyancy to displacement, and freeboard to draught, than in any previous British dreadnought battleship. The armour protection was considered equal to that of *Queen Elizabeth* although the hull armour was not of equal maximum thickness. Underwater protection was provided by bulges, below the waterline, extending the full length of the magazine and machinery spaces. The form of these bulges – which were part of the ship's structure, and not additions to it – was based on a similar arrangement that was to be tested on the Chatham Float on 6th December. The bulges were divided longitudinally into two groups of compartments. The inboard compartments were filled with five rows of crushing-tubes, the outboard compartments served as air spaces. The air spaces provided in the sketch designs was slightly wider than that employed on the Chatham Float. The form of the bulge, together with a full-length flare of the ship's side above the waterline added considerably to stability in the event of damage.

The chief disadvantage of the design lay in its large external dimensions, for which there was a lack of sufficiently large building and docking facilities. At this time she could have been accommodated in the graving-dock at Rosyth, or in 'C' and 'D' locks at Portsmouth, but no other British naval docks were capable of taking a vessel of this type. (Some of the larger floating docks could have been used, but these would have proved far from ideal, in view of the considerable overhang of the vessel at bow and stern.)

In a memorandum to the Third Sea Lord, dated 6th December 1915, the First Sea Lord, Admiral Sir Henry Jackson pointed out that naval construction would certainly form a part of Britain's post-war economy, and that Britain could ill afford to give the United States of America a ". . . new idea, which they would be able to develop more rapidly than ourselves and an 810ft battleship must be classed as a new idea". The considerable cost of a fleet of these vessels would also have had to include the provision of larger docking and berthing accommodation.

He further considered that at that stage of the war, insufficient experience had been gained, and no major lessons had been learned, other than that it was possible for our capital ships to be incapacitated by a lucky hit, or be sunk by a single mine or torpedo. (The battlecruiser *Lion* had been put out of action during the battle of the Dogger Bank, by a shell which penetrated and exploded in the engine room. The battleship *Audacious* was sunk by a single mine in 1914, but a large part of the blame for this loss can be apportioned to bad damage-control.) Nevertheless, he also made the following comment – showing that the effects of plunging shellfire were not unappreciated before the battle of Jutland: "Long range (gun) fire has improved and been proved to be practicable and, consequently, deck protection (in addition to bulging) seems necessary – as exemplified in *Inflexible* at Dardanelles".

After studying the design, and the arguments against it, the Board asked for a second design to be prepared for a vessel similar to the original design but – for docking purposes – having a beam no greater than that of *Queen Elizabeth*. The DNC produced two sketch designs for battleships with a beam of 90 feet(maximum) but apparently, only one of these (for a 25-knot ship) was submitted to the Board. Designated 'B' – the original became design 'A' – it was completed on 1st January 1916, but was kept back for a short

Below: bow and quarter views of *Hood* on the building slip. Note the recess along the ship's side. This was to take the armour belt which, following normal practice, was added later, during the fitting-out.

period pending the results of the Chatham Float experiments. These demonstrated that the protection of capital ships from underwater attack was a practical proposition, but the form of the bulge fitted to the Float was shown to be only just adequate to resist the explosion of a torpedo warhead containing 400 pounds of TNT. As the bulge protection in design 'A' was superior to that fitted to the Float, and the bulge in design 'B', inferior, the DNC strongly urged the adoption of the broader ship, despite the docking restrictions, as this was the only one he could confidently recommend as being reasonably secure against submarine attack. In addition, many of the advantages gained in design 'A' had been reduced in design 'B'. Clearly a reduction in beam was undesirable and the Board decided that a reduction in length would at least allow the ship to be safely accommodated in larger floating docks. On 6th January, two more designs, 'C1' and 'C2', were asked for, in which the speed was to be reduced to 22 knots to allow a reduction in weight and therefore in length. Design 'C1' was to have full bulge protection but 'C2' was to have the best bulge protection possible on a length not exceeding that of *Queen Elizabeth*, and both ships were to be given the minimum possible draught.

The two sketch designs were completed on 18th January and were then submitted to the Board. Design 'C1' had the same beam and draught as Design 'A' but was 100 feet shorter. Design 'C2' was only 610 feet in length, which necessitated an increase in draught of 1 foot 3 inches. Underwater protection in both designs was similar to that in Design 'A' with five rows of tubes, which were considered adequate against the most powerful torpedoes then in existence. To save weight, it had been found necessary to reduce the thickness of some of the armour and to reduce the number of guns in the secondary battery.

After examining these designs, the Board asked the DNC to prepare a modified 'A' design (Design 'D') with the same draught, beam, armour and armament but of reduced length and with a speed equal to that of *Queen Elizabeth*. It was also decided that the introduction of a new calibre gun, the 5-inch, was "unnecessary and undesirable", and that the 5.5-inch gun should be employed in the new ships. The legend particulars of the designs which the Board now had under consideration, are given in Table 16.

Some, or all of these designs, were forwarded to Admiral Jellicoe, Commander-in-Chief, Grand Fleet, for his appreciation. His reply made it clear that, in his opinion, the Admiralty were proceeding along entirely wrong lines. He pointed out that the British superiority in battleships was great and that there was, at this time, no requirement for the construction of ships of this type. There was, however, a great need of battlecruisers. Germany was known to be building at least three fast battlecruisers and it was considered probable that their speed would approach 30 knots and that their armament would consist of guns of 15.2-inch calibre. (In 1915, Germany laid down four battlecruisers – *Mackensen*, *Ersatz Freya*, *Graf Spee* and *Ersatz Friedrich Carl* – apart from the last named ship, all were launched but none was completed. The armament was to consist of eight 35-cm (13.77-inch) guns and the design speed was 27 knots. Three more battlecruisers – *Ersatz Yorck*, *Ersatz Gneisenau* and *Ersatz Scharnhorst* – were laid down in 1916 but were never launched. The armament was to have been eight 38-cm (15-inch) guns and the speed, 27.3 knots.) *Renown*, *Repulse* and the light battlecruisers of the *Courageous* type, then under construction, possessed the necessary speed to counter the German ships, but unfortunately, they would be unable to compete with them because of inadequate protection. Noting the 25- to 27-knot speeds in some of the designs, Jellicoe pointed out that his experience of the 25-knot *Queen Elizabeth* class had convinced him that an intermediate speed was of little use, and he suggested that the new design should be for a battlecruiser of 30 knots or a battleship of 21 knots, but preferably the former.

Having thus had a considerable amount of cold water thrown over the original designs, the DNC prepared six specifications for battlecruisers with a speed of 30 knots or more, to suit the requirements of the C in C. As the beam and length could not reasonably be increased, the extra machinery weight had to be accommodated by an increase in the draught, and much of the advantage gained by the shallow draught of the earlier designs was therefore lost. The specifications for the first two designs were completed on the same day as Design 'D', and the remaining four were completed on 17th February 1916.

In the first three designs, six 18-inch guns could have been mounted as an alternative armament, but this would have increased the

Table 16: Legend particulars of battleships A to D, 1915 to 1916

	A	B	C1	C2	D
	29th November 1915	1st January 1916	18th January 1916	18th January 1916	1st February 1916
Length (oa)	810 feet	800 feet	707 feet	657 feet	757 feet
Length (pp)	760 feet	750 feet	660 feet	610 feet	710 feet
Beam	104 feet	90 feet	104 feet	100 feet	104 feet
Draught (forward)	23 feet	25 feet 3 inches	23 feet	24 feet 3 inches	23 feet
Draught (aft)	24 feet	26 feet 3 inches	24 feet	25 feet 3 inches	24 feet
Displacement	31,000 tons	29,500 tons	27,600 tons	25,250 tons	29,850 tons
Freeboard (forward)	28 feet	26 feet	28 feet	26 feet 9 inches	27 feet
Freeboard (aft)	20 feet	19 feet	20 feet	19 feet	19 feet
Deep load draught (mean)	26 feet 3 inches	28 feet 3 inches	26 feet 6 inches	28 feet 3 inches	26 feet 6 inches
Shaft horse-power	75,000	60,000	40,000	40,000	65,000
Speed at load draught	26·5–27 knots	25 knots	22 knots	22 knots	25·5 knots
Oil fuel at load draught	1,000 tons	1,000 tons	1,000 tons	1,000 tons	1,000 tons
Oil fuel capacity	3,500 tons	3,000 tons	3,000 tons	3,000 tons	3,000 tons
Armament:	eight 15-inch twelve 5-inch two 3-inch HA	eight 15-inch twelve 5-inch two 3-inch HA	eight 15-inch ten 5-inch one 3-inch HA	eight 15-inch ten 5-inch one 3-inch HA	eight 15-inch twelve 5·5-inch one 3-inch HA
Torpedo tubes	four	four	two	two	two
Weights:					
General equipment	750 tons	750 tons	700 tons	700 tons	750 tons
Machinery	3,550 tons	3,250 tons	2,450 tons	2,450 tons	3,350 tons
Armament	4,750 tons	4,750 tons	4,650 tons	4,650 tons	4,700 tons
Armour & protective plating	9,150 tons	8,600 tons	7,860 tons	7,770 tons	8,500 tons
Hull	11,650 tons	11,000 tons	10,800 tons	9,500 tons	11,400 tons
Fuel	1,000 tons	1,000 tons	1,000 tons	1,000 tons	1,000 tons
Board margin	150 tons	150 tons	140 tons	130 tons	150 tons
Total:	31,000 tons	29,500 tons	27,600 tons	26,250 tons	29,850 tons

Armour:	A and B	C1 C2 and D
Belt	10-inch	10-inch
Bulkheads	3-inch to 6-inch	3-inch to 5-inch
Barbettes	10-inch maximum	9-inch maximum
Gun-houses	11-inch to 9-inch	11-inch to 9-inch
Conning-tower (forward)	11-inch	10-inch
Torpedo conning-tower (aft)	6-inch	6-inch
Conning-tower tube	4-inch	—
Backing behind armour	1-inch minimum	1-inch minimum
Vertical protective plating:		
Bulkheads in wake of citadel	1½-inch and 1-inch	1½-inch and ¾-inch
Funnel-uptakes	1½-inch	1½-inch
Horizontal protective plating:		
Forecastle-deck	1½-inch	1½-inch
Upper-deck (amidships)	1-inch	1-inch
Main-deck	½-inch	1½-inch
Lower-deck (forward)	1-inch to 2-inch	1-inch to 1½-inch
Lower-deck (aft)	2½-inch to 3-inch	2½-inch

Note: The other design completed on 1st January 1916 was generally similar to design 'B' except for the following details. Legend draught, 26 feet 3 inches; deep draught, 29 feet 3 inches; displacement, 30,350 tons; 75,000 SHP = 27 knots.

Table 17: Particulars of battlecruiser Designs 1 to 6, 1916

	1	2	3	4	5	6
	1st February 1916	1st February 1916	17th February 1916	17th February 1916	17th February 1916	17th February 1916
Length (oa)	885 feet	840 feet	860 feet	757 feet	830 feet	880 feet
Length (pp)	835 feet	790 feet	810 feet	710 feet	780 feet	830 feet
Beam	104 feet	104 feet	104 feet	104 feet	104 feet	104 feet
Load draught	26 feet	25 feet	26 feet	25 feet	25 feet	26 feet
Deep draught	29 feet 6 inches	28 feet 6 inches	29 feet 6 inches	29 feet	28 feet 6 inches	29 feet 6 inches
Displacement	39,000 tons	35,500 tons	36,500 tons	32,500 tons	35,500 tons	39,500 tons
SHP	120,000	120,000	160,000	120,000	120,000	120,000
Speed	30 knots	30·5 knots	32 knots	30 knots	30·5 knots	30 knots
Armament:	Eight 15-inch Twelve 5·5-inch Two torpedo tubes } Designs 1, 2, 3			Four 18-inch Twelve 5·5-inch Two torpedo tubes } Designs 4, 5, 6	Six 18-inch	Eight 18-inch
Armour belt	8-inch	8-inch	10-inch	8-inch	8-inch	8-inch
Armour barbettes	9-inch	9-inch	9-inch	9-inch	9-inch	9-inch

draught by 6 inches, and slightly reduced the speed. In all the designs, except No. 1, small-tube boilers and forced-draught were specified in order to obtain the highest speed possible on the displacement. The specifications, for which no sketch designs had been prepared, were examined by the Board in March, and Design '3' was chosen to be worked out in detail. Two alternative arrangements of this design were drawn up; the first, proposal 'A', having twelve 5.5-inch guns and the second, proposal 'B', sixteen 5.5-inch guns. The legend and sketch designs were submitted to the Board on 27th March 1916 and, after examining a model and the drawings, the Sea Lords generally favoured proposal 'B'; the extra weight involved being acceptable. The design was officially approved by the Board on 7th April 1916, and on the same day, orders were placed for three ships. The accepted tenders were from John Brown (*Hood*), Cammell Laird (*Howe*) and Fairfields (*Rodney*). An order for a fourth ship (*Anson*) was placed with Armstrong Whitworth, in July 1916.

On 31st May 1916, the day that *Hood* was laid down, the Battle of Jutland took place in the North Sea. Three British battlecruisers blew up during this action; a forceful indication that something was very wrong with the protection of British ships. Work on the new ships was suspended pending an investigation into the possible effects of the results of the battle on *matériel*. Early in June, Jellicoe set up a number of committees, within the Grand Fleet, to study and report on the various problems encountered at Jutland. The committee studying protection, concluded that the loss of the three battlecruisers was almost certainly the result of cordite fires in the turrets or hoists reaching the magazines, and recommended the adoption of anti-flash equipment in magazines and handing rooms. They also urged the improvement of deck protection over magazines which, especially at long ranges, were vulnerable to penetration by shells and shell fragments. These views were put forward by Jellicoe and Beatty during a conference held at the Admiralty on 25th June 1916, and they were accepted by the Sea Lords. The Director of Naval Construction, however, was strongly opposed to the fitting of additional deck protection, and in this, he was supported by the Third Sea Lord. From the many reports available, he had concluded that there was no evidence to indicate that magazines had been penetrated directly by enemy shells, and the losses were entirely due to cordite fires. This is probably why, in the new design for the *Hood* class – modified as a result of Jutland and approved by the Board on 4th August – very little additional deck protection was provided. In the modified

Table 18: Legend of particulars of proposed battlecruiser, 27th March 1916

Length	860 feet (oa), 810 feet (pp)
Beam	104 feet
Draught	25 feet (forward), 26 feet (aft)
Displacement	36,250 tons (36,300 tons in proposal 'B')
Deep draught	29 feet
SHP	144,000
Speed at load draught	32 knots
Oil fuel at load draught	1,200 tons
Oil fuel capacity	4,000 tons

Armament:
Eight 15-inch 42-cal breech-loading: 80 rounds per gun.
Twelve (sixteen in proposal 'B') 5.5-inch 50-cal breech-loading, 150 rounds per gun.
Two 3-inch high-angle.
Two or four (two in proposal 'B') torpedo tubes.

Armour:	
Belt (amidships)	8-inch, 5-inch, 3-inch (1½-inch or 2-inch skin) 5-inch and 4-inch forward and aft
Bulkheads	4-inch and 3-inch
Barbettes	9-inch (maximum)
Gun-houses	11-inch, 10-inch and 4¼-inch (roof)
Conning-tower	10-inch
Conning-tower tube	3-inch – 3½-inch
Torpedo conning-tower	6-inch
Torpedo conning-tower tube	4-inch

Vertical protective plating:	
Torpedo bulkheads	1½-inch and ¾-inch
Funnel-uptakes	1½-inch

Horizontal protective plating:	
Forecastle-deck	1½-inch and 1-inch
Upper-deck (aft)	1-inch
Main-deck	1½-inch
Lower-deck (forward)	1-inch to 2-inch
Lower-deck (aft)	1-inch to 2½-inch

Weights (tons):	Proposal 'A'	Proposal 'B'
General equipment	750	750
Armament	4,750	4,800
Armour and protective plating	10,100	10,100
Oil fuel	1,200	1,200
Hull	14,070	14,070
Machinery	5,200	5,200
Board margin	180	180
Total:	36,250	36,300

Note: Details given above are for Proposal 'A'. Proposal 'B' was the same except where stated.

design, the main 8-inch belt was increased in depth by 1 foot 8 inches, and the strake of armour above this was reduced in thickness from 5 inches to 3 inches. The front plates of the gun-houses were increased to a thickness of 15 inches, and the roofs were increased from $4\frac{1}{4}$ inches to 5 inches. The barbette armour was increased in thickness between the decks but retained its original maximum thickness. Improvements were also made in the protection to the funnel-uptakes, decks and conning-tower. The 5.5-inch ammunition working spaces on the main-deck were enclosed by 1-inch bulkheads; the anti-aircraft armament was increased from two 3-inch guns to four 4-inch guns and the number of dynamos was increased from four to eight. These modifications added 1,200 tons to the displacement and increased the draught by 9 inches.

In July, the DNC put forward a suggestion for still further increases in protection that – with comparatively small modifications to the design – would result in a fast battleship of the same dimensions, but with the draught increased by two feet. The thickness of the armour would be increased generally by about 50 per cent; the 8-inch belt would become 12-inch, the 3-inch armour above it, 6-inch and the barbettes, 12-inch. The loss of speed would be only 1 knot, resulting in a 31-knot ship, better protected above and below water than the *Queen Elizabeth* class and having two feet less draught. The Board agreed generally to this proposal, but before the design was approved, the First Sea Lord asked for some proposals for the possibility of mounting four 15-inch triple turrets in the new ships. The DNC prepared details for three arrangements: twelve guns in four triple turrets, nine guns in three triple turrets and ten guns in two twin and two triple turrets. The designs were designated 'A', 'B', 'C' and 'D' and were submitted to the Board in August 1916.

Design 'A' was approved by the Board in August, and *Hood* was laid down again on 1st September 1916. In the same month, however, probably at the instigation of Admiral Jellicoe, the protection was again modified in the light of further consideration of the lessons learned at the battle of Jutland. Most of the additions were to the deck protection:

1. Belt armour (upper-deck to forecastle-deck) was reduced from 6 inches to 5 inches.
2. Belt armour (main-deck to upper-deck) was increased from 6 inches to 7 inches.
3. Upper-deck (forward) was increased from 1 inch to 2 inches.
4. 2 inch and 1 inch protection on upper-deck (aft) was increased in area.
5. Thickness of main-deck over magazines was increased from 2 inches to 3 inches.
6. Thickness of main-deck (aft) was increased from $\frac{3}{4}$ inch to 1 inch.

Table 19: Modified legends for *Hood* class, 1916

	Modified design	A	B	C	D
Length (oa)	860 feet (oa), 810 feet (pp)	All versions			
Beam (max)	104 feet	All versions			
Draught (forward)	25 feet 9 inches	27 feet 9 inches	29 feet 6 inches	28 feet 6 inches	28 feet
Draught (aft)	26 feet 9 inches	28 feet 9 inches	30 feet 6 inches	29 feet 6 inches	29 feet
Displacement (tons)	37,500	40,600	43,100	41,700	40,900
Deep draught (mean)	29 feet 6 inches	31 feet 6 inches	33 feet 3 inches	32 feet 3 inches	31 feet 9 inches
Speed (knots) at load draught	31.75–32	nearly 31	30.5	30.5–30.75	30.75
SHP	144,000	All versions			
Oil fuel at load draught	1,200 tons	All versions			
Oil fuel capacity	4,000 tons	All versions			
Armament:	Eight 15-inch	Eight 15-inch	Twelve 15-inch	Ten 15-inch	Nine 15-inch
	Sixteen 5·5-inch (all versions)				
	Two 3-inch HA, Two torpedo tubes (Modified design and A)		Four 4-inch HA, Four torpedo tubes (B, C, D)		
Armour:	Modified design	A, B, C, D			
Belt (amidships)	8-inch and 3-inch	12-inch and 6-inch			
Belt (forward)	5-inch, 4-inch and 3-inch	7-inch and 6-inch			
Belt (aft)	4-inch	6-inch			
Bulkheads	4-inch and 3-inch	6-inch and $4\frac{1}{2}$-inch			
Barbettes	9-inch	12-inch			
Gun-houses	15-inch, 11-inch and 5-inch (roof)	15-inch, 12-inch and 5-inch (roof)			
Conning-tower	10-inch	12-inch			
Conning-tower tube	3-inch	3-inch			
Torpedo conning-tower	6-inch	6-inch			
Torpedo conning-tower tube	4-inch	4-inch			

Vertical protective plating (all versions):
Torpedo bulkheads $1\frac{1}{2}$-inch–$\frac{3}{4}$-inch; Funnel-uptakes $2\frac{1}{2}$-inch
Horizontal protective plating (all versions):
Forecastle-deck, $1\frac{1}{4}$-inch–2-inch; Upper-deck (aft), $\frac{3}{4}$-inch–1-inch; Main-deck, 1-inch, $1\frac{1}{2}$-inch, 2-inch; Lower-deck forward, 1-inch, $1\frac{1}{2}$-inch and 2-inch; Lower-deck (aft), 1-inch–$2\frac{1}{2}$-inch.

Weights (tons):	Modified design	A	B, C, D
General equipment	750	750	
Armament	4,950	5,000	
Machinery	5,300	5,300	
Oil fuel	1,200	1,200	
Armour and protective plating	10,600	13,400	B, C, D: weights not known
Hull	14,520	14,750	
Board margin	180	200	
Total:	37,500	40,600	

7. Thickness of lower-deck (aft) was increased from 1 inch to 1 inch and 1½ inches.

This re-arrangement was intended to ensure that a total minimum thickness of 9 inches would be available to oppose a projectile striking the sides or decks at an angle of descent of up to 30°.These modifications were approved by the Board on 2nd October, but a number of other alterations and alternatives were later considered, in consultation with the Commander-in-Chief, Grand Fleet, and the final legend was not submitted until 20th August 1917; it received Board approval on 30th August.

Table 20: Final legend for HMS *Hood*, August 1917

Length	810 feet (oa), 860 feet (pp)
Beam (maximum)	104 feet
Draught	28 feet (forward), 29 feet (aft)
Displacement	41,200 tons
Deep draught (mean)	31 feet 6 inches
SHP	144,000
Speed at load draught	31 knots
Oil fuel at load draught	1,200 tons
Oil fuel capacity	4,000 tons
Armament:	
Eight 15-inch 42-cal	
Sixteen 5.5-inch 50-cal	
Four 4-inch HA	
Two 21-inch submerged torpedo tubes	
Eight 21-inch above-water torpedo tubes	
Armour:	
Belt (amidships)	12-inch, 7-inch and 5-inch
Belt (forward)	6-inch and 5-inch
Belt (aft)	6-inch
Bulkheads (forward)	5-inch and 4-inch
Bulkheads (aft)	5-inch and 4-inch
Barbettes (max)	12-inch
Gun-houses	15-inch front, 12-inch and 11-inch sides, 11-inch back, 5-inch roof
Conning-tower	11-inch, 10-inch, 9-inch and 7-inch
Conning-tower tube	3-inch
Torpedo conning-tower	6-inch
Vertical protective plating:	
Bulkheads	1½-inch, 1-inch and ¾-inch
Funnel-uptakes	2½-inch and 1½-inch
Horizontal protective plating:	
Forecastle-deck	1¼-inch to 2-inch
Upper-deck	¾-inch, 1-inch and 2-inch
Main-deck	1-inch, 1½-inch, 2-inch and 3-inch
Lower-deck (forward)	1½-inch to 1-inch
Lower-deck (aft)	1½-inch, 1-inch and 3-inch
Weights (tons):	
General equipment	800
Armament	5,255*
Armour and protective plating	13,550
Oil fuel	1,200
Hull	14,950
Machinery	5,300
Board margin	145*
Total:	41,200

* An additional 55 tons for heavier gun shields was allocated from the Board Margin.

Armament

The 15-inch guns and mountings would have been identical with those in earlier ships, but after Jutland, it was decided to increase the maximum elevation of the guns from 20° to 30°. This necessitated lengthening the elevating-cylinder, strengthening its supporting structure and bearings, and increasing the height of the roof at the front of the gun-house. In other respects, the gear was the same in principle as before and for this reason, the gun could not be loaded beyond 20°. A hydraulically-operated stop was fitted to prevent elevation beyond this angle when the breech was open, and an interceptor-valve prevented the gun loading-cage being raised until the breech was fully open. The modified mounting was known as the Mk II.

Armament protection

The armour of the gun-houses consisted of Krupp cemented plates. The front plates were 15-inches thick, the forward sides were 12-inches thick and the rear sides and back were 11-inches thick. The centre front plate was stepped into a heavy 17-inch glacis plate keyed to the floor plate of the gun-house. The glacis plate was of KC quality but was not hardened. The roofs consisted of three 5-inch Krupp non-cemented plates, and the floors of 3-inch high-tensile steel with an extra KNC plate under the overhang. The officers' cabinet was constructed of 3-inch KNC plates with a 3-inch high-tensile steel shield-support in front of it. The range-finder hoods were of armour-quality cast steel. The sighting-hoods of earlier turrets, that had proved weak points in the roof armour, were abandoned in favour of sighting-ports in the front shield. The total revolving weight of each turret was 860 tons compared to 750 tons in *Queen Elizabeth.* In July 1917, it was approved to increase the thickness of the roof plates to 6-inches (after a firing trial had been carried out) but as the 5-inch plates for *Hood* had already been rolled and tested, it was decided to accept these for that ship only. In the other three ships of the class, the additional weight incurred (60 tons) was met from the Board Margin.

The 5.5-inch 50-calibre breech-loading Mk I gun was first introduced into British service in the cruisers *Birkenhead* and *Chester* (At the outbreak of war, these two vessels were being built at Armstrongs for the Greek Navy, and were later purchased by the British Government.) and was later fitted in the light battlecruiser *Furious.* The gun fired an 82-pound shell at a muzzle velocity of 2,725 feet per second with a full charge of 22¼ pounds of MD cordite. It lacked the striking power of the 6-inch gun (which fired a shell 18 pounds heavier, containing 30 per cent more high explosive) but it was considered to have sufficient stopping power for use against destroyers – its primary role in a capital ship. Moreover, it was easier to handle than the 6-inch gun, and the lighter projectile facilitated loading. The CP II mounting provided a maximum elevation of 30° (compared to 15° in the earlier PI mounting) giving the gun a maximum range of about 18,500 yards – 5,000 yards more than the 6-inch Mk XII, mounted in a casemate. The new guns, however, were not so well protected from damage or weather, having only 1-inch splinter shields. In October 1917, the possibility of enclosing the guns was discussed, but was objected to on the grounds that it would restrict local control and supervision, and would incur a large amount of additional weight.

The 5.5-inch ammunition was supplied from the magazines and shell rooms by dredger-hoists to working spaces forward and aft on

Below: *Hood* in late 1932.

the main-deck. From these spaces, ammunition was transported along ammunition passages on each side of the ship and then up to each gun by dredger-hoists positioned at intervals along the passages. The fitting of dredger-hoists was approved after the final legend was complete, and the additional weight incurred (80 tons) was met from the Board Margin. The gun trials were carried out on 26th March 1920 and, apart from a few minor problems, were completely satisfactory.

The final design allowed for eight 21-inch above-water torpedo tubes on the upper-deck amidships, and two 21-inch submerged torpedo tubes each with its own compartment, on the platform-deck forward. The submerged tubes

PARTICULARS OF *HOOD*, AS COMPLETED, 1920

Displacement
Load displacement: 42,670 tons.
Deep displacement: 46,680 tons.
Tons per inch: 126.8 tons at load draught.

Dimensions
Length: 860 feet 7 inches (overall), 850 feet 7 inches (waterline), 810 feet 5 inches (between perpendiculars).
Beam: 104 feet 2 inches (maximum).
Draught: 27 feet 11 inches (forward), 30 feet 7 inches (aft), 32 feet (mean deep).

Armament
Eight 15-inch 42-cal breech-loading Mk I: twin mounting Mk II.
Twelve 5.5-inch 50-cal breech-loading Mk I: CP II single mounting.
Four 4-inch quick-firing Mk V: high-angle single mounting Mk III.
Four 3-pounder Hotchkiss saluting guns: Mk I mounting.
Six 21-inch torpedo tubes, two submerged, four surface.

Ammunition stowage
Maximum:
15-inch: 120 rounds per gun (36 CPC, 84 APC); 82 practice and 30 shrapnel for ship.
5.5-inch: 200 rounds per gun (150 Lyddite, 50 common); 464 practice and 96 shrapnel for ship.
Normal:
15-inch: 100 rounds per gun plus 6 shrapnel.
5.5-inch: 150 rounds per gun.
4-inch: 150 rounds per gun.
3-pounder: 64 rounds per gun.

Armour
Belt: 12 inch, 7 inch and 5 inch amidships, 5 inch and 6 inch forward, 6 inch aft.
Bulkheads: 5 inch and 4 inch forward and aft.
Barbettes: 12 inch to 3 inch.
Gun-houses: 15 inch front, 12 inch and 11 inch sides, 11 inch back, 5 inch roof.
Conning-tower: 11 inch to 3 inch.
Conning-tower director-hood: 6 inch front, 2 inch sides, 3 inch roof.
Conning-tower tube: 3 inch.
Torpedo conning-tower (aft): 1½ inch sides, 3 inch roof.
Torpedo conning-tower hood: 4 inch front, 3 inch sides and roof.
Torpedo conning-tower tube: ¾ inch.

Protective plating
Vertical:
Torpedo bulkheads, 1½ inch and 1¾ inch.
5.5-inch working spaces, 1 inch aft, 2 inch forward.
5.5-inch ammunition passages, 1 inch.

Horizontal:
Forecastle-deck, 1½ inch, over forward magazines, 1¼ inch to 2 inch amidships.
Upper-deck, 2 inch over magazines, 1 inch and ¾ inch amidships and aft.
Main-deck (flat), 3 inch over magazines, 1½ inch and 2 inch amidships, 1 inch forward, 2 inch aft.
Main-deck (slope), 2 inch.
Lower-deck, 1 inch forward, 1½ inch over submerged torpedo rooms, 2 inch over magazines, 1 inch and 1½ inch aft, 3 inch over steering gear.

Machinery
Brown Curtis, single-reduction, geared turbines, four shafts.
144,000 SHP = 31 knots at 210 rpm.
24 Yarrow small-tube boilers; maximum working pressure 235 pounds per square inch.

Fuel and endurance
3,895 tons oil fuel (normal).
Fresh-water stowage (for boilers), 572 tons.
58 tons coal capacity.
Endurance: 7,500 nautical miles at 14 knots (estimated from trials).

Fuel consumption: 7½ tons per hour at 14 knots.

Complement 1,397.

were provided with power loading and traversing, and lifts were installed to transport torpedoes, in the horizontal position, from the torpedo-body room on the main-deck to the submerged torpedo rooms.

Arrangements were made in 1918 or 1919, for the fitting of aircraft platforms on 'B' and 'X' turrets and these were fitted shortly after completion.

Fire-control equipment

The main armament-control tower was fitted over the conning-tower. Above this, an armoured, revolving hood contained a director and a 30-foot range-finder. The tower consisted of a 6-inch armour tube. The thickness of the face of the hood was 6 inches; that of the sides, 2 inches and of the roof, 3 inches. The 5.5-inch control-tower was positioned around the base of the main control-tower and was also protected by 6-inch armour. A second director, and a 15 foot range-finder, were fitted in a revolving director-hood on the fore-top. Each turret was fitted with a 30-foot range-finder and an open director-sight for local control.

The forward section of the fore-top served as a 15-inch control-top; the after section served as port and starboard 5.5-inch control-tops, each having a 9-foot range-finder. The two 5.5-inch director-towers were fitted abreast the bridge, in the submarine look-out positions.

Four torpedo-control positions were provided; one under the conning-tower and behind its armour, two between the funnels, and the fourth being the torpedo-control tower aft. The last three positions had 15-foot range-finder hoods. A 2-metre high-angle range-finder was fitted on the after superstructure for controlling the 4-inch anti-aircraft guns.

Protection

The main 12-inch belt extended from 'A' to 'Y' barbettes and was 562 feet long and 9 feet 6 inches deep. It was continued by 6-inch and 5-inch armour forward, and by 6-inch armour aft. Above the main belt, the side armour was carried up to the forecastle-deck by a 7-inch belt, seven feet deep, and a 5-inch belt, nine feet deep. The 7-inch belt was continued forward by a strip of 5-inch armour. As completed, the lower edge of the main belt was four feet below the load-waterline. Beneath the belt, however, was a strip of armour, 3 inches thick abreast the boiler rooms, and continued forward and aft by ¾-inch plating. The lower edge of this strip was seven feet below the loadline. The side of the belt was angled outwards at 12° in order to increase the angle of impact of a projectile and, thereby, increase the thickness to be penetrated. Behind the armour, the skin plating was 2 inches thick, reducing to 1½ inches forward and aft, and it was carried down to the ship's bottom, to form the torpedo bulkhead inboard of the bulge. The ends of the belt armour were closed by 5-inch and 4-inch bulkheads.

The upper sections of the barbettes were of a uniform thickness of 12 inches, unlike earlier designs in which, certain sections had been thinned to save weight. Between decks, the barbette armour reduced to 6 inches and 5 inches, but the fore face of 'A' barbette was thickened to 10 inches, and the after face of 'Y' was thickened to 12 inches and 9 inches. The conning-tower was the largest ever fitted in a British capital ship and its massive structure was heavily protected by armour weighing approximately 600 tons. The tower had been designed to form a compact control-centre containing the main control and communication offices. The upper section contained the conning-tower proper, gun-control positions, admiral's tower and admiral's exchange. Below this were the torpedo-control tower, signal-distribution office and intelligence office (all at different levels) and at the base, on the upper-deck, the auxiliary coding office and third wireless-transmitting office. The conning-tower proper, and the upper half of the torpedo-control tower were protected by plates of a thickness of 11 inches on the sides, 10 inches at the front, 9 inches at the rear and 5 inches on the roof. The lower half of the torpedo-control tower was protected by plates, 7 inches thick at the front and rear, and 9 inches thick on the sides. Below this, armour of a uniform thickness of 6 inches was fitted down to the forecastle-deck, and 3-inch armour was fitted between the forecastle-deck and the upper-deck. The admiral's tower was protected by 10-inch thick walls and a 5-inch thick roof. Inside the tower, a 3-inch thick armoured communication tube extended from the upper conning-tower to the main-deck, where it allowed access to the lower conning-position.

In 1917, approval was given for alterations to the armour bulkheads of *Anson*, *Howe* and *Rodney*, involving an extra weight of 152 tons. This modification, together with the provision of 6-inch roof plates for the turrets and the fitting of dredger-hoists for the 5.5-inch guns, caused the legend displacement of these three ships to be exceeded by 147 tons. Also at this time, it was approved to fit lagging to the crowns and walls of the 15-inch magazines in *Hood*, as a safeguard against fires in adjacent compartments. This involved an additional 45 tons which, with the dredger-hoists, reduced the Board Margin to 20 tons.

As in earlier ships, deck protection was widely distributed and, despite the many additions made after Jutland, did not come up to post-war standards. The protection provided by the forecastle-deck, the side plating and some other sections of the hull, was incidental, their thickness being necessary for structural purposes.

In 1918, Admiral Beatty, Commander-in-Chief, Grand Fleet, proposed that the crowns of the magazines be increased in thickness to a total of 2 inches, by fitting additional 1-inch plating. This was approved by the Board in August 1918, and to compensate the added weight, the 1-inch and 2-inch high-tensile protection to the funnel-uptakes above the forecastle-deck was omitted. In May 1919, approval was given to increase the protection to 3 inches on the sides of the main-deck over the magazines. The thick plating was thus carried out to the ship's side as well as down the slope. To compensate the additional weight (approximately 100 tons), the four aftermost 5.5-inch guns (two from the shelter-deck and two from the forecastle-deck) and their associate dredger-hoists and equipment were omitted.

In 1919, firing trials, with an improved design of 15-inch projectile, were carried out against a target representing the protection of *Hood* in way of her magazines. The trials demonstrated her vulnerability to long-range gunfire and, in July 1919, it was decided to increase the thickness of the main-deck over the after magazines to a total of 6 inches, and over the forward magazines, to 5 inches. The following items were removed to compensate the extra weight, but the additional plating was deferred, pending the results of further firing trials, and was never fitted.

1. Four forward above-water torpedo tubes.

2. Box protection to four after above-water torpedo tubes. (This was an armoured box that had enclosed the forward end of the tubes and, therefore, the torpedo warheads. When the protection had been removed, the tubes were no longer regarded as 'war fittings' i.e. it was not intended that they be carried in wartime. They had been retained for trial purposes in peacetime, and were still fitted in *Hood* when she was sunk in 1941.)

3. The 6-inch armour wall of the after torpedo conning-tower. (Replaced by 1½-inch steel plating.)

Firing trials of the new shell also demonstrated the advisability of positioning magazines below shell rooms – the reverse of the usual arrangement – where they would be less vulnerable to long-range gunfire. Here, however, they would be in greater danger from mine and torpedo explosions, and to determine the extent of this danger, it was decided to conduct a series of experiments on the Chatham Float, with a representation of the new arrangement. But first, it was decided to interchange the forward magazines and shell rooms in all the ships of the class except *Hood*; her construction being too far advanced to incorporate the necessary modifications. Initially, the after magazines remained unaltered, largely because of the lack of space in the hold caused by the fine hull lines and the position of shafting. This made it difficult to fit 'X' magazine, and almost impossible to fit 'Y' magazine into the available area. Admiral Beatty, however, wished to extend the modification to the after magazines, and pointed out that the underwater protection of 'X' and the after 5.5-inch magazines, compared well to that of the forward magazines, and that the danger from gunfire was greater in the after magazines. His proposal was later approved, and resulted in a loss in the ammunition stowage of 20 rounds per gun compared to 10 rounds per gun from 'A' and 'B' turrets. The underwater protection to 'Y' magazine was much weaker, and no decision was made until the results of the Chatham Float experiments were available. Apparently, these showed that the danger from underwater explosions was acceptable for it was concluded that it would ". . . undoubtedly, be the safer course to place the magazines below the shell rooms wherever possible". In August 1918, the Board approved the interchange of all the magazines and shell rooms which, for 'Y' magazine, necessitated widening the hull aft, to accommodate the handing room. It was estimated that this alteration to the hull form would result in a loss of speed of a little under a knot. Other disadvantages that had to be accepted as a result of this alteration were a new design of turret trunk, walking pipes below the platform-deck and a less convenient arrangement for embarking ammunition.

Underwater protection

The bulges were approximately 10 feet deep amidships, and extended the full length of the magazine and machinery spaces, the same distance as the main armour belt i.e. 562 feet. They were divided longitudinally into an outer air space and an inner tube space, and transversely into compartments approximately 20 feet long. The outer skin of the bulge consisted of ⅝-inch plating and the outer bulkhead of the tube space, of ½-inch plating. The torpedo bulkhead, which was also the inboard wall of the tube space, was 1½ inches thick, made up of two thicknesses of ¾-inch plating, and was strongly supported by 12-inch 'I' girders. Wing bulkheads, ¾-inch thick, were fitted well inboard of the torpedo bulkhead, abreast the boiler rooms and magazines, and the wing compartments thus formed, were used for oil-fuel stowage. It was not possible to provide similar wing compartments abreast the engine rooms, because the space was occupied by machinery, but the outer bulkheads of the tube space in this area were increased to ¾-inch thickness and narrow wing compartments were provided abreast the middle and after engine rooms.

Machinery

Four sets of Brown Curtis single-reduction geared turbines, one per shaft, were arranged in three engine rooms. The forward engine room contained the two sets for the outer shafts; the middle engine room contained the set for the port inner shaft and the after engine room contained the set for the starboard inner shaft. Each set consisted of one low-pressure and one high-pressure turbine and, in addition, a cruising turbine was coupled to the fore end of each wing high-pressure turbine. The use of all geared turbines allowed a reduction in the shaft speed to 210 rpm so that propellers of greater efficiency than in earlier designs could be used. In deep water, the speed obtainable with this machinery was estimated as 31 knots at load draught and 30.25 knots at deep draught.

The twenty-four Yarrow small-tube boilers, with forced draught, were divided equally between four boiler rooms. Small-tube boilers required more frequent and extensive repairs to their tubes than the large-tube type, and although employed in cruisers and smaller craft, they had not – until *Hood* – been fitted in British capital ships. The Director of Naval Construction had, for some time, "strongly advocated" their adoption in big ships on the grounds that they saved weight, occupied much less space and their initial cost was less.

Right and overleaf: four views of *Hood* during her final fitting-out at John Brown's dockyard.

They had been fitted in ships of the *Courageous* type. These were classed as large, light cruisers and consequently, their boiler rooms occupied much less space than, and their underwater protection was superior to that of *Renown* and *Repulse*. Presumably the Engineer-in-Chief's department had been opposed to their use in big ships, but weight became an extremely important consideration in the designs leading up to *Hood*, and the objections to small-tube boilers were therefore overruled.

The total heating surface was 174,960 square feet compared to 157,206 square feet in *Renown* and *Repulse*, and the maximum working pressure was 235 pounds per square inch.

The main machinery was fitted on board at Clydebank in 1919. In March 1920, steam trials were carried out on the deep-water measured-mile course off Arran in the Firth of Clyde. The results were entirely satisfactory and the subsequent examination of the machinery revealed no defects.

Table 21: Trials at load displacement, March 1920

Trial	Speed (knots)	SHP	rpm	Displacement (tons)
	13.53	9,103	80.05	42,090
	15.60	14,630	93	41,700
	17.20	20,050	103	41,700
1/5 power	20.37	29,080	124	41,600
2/5 power	25.24	58,020	154	41,850
3/5 power	27.77	89,010	176	42,100
4/5 power	29.71	116,150	191	42,150
Full power	32.07	151,280	207	42,200

3-hour full-power trials, 8th March 1920:

Speed (knots)	SHP	rpm	Remarks
31.79	150,473	205	All turbines in use, closed exhaust.
31.35	144,984	202	All turbines in use, open exhaust.

Trials at deep displacement, 22nd and 23rd March 1920:

Speed (knots)	SHP	rpm	Displacement (tons)
13.17	8,735	81	45,000
15.795	14,020	96	45,000
19.11	24,720	116	45,000
22.006	40,780	136	44,600
25.737	69,010	161	44,600
28.37	112,480	185	44,600
31.888	150,220	204	44,600

Auxiliary machinery

Electricity was supplied at 220 volts DC into a common ring main by eight 175-kilowatt dynamos – two diesel, two turbo- and four reciprocating. The total capacity was 1,400 kilowatts compared to 775 kilowatts in *Renown* and *Repulse*. The dynamos could also provide an alternative AC supply and *Hood* was the first ship in the Royal Navy to possess this capability.

Four main condensers were fitted, one for each set of turbines, and two auxiliary condensers, one in the middle and one in the after engine room. The distilling machinery which consisted of six evaporators and two distilling condensers had a combined normal output of 480 tons of fresh water per day. This machinery was arranged in four sets; two sets in each of the middle and after engine rooms.

Four steam-driven hydraulic pumping-engines were fitted to supply power for working the turrets.

Stability

The original requirement for a vessel of high freeboard and reserve of buoyancy, was completely lost in the completed ship, whose displacement exceeded the original displacement by more than 6,000 tons. The final legend displacement, however, was exceeded by less than 1,500 tons. The actual freeboard figures in the legend condition are given in Table 22.

Table 22: Freeboard of *Hood*

	As designed 1916	As designed 1917	As completed 1920
To forecastle-deck at side, forward	32 ft	29 ft	29 ft
To forecastle-deck at side, amidships	23 ft 6 in	21 ft 11 in	21 ft
To upper-deck at side, aft	19 ft	18 ft 9 in	17 ft

The calculated stability figures for the final design, and the actual figures for the completed ship that were established from an inclining experiment performed on 21st February 1920, are given in Table 23.

Table 23: Stability particulars of *Hood*

Load displacement*	As designed	As completed
Displacement	41,200 tons	42,670 tons
Mean draught	28 feet 4 inches	29 feet 3 inches
GM	4.15 feet	3.25 feet
Angle of maximum stability	—	36°
Range	69°	66°

* Ship when fully equipped with reserve feed-tanks empty and 1,200 tons of oil fuel.

Deep displacement*	As designed	As completed
Displacement	45,500 tons (approx)	46,680 tons
Mean draught	31 feet 4½ inches	32 feet
GM	4.9 feet	4.2 feet
Angle of maximum stability	—	37°
Range	76°	73°

* Fully equipped with fresh water and reserve feed-tanks full and 3,895 tons oil fuel and 58 tons of coal.

Light displacement	As designed	As completed
Displacement	39,500 tons (approx)	41,000 tons (approx)
Mean draught	27 feet 3½ inches	28 feet 3 inches
GM	4.4 feet	3.2 feet
Angle of maximum stability	—	36°
Range	—	64°

The actual weight distribution in the completed ship is shown in Table 24.

Table 24: Weights of *Hood*

	As completed	1917 design
Equipment	913	800
Armament	5,302	5,255
Machinery	5,969	5,300
Fuel	1,200	1,200
Armour and protection	13,650	13,550
Hull	15,636	14,950
Board margin		145
Displacement	42,670 tons	41,200 tons

Having exceeded the original designed draught by 3 feet 9 inches, the ship tended to be wet, particularly aft, where at high speed or in heavy weather the quarter-deck was constantly awash. The comparatively low GM, however, made her a good sea boat and a

Below: *Hood* during final fitting-out.

Table 25: Construction of *Hood* class

	Ordered	Laid down	Launched	Commissioned	Builder	Cost
Hood	7th April 1916	1st September 1916	22nd August 1918	15th May 1920	John Brown	£6,025,000
Howe	7th April 1916	16th October 1916			Cammell Laird	
Rodney	7th April 1916	9th October 1916	Suspended, 9th March 1917 Cancelled, October 1918		Fairfield	£860,000 (total)
Anson	July 1916	9th November 1916			Armstrong	

steady gun platform. The following details are taken from a report of observations made during *Hood*'s passage from John Brown to the Firth of Forth on 12th and 13th January 1920:

"After rounding the Mull of Kintyre the sea was choppy with a moderate beam swell, waves were judged to be about 15 feet high, (and) a strong wind, about Force 8, was blowing from the west. A good deal of water was taken over the forecastle and some of this washed over the forward breakwater. 'A' Barbette was continually deluged with spray. The pitching period was about 9 seconds. Off Islay the ship rolled to about $3\frac{3}{4}°$ maximum from the upright, water occasionally washed over the upper deck just abaft the break of the forecastle, the rolling period was about 17 seconds."

"The ship was comparatively light, mean draught 29ft. 10in., hence if in any new design less freeboard is accepted than that of *Hood* we must be prepared for complaints that the vessel is wet."

"The ship's speed did not exceed 21 knots and nowhere was the vibration of the structure at all noticeable except at the fore end of the 15-inch spotting top where the overhang is considerable. The commander said that at 28 knots the vibration in this position was excessive, if this is concurred in, Rosyth might be able to do something before the full power trials. The standard compass and Pelorus vibrated appreciably. Both these platforms should have some additional stiffening but in my opinion the standards of the instruments themselves are not sufficiently rigid and it is considered that this should be pointed out to D.C.D." (Ship's Cover)

Her deep draught also led to anxiety about docking. In 1920, she could be accommodated at Portsmouth, (after the dock had been modified at the bilges) Rosyth and in the privately owned Gladstone dock at Liverpool.

Construction

Work on *Anson, Howe* and *Rodney* was suspended in March 1917 so that the labour and materials employed in their construction could be utilised for what were regarded as more important projects, i.e. merchant ships, escorts, torpedo-craft, etc. The seven battle-cruisers under construction in Germany were also suspended in 1917, but this was not known at the Admiralty who, like the Commander-in-Chief were strongly in favour of expediting the completion of *Hood* and re-starting her three sisters. To do this, however, would have paralysed output elsewhere and nothing could be done. The C in C expressed the view that *Hood*, at least, should be expedited whatever the sacrifice, but the Naval Staff were unable to suggest any items that could be sacrificed from the shipbuilding programme except the transfer of labour from the cruisers *Raleigh* and *Effingham*. In October 1917, it was decided that it would be ". . . undesirable that *Hood* should be expedited in view of the sacrifices, with regard to other important items on the shipbuilding programme". Work on *Hood*, therefore, proceeded at a fairly leisurely pace and her sister ships remained suspended until the armistice in November 1918, when they were cancelled.

Hood was launched on 22nd August, 1918. Her displacement, as launched, was 21,720 tons. The following equipment weights were already on board:

Armament:	74 tons
Machinery:	1,620 tons
Armour and backing:	1,184 tons
Men, ballast, plant, etc., to be removed	310 tons
Total	3,188 tons
Launch weight	21,720 tons
Less	3,188 tons
Hull and protective plating	18,532 tons

The ship left Clydebank in January 1920, and proceeded to Rosyth where she was dry-docked for inclining experiments and preparation for trials. She returned to the Clyde and was completed by John Browns on 5th March. She was completed to full complement on 29th March and machinery, steering and gun trials were held between March and May 1920.

She was inspected at Rosyth on 14th May and handed over on the following day.

General features

In the original design the main tripod mast served chiefly as a derrick post, having no yards or topmast. In February 1919, it was decided to fit a main-topmast and topgallant-mast with a wireless-transmitting aerial yard 175 feet above the waterline. The original fore-topmast was retained, with a combined signal and wireless-transmitting yard at 130 feet above the waterline. The main-topgallant-mast was removed in March 1920 and was not replaced until 1923.

She was taken into dockyard hands for minor refits and alterations between 20th and 25th May, 1920, 7th September and 8th October 1920 and 6th December 1920 and 6th January 1921. During this period, the fore-bridge was modified and an after control-position was added under the after searchlight-platform.

During a refit at Rosyth between June and July 1921, the fore bridge was again modified and an 8-foot range-finder was added above it. At the same time, two of the four 36-inch searchlights between the funnels were removed.

5. From the Armistice to Washington, 1918 to 1921

1: POLICY

The most immediate post-war requirements of the Navy were demobilisation, the reduction of war expenditure, and the reorganization of the Fleet on a peacetime basis. Of the existing dreadnoughts, only three, *Dreadnought* herself, and the battlecruisers *Indomitable* and *Inflexible* were listed as not required in the post-war fleet. Most of the remaining 12-inch gun dreadnoughts, however, were placed in reserve or employed on subsidiary duties, and two of them, *Colossus* and *Hercules*, were sold in 1920. During the early post-war period, therefore, Britain possessed a total of twenty-seven front-line capital ships, armed with 13.5-inch and 15-inch guns. (Battleships with 13.5-inch guns: four *Orion* class, three *King George V* class and four *Iron Duke* class; with 15-inch guns: five *Queen Elizabeth* class and five *Royal Sovereign class.* Battlecruisers with 13.5-inch guns: *Lion*, *Princess Royal* and *Tiger*; with 15-inch guns: *Renown* and *Repulse.* The light battlecruisers *Courageous* and *Glorious*, and *Erin* (13.5-inch) and *Canada* (14-inch) are not included.) There were also *Hood*, still under construction, and her three suspended sister ships. These were the only post-Jutland designed ships in the fleet, but they were not regarded as embodying all the lessons of the war and the decision to cancel *Anson*, *Howe* and *Rodney* was taken with few regrets at a Board meeting in February 1919. There was, however, the question of the existing capital ships being out of date particularly as regards protection. Before considering Britain's post-war capital ship policy it is necessary to examine the progress of the USA and Japan.

In 1916, the US Congress approved a construction programme of ten battleships and six battlecruisers. Four of the battleships of this programme – the *Colorado* class – were authorised in the same year. They were of 32,600 tons, armed with eight 16-inch guns and capable of a speed of 21 knots. *Maryland*, the first ship of the class, was laid down on 24th April 1917, but the entry of the USA into the war effectively suspended the entire programme, as the shipyards were required for other purposes. Before the war had ended, however, the Navy Department was considering the expansion of the 1916 programme, and in October 1918, asked Congress to authorise the construction of a further ten battleships and six battlecruisers over a three-year period. This would have doubled the size of the 1916 programme, and, if it had been carried through, would have given the US Navy a fleet of forty-nine dreadnoughts by 1925. (This figure increases to fifty-one if the 18.5-knot *South Carolina* and *Michigan* class be included.)

In proposing this enormous fleet, the Navy Board had in mind two potential enemies – Japan and Great Britain, individually or – in view of the Anglo-Japanese Alliance – together. This necessitated, in the opinion of the Board, a fleet "second to none", capable of defending the USA in the Pacific and Atlantic Oceans, simultaneously. The background to this seemingly aggressive policy, was the growing and potentially dominant world trade of the USA (which it was thought would antagonise the British) and the conflict of American and Japanese interests in Asia and the Western Pacific. Without doubt, the threat of a future war with Japan was a real one, but a war with Britain seems to have been seriously considered for planning purposes only, by the Navy Department and the Admiralty. The Navy Department did not, at that time, regard Japan as an individual threat.

The USA, however, was not entirely populated by anglophobic 'Big Navy' men, and a large body of opinion was strongly opposed to such a large and expensive building programme. Not surprisingly, therefore, the 1918 programme was not passed through Congress. The 1916 programme remained in force, however, and work on it recommenced in 1919. *Maryland*'s three sister ships, *Colorado*, *Washington* and *West Virginia* were laid down in May 1919, June 1919 and April 1920, respectively. The second group of ships, the *South Dakota* class battleships, authorised in 1917, were enlarged versions of the *Colorado*s, with twelve 16-inch guns in four triple turrets, compared to four twins in the earlier design. They had a displacement of 43,200 tons and were designed for a speed of 23 knots. The six ships of this class, *South Dakota*, *Indiana*, *Montana*, *North Carolina*, *Iowa and Massachusetts* were laid down between January 1920 and April 1921. The last six ships of the programme, the battlecruisers of the *Lexington* class, were designed to carry eight 16-inch guns on a displacement of 43,500 tons and, with 180,000 shaft horse-power, were intended to achieve a speed of 33.25 knots.

The main purpose of the Japanese fleet was the protection of Japanese interests in the Far East and the Pacific Ocean. The conflict of these interests with those of the USA naturally led to a naval policy designed to give security in the event of war with that nation. The programmes and capital ship designs of the USA were studied carefully by the Japanese and matched as far as possible, ship for ship. After the 1916 programme had been authorised in Congress, the Japanese Diet approved the '8 - 8 Fleet' programme. This was designed to provide the Japanese Fleet with eight battlecruisers and eight battleships, none of which was to exceed eight years in age. Only two ships of this programme were commenced during the war; *Nagato*, laid down in August 1917, and *Mutsu*, laid down in June 1918. They displaced 32,700 tons, were armed with eight 16-inch guns and were capable of a speed of 26.75 knots. The next two ships, *Kaga* and *Tosa*, were ordered under the 1918 programme but were not laid down until February and July, 1920, respectively. They were enlarged versions of the *Nagato* class, carrying two additional 16-inch guns on a displacement of 38,500 tons. These were followed by four battlecruisers of the *Amagi* class. Like *Tosa*, they carried ten 16-inch guns and, on a displacement of 40,000 tons were capable of 30 knots. *Amagi* and *Akagi* were ordered in 1919 and laid down in December 1920; *Atago* and *Takao* were ordered in 1920 and laid down in November and December 1921, respectively. In 1921, plans were made to complete the 8 - 8 Programme; the USA having, by this time, laid down and committed herself to the ships of the 1916 programme. The remaining eight ships were divided equally between two classes of fast battleships. The first group, the *Kii* class, *Kii*, *Owari* and two unnamed ships, were ordered in 1921 but were not laid down; the second group, all unnamed, were never ordered. The *Kii* class were virtually repeats of the *Amagi* design with slightly improved protection, but in the second design, the displacement was increased to 47,500 tons to allow for an armament of eight 18-inch guns, improved protection and a speed of 30 knots with 150,000 shaft horse-power. The Japanese had thus not only equalled the USA programme numerically but had, on paper at least, exceeded it.

During 1919, the British Admiralty had formed no definite capital-ship policy but were, nevertheless, quick to recognise the threat of the USA programme to Britain's long-standing naval supremacy. Before any definite proposals could be made for a new construction programme to counter this threat, there were two major obstacles to be overcome. First, there was a strong body of opinion in the country, and even inside the Admiralty itself, that the capital ship was far too vulnerable to under-water and aerial attack and that submarines and aircraft were the new arbiters of sea warfare. In August 1919, a Post-War Questions Committee was formed, to examine and report on this and other matters related to the war's effect on future warship design. In their report, made in March 1920, the committee stated that it considered the capital ship had not been made obsolete by the recent developments in aerial warfare. It also recommended the construction of 35,000-ton battleships armed with 15-inch guns. Although the committee was somewhat biased, one cannot entirely disagree with this conclusion for it was to be some years before aircraft and aerial tactics were developed sufficiently to overcome the equivalent anti-aircraft defences developed after the war. In March 1920, this conclusion was echoed in the "First Lord's Statement Explanatory of Navy Estimates 1920–1921" under "Remarks on the Capital Ship":

"There has been some criticism of the maintenance in commission of the present types of vessels, especially in regard to the capital ships. A contrary policy has been openly advocated, this policy being based, it is presumed, on the idea that the battleship is dead and that submersible, and air vessels are the types of the future. The Naval Staff has examined this question with extreme care and as a result we profoundly dissent from these views . . . the immediate abandonment of the capital ship in favour of a visionary scheme of aircraft and submarines, would leave the British nation destitute of sea power and without the means of progressive training."

Second, there was no positive government directive regarding the strength of the Royal Navy in relation to other navies, on which the Admiralty could formulate a policy. In August 1919, however, in response to demands from all three services for some definite ruling on which to base their programmes for 1920 to 1921, the Government introduced the "Ten Year Rule". This required the services to revise their estimates on the assumption that the British Empire would not be engaged in a major war during the next ten years.

This ruling was based entirely on economic considerations. It set the scene for the next decade in which the services, on one hand, attempted to obtain the funds they considered essential for the defence of the Empire, while the Treasury, on the other, did all it could to limit that expenditure. So far as the Navy was concerned, the feud between the Treasury and the Admiralty was long and on occasions very bitter, but the blame for this must lie with those who gave these two government departments directives that were diametrically opposed. Probably the worst effect of these financial restrictions between the wars, was the delay in and the cutting back of the development and testing of new equipment and ideas, particularly in the fields of anti-aircraft defence and naval aviation, and the delays caused in modernising older ships.

In August 1919, the Cabinet directed the Admiralty to aim at a maximum of £60,000,000 for the 1920 to 1921 Estimates. In October 1919, the Admiralty informed the Cabinet that this would not allow for the laying down of any new capital ships, and that if the USA completed her 1916 programme, Britain would, by 1923, become the world's second naval power. To prevent this, the only alternative to a new building programme would be to invite the US authorities to discuss the possibility of an agreed parity in naval strength. When the 1920 to 1921 Estimates (£84,000,000) were submitted to the Cabinet in February 1920, they included no provision for new capital ships and were passed by the Cabinet and Parliament in March 1920 without difficulty, but as stated earlier, the Admiralty re-affirmed their belief in the capital ship as the prime unit of the fleet. At the same time, the "One Power Standard" was given as the criteria on which future British naval strength was to be built; that is, a navy as strong as any other in the world.

The most likely reason for the Cabinet's lack of enthusiasm for a new building programme, apart from the cost, was the likelihood of such a programme providing the 'Big Navy' men in the USA with an additional and very strong argument with which to further their aims. Whatever the Cabinet thought, however, the Admiralty regarded the construction of new capital ships as essential and Table 26 shows why.

Table 26: Capital ship strength at end of 1919*

	Gun calibre	Britain	USA	Japan
Ships completed	13.5-inch	14		
	14-inch		9	8
	15-inch	12		
Ships under construction	15-inch	1		
	16-inch		4	2
Projected		None	12	14
Total:		27	25	24

* The 12-inch gun dreadnoughts are not included in this list (nor the light battlecruisers *Courageous* and *Glorious*, which were shortly to be converted to aircraft carriers, and the foreign dreadnoughts *Erin* and *Canada* taken over in Britain in 1914) which in the circumstances, could not be regarded as effective units.

As can be seen, although Britain still possessed a superiority in numbers, the majority of her ships were of pre-war design, but the 1916 programme would give the USA sixteen post-Jutland ships by 1923, against one, *Hood*, in the British fleet. All of these American ships moreover, would be armed with 16-inch guns; but the largest gun in a British capital ship was of 15-inch calibre. The extent of the Japanese programme was not at this time fully appreciated in either country, but as more information became available it gradually gained the attention it deserved.

During 1920, the Board began to formulate a positive capital-ship policy and the Director of Naval Construction's department started work on new battleship and battlecruiser designs. As a result, in November of the same year, the Admiralty forwarded to the Cabinet a proposal to lay down four such ships in 1921, to be followed by a further four in 1922. The eight ships were to be completed between 1924 and 1927. In December 1920, a 'Naval Shipbuilding' sub-committee of the Committee of Imperial Defence was appointed to investigate the Admiralty's submissions regarding Britain's naval strength. After taking evidence from both inside and outside the Admiralty, the committee concluded early in 1921 that the capital ship was, after all, obsolete. This needless to say, produced a very strong reaction from the Admiralty and after representations by Beatty, Long (the First Lord) and Churchill, the committee's report was rejected, but the Admiralty was still not provided with the necessary authority to begin the new construction programme. This could have been nothing short of extremely annoying to the Board, for one of their strongest arguments for the early commencement of the new ships was the rapid run down of the ordnance and armour-plate industry and the loss of its skilled labour which, if not checked, would result in excessive delays in the construction of any new capital ships.

The Admiralty, however, achieved its goal in a somewhat unusual manner involving a disagreement over the 1921–1922 Estimates. The original Estimates for £85,500,000 were forwarded to the Cabinet in December 1920 and were rejected, the Admiralty being requested to reduce them to a sum not exceeding £60,000,000. Their Lordships were apparently not impressed and re-submitted the Estimates in January, at £85,000,000. The subsequent debate continued until March 1921 when an amount just below £80,000,000 was accepted. In addition to this sum, however, the Admiralty extracted from the Cabinet a further £2,500,000 for the replacement of obsolete ships, that provided the necessary funds to commence work on the new ships. This money was voted only on condition that no supplementary estimate would be submitted later in the financial year. Therefore, when, in August 1921, the Admiralty asked for an additional £12,000,000 they were, to say the least, very unpopular.

2: MATÉRIEL

Before discussing the 1921 capital ships, it is necessary to examine the effects of the lessons of the First World War on the design of British capital ships and their equipment. The developments in all branches of naval science had, particularly in the latter years of the war, been rapid and extensive. In 1919, the Royal Navy was the only existing navy that had any experience of a modern fleet action; and in practically all other types of naval warfare, it had gained far more experience than any of her enemies or allies. Naval aviation, fire-control, protection, damage-control, had all moved forward, at a rate impossible in peacetime, until the navy was in a position years ahead of its contemporaries.

Financial restrictions between the wars, however, slowed the development of this newfound knowledge, and a considerable amount of ground was lost. This was particularly so with regard to naval aviation in which Britain was to be overtaken by the USA and Japan, partly because of Royal Air Force control of Fleet Air Arm aircraft and partly because shortage of money resulted in a lack of RAF interest in naval flying. There were also the naval limitation treaties which resulted in reliance on a battle fleet largely composed of battleships of pre-war design and in which it was impossible, even with drastic modernisation, to incorporate the full lessons of the war.

Fire-control equipment

In 1914, a virtually standard fire-control system was in use in the majority of British dreadnoughts. Briefly, this consisted of a spotting-top containing a 9-foot range-finder, rate and deflection instruments, bearing indicator and communication equipment. This gear was used to feed information to a Dreyer fire-control table (Detailed descriptions of this and other equipment mentioned in this section can be found in the appendix on gunnery) or, in earlier ships, to a range-clock, which in turn fed the guns with the required range, bearing and deflection for attack on a moving target. There was also a second 9-foot range-finder fitted on the superstructure, or, in later ships, in an armoured hood on the conning-tower, which served as either a back-up or an alternative instrument to that in the spotting-top. In the *Iron Duke* class, main and secondary armament-control positions were provided in the armoured conning-tower – a practice that was to be continued in later capital ship designs.

This system was in the process of being revolutionised by the introduction of director-control, which was first tested in its modern form in 1910. In that year, the battleship *Neptune* was fitted with an experimental director-control system, designed by Admiral Sir Percy Scott, and developed by Vickers. This was the first serious attempt to control both the elevation and training of turret guns from a position independent of the turrets. The gear was very compact and could be universally applied to modern turrets largely because of the adoption of Vickers' 'follow the pointer' transmission system. The director had a crew of four – sight-setter, trainer, layer and telephone number – arranged in a semi-circle with their feet towards the centre. The trainers' and layers' telescopes had independent elevation, a feature not repeated in later director-sights in which both telescopes elevated as a unit.

The trials of the director gear were carried out in the Mediterranean early in 1911, under the supervision of Percy Scott. They demonstrated the great advantages of director firing, and Jellicoe, who had attended the trials with Commander F. C. Dreyer, recommended its adoption in all the ships of the fleet. (At that time, Jellicoe was Commander-in-Chief, Atlantic Fleet. Both he and Dreyer were eminent gunnery experts.) Faults were found in the equipment but nothing that could not be corrected by modification. The most important of these faults was revealed by an analysis of the results of the firing trials. These showed that some form of correction to the elevation was necessary to compensate discrepancies between the horizontal level of each turret-roller path and the director-platform. The matter was carefully studied, and instruments known as 'tilt correctors' were developed which gave the exact correction necessary for any given turret bearing. These instruments, and other alterations considered necessary as a result of the *Neptune* trials, were incorporated in a modified version of the director system.

The new installation was fitted in the appropriately named, battleship *Thunderer* in 1912, and trials were carried out in October of that year. The results were conclusive and, in 1913, two orders for a total of twenty-nine main armament-director systems were placed with Vickers. Delivery of the equipment, however, was to be spread over several financial years, and on the outbreak of war in 1914, only eight battleships, including *Neptune* and *Thunderer*, were complete with main armament-directors. All the battleships and battle-cruisers of the Grand Fleet, except *Erin* and *Agincourt* were fitted with them before the Battle of Jutland in May 1916.

Although the director systems employed during the war, varied in detail from ship to ship, the design was in all cases, basically similar to that fitted in *Thunderer* in 1912. The director, known as the 'tripod-type director' was to remain in use with some small modifications up to and during the Second World War. The *Queen Elizabeth* class and subsequent ships were designed with an armoured director and range-finder hood on the conning-tower in addition to the aloft director-position.

Late in 1914, it was decided to fit secondary armament-directors in all new ships, but their supply was greatly delayed because production capacity was fully occupied in the manufacture of gear for the main armaments of capital ships and cruisers. Temporary installations were fitted in *Emperor of India*, *Benbow* and *Queen Elizabeth* at the end of 1916, and the full gear was fitted in all dreadnoughts of the *Iron Duke* and subsequent classes, between 1916 and 1918.

In September 1914, designs for an open director-sight for gun turrets were called for. These were mainly intended to provide the officer of the turret with the means to control the fire of his own guns, should the turret be isolated. An order for twenty-two sights was placed with Vickers in October, and additional orders in December 1914, March 1915 and finally, in July 1915 provided sights for the entire dreadnought fleet. Deliveries of these sights had been completed by January 1917.

During the war, some difficulty was encountered in keeping the director-sight on its target, which resulted in the provision of spotting aids and, more importantly, the increased development of the 'Evershed' system of target indication. Basically, this consisted of a bearing-sight (usually called the Captain's sight) which, when trained on a target, automatically indicated to the director (or to a gun), the direction in which the target was to be found. Two other important innovations were under development at the end of the war; aircraft-spotting and the inclinometer. The latter was an instrument for measuring the inclination of a target ship, i.e. the angle between the fore-and-aft line of the enemy, and the line of sight. Post-war developments were mainly directed towards improving the equipment already in use and, for new construction, the development of a director-control tower in which director-sight, range-finder and spotting facilities could be concentrated.

Range-finders

Although the fire-control system depended on the observation of fire rather than on range-finder ranges, these instruments were important for obtaining the initial target range, and as an aid to keeping the range. Consequently, great efforts to increase their efficiency were made during the war. In the *Queen Elizabeth* class, the 9-foot range-finders of earlier ships were replaced by 15-foot range-finders, but even these were insufficiently accurate to cope with actual battle ranges. In 1915, a 28-foot Barr and Stroud range-finder was tested by *Excellent*, but for some strange reason the Director of Naval Ordnance recommended the adoption of a 22-foot instrument for the designs, then under consideration, that were to lead to the construction of *Hood*. The 30-foot range-finder, however, was eventually adopted and these began to be fitted in capital ships in 1919. It should be noted that the British used coincidence range-finders which were not so accurate as the stereoscopic type used by the German navy. (See Appendix 2.)

Fire-control

The system of fire-control used in 1914 was considered highly efficient, and great confidence was felt in its ability to deal with the ranges expected in general battle conditions. Basically, the system relied on obtaining the maximum information from the initial observation of the target's course and speed, using the range-finders and bearing instruments, and passing the results to the guns through the fire-control table or clock. Fire was then directed by observation of the fall of shot, using the 'bracket' system. In this system, the first salvo was fired at the best mean range and subsequent salvos were corrected up or

Below: *Revenge* in the early 1920s. Note the 9-foot range-finders on the compass-platform—a torpedo range-finder on the centreline and a tactical range-finder on each beam.

down until 'spotted' both over and short of the target. The corrections were then halved to reduce the bracket until the target was straddled. Corrections for line were similarly made. As each salvo was spotted before firing the next one, the rate of fire was slow, though rapid firing was used when straddling. Nevertheless, the system was regarded as sufficient to meet the needs of war. This erroneous conclusion was reached principally because of the unrealistic battle practices carried out before the war. In these, targets were towed at a constant slow speed, under good conditions of visibility and sea, at comparatively short ranges and on a straight course. (To be fair, it was difficult to introduce alterations of course of the target during the short battle-practice runs.) Moreover, ample time was allowed for range-finding before opening fire.

The earliest engagements of the war gave little indication that the existing firing rules were inadequate. The battle of Heliogoland Bight in August 1914 did, however, demonstrate the impossibility of taking ranges in low visibility, but did not produce any other reliable information. The battle of the Falklands, on 8th December 1914, provided the first real indication that the British fire-control system was not entirely satisfactory. The main part of this action consisted of a gun duel between the battlecruisers *Invincible* and *Inflexible* and the German armoured cruisers *Scharnhorst* and *Gneisenau*. Theoretically, the British ships should have made short work of the German cruisers. Their armament was superior – eight 12-inch as opposed to eight 8.2-inch guns – and they had a 4-knot advantage in speed. In fact, it took three hours to sink *Scharnhorst* and five hours to sink *Gneisenau*, during which time, the British ships fired a combined total of 1,174 12-inch shells. (*Gneisenau* was, in fact, scuttled after firing her entire supply of ammunition and losing all her motive power.) The main reasons for this poor performance were these. First, the attempt by the British ships to keep outside the range of the German guns (13,500 yards) which led to the action being fought at a much greater range than had been anticipated in pre-war practices; second, the zigzag tactics employed by the Germans and the frequent changes of course that occurred during the battle; third, the great difficulty of keeping on the correct target experienced by observers and gun-layers. The range-finders failed to provide sufficient information chiefly because of the long range, which outclassed the 9-foot range-finders, and also because of interference from cordite and funnel smoke. The use of zigzag tactics made the control of fire extremely difficult and placed a high premium on rapid fire as soon as the target had been straddled. The problem of keeping on target was, to a certain extent, already being solved by the introduction of director firing (*Invincible*, in fact, had been fitted with a director at the time of this action) but even this was to prove insufficient and later had to be supplemented by spotting aids and the increased development of the Evershed system.

The battle of Dogger Bank in January 1915 provided the first experience of modern battle conditions, where capital ships of similar type, engaged one another in line ahead formation. This action, which was basically a long stern chase, was fought at long range (hits being obtained at 19,000 yards) and confirmed the lessons of the Falkland Islands battle. Range-finders again proved insufficiently accurate and the ranges obtained from them were generally received too late to be applicable because of the frequent course alterations. It was discovered also that rate-finding, using range-finders and bearing instruments, was not sufficiently dependable so spotting was employed to find the rate but this presented a new difficulty. Shots which fell beyond the target could not be seen, and hits were seldom observed, so it was necessary to depend almost entirely on 'shorts' for the correction of fire. This made a high rate of fire absolutely essential, but with the bracket system, this could not be achieved. It also became evident as a result of this action that, the great range at which future actions were likely to be fought, necessitated some form of additional adjustment to gun- and director-sights, which were not calibrated for use at these long distances. This problem was overcome by the '6° prism attachment' which was fitted to the telescopic sights of directors and to the centre sights of turrets. It effectively added 6° to the elevation adjustment available on the sights, which, instead of being elevated to the horizontal position, would be pointing 6° down. The prism then served to deflect the target image from the horizontal plane. This fitting had been added in all the ships of the Grand Fleet by May 1916, and it was generally considered that without it, few hits would have been obtained during the battle of Jutland. Again, conditions during this action were extremely difficult, mainly because of very poor visibility. In many cases, enemy ships were in sight for such short periods that it was impossible to obtain a single range, still less a range or bearing plot. In these circumstances, about six salvoes was the maximum that could be fired before the target disappeared. These experiences led to two lines of development which – between 1916 and 1918 – improved the gunnery of the fleet to an enormous extent.

The first, emanated from the post-Jutland gunnery committees of the Grand Fleet which recommended the adoption of new spotting rules based on the 'ladder system' instead of the existing 'bracket system'. (The German Navy already used the ladder system and, at Jutland, had been much more successful in finding the range quickly, but in this, they were assisted by their stereoscopic range-finders.) The ladder system increased the rate of fire and the number of hits obtainable in a given time, and reduced the time required to find the target. It also reduced the dependence on range-finder ranges. The new spotting rules were introduced by the C in C, Admiral Jellicoe, in September 1916, and were adopted for the control of the main armament of capital ships in 1917, and for secondary armaments in 1921. The "1916 Spotting Rules" for capital ships were as follows:

"(a) First find the target by firing double salvoes, each consisting of half the number of guns in the ship, spread for direction by one third the length of the target on each side of the estimated deflection. Deflection salvoes to be repeated as necessary.
(b) Having found the target for line continue to fire double salvoes spread for range towards the target, spotting each double before firing the next. This is termed firing a ladder.
(c) Having found the target for both line and elevation continue to fire doubles but without spreading them for either line or direction and without necessarily waiting to spot between doubles.
(d) When the target is again lost for elevation it is found by firing doubles spread for range towards the target as in (b). In general the range spread or ladder concentration between doubles and between salvoes of a double is 400 yards and when regaining the target somewhat smaller this being governed more or less by the spread of the salvoes. In each case if the smaller spread of the ladder fails to regain the target the 400 yard ladder is reverted to. A revision to a ladder is always to be accompanied by a rate correction."

These rules may seem rather complicated and the following example will help to clarify the procedure. Assuming that the ship carried eight guns, she would fire four-gun salvoes – two four-gun salvoes constituting a double. If the estimated range of the target was 14,200 yards, the first salvo was fired at this range, to the left of the estimated deflection. The second salvo was fired to the right of the estimated deflection without waiting to spot the fall of shot of the first salvo. The first salvo fell to the left of the target, the second fell in line but short of the target. The third salvo was fired with the same deflection as the second but with a correction of 'up 400' (14,600 yards) and the fourth salvo – which completed the second double – was corrected by another 'up 400' bringing the range to 15,000 yards. The third salvo fell short of the target, the fourth fell beyond the target, which was then bracketed; the next double being fired 'down 200' at 14,800 yards. Both salvoes straddled the target and doubles were fired on this bearing and elevation until the target was lost. The process was then repeated, but with smaller corrections – in 200-yard steps, for example. If the target were not regained quickly, the 400-yard step was reverted to. Admiral Jellicoe estimated that the ladder system enabled the target to be located in half the time of the bracket system.

The second line of development undertaken after Jutland, concerned the concentration of fire of two or more ships on one target, in order to achieve their maximum effective volume of fire, and also to allow ships to fire at a target they could not see. Early in 1917, the battle squadrons of the Grand Fleet began to establish the best method of concentrating the fire of not only two, but three or four ships. During the year, each squadron tested a different system, and during the third quarter of 1917, the various systems were tried with full-calibre firings, to determine the best system for adoption throughout the fleet. The final choice was basically as described below:
1. Concentration of fire was generally by pairs and depended on the efficient communication of information between the ships of a pair.
2. With four-ship concentration, the ships worked in two pairs, linked by communication between the rear ship of the leading pair and the leading ship of the rear pair.
3. With three ships, the two most accustomed to working together formed a pair, while the third ship exchanged information with the ship ahead or astern, depending on her position.
4. The firing was by sequence, each ship having a definite firing time so that her fall of shot could be spotted and not be confused with that of another ship.

The system was based on a rate of fire of one round per gun per minute. Thus, for two-ship concentration, the interval for a double salvo was 30 seconds; for three ships, 20 seconds and for four ships, 15 seconds. This last was found to be too short to be strictly adhered to, but each pair of ships was expected to keep to the 30-second interval.

In 1917 and 1918, the most obvious external sign of the adoption of concentrated fire by the ships of the Grand Fleet, was the appearance of range-clocks and training scales for the rapid communication of target information. The improvement of concentrated fire, particularly with the aid of short-range wireless communication, and use of the 1916 Spotting Rules, formed the main work of development in fire-control during the post-war period.

Ordnance

The production of heavy guns and mountings was brought to a fairly high state of efficiency before 1914, and the war revealed no fundamental weaknesses in their design. Some defects were found, particularly in the hydraulic systems, which were corrected during the war, but no major alterations were required. The same, however, could not be said of the heavy armour-piercing shells that were in use at this time.

Before the war, British armour-piercing capped shells were proof tested at normal impact, a situation unlikely to occur in battle where varying degrees of oblique impact would be the norm. As early as 1910, Jellicoe, who was then the Third Sea Lord, had instigated trials in which 12-inch APC shells were fired at oblique angles of attack against a modern armoured structure built into the old Victorian turret ship *Edinburgh*. The defects revealed by these trials caused Jellicoe to ask for new designs of heavy APC, capable of exploding efficiently after having penetrated armour at oblique impact without breaking up. The Ordnance Board, however, considered that a shell capable of penetration at normal impact would be equally capable at oblique impact, and that the rules governing the existing proof trials were, therefore, adequate. Unfortunately, Jellicoe, who was the driving force in this matter, had left the Admiralty shortly after the request was made and as, apparently, nobody was willing to argue the point, the project was dropped. Thus was lost the opportunity to remedy the defects in the APC shell

Left: Ammunition on *Royal Oak* in 1917. **Above**, a 15-inch common shell on board *Royal Oak* in 1917 being wheeled across the deck. **Below**, the process of ammunitioning. The shells being brought aboard are probably 15-inch common, as in the top photograph.

before the war, and it was not until after Jutland that this matter was again investigated.

At Jutland, a high percentage of the hits on enemy vessels were seen to explode on contact. This was spectacular, but unlikely to cause vital damage, the force of the detonation being expended outside the target's protection. The cause was attributed to the APC shell and its fuze being unsuitable for oblique impact, and the Lyddite bursting-charge being too sensitive to withstand the shock of impact. These faults had been overcome in German shells by the use of an efficient delayed-action fuze and a Trotyl (TNT) burster. In July 1916, Jellicoe suggested the adoption of Trotyl bursters and fuzes based on the German design. Their Lordships were not entirely convinced that British shells were faulty, and the problem was not tackled seriously until Jellicoe himself became First Sea Lord in December 1916, and his former flag-captain, F. C. Dreyer became Director of Naval Ordnance on 1st March 1917. Dreyer dissolved the existing shell committees and formed a new committee, with himself as president. Other members of the committee included Lieutenant-Colonel Haynes, superintendent of experiments at Shoeburyness, Commander W. F. French and Dreyer's brother, Lieutenant-Colonel J. Dreyer.

Under the direction of Haynes, firing trials were carried out at Shoeburyness with the existing 12-inch, 13.5-inch and 15-inch APC shells. The bursting-charge was replaced by salt, and the shells were fired at an angle of 20° to the normal, through a 6-inch Krupp cemented armour plate, at striking velocities equal to those that could be expected at battle ranges. All these shells, including the 15-inch, broke up in perforating the plate. In May 1917, therefore, urgent steps were taken to obtain a new design of APC shell. Fifteen shell designs were considered by the committee and on 14th May, orders were placed with Vickers, Hadfields and Firth, for special trial shells. The old-type shells had soft AP caps whose weights varied from 3.7 per cent to 9 per cent of the total shell weight; the trial shells were fitted with hard AP caps whose weights varied from 11 per cent to 12 per cent of the total. In addition, the bursting-charge in the trial shells was reduced to 2 per cent or 2½ per cent of the total weight compared to over 3 per cent in the older types. Most of the early trials were carried out with 13.5-inch shells because it was considered that this calibre, midway between the 15-inch and 12-inch, would produce results that could be fairly easily applied to other calibres. The trials demonstrated that it was unnecessary to reduce the burster to 2 per cent, and a burster capacity of 2½ per cent was decided upon. More orders were then placed with Hadfield, Firth, Vickers, Elswick and Cammell, for trial shells of all sizes.

By August 1917, sufficient information had been obtained from the trials of the 2½ per cent-capacity shells, to produce a specification for plate and proof tests, and further trials were carried out in accordance with this specification. At the same time, other trials – begun earlier – were still being conducted with the old-type 13.5-inch and 15-inch APC fitted with special caps designed by Hadfields and Firth. These were concluded without success on 3rd August 1917, and, thereafter, effort was concentrated on the new design.

On 16th July 1917, the adoption of the new shells for guns of 12-inch calibre and upwards, was approved. The outfit of shells in capital ships was to be in the proportion of 70 per cent of the new APC and 30 per cent Common pointed capped. As these two types of shell ranged differently (i.e. they travelled different distances) it was decided to carry out ballistic trials with the new APC in an attempt to get them to range the same. The weights of the APC were modified slightly to give the same muzzle velocity as the CPC, and the length of the ballistic cap was altered. Some success was achieved, but the drift of the APC and CPC shells was not the same, and no solution for this problem could be found.

The first firm to submit 'lots' of shell for proof, was Firth, who had also been the first to achieve success with the 13.5-inch heavy (1,400-pound) shell. Their new shells (also 13.5-inch heavy) failed to pass proof as did the shells from other firms. The results of the proof tests varied widely but failures followed the earlier successes. The bulk manufacture of shells, therefore, was seriously delayed while the manufacturing process was investigated in more detail. Other delays were caused by the discovery that the new hard caps were liable to crack, and by the need to erect new plant for the heat treatment of the caps, which were made of special steel. The difficulties, however, were overcome and the first success was obtained by Vickers with the first half of their 'lot one' of the 13.5-inch heavy Mk IIA, which passed proof as APC shell on 27th February 1918. By 18th May 1918, 4,000 shells had passed proof, and by the end of the war, 12,000 had been supplied to the Grand Fleet. Trials and tests with the shells continued until well after the war and included firing trials against the *Baden* in 1921 and *Monarch* in 1924. The shells, apart from having a hard cap and a smaller burster, were equipped with a new delayed-action fuze, designated '16D' that was designed to give a normal length of delay of 35 feet from the point of impact and the Lyddite bursting-charge of earlier shells, was replaced by the less sensitive Shellite in APC and Trotyl in CPC shells.

Armour and protective plating

British armour plate stood up well to the test of war, but two important points were emphasised. First, the need of improvements in the fixing of armour plate to ships' structures and second, that greater care was necessary in arranging the distribution of armour so as to eliminate weak points in the protection. The provision of thin high-tensile plating for protective decks was completely inadequate against long-range gunfire. Most of the lessons regarding protection had been learnt at Jutland, but further information was obtained from the trials of the new APC shell, particularly against a target representing the protection of *Hood*.

Manufacturers had always endeavoured to increase the size of armour plates so as to reduce the number of butts and rivetted edges that, obviously, represented weak points in any area of armour. The experiences of Jutland justified the recommendation made after this battle that, "steel plate manufacturers and shipyards should be continuously pressed to make and work still larger plates". Later attempts to reduce the weakness of armour joints, resulted in the adoption of plates keyed and scarfed at the butts.

After Jutland, considerable amounts of additional high-tensile plating were added to the decks of British capital ships. This was particularly marked in the modified design for *Hood* which had more protective plating over her magazines than any other ship in the fleet. The trials carried out with the new APC shell against the *Hood* target, therefore, had particular significance. They showed that *Hood*'s magazines were vulnerable to long-range gunfire, and that at 25,000 yards, a 15-inch APC shell could penetrate all the decks, and burst in her magazines. Consequently, steps were taken to obtain armour plating – as opposed to protective plating – for the horizontal protection of future capital ships.

It had been originally intended that deck armour should be fitted in *Hood* when it became available, but this was never done. It was, however, incorporated in several other ships of the fleet when they were reconstructed during the 1930s.

From a study of the damage received by various ships at Jutland, a considerable number of other deductions was made. The more important of these are listed below.

1. Hits on the waterline belts of British ships were few, and it was concluded that with battle ranges increasing, hits on or near the waterline were likely to decrease still further in the future.

2. The use in battlecruisers of barbette armour thinner than that of similar mountings in battleships, was regarded as undesirable, though the lighter hull protection was considered acceptable in order to obtain sufficient machinery weight for the speed.

3. The thickness of turret roof plates and the strength of their fixings needed improvement. The sighting-hoods in the turret roofs were also found to be insufficiently secure and constituted a weak point in the protection.

4. It was found that the fixings of armoured structures to decks, i.e. barbettes, conning-towers and communication tubes, were insufficiently secure. The normal practice at this time, was to connect the armour to the deck by means of angle-connections rivetted to the deck and tap-rivetted to the armour. This type of fixing was too weak to withstand the impact of a projectile and it was recommended that additional support be provided, particularly for barbettes.

5. Vertical protective plating above the weather-decks was found to be of little value and, if anything, was dangerous as it was liable to burst shells that otherwise would have passed through the structure without exploding. Vertical protective plating between decks, however, was regarded as good protection against shell splinters created by shells exploding on the decks or against the ships' sides.

6. Armour gratings for funnel-uptakes, and the supports provided for them, proved of great value.

7. Framing behind armour was found to be sufficiently strong, but it was recommended that the framing at the waterline should be stiffer than that above the waterline. This was based on the discovery that when shells struck above water, they tended to perforate armour without exploding and that the framing absorbed the impact well. Below water, however, shells were liable to explode outside the armour where the tamping effect of the water produced a very high pressure. Consequently a large area of the armour was likely to be forced inwards for a relatively large distance. It was recommended also, that transverse bulkheads, where they came in behind armour, be stiffened, as they were not so strong as the frames.

8. Openings for ventilation trunks in the decks around barbettes, were found to be a dangerous source of weakness. Shells striking the decks in the vicinity of these openings could penetrate easily and strike the barbette armour, beneath.

9. No additional protection appeared to be afforded by the wooden decks – which is hardly surprising – and there was no instance of them burning when struck by shells. The opinion was expressed, however, that the wood probably assisted in holding the point of a shell, allowing it to penetrate, and that a plain steel deck, like those in *Renown* and *Repulse* would, in many cases have deflected the shell.

Protection against magazine explosions

During the war, eight ships were lost as a direct result of magazine explosions. In addition to these ships, two pre-dreadnoughts, *Russell* and *Britannia*, suffered magazine explosions after being mined and torpedoed respectively. It is probable also, that magazine explosions contributed to the loss of two armoured cruisers at the battle of Coronel in 1914. These explosions fall into two groups: (a) those thought to be (though not absolutely proved to be) caused by the deterioration of cordite – which rendered it unstable, and (b) those caused by direct enemy action.

In April 1917, considerable improvements had been introduced in the control of the production of cordite to strict specifications, and inspectors were appointed to watch over all stages of its manufacture. Arrangements were also made to withdraw 6,000 tons of old cordite from the ships of the fleet. In July 1917, the battleship *Vanguard* blew up at her anchorage in Scapa Flow, after which, the provision of the new cordite was expedited. All the old cordite in the Grand Fleet had been replaced by March 1918, and in the remaining ships of the Navy, by September 1918. Measures taken to improve the safety of cordite under non-battle conditions were:

1. Regulations for the care and stowage of explosives in HM ships were revised.

2. Ventilating and cooling trunks to magazines were modified, stowage arrangements were altered, lagging and drenching arrangements were fitted.

3. Cordite cases were improved and all cases not properly weakened were removed.

4. Improvements were introduced in magazine-locking arrangements and the available means of access. Strict regulations were issued for the supervision of access to and the searching of compartments. (This measure was directed towards the prevention of sabotage.)

Magazine explosions caused by enemy action were not seen as a great danger until after Jutland. During this battle, three battlecruisers and one armoured cruiser blew up while in action, and serious cordite fires almost caused the loss of the battlecruiser *Lion* and the battleship *Malaya*. In *Lion*, an 11-inch or 12-inch shell hit and penetrated the centre of 'Q' turret at the joint of the front plate and the roof. The projectile exploded over the left gun and forced back the breech-operating lever. The breech opened, and the charges and shell slid out and dropped into the well at the rear of the gun. Some small fires had been caused inside the gun-house and, after some delay, the cordite ignited. The resultant flash vented itself through the turret roof and down the trunk to the magazine handing room. Luckily, during the lull between the shell explosion and the cordite fire, the magazine doors had been closed.

In *Malaya*, a 12-inch shell penetrated the forecastle-deck and exploded in the starboard battery near 'S3' gun, which was wrecked. Shell splinters penetrated some of the 'W' cases containing ready-use charges, and started a cordite fire which caused more than a hundred casualties and put the entire battery out of action. The fire also penetrated the 6-inch shell room which was open to the magazine, and but for the quick action of two men, *Malaya* would probably have been lost.

These occurrences were the most important evidence available to the Protection Committee of the Grand Fleet which concluded that the presence of bare charges in the gun-houses, hoists, handing rooms and magazines, was the most probable cause of the loss of the three battlecruisers. The charges – there were, on average, ten between the bottom of the hoist and the gun – constituted virtually a fuse connected to the magazine, and a shell explosion in gun-house or trunk was almost certain to ignite it. The committee recommended the fitting of flash-tight doors at the tops of the hoists, so arranged as to be always shut except when transferring ammunition from the hoist to the loading-cage, and the fitting of flash-tight hoppers in handing-room bulkheads with a door each side, one of which was to be shut at all times. The committee pointed out, however, that the large number of charges that were needed, between handing room and gun-house, to maintain rapid fire, would always entail the risk of an occurrence, similar to that in *Lion*, where the turret would be burnt out, but the magazine would be safe.

The committee's recommendations for the prevention of the spread of cordite fires among the ready-use ammunition for secondary armaments, were less positive. It concluded that the provision of structural arrangements to prevent extensive fires, like that in *Malaya*, was very difficult, but that some improvement in safety could be obtained by enclosing individual casemate-guns, providing fire-proof cases for the charges, and reducing the number of charges stowed round the guns. These and other recommendations were taken into account in the anti-flash arrangements that were introduced immediately after Jutland. The modifications and improvements mentioned below, are biased towards the ships with which this book is particularly concerned. Alterations in other ships were often of a different nature.

1. Trials were begun in HMS *Excellent* to determine the best form of flash-tight scuttle for handing rooms.

2. Handing rooms were built around the ammunition-hoists of secondary breech-loading armaments, and another series of trials was begun in *Excellent* to establish the most suitable type of scuttle for these rooms. Handing rooms for quick-firing magazines were not considered necessary as the cartridges, being in brass cases, were safe from flash; nevertheless, handing rooms were installed.

3. Leather aprons were fitted between the fixed and revolving structures of turret trunks, and the trunks were examined in detail and made as flash-tight as possible.

4. The enclosing of 6-inch casemate guns in the *Queen Elizabeth* and *Royal Sovereign* classes was objected to on the grounds that it would make command of the batteries difficult, but it was decided to provide 'Fearnought' fireproof screens between open battery gun-positions and ammunition passages.

5. Special instructions were issued concerning the supply of charges, so as to reduce as much as possible, the train of cordite from the magazines to the guns.

6. New pattern 'Clarksons' cases were introduced for use with hand-operated breech-loading guns. These cases, when spaced 5 feet apart, prevented the communication of explosions. Together with the introduction of splinter-proof ready-use ammunition boxes of 1-inch steel, they were to prevent a recurrence of the experience in *Malaya*.

All these alterations were made without carrying out shipboard trials, and to ensure that they were satisfactory, the pre-dreadnought *Vengeance* was employed in trials, so that the validity of the measures taken might be ascertained, and the need of additional measures determined. From the results of these trials, which took place in 1917, it was concluded that – with some modifications – the flash-proof fittings introduced after Jutland were satisfactory. In addition, it was discovered that because cordite explosions tended to vent upward, it should be fairly easy to make lower gun-mounting compartments flash-tight, even when tightly closed, and that ventilating trunks were liable to transmit flash to magazines. It was also concluded from these experiments, that some form of venting was essential in any compartment where it was particularly important that bulkheads remain intact.

Early in 1918, experiments were begun to find a magazine door that would be both flash-tight and an efficient vent to the magazine should an explosion occur. These trials, again using *Vengeance*, were unsuccessful and further tests were carried out in 1919 (in the pre-dreadnought *Prince of Wales*) and 1920. The result was a new circular magazine-access door which was flash-proof, watertight and which formed an efficient explosion vent. It was decided, however, that this be adopted only in new capital ships. (In fact it was never used. *Rodney* and *Nelson* were fitted with access doors of a different design.) After more trials in 1919, venting-plates and explosion-trunks, designed to prevent pressure build-ups in magazines, were abandoned, because they were not flash-tight. Also during this year, *Prince of Wales* was used to test the venting qualities of the magazine hatches of battleship secondary armament and cruiser main armament. The results showed that these were also satisfactory. In 1922, a new design of flash-proof magazine-scuttle with vertical revolving twin-compartments was introduced, which provided a saving in space over the previous type.

Apart from these structural arrangements to restrict the spread of cordite fires, efforts were made to render the cordite charges themselves, more flash-proof. After Jutland, trials were carried out in HMS *Excellent* to establish the vulnerability of breech-loading charges to ignition by fire, cordite-flash and shell explosions. It was proved that the main point of danger was the powder-igniter, sewn into the end of cordite charges to provide the first ignition to the cordite, but it was also found that even without the igniter there was a great danger of fire being communicated from one charge to another. The igniters on heavy charges were covered by tear-off discs that provided good protection against fire and flash. Firing trials were carried out, in which the discs were retained on all charges except the rearmost. Subsequently, the drill for guns of 12-inch calibre and greater, was modified to allow the discs to remain on the charges. The disc on the rear charge was removed just before the charge was rammed into the gun. This was not an ideal arrangement, as it was likely to cause delays and mistakes in loading, and by 1920 it had been abolished. Tests carried out to discover the effect of shell-bursts on bare charges, revealed that shell splinters did not ignite the cordite but the explosion of the shell would ignite the charge once its silk cloth covering had been penetrated by the shell fragments.

From 1916 onwards, suggestions for the protection of bare charges resulted in a series of varied and complex experiments, that was conducted over a considerable period. The following – by no means exhaustive – notes, outline the endeavours to immunise charges from fire, flash and explosion.

1. Cloth coverings. During 1917 to 1918, various types of material were investigated with a view to replacing the silk cloth of the bags which enclosed the cordite, by a cloth having greater resistance to fire and flash. Trials were carried out with asbestos cloth, viscous-treated silk and wool-serge and many others, including the material used on charges in the US Navy. None possessed the necessary qualities to replace silk cloth. More promising results were obtained with double-bagging, i.e. enclosing the charge in one silk cloth bag inside another. This was first suggested during the war, but could not be thoroughly investigated because of the difficulty of obtaining material, but in 1920, the Ordnance Committee carried out various trials with double-bagged charges. The results were satisfactory, but were not recommended for use in guns of up to and including 6-inch calibre because they affected the regularity of ballistics in these guns. In March 1926, further trials in HMS *Excellent*, under the conditions to be expected in a handing room, revealed that the adoption of double-bagging for heavy charges could not be justified. As against a limited protection from flash, the charges reduced the rate of fire, lessened the regularity of the ballistics and left débris in the gun. Additional trials, carried out with 16-inch charges, also proved unsatisfactory and the adoption of double-bagged charges in *Nelson* and *Rodney* was not approved. Trials were continued with tinned silk cloth and other materials but no success was ever obtained and the silk cloth bag was never replaced.

2. Metal envelopes. In the German Navy, charges for heavy guns were made up of four quarter-charges contained in heavy brass cases. Furthermore, to guard against premature ignition, the fore-charge was enclosed in a thin brass case without an igniter. The charges were removed from the heavy case immediately before loading into the gun, but the fore-charge was loaded complete with its thin brass container. The fact that the Germans used brass cartridge cases for their heavy guns was well known, but it was not until 1915 that the British discovered that the fore-charges were separately encased. The details were made available from a German ammunition handbook, translated in *Iron Duke*, but no importance was attached to the information at the time. After Jutland, it was suggested that British charges could be encased in thin metal containers but no action was taken at that time. In 1921, during discussions regarding flash-proof charges for 16-inch guns, the Elswick Ordnance Company proposed the adoption of thin brass envelopes for containing the charges, and at about the same time, details of the charges used in their 11-inch Krupp guns were obtained from the Dutch. Trials were begun using charges totally enclosed in brass sheet, but these were unsuitable and were abandoned in 1922. Trials were also carried out, using tin foil wrapping inside the silk bag, but these were also unsuccessful. The lack of success, however, is not surprising because the arrangements tested by the British were very different from those employed in the Krupp guns. The containers were made of thicker material than that enclosing the German fore-charges, but thinner than the main brass case. The trial cases, moreover, were joined by solder whereas those of the foreign guns were joined by mechanical pressure. Consequently they were too weak to withstand normal usage and, though immune from passing flash, they could not withstand the close proximity of a burning cordite charge. Firing trials with a 4-inch breech-loading charge in a brass case, resulted in the container being left almost whole in the chamber of the gun, and the chamber and bore were fouled by solder and pieces of brass. Tests with tin foil produced much better results, but these were still not up to the requirements and could not be guaranteed against cordite fires.

3. Igniters. In 1920, the question of reducing the number of igniters was considered, and in 1923 it was decided that two igniters per full charge was acceptable. In guns of up to 6-inch calibre, this meant one at each end of the charge, but in heavier guns in which charges were made up in fractions, it necessitated placing the charges in the correct order at the hoist in the handing room. In October 1924, the Ordnance Committee recommended the adoption of one 2-pound igniter per half-charge for 15-inch guns, and in May 1926, it was approved to adopt this arrangement in all guns of 12-inch calibre and greater. To reduce the possibility of mistakes, the igniter covers were painted red. In 1919, various trials were carried out with igniter covers and it was found that a double silk cloth cap reduced the flash danger to the same as that in any other part of the charge. These were adopted in guns of up to 8-inch calibre and the tear-off discs on heavy charges were retained. Arrangements were also made for the igniter covers not to be removed until the charge was ready for loading into the hoist in heavy guns, or into the gun, in hand-operated breech-loading weapons. In some guns, non-removable covers were provided.

4. Igniter-less charges. In 1921, a proposal was put forward to abolish igniters on charges and to place the igniter in a brass case which could be fixed to the breech of the gun. Preliminary trials with a compressed-powder igniter-charge placed in an enlarged breech-vent produced satisfactory results and further trials were carried out with a 6-inch Mk XII in November 1921 and early in 1922. In the latter year, a proposal was made for a 1-inch vent-tube in which the functions of primer and igniter could be combined. The first design of 1-inch tube was tested in 1924, and others followed in 1925 and 1926. As a result, the 1-inch vent-tube and igniter-less charge was approved for use in new breech-loading guns, and the design was put in hand in June 1926. It was not introduced for existing guns because the necessary alterations would have been very costly.

5. Water-jacketing. Between 1918 and 1924, various trials were carried out, in which magazines and individual charges were surrounded by a water-jacket. The success of the trials was very limited, and, in 1925, the Board decided that its advantages were not commensurate with the complications of construction and reduction in ammunition stowage (or, alternatively, the increase in space required) and the project was dropped.

6. Drenchers and sprayers. The original proposal to fit magazines with sprayers had been made in 1905, but was not taken up at that time. It was suggested again after Jutland, and, in 1917, approval was given for the fitting of sprinklers in all ships. The system employed was tested during the *Vengeance* trials in the same year.

In conclusion, it must be said that the arrangements adopted for rendering charges flash-proof, only reduced the risks of cordite fires, and it was fully realised that the likelihood of providing complete protection was very remote.

Underwater protection

Before the war, experiments were carried out with the old pre-dreadnoughts, *Hood* and *Royal Sovereign*, in order to gauge the effects of mine and torpedo explosions and to find a means by which the hull protection from such explosions might be improved. These tests resulted in the improvement of longitudinal torpedo bulkheads, and the introduction of the bulge. The latter was first fitted in some old cruisers of the *Edgar* class, and consisted of an outer air space and an inner, free-flooding, water space. Although these early experiments were obviously of great value, the results obtained were not completely reliable, and early in the war, a more scientific series of tests was begun. The most important of these were carried out on the 'Chatham Float, in which charges were detonated underwater against floating scale and full-size models, representing ships' structures. These experiments continued throughout the war, and for many years afterwards, providing invaluable information.

The main principles of bulge protection as developed during the war were these:

"(1) The damaging effect of an underwater explosion falls off very rapidly with distance and the first requirement of all underwater protection is to ensure that the explosion takes place at the maximum distance from the main protective structure of the ship. The longitudinal protective bulkhead is therefore fitted as far inboard as possible, the space between this and the outer skin is divided into two longitudinal groups of compartments.

(2) It is essential that the outer compartments should be empty as this air space serves to cut off the heavy pressure pulse which the explosion sets up in the water.

(3) The gaseous products of the explosion and large masses of spray are projected at high velocity into the air filled compartment. Their damaging effect can be greatly reduced by distributing their momentum over as large an area of the protective bulkhead as possible. This is efficiently done by a buoyancy space, containing either crushing tubes or water, which not only distributes the blow, but reduces the momentum of splinters and débris which might with mere projectile effect pierce the main protective bulkhead.

(4) Flooding the outer water tight compartments or emptying buoyancy spaces containing water for purposes of correcting heel and trim would considerably reduce the protective efficiency of the bulge and should only be resorted to when essential.

(5) A certain amount of fuel oil is often carried in side tanks immediately inboard of the protective bulkhead. In the event of a severe underwater explosion abreast such a position it is possible that, although the protective bulkhead would remain intact, the secondary pressure wave set up in the oil fuel, due to the sudden distortion of the bulkhead, would cause these tanks to leak into adjacent compartments. To minimise this possibility it is desirable to use the fuel in these tanks first."

The bulge provided good protection to a ship's sides, but parts of a ship's bottom could also be damaged by mines or by distant explosions. In this respect, it was found that double-bottom compartments half-filled with liquid helped to minimise such damage. Instructions were issued that double-bottom oil-fuel compartments should be brought to this condition whenever possible and, after the war, arrangements were put in hand for certain double-bottom compartments, particularly in the vicinity of magazines, to be half-filled with water. These compartments became known as 'water-protection compartments'.

Another important development of the war, with regard to protection from mines, was the introduction of the paravane. This minesweeping device, invented by Commander C. D. Burney, was fitted in a destroyer for trials in May 1915 and was fitted in all the major ships of the Navy between 1915 and 1917.

Aircraft

In 1916, Admiral Jellicoe set up a Grand Fleet Aircraft Committee, to consider the question of providing the ships of the Fleet with scouting and anti-Zeppelin aircraft. These were to be specifically for the fighting ships of the fleet; aircraft carriers had already been under development for some time. At first, efforts were concentrated on fitting aircraft flying-off platforms on light cruisers, mainly to provide the fleet with anti-Zeppelin aircraft. Demands were soon being made, however, for

Below: views of the aircraft platforms on 'B' and 'Y' turrets of *Repulse* in October 1917. The platform on 'B' turret (top photograph) was a temporary affair, fitted for trials only, and was different from later ones in that it had a pronounced downward slope. Note the training scale on 'Y' turret.

similar arrangements to be provided in capital ships for anti-Zeppelin use, but this was not considered practical because the ship would have to leave the line in order to fly-off its aircraft. This objection, however, was countered by a suggestion that flying-off platforms might be fitted on the turret roofs, as these could be trained into the wind without the ship having to leave its station. This technique was first tested in *Repulse*, in October 1917, and proved successful. It was practical and did not interfere with the operation of the turrets or the efficiency of the ship. It was decided to fit platforms for single-seater fighters in all the battlecruisers, and by early 1918, this had been successfully achieved.

Early in 1918, consideration was given to the possibility of improving the air-reconnaissance capability of these ships by equipping them with two-seater aircraft. The main problem was that these heavier machines required a longer platform from which to take off, but this was overcome by providing portable extensions to the existing platforms, that could be attached to the barrels of the turret guns. The first successful flight using this type of platform, was made from the *Australia* on 4th April 1918, in a Sopwith 1½-strutter. A programme was quickly put in hand, to fit lengthened platforms for two-seater aircraft on the forward turrets of all battlecruisers, and a single-seater fighter was carried on the after turrets. (This arrangement was not strictly adhered to; in the earlier battlecruisers, for example, the flying-off platforms were fitted on the wing turrets, and some ships carried fighters only.) Carrying aircraft in this manner soon proved very advantageous and it was eventually approved to fit similar platforms in the battleships. By the end of 1918, all the capital ships of the Grand Fleet had been equipped with aircraft.

By 1919, the carrying of spotter/reconnaissance aircraft by capital ships was considered essential. The development and use of flying-off platforms continued throughout the 1920s, but, as aircraft became heavier, the comparatively short platforms became less and less

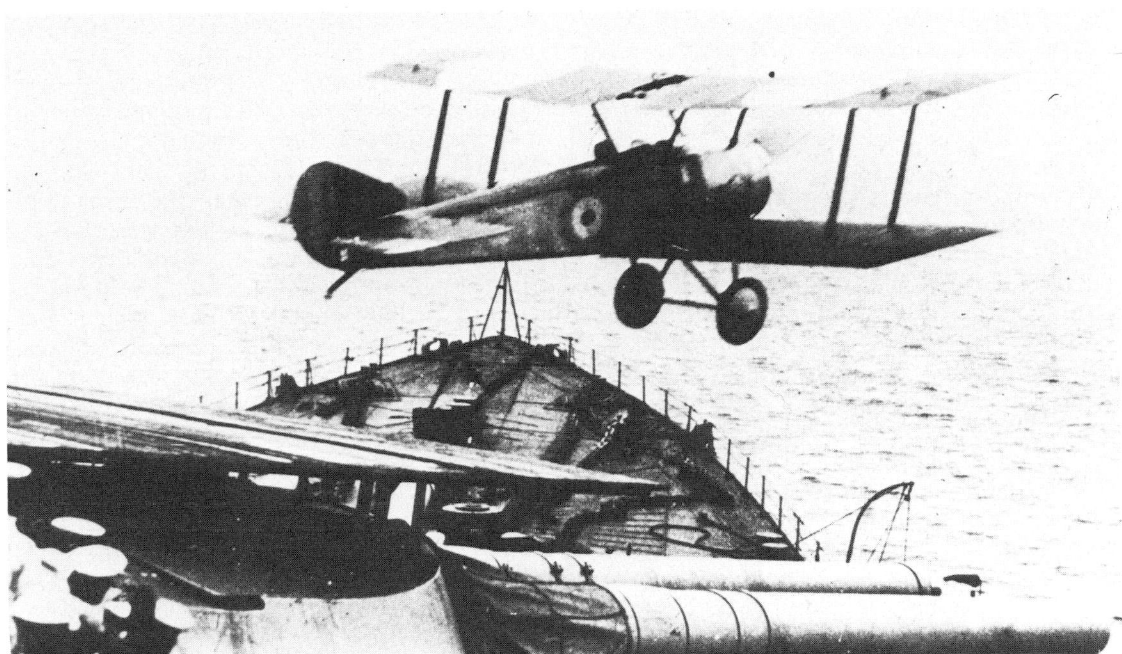

adequate. Attention, therefore, was directed towards the development of aircraft catapults, but as these did not come into general use until the 1930s the story of their introduction has been left for a later chapter.

Anti-aircraft defence

The need of a high-angle gun-mounting for anti-aircraft use had been realised before 1914, and to fulfill this need, an AA mounting for the 3-inch quick-firing gun was introduced. Few ships had been equipped with these weapons before the war, but by 1916, most of the dreadnoughts carried two 3-inch AA guns. The increasing activity of enemy airships over the North Sea during 1916, led to a demand for a larger calibre AA gun, and as production of 3-inch high-angle mountings had exceeded that of the guns, it was decided to convert forty-four of the spare mountings to carry a 4-inch breech-loading Mk VII or a 4-inch quick-firing Mk V. Strangely, none of these larger weapons was mounted in the more modern dreadnoughts; the ships of the *Queen Elizabeth* class and later designs, retained their 3-inch guns until well after the war. The final development of these early mountings was the 4-inch high-angle Mk III, which became the standard AA weapon of the battle fleet during the 1920s and early 1930s.

Although the provision of AA guns was a positive advance, their value during the war was very limited. The only likely target was the Zeppelin, and even if one of these came within range, the possibility of scoring a hit was remote. Some idea of the difficulties involved, is given by the fact that during the period 1914 to 1915, it was estimated that 100,000 AA rounds were fired, for every aircraft brought down by the army. By the end of the war, this figure had been reduced to 4,000 rounds, which, though a great improvement, was still not encouraging, particularly as the Army had far greater opportunities than the Navy, to fire at enemy aircraft. Towards the end of the war, the fighter aircraft carried by the ships of the fleet were available to deal effectively with the scouting Zeppelins, and the shortcomings of the AA gun became relatively unimportant. It was realised, however, that the rapid development of aircraft, the aerial-torpedo and the armour-piercing bomb, would, in the near future, present a substantial threat to the security of the capital ship. The main fear was that an aerial attack would disable, rather than sink, a large ship, and for this reason the development of an efficient air-defence system was of major importance. After the war, a Naval Anti-Aircraft Gunnery Committee was set up to look into this question, and to make recommendations on the provision of AA armaments in new ships. In addition, projects were put in hand for the development of a high-angle fire-control system, 5.5-inch and 4.7-inch quick-firing AA guns and, in 1921, a multi-barrel close-range AA mounting. The control-system and the close-range AA weapon were developed at a very slow pace, and appeared in the early 1930s as the High-Angle Control-System Mk I and the eight-barrel 2-pounder pom-pom respectively. Of the two heavy AA guns, only the 4.7-inch actually came into service, and then, only a few were manufactured.

3: THE NEW GENERATION*

The new capital ship designs considered during 1920, and those decided upon and worked out in detail in 1921, were without doubt, the most advanced and powerful capital ships – for their time – ever conceived. Their specifications were comparable to those of ships constructed during the Second World War, and had they been built, no other capital ship in existence could have faced them with any confidence. Needless to say, the design requirements for the new ships were based upon a detailed study of war experience, together with the examination of the available details of foreign construction; including that of the German Navy. (The German battleship *Baden* received a particularly detailed examination after being re-floated at Scapa Flow.) Although the Admiralty did not receive the necessary authority to begin a capital ship replacement programme until 1921, the requirements for future designs were being worked on as early as 1919, and were virtually complete in late 1920.

*Unfortunately, the authors were unable to locate the 'Battleship Cover' for the designs of 1920 to 1921. The amount of detail available for these designs, therefore, is not so extensive as that for the battlecruisers.

General Requirements for the 1921 and 1922 capital ships

General features. Two designs were required for the new ships; one, for a class of four battlecruisers to be laid down in 1921, and one, for a class of four battleships to be laid down in the following year. The only major difference between the two types was the question of speed; and the old definition of the battlecruiser gave way to what can be best described as a fast battleship. The armour protection was only marginally inferior to that of the battleship; the main armament was somewhat less powerful, and the speed was considerably greater, but otherwise, the two types were basically similar.

The necessity to counter the large ships under construction in the USA and Japan, and the heavy weights of the armour and armament specified, meant that considerable size would be unavoidable. The only restrictions imposed on the new ships in this respect, were the available docking facilities and the ability of the ships to pass through the Panama and Suez canals, but even so, the dimensions were expanded to the absolute limit. Even *Hood*, then the largest warship in the world, would have been dwarfed by the new ships which were the largest capital ships ever designed for the Royal Navy.

Primary armament. Early in 1920, three calibres of gun were under consideration. Their characteristics are shown in Table 27.

The general requirement was for a gun capable of defeating a ship protected by a 15-inch belt and a 7-inch deck. The design for the 18-inch gun was regarded most favourably

Table 27: Particulars of proposed guns

Calibre	Length	Weight of Projectile	Weight of Gun*
15-inch	50-cal	1,920 pounds	110 tons
16.5-inch	45-cal	2,552 pounds	130 tons
16.5-inch	50-cal	2,552 pounds	140 tons
18-inch	45-cal	3,320 pounds	159 tons**

* Approximate weights, Vickers designs. ** For the purposes of secrecy the 18-inch gun was always referred to as the 16-inch, 50-cal.

as the one least likely to be outclassed by foreign designs. It was known that the *South Dakota* class battleships were to carry a 16-inch 50-cal high-velocity gun, firing a 2,100-pound projectile at a muzzle velocity of 2,800 feet per second. It was rumoured also, that the Americans were producing an 18-inch 47-cal gun for trial, and that plans for 20-inch guns had been prepared, and plant for making them had been obtained. In June 1920, the American newspaper *The Globe* published details of the *Lexington* class battlecruisers and incorrectly claimed that they were to be armed with 18-inch guns, with an estimated range of between 26 and 27 miles. Strangely, the names of six ships (*Lexington*, *Constellation*, *Saratoga*, *Ranger*, *Constitution* and *United States*) their displacement, shaft horsepower and speed were all given correctly. Less was known of Japanese plans, but the Director of Naval Ordnance had been personally informed by his Japanese opposite number that they were considering guns larger than 16-inch calibre.

All the heavy gun designs considered early in 1920 and listed above, followed the practice that had begun with the 13.5-inch gun of having a heavy shell/low velocity combination, but in March 1920, the DNO issued a memorandum in which he cast serious doubts upon the advisability of this system. His arguments were based on the results of the proof tests of the 13.5-inch, 1,250-pound and 1,400-pound projectiles, which demonstrated that it was by no means certain that, at oblique attack, the heavier shell was the more efficient armour piercer. Both the light and the heavy 13.5-inch shell had to pass the same proof tests at the same striking-velocities, and while there were no failures with the 1,250-pound projectile, there were many, at first, with the 1,400-pound projectile. The failed shells usually passed through the plate but not in a fit state to burst, probably – it was thought – because of the greater length of the heavy shell. When penetrating armour at oblique angles of attack, the projectile was deflected from its line of flight, which produced a whip in the base portion. The stresses set up by this whip were greater in the long-bodied shell than in the short one, and its chances of breaking up during penetration were, therefore, greater.

It was also pointed out by the DNO that the existing 15-inch armour-piercing capped shell was not, as was commonly believed, capable of penetrating whole, any armour then carried afloat. Under proof conditions, only two such shells had successfully penetrated, in an unbroken condition, a 12-inch plate at 20° to the normal. The first was fired with a striking-velocity of 1,690 feet per second, equal to a range of 12,300 yards, at a standard armour plate, and the second, with 1,347 feet per second, equal to 25,000 yards, at a Vickers trial plate.

Trials against turret roofs showed that 5-inch and 6-inch armour when struck at 60° to the normal, could keep out a 15-inch shell, though a hole was punched in the armour. From these results, it was deducted that a 7-inch armour deck would defeat a 15-inch armour-piercing capped shell at 60°, that is up to a range of 25,000 yards. Only one trial at a steeper angle had been held, in which a 15-inch APC shell penetrated a 7-inch plate, at 45°, with a striking-velocity of 1,465 feet per second. Again, the DNO intimated that a shorter-bodied 15-inch shell would probably have better powers of penetration, and for future designs, he proposed the adoption of a high-velocity gun, firing a light shell. The theoretical advantages of a gun of this type were, a high striking-velocity at short range, a steep angle of descent at long range and a greater danger-space up to certain ranges. The loss in striking-energy resulting from the lower weight of a short shell compared to a long one of the same calibre and type, were considered by the DNO to be far more important in small and medium calibre guns than in heavy guns. Calculations showed, that for an equal maximum chamber pressure, a 1,690-pound 15-inch shell would have a muzzle velocity of 2,650 feet per second compared to 2,450 feet per second in the existing 1,920-pound shell. This gave the lighter shell a greater danger-space up to 22,000 yards, or 25,000 yards with a modified ballistic cap (6 crh instead of 8 crh). In the opinion of the DNO, the greater striking-energy of the heavy projectile would have little effect on the ability of the shell to perforate in a fit state to burst. Calculations were also made for the 18-inch gun with 8 crh projectiles of 3,353 pounds and 2,837 pounds and muzzle velocities of 2,500 feet per second and 2,700 feet per second respectively. The remaining velocities were found to be the same at 23,000 yards and only differed by 25 feet per second at 30,000 yards.

To test these theories, experiments were conducted with short-bodied 15-inch armour-piercing capped shells. The detailed results of these trials are not known, but they must have vindicated the DNO's arguments, for the 16-inch Mk I gun mounted in *Nelson* and *Rodney* used the high-velocity/light shell combination; in the event it was to prove a mistake.

It was considered that the best distribution of the main armament was in four twin turrets, arranged as in the *Queen Elizabeth* class. This system was ideal for efficient fire-control, and twin mountings allowed for turret designs of maximum simplicity and reliability. It was realised, however, that it might be necessary to adopt triple turrets in order to keep the displacement of the new ships within reasonable limits. Designs for both twin and triple mountings were obtained from Vickers and the Elswick Ordnance Company, for inclusion in the sketch designs of the 1921 to 1922 capital ships. These turret designs were given a maximum gun-elevation of 40° or 45°, which, it was thought, was necessary in order to obtain the maximum possible range.

Although at very long ranges, the danger-space of a broadside target would be so small as to be practically negligible, it was thought that the high elevation would be useful when the target was end on or near so; an important consideration in a stern chase, or when an enemy ship was closing or drawing away.

Secondary armament. The choice of calibre for the secondary armament was between the 6-inch and the 5.5-inch breech-loading guns. New designs were put in hand for both types, but by July 1920, the Staff had decided in favour of the 6-inch, and work on the new 5.5-inch design was suspended. (On the recommendation of the Ordnance Committee, the new 5.5-inch gun was to have been provided with a 90-pound shell as compared to the 82- pound shell of the existing gun of this calibre.)

Consideration was later given to combining the secondary and long-range AA requirements in one high-angle/low-angle gun, but it was decided that this was impracticable. Nevertheless, comparative trials were carried out in 1921, to test the stopping-power of the 6-inch and 4.7-inch guns against destroyers, it having been decided that the 4.7-inch calibre was ideal for the long-range AA armament. The general requirement was that one hit should have a moderately good chance of stopping a destroyer. The trials clearly demonstrated that the 6-inch common pointed capped shell, with Shellite burster, and the 6-inch high-explosive shell had much greater stopping power than the 4.7-inch semi armour-piercing shell. The 5.5-inch gun was not included in these trials, but its burst effect was considered to be approximately 30 per cent less than that of the 6-inch gun.

A comparison of the new 6-inch gun – which became the Mk XXII – with the existing Mk XII, is shown in Table 28.

Table 28: Comparison of 6-inch guns, Mk XII and XXII

Calibre	Wt. of gun	Mark	Length	MV	Wt. of shell	Wt. of charge
6-inch	6.7 tons	XII	45-cal	2,800 fps	100 pounds	
6-inch	8.8 tons	XXII	50-cal	2,945 fps	100 pounds	30 pounds

Neither of the existing methods of mounting secondary batteries in capital ships was regarded as ideal. The casemate, because of its adverse effect on stability and sea-keeping qualities, and the open battery, because of its lack of protection against gunfire and weather. The alternative was the turret, but to carry guns in sufficient numbers in this way necessitated the employment of twin mountings. This type of mounting had been out of favour in the Royal Navy, ever since the failure of the 6-inch twin turrets of the *County* class armoured cruisers, but the DNO pointed out that none of the drawbacks of this early design need be repeated in a new twin mounting. (The turrets of the *County* class were cramped, equipped with unsatisfactory training and ammunition-hoist machinery and poor gun-sights. The two guns were fitted in a single cradle without means of relative adjustment.) The turret would provide high and wide arcs of fire, lend itself to director-control, was easier to make flash-proof, provided better protection to gun-crews from gunfire and weather than the open battery, and had none of the disadvantages of the casemate, with regard to water-tightness. It would not be so well protected as the casemate and would absorb more weight than the open battery, but the advantages far outweighed these considerations, and by mid-1920, the Staff had decided in favour of the twin mounting for the secondary armament of capital ships, and the main armament of light cruisers.

Anti-aircraft armament. An AA armament was provided in accordance with the recommendations of the Naval AA Gunnery Committee. Its interim report was made on 13th September 1920, and the final report on 18th June 1921, but the committee was consulted before either report was submitted, in order that its recommendations might be included in the first sketch designs. As it was considered impracticable to combine the secondary and AA armaments, it was decided that the 4.7-inch gun was the best available calibre for the long-range AA armament. This conclusion was reached after comparing the rate of fire, burst-effect and weights of four calibres – the 3-inch, 4-inch, 4.7-inch and 5.5-inch. The first two guns were already in use, but the latter two were new designs. Work on the 5.5-inch quick-firing gun was suspended when the 4.7-inch was accepted.

The general recommendations of the committee for the AA armament of the new ships were: (a) Five or six 4.7-inch high-velocity AA guns firing a 60-pound projectile, at least four of the guns should be able to bear on any point in the sky. (In their final report the committee modified this statement saying that eight 4.7-inch guns would probably be necessary to allow four guns to be brought to bear on any target.) (b) The director-control position to be above all other control-positions with an absolutely clear view of the whole sky. (c) Secondary AA to consist of four multiple pom-pom mountings, with 90° elevation and after-training of about 180°, disposed two on each side. (d) Two secondary director-positions to control the pom-poms, one on each beam, with 200° arcs of training.

Armour. The war having demonstrated the the limited value of medium thickness of armour, it was decided that the new ships should be protected on the 'all or nothing' principle. This system was first employed in a dreadnought by the USA, in the battleships of the *Nevada* class of 1912. Briefly, the idea was that the vital areas of the ship – magazines, machinery and armament – should be protected by the thickest possible armour, while all other areas were unarmoured or 'soft'. One important requirement of this system was that the armoured citadel should have sufficient reserve of bouyancy to keep the ship in a stable condition should the 'soft' areas of the hull be riddled by gunfire or other forms of attack.

For the first time in a dreadnought, armour was specified for the horizontal protection. It was to be concentrated in single thick decks over the citadel and forward and after compartments, in order to provide the maximum protection against long-range gunfire and bombs. Although bombs had not constituted a danger to ships during the war, it was realised that there would be a steady progress in the size of bombs and in the methods of their use. To gauge the likely effects of bombing on future ships was difficult, however, as extensive bombing trials against actual ships were impracticable. Attempts were made to evolve a system of testing bombs in the same way as shells, that is, by firing them at a plate, at short range but with the velocity and angle of attack so adjusted as to resemble the conditions to be expected in battle. In 1920, the first experiments were conducted, to see if a bomb fired from a howitzer could be made to drop in the same way as from an aircraft. It was found that true conditions could be simulated, and a proper series of trials against armour plates was started in 1921. They continued throughout the inter-war period; all sizes and types of bombs being used, up to 2,000 pounds weight. It was from these trials that much of the information regarding protection from bomb attack was obtained.

Live trials were carried out against the radio-controlled target-ship, *Agamemnon* from 1921 to 1922 and *Monarch*, in 1924 but they were of short duration, poorly organised and only dummy bombs were used, and the results obtained were of limited value.

Underwater protection. The underwater bulge protection was to be based on that of *Hood* but with some important differences. Between 1920 and 1921, two experiments were conducted on the Chatham Float, when a 500-pound charge was detonated against the proposed bulge structure. In the first of these experiments, the buoyancy space was filled with crushing-tubes as in *Hood*, but in the second, water was substituted. The results showed that a water-jacket was less expensive than tubing and equally effective and it could therefore be adopted in new construction. Sufficient knowledge was also obtained to enable the depth of the bulge to be so arranged as to provide protection against 750-pound instead of 500-pound warheads.

As with *Hood*'s cancelled sister ships, it was decided to place the magazines below the shell rooms, where they would be less vulnerable to shell and bomb attack. Here, however, they were more vulnerable to underwater attack, and a third experiment was conducted at Chatham when a 320-pound charge was exploded under a structure representing a ship with a 7-feet deep double bottom. A compartment, representing a magazine containing various charges, was placed immediately over the position to be attacked. It was concluded that a 7-feet double bottom would provide a good protection, and that a 5-feet double bottom could be accepted with suitable magazine venting arrangements – even though charges larger than 320 pounds could be expected.

Machinery. A fairly conventional speed was envisaged for the future battle fleet, and although 25 knots was considered in the early sketch designs, 23 knots was eventually decided upon for the battleships. In the case of the battlecruisers, a speed equal to that of the US *Lexington* class was asked for but some difficulty was experienced in providing for this requirement plus the heavy weights of the armour and armament. The speed of the *Lexington* class was to be 33.25 knots; in the battlecruiser sketch designs, the speeds varied from a little under 30 knots to 33.75 knots. The Staff requirement for endurance was 7,000 miles at 16 knots, but here again, this was not strictly adhered to in the sketch designs.

The 1921 battlecruisers

The eight legends, sketch designs and particulars that were considered for the 1921 battlecruisers, are given in Table 29 overleaf.

The first two designs, 'K2' and 'K3', were very similar in general layout to *Hood*, particularly in 'K2' which was armed with four twin turrets. In 'K3', the use of three triple turrets produced a saving in weight of 1,100 tons, and thereafter, all the battlecruiser designs carried turrets of this type. The great size of the ships necessitated a transom stern in order to keep the overall length within reasonable limits. Even so, they could only just fit in the larger docks at Rosyth and Portsmouth, and their draught was too deep for the Suez Canal. (The maximum permitted draught in the Canal at that time, was 31 feet, but it was to be deepened sufficiently for the 'K3' design.) The 'K3' hull design was later modified to allow a ½-knot increase in speed and this involved increasing the beam to 115 feet 3 inches, the length to 855 feet (pp) and the displacement to 52,500 tons. (Later, the beam was increased still further to 115 feet 9 inches and the displacement to 52,800 tons.) This modification made it impossible for the ship to pass through the Panama Canal (maximum width 110 feet) or the Suez Canal. Furthermore, she could only be accommodated at the Gladstone Dock, Liverpool and in a newly acquired German floating dock. Both the designs were provided with a flush deck, by continuing the forecastle right aft. This increased the freeboard at the after end, and provided more accommodation. It also improved security against damage and obviated any repetition of the troubles in *Hood*, whose quarter-deck became awash in a heavy sea, or when travelling at speed.

In the next design, 'J3', the dimensions were reduced by providing an armament of nine 15-inch 50-cal guns, and by thnning the main armoured-deck to 4 inches. This reduced the displacement by nearly 10,000 tons permitting a length of 850 feet without the need for a transom stern. She could have been accommodated in any of the docks capable of taking *Hood* and she would have been able to pass through the Panama and Suez canals. The general layout was similar to that of 'K3' but the bulges and side armour were arranged as in *Hood* and not internally, and the forecastle-deck was not continued aft. 'X' turret, however, was raised well clear of the quarter-deck to the level of 'A' turret.

The 'J3' design was somewhat retrograde in character, and in 'I3' the problem of size was approached in a different way. The positioning of magazines below shell rooms necessitated very long ammunition compartments in order to keep the magazines away from the ship's side thereby providing them with sufficient protection from underwater attack. In 'I3', weight was saved by concentrating the main armament amidships, where the greater width of the hull, allowed a reduction in the length of the magazines and shell rooms, and therefore kept to a minimum the armour required to protect them, and ensured that the underwater protection was the best that could be provided. Thus, 'X' turret was placed between the bridge and the funnels, and the engine and boiler rooms were concentrated in the after part of the ship. The only major disadvantage of this system, was a 40° blind arc of fire across the stern which would probably have been even greater in battle because of blast effect on the after superstructure. The deck protection over the magazine spaces was slightly heavier than that in 'K3' but over the machinery and outside the citadel, the armour was generally reduced in order to save weight. These savings, however, were absorbed in the increased hull and machinery weight and the result was a displacement only a little under that of 'K3'. The ship could not have been docked at Rosyth or Portsmouth, but the beam and draught were restricted sufficiently to allow passage through the Panama Canal, and through the Suez Canal when it had been deepened.

In the December designs, more drastic methods of saving weight were employed. In the three variants of the 'H3' design, the main armament was reduced to six 18-inch guns in two triple turrets, and the weight thus saved, not only allowed for a reduction in size but also for an increase in the armour protection over the magazines. The speeds varied from 33.25 to 33.75 knots and therefore, were equal to the *Lexington* class. In 'H3a', the armament was concentrated forward, and in 'H3b', one turret was forward and one aft of the bridge structure. This, together with an increase in beam to 106 feet, resulted in a displacement of 45,000 tons. In 'H3c', the same layout as in 'H3b' was employed, but the turrets were lowered one deck, and the beam was reduced to 104 feet, bringing the displacement down to 43,750 tons.

In the 'G3' design, the calibre of the heavy guns was reduced (instead of their number), the main armament consisting of nine 16.5-inch guns in three triple turrets. The Director of Naval Construction pointed out that if this calibre of gun was unacceptable, three 18-inch twin turrets could be substituted and the resulting displacement and sketch design would be practically the same. The horizontal protection over the magazine was – as in the 'H3' design – equal to that of the battleship designs, then under consideration, and over the machinery spaces, it was similar and slightly superior to that in *Hood*. The obtainable speed was estimated as 33 knots, based on the assumption that eighteen high-power small-tube boilers could be forced to give 180,000 shaft horse-power.

On 13th December 1920, the 'G3' and 'H3' designs were discussed at a conference presided over by the Third Sea Lord. It is pro-

Table 29: Battlecruiser designs, 1920

	K2	K3	J3	I3	H3a	H3b	H3c	G3
Date	Oct. 1920	Oct. 1920	Nov. 1920	Nov. 1920	Dec. 1920	Dec. 1920	Dec. 1920	Dec. 1920
Length (pp) feet	850	850	810	890	825	825	825	825
Length (oa) feet	885	885	860	925	860	860	860	860
Beam (max) feet	106	106	104	108	105	106	104	106
Draught (for'd) feet	33	32½	29	32½	32½	32½	32½	32½
Draught (aft) feet	34	33½	30	33½	33½	33½	33½	33½
Displacement (tons)	53,100	52,000	43,100	51,750	44,500	45,000	43,750	46,500
Shaft horse-power	144,000	144,000	151,000	180,000	180,000	180,000	180,000	180,000
Speed at lwl (knots)	30 (nearly)	30	32	32.5	33.5	33.25	33.75	33
Fuel at lwl (tons)	1,200	1,200	1,200	1,200	1,200	1,200	1,200	1,200
Coal capacity (tons)	60	60	58	60	60	60	60	60
Oil fuel capacity (tons)	5,000	5,000	3,895	5,000	5,000	5,000	5,000	5,000
Armament:	8 18-inch 16 6-inch 6 4.7-inch 4 pom-poms	9 18-inch 16 6-inch 6 4.7-inch 4 pom-poms	9 15-inch 12 6-inch 6 4.7-inch 4 pom-poms	9 18-inch 16 6-inch 5 4.7-inch 4 pom-poms	6 18-inch 16 6-inch 5 4.7-inch 4 pom-poms	H3a, H3b, H3c		9 16.5-inch 16 6-inch 5 4.7-inch 4 pom-poms
Torpedo tubes	2	2	2	2	2			2
Armour:								
Belt	12-inch	K2 & K3	12-inch	12-inch	14-inch (over magazines) 12-inch (over machinery)			H3a, H3b, H3c, G3
Bulkheads	11-inch		12-inch	11-inch (forward) 10-inch (aft)	12-inch forward, 10-inch aft			
Barbettes	12-inch and 10-inch		12-inch	12-inch	14-inch			
Turret fronts	15-inch		15-inch	15-inch	18-inch			
Turret sides	12-inch		12-inch	12-inch	14-inch			
Turret roofs	8-inch		8-inch	8-inch	8-inch			
Conning-tower	10, 12, 15-inch 8 inch roof		10, 12, 15-inch 8 inch roof	12-inch 6-inch roof	12-inch 6-inch roof			
Conning-tower tube	11-inch		11-inch	8-inch	8-inch			

bable that 'H3' was not liked because the reduced number of guns in the main armament would make fire-control difficult and restrict the amount of all-round fire available. The conference liked the general features of 'G3' but objected to the thin armour-deck over the machinery compartments. They also thought that an unacceptably large number of men would be needed for supplying ammunition from the after magazines to the after 6-inch guns. The possibility of a 6-inch triple turret was discussed, but it was decided that a redistribution of the existing turrets would suffice. Finally, the DNC was requested to prepare a new legend for the 'G3' design, with the upper-deck armour over machinery increased from 2-inch and 3-inch to 3-inch and 4-inch. To compensate the additional weight of 1,125 tons, the following reductions were made.

1. The number of 6-inch twin turrets was reduced from eight to six, saving 100 tons. The turrets were to be arranged to give rapid supply of ammunition without a large increase in personnel.

2. The 14-inch armour belt was reduced in depth by 1 foot, saving 115 tons. The depth of the belt below the loadline was to be 4 feet 6 inches instead of 5 feet 2 inches and above the loadline, 9 feet 2 inches instead of 9 feet 6 inches.

3. Turret armour thickness was reduced; the Staff being willing to accept 16-inch front plates and 12-inch sides, which would save 75 tons.

4. The 8-inch and 9-inch deck over the magazines was to be reviewed in an endeavour to reduce weight, but without endangering the magazine protection which was generally to remain at its original thickness. This would save 125 tons and leave an adverse balance of 710 tons, and it was decided that the legend displacement should be increased from 46,500 tons to 47,500 tons.

In the new legend, the upper-deck over the machinery was actually given a uniform thickness of 4 inches and in addition to this, and the other alterations above, the following armour thicknesses were modified:

Conning-tower tube, from 8-inch to 8-inch and 6-inch.

Lower-deck (forward), from 7.5-inch and 4-inch to 7.5-inch and 3-inch.

Lower-deck (aft), from 7.8-inch and 3-inch to 7.5-inch and 3-inch.

After bulkhead, from 10-inch to 12-inch.

The legend was the same as before but the weights were changed; the armament was reduced to 7,300 tons, the armour was increased to 14,050 tons and the hull to 17,290 tons.

Early in 1921, the design was again modified. The main armament was reduced in calibre to 16-inch, and the machinery was reduced in power to 160,000 shaft horse-power for a speed of 31 to 32 knots. The reason for these changes are not clear, but it seems that the forcing of the high-power small-tube boilers was not possible. The original eighteen boilers providing 180,000 SHP (10,000 SHP each) were replaced by twenty boilers giving 160,000 SHP (8,000 SHP each). Despite the increased number of boilers, the machinery weight was less than in the previous legend, and it is likely that the boilers were of less weight than anticipated in the original estimates, which were based on the machinery weights of *Hood*. The change in gun calibre could have been merely a weight-saving exercise but it is also possible that the 16.5-inch calibre was disliked.

	K2	K3	J3	I3	H3a	H3b	H3c	G3
Director-hood	6-inch and 4-inch	K2 & K3	6-inch and 4-inch	5-inch and 3-inch	5-inch and 3-inch			H3a, H3b, H3c, G3
Vertical protective plating	$1\frac{3}{4}$-inch, 1-inch and $\frac{3}{4}$-inch		$1\frac{1}{2}$-inch, 1-inch and $\frac{3}{4}$-inch	$1\frac{3}{4}$-inch, 1-inch and $\frac{3}{4}$-inch	$1\frac{3}{4}$-inch, 1-inch and $\frac{3}{4}$-inch			
Funnel-uptakes	None		None	None	None			
Main-deck	1-inch (over magazines)		$1\frac{1}{4}$-inch	None	1-inch			
Forecastle-deck	$1\frac{1}{4}$-inch and $1\frac{1}{2}$-inch		2-inch, $1\frac{1}{2}$-inch and $1\frac{1}{4}$ inch	2-inch	2-inch			
Upper-deck	7-inch and 6-inch		4-inch	7-inch and 8-inch (over mags) 4 and 5-in (over mach)	9 and 8-inch (over mags) 4 and 5-inch (over mach)		H3a, H3b, H3c	9–8-inch (over mags) 2–3-inch (over mach)
Lower-deck (forward)	6-inch, 3-inch and 2-inch		4-inch, 3-inch and 2-inch	7, 5 and 4-inch	7-inch, 5-inch and 4-inch			7-inch, 5-inch and 4-inch
Lower-deck (aft)	6-inch and 3-inch		4-inch, 3-inch and 2-inch	6-inch, 7-inch, 5-inch and 4-inch	6-inch, 7-inch, 4-inch and 5-inch			7-inch, 8-inch and 3-inch
Weights (tons):								
General equipment	1,000	1,000	910	1,000	1,000	1,000	1,000	1,000
Armament	8,770	8,670	6,740	8,670	6,150	6,150	6,150	7,400
Machinery	5,670	5,670	5,670	6,430	6,430	6,430	6,430	6,430
Fuel	1,200	1,200	1,200	1,200	1,200	1,200	1,200	1,200
Armour and protective plating	17,310	16,060	12,780	14,600	13,250	13,600	12,800	13,350
Hull	18,900	19,150	15,640	19,590	16,250	16,400	15,950	16,890
Board margin	250	250	160	260	220	220	220	230
Totals:	53,100	52,000	43,100	51,750	44,500	45,000	43,750	46,500

Note. The number following the letter designation of the designs refers to either twin (2) or triple (3) main armament mountings

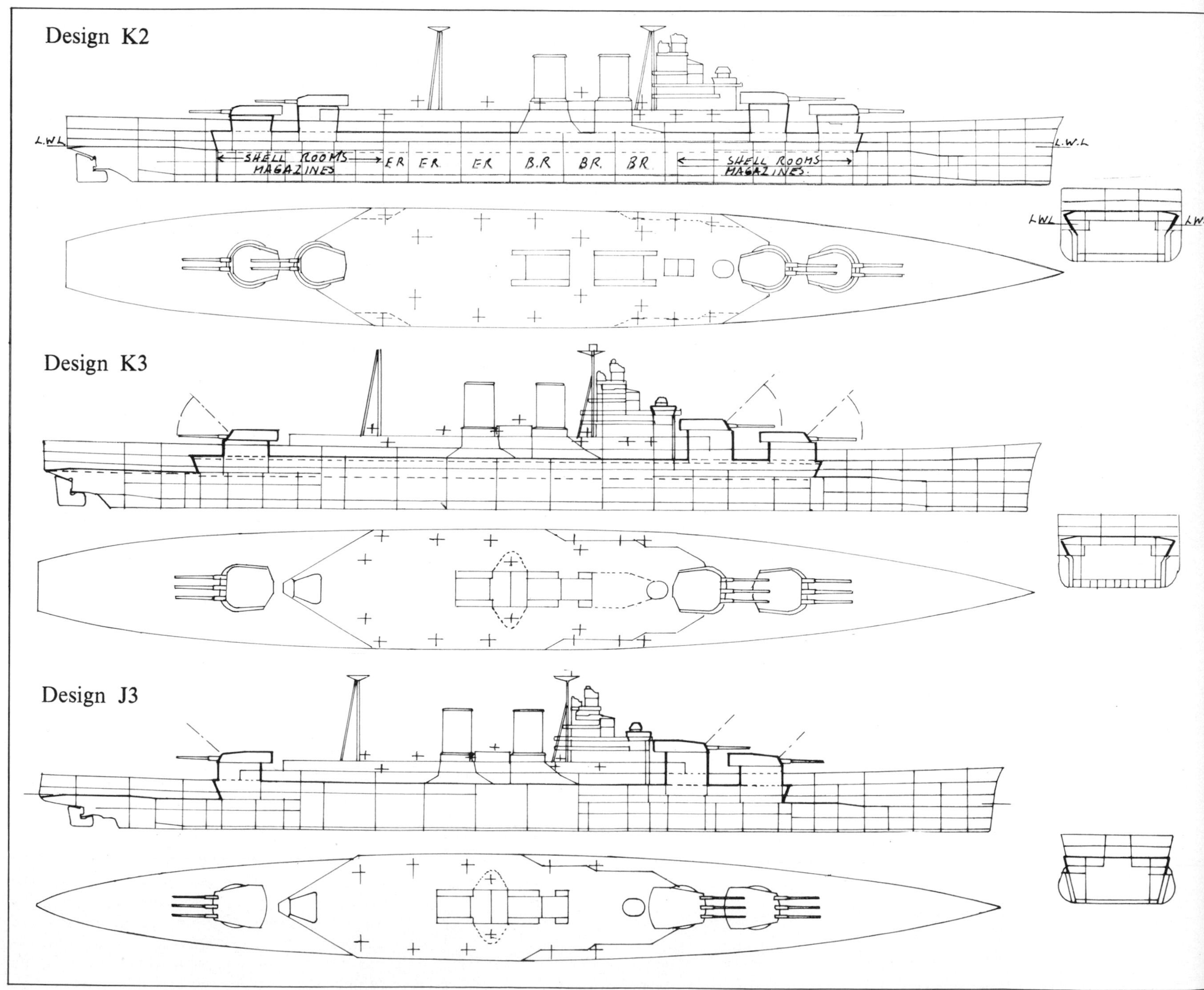

Design K2
L.W.L
SHELL ROOMS
MAGAZINES
ER
ER
ER
B.R
BR
BR
SHELL ROOMS
MAGAZINES
L.W.L
LWL
LWL
Design K3
Design J3

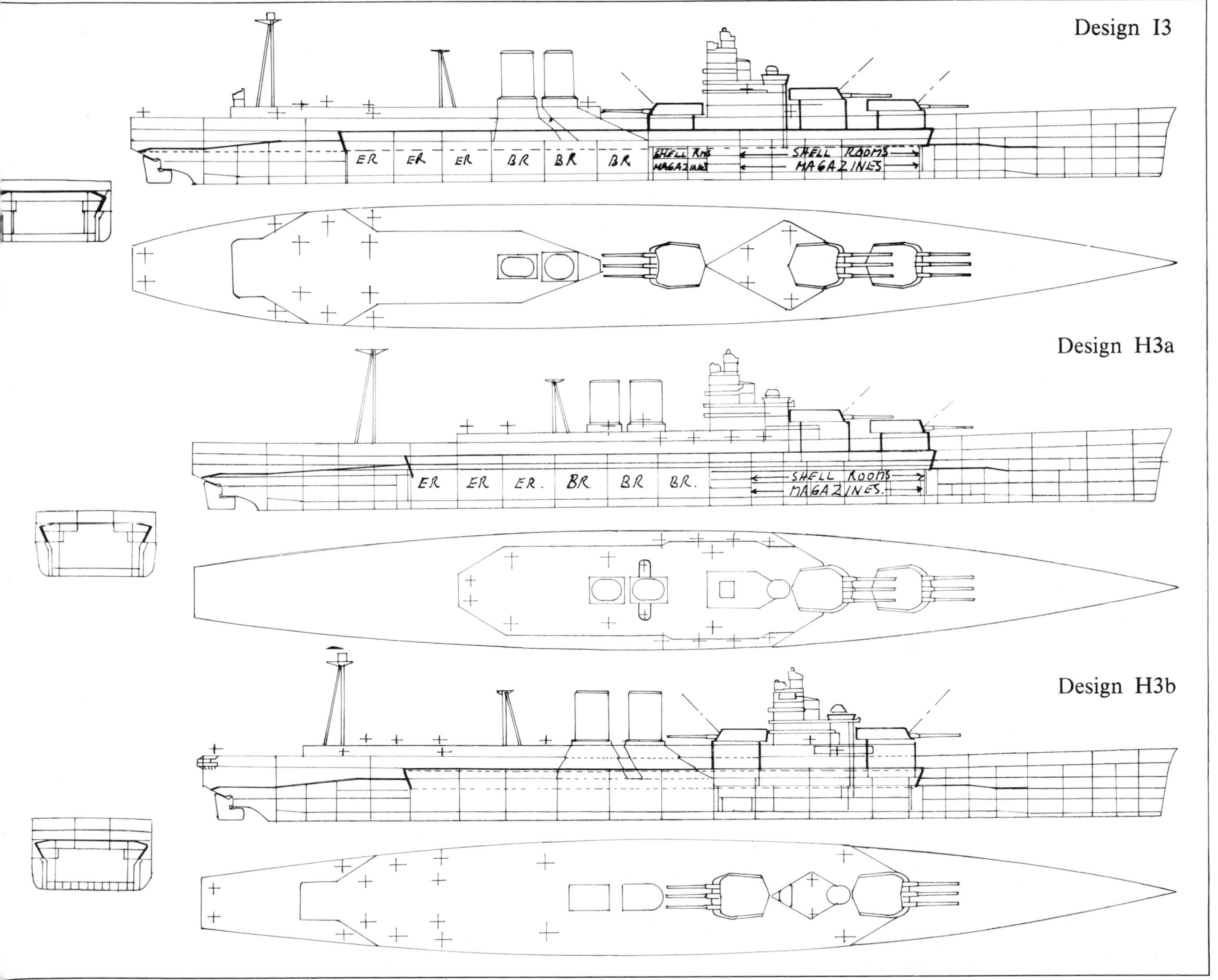
Design I3
ER
ER
ER
BR
BR
BR
SHELL ROOMS
MAGAZINES
Design H3a
ER
ER
ER.
BR
BR
BR.
SHELL ROOMS
MAGAZINES.
Design H3b

The weight saved, was utilised to increase the secondary and AA armaments to sixteen 6-inch and six 4.7-inch guns respectively, and to generally improve the armour protection, which required the reversal of some of the previous alterations. The belt was increased in depth to extend from 4 feet 6 inches below, to 9 feet 9 inches above the loadline. The after bulkhead reverted to a thickness of 10 inches and two additional armour bulkheads were installed; one, of 5-inch across the fore end of the forward submerged torpedo room and one of 4-inch, abaft the steering compartment. The main belt and deck armour were extended aft to include the after 6-inch magazines, and the turret thicknesses were increased to 17-inch (front plates) and 13-inch (sides). The armour on the lower-deck fore and aft of the citadel, was slightly rearranged and the conning-tower tube was returned to its original overall thickness of 8 inches. The effect of these changes was a reduction in length to 820 feet (pp) and an increase in displacement to 48,000 tons, the weights being modified as shown below.

General equipment	1,000 tons
Armament	7,050 tons
Machinery	5,950 tons
Fuel	1,200 tons
Armour and protective plating	14,700 tons
Hull	17,860 tons
Board Margin	240 tons
Legend displacement	48,000 tons

Some concern was expressed about the reduction in speed to 31/32 knots and the possibility of increasing this was discussed in February 1921. A ½-knot increase required 180,000 shaft horse-power and would have resulted in an increase of 200 tons in the displacement. The length would have had to be increased by 25 feet, which would have added to the difficulties of docking and passing through the canals. (The vessel could have docked at Portsmouth only if the caisson were in the outer stops, and this was considered unsafe.) The additional space required for the machinery would have reduced the underwater protection abreast the engine and boiler rooms. There would also have been an increase in building costs of £350,000, plus an increase in the running costs, because of the need of more fuel and a larger complement. The question to be resolved was, would a speed of almost 32 knots suffice to counter the *Lexington* class; the Assistant Chief of Naval Staff having asked originally for 33 knots for this purpose. The American ships, however, were considered to be of a very inferior type – in regard to protection – when compared to the 'G3' design, but there were also the new Japanese battlecruisers to consider. Nothing was known about their speed or protection, but it was thought that the Japanese were more likely to follow the British than the American type, in which case they were unlikely to achieve a speed of more than 32 knots. Regarding the *Lexington* class, one knot seemed a small tactical advantage if one considered the likely loss of speed resulting from a foul bottom. It was generally agreed by the Staff, that the existing design could be accepted; the advantages of a slight increase in speed would not be worth the increase in size.

These arguments regarding the acceptance of a 32-knot ship, were set out by the ACNS, Rear-Admiral E. Chatfield, in a memorandum dated 18th February 1921. It was circulated to the Naval Staff between 18th and 23rd February. The lack of information about the Japanese ships was viewed with some concern by the ACNS, and he suggested that a telegram be sent to Japan, asking the British Naval Attaché to find out more about their plans, or alternatively, that some information – on an exchange basis – might be obtained from the Japanese Naval Attaché in London.

In February 1921, the sketch designs and legend for the 'G3' design received the approval of the Board, and the Director of Naval Construction was requested to proceed with the detailed design. The final legend, midship section and sheer drawing were approved by the Board six months later on 12th August 1921. Invitations to tender for the hull and machinery were sent out on 3rd September 1921, to Beardmore, John Brown, Cammell Laird, Vickers, Fairfield, Armstrong, Harland and Wolff and Swan, Hunter. The tenders accepted were £3,786,332 from Beardmore, £3,879,000 from John Brown, £3,900,000 from Fairfield and £3,977,175 from Swan, Hunter. In all cases, the costs included fixed establishment charges and a profit of £700,000. The propelling machinery for the Swan, Hunter ship was sub-contracted to Parsons but in the other three it was to be manufactured by the builders. The orders were placed on 26th October 1921.

Armament. Early in 1921, the Elswick Ordnance Company was asked to produce a design for a 16-inch 45-cal triple turret based on the design of the triple 18-inch. In the same year, the designs submitted were approved and orders were placed for the necessary mountings for the first two battlecruisers.

War experience, and recently acquired details of German and American turrets were carefully considered when preparing the main armament designs. The flash-tightness was exceptionally complete – even excessive – and the armour protection was such that the turrets were virtually immune from penetration by existing guns or bombs. The magazine, shell room and loading arrangements were so disposed as to provide an estimated rate of fire of two rounds per gun per minute, and stowage of 100 rounds per gun was provided. The large increase in the revolving weight and barbette diameter, compared to previous turrets, required very careful investigation and extensive calculations were made. This particularly applied to the design of the ring-bulkhead and its supports, which had, also, to withstand the simultaneous discharge of three 16-inch guns.

The 16-inch guns were provided with the light shell/high-velocity combination, being designed to fire a 2,048-pound shell at 2,670 feet per second with a full charge of 525

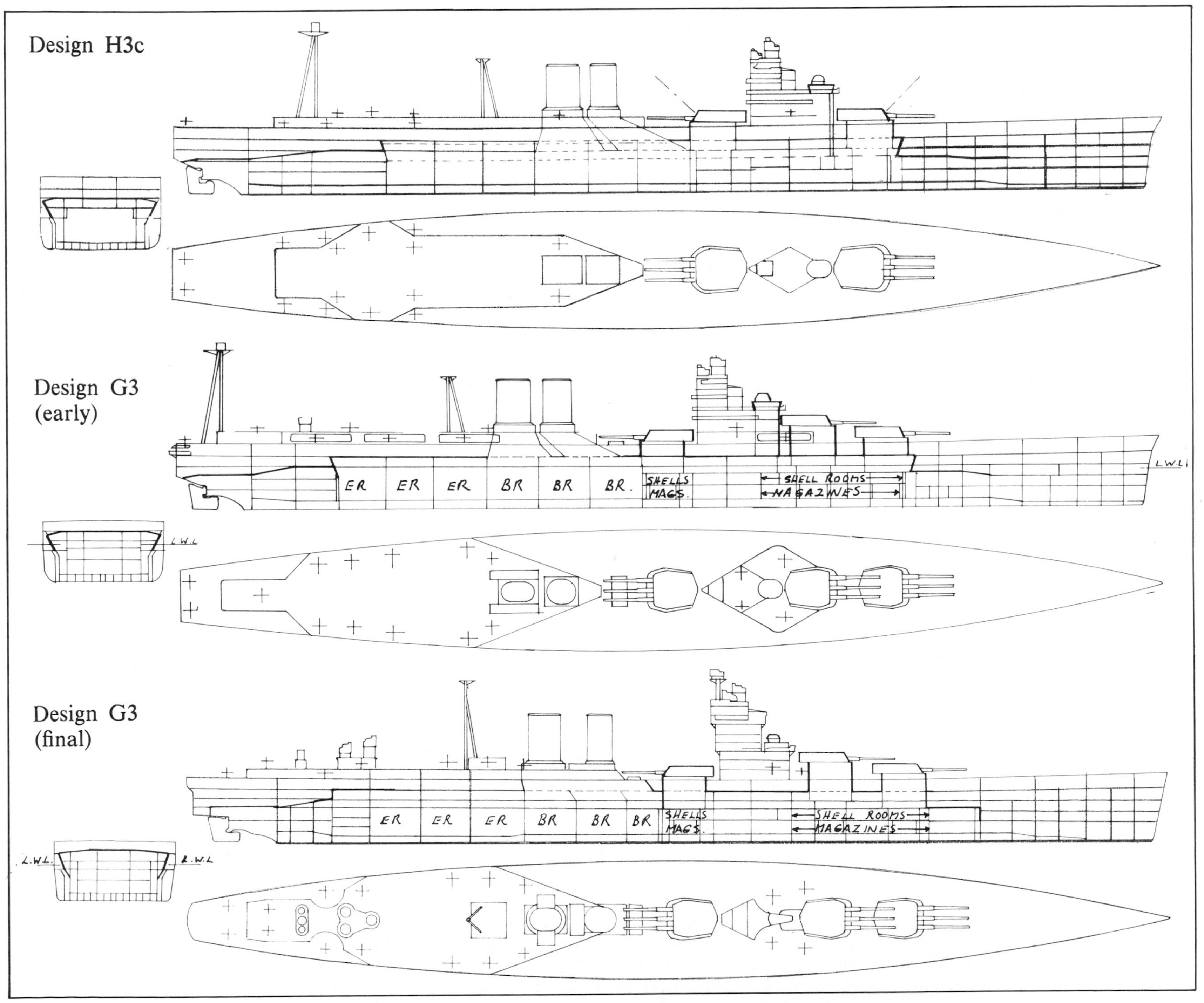
Design H3c
Design G3
(early)
L.W.L
ER
ER
ER
BR
BR
BR.
SHELLS
MAGS.
SHELL ROOMS
MAGAZINES
Design G3
(final)
L.W.L.
R.W.L
ER
ER
ER
BR
BR
BR
SHELLS
MAGS.
SHELL ROOMS
MAGAZINES

pounds of cordite. At the maximum elevation of 40°, this would give the guns a range of almost 42,000 yards (23½ miles).

The secondary armament of sixteen 6-inch guns, mounted in eight twin turrets, was so arranged as to receive a very direct supply of ammunition from the magazines and shell rooms. Stowage was provided for 150 rounds per gun for the forward, and 110 rounds per gun for the after turrets. As with the main armament, the ammunition supply was provided with several breaks and other safeguards to prevent cordite flash from passing down to the magazines. Economy of personnel was carefully considered when designing the main and secondary armaments.

The AA armament followed the recommendations of an interim report, by the Naval AA Gunnery Committee, and consisted of six 4.7-inch high-angle single mountings, and four multiple pom-poms. The latter were, at this time, envisaged as having ten guns per mounting.

The torpedo armament was to consist of two 24.5-inch submerged torpedo tubes, generally similar in design to those in the German battleship *Baden.* The torpedo tube compartment was in the usual position on the platform-deck, just forward of 'A' shell room.

Aircraft could be carried on the roofs of 'B' and 'X' turrets, but it had not been decided definitely that these would be carried.

Fire-control equipment. The bridge tower carried a main director-control tower, two secondary director-control towers and a high-angle director-control tower high up and well clear of smoke. (In the original sketch designs, the high-angle director was positioned on the starfish of one of the masts.) A small structure aft, carried a second main DCT and another two secondary DCTs, and abaft this, was an after anti-aircraft-control position. An alternative main armament-director was to be provided in the armoured hood on the conning-tower.

Protection. Basically, the sloping side armour and bulge protection was similar to that of *Hood*, but, as the bulge plating was carried vertically upward to join the forecastle-deck, the belt had become internal, and there was no external evidence of the bulge – though its requirements were maintained. This arrangement tied in well with the bulge-protection system and provided protection against attack from radio-controlled boats carrying large explosive charges (the belt being inboard of the point of impact). Abreast the magazines, the main belt was 14 inches thick, from the end of 'A' barbette, to the after bulkhead of 'A' boiler room; abaft this, over the remaining machinery compartments and after magazines, it was 12 inches thick. The ends of the citadel were enclosed by a 12-inch bulkhead forward, and a 10-inch bulkhead aft; in the original sketch design these were sloped like the side armour but in the final design they were made vertical. The citadel's horizontal protection was provided by an 8-inch deck over the main magazines, a 4-inch deck over the machinery and a 7-inch deck over the after magazines. It had been realised, at an early date, that such heavily-protected decks would have weak points at the openings for boiler-uptakes and ventilator shafts, and that substantial protection would be necessary for these openings if they were not to be a hazard to the safety of the ships. When the earlier designs were under consideration it was thought that it would be possible to provide deck-openings on two levels, each opening having an armour grid and being staggered relative to the opening on the next level, so arranged that a projectile would be bound to hit a grid on either the upper or lower level. The construction of a model demonstrated that this system would be very difficult to arrange in the battleships, and impossible in the battlecruiser because of the very large openings. It was then decided to reduce the size of the openings as much as possible, by omitting the armour gratings and increasing the velocities of the gases passing through these openings. Although reduced in area, however, they were still relatively large, and it was decided to protect them with sloping armour between the upper-deck and forecastle-deck and, on top of this, to fit armour gratings of special design, resting on cast steel bars of streamlined form. It was hoped that the gratings would deflect a short-range projectile and cause a long-range projectile to explode on contact, or before it penetrated very deeply. Financial stringency, however, prevented this from being tested practically.

In the 'G3' design, the accepted principle of the protection was, that the magazines should be absolutely safe, but that protection over the rest of the ship should be reduced. The funnel protection was therefore arranged with heavy armour and gratings at the fore end. This was designed to prevent a delayed-action shell detonating in the vicinity of 'X' magazine. At the after end, the armour thickness and gratings were reduced in order to save weight, but even so, the total weight of the funnel protection was 766 tons. In the words of the Director of Naval Construction: "The arrangement of reduced armour at the after end is not logical except that it conforms with the natural illogical protection of a battlecruiser".

Forward of the citadel, the submerged torpedo rooms were protected below the waterline by a heavy belt, tapering in thickness towards the stem, a 6-inch deck and a 6-inch bulkhead. This armour also provided additional security to the forward magazines. Abaft the citadel, the steering compartment was protected by a 5-inch deck and a 4½-inch bulkhead and forward of this, a 3-inch and 5-inch deck protected the after magazines from raking fire.

The barbette armour was 14 inches tapering to 12 inches or 11 inches at the middle-line and the turrets had 17-inch front plates, 13-inch sides and an 8-inch roof. The conning-tower had 14-inch sloping sides, 4-inch back, 10-inch front, 6-inch roof and 4-inch floor, with an 8-inch communication tube down to the armoured-deck. The armoured director-hood had 3-inch sides and roof and a 5-inch face, and rested on a tube, 6 inches thick outside and 2 inches thick inside the conning-tower. The working spaces for the 6-inch turrets, conning-tower support, bridges and director-control tower were protected by 1-inch protective plating, and the secondary armament and control-positions, with the exception of the one armoured director-hood, were, therefore, relatively poorly protected.

Underwater protection. The bulge protection was designed to withstand the explosion of a 750-pound torpedo warhead. It consisted of an outer air space, an inner bouyancy space and a 1¾-inch torpedo bulkhead. The overall width of the protection was approximately 14 feet on each side. To fill the buoyancy spaces, a total of 2,630 tons of water was required, but it was considered necessary to flood them only during wartime or for purposes of tests and exercises. This reduced the load carried by the ship in peacetime and offered some economy in fuel consumption. In order to correct heel rapidly in the event of damage, an air-compression system for blowing out the tanks was to have been fitted – similar to those in submarines. With this arrangement, it would have been possible to return the ship to the upright in not more than fifteen minutes after having been struck by two torpedoes. In addition, oil-fuel pumps, larger than those of *Hood* were specified, in order to improve the transference of oil fuel from one compartment to another for the purposes of correcting heel and trim. Protection from mines was provided by a double bottom, seven feet deep.

Machinery. The propelling machinery was similar to that fitted in *Hood,* and consisted of four sets of geared turbines driving four shafts, arranged in three engine rooms, and twenty boilers arranged in nine boiler rooms. Fuel economy at cruising speed was to be achieved by cruising turbines developing 20,000 shaft horse-power for an estimated 17 knots. Oil-fuel stowage was 5,000 tons, sufficient for the Staff requirement of an endurance of 7,000 miles at 16 knots.

Stability. The 'all or nothing' protection system required a fairly substantial level of stability in order to ensure the safety of the ship in riddled condition. The GM, therefore, was higher than any yet specified for a British dreadnought, being 4.9 feet in the light condition, 5.63 feet in the legend condition, 7.786 feet in the deep condition and 8.48 feet in the extra deep condition. To ensure that the stability was adequate, the triangular spaces between the belt armour and the ship's side were to be filled with light tubes. With these

PARTICULARS OF 'G3' BATTLECRUISERS AS FINALLY DESIGNED, NOVEMBER 1921

Displacement and weights

Hull	18,600 tons
General equipment	1,000 tons
Armour and protective plating	14,440 tons
Main armament	6,120 tons
Minor armament	1,040 tons
Oil fuel	1,200 tons
Machinery and engineers' stores	6,000 tons
Legend displacement	48,400 tons

Additions for deep condition:

General equipment	320 tons
Main armament	437 tons
Minor armament	177 tons
Oil fuel	3,800 tons
Machinery and engineers' stores	775 tons
Deep displacement	53,909 tons

Additions for extra deep condition:

Water in buoyancy spaces	2,630 tons
Extra deep displacement	56,540 tons

Subtractions from legend displacement for light condition:

Oil fuel	1,200 tons
Engineers' stores	60 tons
Stores	30 tons
Officers' stores	70 tons
Provisions	100 tons
Fresh water	110 tons
Total	1,570 tons

Legend light condition = 48,400 tons – 1,570 tons = 46,830 tons.

Tons per inch: 144.4 tons at load line.

Dimensions

820 feet (between perpendiculars), 850 feet (waterline). 856 feet (overall) × 106 feet (maximum).

Draught:	Forward	Aft	Mean	Trim
Load	31ft 7½in	33ft 3in	32ft 5¼in	1ft 7½in by stern
Deep	35ft 4in	36ft	35ft 8in	8in by stern
Extra deep	37ft 4in	37ft 1in	37ft 2½in	3in by bow
Light	31ft 1in	32ft 1in	31ft 7in	1ft by stern

Armament

Nine 16-inch 45-cal breech-loading: three triple mountings.
Sixteen 6-inch 50-cal breech-loading: eight twin mountings.
Six 4.7-inch 43-cal high-angle quick-firing: single mounting.
Forty 2-pounder pom-poms: four mountings.
Two 24.5-inch torpedo tubes.
Two aircraft.

Ammunition stowage

16-inch: 80 rounds per gun normal; 100 rounds per gun maximum.
6-inch: 150 rounds per gun forward turrets; 110 rounds per gun after turrets.
4.7-inch: 200 rounds per gun.
2-pounder: 1,225 rounds per barrel.
16 torpedoes peacetime; 20 torpedoes wartime.

Armour

Belt: 14 inch at 72° abreast magazines, 12 inch at 72° abreast machinery and after magazines.
Bulkheads: 12 inch and 5 inch forward, 10 inch and 4 inch aft.
Barbettes: 14 inch, 13 inch, 12 inch and 11 inch.
Turrets: 17 inch front, 13 inch sides, 8 inch roof.
Conning-tower: 14 inch sides, 10 inch front, 4 inch back, 6 inch roof, 4 inch floor.
Conning-tower tube: 8 inch.
Conning-tower support: 1 inch.
Director-hood: 5 inch and 3 inch.
Director-hood support: 6 inch and 2 inch.
Funnel-uptakes: 4 inch and 5 inch forward, 12 inch, 9 inch, 6 inch, 5 inch and 4 inch sides, 3 inch aft on ½ inch plating.

Protective plating to 6 inch working spaces, bridges and DCTs: 1 inch.
Forecastle-deck: 1 inch.
Upper-deck: 8 inch over main magazines, 7 inch over after magazines, 4 inch over machinery.
Lower-deck: 6 inch forward, 5 inch and 3 inch aft.
Torpedo bulkheads: 1¾ inch.

Machinery

Single-reduction geared turbines, four shafts.
160,000 SHP = 31/32 knots.
Twenty small-tube boilers.

Fuel

5,000 tons oil fuel capacity.
50 tons coal capacity.

Complement 1,716.

in place, it was calculated that the whole of this structure on either side of the ship would have to be blown away before the ship lost its stability.

The 1922 battleships

The first sketch designs for the 1922 battleships were drawn up in June 1920, before the Staff requirements had been fully settled. These two designs, 'L^{II}' and 'L^{III}' are of interest, primarily because of the strange arrangement of their main armament, all the turrets being positioned at the same level. It is difficult to see any advantage in this layout apart from a saving in top-weight and a possibility that the guns would be easier to calibrate. Although the blocked turrets could fire over the adjacent turrets, if the guns were elevated to 12° or more, the resulting blast effects would probably have precluded their use in this manner. Other interesting features are the omission of an armoured conning-tower, the midship section, which varies in several points from that of the later designs, and the retention of a quarter-deck in Design 'L2'. The general particulars of the two designs are given in Table 30.

Table 30: Legend of particulars of Designs L^{II} and L^{III}

	L^{II}	L^{III}
Length (wl) (feet)	850	850
Beam (feet)	106	106
Draught (feet)	31	30½
Speed (knots)	25	26
Armament	Eight 18-inch Sixteen 6-inch Four 4.7-inch	Nine 18-inch Sixteen 6-inch Four 4-inch
Armour:		
Belt	18-inch	
Bulkheads	15-inch	
Barbettes	18-inch	
Turret fronts	18-inch	
Turret roofs	9-inch	
Upper-deck (flat)	8¾-inch	
Upper-deck (slope)	13-inch	
Lower-deck (forward)	3½-inch, 5½-inch and 8¾-inch	
Lower-deck (aft)	8¾-inch	
Torpedo bulkheads	1½-inch	
Weights (tons):		
General equipment	1,000	1,000
Armament	8,850	8,000
Machinery	3,350	3,560
Oil fuel	1,200	1,200
Armour and protective plating	17,600	17,000
Hull	18,500	18,100
Board margin	250	240
Displacement:	50,750	49,100

In October 1920 these two designs were heavily modified and put forward at the same time as the first two battlecruiser designs, 'K2' and 'K3'. They were followed by Designs 'M3' in November 1920, and 'M2' in December 1920. The particulars of the four designs considered, are given in Table 31.

Table 31: Battleship designs, 1920

	L2	L3	M3	M2
Date	October 1920	October 1920	November 1920	December 1920
Length (pp) feet	825	825	740	780
Length (oa) feet	860	860	775	815
Beam (maximum) feet	106	106	106	106
Draught (mean) feet	33½	33	33	33
Displacement, tons	52,100	51,100	46,000	48,750
SHP	70,000	70,000		
Speed at lwl (knots)	25	25	23.5	23
Fuel at lwl tons	1,200	1,200	1,100	1,100
Oil fuel (capacity) tons	5,000	5,000		
Armament:	Eight 18-inch	Nine 18-inch	Nine 18-inch	Eight 18-inch
	Sixteen 6-inch Six 4.7-inch Four pom-poms Two torpedo tubes	} L2, L3	Sixteen 6-inch Five 4.7-inch Two pom-poms Two torpedo tubes	} M3, M2
Armour:				
Belt	15-inch	} L2, L3	15-inch	} M3, M2
Bulkhead	14-inch		14-inch and 12-inch	
Barbette	15-inch		15-inch	
Turret front	18-inch		18-inch	
Turret back	9-inch		9-inch	
Turret roof	8-inch		8-inch	
Conning-tower	15-inch, 8-inch roof		15-inch, 8-inch roof	
Director-hood	6-inch and 4-inch		6-inch and 4-inch	
Upper-deck	8-inch flat, 9-inch slope		6-inch, 7-inch and 8-inch flat 7-inch, 8-inch and 9-inch slope	
Lower-deck (forward)	2-inch, 4-inch, 6-inch and 8-inch		4-inch, 6-inch and 8-inch	
Lower-deck (aft)	8-inch and 5-inch		6-inch, 7-inch and 8-inch	
Torpedo bulkheads	1¾-inch		1¾-inch	
Weights (tons):				
General equipment	1,000	1,000	1,000	1,000
Armament	8,950	8,850	8,850	8,950
Machinery	3,250	3,250	2,720	2,720
Fuel	1,200	1,200	1,100	1,100
Armour and protective plating	18,850	17,800	15,400	17,200
Hull	18,600	18,750	16,700	17,530
Board margin	250	250	230	250
Totals:	52,100	51,100	46,000	48,750

The problems of battlecruiser Designs 'K2' and 'K3' regarding the difficulties of docking and passing through the Panama and Suez canals, also applied to Designs 'L2' and 'L3'. The general principles of the designs were similar but had some important differences.

Naturally, the armour protection was heavier.

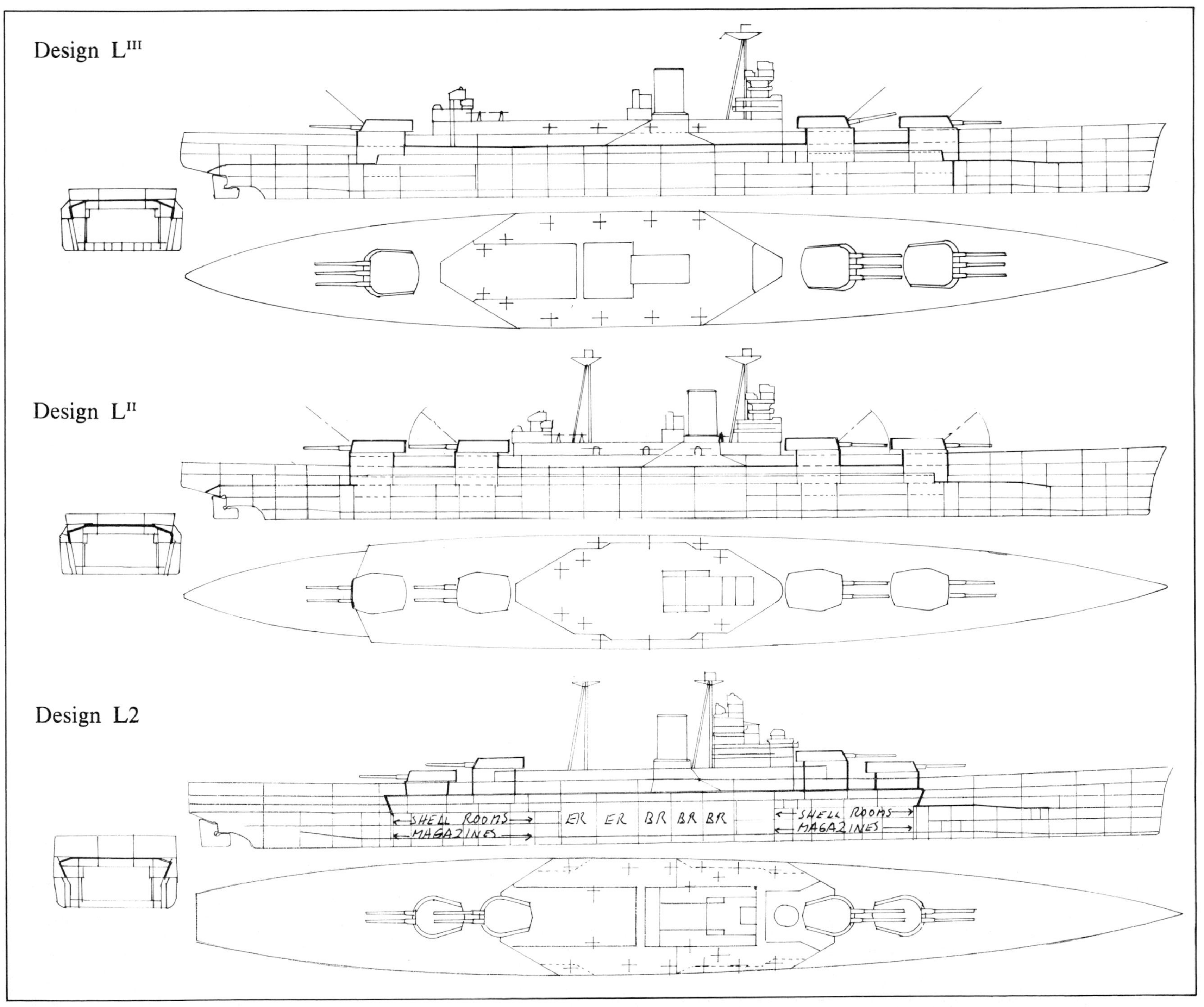
Design L^{III}
Design L^{II}
Design L2
SHELL ROOMS
MAGAZINES
ER ER BR BR BR
SHELL ROOMS
MAGAZINES

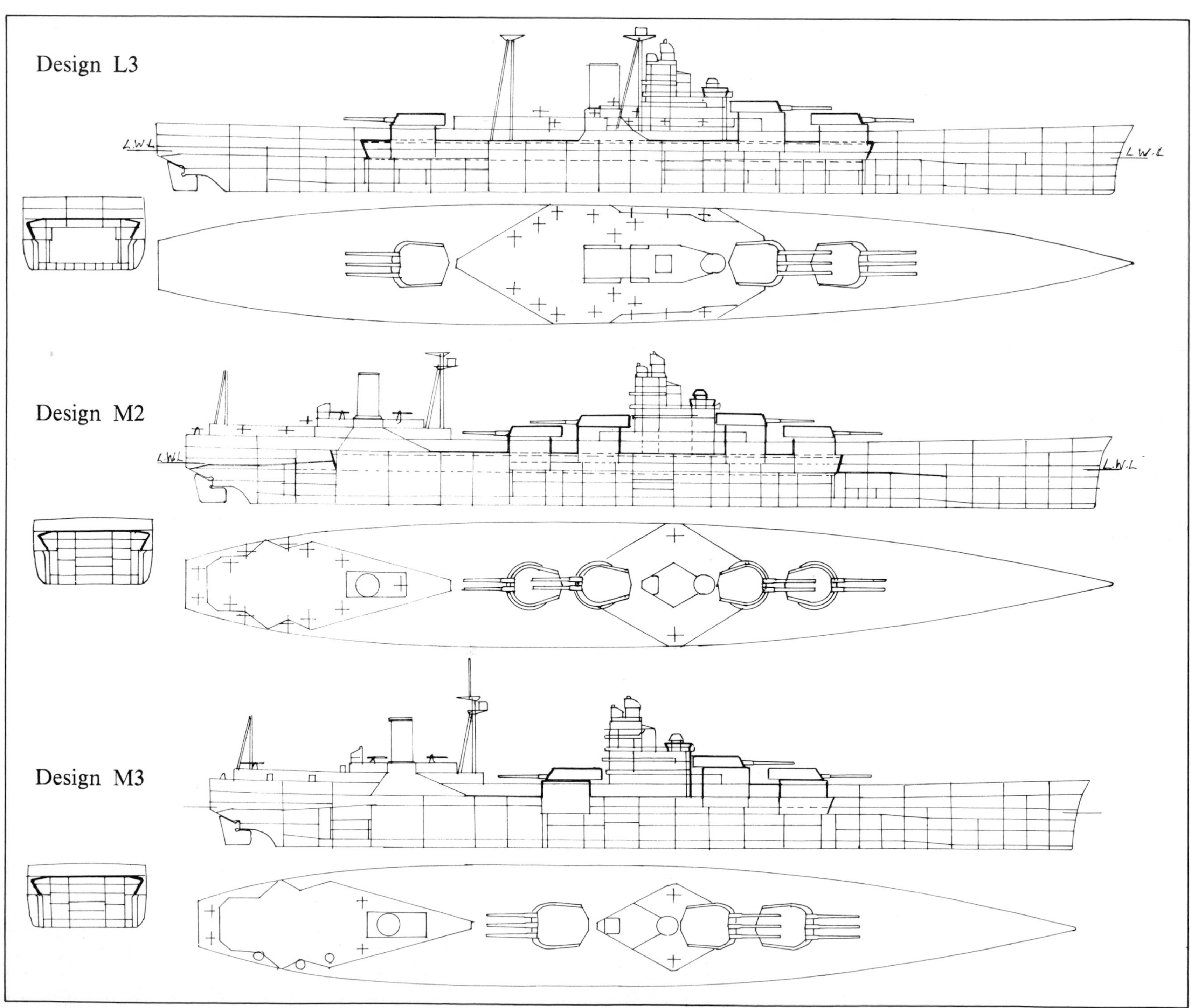
Design L3
L.W.L
L.W.L
Design M2
L.W.L
L.W.L
Design M3

PARTICULARS OF 'N3' BATTLESHIPS AS DESIGNED, NOVEMBER 1921

Displacement 48,500 tons.

Dimensions
820 feet (oa), 815 feet (wl), 790 feet (pp) × 106 feet × 32 feet to 33 feet.

Armament
Nine 18-inch 45-cal breech-loading: three triple mountings.
Sixteen 6-inch 50-cal breech-loading: eight twin mountings.
Six 4.7-inch 43-cal high-angle quick-firing: single mountings.
Forty 2-pounder pom-poms : four mountings.
Two 24.5-inch torpedo tubes.
Two aircraft.

Armour
Belt: 15-inch at 72° abreast magazines, 13.5-inch at 72° abreast machinery.
Bulkheads: 14-inch and 9-inch forward, 14-inch and 6-inch aft.
Barbettes: 15-inch.
Turrets: 18 inch front, 14 inch sides, 14 inch back, 8-inch roof.
Conning-tower: 15-inch walls, 8-inch roof, 6-inch floor.
Conning-tower tube: 8-inch.
Director-hood: 4-inch and 6-inch.
Director-hood support: 6-inch.
Protective plating to 6-inch working spaces, bridges and DCTs : 1 inch.
Upper-deck: 8-inch.
Lower-deck: 8-inch forward, 8-inch and 6-inch aft.
Torpedo bulkheads: 2-inch.

Speed 23/23.5 knots.

The great weight involved was largely necessitated by the thick deck, which was 8 inches on the flat and 9 inches on the slope, over the entire length of the citadel. At that time, it was thought that any less thickness would be penetrable by heavy projectiles, at long range. The speed of 24 knots in the deep condition, and 25 knots in the light condition, was to have been provided – for the first time in a dreadnought – by twin-screw machinery. The two larger screws would have given better manoeuvring power than four small screws.

The 'M3' design was contemporaneous with the 'I3' batlecruiser, and, as in that ship, weight was saved by concentrating the main armament amidships. A considerable amount of weight was also saved by reducing the speed to 23.5 knots, which produced an overall reduction of 5,000 tons on the 'L3' design. The docking restrictions still remained however, although she could have passed through the Panama and Suez canals. One important difference between 'M3' and 'I3', was the positioning of the boiler rooms abaft the engine rooms, which was not practical in the battlecruiser because of the great length of shafting required. This allowed the funnel to be placed aft, and reduced the blind arc of fire of 'X' turret to 15° on either side of the middle-line aft, and placed the engine rooms in a wider part of the ship, where it was possible to provide better underwater protection. Some saving was also made on the protection by reducing the armoured deck thickness to 7 inches and 8 inches over the engine rooms, and 6 inches and 7 inches over the boiler rooms. The 'M2' design was a modified version of 'M3', with an extra turret sited between the bridge and the after superstructure, a $\frac{1}{2}$-knot reduction in speed, and an increase in displacement of 2,750 tons.

The results of the discussions of these designs are unknown, but it appears that Design 'M3' was chosen to be worked out in detail. The final sketch design was a slightly larger and longer version of 'M3', that was generally similar in layout to the 'G3' design. The approved version was designated 'N3', and was dated November 1921. The following description is based mainly, but not entirely, on the sketch design.

Armament. The 18-inch 45-cal gun and its triple mounting, were designed by Armstrongs

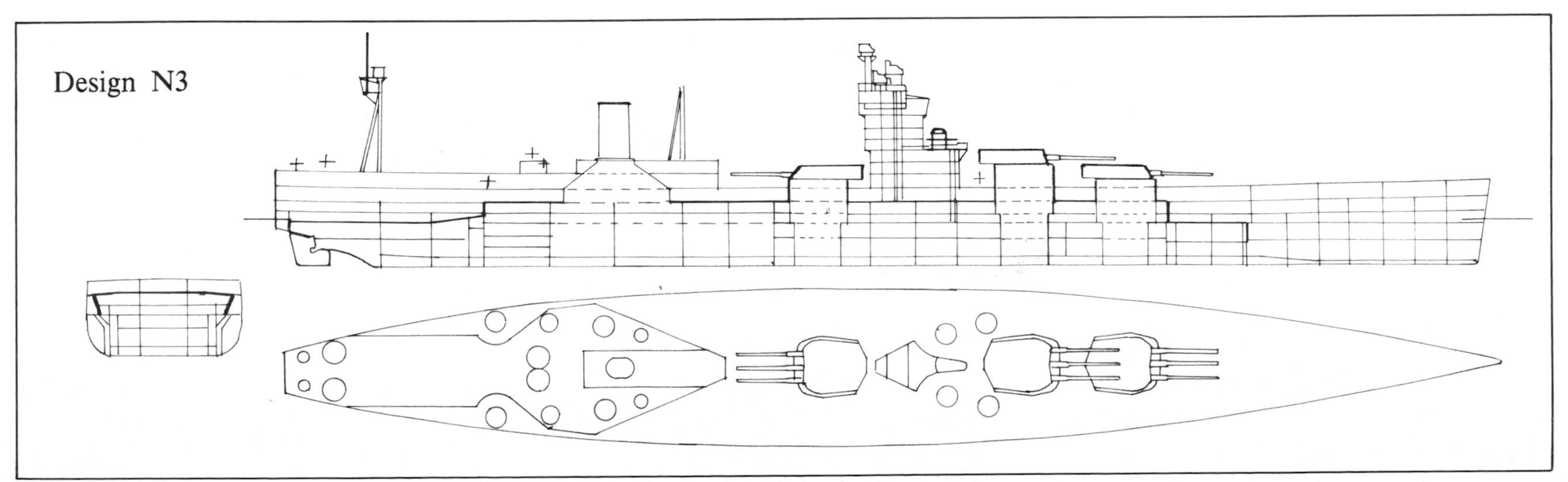

to fire a 2,837-pound projectile at a muzzle velocity of 2,700 feet per second, giving a muzzle energy of 143,300 foot-tons. It was, therefore, the most powerful gun ever proposed for a British warship. In view of the problems of blast effects and high velocity, later encountered with the 16-inch gun, however, the theoretical value of the 18-inch was probably much greater than its actual value. The maximum elevation of the gun was reduced from 45° in the original designs, to 40° in Design 'N3'. It is interesting to note that the magazines extended for nearly 40 per cent of the length of the ship – twice the length of the space occupied by the engine and boiler rooms.

The secondary, AA and torpedo armaments were the same as those provided in 'G3'. The fire-control equipment was also the same except that the after main and secondary directors were omitted, and the after high-angle control was positioned on the starfish of the mizzenmast.

Protection. The main belt was 15 inches thick abreast the forward and after magazines, and 13½ inches abreast the machinery spaces. The 15-inch thickness, however, overlapped the machinery spaces, forward and aft. The ends of the belt were closed by 14-inch bulkheads, and the central armoured citadel was completed by an armoured deck of a uniform thickness of 8 inches. Forward of the citadel, an 8-inch deck and a 9-inch bulkhead protected the submerged torpedo rooms and forward magazines. The steering gear was protected by a 6-inch deck and bulkhead, and the after magazines were protected from fire, abaft the beam, by an 8-inch deck.

The barbettes were of a uniform thickness of 15 inches down to the armoured deck. The turrets had 18-inch front plates, 14-inch backs and 8-inch roofs. The exact thickness of the sides is not known, but they were probably 14-inch. The conning-tower had 15-inch walls, an 8-inch roof and a 6-inch floor, with an 8-inch communication tube down to the armoured deck. The armoured director-hood had 4-inch sides and roof and a 6-inch face, and rested on an armoured tube of a uniform thickness of 6 inches. The arrangement of the vertical protective plating was generally similar to that of the battlecruisers, except that the torpedo bulkheads were 2 inches thick instead of 1¾ inches.

Machinery. Little is known about the machinery except that it was a two-shaft arrangement, designed for a speed of 23 to 23.5 knots. The turbines occupied a greater width than the boilers, and in order to provide them with the best possible underwater protection, the engine rooms were positioned forward of the boiler rooms so as to be in a wider part of the ship. This also allowed the funnel to be placed farther away from 'X' turret.

Stability. This would have been generally similar to that of the battlecruiser.

Below: an artist's impression of battleship M3 and battlecruiser H3c as they might have appeared. This illustration is based on the sketch designs, although it is unlikely that the ships would have been completed strictly according to them. (Reproduced by kind permission of G. W. Hunt.)

6. The Washington Conference, 1921 to 1922

Table 32 gives the basic particulars of the newest designs of USA, Britain and Japan, in 1921. The USA had the earliest designs and as their ships were well advanced, were already at a disadvantage. In the Western world very little was known about the Japanese designs until 1921, and when the details became available they caused something of a shock. The ships of the *South Dakota* class were well armed and well protected by vertical armour, but by comparison, their deck protection was weak and their speed insufficient to counter the Japanese ships. The *Lexington* class ships had the necessary speed but were otherwise completely outclassed, and their slight advantage in speed would have been best employed in putting as much water as possible between themselves and the Japanese ships. The very weak protection of the *Lexington* class – which was little better than that provided in the early British battlecruisers – is all the more surprising when one considers that the USA was the first nation to employ the 'all or nothing' protection system in a dreadnought, and in this matter were well ahead of every other naval power in the world. It is interesting to note, however, that the design compares much more favourably to the original design for *Hood*.

The 'N3' design was better protected than the *South Dakota* class, but the two classes were otherwise comparable, having equal speeds; the larger calibre of the British guns being offset by the greater number of guns in the American ships. Like the *South Dakota* class, the 'N3' had insufficient speed to counter the Japanese ships but, otherwise, compared well. The 'G3's compared very favourably to the Japanese ships and had a positive advantage in speed and protection, but there were to be only four of these ships against the Japanese twelve. Again, the ships of the *Lexington* class were completely outclassed by the 'G3' design.

This then was the state of affairs in 1921, and one can safely assume that Japan was the only nation reasonably happy with the situation. The USA was faced with the prospect of having their ships outclassed before they were even completed, and Britain, with having an insufficient number of new ships to maintain the one-power standard. One solution, for both nations, would have been an even larger building programme, which for the USA would have meant also, larger and more powerful ships. If this had occurred, the Japanese would almost certainly have expanded their own construction programme, and the result would have been a naval race of gigantic proportions, leading ultimately to a Pacific war. The US Navy Board firmly believed that in such a conflict, Britain would side with the Japanese. Furthermore, in the USA, there was strong opposition to the vast expense of the existing programme, and a distinct possibility of a cut-back. The prospect of a yet larger programme was, therefore, extremely remote and there remained but one other way to extract the USA from her uncomfortable predicament.

Table 32: Comparison of capital ship designs, Britain, USA and Japan

	Britain		USA		Japan		
	G3	N3	*Lexington*	*South Dakota*	*Amagi*	*Kii*	13 Class
Displacement (tons)	48,400	48,500	43,500	43,200	40,000	41,400	47,500
Speed (knots)	31/32	23	33.25	23	30	29·75	30
Main armament	9 16-inch	9 18-inch	8 16-inch	12 16-inch	10 16-inch	10 16-inch	8 18-inch
Belt armour (maximum)	14-inch	15-inch	7½-inch	13½-inch	10-inch	11½-inch	13½-inch
Deck protection (maximum)	8-inch	8-inch	2-inch	3½-inch	6-inch	6-inch	5-inch

In July 1921, the USA invited the largest naval powers of the world to take part in a conference on Pacific and Far Eastern affairs and the limitation of naval armaments. The invitation was immediately welcomed by Britain who, like the USA, wished to reduce the enormous financial outlay of the new construction programme and, together with Japan, France and Italy, sent a delegation to Washington where the conference began on 12th November 1921. Britain was represented by Arthur Balfour, Lord Lee of Fareham (the First Lord of the Admiralty) and Sir Auckland Geddes (the British ambassador in Washington) and there were also representatives from Australia, Canada and New Zealand. The naval advisers were Admiral Beatty (the First Sea Lord), Rear-Admiral Chatfield (the Assistant Chief of Naval Staff) and Captains B. Domville and C. Little. Admiral Beatty returned to the Admiralty shortly after the conference had begun and his place was taken by Chatfield.

The chairman of the conference was the US Secretary of State, C. E. Hughes, and in his opening speech he put forward his country's proposals for the reduction of naval armaments. These were: (a) The USA was willing to scrap fifteen of the sixteen ships of the 1916 programme (the *Maryland* was already completed) if commensurate action was taken by the British and Japanese. (b) Strength should be further reduced by the scrapping of older ships. (c) No capital ships should be replaced for at least 10 years. (d) New ships should displace no more than 35,000 tons. (e) Overall battleship tonnage was to be the yardstick by which naval strength was to be measured. In detail, Hughes proposed the following distribution of capital-ship strength.

USA: Scrap fifteen ships under construction and fifteen pre-dreadnoughts, leaving eighteen ships in service.

Britain: Scrap proposed new construction and nineteen old ships, leaving twenty-two ships in service.

Japan: Scrap fifteen ships proposed and under construction and ten pre-dreadnoughts, leaving ten ships in service.

Britain was to be allowed the greatest number, so as to offset the greater age of her ships, compared to those of the USA and Japan. Generally, however, the proportion of strength between the three major naval powers was to be 5: 5: 3.

These proposals were much more drastic than anybody had expected, and although Britain agreed with them in principle, there were certain points which caused some concern. The most important of these was the proposed 10-year break in capital-ship construction, which would necessitate subsidising British armament firms to prevent them from running down excessively. There was also the question of the greater age of the British ships, and Balfour wished to propose a slow replacement programme in place of the ten-year break, but in this, he was overruled by the Prime Minister. The Japanese delegation, led by the Minister of the Navy, Baron T. Kato, were also unhappy about the proposals and wished to increase the Japanese ratio and complete the *Mutsu*, sister of the already-commissioned battleship *Nagato*. In the debate which followed, a compromise was reached. Japan would be allowed to complete *Mutsu*, but to compensate this, the USA was to complete *Colorado* and *West Virginia*. Britain would be allowed to construct two new ships, within the limits of 35,000 tons maximum displacement and 16-inch maximum gun calibre. In addition, Japan was to scrap one more old ship and the USA two; Britain was to scrap four old ships as soon as the two new battleships were completed. The 35,000-ton limit was agreed, despite the wishes of the Admiralty who wanted to complete two of the 'G3' battlecruisers, and who regarded 43,000 tons as the minimum displacement for a satisfactory 16-inch gun ship.

The conference came to an end on 6th February 1922, the following points having been agreed by the participants.

1. The Anglo-Japanese Alliance was to be dissolved.

2. No new capital ships were to be constructed for ten years, except for the two new ships allowed to Britain.

3. The ratio of naval strength between the USA, Britain, Japan, France and Italy was to be in the proportion 5: 5: 3: 1.75: 1.75.

4. After the expiration of the 10-year break in battleship construction, no capital ship was to be replaced by new construction until it was at least twenty years old.

5. The maximum displacement was to be 35,000 tons for capital ships, 33,000 tons for aircraft cariers and 10,000 tons for cruisers. The displacements were to be taken as being the displacement of the ships fully equipped for war, but without oil fuel or reserve feed-water and carrying their normal (as opposed to maximum) ammunition stowage.

6. The maximum gun calibre of capital ships was to be 16 inches, and of cruisers, 8 inches.

7. The signatory powers had the right to add 3,000 tons to the displacement of existing ships for the purpose of improving their defence against aerial and submarine attack. No improvement in the offensive powers of the existing ships was allowed.

8. Certain areas of the Pacific Ocean were specified as areas in which no expansion of existing fortifications or naval bases was to take place. Singapore was excluded from these areas.

The terms of the limitation treaty were rapidly implemented by the nations concerned. In Britain, the 'G3' battlecruisers, which had been suspended on 18th November 1920, were cancelled on 13th February 1921. (Under the terms of the treaty, Britain could have converted two of the 'G3's to aircraft carriers, but the Admiralty considered them unsuitable for this purpose.) The design of the two new ships (*Nelson* and *Rodney*) was already well under way. Four of Britain's older dreadnoughts had been sold during 1920 and 1921; another twelve were sold in 1922, and the battlecruisers *Lion* and *Princess Royal* were sold in 1924 and 1926, respectively. The battleship *Monarch* was used as a target for bombs and gunfire, and was eventually sunk, deliberately, by *Revenge*, in January 1925. The battlecruiser *Australia* suffered a similar fate. She was towed out to sea and sunk off Sydney, Australia in 1924. Thus, twenty dreadnoughts were disposed of and another two, *Courageous* and *Glorious*, were converted to aircraft carriers, leaving the following capital ships in service: 5 *Royal Sovereign* class, 5 *Queen Elizabeth* class, 4 *Iron Duke* class, 3 *King George V* class, 1 *Hood*, 2 *Repulse*, 1 *Tiger*, 1 *Thunderer* (training-ship for cadets).

The three *King George V* class ships and *Thunderer* were to be scrapped on completion of *Nelson* and *Rodney*. Three were sold in November and December 1926, but *Centurion* was saved from the scrap-yard to become a radio-controlled target-ship.

The USA suspended all her new construction on 8th February 1922, except for *Maryland*, which was already completed, and her two sister ships, *Colorado* and *West Virginia*, which were completed in August and December 1923, respectively. The fourth ship of the class, which was 75 per cent complete, was sunk as a target in 1924, and the six *South Dakota*s and four of the *Lexington*s were scrapped on the stocks during 1923 to 1924. *Lexington* and *Saratoga*, however, were redesigned, and were completed as aircraft carriers. Nineteen pre-dreadnoughts and four dreadnoughts were scrapped or otherwise removed from the effective list, during 1923 to 1924, leaving eighteen capital ships in service with the US Navy.

All the Japanese ships, under construction or projected, were cancelled in 1922 except *Mutsu*, which was completed in October 1921, and *Kaga* and *Akagi* which were completed as aircraft carriers. All pre-dreadnoughts were removed from the effective list during 1922 to 1923, and one early dreadnought, *Settsu*, was converted to a target-ship in 1924, which left ten capital ships in service.

7. Nelson and Rodney, 1922 to 1930

Nelson and *Rodney* were unique in many ways, in the fleet and in the world. They were the only British dreadnoughts to carry 16-inch guns, and until the appearance of the *King George V* class, were the only new ships to reflect the lessons of the First World War. Their unusual appearance, with the entire main armament forward and the superstructure aft, was unmatched, and though many thought them ugly, and hardly a fitting successor to the handsome lines of *Hood*, they did give a distinct impression of power. Their design was based directly on that of the 'G3's of which they were virtually 23-knot versions.

As soon as the 35,000-ton limit on capital ships, proposed at Washington, seemed as though it might be accepted, the Director of Naval Construction was asked to produce a battlecruiser design that would be in accordance with this requirement. Two designs were worked out, one with twin turrets and an alternative, with triple turrets. The legend and sketch designs were placed before the Board on 30th November 1921.

In both designs, all three 15-inch turrets were placed forward of the bridge. This concentrated the magazines amidships, and reduced the weight of armour required for their protection. In 'F2', the secondary armament was carried in four twin and four single turrets; in 'F3', the four singles were omitted, to save weight. Both were provided with four pom-pom mountings, but no 4.7-inch guns were specified. The armour was generally reduced compared to 'G3', slightly more so in 'F3', but shell trials carried out on 29th November showed that an improvement in the deck armour – above that assumed for 'G3' – could be expected. The lower speed of 'F3' resulted from the greater weight of her triple turrets, but the DNC pointed out that if the Engineer-in-Chief would agree to force the boilers and provide light machinery (following the practice adopted in the *E* class cruisers and the *Courageous* class) a speed of 30 knots could be obtained.

These two battlecruiser designs were shortlived, and were abandoned when it was decided

Table 33: Legend for battlecruiser designs, November 1921

	F2	F3
Displacement tons	35,000	35,000
Length (pp) feet	720	700
Length (oa) feet	760	740
Beam (maximum) feet	106	106
Draught feet	28½	28½
Armament:	Six 15-inch 50-cal Twelve 6-inch 50-cal 4 pom-poms	Nine 15-inch 50-cal Eight 6-inch 50-cal 4 pom-poms
Oil fuel capacity	4,000 tons	4,000 tons
SHP	112,000	96,000
Speed (deep)	29.5 knots	28.5 knots
Speed (light)	30 knots	29 knots
Armour:		
Belt	13-inch at 72° (over magazines) 12-inch at 72° (over machinery)	12-inch at 72° (over magazines) 12-inch at 72° (over machinery)
Bulkheads	11-inch, 10-inch and 8-inch	10-inch, 9-inch and 5-inch
Barbettes	13-inch	12-inch
Turrets (front)	16-inch	16-inch
Turrets (side)	12-inch	12-inch
Turrets (rear)	9-inch	9-inch
Turrets (roof)	7-inch	7-inch
Conning-tower (wall)	12-inch	9-inch
Conning-tower (roof)	6-inch	6-inch
Communications tube	6-inch	5-inch
Forecastle-deck	1-inch	1-inch
Upper-deck	7-inch (over magazines) 3¼-inch (over machinery)	7-inch (over magazines) 3¼-inch (over machinery)
Weights (tons):		
General equipment	850	850
Hull	13,500	13,500
Machinery	4,660	4,100
Armour and protection	10,210	9,970
Armament	4,600	5,400
Fuel	1,000	1,000
Board margin	180	180
Legend displacement:	35,000	35,000

at Washington that Britain was to be allowed to build two new ships armed with 16-inch guns. As the new ships would have to counter the 16-inch guns of the *Nagato* and *Maryland* classes (both of moderate speed) and as it was impossible to design an adequately protected ship combining a high speed and a 16-inch gun armament, it was decided to build two battleships having a speed of 23 knots, designed to carry the 16-inch guns and mountings ordered for the first two 'G3's. On 17th December 1921, the following outline details on which the new design was to be based, were passed, by the DNC, to the constructor, Attwood.

Displacement: 35,000 tons (to Washington standard).
Armament: Nine 16-inch guns; secondary and AA armaments not decided but twelve 6-inch and four 4.7-inch to be allowed for.
Armour: Belt, 14-inch over magazines, 13-inch over machinery; barbettes, 15-inch; conning-tower, 15-inch; funnel, 10-inch, deck, 8-inch over magazines, 5-4-inch over machinery.
Underwater protection: To withstand a torpedo warhead of 750 pounds.
Machinery: 46,000 shaft horse-power; E in C will oppose the use of fewer than eight boilers.
Dynamos: If difficulty is experienced in finding space for eight, these may be reduced to six.
Special instruction: In order to keep the displacement to 35,000 tons, everything is to be cut down to a minimum.

From this specification two preliminary sketch designs were prepared. The first design covered all the requirements but resulted in a displacement of 35,500 tons. In the second, only six boilers were provided and the bridge and fire-control arrangements were in accordance with those recommended by the Fire-control Committee, instead of those of Design 'G3'. In this way, the length of the citadel was reduced, and the displacement was brought down to 35,000 tons. The rough drawings were inspected by the DNC on 19th December, and the following, possible ways of meeting the requirements of the first design while reducing the displacement, were put forward.

1. Reduce the calibre of the main armament to 15-inch 50 cal.
2. Reduce the deck protection by 1 inch.

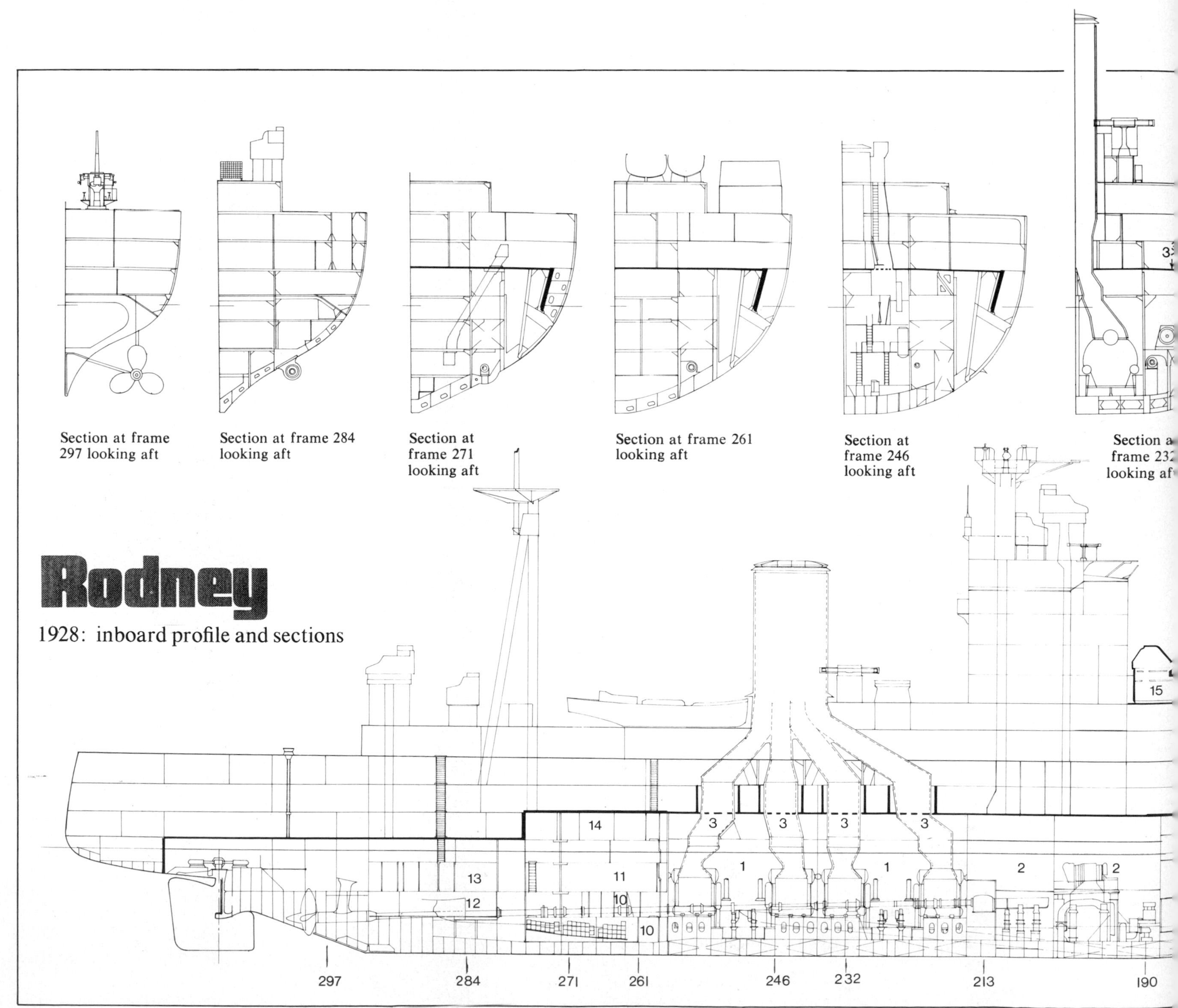
Section at frame 297 looking aft
Section at frame 284 looking aft
Section at frame 271 looking aft
Section at frame 261 looking aft
Section at frame 246 looking aft
Rodney
1928: inboard profile and sections
15
14
3
3
3
3
13
11
1
1
2
2
12
10
10
297
284
271
261
246
232
213
190

Left: *Nelson* in 1934 at Plymouth.

3. Adopt the Fire-control Committee's bridge arrangement.
4. Reduce the hull weight, by accepting higher stresses and different materials.

The DNC ruled out the first suggestion because he had received definite instructions from the First Sea Lord that the main armament must be 16-inch. For the second, he allowed a reduction of ½-inch in the deck armour. With regard to the bridge arrangements, he preferred to adhere to that of the 'G.3's, but said that it might be possible to reduce this in minor ways. The reduction in hull weight by the use of new materials was thought to be worthy of investigation, and this led to the extensive use of 'D' steel in the final design and accounted for the largest part of the weight saved in the ships.

The DNC inspected the designs on 21st December, and decided to lower the upper-deck slightly, and, if possible, work in two decks between this and the top strength-deck in order to provide more living space, and a deeper girder. He also required, if possible, that buoyancy spaces be fitted forward and aft of the citadel with arrangements for blowing out the contained water by compressed air. Lastly, he decided to reduce the depth of the belt, and on the following day, he fixed this depth as sufficient to extend from 5 feet above the deep waterline to 2 feet 3 inches below the loadline. On the same day he directed that the hull form for the new ships be based on that of *Hood*, but later modified this statement, saying that the form could be fined forward and aft as necessary.

The first legend and sketch design for the battleships were completed in January 1922, the design being designated 'O3'. In addition, two sketch designs, 'P3' and 'Q3' (both for ships carrying 15-inch guns) were prepared for the purposes of comparison. The three designs were to have been discussed with the Assistant Chief of Naval Staff, on his return from Washington, but, as 'O3' was approved by the Board before the ACNS returned, it seems that 'P3' and 'Q3' did not receive serious consideration.

Table 34: Legend of battleship designs, January 1922

	O3	P3 and Q3
Displacement	35,000 tons	All versions
Length	670 feet (pp) 717 feet (oa)	All versions
Beam (maximum)	104 feet	All versions
Draught	30 feet (mean) 36 feet (maximum)	All versions
SHP	45,000	All versions
Speed	23 knots	All versions
Oil fuel capacity	3,500 tons	All versions
Endurance	5,500 miles at 16 knots	All versions
Complement	1,550	1,600
Armament:	9 16-inch 45-cal 12 6-inch 50-cal 4 4.7-inch HA 4 pom-poms 2 24.5-inch torpedo tubes	9 15-inch 50-cal 16 6-inch 50-cal 5 4.7-inch HA 4 pom-poms 2 24.5-inch torpedo tubes
Armour:		
Belt	14-inch (over magazines) 13-inch (over machinery)	14-inch (over magazines) 10-inch (over machinery)
Turrets	16-inch front, 12-inch sides 9-inch back, 7½-inch roof	All versions
Barbettes (max)	15-inch	All versions
Bulkheads	12-inch and 8-inch (forward) 10-inch and 4-inch (aft)	All versions
Conning-tower	15-inch (max) 7-inch (roof).	All versions
Conning-tower tube	6-inch	All versions
Armoured director-hood	5-inch and 3-inch	All versions
Main director-control tower	2-inch to 1-inch	All versions
Secondary director-control tower	1½-inch to 1-inch	All versions
Main-deck	7½-inch (over magazines) 5½-inch (over machinery)	All versions
Lower-deck	5-inch	All versions
Funnel base	8-inch (mean)	All versions
Weights (tons):		
General equipment	1,000	1,050
Armament	6,900	6,550
Machinery	2,600	2,600
Fuel	0	0
Armour	11,100	11,400
Hull	13,400	13,400
Board margin	0	0
Standard Displacement:	35,000	35,000

The 'O3' design was discussed during January and February 1922, and various alterations were made, principally on the instructions of the Third Sea Lord. The new legend, known as 'O3 modified' was approved by the Board on 6th February, the day the Washington Conference ended. The details of the ship were the same as those given in the previous legend with the following exceptions:

Table 35: '03 Modified', 6th February 1922

Dimensions	660 feet (pp) 710 feet (oa) × 106 feet (max)
Armament	Six 4.7-inch HA
Armour:	
Turrets	16-inch front, 11-inch sides, 9-inch back, 6¼-inch roof
Conning-tower	14-inch (max) 6½-inch roof
Main-deck	6¾-inch over magazines, 4¼-inch over machinery
6-inch turrets	1½-inch front plates
Director-control tower	2-inch front plates
Weights (tons):	
General equipment	1,050
Armament	6,950
Machinery	2,600
Fuel	0
Armour	10,250
Hull	14,150
Board margin	0
Total:	35,000

The final legend and rig drawing were approved by the Board on 11th September 1922, and the remainder of the building drawings were approved on 16th October. The basic design had received few modifications since February – the maximum draught was reduced to 35 feet and the oil-fuel capacity was increased to 4,000 tons. The complement was reduced to 1,560. The weights were correspondingly adjusted as shown in Table 36.

Table 36: '03' modified – new weights

Equipment	1,050 tons
Armament	6,900 tons
Machinery	2,550 tons
Armour and protective plating	10,250 tons
Hull	14,250 tons
Total:	35,000 tons

PARTICULARS OF *NELSON* AND *RODNEY* AS COMPLETED, 1927

Displacement

	Nelson	*Rodney*
Light	32,800 tons	
Standard	33,313 tons	33,730 tons
Deep	37,800 tons	
Extra deep	38,400 tons	38,316 tons
Extra deep (with buoyancy spaces filled)	41,250 tons	

Tons per inch: 126.6 tons at 40 foot draught, 124.3 tons at 35 foot draught, 121.2 tons at 30 foot draught, 116.6 tons at 25 foot draught.

Dimensions

Length:
Nelson, 710 feet (oa), 660 feet (pp).
Rodney, 710 feet 2½ inches (oa), 660 feet ⅛ inch (pp).

Beam:
Nelson, 106 feet.
Rodney, 106 feet 1/16 inches.

Draught:
Standard displacement, 26 feet 8 inches (forward), 29 feet 6 inches (aft).
Extra deep displacement, 30 feet 6 inches (forward), 32 feet 10 inches (aft).
Extra deep displacement (with buoyancy spaces filled), 32 feet 5 inches (forward), 34 feet 7 inches (aft).

Armament

Nine 16-inch 45-cal breech-loading Mk I: three triple mountings Mk I.
Nine 6-pounder sub-calibre.
Twelve 6-inch 50-cal breech-loading Mk XXII*: six twin mountings Mk XVIII.
Twelve 3-pounder sub-calibre.
Six 4.724-inch (120-mm) 40-cal quick-firing Mk VIII*
Six high-angle single mountings Mk II.
Six 2-pounder sub-calibre.
Eight 2-pounder pom-poms: eight single mountings Mk II.
Four 3-pounder Hotchkiss quick-firing saluting guns Mk I.
One 12-pounder 18-cwt quick-firing field-gun and carriage.
Five 0.303-inch Vickers machine-guns on cone mountings.
Ten 0.303-inch Lewis machine-guns: five twin mountings.
Four 0.303-inch Lewis machine-guns: single mountings.
Two 24.5-inch barless submerged torpedo tubes.

Ammunition stowage

Maximum as designed:
16-inch: 95 APC rounds per gun; 10 practice rounds per gun.
6-inch: 168 rounds per gun; 20 practice rounds per gun; 72 smoke shell per ship.
4.7-inch: 211 rounds per gun; 20 smoke shell per ship.
Maximum as completed:
16-inch: 100 APC rounds per gun; 10 practice rounds per gun.
6-inch: 135 CPBC rounds per gun; 15 HE rounds per gun; 24 practice rounds per gun; 72 smoke shell per ship.
4.7-inch: 175 HE rounds per gun; 150 star shell per ship; 20 target smoke shell per ship.

Normal:
16-inch: 80 rounds per gun.
6-inch 100 rounds per gun.
4.7-inch: 100 rounds per gun.
10 24.5-inch torpedoes Mk I.
Pom-poms: 1,000 rounds per mounting.

Paravanes

Four Type BV. (Two Type BIII** were to be carried in lieu of two of the Type BV until the stocks of BIII** were exhausted.)

Armour

Cemented (C):
Belt: 14 inch at 72° abreast magazines, 13 inch at 72° abreast machinery and after magazines.
Barbettes: 15 inch, to 12 inch.
Turrets: 16 inch face, 11 inch and 9 inch sides, 9 inch back, 7¼ inch roof.
Conning-tower: 14 inch sides, 12 inch front, 10 inch back, 6½ in roof, 4 inch floor.
Conning-tower tube: 6 inch.
Conning-tower hood: 5 inch and 3 inch.
Funnel-uptakes: 9 inch sides, 8 inch and 7 inch forward and aft.

Non-cemented (N.C.):
Bulkheads: 12 inch and 8 inch forward, 10 inch and 4 inch aft.
Middle-deck: 6¼ inch over magazines, 3¾ inch over machinery.
Lower-deck (aft): 4¼ inch.
Torpedo bulkheads: 1½ inch, D steel.
Director-control towers: 2 inch front and 1 inch, D steel.
6-inch turrets: 1½ inch front and 1 inch, D steel.
Secondary Director-control towers: 1½ inch front and 1 inch, D steel.

Protective plating

Fore-bridge: 1 inch high-tensile.
6 inch working spaces: 1 inch high-tensile.

Machinery

Brown Curtis single-reduction geared turbines, two shafts.
45,000 SHP = 23 knots at 160 rpm.
Maximum sea-going speed 40,500 SHP = 22 knots.
Eight Admiralty three-drum boilers with superheaters.
Maximum working pressure 250 pounds per square inch.

Speed:

	SHP	rpm
10 knots	3,650	64
12 knots	6,250	75
14 knots	9,900	88
16 knots	14,350	100
23 knots	45,000	160

Fuel and endurance

Oil fuel (normal maximum), 3,805 tons (*Nelson*), 3,770 tons (*Rodney*).
Diesel fuel, 162 tons (*Nelson*), 161 tons (*Rodney*).

Endurance:
5,500 nautical miles at full speed (actual).
7,000 nautical miles at 16 knots (designed).

Fuel consumption:
16 tons per hour at full speed (actual).
7½ tons per hour at 16 knots (designed).

Complement 1,314 (1,361 as a flagship).

Weights (as designed)
Weights given in tons.)

EQUIPMENT:	
Mast, derricks and rig	118
Fresh water	75
Provisions	220
Canteen stores	25
Officers', stores and slops	34
Officers, Men and effects	205
Anchors, cables and hawsers	197
Boats	53
Stores	120
	1,047
Taken in legend:	1,050
Additions for extra deep:	
Fresh water	75

Boats	30
Coal	40
Admiral's stores	10
	155
Total equipment for extra deep:	1.205

ARMOUR AND PROTECTION	
Side armour	2,190
Side armour chocks	117
'A' barbette	543
'B' barbette	823
'X' barbette	547
Barbette chocks	129
Middle-deck	2,930
Lower-deck, forward	30
Lower-deck, aft	420
Armour bulkheads	365
Conning-tower	222
Funnel-uptakes	177
Torpedo bulkheads	950
Buoyancy space	186
Protection to 6-inch working spaces	182
Protection to fore-bridge	44
Protection to director-control tower	92
Splinter gratings in boiler-uptakes	5
Armour bolts	150
	10,102
Taken in legend:	10,250

MACHINERY	
Main machinery (dry weight)	1,924
Water in boilers, condensers, pipes, feed tanks ½-full	130
Engine-room fans	10
Engineers' stores and oil	130
Boat-hoists	20
Dynamos	160
Refrigerating and magazine-cooling machinery	75
High-pressure air-compressors	20
Electric winches	36
Workshop motors	3
	2,508
Taken in legend:	2,550

MAIN ARMAMENT	
Revolving weight, 'A' turret	1,463
Revolving weight, 'B' turret	1,463
Revolving weight, 'X' turret	1,463
16-inch cordite and cases (80 rounds per gun)	346
16-inch shell (80 rounds per gun)	726
Hydraulic-engines	120
Water in hydraulic-tanks	30
Shell room machinery	100
Training-racks	24
Lower roller path	39
½-weight of rollers and rings	22
Piping and supports	90
Spare gear and miscellaneous	50
Total:	5,936

MINOR ARMAMENT	
Six 6-inch mountings	450
Six 4.7-inch high-angle guns	84
Four pom-poms Mk M	32
6-inch shell (100 rounds per gun)	58
6-inch cordite and cases (100 rounds per gun)	22
4.7-inch high-angle ammunition (100 rounds per gun)	34
Pom-pom ammunition (1,000 rounds per mounting)	6
6-pounder sub-calibre and ammunition	19
3-pounder sub-calibre and ammunition.	10
2-pounder sub-calibre and ammunition	3
Field-gun and ammunition	5
Aiming-rifles and ammunition	2
Vickers machine-gun and ammunition	2
Lewis machine-gun and ammunition	2
Four Hotchkiss 3-pounders and ammunition	4
Fuzes	4
Small arms and ammunition	18
Torpedo stores	13
Ten torpedoes	24
Torpedo tubes and fittings	33
Air bottles	26
No. 1 air-compressing machinery	20
Paravanes and stores	7
Two aeroplane hangars and stores	15
Gunners' stores	40
	933
Main armament:	5,936
Minor armament:	933
	6,869
Taken in legend:	6,900

ADDITIONS TO ARMAMENT WEIGHT FOR EXTRA DEEP	
16-inch shell (15 rounds + 10 practice per gun	227
16-inch cordite (15 rounds per gun)	65
6-inch shell (88 rounds per gun)	51
6-inch cordite (68 rounds per gun)	15
6-inch smoke shell (72 rounds)	4
4.7-inch ammunition (666 rounds)	38
4.7-inch smoke shell (20 rounds)	1
Pom-pom ammunition (970 boxes)	73
Total addition:	474

Hull weight:	14,248
taken in legend:	14,250
Oil fuel:	3,956
taken in legend:	4,000
Overflow and reserve feed-water:	246
taken in legend:	245

Displacement (tons)

Standard:	
Equipment	1,050
Armament	6,900
Machinery	2,550
Armour and protection	10,250
Hull	14,250
Total:	35,000

To convert the above figures to the legend displacement used before the Washington Conference, it is necessary to subtract from the equipment figure 110 tons of provisions (½ of total), 25 tons of canteen stores and 15 tons of admiral's boats, and to add 30 tons of boats. It is also necessary to add 1,200 tons of oil fuel, = 35,000 tons − 120 tons equipment + 1,200 tons oil fuel = 36,080.

Deep displacement:	
Hull	14,250
Equipment	1,050
Armour and protective plating	10,250
Armament	6,900
Machinery and engineers' stores	2,550
Oil fuel	4,000
Reserve feed-water	200
Overflow feed-water	45
Total:	39,245

Extra deep displacement:	
Deep displacement	39,245
Equipment	155
Armament	474
Total:	39,874

Extra deep displacement (with buoyancy spaces filled):	
Extra deep displacement	39,874
Water in buoyancy space (to 35 feet above keel)	2,870
Total:	42,744

Light displacement:	
Weights to be deducted from deep condition	
Equipment:	414
½ engineers' stores:	65
Oil fuel:	4,000
Reserve feed-water:	200
Overflow feed-water:	45
	4,724

Light displacement = 39.245 − 4,724 = 34,521 tons.

Left: close-up views of *Rodney* shortly after completion in 1928. **Above,** the main armament; **below,** the secondary armament.

Invitations to tender were sent out on 16th October, and on 11th November, those from Cammell Laird, at £1,563,000, and Armstrongs, at £1,479,000, were accepted. Both vessels were laid down on 28th December and the orders were officially placed on 1st January 1923.

Table 37: Construction of *Nelson* and *Rodney*

	Nelson	*Rodney*
Laid down	28th December 1922	28th December 1922
Launched	3rd September 1925	17th December 1925
Completed	June 1927	August 1927
Builder	Armstrong	Cammell Laird
Cost	£7,504,055	£7,617,799

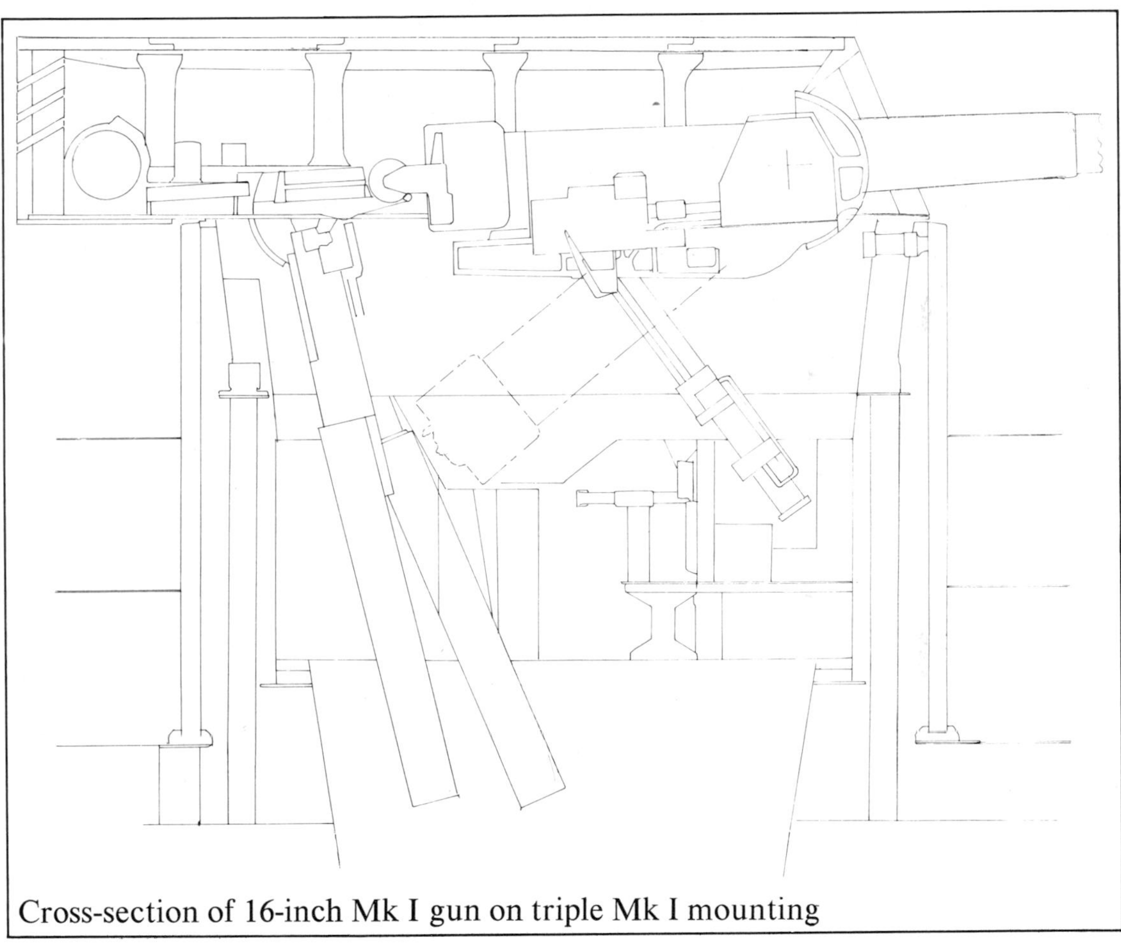

Cross-section of 16-inch Mk I gun on triple Mk I mounting

Armament

As has been stated, the 16-inch guns and mountings for *Nelson* and *Rodney* were originally ordered in 1921 for the first two of the 'G3' battlecruisers. All six mountings were manufactured by Armstrongs. The guns were designed to fire a 2,048-pound projectile with a muzzle velocity of 2,670 feet per second. The first indication that this light shell/high-velocity combination was not going to be an unqualified success, came on 15th March 1926, when the first 16-inch Mk I gun was subjected to firing trials. Using a charge of 525 pounds S.C. cordite, the gun achieved the exact muzzle velocity for which it had been designed, i.e. 2,670 feet per second, but it also gave a drop in muzzle velocity between rounds, of 1.5 feet per second indicating a very rapid rate of wear, and a maximum barrel life of 180 full charge firings. Later trials showed that there was also a considerable loss of accuracy during firing, and a tendency for the projectile to strip the rifling of the gun ". . . due to the hammering action of the short bodied, long headed projectile on its way down the bore . . .".

To remedy this situation, trials were carried out with a view to improving the rifling and the size and the form of the gun-chamber. As a result, the chamber size was reduced from 35,000 cubic inches to 30,000 cubic inches, and the charge was reduced from 525 pounds to 510 pounds giving a barrel life of 200 full charges, and a drop in muzzle velocity between rounds, of 1 foot per second. The rifling was modified, and the accuracy was improved, but the gun never reached the standard of efficiency achieved in the 15-inch Mk I.

The 16-inch Mk I triple mounting was to prove even more troublesome. The need to carry three guns naturally made the mounting more complex than the earlier 15-inch twin mounting, but this complexity was considerably increased by the need of flash-tightness, the excessive use of interlocks in the ammunition supply and loading system, and by the use of a large number of swash-plate engines. Unlike earlier mountings, cordite and shell were supplied to the gun-house, in the vertical position by pusher hoists. The cordite hoists were fitted with flash-tight scuttles at top and bottom, and venting-plates at the sides of the trunks. The cordite was exposed only when in the handing room between the magazine scuttles and the hoist, and immediately after having been loaded into the gun; it was completely invisible between these two points. The magazine-access doors were 18 inches square and had a light plate covering; they were flash-tight and water-tight. No explosion venting-plates were fitted to the magazines because of the decision made in 1919 to abandon venting-plates and explosion trunks as they were not flash-tight.

Below: amidships view of *Nelson* in 1929.

During the period of construction, a number of modifications was made to the turret design. The most important of these were: (a) The pressure medium for the hydraulic system was changed from water to oil. This allowed the use of steel pipes in the hydraulic system instead of the heavy-duty brass pipes used in earlier designs, and provided a saving in both weight and expenditure. (b) Independent shell-bogies were originally fitted in the shell handing room at the base of the shell hoists, but, owing to the impossibility of organising the loading-cycle, they were replaced by three fixed shell-bogies, mounted 90° apart on a shell-bogie ring. As a result the three guns could only be loaded more or less simultaneously with the shell handing room loading-cycle. (c) The cordite-bogies – which had been arranged in a similar manner to the shell-bogies – were replaced by cordite-hoppers in the revolving structure. This necessitated increasing the handing-room complement as the cordite had to be transferred from the fixed to the revolving structure by hand. (d) Modifications to the size of the driving-band on the 16-inch projectile, involved making provision for the increased diameter in all parts of the shell-supply system.

Unfortunately, it was not possible to carry out a pit trial of the fixed and revolving machinery of the shell handing rooms, and when the mountings were installed in the ships during 1926 to 1927, this gear began to give considerable trouble. Some degree of improvement was effected by modifying the existing gear but the most satisfactory solution of the problems would have involved extensive modifications and had to be deferred for financial reasons.

The designed loading-cycle for the mounting was 30 seconds, but in practice, it was 35 seconds for one gun. As, however, the shell-loading in the handing rooms required 50 seconds, the maximum sustained rate of fire was one round per gun every 50 seconds and because of the necessity of firing wing and centre guns of turrets in different salvoes, this was further increased to one round every 60 to 65 seconds. Even with modifications, the Director of Naval Ordnance considered it exremely doubtful that a greater rate of fire than one round every 40 seconds for the first four rounds, and one round every 45 seconds thereafter would ever be achieved, which compared very unfavourably to the one round per gun every 25 seconds of the 15-inch Mk I mounting.

In July 1927, an inspection of *Rodney*'s turret-roller paths revealed that the inner edge of the lower roller path was cutting into the flanges of the turret-rollers and a similar state of affairs was discovered in *Nelson* when she was inspected. It was caused by the great weight of the revolving structure of 1,480 tons, and the lateral thrust it produced when the turrets were trained, particularly in a seaway. Restrictions were applied to the maximum speed of turret training, and various modifications were made to the turret-rollers but it soon became clear that these modifications were inadequate. It was then decided to fit an entirely separate set of vertical rollers mounted on the revolving structure and bearing against the inner face of the lower roller path. They were designed to take the lateral thrust off the horizontal roller flanges; to maintain the concentricity between the upper and lower roller-paths, some of the vertical rollers were spring-loaded and so fitted that no two fixed rollers were diametrically opposite. Fitting of the vertical rollers commenced in August 1928, and was completed by October 1929. They proved successful, and the restriction on the maximum speed of turret training was lifted.

Shipboard firing trials revealed yet another problem – that of the blast effect of the 16-inch guns. When 'A' and 'B' turrets were fired on forward bearings, many weather-deck fittings were damaged, and conditions in the mess-decks became very uncomfortable. Similarly, when 'X' turret was fired abaft the beam, considerable damage was caused to the superstructure and the bridge was almost untenable, particularly when the guns were at high elevation. As a temporary measure, the

Below: bow view of *Nelson* in April 1930. Note the short-range WT aerials fitted in 'B' turret roof.

arcs over which the main armament could fire, were restricted to areas where little damage would be incurred.

In an attempt to reduce the blast effect on bridge personnel and instruments, the openings in the bridge structure of *Rodney* were fitted with curtain-plates at top and bottom to reduce the aperture, and small plate-glass windows were fitted in the compass-platform. This work was carried out at Portsmouth, and, on 24th/25th November 1930, gun trials were carried out south of the Isle of Wight, under the direction of the gunnery experts from HMS *Excellent*. The result came near to being a complete failure – when 'X' turret was fired abaft the beam, the windows disintegrated and filled the compass-platform with bits of flying plate-glass and the bridge structure was damaged. The curtain-plates must have been partially successful because they were retained in *Rodney*, and later, they were also fitted in *Nelson*. Eventually, in both ships, baffles were fitted under the bridge-openings in addition to the curtain-plates, and the lower row of windows in the compass-platforms were plated over. Although these measures eased the situation, they by no means solved it and the restrictions on the permissible arcs of fire of the main armament remained in force throughout their peacetime careers.

In May 1934, all the 16-inch mountings in *Nelson* were – for the first time – subjected to the prolonged simultaneous firing of sixteen rounds per gun. A number of breakdowns occurred, which were carefully investigated, and in December 1934, became the subject of a conference in *Nelson* at which the Fleet, the Admiralty and HMS *Excellent* were represented. The conference discussed all the known weaknesses of the mountings, and a number of recommendations was made as to how these might be remedied. Energetic steps were taken to implement these recommendations, but although considerable improvements were made, the mountings were never completely trouble-free.

The details of the 16-inch guns and mountings compared to the 15-inch armament of *Hood*, are given in Table 38. As can be seen, in power at least, the 16-inch gun is superior, but in view of the higher rate of fire of the 15-inch gun, and its greater accuracy, it is difficult to make a positive judgement of their relative merits.

Table 38: Comparison of 16-inch and 15-inch guns

	16-inch	15-inch
Mark of gun	I	I
Mark of mounting	I	II
Length of bore	45-cal	42-cal
Weight of shell	2,048 pounds	1,920 pounds
Weight of charge	510 pounds	428 pounds
Muzzle velocity	2,700 fps	2,450 fps
Muzzle energy	103,500 f-t	80,000 f-t
Life of barrel (full charges)	200	350
Weight of gun	108 tons	97 tons 3 cwt
Maximum range	41,923 yards	30,500 yards
Maximum elevation	40°	30°
Weight of revolving structure	1,480 tons	860 tons

The secondary armament which, like the main armament, was originally designed for the 'G3' battlecruisers, consisted of twelve 6-inch 50-cal, breech-loading Mk XXII guns, mounted in six Mk XVIII twin turrets. The details of the gun, compared to those of the 6-inch Mk XII are given in Table 39.

In the original sketch designs, the 6-inch turrets were arranged around the base of the bridge, but by September 1922, they had been moved farther aft, to keep them clear of the blast from the main armament. The 6-inch magazines and shell rooms were abaft the machinery spaces, and almost immediately below the turrets, providing a very direct supply of ammunition. Shell was supplied by pusher-hoist, and the cordite, in Clarksons' cases, by endless-chain hoist to the 6-inch working spaces below the turrets on the main-deck. Flash-tightness in the cordite-supply system was very nearly complete and included flash-tight scuttles in the magazine bulkheads, flash-tight heads on the cordite-hoists, vent-plates in the sides of hoists, and venting-valves in the heads of the hoists, which vented upwards and were automatically closed when the heads were on their downward journey.

The general arrangement of the secondary armament had one major disadvantage in that the turrets and their working spaces were concentrated in one area, and, as they were protected by 1-inch high-tensile plating only, they were extremely vulnerable to shell-fire. One or two shells could very easily have put the entire battery out of action, on one side of the ship.

A pilot 6-inch twin turret was fitted in the cruiser *Enterprise* (completed in 1926) for sea trials and proved successful. This mounting was the Mk XVII which was generally similar to those in *Nelson* and *Rodney* except that it carried a much longer trunk. Originally, the Mk XVIII turret was to have been provided with 40° elevation, like the mounting in *Enterprise*, but in November 1922, Board approval

Table 39: Comparison of 6-inch guns, Mk XII and Mk XXII

	6-inch Mk XII	6-inch Mk XXII
Length of bore	45-cal	50-cal
Weight of gun	6.7 tons	8.8 tons
Weight of shell	100 pounds	100 pounds
Weight of charge	27 pounds	30 pounds
Rate of fire	7 rounds per minute	8 rounds per minute
Range at 45° elevation	22,100 yards	25,100 yards
Muzzle velocity	2,800 fps	2,945 fps
Muzzle energy	5,430 f-t	6,010 f-t

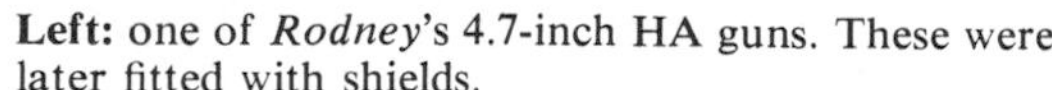

Left: one of *Rodney*'s 4.7-inch HA guns. These were later fitted with shields.

was given to increase the elevation to 60° so that the guns could be used against aircraft at long range. The AA capability, however, was of secondary importance to the low-angle requirements.

Rodney's 6-inch mountings were manufactured by Vickers, and those of *Nelson*, by Armstrongs.

The long-range AA armament consisted of six 4.7-inch 43-cal Mk VIII guns, on single, unshielded high-angle Mk XII mountings which provided a maximum elevation of 90°. Two were mounted on the quarter-deck and four on the shelter-deck. They gave good all-round arcs of fire, but did not meet the requirements of the AA Gunnery Committee which stipulated that at least four guns should be capable of bearing on any point in the sky. The maximum number of guns that could fire on either beam was three, and on some bearings, two. Four guns could fire directly ahead, but they could not track aircraft across the bow. Six could fire directly aft, and the two on the quarter-deck could track to a maximum of 41° across the stern.

The intended close-range AA armament was four eight-barrelled pom-pom mountings but these were not available at the time the ships were completed and eight single 2-pounder Mk II mountings were fitted instead. Four were fitted on the conning-tower platform abreast the bridge, and four at the after end of the superstructure.

The AA armament for both ships was manufactured by Vickers.

In the 'G3' design, some difficulty was encountered in arranging the broadside submerged torpedo tubes. Tubes of this type carried a bar which, when extended, guided the torpedo during its launching. The bar prevented the torpedo from being deflected from its path, or jammed in the mouth of the tube by the motion of the ship, but in high-speed ships, this problem was much more difficult to overcome. In *Rodney* and *Nelson*, the difficulties were completely avoided by arranging the two forward torpedo tubes at a slight angle to the fore and aft line and abandoning use of the bar. Trials with this equipment were satisfactory and the arrangement was definitely preferred to the broadside system. The torpedo tubes were 24.5-inch and *Rodney* and *Nelson* were the only ships in the Royal Navy to be equipped with tubes of this size. The 24.5-inch torpedo weighed 5,628 pounds, had a range of 30,000 yards at 30 knots or 15,000 yards at 35 knots. The running times were 20 minutes and 12.85 minutes, respectively.

Fire-control equipment

Two director-control towers were provided for the main armament, one on the bridge and one at the after end of the superstructure. Each tower contained a 15-foot range-finder. The four secondary armament-directors were arranged two abreast the main DCT on the bridge and two abreast the after main DCT, each of these contained a 12-foot range-finder. An alternative main armament-control position was provided in the armoured hood on the conning-tower. The transmitting-station contained one Admiralty fire-control table (AFCT) Mk I (a more sophisticated version of the Dreyer table used in earlier ships) for the main armament, and two Type 'S' fire-control clocks for the secondary armament. Transmission between the DCTs and the fire-control gear, and between the fire-control gear and the guns, was provided by a new system. This was known as the auto-synchronous transmission system and it provided a number of advantages over the 'step-by-step' system already in use. The transmitters could be driven fast without the system getting out of step. A large number of transmitters could be used (in 'step-by-step' the number of transmitters was limited). The system did not need lining-up when changing from one director to another. (With 'step-by-step' it was necessary to ensure that both transmitters were in line before the change over could be effected.) If electric power failed, the system did not get out of step, provided the transmitters were not moved. (In the 'step-by-step' system, a fault in one transmitter was sufficient to throw the entire system out of gear.) However, there were disadvantages to the synchronous system; it was more expensive and complicated, not so accurate and, at high speed, was not so smooth in operation as 'step-by-step'.

The AA control-position was on a small tower mounted at the after end of the DCT platform on the bridge. The platform on top of this tower contained two, sided, high-angle directors and on the centre-line, a 12-foot high-angle range-finder, an Evershed bearing-indicator and a Dumaresq rate instrument. The high-angle calculating position was at the base of the tower on the DCT platform.

For control of the torpedo armament, two towers containing 15-foot range-finders were provided abreast the funnel, and a torpedo-sight was fitted on each side of the admiral's bridge.

The fire-control equipment also included the following instruments:

1. A 41-foot range-finder in each of the 16-inch gun-houses.
2. Two 9-foot tactical range-finders on the DCT platform.
3. Six enemy bearing-indicators, two on the compass-platform, two on the captain's bridge and two on the admiral's bridge.
4. Four Evershed searchlight transmitters, two on the DCT platform and two on the captain's bridge.
5. Two Evershed transmitters for star shell on the captain's bridge.

Protection

The main armament was concentrated amidships, in order to keep to a minimum the area of heavy horizontal and vertical armour protecting the magazines. It also confined the magazines to the widest part of the ship, and ensured that the underwater protection for these compartments was the best that could be provided.

The main armour belt was arranged internally and set at an angle of 72° to the horizontal in a position about half-way between the skin plating and the protective bulkhead. This arrangement was preferred to that of *Hood* for two main reasons. First, the belt had to be set back from the maximum beam to allow an underwater explosion to vent itself outboard of the citadel, and as the side plating was kept flush with the maximum beam – to improve stability – the belt automatically became internal. Second, the required width of the bulge protection was such, that if the belt armour had been kept flush with the protective bulkhead, as in *Hood*, the armoured beam would have been insufficient to provide the required armoured stability. From a structural point of view, this system was not ideal, because the armour belt had to be provided with a special supporting structure, whereas, in earlier ships, the existing hull structure – specially arranged and strengthened for the purpose – provided most of the required support.

The belt armour was 13 feet in depth and extended from the fore end of 'A' barbette to the after end of the 6-inch magazines. It was fourteen inches thick abreast the main magazines and the main control-positions below the armoured deck, and thirteen inches thick abreast the machinery spaces and 6-inch magazines. The belt armour was backed by ½-inch plating. As with the armour elsewhere in the ship, the plates were made as large as possible, and heavy bars were fitted behind the butts which were 'keyed'. The upper edge of the belt was supported by the armoured deck and the lower edge rested on a heavy, armour-quality 'chock' casting. This, in turn, rested on the outer edge of a strongly supported sponson, set at an angle of 30° to the horizontal. A shell striking the belt would tend to push the belt up this sloping sponson and, therefore, wedge it more firmly onto its seating. This arrangement, together with the keyed and supported butts, greatly reduced the likelihood of the plates being displaced by the impact or explosion of a projectile.

The deck armour over the citadel was 6¼ inches thick, on ½-inch plating, over the main and secondary magazines, and 3¾ inches thick, on ½-inch plating, over the machinery spaces.

In 1922, a target representing the arrangement of the deck and belt armour of the

'O3' design was built into the old dreadnought *Superb* and was subjected to trial. Briefly, the results showed that a 6¾-inch deck and 14-inch belt would be capable of withstanding 16-inch projectiles at such striking-velocities and angles of attack as might reasonably be expected in battle conditions. It was considered that the same was probably true of the 13-inch belt, and that if a shell struck the 4¼-inch deck over the machinery spaces, the likelihood of complete penetration followed by a burst far beyond, was remote. During the trials, a shell was exploded on the target to ascertain whether the protective bulkhead would be pierced by fragments if the projectile, after striking the belt, was deflected in a certain manner. The results were satisfactory and it was concluded that the armour arrangement was the best that could be provided, on the displacement.

The forward end of the citadel was closed by a 12-inch thick bulkhead between the middle-deck and the lower-deck. At the base of this bulkhead was a horizontal shelf of armour, seven inches thick, which extended forward three feet to meet the top of an 8-inch bulkhead which extended down to the platform-deck and protected the magazines from 'end-on' fire. Forward of the citadel, the hull was completely unprotected. The after end of the citadel was closed by a 10-inch thick bulkhead between the middle-deck and the lower-deck. From the base of this bulkhead to the after end of the steering-gear compartments, the lower deck was 4¼ inches thick, on ½-inch plating, on both flat and slope. The lower edge of the slope of this deck was level with the lower edge of the armour belt. The after end of the steering-gear compartment was protected by a 4-inch thick bulkhead.

The barbette armour, like the side armour, rested on heavy 'chock' castings and was therefore very firmly fixed to the armoured middle-deck and unlikely to be displaced by shell hits or explosions. The armour was 15 inches thick on the sides and became progressively thinner as it approached the centre-line.

This thinning of the armour was designed to save weight, and was considered acceptable on the grounds that the barbettes protected each other – to a certain extent – on forward and after bearings. The internal diameter of the barbettes was 37 feet 6 inches compared to 30 feet for the 15-inch Mk I twin mounting.

The front plates of the gun-houses were 16 inches thick, angled at 67° to the horizontal and measured 28 feet x 10 feet. The gunports were 4 feet wide and 7 feet 6 inches high. Curved corner-plates, 11 inches thick, joined the front plates to the 11-inch armour at the forward sides of the gun-houses. The after sides and backs of the gun-houses were 9 inches thick. The back plate was curved so as to provide additional room in the gun-house, and was pierced by seventy-two 4½-inch diameter vent-holes which were hidden externally by light plate covers. The underside of the gun-house, where it overhung the barbette, was protected by a 3-inch thick plate. The roof consisted of five transverse armour plates, 7¼ inches thick, secured to each other by bolts and supported by eight steel columns, in addition to the front and side armour plates.

The funnel-uptakes between the armoured middle-deck and the main-deck, were protected by four armour tubes of 8 inch(mean) and 9 inch (maximum) thickness.

The conning-tower had 14-inch thick sloping sides, 12-inch front and 10-inch rear plates. The floor was 4 inches thick, and the roof, 6½ inches thick. The revolving hood was 3 inches thick, but had a 5-inch face. The communication tube, which connected the conning-tower to the lower conning-position on the platform-deck, was protected by 6-inch armour down as far as the armoured-deck.

Splinter protection for the 6-inch turrets and their working spaces, the bridge and the DCT was provided by thin high-tensile protective plating.

The complete lack of protection forward of the citadel, the weakness of the protection of the secondary armament and control-positions, and the narrowness of the belt armour are features that invite criticism of this system of protection. Little improvement could be effected, however, without drastic reductions in weight elsewhere. This would not have been possible without seriously affecting the overall balance of the design, with, perhaps, one exception – the armoured conning-tower. This weighed 222 tons and its ommission would not have seriously affected the quality of the ships.

Underwater protection

The internal bulge protection was similar to that provided in the 'G3' design, and consisted of an outer air space, an inner buoyancy space and a protective bulkhead. This bulkhead was 1½ inches thick, made from two ¾-inch thicknesses of 'D' steel, and was 12 feet inboard of the ship's side. As designed, 2,870 tons of water were necessary to flood the buoyancy spaces, and this increased the draught by 23 inches and reduced the speed by approximately ⅓ knot. The arrangements in the 'G3' design for blowing the water out of the buoyancy spaces by compressed air could not be provided because of displacement limitations, and a system of pumping and flooding was reverted to. Special attention, however, was paid to the detailed design of this feature and the arrangements showed some improvement on earlier practice. Except for exercises and compartment testing, the buoyancy spaces were to be flooded in wartime only, which provided a saving in weight and, therefore, fuel consumption, in peacetime. The framing of the air space was kept as light as possible, consistent with strength considerations, and arrangements were provided for the venting of explosions through circular venting-plates, bolted to the outer hull at the top and bottom of the buoyancy space, and at the top of the air space.

During 1922, trials were held on the Chatham Float, using models to test the underwater protection system described above. From these trials, it was deduced that *Nelson* and *Rodney* would be safe against a 750-pound charge, but to confirm this it was decided to carry out a full-scale trial. A 1,000-pound charge was exploded against a structure representing the underwater protection. A very large hole was made in the outer bottom plating but the leakage into the hull proper proved to be negligible. It was concluded that the underwater protection was satisfactory, and that even a hit by a torpedo carrying a 1,000-pound warhead would be unlikely to prevent a ship so protected, from continuing in action at a reasonable speed.

Either as a result of these or later experiments, the venting-plates were sealed off, because it was found that they were ineffective during the time the maximum pressure was exerted.

The 7-foot double bottom of the 'G3' design could not be provided, and in *Nelson* and *Rodney* the depth was reduced to 5 feet. Earlier experiments had shown that this depth would provide sufficient protection from explosions under the ship.

Machinery

The need to save weight in the machinery was paramount in order to keep within the 35,000-ton displacement limit, and the efforts made to this end were unprecedented either before or since. Three machinery-space plans were originally considered for the 'O3' design.

'A': Engine room forward of the boiler rooms, eight boilers, two shafts, 150 rpm – based on the machinery layout of the 'N3' design.
'B': Engine room abaft boiler rooms, eight boilers, two shafts, 160 rpm – based on the machinery layout of design 'G3'.
'C': Steam and electric installation which, owing to the size of the motors and restrictive dimensions, employed four shafts at 220 rpm.

These three layouts were discussed by the Director of Naval Construction and the Engineer-in-Chief early in January 1922 and plan 'A' was preferred. The second layout though less desirable, was less cramped and required less weight, and might have been adopted if the requirements of other departments had exceeded the displacement laid down. The turbo-electric drive, employed at that time in certain battleships of the US Navy, does not seem to have been seriously considered.

The E in C was requested to investigate layout 'A' in greater detail and supply the weight required for the main machinery, bearing in mind that it did not seem possible to allow for more than 2,000 tons. He replied on 5th January, stating that layout (A) was acceptable, with slight modifications, at 45,000 SHP, 160 rpm and with two shafts. The machinery weight would be 2,000 tons excluding the auxiliary machinery, and subject to any modifications as the design developed. On 9th February, the first modification to the layout took effect when the E in C informed the DNC that an increase in the length of the propeller shafting would increase the weight of the main machinery to 2,030 tons. The shafting was later reduced, and the DNC asked if the weight might be reduced to its original figure but was informed by the E in C that this would not be possible. On 19th May, the weight was further increased to 2,080 tons because of various alterations in the machinery design. On 30th May, the DNC again asked if it were possible to reduce the weight to 2,000 tons. The E in C replied on 17th June, that although the earlier figure was a rough approximation, 2,080 tons had now been calculated in detail and no reduction to this figure was possible with a two-shaft, 160 rpm arrangement, if the quality were to be maintained. He suggested, but did not recommend an increase in the propeller revolutions to 180 or 200, which would save 25 tons or 40 tons respectively and would give equal turbine efficiency but reduced propeller efficiency. This proposal was seriously considered but was not taken up. By September 1922, when the final design was passed by the Board, the main machinery weight had been reduced to 2,054 tons by reductions in the machinery fittings, spare gear, workshop machinery, the use of aluminium and the storage ashore of turbine lifting-gear. It was also suggested that a further saving in weight of 30 tons could be achieved if the oil-fuel heating pipes were stored ashore. These heaters were fitted in oil-fuel tanks to make heavy oil fuels flow more easily. Their omission would mean that certain oil fuels could not be used. This modification was approved by the Board in September 1922, but it was not taken up. Despite all the efforts made, the final design weight was taken as 2,054 tons. As completed, *Nelson*'s main machinery weighed 2,150 tons, and though this is higher than the design figure, the difference is slight and the achievement of such a low figure was very creditable. The emphasis on weight saving, however, had a detrimental effect on the long-term performance of the machinery, and *Rodney*, particularly, was continually beset by machinery problems.

The relatively low shaft horse-power required to provide the desired speed of 23 knots was mainly due to the low propeller speed of 160 rpm (maximum) which allowed the use of propellers of greater efficiency than was possible in installations of higher speed. The two propellers were 16½ feet in diameter with a 19½-foot pitch and were driven by two sets of Brown Curtis impulse turbines, via single-reduction gears. No separate cruising turbines were fitted, but special cruising stages, with their own steam nozzles, were incorporated in the main turbines. As with cruising turbines, this reduced the amount of steam, and therefore fuel, required for low (cruising) speeds. A transverse bulkhead separated the turbine and gearing compartments which were subdivided into port and starboard engine rooms by a longitudinal centre-line bulkhead.

Steam was supplied by eight Admiralty three-drum boilers with superheaters and a maximum working pressure of 250 pounds per square inch. Like the engine rooms, the boiler rooms were divided transversely and longitudinally into four compartments, each compartment containing two boilers.

The boiler rooms were positioned abaft the engine rooms, so that the latter compartments, which occupied more width than the boilers, would be in a less fine section of the hull and consequently, would, be better protected.

Table 40: Trials of *Nelson* at standard displacement (May 1927)

Date	Wind	Sea	SHP	rpm	Speed (knots)	Displacement (tons)
21st	W.4.	Choppy	6,296	83·35	12·605	33,859
21st	W.4.	Choppy	9,218	94·96	14·41	33,870
21st	W.4.	Choppy	14,605	110·9	16·83	33,884
21st	W.4.	Choppy	18,662	121·19	18·3	33,913
23rd	S.W.1.	Smooth	27,492	136·97	20·44	33,873
24th	S.W.1.	Smooth	36,920	150·67	22·4	33,624
26th	E.N.E.4.	1–2	46,031	161·6	23·55	33,636

This kept the openings for the boiler-uptakes in the armoured-deck farther away from the main magazines, and the funnel, farther away from the bridge structure. It was hoped that the distance between the funnel and the bridge would prevent smoke interference but, in practice, the funnel was too short, and under certain conditions, smoke was drawn into the bridge and control-positions by the back-draught of the tower structure.

Nelson carried out her steam trials on the measured mile at West Looe, Cornwall between 21st and 28th May 1927 with the results shown in Tables 40 and 41.

Nelson was handed over on 10th August 1927, and was brought to full commission at Portsmouth on 15th August for service with the Atlantic Fleet. On 21st October 1927, (Trafalgar Day) the flag of Vice-Admiral Sir H. Brand, Commander in Chief Atlantic Fleet, was transferred from *Revenge* to *Nelson.*

Table 41: Trials of *Nelson* at deep displacement, 27 May 1927

Wind	Sea	SHP	rpm	Speed (knots)	Displacement (tons)
E.S.E.2.	1	6,194	18.72	12.315	37,860
E.S.E.2.	1	9,223	95.31	14.29	
E.S.E.2.	1	15,197	112.7	17.01	
E.S.E.2.	1	18,742	120.44	18.07	
E.S.E.2.	1	27,402	135.84	20.15	
E.S.E.3.	2	36,720	149.2	21.66	
E.S.E.3.	2	45,803	160.3	23.05	37,748

Rodney also carried out her steam trials at West Looe, with the results shown in Table 42.

Rodney was commissioned by a Devonport navigation-party at Birkenhead on 8th November 1927, for passage to Devonport. She was brought to full commission at Devonport on 7th December, for service as a private ship in the Atlantic Fleet.

Auxiliary machinery

In the 'G3' design, several departures from previous practice were instituted in the matter of auxiliary machinery. These alterations – mainly the substitution of electric power for steam power – were repeated in the 'O3' design. Because of the restrictions on space and weight, it was impossible to provide eight dynamos and only six were fitted. Each of these had a capacity of 300 kilowatts; four were driven by geared turbines and two, by diesel-engines. It was considered, however, that these would provide ample electric power for all shipboard purposes.

Table 42: Trials of *Rodney* at standard displacement

Date	No. of runs	SHP	rpm	Speed (knots)	Displacement (tons)	Fuel consumption (tons/hour)
30th August 1927	4	6,590	87.7	13.3	33,765	
30th August 1927	4	9,982	97.94	14.99	33,717	
30th August 1927	4	14,931	114.4	17.44	33,775	
30th August 1927	4	18,274	123.1	18.59	33,785	7.4
1st September 1927	4	28,030	140.1	21.02	33,660	10.5
2nd September 1927	4	36,766	153.44	22.66	33,430	14
7th September 1927	6	45,614	163	23.8	33,660	16

Stability

Due mainly to the adoption of the 'all-or-nothing' protection system, the level of stability provided was much higher than in any previous British dreadnought, and *Rodney* and *Nelson* had the distinction of possessing a higher GM than any other British dreadnought battleship. This, of course, gave them a comparatively quick roll, but the adverse effect that this would have had on fire-control was compensated by the introduction of the stabilised director sight, and the general post-war improvement of fire-control equipment. In addition to the high GM, the reserve of buoyancy was substantially greater than in earlier vessels, and this was further improved by extending the forecastle-deck aft. The stability calculations gave the results shown in Table 43.

Table 43: Calculated stability of Design 03

Light condition (Ship with all oil fuel, officers' stores, canteen stores, provisions, fresh water, reserve and overflow feed-water consumed. Half engineers' and W.O.'s stores on board):	
Displacement	34,521 tons
Draught (forward)	26 feet 2 inches
Draught (aft)	31 feet 5 inches
Trim by stern	5 feet 3 inches
GM	7 feet
Angle of maximum stability	37½°
Range	65°
Deep condition (Ship in standard condition but with all oil fuel, reserve feed-water and overflow feed-water on board):	
Displacement	39,245 tons
Draught (forward)	30 feet 4 inches
Draught (aft)	33 feet 11 inches
Trim by stern	3 feet 7 inches
GM	9.4 feet
Angle of maximum stability	38½°
Range	74½°
Extra deep condition (Ship with buoyancy spaces filled to 35 feet above keel):	
Displacement	42,744 tons
Draught (forward)	32 feet 8 inches
Draught (aft)	36 feet 4 inches
Trim by stern	3 feet 8 inches
GM	10.2 feet
Angle of maximum stability	38°
Range	77½°

Table 44: Effect of theoretical damage on freeboard and draught

	Deep fighting condition			Light fighting condition		
	Draught		Freeboard	Draught		Freeboard
Damage	Forward	Aft		Forward	Aft	
Whole of fore end forward of citadel and below the upper-deck, open to the sea	53 feet	28½ feet	5.8 feet (forward)	46½ feet	25½ feet	9.5 feet (aft)
Whole of after end abaft the citadel and below the upper-deck, open to the sea	52 feet	26 feet	6.8 feet (aft)	22 feet	45½ feet	10.5 feet (aft)

Calculations were also made to establish the stability of the vessels in the riddled condition. These were made for the ships in two states:

"1. Deep Fighting Condition. In this condition the ship is completely loaded as in the extra deep condition shown in the calculations and all buoyancy spaces are flooded."

"2. Light Fighting Condition. This is the condition which the ship might be in towards the close of an action. It has been assumed that [the] machinery is in [a] steaming condition with water in [the] boilers, condensers, etc., and with half reserve feed water and half oil fuel. Half provisions, half fresh water, half stores and half normal ammunition (40 rounds per gun) are assumed on board: the buoyancy spaces are flooded."

The calculations were based on the assumption that the soft ends, forward and aft of the citadel, were open to the sea above the lower-deck; the sides amidships, outside the armour belt were open to the sea, the structure above the middle-deck riddled and gutted but with the bulge compartments intact. In this condition, the vessel was found to have a positive metacentric height, but in the case of the light condition, this was very small. The range of stability both for the deep and light fighting conditions was small, and thus with this extreme damage, the ship was just stable.

Table 45: Angle of heel with theoretical damage

Damage	Fighting condition	Angle of heel
The compartments between stations '134' and '172' outside the armour belt, the five bulge compartments between stations '124' and '184' and the space above the middle-deck, between stations '127' and '165', open to the sea	Deep Light	11½° 15°

With the damage restricted to less extensive areas, the effect on heel and trim was as shown in Tables 44 and 45.

The actual stability of *Nelson* was established from an inclining experiment carried out on 19th March 1927. The results are shown in Table 46. As can be seen, figures are higher than those established in the calculations, which is largely accounted for by the reduced displacement of the completed ships.

Table 46: Stability of *Nelson*, March 1927

Load displacement (Ship fully equipped with 1,000 tons of oil in double bottom tanks, 1,000 tons of oil in wing tanks and reserve feed-tanks full):	
Displacement	36,200 tons
Mean draught	30 feet 4 inches
GM	9·3 feet
Angle of maximum stability	39°
Range	73°
Deep displacement (Ship fully equipped with reserve feed-water tanks full and oil tanks full to 95 per cent capacity [3,900 tons]):	
Displacement	38,400 tons
Mean draught	31 feet 8 inches
GM	10·2 feet
Angle of maximum stability	40°
Range	77°
Standard displacement:	
Displacement	33,500 tons
Mean draught	28 feet 1 inch
GM	7·7 feet
Angle of maximum stability	38°
Range	67°
Extra deep condition (Ship as in deep condition, but with buoyancy spaces flooded):	
Displacement	41,250 tons
Mean draught	33 feet 6 inches
GM	11 feet
Angle of maximum stability	40°
Range	81°

Handling

The twin screws gave *Nelson* and *Rodney* a comparatively small turning circle of 670 yards at full speed, but in other respects their manoeuvring capabilities left much to be desired. They were slow to answer the helm, tended to turn into the wind and were difficult to hold on a steady course when any sort of wind was blowing. One commanding officer reported that he did not consider the ships could be regarded as under complete control at speeds of less than 10 knots. Nevertheless, the history of the class, in the 'Ship's Cover', contains the following passage:

"The manoeuvring capabilities of these vessels was affected at less than 7 or 8 knots and the high superstructure aft caused difficulties until the commanding officers gained experience in handling these ships. The C.O. of *Rodney* on relinquishing his command in 1930 stated that it was a misconception to say that the ships were unhandy and difficult to manoeuvre. In calm weather the ships' manoeuvring capabilities were, in many ways, considered superior to those of the *Queen Elizabeth* and *Royal Sovereign* classes and their astern power was much better than that of the *Queen Elizabeth* class."

The high GM gave the ships a comparatively quick roll. Experiments at the Admiralty Experimental Works at Haslar gave them a rolling period of 14 seconds with a GM of 7.5 feet and a displacement of 35,600 tons. Actual rolling observations provided the figures given in Table 47.

Signalling arrangements

Because of the large amount of space required for the armament it was not possible to provide wireless-transmitting arrangements that met with the full approval of the Director of the Signal Division (DSD). All the WT offices were below the armoured-decks. The main WT office was on the lower-deck, immediately under the mainmast. The main aerial-trunk led to a position on the shelter-deck just abaft the mainmast, and the WT aerials ran from this position to a 50-foot WT yard on the

Table 47: Rolling observations

Ship	Date	No. of rolls observed	Period (seconds)	Maximum angle of roll	Mean angle of roll	Displacement (tons)	State of sea
Nelson	14th January 1931	96	12.5	10°	3.65°		Waves 100 feet long, 15 feet high
Rodney	14th January 1931	106	11.3	7½°	2.96°	37,100	Moderate sea, considerable swell
Rodney	18th March 1931	88	13.6	10°		36,550	Moderate swell

main-topgallant-mast and from there to two spreaders on the high-angle control-position. There were also several receiving-aerials and a low-power aerial rigged between the base of the mainmast and its starfish. The second WT office was on the upper platform-deck below the after director-control tower. From this office, two aerial-trunks led to a position at the after end of the superstructure. One carried the second WT aerial that was rigged to the main-topgallant-mast and the other carried another low-power, aerial that was rigged to the starfish. A small sets WT office was provided on the lower-deck below the conning-tower, with four trunks (three to port and one to starboard) and four aerials that were rigged to spreaders extending from the upper bridge and high-angle control position. A Type '71' WT set was provided for fire-control with two transmitting-aerials (one horizontal, one vertical) on the roof of the high-angle calculating-position at the after end of the director-control tower platform on the bridge. There were four Type '71' receiving-aerials, one on each of the 36-inch searchlight-platforms on the funnel and mainmast. The medium-frequency direction-finder aerials (similar to *Hood's*) were rigged between the funnel and the bridge.

The flag-signalling arrangements were not particularly unusual, apart from their position. The main flag-deck was at the base of the mainmast, some distance from the normal position in the bridge structure. The main signal-yard was under the starfish, and the signal-distributing office was on the shelter-deck, at the base of the mainmast.

Six 18-inch signalling-searchlights were provided on the projector-platform in the bridge, and two Aldis lamp positions on the director-control tower platform.

Four 36-inch searchlights were provided on platforms on the funnel and mainmast, each having a separate manipulating-hut below.

General features

The tower-type bridge structure that was such a prominent feature of the *Nelson* class, and all future newly-constructed and re-constructed British battleships, was, without doubt, a considerable improvement on the open platform tier-type bridge. The large block structure was peculiarly British, and no equivalent was ever produced in a foreign battleship. Its main purpose was to provide a solid and rigid support for the heavy armament-directors, but it also gave greatly improved accommodation for the various bridge functions, and the enclosed platforms provided better protection from the weather and generally improved the comfort of the bridge personnel.

Sandwiched between 'X' magazine and the engine rooms and below the armoured-deck, was what might be called the central control-position. In this area were the lower conning-tower (with a communication tube to the armoured conning-tower) the main switch-board, the tactical plot, the 6-inch gun switch room and telephone-exchange on the platform-deck, and the transmitting-station, gyroscope room and dummy plot in the hold. All these compartments were gas-tight.

Weight savings

The adoption of weight-saving innovations resulted in a total saving of 2,000 tons in *Nelson* and 1,600 tons in *Rodney*. Most of this resulted from the adoption of a new type of high-tensile steel, known as 'D' steel, which had an ultimate tensile strength of 37 to 44 tons per square inch compared to 26 to 30 tons for mild steel. This meant that thinner and, therefore, lighter plates could be used in the hull structure.

When account was taken of *Nelson* in January 1926, the mean estimated standard displacement, including only such ammunition and fresh water as given in the approved legend, was 33,000 tons. After considering the DNC's report of the estimated displacement, the Board approved a re-arrangement of the ammunition stowage and an increase in the amount of fresh water to be carried. The maximum stowage of 16-inch shell was increased from 95 to 100 rounds per gun and the 6-inch and 4.7-inch ammunition stowage was reduced. This increased the estimated standard displacement to 33,600 tons. The exact figures are given in Table 48.

Table 48: Weight comparisons

	As designed* 1923 (tons)	*Nelson* 1927 (tons)	*Rodney* 1927 (tons)
Hull	14,248	13,073	13,167
Armament	6,869	7,308	7,308
Equipment	1,047	1,172	1,172
Armour and protection	10,102	9,528	9,638
Machinery	2,508	2,500	2,500
Total:	34,774	33,580	33,785

* In the legend, these figures were rounded up to give 35,000 tons

The figures given above are based on the weighed weights of the ships while building. The figures calculated from the draughts of the completed ships were about 200 tons less in *Nelson* and about 50 tons less in *Rodney*. After being inclined on 19th March 1927, *Nelson's* displacement was estimated at 33,313 tons. Allowing for the addition of four multiple pom-poms in place of the singles, and two air-craft and their equipment, increased this figure to 33,413 tons. The standard displacements of the two ships were published, therefore, as 33,500 tons for *Nelson* and 33,900 tons for *Rodney*.

8. The Modernisation of the Battle Fleet I: 1922 to 1930

At the Washington Conference, it had been agreed that 3,000 tons could be added to the displacement of existing capital ships, for the purpose of improving their protection against aerial and underwater attack. As the majority of the capital ships of the British fleet were of pre-1916 design, this concession was of considerable importance in maintaining the strength of the battle fleet with regard to the number of ships that could be considered fit to take part in a modern naval war, when aircraft would certainly be more extensively employed than during the First World War.

Immediately after the Washington Conference, an Admiralty sub-committee was appointed, to consider the possible improvements that might be made in the protection of capital ships. Its report, in May 1922, concluded that "at present underwater protection is more important than deck protection, though the position in future may be reversed if there is any great development in bomb dropping from aeroplanes". In the light of this report, the Naval Staff were ordered to consider the relative merits of adding bulges and deck armour to the *Queen Elizabeth* class and later ships, and to prepare a modernisation programme for the ships in question. The Admiralty would have liked to improve underwater and deck protection but the Staff considered correctly, that the possibility of war was remote and the necessary finance would not be made available for both. Bearing this in mind, they concluded, that the progress in aerial warfare and the necessity of providing protection against torpedo attack from aircraft and submarines, was sufficient to justify a policy of bulging all capital ships at the earliest practical date.

With regard to the addition of deck armour to provide protection from armour-piercing bombs, the Staff considered that "if, at some future date, the possibility of a war with a first class naval power were brought closer than is now reflected by the present international situation we could press for the additional armour protection, allowed by the Washington Conference, to the decks of these ships. This additional armour is ostensibly for the purpose of protection against aircraft but will also provide additional protection against plunging shell".

The arguments for bulging, rather than re-armouring, were further strengthened by the fact that the former would cost much less – £200,000 per ship, compared to £350,000 per ship – and that six of the capital ships of the fleet were already fitted with bulges. (*Hood*, *Repulse* and four of the *Royal Sovereign* class.) It was considered that these latter points "would not provide strong grounds for putting forward proposals for an immediate programme of re-armouring" and it was decided to proceed with the bulging and leave the deck protection until later. It is also worth mentioning, that the addition of deck armour to the unbulged ships would have had a detrimental effect on their stability.

The Staff also considered in detail the value of deck armour in relation to aircraft attack, and concluded that:

"1. The total weight of bombs an aircraft flying from an aircraft carrier can carry is about 1,600 lb. It is probable that if light case bombs are developed, for underwater bursting, the whole available weight will be carried in a single bomb of 1,600 lb. If heavy case bombs, for armour piercing, are developed it is probable that the available weight will be distributed into three bombs of about 550 lb each.

2. Aircraft flying from the shore can carry a much greater total weight of bombs than 1,600 lb and may therefore be armed with either heavier or a greater number of bombs.

3. It is essential to provide protection as far as possible against bomb attacks but, since the Washington Conference has limited the total weight which can be added, it is considered that protection should aim at meeting the attack of aircraft flying from ships. That is of 1,600 lb light case bombs and 550 lb AP bombs.

4. Underwater protection against light case bombs is being met by bulging ships when possible.

5. The scheme of additional deck protection should be sufficient to prevent a 550 lb AP bomb from bursting below the main deck in the vicinity of the magazines.

6. It appears that the additional protection to magazines will not increase the displacement to a greater extent than 3,000 tons but no margin can be allowed for any further additions.

7. The existing protection to the engine and boiler rooms in the *Queen Elizabeth* and *Royal Sovereign* classes is as follows:

Except where there are uptakes and ventilator openings there is everywhere at least 3 inches of steel deck to be pierced. The decks are generally of about 1 inch thickness. The protection fitted in funnel hatches and ventilators consists of tiers of gratings, the area so protected being about 2.8% of the total deck area of the target. It is not possible to say definitely what the equivalent in inches of armour plate is to this grating protection but it has been roughly estimated as from ½ inch to 2 inches.

8. It is not practical to improve the protection in the funnel hatches and ventilators in existing ships in view of the necessity of maintaining the area necessary for the passage of funnel gases and air."

These notes are interesting in that they demonstrate the Admiralty's awareness of the fact, that the capital ships of the fleet were vulnerable to bomb attack, and that even if additional deck protection were fitted, the 3,000-ton limit would prevent the provision of anything better than magazine immunity from 550-pound armour-piercing bombs. The Admiralty's view was that "unless adequate counter measures are employed it is quite clear that a concentrated attack by aircraft may [cause the destruction or disablement] or at any rate seriously effect the control of the main or secondary armaments and possibly render the manoeuvring of capital ships in close order a matter of hazard and danger. Immunity or inter-immunity from aircraft attack is therefore a matter of vital importance . . .". The "adequate counter measures" mentioned above were to be provided by replacing the existing AA armaments, which were known to be totally inadequate, by four 4-inch high-angle guns, two multiple pom-poms and a modern high-angle control system (HACS). These proposals may well have been sufficient to meet the needs of the 1920s, but they showed little appreciation of the future development of aircraft, and certainly over-estimated the power of anti-aircraft guns. The Admiralty believed, nevertheless, that with modern high-angle equipment, there were "no grounds for believing that air attack alone will often cause the destruction or disablement of capital ships".

Most of the work involved in the modernisation could be made while the ships were afloat, and only the seven ships requiring bulges needed the use of a dry dock. This latter consideration was of major importance in arranging the modernisation programme because of the limited number of suitable docks available.

The modernisation of *Royal Oak* and *Renown*, whose large refits had actually been authorised before the Washington Conference, would occupy the only suitable dock at Portsmouth until 1924. Another dock was available at Rosyth, but it was not desired to use this. It would have been possible to carry out the necessary work in a floating dock at Devonport, but this would have necessitated dredging, and it was thought that this would be unsuitable. *Warspite* was due for a large refit in July 1923, the principal work involved being the renewal of the water-pockets in her boilers. The Engineer-in-Chief, however, agreed to her continuing in service until April 1924, and it was hoped that her boilers would remain efficient until this date. By that time, *Royal Oak* would have completed her refit at Portsmouth, and *Warspite* could then be taken in hand in the same dock. The remaining ships of the class were to follow at eight-month intervals.

This was the programme that was finally decided upon, but its implementation was seriously hampered by financial restrictions, and it was almost two years before the programme was fully implemented. Much of the work on individual ships was spread over several refits, and inevitably, there were minor differences in the alterations carried out on the ships within a class. To avoid confusion, therefore, the modifications to each class, and to each ship within a class, are described separately, without reference to the chronological order of refits.

THE QUEEN ELIZABETH CLASS

The *Queen Elizabeth* class were the oldest ships in the reconstruction programme, and, as a group, represented the most expensive part thereof; the total cost of fitting bulges and providing the new AA armament was £195,000 per ship.

Bulges

Apart from a considerable improvement to underwater protection, the bulges added substantially to the freeboard, reserve of buoyancy and stability. The overweight condition of the ships as completed – which had been worsened by subsequent additions – was compensated almost completely, the draught being reduced to that specified in the original legend. There were eight docks in Home Waters capable of taking the *Queen Elizabeth*s after bulging, but no dock at Devonport was adequate for this purpose.

The bulges were divided horizontally into upper and lower compartments. The upper bulge which extended three feet from the ship's side and covered the full depth of the main armour belt, was divided transversely by watertight bulkheads, sixteen feet apart. The lower bulge which extended six feet from the ship's side, and covered the area from the base of the belt to the ship's bottom, was divided by bulkheads twenty feet apart. The distance inboard of the protective bulkhead was consequently increased from ten feet to sixteen feet amidships, which was sufficient to provide protection from a 750-pound torpedo warhead. Between the outer plating of the bulge, over the midships portion, and the protective bulkhead there were three longitudinal groups of compartments, the bulge, the double bottom and the wing compartments. Both the wing and double bottom compartments were arranged as oil-fuel tanks and, as such, formed a part of the protective system. It was considered desirable to retain the oil in these tanks as long as possible and, if the oil was used, to flood the side double bottom compartments in order to maintain the protective system. Abreast the boiler rooms, oil fuel was also carried directly inboard of the protection bulkhead. In the event of an underwater explosion, it was considered that, though the protective bulkhead would remain intact, the secondary pressure-wave set up in the oil fuel by the sudden distortion of the bulkhead would cause these tanks to leak into adjacent compartments. In order to minimise this possibility, it was directed that the oil fuel inboard of the protective bulkhead be used first.

Abreast the main magazines, both forward and aft, where no oil fuel was carried, and where the depth of the underwater protection was less than that amidships, water protection compartments were provided. These compartments, which were fitted for flooding and pumping, or draining, were in the side, double-bottom and wing compartments, and entailed the addition of new transverse watertight bulkheads at stations '33' and '232'. The flooded side double-bottomed compartments formed an air-water-air sandwich between the outer bulge plating and the protective bulkhead, and provided a very efficient form of underwater protection. The area under the magazines was protected by double bottom compartments intended to be half-full of water. (Instructions were also in force for bringing double bottom oil fuel compartments to this condition wherever practical. For protective purposes, it was necessary for compartments to be no more than 75 per cent and no less than 25 per cent full; 50 per cent was the ideal.) The total capacity of the water protection compartments was 815 tons.

Below: *Queen Elizabeth* in November 1927, after refit. Note the early MFDF aerial frame at the rear of the spotting-top, range-clocks on 'X' turret and the modified after superstructure.

High-angle armament

Replacing the existing 3-inch high-angle guns by four 4-inch high-angle guns entailed few difficulties, and the only dockyard work needed was placing the guns on board and modifying the magazines. This was not the case with the high-angle control-position, however, which involved more complex modifications. Ideally, the high-angle control required a clear all-round view of the sky, to allow alignment of the various high-angle instruments on any attacking aircraft in the minimum space of time. The only position that fulfilled this requirement was the roof of the fore-top, but this area was already occupied by the 15-inch director-tower. The space could be cleared by re-positioning the director on the foremast under the fore-top, as in the *Royal Sovereign* class, but this had a number of disadvantages:

1. Wooding of the 15-inch director on after bearings, this being at 156° for one telescope and at 164° for both.
2. Added cost of major alterations to fore-top.
3. Increased weight on fore tripod mast.
4. Delay in installing the high-angle control-system because of the additional work involved.
5. When a target was on an after bearing, the main armament had to be controlled from 'X' turret instead of from the director. In practice, the change over took time because the step-by-step transmission system had to be re-aligned. In 1924, the synchronous transmission system was being tried in *Tiger*. It was thought that its introduction might solve the problem.

Meanwhile, the alternative would be to place the high-angle control-position aft, over the torpedo conning-tower. This – though far from ideal – would be cheap, and would quickly enable several ships to gain experience of high-angle fire-control.

It was eventually decided to adopt the fore-top position in *Warspite*, which was then undergoing her bulging refit, and to fit the remainder of the class with a temporary after high-angle control-position during their ordinary refits. The fore-top control, however, was to be fitted in the rest of the class when they were taken in hand for the full bulging refit.

On 16th March 1925, the Admiral Superintendent of Portsmouth Dockyard was informed that the Board had approved the fitting of temporary after HACPs in *Queen Elizabeth*, *Malaya*, *Valiant* and *Barham*. Apparently only *Barham* was actually fitted with a temporary control-position, but several ships of the class were fitted with the fore-top high-angle control, in advance of the bulging.

Bridge modifications

A new fore-top was installed to contain the HACP and to generally improve the main and secondary armament spotting-positions. The control-positions were re-arranged on up-to-date lines to give improved efficiency, and the 6-inch control-positions were separated from the 15-inch control-position. This was a "long felt want and will meet the requirements which have been put forward by the fleet on many occasions during recent years". The 15-inch position occupied the forward part of the top; the high-angle control occupied the after part, between the two 6-inch positions. Access was provided between the sided 6-inch positions so that the control officer could cross to the engaged side.

A new platform for the 15-inch director was constructed under the fore-top, and a new enclosed torpedo-control position, with a 9-foot range-finder hood, was provided above the chart-house. The torpedo-plotting room was behind the chart-house. The guard rails and canvas screens of the compass-platform were replaced by a steel bulwark, and this and the remaining bridge-platforms were slightly modified.

It was stipulated that, in extending and re-arranging the bridge structure, the structural weights be kept to a minimum and, as far as possible, any additional weights be carried to the decks and bulkheads below, by means of additional supports, in order to avoid excessive weights on the tripod. It was also required that the existing structure be incorporated as far as possible and that all unnecessary structures and fittings thereon, be removed.

Funnels
One of the problems encountered when modifying the bridgework, was that the new structures were likely to cause a back-draught that would draw the funnel gases into the rear of the bridge. In February 1924, the Director of Naval Construction considered that this could be prevented by trunking the fore funnel into the after funnel. Despite the additional time and expense involved, the proposal was later approved by the Board.

Warspite
The large refit of *Warspite* was carried out at Portsmouth between November 1924 and 6th April 1926. The modifications carried out during this period are summarised below:
1. Bulges were fitted, and water-protection compartments were arranged abreast magazines.
2. Two 3-inch high-angle guns were removed and were replaced by four 4-inch HA guns.
3. A new fore-top was fitted with a HACP containing a 12-foot high-angle range-finder, Type 'UB4'.
4. The original 15-inch director was refitted on a new platform below the fore-top.
5. The torpedo-control position on the chart-house was remodelled and enclosed.
6. Bridgework modified: compass-platform enlarged and fitted with steel screen, admiral's platform enlarged, searchlight-platform enlarged and the two 36-inch searchlights replaced by two 24-inch signalling-projectors, flag-deck extended aft to base of trunked funnel.
7. Fore-topmast replaced by short stump mast with its truck thirteen feet above the floor of the spotting-top. This modification was necessary to clear the field of vision of the HACP. The stump mast was needed to carry the main wireless-transmitting aerials.
8. The searchlight and searchlight control-position were removed from the mainmast.
9. Short-range fire-control wireless-transmitting set was fitted; the aerials were fitted on the after searchlight-towers on the funnel.
10. Collective protection was fitted, i.e. the transmitting station lower conning-tower etc., were made gas-tight.
11. Funnels trunked.

Queen Elizabeth
During a short refit, between August and September 1924, *Queen Elizabeth* was fitted with two of her 4-inch high-angle guns. The two 3-inch high-angle guns together with the searchlight and searchlight-control position on the mainmast were removed. The second pair of 4-inch high-angle guns were fitted between November 1925 and January 1926. *Valiant* was to have been taken in hand for bulging when *Warspite* had been completed, but it was decided to substitute *Queen Elizabeth.* She was taken in hand at Portsmouth in June 1926, and the refit was completed in October 1927. The modifications were similar to those of *Warspite* but with some minor variations:

Below: close-up views of *Queen Elizabeth* in 1930. Note the inspection covers along the top of the bulge and the box-like after conning-tower that replaced the original, and heavier, torpedo control-tower.

1. Bulges and water protection were fitted.
2. New fore-top with HA control-position.
3. 15-inch director was re-positioned below fore-top.
4. Torpedo-control position on chart-house, as in *Warspite*.
5. Bridgework modified – the admiral's platform was enlarged and, unlike *Warspite*, was extended forward and fitted with a steel screen. Other alterations were the same as those in *Warspite*.
6. Fore-topmast was removed and the main wireless-transmitting aerials were rigged to rear of fore-top.
7. Medium-frequency direction-finder rotating-frame coil fitted at rear of fore-top with direction-finder office below at after end of 15-inch director-platform.
8. After topedo conning-tower removed and a lighter torpedo conning-tower fitted in same position but one deck higher. The original armoured range-finder hood was retained.
9. After superstructure was remodelled and increased in height.
10. Short-range fire-control wireless-transmitting set fitted, with aerials on searchlight-towers on funnel.
11. Collective protection fitted.
12. Funnels trunked.
13. Aircraft-platform on 'X' turret was removed.
14. Stowage for aviation-spirit. Two tanks (that could be jettisoned) were fitted at the edge of the forecastle-deck, abreast the mainmast.

Malaya

The first pair of 4-inch high-angle guns was fitted during April and May 1924. At the same time, the 3-inch guns and the searchlight-platforms on the mainmast were removed. The second pair of 4-inch guns, the HACS, the new fore-top, stump fore-topmast and re-positioned 15-inch director were fitted during a refit, between July and September 1926. As in *Warspite*, a short-range wireless-transmitting set was fitted during this refit, or possibly, earlier.

Below: *Malaya* after her 1926 refit, with new fore-top, re-positioned 15-inch director and stump fore-topmast.

Bottom of page: *Malaya* in July 1930. Note the yardarm fitted fore and aft on the centreline on the mainmast starfish, to carry the aerials for the MFDF outfit. To complete the aerials, a second yard is fitted on the same level athwartships. An 'R' class destroyer is lying alongside, and in the background can be seen the bridge and forward funnels of the battlecruiser *Tiger*.

Below right: a close-up of the back of *Malaya*'s bridge in 1930. The covering over the lower fore part of the funnel trunking is a heat shield.

In 1927, reports were received that the forward ends of the bulges in *Warspite* and *Queen Elizabeth* had developed leaks. It was decided, therefore, to modify the form of the forward and after portions of the bulges in subsequent ships, by substituting curved sections for flat ones, so as to provide access for hot riveting (instead of tap riveting) the boundary of the bulge. It was also decided to fill the extreme ends of the bulge with wood bounded by watertight frames, and to lower the top of the bulge at the forward end, as in the *Royal Sovereign* class.

On 4th January 1928, the DNC inspected wooden models of the forward ends of the existing bulge, and the modified form proposed for *Malaya.* He also inspected the drawings of the modified fore end and the proposed stiffening to bulge and hull. He approved the proposals, but, discovering that *Queen Elizabeth* and *Warspite* had a trim by the bow in the deep condition, he decided to move the bulge, as a whole, fourteen feet farther forward in *Malaya*, *Valiant* and *Barham.* This

Below: *Valiant* in 1931.

Right: *Valiant* in a floating dry-dock in October 1932.

distance was subsequently modified to twelve feet. Approval to fit the modified bulges in *Malaya* was given on 2nd February 1928.

The DNC considered that the leakages were probably caused by slight panting, abaft the section of side plating that had been stiffened during 1915 (see page 30) and he decided to fit further stiffening to the ships' framing in the areas in which leakage to the bulges had been reported.

Malaya was taken in hand for her large refit in September 1927. As completed, in March 1929, she was virtually identical in appearance with *Warspite*.

1. Modified bulges and water protection fitted.
2. Torpedo-control position fitted on chart-house, as in *Warspite*.
3. Bridgework modified, as in *Warspite*.
4. HACS Mk I director fitted in existing HACP in fore-top.
5. Stowage for aviation-spirit provided, as in *Queen Elizabeth*.
6. Six-inch ammunition supply improved.
7. Collective protection fitted.
8. Stump fore-topmast removed and main wireless-transmitting aerials rigged to rear of fore-top.
9. Funnels trunked.

Valiant

The two 3-inch high-angle guns were replaced by two 4-inch guns during January to March 1925. The second pair of 4-inch guns were fitted during June to August 1926. During these periods the searchlight-platforms on the mainmast were removed, a short-range wireless-transmitting set was fitted, and a range-finder (originally fitted on the conning-tower hood during 1923 – 24) was moved to a position above the raised compass-platform. She was refitted again during March to July 1927, when the 15-inch director was re-positioned and the new fore-top and HACS was fitted. Her large refit began at Portsmouth in March 1929, and was completed in December 1930. The following alterations and additions were made:

1. Modified bulges and water protection fitted.
2. HACS Mk I director was fitted in existing HACP in fore-top.
3. Torpedo-control position fitted on chart-house, as in *Warspite*.
4. Bridgework modified, as in *Warspite*.
5. Stowage for aviation-spirit provided, as in *Queen Elizabeth*.
6. Six-inch ammunition supply improved.
7. After torpedo conning-tower removed and replaced by new torpedo conning-tower. The original range-finder hood was retained.
8. Collective protection fitted.
9. Funnels trunked.
10. Medium-frequency direction-finder rotating-frame coil fitted at rear of fore-top with office below, on 15-inch director-platform.
11. McTaggart aircraft catapult Type 'EIH' for Fairy IIIF seaplane fitted on quarter-deck.
12. Four-ton crane, for handling aircraft, fitted on the extreme after end of the quarter-deck.
13. Aircraft-platform on 'X' turret removed.
14. One multiple pom-pom mounting Mk V fitted on conning-tower platform; two pom-pom director-positions fitted abreast and below fore-top, but only one pom-pom director Mk I fitted; it was intended to fit two mountings and directors, but the complete outfit was not available at the time of the refit.
15. After submerged torpedo tubes removed, compartment sub-divided and converted to store-rooms.
16. Searchlight-towers on funnel modified and remote power-control for searchlights fitted.

In November 1930, *Valiant* carried out trials, during which opportunity was taken to study the effects of vibration and conditions on the bridge, at speed.

No serious vibration was found in any part of the vessel and the bridge was found to be particularly free of any movement. Aft, in the vicinity of the shaft-brackets, vibration was more noticeable on the main-deck than on the middle-deck, but even in the cabins in this area, it was insufficient to prevent comfortable writing. At full speed, the aircraft catapult, which was right aft, "chattered" a fair amount, but this was regarded as inevitable.

The trials took place in cold and windy weather, and conditions on the bridge were anything but satisfactory, though why this had not been discovered in the ships previously modified, is not entirely clear. The raised compass-platform was protected by a screen 5 feet 6 inches high, with an outward flare at the top, to deflect the wind upwards. This flare successfully sheltered the area immediately behind the screen, but it was found that

Below: *Valiant*'s starboard quarter in 1933, showing the aircraft arrangements on the quarter-deck.

the wind was then forced down again, probably by the torpedo-control position immediately abaft and above the raised compass-platform. The draught descended at the level of the Pelorus – making it extremely difficult to take a sight from this instrument – and about five to six feet abaft the screen. It then divided at the chart-house and swept down each side of the compass-platform, with such force that it was difficult to stand without hanging on. This caused considerable difficulty in operating the instruments located along the sides of the compass-platform. One amusing note was made at the end of the report on these trials to the effect that "a certain amount of backdraught which blows up the tails of coats, is noticeable in the forward parts of the raised compass platform".

Portsmouth Dockyard tried to solve this problem by fitting semi-permanent extensions, six inches wide, to the flare around the compass-platform. They were secured by bolts and nuts so that if they proved unsatisfactory, they could be removed. These extensions alleviated the discomfort to some extent, but eventually, it was realised that only by enclosing the platform completely could the navigating-position be made comfortable when proceeding at high speed, in cold weather.

Shortly after this, a wooden roof was fitted on the raised compass-platform, and later, this modification was extended to the other ships of the class.

Barham

During November 1924 to January 1925, *Barham* was fitted with two 4-inch high-angle guns in place of the two 3-inch high-angle. The searchlight and the searchlight-control positions on the mainmast were removed and a short-range fire-control wireless-transmitting set was fitted. The other two 4-inch high-angle guns were fitted, between October and November 1925, and at the same time she was fitted with a temporary after HACP, on a platform above the torpedo conning-tower. Between February and July 1928, she received her new fore-top with HACP and stump fore-topmast, and a re-positioned 15-inch director. A redundant platform on the fore-mast, formerly occupied by a 36-inch searchlight, was removed. The temporary after high-angle control was converted to a torpedo-control position.

Barham's large refit did not begin until January 1931, and was more extensive than those of the earlier ships. For this reason the description of this refit has been included in the chapter on the modernisations of the 1930s where it fits more neatly into the reconstruction story.

ROYAL SOVEREIGN CLASS

The modifications to the *Royal Sovereign* class generally followed those of the *Queen Elizabeth* class except that the majority of the ships had already been bulged.

During 1922, the placing of the magazines below the shell rooms was discussed, but was decided against on the grounds that (a) it would reduce the rate of fire of the 15-inch guns, (b) it would reduce shell stowage, (c) it would be expensive, (d) such a modification would be outside the terms of the Washington Treaty.

Royal Oak

Royal Oak was the last ship of the class to be bulged. Three ships had been so fitted

Below: *Barham*, in January 1930, still retains her twin funnels, but has been fitted with her new fore-top. Note the torpedo range-finder on the after superstructure in the position formerly occupied by the temporary HA control-position.

Below: amidships view of *Ramillies* in 1932.

before 1919, and the fourth, *Royal Sovereign*, had started her bulging refit in December 1920. Reports had been received that the bulged ships rolled excessively in a seaway and various experiments were carried out at Haslar, to establish a form of bulge for *Royal Oak* which, together with improved bilge keels, would eliminate the problem. The new bilge keels were later fitted to the remainder of the class.

The new-type bulges were fitted to *Royal Oak* between October 1922 and May 1924, during a refit at Portsmouth. They had separate, upper and lower compartments and contained no tubes or other filling. They weighed 1,100 tons, and generally followed the protective principles of those fitted in the *Queen Elizabeth* class. The bulge increased the GM in the deep condition to 5.5 feet. The following modifications were also made during this refit:

1. Water protection was fitted abreast magazines.
2. A new torpedo-control position was fitted on the chart-house.
3. The search-light tower was removed from the mainmast.
4. The upper searchlight-platform on the bridge was enlarged, and two 24-inch signalling searchlights were fitted.
5. Two 4-inch high-angle guns were fitted (in March 1924) and two 3-inch high-angle guns were removed.
6. Abaft the funnel, the range-finder on the searchlight-tower was removed.

A main-topgallant-mast was added during 1925 or 1926, and between April and June 1927, she received her new fore-top with HACP, stump fore-topmast, collective protection and the second pair of 4-inch high-angle guns. At about this time, the two 6-inch guns were removed from the forecastle-deck.

Ramillies

In March 1923, the deep displacement of *Ramillies* was 36,140 tons, 2,600 tons greater than when inclined in April 1917. Her deep draught was about 34 feet 6 inches and her stability was much lower than that of the other ships of the class. She had been the first modern capital ship to be bulged, this having been carried out while she was building during the First World War. The upper part of her bulge consisted of separate compartments about fifteen feet long. By 1923, the fastenings securing the top part of the bulge had deteriorated to such an extent that they required complete renewal. Portsmouth Dockyard reported that it would take two and a half months to carry out repairs, and in view of this, and the great expense involved, it was decided that it would be more advantageous to fit a new bulge top, similar to that fitted in *Royal Oak*. It was also decided to remove 800 tons of steel tubes and wood (all except 167 tons in way of the magazines) from the lower bulge, to lighten the ship. It was estimated that these modifications would reduce the draught by approximately two feet, improve the stability and provide a slight increase in speed.

Although this matter was discussed in July 1923, *Ramillies* was not taken in hand for modifications to her bulges until August 1926, and it seems more than probable that the original upper bulges were repaired. She was fitted with her first pair of 4-inch high-angle guns and a modified upper-bridge with a new torpedo-control position, during May to September 1924. At the same time, her two 3-inch high-angle guns and the searchlight-tower on the mainmast were removed. During her refit, from August 1926 to March 1927, the following modifications were made.

1. A new upper bulge was fitted and tubes were removed from the lower bulge except in way of the magazines.
2. Water protection was fitted abreast the magazines.
3. Collective protection was fitted.
4. Two 4-inch high-angle guns were fitted.
5. A new fore-top with HACP and stump fore-topmast were fitted.
6. A main-topgallant-mast was added.
7. Two 6-inch guns were removed from the forecastle-deck.

Below: a view of the port quarter of *Revenge* in 1926. Note the four yardarms on the fore-masts: the lower three are signal yards, while the top yard is carrying the main WT aerials.

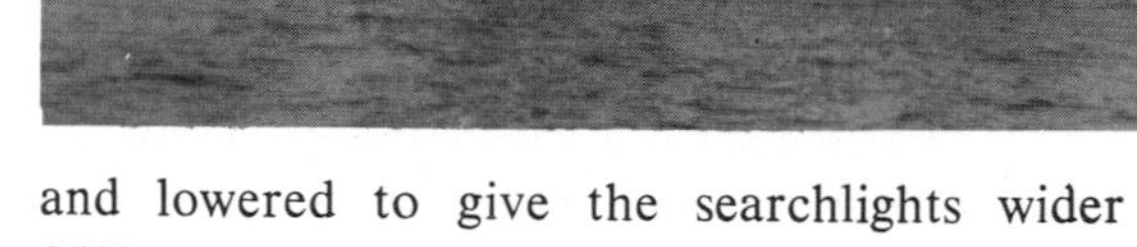

The 6-inch ammunition supply was improved during July to September 1929.

Resolution

Refit of November to December 1924:
1. Two 4-inch high-angle guns were added and two 3-inch high-angle guns were removed.
2. A clinker screen was fitted to the funnel.
3. A torpedo-control position was fitted over the chart-house.
4. A flagstaff was added to the fore-topmast.
5. Two 36-inch searchlights on the upper searchlight-platform on the bridge were replaced by two 9-foot range-finders.

Refit of December 1926 to January 1928:
1. A new fore-top with HACP and stump fore-topmast.
2. Two 4-inch high-angle guns were added.
3. Two 6-inch guns were removed from the forecastle.
4. Collective protection was fitted.
5. Searchlight-tower was removed from the mainmast.

Revenge

Revenge was fitted with her first pair of 4-inch high-angle guns, during April to May 1925. At the same time, she was fitted with a main-topgallant-mast, a new control-position above the chart-house and abaft the fore-mast, and the searchlight-tower was removed from the mainmast. Between January and December 1928, she was refitted at Devonport and the following alterations were made.
1. A new fore-top with HACS Mk I director was fitted.
2. Two 4-inch high-angle guns were fitted.
3. MF/DF rotating-frame coil was fitted at the rear of the fore-top with a direction-finder office below, on the 15-inch director-platform.
4. Collective protection was fitted.
5. The 6-inch ammunition supply was improved.
6. Two 6-inch guns were removed from the forecastle-deck.
7. Visual signalling arrangements were fitted aft (new flag-deck over after superstructure).
8. Searchlight-towers on the funnel were modified, the foremost towers being moved out and lowered to give the searchlights wider arcs.

Royal Sovereign

During her bulging refit of 1920 to 1922, the compass-platform was modified, a torpedo-control position – similar to that of *Royal Oak* – was added, and the searchlight-tower was removed from the mainmast. The first pair of 4-inch high-angle guns were fitted during August to September 1924. The following alterations were carried out between September 1927 and April 1928:
1. A new fore-top with HACP was fitted.
2. Two 4-inch high-angle guns were added.
3. Collective protection was fitted.
4. Two 6-inch guns were removed from the forecastle-deck.

Tropical cruise of *Barham* and *Ramillies*

In 1928, *Barham* and *Ramillies* made a tropical cruise, during which time, opportunity was taken to study the ventilation arrangements. While not a very exciting subject, this it is of interest in that it demonstrates the conflicting requirements for ventilation under tropical and North Sea conditions. The DNC commented that "the experience gained on this cruise is of considerable interest and value and while among these there are a fair number of comparatively minor matters susceptible of improvement no defects of a fundamental nature have been revealed". He also made the following observations based on the information gathered during the cruise.
1. Movement of Air: Under tropical conditions, a noticeable movement of air is essential to cause evaporation of perspiration and consequent cooling. Under Home conditions a supply of fresh air without draughts is the ideal.
2. Ventilation of hot spaces: e.g. the galley – under tropical conditions some artificial air supply is very desirable to provide a noticeable current of air where men are working, artificial exhausts being retained.
3. Lagging of steam pipes: Under tropical conditions this lagging needed to be more

Below: the after decks of *Renown* in 1930.

Bottom of page: *Renown* after her 1923/6 refit.

efficient and, to avoid unnecessary heating, steam pipes in living spaces would ideally be replaced by electric heaters. Under Home conditions the lagging could be limited to that necessary to prevent excessive condensation. The heat was often a welcome addition to personal comfort.

4. Conclusion: Although it was found that the ventilation system, in the sense of the quantities of air supplied and exhausted, was adequate on the whole, the actual movement of air was found to be inadequate.

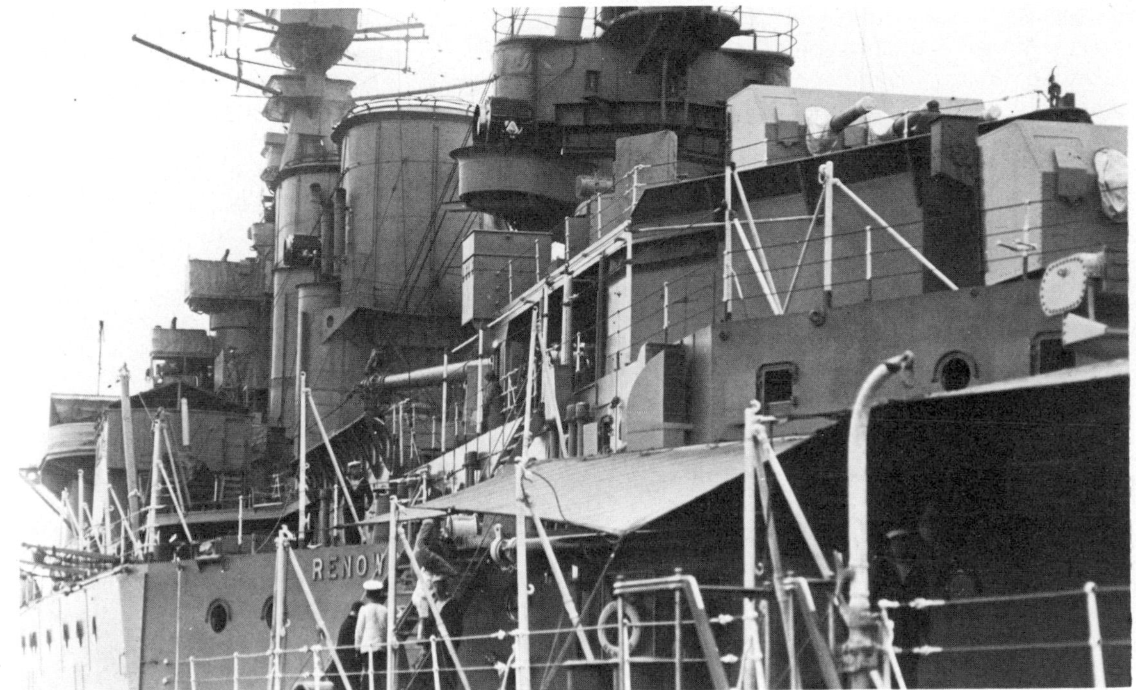

RENOWN

It was originally proposed to re-armour and bulge *Renown* along similar lines to *Repulse*, as refitted during 1918 to 1921. Early in 1922, however, the DNC's department studied the possibility of improving these proposals in the light of the latest armour and bulge experiments, without entailing undue work or expense. The proposals put forward by the DNC on 16th February, differed from the *Repulse* arrangement as shown below:

1. The new 9-inch belt was to be placed higher to allow for the increased draught caused by the various alterations and additions that had already been made.
2. The ship's original 6-inch belt, which was to have been fitted between the main-deck and upper-deck, was to be omitted.
3. The thickness of the main-deck was to be increased to 4 inches over the magazines and 2½ inches amidships, compared to 3 inches and 1 inch respectively in *Repulse*. Some additional plating was also to be added to the lower-deck, as protection against raking fire, and two longitudinal splinter bulkheads were to be added on the main-deck.
4. The bulge was to be lightened by structural modifications, and by the omission of crushing-tubes, except abreast the magazines.

It was anticipated that these proposals would provide a considerable improvement to the ship's protection against both long- and medium-range gunfire. It was estimated that the deck over the magazines would deflect

15-inch shells, at all ranges and angles of descent, under ordinary conditions, and that the deck over the machinery would deflect 15-inch shells at 15,000 yards and below. The 9-inch thick belt was not quite equal in protective value to the 4-inch deck, but it was considered that, except at close range, a 15-inch shell would be broken up in passing through the armour, or would explode at a moderate distance inside the belt. As a result of the experiments carried out on the Chatham Float during 1921 to 1922, it was concluded that the omission of the crushing-tubes from the bulge would not seriously weaken the underwater protection. It was estimated that the net effect of the alterations would be to increase the draught by 3 inches compared to 12 inches in *Repulse* – the difference of 9 inches being mainly due to the saving in weight in the bulge.

The rough estimated cost of *Renown*'s refit was £750,000. This was greater than that spent on *Repulse*, chiefly because of the great amount of work required on her main-deck. Important economies were made by utilising the 9-inch armour that had been ordered for the Chilian battleship *Almirante Cochrane* (completed as the aircraft carrier *Eagle*) and by simplifying the bulge design.

Wages and costs of materials were lower (in 1922) than when *Repulse* was reconstructed, but the final cost exceeded the rough esimate by over £200,000.

The Assistant Chief of Naval Staff examined the DNC's recommendations and expressed a preference for the protection proposed for *Renown* rather than that fitted in *Repulse*, except that the latter ship had additional 2-inch plating on the slope of the main-deck abreast the magazines. He asked if this might also be provided in *Renown* in order to furnish additional protection against the possibility of a heavy APC shell passing through the 9-inch belt armour. The DNC said that this would not be difficult, but the addition would absorb about 150 tons in weight and sink the ship a further 1½ inches. There would be a corresponding increase in cost, however, and as this portion of the belt above the water presented a target – to a projectile at 20° angle of descent – that was only about 4 per cent of the whole, it might be better to omit the 2-inch plating from this comparatively small area of weakness. Nevertheless, the addition was approved in March 1922.

The ACNS also pointed out that his "instructions at Washington were to alter the *Renown* similarly to the *Repulse* and this was the main argument [for modernising the *Renown*] that I used, . . . I do not think this is really very important so long as the fact that some of the entirely novel alterations now intended are not advertised so as to cause suspicion."

Subsequent modifications to the deck-armour proposals, increased the expected draught until – in the revised legend approved by the Board in July 1923 – it was only a few inches less than that of *Repulse*. *Renown* began her refit at Portsmouth in May 1923. It was completed in August 1926, when the following modifications had been made:

1. Belt armour: The 6-inch armoured belt was removed and replaced by a 9-inch belt positioned about three feet higher than the original. The space between the lower edge of the belt and the armour shelf was fitted with tapered armour, 9 inches thick at the top edge and 2 inches thick at the lower edge. At the extreme ends of the belt, this tapered armour was replaced by non-cemented armour of a uniform thickness of 2 inches. The length of the belt and the 4-inch and 3-inch extensions to the belt, forward and aft, remained unaltered. Twenty-four of the 9-inch armour plates were originally intended for *Almirante Cochrane*. The remaining twenty-eight 9-inch plates and the tapered armour (about 200 tons in weight) were new plates, specifically ordered for *Renown*. The total weight of the new side armour was 1,430 tons for the 9-inch and tapered plates, 40 tons for the 2-inch plates and 35 tons for additional framing behind the armour. The weight of the removed 6-inch belt was 896 tons.

2. Deck armour: 2-inch non-cemented armour was fitted on the flat and slope of the main-deck over the magazine, and 4-inch non-cemented armour, extended horizontally, outboard from the top of the slope to within about two feet of the ship's side. 1½-inch non-cemented armour was added to the flat of the main-deck, over the boiler rooms outboard of the new longitudinal bulkheads between the main-deck and the upper-deck. 2½-inch non-cemented armour was fitted horizontally between the top of the slope and the ship's side, over the engine and boiler rooms. The original 3-inch high-tensile plating on the main-deck over the engine room, was retained without additions. None of the original high-tensile plating was removed, and the new armour was added to the existing deck thicknesses. To protect the magazines from raking fire, the lower-deck, for 15 feet forward of 'A' barbette and 25 feet abaft 'Y' barbette, was strengthened by the addition of 3-inch (over ¾-inch high-tensile plating) and 1½-inch (over 2½-inch high-tensile plating) non-cemented armour. The new deck armour was fitted in large plates between the watertight bulkheads, all the minor bulkheads and fittings being temporarily removed, for this purpose. Although this added substantially to the cost of the alterations, it was regarded as absolutely necessary in order to ensure the full protective value of the deck being realised. This was not possible when plates were worked in small pieces around fittings, as had been necessary during the First World War. *Renown* was the first British capital ship to be fitted with non-cemented deck armour. The weight of the additional deck protection was 1,020 tons for the decks (and 2-inch bulkheads, see section 3), 127 tons for the slopes of the main-deck and a further 40 tons for the additional deck supports.

3. Two 2-inch non-cemented longitudinal bulkheads were fitted between the main-deck and the upper-deck. Each was fifteen feet from the centre-line of the ship, and extended from the base of the conning-tower to the after end of the boiler rooms.

4. Bulges and water-protection compartments

Below: *Repulse* in 1928. Note the HA control-position on her fore-top.

were fitted. The underwater protective system worked on the same principle as that provided in the *Queen Elizabeth* class. No crushing-tubes were fitted in the bulge. The bulges added 1,100 tons to the displacement.

5. In 1922, approval was given to fit eight 21-inch, fixed, above-water torpedo tubes similar to those in *Hood*, but – presumably to save weight – they were omitted.

6. Two 3-inch high-angle guns abreast the funnel and two 4-inch low-angle guns on the forward shelter-deck were replaced by four 4-inch high-angle guns.

7. A high-angle control-position was fitted on the fore-top roof.

8. Collective protection was fitted.

9. Fore-topmast and wireless-transmitting yard were removed, the main wireless-transmitting aerials were rigged to the rear of the fore-top.

10. The bridge was slightly modified.

11. Two 36-inch searchlights in the after searchlight-towers on the funnel were taken off.

REPULSE

In 1922 the two 36-inch searchlights were removed from the after searchlight-towers on the funnel. During November to December 1924, the two 3-inch high-angle guns abreast the funnel and the two single low-angle 4-inch guns on the forward shelter-deck were removed and were replaced by four single 4-inch Mk V guns on Mk III high-angle mountings. In 1925, *Repulse* was employed to carry HRH the Prince of Wales on a tour of South Africa and South America, and during this time, she carried a fairly large cabin on the starboard side of her superstructure, between the funnels. On her return, she was taken in hand for a refit, which began in November 1925 and ended in July 1926. During this period, she was fitted with a HACP on the fore-top, and collective protection, and the cabin between the funnels, the fore-topmast and the fore-main wireless-transmitting yard were removed. The bridge, also, was slightly modified. By 1926, *Repulse* and *Renown* were, externally, virtually identical, the only substantial visible difference being the 6-inch armour belt in *Repulse* and the more prominent bulge and second row of side scuttles in *Renown*.

HOOD

Hood was one of the newest ships in the Fleet, and was not modified to any appreciable extent during the 1920s. The following list gives the more important alterations:

June to July 1921, at Rosyth: Foremost pair of 36-inch searchlights on tower between funnels removed.

August to November 1923, at Devonport: Two 36-inch searchlights replaced and main-top-gallant-mast rigged.

October to December 1924, at Devonport: The two open 9-foot range-finders abreast the 5.5-inch spotting-positions of the fore-top were replaced by two 9-foot range-finder-towers. Main-topgallant-mast was taken down and two 36-inch searchlights between the funnels again removed.

November 1925 to January 1926, at Rosyth: High-angle control was improved, the 2-metre high-angle range-finder on the after superstructure was replaced by a 15-foot high-angle range-finder. The control-platform was re-arranged to accommodate the new gear, and the two 36-inch searchlights thereon, originally fitted fore-and-aft, were re-positioned athwartships. The cost of improving the high-angle control was £6,500.

In 1927, the DNC raised the question of improving *Hood*'s deck protection against shellfire by fitting non-cemented armour. The importance of this matter had greatly increased since 1919, when the original deck armour proposals had been made, principally because of the rapid development of aircraft bombing techniques. The ship was too deep, however, to absorb any substantial additions to her displacement without major reconstruction, and – probably with cost in mind – the matter was dropped.

Summary of major modifications, 1922 to 1930

PARTICULARS OF *QUEEN ELIZABETH* CLASS, 1926 to 1930 (EXCLUDING *BARHAM*)

Displacement

	Deep	Standard
Queen Elizabeth (August 1927)	35,480 tons	31,210 tons
Malaya (March 1929)	35,380 tons	30,930 tons
Valiant (December 1930)	35,710 tons	31,140 tons
Warspite (February 1926)	35,060 tons	30,800 tons

For extra deep with water-protection compartments filled, add 815 tons to deep displacement.

Tons per inch (bulged): 103.

Weights (from legends of *Warspite* 1925, and *Queen Elizabeth* 1926).

General equipment	700 tons
Armament	4,950 tons
Machinery	3,890 tons
Oil fuel	650 tons
Armour, hull and protective plating	21,110 tons
Legend displacement	31,300 tons

Dimensions
Length: as before.
Beam (maximum bulged): 104 feet (over rubbers).

Draught (*Warspite* at load draught): 28 feet 4 inches (forward), 29 feet (aft), 31 feet 8 inches (mean, deep).

Armament
Eight 15-inch Mk I.
Eight 6-pounder sub-calibre.
Twelve 6-inch Mk XII.
Six 3-pounder sub-calibre.
Four 4-inch quick-firing Mk V: four high-angle mountings Mk III.
Four 3-pounder saluting guns Mk I and Mk I* (Mk I* only in *Malaya*).
One 2-pounder eight-barrel pom-pom: Mk V mounting in *Valiant* only, 1930.
Four 21-inch submerged torpedo tubes (*Valiant*, two, 1930).

Ammunition stowage (normal)
15-inch: 100 rounds per gun; 6 shrapnel rounds per gun.
6-inch: 130 rounds per gun; 100 star shell per ship.
4-inch: 150 rounds per gun; 100 star shell per ship.
3-pounder (saluting): 64 rounds per gun.
Twenty 21-inch torpedoes.

Fire-control equipment
Main armament: two tripod-type directors, one Dreyer table.

Secondary armament: two directors with pedestal-type sights, two Admiralty fire-control clocks.

High-angle armament (1930): High-angle control-system with open range-finder in *Warspite* and *Queen Elizabeth*, one high-angle control-system Mk I director in *Malaya* and *Valiant*, one pom-pom director Mk I in *Valiant* only.

Range-finders
Two 13-foot in 'B' and 'X' turrets.
Two 15-foot in 'A' and 'Y' turrets.
One 15-foot in armoured director-hood.
One 12-foot in HACP or high-angle director.
One 12-foot in bridge torpedo-control position.
One 12-foot in after torpedo-control tower.
Two 9-foot on admiral's bridge.

Seachlights
Four 36-inch; four 24-inch (signalling).

Armour and protective plating
As before, except that the after torpedo-control tower was removed from *Queen Elizabeth* and *Valiant*.

Machinery
Generally as before. Speed 23.5 knots.

Cost of modernisations
Warspite £195,000; *Queen Elizabeth* £195,000; *Malaya* £195,000; *Valiant* £276,000. Of these costs, £4,000 was for the four 4-inch guns, and £9,000 for the high-angle control-systems.

Complement 925.

PARTICULARS OF *ROYAL SOVEREIGN* CLASS,

Displacement *Royal Oak* (as bulged)
Load displacement: 29,000 tons (designed).
Deep displacement: 33,240 tons (designed).
Standard displacement of class as officially published: 29,150 tons.

Weights (from legend of *Royal Oak* 1923).

General equipment	720 tons
Armament	5,020 tons
Machinery	2,710 tons
Armour, hull and protective plating	19,650 tons
Fuel	900 tons
Legend displacement	29,000 tons

Dimensions
Length and beam as before.
Draught, *Royal Oak* (as bulged): 31 feet 6 inches (mean) at deep draught; 26 feet 6 inches (forward); 29 feet 6 inches (aft) at load draught.

Armament
Eight 15-inch Mk I.
Eight 6-pounder sub-calibre.
Twelve 6-inch Mk XII.
Six 3-pounder sub-calibre.
Two (later four) 4-inch quick-firing Mk V: single high-angle mounting Mk III.
Four 3-pounder saluting guns Mk I*
Four 21-inch submerged torpedo tubes.

Ammunition stowage (normal)
15-inch: 100 rounds per gun; 6 shrapnel rounds per gun.
6-inch: 130 rounds per gun; 100 star shell per ship.
4-inch: 250 rounds per gun; 100 star shell per ship.
3-pounder saluting guns: 64 rounds per gun.
21-inch torpedoes: 20.

Fire-control equipment
Main armament: two tripod-type directors, one Dreyer table.

Secondary armament: two directors with pedestal-type sights, two Admiralty fire-control clocks.

High-angle armament: high-angle control-system with open range-finder.

Range-finders
Two 30-foot in 'B' and 'X' turrets.
One 15-foot in armoured director-hood.
One 12-foot in high-angle control position.

1922 to 1930

One 12-foot in bridge torpedo-control position.
One 12-foot in after torpedo-control position.
Two 9-foot on bridge.

Armour and protective plating as before.

Machinery as before.

Searchlights
Four 36-inch; four 24-inch (signalling).

Cost of modernisations 1922 to 1928
£4,000 per ship for four 4-inch high-angle; £9,000 per ship for high-angle control-system.
£160,000 fitting of bulges in *Royal Oak*

PARTICULARS OF *RENOWN* AS RECONSTRUCTED, 1926

Displacement
Load displacement: 32,520 tons.
Deep displacement: 37,150 tons.
Published standard displacement 32,000 tons.

Weights (given in legend 1922)

General equipment	800 tons
Armament	3,400 tons
Machinery	5,890 tons
Fuel	1,000 tons
Armour, hull and protective plating	21,430 tons
Load displacement	32,500 tons

Dimensions
750 feet (pp); 794 feet 1½ inches (oa) × 102 feet 4 inches (maximum) × 27 feet 9 inches (mean) load draught; 31 feet 3 inches (mean) deep draught.

Armament
Six 15-inch Mk I.
Six 6-pounder sub-calibre.
Fifteen 4-inch Mk IX.
Four 2-pounder sub-calibre.
Four 4-inch quick-firing Mk V: single high-angle mountings Mk III.
Four 3-pounder saluting guns Mk I.
One 12-pounder field-gun mounting.
Five Maxim machine-guns.
Two 21-inch submerged torpedo tubes.

Ammunition stowage
15-inch: 126 rounds per gun (24 CPC, 96 APC, 6 shrapnel); 70 practice rounds per ship.
4-inch low-angle: 200 rounds per gun; 100 star shell per ship.
4-inch high-angle: 150 rounds per gun.
3-pounder saluting guns: 64 rounds per gun.
12-pounder field-gun: 200 rounds per gun (50 shrapnel + 150 common).
0.303-inch Maxim machine-guns: 5,000 rounds per gun.
16 torpedoes.

Fire-control equipment
15-inch: two tripod-type directors, one Dreyer table.
4-inch low-angle: two directors with pedestal-type sights, two transmitting-clocks.
4-inch high-angle: high-angle control-system.

Range-finders
Two 30-foot in 'Y' turret and on armoured director-hood.
Three 15-foot in 'A' turret, 'B' turret and armoured director-hood.
One 12-foot high-angle on fore-top.
Four 9-foot on bridge.
One 9-foot in after torpedo-control tower.

Searchlights
Six 36-inch (two on bridge, two abreast second funnel, two on after superstructure); four 24-inch (signalling).

Armour and protective plating
Belt: 9 inch amidships, 4 inch forward, 3 inch aft.
Bulkheads: 4 inch and 3 inch.
Turrets: 9 inch, 7 inch, 11 inch and 4¼ inch.
Barbettes: 7 inch (maximum).
Conning-tower: 10 inch (maximum).
Conning-tower tube: 3 inch and 2 inch.
Torpedo conning-tower: 3 inch.
Side above belt: 1½ inch high-tensile.
Funnel-uptakes: 1½ inch high-tensile.
Longitudinal bulkheads (main-deck to upper-deck): 2 inch NCD.
Forecastle-deck: 1⅛ inch amidships.
Main-deck (flat): 4 inch (2 inch NCD + 1 inch high-tensile + 1 inch high-tensile) over magazines, 2½ inch (1½ inch NCD + 1 inch high-tensile) over boilers, 3 inch (1 inch = 1 inch + 1 inch high-tensile).
Main-deck (slope): 4 inch (2 inch NCD + 1 inch high-tensile + 1 inch high-tensile) over magazines, 3 inch and 1 inch (1 + 1 + 1 or 1 inch high-tensile) over machinery.
Main-deck (flat over slope): 4 inch NCD abreast magazines, 2½ inch NCD abreast machinery.
Main-deck (flat): 1¾ inch high-tensile forward of 'A' and abaft 'Y' barbettes.
Lower-deck: 2½ inch high-tensile (forward and aft of citadel), 1½ inch NCD on 2½ inch high-tensile and 3 inch NCD on ¾ inch high-tensile (forward of 'A' and abaft 'Y' barbettes), 2 inch high-tensile (over magazines).

Machinery
As before, except speed at loadline 30.25 knots (designed).

Complement 1,238 as a private ship.

Hood in American waters, July 1924. **Below**, an aerial view; **right**, passing through the locks of the Panama canal.

Overleaf: looking down on 'A' and 'B' turrets of the battlecruiser, as she lies in dry-dock at Portsmouth in 1929.

9. Replacement plans and the London Naval Treaty, 1927 to 1930

The ten-year break in battleship construction, agreed at Washington, was due to end in 1931, when the signatories of that agreement would be free to replace, with new construction, any of their capital ships that were twenty or more years of age. The oldest capital ships in the British fleet were the four *Iron Duke* class battleships that were due to be scrapped in 1934, and in that year, the replacement ships would need to be nearing completion. The Admiralty intended to lay down the first two replacement ships in 1931, and discussions of the designs of these vessels began as early as 1926.

The Admiralty were becoming more and more concerned about the increasing size and cost of warships and, in the prevailing mood of economy, favoured a return to capital ships of more moderate dimensions. This would not be possible, however, without an international agreement to reduce the 35,000-ton limit set at Washington. It was also desired to extend the agreed lives of capital ships, for replacement purposes, from twenty to twenty-six years. An opportunity to put forward these proposals came in March 1927, when President Coolidge of the USA invited Britain, Japan, France and Italy to take part in a disarmament conference at Geneva. The Conference began in June 1927, but without official delegates from France or Italy as these countries had refused to participate. When the Conference ended in August, no agreement had been reached concerning the limitation of cruiser sizes and numbers. Britain's proposal to limit capital ships to 28,500 tons displacement and 13.5-inch gun calibre appears to have been received with scant enthusiasm by the USA; little time was spent on the question of capital ships, and the future limitation of such vessels was as uncertain as before.

At the beginning of 1927, the Director of Naval Construction prepared a legend and sketch design for a battleship, generally similar to *Nelson* but armed with nine 14-inch guns, instead of 16-inch. The ship was of 28,000 tons displacement but it seems this was later modified to 28,500 tons and 13.5-inch guns, it having been decided by the Admiralty that these figures should be proposed at Geneva. (For some strange reason, the legends, sketch designs and Staff requirements always refer to the 14-inch gun, whereas papers on general policy usually refer to the 13.5-inch gun. It is clear, however, that the Admiralty was designing a 14-inch gun.) In June 1927, the DNC produced a second 14-inch gun battleship design, this time with the more usual arrangement of eight guns in four turrets – two forward and two aft. This distribution of the main armament was preferred to that employed in *Nelson*, but as it required a longer citadel, it resulted in an increase in the displacement of 1,200 tons. It appears that this design was produced for purposes of comparison with the earlier design.

Table 49: Legends of 1927 battleship designs

	January 1927	June 1927
Length (pp)	600 feet	630 feet
Length (wl)	630 feet	660 feet
Beam (maximum)	100 feet	100 feet
Draught (mean)	28 feet	28 feet
Draught (deep)	33 feet	33 feet
Standard displacement	28,000 tons*	29,200 tons*
SHP	45,000	45,000
Speed at standard draught	23·25 knots	23·25 knots
Speed at deep draught	22·75 knots	22·75 knots
Oil fuel capacity	3,000 tons	3,000 tons
Armament:	9 14-inch guns in three triple turrets (100 rpg)	8 14-inch guns in four twin turrets (100 rpg)
	12 6-inch guns in six twin turrets (176 rpg)	12 6-inch guns in six twin turrets (176 rpg)
	8 4·7-inch HA guns in four twin turrets (200 rpg)	6 4-inch single HA guns (200 rpg)
	4 multiple pom-poms (1,000 rpg)	2 multiple pom-poms (1,000 rpg)
	2 24·5-inch submerged torpedo tubes (10 torpedoes)	2 24·5-inch submerged torpedo tubes (10 torpedoes)
	2 aircraft	2 aircraft
Armour:		Both versions
Belt	12-inch abreast main magazines; 10-inch abreast machinery and secondary magazines	
Bulkheads	10-inch and 7-inch (forward); 9-inch and 4-inch (aft)	
Barbettes	12-inch (maximum)	
Turrets	14-inch (front); 10-inch and 9-inch (sides and rear); 6½-inch (roof)	
Secondary turrets	1-inch NC	
Conning-tower	12-inch (maximum); 6-inch roof	
Conning-tower tube	5-inch	
Conning-tower hood	4-inch and 3-inch	
Director-control towers	2-inch and 1-inch NC	
Main-deck	6¾-inch (over magazines); 4½-inch (over machinery)	
Lower-deck (aft)	4¾-inch	
Torpedo bulkheads	1½-inch	
Funnel-uptakes	8-inch	

* 500 tons was later added for protection from diving shell.

The purpose of these two designs seems to have been twofold. They furnished a guide, enabling the Admiralty to recommend a displacement for future ships, and provided the Naval Staff with discussion material when deciding the 1931 capital ships requirements.

Staff Requirements for the 1931 capital ships

During 1928, the general features of the 1931 capital ships were considered by the Naval Staff. It was necessary to decide the requirements for these ships, particularly the armament, by about February 1929 in order to allow sufficient time for the design work to be completed by 1931. The Geneva Conference had not clarified in any way, the possibility of a future reduction in capital-ship displacement, and consideration was given to both 16-inch and 14-inch gun ships.

1. Main armament: The Director of Naval Ordnance put forward his proposals for the armament of the replacement capital ships between February and March 1928. The 16-inch guns of *Nelson* and *Rodney* had not proved an unqualified success, and he strongly recommended a return to a low-velocity weapon, employing a heavy shell. The new guns would be of all-steel construction, and the 16-inch calibre would fire a shell of 2,250 to 2,200 pounds weight at a muzzle velocity of between 2,575 and 2,550 feet per second. It was estimated that the gun would have a life of 250 effective full charges, and a low loss of muzzle velocity per round of approximately 0.4 feet per second. The lower velocity reduced the possibility of the rifling being stripped – as had occurred with the 16-inch Mk I – but it was thought that the margin of safety against this possibility was far too small. It was, however, expected that the gun would possess exceptionally good accuracy and that the projectiles would have armour-piercing quality equal to the existing 16-inch armour-piercing shell. For the 14-inch calibre, it was hoped to produce a gun that would fire a 1,500-pound shell at a muzzle velocity of 2,550 feet per second, have a life of approximately 300 effective full charges, a low loss of muzzle velocity per round and a good accuracy.

The DNO pointed out that the adoption of a new 16-inch gun would mean that its ammunition would not be interchangeable with that of the 16-inch Mk I. This would lead to complications in the supply system, and make it difficult to concentrate fire between *Rodney* and *Nelson* and the new ships. It was considered desirable, however, for *Rodney* and *Nelson* to concentrate fire together, rather than with other capital ships, but as this could not always be arranged, it was thought that the different ballistics of the two types of 16-inch gun could be allowed for and that the concentration results would not materially suffer.

With regard to the mountings for the new guns, it was stated that: "Sufficient experience has been obtained in the *Nelson* and *Rodney* turrets to enable the DNO to recommend, definitely, that these turrets should not be reproduced". Consideration was being given to an improved design of 16-inch triple turret in an endeavour to overcome the drawbacks of the Mk I mounting, and to increase the rate of fire. If a twin mounting were to be adopted, it was proposed that the design be based on the 15-inch twin turret but with some modification to the gun loading-trays and transfer-positions in the working chamber so as to improve flash-tightness and to take account of the shell rooms being above the magazines. As with the 16-inch Mk I, it was intended to use a fixed loading-angle. A rate of loading of one round per gun every thirty seconds was anticipated. This would be slower than that of the 15-inch twin mounting because of the increased flash-tightness and higher elevation. In this regard, the DNO pointed out that the higher the elevation, the longer must be the hoist for the loading cage and consequently, the greater the loading interval. He recommended that the maximum elevation be reduced to 35° or even 30° provided that this did not seriously affect the range of the main armament if the ship was listing as a result of up to four torpedo hits on the engaged side.

For the main armament disposition, the *Queen Elizabeth* class system of four twin turrets was preferred, rather than that used in *Nelson*. This would mean a longer and heavier ship, and would reduce the underwater protection to the magazines, but these disadvantages were not considered sufficient to prevent the adoption of eight guns, disposed fore and aft.

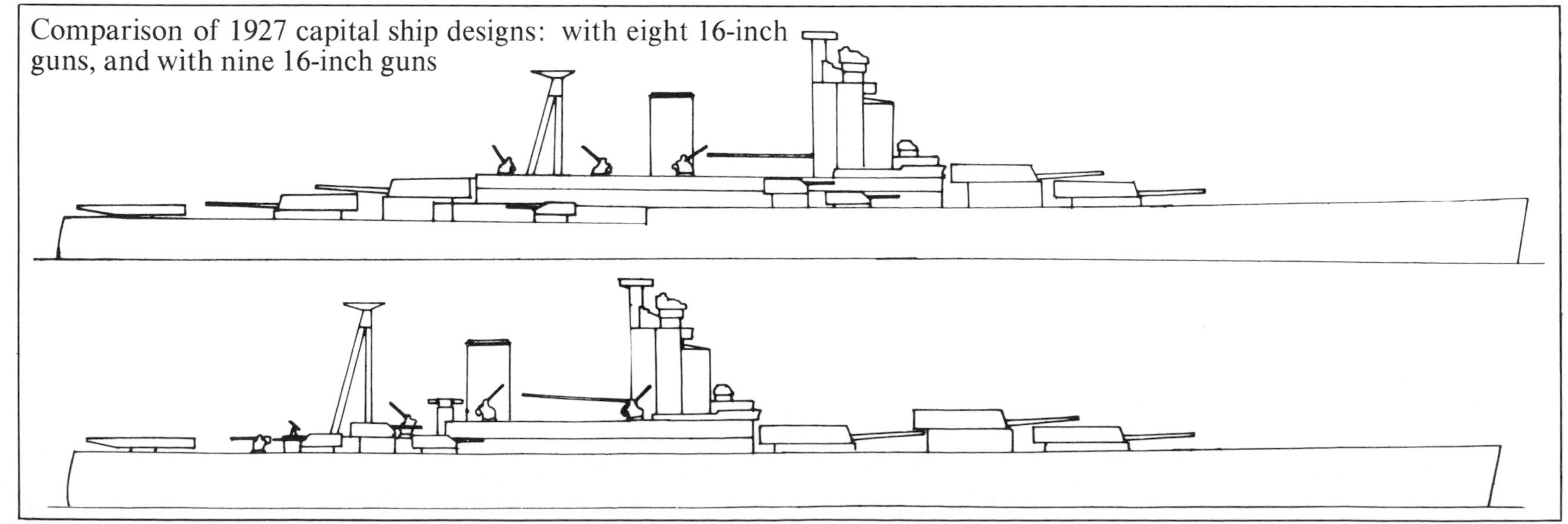
Comparison of 1927 capital ship designs: with eight 16-inch guns, and with nine 16-inch guns

All the DNO's proposals were accepted, though the DNC expressed concern about the reduced underwater protection to magazines and proposed that the magazines be placed above the shell rooms, as in earlier ships. This proposal was not adopted.

2. Secondary armament: The 6-inch Mk XXII gun had proved a reliable weapon, and it was proposed to adopt an all-steel version of this gun for the new ships. Six such guns on each side was considered the minimum acceptable number because of the need of obtaining early hits, thereby fulfilling adequately, the function of a secondary armament. Eight guns on each side was ideal provided that they could be adequately protected. Again, the possibility of combining the secondary and long-range anti-aircraft armaments was considered but, as in 1921, the arrangement was not favoured. The 4.7-inch gun was the largest high-angle weapon that could be loaded by hand with quick-firing ammunition, but it was not large enough to serve as a secondary-armament weapon. Experiments had demonstrated that the 5.5-inch quick-firing high-angle gun might prove a practical proposition but, even so, it was not so effective against aircraft as the 4.7-inch. Keeping the two requirements separate was, undoubtedly, advantageous in that the most efficient weapons for each purpose could be provided. It was realised, however, that it might be necessary to combine the functions, if the displacement of the new ships were reduced below 35,000 tons.

Twin turret mountings were preferred rather than the broadside battery, but it was specified that these be better protected, and spaced farther apart than in *Nelson*. It was hoped, also, to increase the rate of fire by improving the loading arrangements and increasing the speed of elevation, provided that no undue complication or expense were involved, and for this purpose, a reduction in the elevation from the 60° provided in the Mk XVIII mounting was considered acceptable.

3. Anti-Aircraft armament: For the long-range AA armament, the DNO proposed a 4.7-inch quick-firing gun, with a performance equal to a new destroyer gun, (the Mk IX, with a muzzle velocity of 2,650 feet per second.) The Staff required that the gun be capable of achieving 12,000 yards plan range and 20,000 feet in height. The time of flight at these distances, was to be not more than 32 seconds, and the rate of fire 8 rounds per gun per minute. The guns were to be mounted in between-deck twin turrets, so as to provide good protection to gun-crews from weather, gun-blast and shell and bomb splinters. Two such mountings were to be fitted on each beam, with the largest possible arcs of fire, and elevation up to 90°.

The close-range AA armament was to consist of four eight-barrel pom-pom mountings and two 0.5-inch machine-gun quadruple mountings.

4. Torpedo armament: The possibility of returning to the 21-inch calibre was considered. The latest 21-inch Mk VII torpedo had a performance nearly equal to that of the 24.5-inch, with a range of 16,000 yards at 33 knots, and a running time of 14.54 minutes. The 24.5-inch, however, carried a charge of 1,000 pounds. It was thought that the Mk VII might also be capable of carrying a charge of this weight, and a decision was deferred, pending the results of trials of the 21-inch torpedo, carrying the larger charge. The forward, barless torpedo tubes of the *Nelson* class had proved successful, and it was decided, not only to repeat the arrangement, but to expand it. The Captain of HMS *Vernon* (the torpedo school) proposed an arrangement similar to that used in the 'O' class submarines. This consisted of a nest of three tubes on each side, either in the fore-and-aft line or at 5° from the bow. It was decided to adopt this system if it proved practicable.

5. Fire-control positions: The Staff required that these be as in *Nelson*, but with the after position simplified by omitting the two secondary director-towers.

6. Protection: The magazines were to withstand 16-inch plunging shells, at ranges up to 30,000 yards, and the machinery spaces, up to 26,000 yards. The side armour was to be impenetrable at ranges greater than 12,000 yards, or at a striking angle of 70°. The magazines were to withstand 2,000-pound bombs dropped from heights up to 10,000 feet, and the machinery spaces, 2,000-pound bombs from 4,000 feet and 500-pound bombs from 10,000 feet.

7. Steering gear: This was to be covered by a deck, 5 inches thick as against 4½ inches in *Nelson*. The main turrets were to have 15-inch front plates and 11-inch to 9-inch sides. The secondary turrets were to have 2-inch protection as opposed to 1-inch in *Nelson*.

8. Underwater protection: A five-foot double bottom as in *Nelson* unless this could be improved upon. Bulge protection against a 750-pound torpedo warhead and a torpedo bulkhead extending as far forward as possible.

9. Aircraft: One spotter/reconnaissance and one fighter or fighter/reconnaissance.

10. Endurance: 7,000 miles at 16 knots.

11. Speed: 23 knots at standard displacement. Six boilers of 7,000 shaft horse-power each.

The 1928/29 sketch designs

On 15th March 1929, the Sea Lords met to discuss future battleship policy and concluded that a 25,000-ton ship armed with 12-inch guns would meet British requirements, provided that other naval powers could be induced to agree to this limitation. It was known that the USA were not anxious to discuss alterations to the Washington Agreement before January 1931, and unless they could be persuaded to modify this attitude and agree to a conference that would further limit the displacement of capital ships, it would be necessary to proceed with ships comparable to *Nelson* and *Rodney*. Furthermore, if a conference were not held at an early date, insufficient time would be available to prepare a new design conforming to any new limitation agreed at such a conference. It was decided that the Cabinet be informed of these views, so that it might initiate action, if and when required. It was also decided that Britain's proposal at Geneva, to extend the lives of capital ships to twenty-six years, might be put forward again, though this would entail putting back and re-drafting the replacement programme. To cover all possible future developments, as far as possible, it was decided to prepare designs for 16-inch, 14-inch and 12-inch gun ships of 35,000, 28,000 and 25,000 tons respectively, so that, if necessary, building could begin as soon as the conference reached a conclusion.

In 1928, the DNC had produced a legend and sketch design for a 16-inch gun ship, and it appears that this design '16A' was the only 35,000-ton ship included in the preparations for the replacement programme. The Staff requirements for this design were also applied to the 12-inch gun designs, but the DNC was asked to determine the sacrifices necessary, if a speed of 23 knots were to be exceeded, and to what extent the side armour could be reduced, if intended to withstand 12-inch shells only. Of the many designs produced, the following received serious consideration:

1. Design '16A': This design met the Staff requirements for the 16-inch gun ship, as set out in 1928. The main armament was provided with a maximum elevation of 35° and the arc of fire of 'B' turret, abaft, and 'X' turret, forward of the beam, was restricted to 45°, in order to reduce the effect of blast on the superstructure. 'A' and 'Y' turrets retained the full arc of 300°. The 6-inch turrets were spaced forty feet apart as opposed to thirty feet in *Nelson* and they were supplied with ammunition from two sets of magazines (one forward and one aft) instead of one.

2. Designs '12B', '12D', '12G' and '12J': Eleven 12-inch gun battleship designs were drawn up, with speeds ranging from 23 to 27 knots, and main armaments arranged in four twin turrets, three triple turrets, two triple turrets and even two triples and one twin. The four designs listed above, were considered the most promising and were presented to the Board for examination. Designs '12B', '12G' and '12D' had speeds of 23, 24 and 25 knots respectively, and were all armed with eight 12-inch guns in four twin turrets. The armour protection followed the system employed in *Nelson* except that the side armour offered better protection

Table 50: Legend of particulars of Design 16A

Length (pp)	692 feet
Beam (max)	106 feet
Draught (mean)	30 feet
Displacement (standard)	35,000 tons
SHP	45,000
Speed	23 knots
Oil fuel capacity	3,000 tons
Armament:	8 16-inch guns (4×2) 12 6-inch guns (6×2) 8 4·7-inch HA guns (4×2) 6 multiple pom-poms (6×8) 2 aircraft 2 aircraft catapults
Armour:	
Belt	13-inch and 4-inch (abreast magazines) 11-inch and 4-inch (abreast machinery)
Bulkheads	11-inch and 7-inch (forward) 11-inch and 4-inch (aft)
Barbettes	13-inch to 10-inch
Turrets	15-inch (front) 6-inch (roof)
Conning-tower	12-inch and 8-inch, 6-inch (roof)
Decks	6¼-inch (over magazines) 4¼-inch (over machinery) 4-inch (over steering gear)
Director-control towers	2-inch
6-inch gun working spaces	6-inch
Funnel-uptakes	9-inch to 7-inch
Bridge	1-inch
Torpedo bulkheads	1½-inch
Complement	1,342
Weights (tons):	
Equipment	1,100
Armament	6,900
Machinery	2,450
Armour	11,150
Hull	3,400
Standard displacement:	35,000 tons

Table 51: Legend of particulars of Designs 14A and 14B

	14A	14B
Length (pp)	660 feet	620 feet
Beam (maximum)	104 feet	104 feet
Draught (mean)	27 feet	27½ feet
Displacement (standard)	30,700 tons	29,070 tons
SHP	60,500	43,500
Speed		23 knots
Oil fuel capacity	3,500 tons	3,000 tons
Armament:	8 14-inch guns (4×2) 12 6-inch guns (6×2) 8 4·7-inch HA guns (4×2) 4 multiple pom-poms (4×8)	Both versions
Armour:		
Belt	11-inch and 3-inch (abreast magazines) 10-inch and 3½-inch (abreast machinery)	Both versions
Bulkheads	10-inch and 7-inch (forward) 10-inch (aft)	Both versions
Barbettes	12-inch, 11-inch and 10-inch	Both versions
Turrets	14-inch (front) 9½-inch (side) 7¾-inch (rear) 6-inch (roof)	Both versions
Conning-tower	11-inch and 8-inch 4¾-inch (roof)	Both versions
Decks	6¼-inch (over magazines) 4¼-inch (over machinery) 4-inch (over steering gear)	Both versions
Director-control tower	2-inch	Both versions
6-inch gun working spaces	6-inch	Both versions
Funnel-uptakes	8-inch to 6-inch	Both versions
Bridge	1-inch	Both versions
Torpedo bulkheads	1½-inch	Both versions
Complement	1,200	1,300
Weights (tons):		
Equipment	1,100	1,090
Armament	5,680	5,680
Machinery	2,950	2,350
Armour	8,970	8,700
Hull	12,000	11,250
Standard displacement:	30,700	29,070

Table 52: Legends of particulars of battleship Designs 12A to 12L*

	12A	12B	12C	12D	12E	12F	12G	12H	12J	12K	12L
Length (pp) feet	610	610	620	620	610	610	612	600	620	630	620
Beam (max) feet	96	100	100	102	100	104	102	100	102	102	102
Draught (mean)	27 ft	26 ft	26 ft 8 in	26 ft 2 in	25 ft 5 in	25 ft	26 ft	25 ft 3 in	26 ft 6 in	27 ft	27 ft
Standard displacement (tons)	25,040	25,430	26,700	26,800	24,690	24,930	26,070	24,230	26,700	28,150	27,750
SHP	37,000	40,000	53,200	55,000	39,000	38,000	48,000	37,500	55,000	80,000	80,000
Speed (knots)	23	23	25	25	23	23	24	23	25	27	27
Oil fuel capacity (tons)	2,700	2,700	3,000	3,000	2,700	2,700	2,700	2,700	3,000	3,000	3,000
Armament**	8 12-in (4 × 2) 12 6-in (6 × 2) 8 4.7-in HA (4 × 2) 4 pom-poms (4 × 8) (12A, 12B, 12C, 12D) 1 aircraft, 1 catapult				8 12-in 8 6-in (4 × 2) 8 4.7-in HA (4 × 2) 2 pom-poms (4 × 2)	6 12-in (2 × 3) 12 6-in (6 × 2) 8 4.7-in HA (4 × 2) 4 pom-poms (4 × 8)	8 12-in (4 × 2) 12 6-in (6 × 2) 8 4.7-in HA (4 × 2) 4 pom-poms (4 × 8)	8 12-in (2 × 3 + 1 × 2) 12 6-in (6 × 2) 8 4.7-in HA (4 × 2) 4 pom-poms (4 × 8)	9 12-in (3 × 3) 12 6-in (6 × 2) 4 pom-poms (4 × 8)	8 12-in (4 × 2) 24 4.7-in HA (12 × 2) 4 pom-poms (4 × 8)	9 12-in (3 × 3) 24 4.7-in HA (12 × 2) 4 pom-poms (4 × 8)

Armour (all versions):

Belt	10-inch and 3-inch (abreast magazines) (12K and 12J 10-inch and 5-inch) 8-inch and 3-inch (abreast machinery) (12K and 12J 10-inch and 5-inch)
Bulkheads	10-inch and 7-inch (forward) 10-inch (aft)
Barbettes	11-inch and 9-inch
Decks	6-inch over magazines, 4-inch over machinery and steering gear
Turrets	12½-inch (face) 8½-inch (sides and rear) 5¾-inch (roof)
Conning-tower	10-inch and 7-inch, 4½-inch (roof)
Director-control tower	2-inch
Secondary armament working spaces	1-inch (12K and 12J 2-inch)
Funnel	7-inch and 5-inch
Bridge	1-inch
Torpedo bulkheads	1½-inch

Weights (tons):	12A	12B	12C	12D	12E	12F	12G	12H	12J	12K	12L
General equipment	1,060	1,060	1,080	1,080	1,015	1,060	1,070	1,060	1,080	1,050	1,050
Armament	4,190	4,190	4,190	4,190	3,810	4,020	4,190	4,020	4,380	4,250	4,400
Machinery	2,050	2,180	2,800	2,840	2,150	2,090	2,500	2,050	2,840	2,880	2,880
Armour	7,230	7,400	7,530	7,600	7,240	7,090	7,510	6,800	7,400	8,470	8,100
Hull	10,510	10,600	11,100	11,090	10,475	10,670	10,800	10,300	11,000	11,500	11,320
Standard displacement:	25,040	25,430	26,700	26,000	24,690	24,930	26,070	24,230	26,700	28,150	27,750
Complement	1,264	1,266	1,286	1,286	1,166	1,264	1,276	1,264	1,300		

* No record has been found of a 12I design, if such a design existed.
** Because of weight restrictions, none of the 12-inch gun ships were provided with torpedo tubes.

Table 53: Legend particulars of battleship Designs 10A, 10C and 11A*

	10A	10C	11A
Length (pp) feet	620	600	600
Beam (maximum) feet	96	98	98
Draught (mean) feet	25	25	26
Displacement (tons)	21,670	22,000	23,300
SHP	54,000	48,000	48,000
Speed (knots)	25	24	24
Oil fuel capacity (tons)	2,700	2,700	2,700
Armament:	8 10-inch guns (4 × 2) in 10A and 10C		8 11-inch guns (4 × 2)
	8 6-inch guns (4 × 2) 8 4·7-inch HA guns (4 × 2) 2 pom-poms (2 × 8) 1 aircraft and catapult (All versions)		
Armour:			
Belt (abreast magazine)	8-inch and 2½-inch		9-inch and 3-inch
Belt (abreast machinery)	6-inch and 2½-inch		7-inch and 3-inch
Bulkheads (forward and aft)	8-inch and 4-inch		9-inch and 5-inch
Barbettes	9-inch, 8-inch and 7-inch		10-inch and 8-inch
Turrets	11½-inch, 8-inch and 6-inch 5¾-inch (roof)		12-inch front. 5¼-inch roof
Conning-tower	9-inch and 6¼-inch, 4-inch (roof)		10-inch and 7-inch 4½-inch roof
Deck (over magazine)	5½-inch		4¾-inch
Deck (over machinery and steering)	3½-inch		3¾-inch
Director-control towers	2-inch		2-inch
6-inch working spaces	1-inch		1-inch
Funnel-uptakes	6-inch and 4-inch		7-inch and 5-inch
Bridges	1-inch		1-inch
Torpedo bulkheads	1½-inch		1½-inch
Weights (tons):			
Equipment	900	950	1,000
Armament	3,010	3,050	3,550
Machinery	2,800	2,500	2,500
Armour	5,500	5,700	6,250
Hull	9,460	9,800	10,000
Standard displacement:	21,670	22,000	23,300

* No details have been found of a 10B Design, if such a design existed

against 12-inch shells than *Nelson*'s armour did against 16-inch shells. Only Design '12B' met the Board requirement of 25,000 tons, but the DNC pointed out that '12G' could also be brought down to this displacement, if the side and deck armour were reduced in thickness. He considered such a reduction inadvisable, however, because of the increased vulnerability that would ensue. In '12J', an attempt was made to save weight by adopting triple turrets for the main armament. The design was for a 25-knot ship and, compared with '12D', showed very little reduction in displacement. Triple turrets for the secondary armament were also considered but it was decided that these would be impracticable because of the large space they would occupy, and the large holes that would be required for the mountings, in the strength-deck, amidships. The DNC concluded that it would be "unsafe to fix the displacement required, below 27,000 tons as further additions and some alterations would almost certainly be required before a complete design was ready for building".

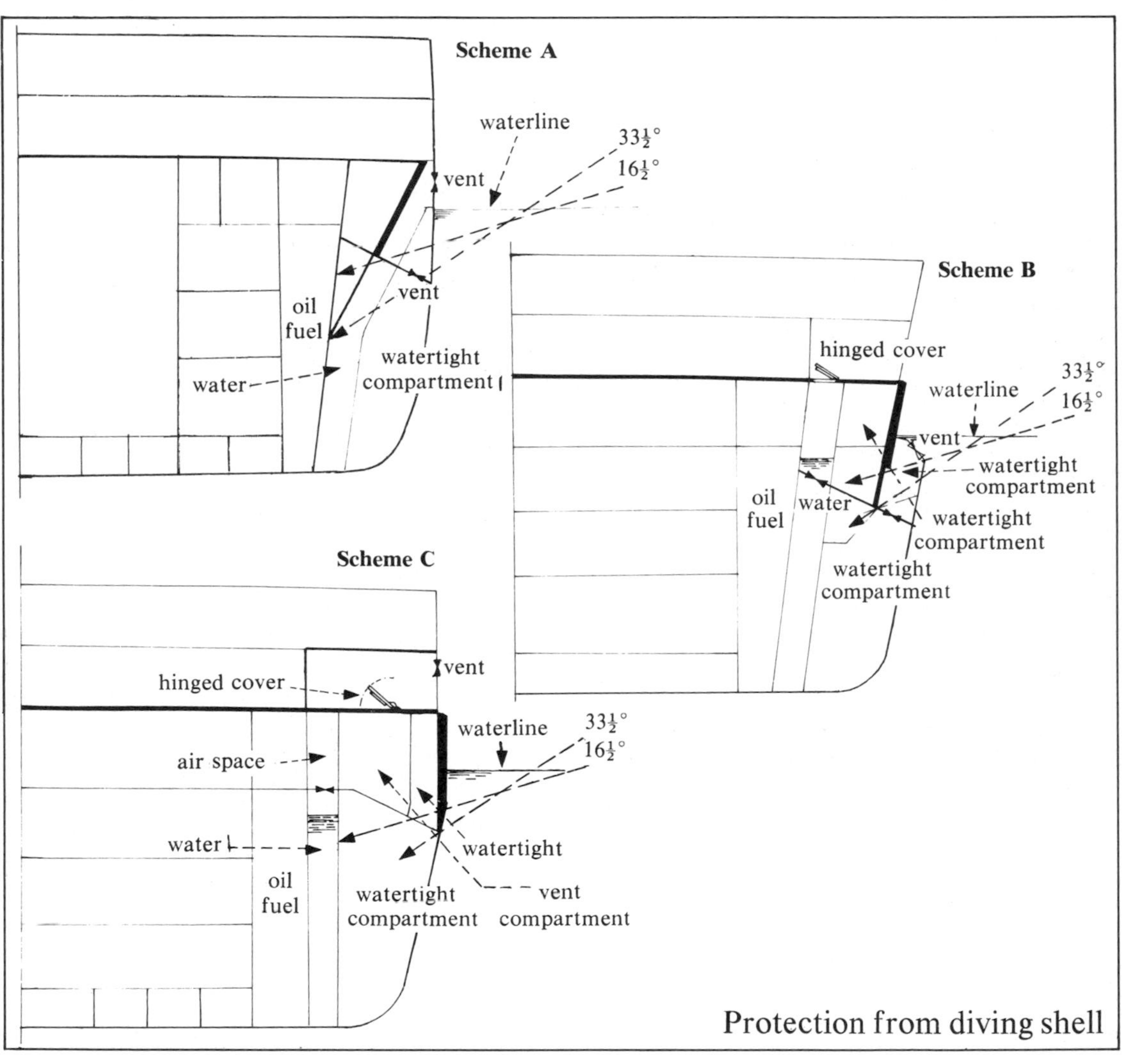

Protection from diving shell

Diving shell

Projectiles fired from guns, on striking the surface of the sea, will either (a) detonate, (b) be deflected from their line of flight, and sink, (c) ricochet off the surface of the sea, or (d) continue underwater approximately along their line of flight. The last possibility, (d) is known as diving, and constitutes a positive danger to capital ships in that such a shell can penetrate a ship's side below the belt armour. Many examples of this phenomenon had been recorded. At Dogger Bank, the battlecruiser *Lion* was struck by five shells, at distances varying from three to eighteen feet below the waterline, and *Malaya*, at Jutland, by two shells, four and twelve feet below the waterline. There were also many cases of battle-practice targets being holed near the keel, and the target-ships *Agamemnon* and *Centurion* had both been holed many times below the waterline, by 4-inch, 6-inch and 9.2-inch projectiles. No serious attempt however, had been made to protect ships from such hits, before 1928. In December of that year, the DNC was asked to investigate the possibility of providing a deeper belt in the new designs, to counteract, as far as possible, the effects of underwater hits by diving shell. He was also asked to investigate the possibility of positioning the belt armour on the ship's side, instead of internally as in *Nelson*.

The Ordnance Committee was given the task of investigating the behaviour of diving shell, but it could not supply any information based on experiment, until the series of trials with small-calibre shells – which it was preparing – had been carried out. However, it could, and did provide the DNC with information and a set of figures based on theoretical considerations, which enabled him to prepare his proposals immediately. The information supplied by the Ordnance Committee was summarised as follows.

"(a) A 16 inch shell at ranges of above 20,000 yards will dive. The path after diving will for moderate depths be approximately a continuation of the path before striking the water.

(b) Estimated velocities of shell at depths of 6 feet and 12 feet below water are given for ranges of 20,000 yards and above as follows:

Table 54: Velocity of diving shell

Range (yards):	20,000	25,000	30,000	35,000	39,500
Angle of descent	16½°	24½°	33½°	44°	59°
Remaining velocity on striking the water (fps)	1,610	1,490	1,430	1,450	1,600
Remaining velocity 6 feet below surface (fps)	1,210	1,175	1,165	1,180	1,245
Remaining velocity 12 feet below surface (fps)	1,070	1,080	1,090	1,115	1,175

(c) The fuze will function on impact with the water and for British shell the delay is 0.024 seconds. For a shell at ranges of above 20,000 yards this is equivalent to a travel of about 30 feet after striking the water.
(d) After travel of the order of 25 feet the shell will lose stability and turn broadside on."

From these figures it was decided that protection should be provided from diving shell, travelling up to thirty feet, after striking the water from a range of between 20,000 and 30,000 yards. The latter range was the maximum at which the Staff required the magazines to be safe.

The DNC prepared three drawings, showing different arrangements of side armour and bulge protection, on which were indicated the lines of descent of a 16-inch shell at 20,000 yards and 30,000 yards. Between these two ranges, the space in which a shell must fall in order to dive and cause damage to a ship, was less than twenty feet in width. The three schemes were designated 'A', 'B' and 'C'.

'A': This arrangement was generally similar to that in *Nelson*, except that the belt was increased in depth to twenty-five feet, by the addition of somewhat thinner armour below the main belt. This necessitated an increase in the slope of the armour in order to retain the outboard venting of the buoyancy spaces.

'B': In this arrangement, the armour belt was placed on the ship's side. From the point of view of protection from shellfire and preservation of stability, this was by far the best system. It did, however, possess a major disadvantage in that the bulge compartments would, in the event of an underwater explosion, vent inboard of the citadel. To facilitate the venting of underwater explosions, hinged armour covers were placed in the armoured-deck, and vent-plates were fitted in the ship's side.

'C': This system was virtually a combination of schemes 'A' and 'B', in which the bulge compartments vented both inboard and outboard, and the underwater protection, as such, was superior to 'B' but inferior to 'A'.

After a careful consideration of these three schemes it was concluded that the inboard-venting arrangements of 'B' and 'C' were a grave disadvantage, and scheme 'A' was to be preferred. This form of protection was employed in all the 1929 designs.

The London Naval Conference, 1930

In June 1929, the Labour Party under Ramsay MacDonald came to power for the second time. The new Government was strongly committed to the principle that continuous peace could be achieved by international negotiation and, at the opening of Parliament, MacDonald announced the Government's intention to reduce the size of the Navy.

Shortly after this, the 1928 programme of new construction was drastically reduced, and the British Government's wish for a new naval limitation conference was communicated to the USA.

The third Naval Disarmament Conference, to which Britain invited the USA, Japan, France and Italy, began in London on 21st January 1930. Hopes of a five-power agreement were quickly dashed when it became clear that France and Italy were unlikely to resolve their differences, and after a number of stormy debates, both these powers withdrew from the Conference. Britain, the USA and Japan, however, succeeded in reaching an agreement, largely because of Britain's accommodating attitude towards the wish of the USA to achieve parity with Britain in all classes of warship. As at Geneva, three years earlier, the negotiations were largely concerned with the limitation of cruisers, and the future of the capital ship was dealt with, comparatively quickly. Britain put forward a proposal to reduce the size of future battleships to 25,000 tons, with 12-inch guns, or 22,000 tons with 11-inch guns. Japan suggested 25,000 tons, with 14-inch guns and the USA expressed the wish to preserve the existing limitations that had been agreed at Washington. These proposals reflected the wishes of the naval elements, rather than of the governing powers, and – the world depression was at its worst – it is not surprising that the politicians aimed for and achieved the complete abandonment of new capital-ship construction for a further five years. Discussions as to the limitation of the size of this type of vessel, therefore became academic.

For Britain, this represented an ascendency of Government views over those of the Admiralty. Admiral Chatfield has written that "The Prime Minister, Mr. Ramsay MacDonald, had been considerably affected by Admiral Richmond's theories that capital ships were unnecessary, and that no ship need exceed 7,000 tons, the size, the distinguished naval writer considered, sufficient to defeat an armed merchant ship. In so far as this argument was purely theoretical, such articles could be written for academic interest and discussion; but the articles went further than that. The other nations of the maritime world, had no intention of adopting such theories and our Navy has to be built to fight other navies. If the Admiral had gone, say, to Washington to lecture on the theory of the small ship, some considerable value might conceivably have been attained and much expense saved to the tax payers." (*The Navy and Defence*, Vol. II, Admiral of the Fleet, Lord Chatfield.)

The Government's view of the future of the capital ship certainly did not agree with that of the Admiralty. In February 1930, the Prime Minister sent a memorandum to Geneva giving the position of HM Government. This paper contained the following passage: "In the opinion of His Majesty's

Government in the United Kingdom the battleship, in view of its tremendous size and cost, is of doubtful utility and the Government would wish to see an agreement by which the battleship would in due time disappear from the Fleets of the World."

The London Naval Conference ended in April 1930, the terms of the Three Power Pact having been agreed. The Treaty was passed through Parliament though not without considerable criticism from both Houses. Churchill expressed the opinion that its signature would be "a memorable and melancholy event in British history". The Treaty was ratified in October; in outline, the terms were as follows:

1. Britain accepted the right of the USA to possess a fleet equal to the Royal Navy.
2. The 5:5:3 ratio accepted at Washington for capital ships and aircraft carriers, was extended to include cruisers and destroyers.
3. The existing battle fleets were to be reduced in size, to fifteen ships each for the USA and Britain, and nine ships for Japan. Britain subsequently scrapped *Emperor of India*, *Marlborough*, *Benbow* and *Tiger* and converted *Iron Duke* to a gunnery training-ship. The USA scrapped the battleship *Florida* and converted *Utah* to a target-ship and *Wyoming* to a training-ship. Japan converted the battlecruiser *Hiei* to a training-ship but, between 1936 and 1940, this ship was reconstructed and rejoined the battle fleet. All ships retained for training, were required to be demilitarised by the removal of a substantial percentage of their armour, armament and machinery.
4. The break in battleship construction, agreed at Washington, was extended for a further five years, until 31st December 1936.
5. It was agreed that another naval limitation conference be held in 1935, with a view to modifying or extending the existing agreement, depending on the circumstances at that time.

So far as the Navy was concerned, this agreement possessed practically no advantages whatever, but it did serve to improve the relationship between the USA and Britain.

Left and **below:** the fore-turrets of *Hood* in July 1932, training to starboard.

10. The Aftermath of the London Naval Treaty, 1930 to 1939

The London Naval Treaty placed the Admiralty in a similar position to that which it had occupied in 1922. The battle fleet was still largely composed of old ships, and although the modernisations of the 1920s had greatly improved their underwater protection, they were still vulnerable to long-range shellfire and bomb attack. With the replacement programme deferred and the strength of the battle fleet reduced, it was essential to begin a further modernisation programme if the Royal Navy were to maintain its position among the world's naval powers. The necessary funds, however, were not available. In 1928, the Cabinet had made the 'Ten-Year Rule' self-perpetuating, which provided the Treasury with a stranglehold on the Service Estimates. With the depression, the Naval Estimates began to fall until they reached their nadir in 1932, at a little over £50,000,000. During this period, the Admiralty was engaged in a bitter conflict with the Chancellor of the Exchequer, particularly during the term of the Labour Government of 1929 to 1931, under Ramsay MacDonald. Some idea of the feelings of the Admiralty at this time can be found in the words of Lord Chatfield, who was the Third Sea Lord during 1925 to 1928 and became First Sea Lord in January 1933.

"We have the strongest Navy in the world, it was stated – where is all the money gone to? Parliament has voted, since the peace, £700,000,000 for the Navy in thirteen years – yet the Admiralty clamours for more. Hearing these things said, when listening to debates from the Stranger's Gallery, I felt a great wish to shout out; 'Let me come down to the Bar of the House and explain to you how little you understand your responsibilities, and the inadequacy of the monies, you grant with such a niggardly hand.

"In 1930 even, after years of retrenchment under the vicious Ten-Year Rule and a policy in international affairs which was based on keeping the world at peace by the undefined defence system called Collective Security, there might still have been time to give the country the defence forces it needed, by adequate financial sacrifice. But the wisest statesmen could not see the precipice that lay ahead and towards which, carrying the banner of mutual security, they were leading the British race." (*It Might Happen Again*: *The Navy and Defence*, Volume II. The autobiography of Admiral of the Fleet, Lord Chatfield.)

There is no doubt that Chatfield was biased. He took a narrow, Admiralty view rather than the broader view necessarily adopted by the Government. Since 1918, national policy, with the support of the people, had been directed towards peace by negotiation, and it would have required some dramatic change in international affairs to shake the belief that the First World War had been the 'war to end wars'. Foreign policy, moreover, demanded that Britain should not offer peace with one hand while obviously re-arming with the other. There was also a real shortage of funds, particularly during the great depression, and the Treasury would not have been doing its job if it had not ensured that the country's available funds were spent to good effect.

In these circumstances, and with the campaign against the battleship in Parliament and press at its height, it is not surprising that the Naval Estimates were cut to the bone.

However, it was not a situation that could continue indefinitely without endangering the safety of the country, and in 1932 came the first sign of change. In that year, the Chiefs of Staff's Report to the Cabinet warned of the dire consequences of assuming that a war was unlikely, and of the dangers of military unpreparedness. The Cabinet was sufficiently impressed to rescind the Ten-Year Rule, and the Treasury's strongest weapon against re-armament was removed. Improvement was slow, but in a steadily-worsening international situation, the Naval Estimates gradually increased, reaching – in 1938 – £93,707,000, the highest figure since 1919.

The matériel developments of the 1920s

Most of the new equipment and matériel that appeared on British warships in the 1930s had been developed during the previous decade. This development had been restricted and slowed by financial considerations, and, in many cases, several years separated the initial design from the final production. This naturally prevented the early evaluation of new equipment, and delayed subsequent improvements.

Experimental work, such as shell and bomb trials, was less affected by financial restrictions and proceeded at a moderate pace in the 1920s and 1930s, providing much valuable information.

Close-range AA defence.

The multiple pom-pom:

In 1921, the Naval AA Gunnery Committee recommended the development of a multi-barrelled, close-range, anti-aircraft gun-mounting. (The Chairman of the committee was Rear-Admiral C. V. Usborne who, according to Lord Chatfield was ". . . an officer of imagination and inventive talent, as well as high technical capacity.")

After a series of trials and experiments, a contract was placed with Vickers for the development of the new weapon. The design involved many difficult problems, not previously encountered in a gun-mounting. Power operation at speeds of up to 15° per second was required and it was necessary to supply the several guns at a minimum rate of 720 rounds per minute without restricting the 90° elevation of the cradle. Designs of mounting with six, seven and ten barrels were considered, but eventually a mounting carrying eight 2-pounder pom-poms was decided upon. Faced with difficult technical problems and lack of funds, the development occupied six years, and it was not until 1928 that two prototype mountings were available. A series of trials was conducted, off Portsmouth, and was sufficiently successful to justify full production. The Board decided that four Mk M pom-poms should be fitted in each capital ship, and wished to order forty-six mountings at a cost of between three and four million pounds. (Mk M was the original, and generally used

Below: The eight guns of a Mk. VI pom-pom mounting (a photograph taken aboard the aircraft carrier *Ark Royal* in 1939).

name of the mounting. The 'M' presumably stood for multiple, but the mountings also possessed individual Mark numbers, following the usual practice.) The Chancellor of the Exchequer, however, refused to allow this addition to the Naval Estimates for 1928. This produced a strong reaction from the Board, who pointed out that Vickers-Armstrong were pressing for an order and that if production did not start soon, this firm would begin to lose skilled labour. It was also necessary to equip the Fleet with the new weapon at the earliest opportunity, in order that men be trained in its use.

After a certain amount of correspondence between the Treasury and the Admiralty, the Prime Minister referred the entire matter to the Committee of Imperial Defence. During the meeting that followed, it was suggested that the Admiralty be allowed to order a limited number of mountings and a small quantity of ammunition, which was a very expensive item. The Treasury eventually agreed to this compromise, and the Navy got at least a few of its badly-needed close-range anti-aircraft weapons with which to gain experience and train gun-crews.

Orders were placed, and production began in 1929. The first multiple pom-pom mounting on a capital ship was fitted in *Valiant* in 1930. It was certainly a very advanced weapon for 1921, slightly less so in 1930, but no equivalent mounting was to be fitted in a foreign warship for some years. However, like many 'firsts', it had a number of disadvantages, and its power to destroy aircraft was certainly greatly over-rated. The reason for choosing the 2-pounder gun was that the ". . . burst from one HE 2-pdr shell, grazed fuzed, is considered to have a good chance (85%) of doing fatal damage whatever part of an aeroplane, excluding the wing tip, is struck". It has also been said that the 2-pounder was chosen because about two million rounds of this ammunition were left over from the First World War.

The muzzle velocity of the gun was only 1,920 feet per second which necessitated a large deflection correction and reduced the effective range. To provide accurate AA fire, a high-velocity gun was necessary and the 2-pounder hardly fulfilled this requirement. Towards the end of the 1930s, an attempt was made to improve the gun, by increasing the muzzle velocity to 2,400 feet per second but this was still too low to be fully effective. The mounting was controlled by 'eyeshooting' which, simply, means that the aiming of the guns relied on the aimer pointing them in the correct direction by eye with the aid of 'forward-area sights.' The original pom-pom director, which was developed in parallel with the mounting, consisted of an eyeshooting sight on a separate pedestal. It did, however, have some simple correction gear. Thus, with an insufficiently-powerful gun and comparatively crude methods of fire-control, the eight-barelled pom-pom was of limited value. During the 1930s a four-barrel version of the mounting was introduced, for use in cruisers and smaller ships, but during the Second World War when there was a shortage of the close-range AA weapons, these were also fitted in battleships.

The 0.5-inch machine-gun:
Production of the 0.5-inch machine-gun was begun by Vickers in 1926, and shortly afterwards, the Admiralty asked the firm to produce a four-barelled mounting for shipboard AA use. At first glance, this weapon had many desirable features. The Mk III gun had a reasonable muzzle velocity of approximately 2,520 feet per second and a high rate of fire of about 700 rounds per minute per barrel. The mounting occupied little space and could be reloaded and brought to action again in 30 seconds. Three mountings were produced, the Mk I, Mk II and Mk III. The latter had an entirely new type of base plate which was more robust and of larger diameter than in the earlier marks. Mk I and Mk II were modified, when opportunity offered, to bring them into line with the Mk III type, and when modified became known as the Mk I** and the Mk II*. The weapon was intended for use against aircraft at ranges of up to about 1,500 yards, but its maximum effective range was 800 yards. The gun fired a solid bullet which

weighed 1.32 ounces. This was unlikely to bring an aircraft down unless it struck a particularly vulnerable spot. The control was by 'eyeshooting' and, generally speaking, the four-barrelled 0.5-inch machine-gun was a very poor AA weapon.

In the mid-1930s development work began on a new type of 1½-pound Mk M pom-pom to replace the 2-pounder and a 0.661-inch calibre machine-gun to replace the 0.5-inch. Both weapons were to have a better performance, and would have been more effective than the existing guns, but neither project was completed.

Long-range AA defence. In 1927, design work began on the development of improved, long-range AA weapons for the fleet. Twin mountings were favoured as providing more guns without a drastic increase in space or weight. It was also required that mountings be shielded or enclosed, so as to protect the gun-crews from weather, gun-blast and shell and bomb fragments.

In 1927, a twin BD (between decks) gun-mounting had been proposed for the AA armament of the 1931 capital ships. Although these ships were not developed beyond the sketch-design stage, the design of the BD mounting was continued. Experimental mountings, carrying two 4-inch guns, were fitted in *Resolution* in 1931, and in *Repulse* in 1936, for sea trials. The production models, carrying two 4.5-inch guns, appeared towards the end of the 1930s and replaced the secondary armaments of *Renown*, *Valiant* and *Queen Elizabeth* when these ships were reconstructed.

As the name suggests, the mounting was carried between decks and had a low cupola turret protruding above the deck. The bulk of the mounting was below the deck. The structure was supported by a roller path on the lower of the two decks, and revolved about a centre-pivot through which power cables and pipes were led. The mounting was power-operated, completely enclosed and very compact. The two guns elevated as a unit, up to a maximum of 85° and could be loaded at all angles of elevation and training. The 4.5-inch 45-cal Mk III gun, fired a 55-pound projectile at a muzzle velocity of 2,490 feet per second. The maximum rate of fire was twelve rounds per minute.

Design work was also begun in 1927, on a 4-inch twin UD (upper-deck) mounting to replace the single 4-inch high-angle mounting. The result was the Mk XIX twin mounting, carrying two 45-cal Mk XVI guns, which first appeared in 1935. It was later fitted in *Barham*, *Malaya*, *Hood*, *Warspite* and the five ships of the *Royal Sovereign* class.

The mounting was hand-operated and provided 80° elevation and 10° depression. The two guns were fitted on a single cradle and could not be elevated independently. The gun fired a 36-pound shell at a muzzle velocity of 2,650 feet per second. The maximum rate of fire was twenty rounds per minute.

Both the 4.5-inch twin BD and the 4-inch twin mountings were dual-purpose, high-angle/low-angle weapons, but their primary function was high-angle.

High-angle fire-control. In 1930, the first high-angle control-system Mk I director was introduced in the ships of the fleet. The director contained a 12-foot range-finder, and the control- and transmitting-instruments that had previously been fitted separately in the open high-angle control-positions. Information from the director was passed through a high-angle calculating-table and thence to the guns, as training, elevation and fuse setting. The system was steadily improved and modified, and before 1939, the Mk II, III and IV HACS were introduced. The Mk I director fitted very conveniently into the existing high-angle control-positions in the fore-tops of the *Queen Elizabeth* and *Royal Sovereign* classes, and it seems likely that the open range-finders were a temporary measure to fill the gap while the director was under development. In 1931, it was estimated that a well-trained crew, using HACS Mk I, could bring down an aircraft with 178 4-inch high-explosive shells. In the following year, this figure was reduced to 136.

Low-angle fire-control. The main developments of the 1920s were directed towards improving the already proven director system. The director-control tower, introduced in *Nelson* and *Rodney*, gathered the functions of director, range-finder and spotter into one revolving structure, which greatly simplified the fire-control communication system. The Admiralty fire-control table (AFCT) and the auto-synchronous transmission-system were also introduced in the *Nelson* class. The AFCT was an improved version of the Dreyer table, incorporating an Admiralty fire-control clock (AFCC) which was also used as an independent calculator for the secondary armaments. The use of gyro-stabilisation for director-sights and many other fire-control instruments, steadily increased between the wars. All this new equipment greatly improved the accuracy of the fire-control system, but in general, it was more delicate and required more expertise to maintain. A good example of this, is the Magslip transmission-system which superseded the synchronous system in 1938. Magslip had practically all the advantages and none of the disadvantages of the synchronous system, but the mechanism was delicate and the Magslip receivers, if damaged, could not – under normal circumstances – be repaired on board ship.

New materials

Before 1919, the principal materials used in shipbuilding had been mild steel and high-tensile steel ('HT' and 'HHT'). The post-war period saw the development and introduction of new steel alloys and new processes for the manufacture and treatment of steel in general. A new type of high-tensile steel known as 'D' steel was developed, and superseded 'HT' and 'HHT' steel for the more important structural members of hulls. Like the earlier 'HT' steel, it permitted the use of lighter frames and plates of lesser thickness, and provided considerable savings in weight. 'D' steel could also be heat treated and in this state was used for armour. The heavy plates of this type, known as 'NCD' armour, were used for such

Below: the aircraft arrangements on the quarter-deck of *Hood*. The catapult is folded and the aircraft is a Fairy IIIF; note also the petrol tank at the extreme stern of the ship.

things as deck protection, and thinner plates, known as DI quality, were used for torpedo bulkheads and to bullet-proof bridges.

In the 1930s, increasing use was made of welding in shipbuilding, but this process was difficult to apply to 'D' steel, the welding of which had to be restricted to plates of ½-inch thickness and less. As a result, a modified 'D' steel known as 'DW' steel – with improved welding qualities was introduced.

Alluminium alloy found increasing use in the 1920s, particularly in *Nelson* and *Rodney* where it provided considerable savings in weight. It could be used in cast form for such items as side scuttle-frames and hand-wheels on valves, and in sheet form, for kit lockers, shelves and many other items not directly associated with the ship's structure.

In 1927, a nickel-chrome steel alloy containing molybdenum, suitable for the production of 'all-steel' guns, was developed. Earlier guns were wire-wound to provide the strength needed to withstand the pressure set up inside the gun when firing the charge. With the new steel, a gun could be manufactured of built-up tubes, sufficiently tough to make the wire unnecessary. Gun barrels of this type were stronger, lighter and less liable to droop, and all guns manufactured for the Royal Navy, from this time onwards, were of "all-steel" construction. The majority of the guns produced in the early 1930s were of small and medium calibre. In order to gain experience in the construction of heavy calibre all-steel guns, a long series of experiments with 12-inch guns, was carried out, from 1929 onwards. The information gained during these experiments was used in the design of the 14-inch guns of the *King George V* class.

The 1920s saw the development of a new type of cordite propellant-charge for heavy guns. The cordite in use at the end of the war, known as MD cordite, was not suitable for use in guns larger than those already in service. The difficulty was, the larger the gun the larger the size of cordite required, and MD cordite was very difficult to manufacture in large sizes. In 1920, therefore, when

guns of 15-inch 50 calibres and above, were being considered for the 1921-22 capital ships, research began into the development of a new type of propellant. The result was SC cordite, which could be manufactured in any size, was easier to produce than MD and whose accuracy of finished dimensions – and therefore its ballistic accuracy was superior to MD.

Aircraft catapults.

British work towards the development of a shipboard catapult for launching aircraft began in 1916. A catapult, operated by compressed air, was subsequently fitted on the converted dredger, HMS *Slinger*, and with it, a series of moderately successful trials were carried out between 1917 and 1918. At the same time, however, a fairly high degree of success had been obtained with the much simpler turret flying-off platform, and experiments with the catapult were abandoned.

After 1918, the utility of the turret platform gradually decreased as the weight of aircraft increased, and in 1922 the development of catapults was resumed. In 1925, the cruiser, *Vindictive* was fitted with one of the first experimental installations, and a successful flight was made from this 'fixed' catapult on 30th October, by Wing Commander Burling, in a Fairy III D floatplane. In 1928, a cordite-operated catapult was introduced, and proved more efficient than the earlier compressed air types. All later British catapults employed a cordite propellant. The types developed included the folding, extending, slider and finally, the cross-deck catapults. The earlier models were fitted on a rotating platform, or were fixed to turret roofs, but the cross-deck catapult was a fixed structure built into the ship. In 1930, *Valiant* and *Resolution* became the first British capital ships to be fitted with catapults. *Hood* was similarly

Above: the aircraft catapult and crane on *Valiant* in 1934. The seaplane is a Fairy IIIF. **Below**, another view, this time of the port quarter, and with a Supermarine Seagull Mk.V, which was carried for trials for a short period of time. In both photographs the catapult is folded.

Left: *Queen Elizabeth* at the 1937 Coronation Review, dressed overall, and with the other ships of the fleet stretching into the distance.

fitted in 1931. All three ships had quarter-deck catapults, but this position was far from ideal as the catapult was susceptible to damage by weather and gun-blast, and could be operated only in calm weather conditions. Subsequent installations were fitted on turret roofs, or amidships.

Protection

Trials and experiments. The resistance of armour to shell and bomb attack and the protection of magazines against cordite explosions, were the subjects of a great deal of research, and many trials and experiments between 1919 and 1930. In 1930, it was decided to carry out full-scale trials to add to, and test the validity of the results already obtained. These trials were conducted in 1931, on battleships due to be scrapped as a result of the London Naval Treaty. *Emperor of India* was used as a target for shell trials and *Marlborough* was subjected to bomb attack. *Marlborough* was also used to ascertain the effect of cordite being ignited in a main magazine. From the results of these experiments the following conclusions were drawn:

"A. *Emperor of India*—shell trials:

1. Underwater protection shall be such that a diving shell should not inflict serious damage such as the flooding of the engine room by hit number 4.
2. Horizontal protection (of new reconstructed ships) should be greater than in *Emperor of India.*
3. Secondary armaments comprising B.D. guns should be isolated so that fragments and blast from one burst should not put a number [of guns] out of action.
4. Provision should be made for venting shell bursts.

B. *Marlborough*—bomb trials: Remarks as per 2, 3 and 4 above.

C. *Marlborough*—magazine venting trials:

1. Magazine contents should be so protected that fragments or flash cannot penetrate to them.
2. The cordite exposed bare should be kept to a minimum.
3. Strength in venting cases is necessary for ships not protected as in 1.
4. Venting arrangements should be provided to magazines and handing rooms of ships not protected as in 1."

In 1932, as a result of these venting trials, it was concluded that armour was the only really effective method of magazine protection, and attempts to immunise the contents of the magazine were abandoned.

The reconstruction programme, 1932 to 1939

From the results of the *Emperor of India* and *Marlborough* trials, it was concluded that out of the fifteen capital ships in service, only two, *Nelson* and *Rodney*, could be regarded as having reasonably satisfactory horizontal protection, and that it was possible for any of the remaining thirteen ships to be blown up by a lucky hit from shell or bomb. It had already been approved to fit extra deck protection over the magazines of *Barham* during her bulging refit, and of the remainder, it was considered that *Hood* and *Renown* had the best deck protection and ". . . the expense involved in bringing these ships up to this standard [protection from 15-inch plunging shell at 24,000 yards and below] could not be justified at the present time".

The need of an extensive modernisation programme was also influenced by events abroad, and at a meeting of the Sea Lords in October 1933, this point was discussed. According to figures produced by the Director of Naval Intelligence, the USA had spent £16,000,000 on the modernisation of capital ships ". . . and were about to spend the whole or a large part of a further £16,000,000 for modernisation under the National Recovery Act". The Japanese had so far allowed £9,000,000 for reconstruction and would probably spend more. Britain however, had spent only £3,000,000 on this work. "The general opinion of the Sea Lords was that the fitting of additional armour to magazine and engine rooms would effect a very great addition in protection and that in the face of the vast sums expended on thorough modernisation by foreign naval powers, it was essential to improve, in the way suggested, the efficiency of those of our capital ships the length of whose remaining life on completion of their next large repair would render it justifiable to incur the extra expenditure". After this meeting it was decided that *Repulse*, *Warspite*, *Royal Oak*, *Malaya*, *Queen Elizabeth* and *Valiant* should be fitted with extra deck protection over the magazines and engine rooms, and this work was later carried out on *Repulse*, *Royal Oak* and *Malaya* during 1933-36.

The addition of deck armour had a major disadvantage in that it reduced stability, reserve buoyancy and speed. Although some weight saving was effected by removing such structures as the armoured conning-tower, it scarcely compensated the considerable additional top-weight of the deck armour. Similarly, it was necessary to restrict the amount of additional equipment and protection that could be included. Hence, no armour was to be fitted over the boiler rooms and, although these compartments possessed a higher degree of watertight sub-division than the engine rooms, this represented a weak point in the horizontal protection. It was clear, therefore, that to provide to the fullest possible extent the required military characteristics without excessive loss of stability it would be necessary to make a substantial compensatory saving in weight. To achieve this a complete reconstruction was necessary, including the provision of new machinery that – because of the progress made in marine engineering – would be considerably lighter than the existing installations. A complete reconstruction of this nature involved considerable expense, and for financial reasons, only one ship, *Warspite*, was completely reconstructed prior to 1936. Subsequently, *Renown*, *Queen Elizabeth* and *Valiant* were taken in hand for similar reconstruction. Proposals were also put forward at various times for *Hood*, *Rodney*, *Nelson* and ships of the *Royal Sovereign* class, but at the outbreak of war in 1939, these were cancelled because the ships and dockyards were too busy to undertake long refits.

11. The Modernisation of the Battle Fleet, II: 1930 to 1946

THE ROYAL SOVEREIGN CLASS, 1930 to 1939

Although consideration was given, at various times, to the possibility of reconstructing the ships of the *Royal Sovereign* class, no major alterations, comparable to those made to other ships, were ever carried out. The usual reason given, is that the ships were too slow, but as they could have been fitted with new machinery during major reconstruction, it seems unlikely that this was the main reason. No definite statements appear in any of the official papers consulted by the authors, but two considerations seem to have influenced the matter. First, there are continual references to the lack of available space between the forward and after turrets, where a new superstructure could be built; the ships of the class were some twenty feet shorter than the *Queen Elizabeth*s. Second, some of the ships of the class do not seem to have been in very good condition, and plans were made to begin scrapping the *Royal Sovereign*s as soon as the first

PARTICULARS OF *ROYAL SOVEREIGN* CLASS, 1930 to 1946

Displacement
Royal Sovereign: September 1943 (after refit at Norfolk Navy Yard, USA) 34,836 tons deep, including 586 tons of water protection and 95 per cent oil fuel; 33,490 tons average action condition, including 586 tons water protection and 1,880 tons oil fuel; 29,950 tons light.
Revenge (1945): 33,560 tons deep.
Resolution (1945): 34,700 tons deep.
Ramillies (1945): 35,390 tons deep.

Dimensions
Length and beam as before.

Draught:	Forward	Aft
Royal Sovereign (1943) deep	35 feet 1 inch	33 feet 3 inches
average action	(32 feet 10 inches mean)	
light	(29 feet 8 inches mean)	
Revenge (1945) deep	33 feet 9 inches	32 feet 3 inches
Resolution (1945) deep	35 feet 2 inches	33 feet
Ramillies (1945) deep	34 feet 1 inch	33 feet 2 inches

Armament (1939)
Eight 15-inch Mk I: Mk I mounting.
Twelve 6-inch Mk XII: P IX mountings (two removed from *Resolution* and four from remainder. 1943).
Eight 4-inch Mk XVI: four high-angle/low-angle twin mountings Mk XIX.
Sixteen 2-pounder Mk VIII: two mountings Mk V or Mk VI.
Eight 0.5-inch Mk III: two mountings Mk I or Mk II (during the period 1931 to 1938, *Resolution* carried two 4-inch Mk V guns in a high-angle/low-angle between-decks twin mounting Mk XVII).

Additions to close-range AA armament, 1941 to 1945
Royal Sovereign
June 1941 (after refit at Norfolk Navy Yard: Ten 20-mm Oerlikons single mountings fitted; two 0.5-inch machine-gun quadruple mountings removed.
Early 1942: Two pom-pom Mk VII quadruple mountings fitted (one on 'B' and one on 'X' turrets).
September 1943 (after refit at Norfolk Navy Yard): Four single 20-mm Oerlikons added; sixteen twin 20-mm Oerlikons added.
1944: Four single 20-mm Oerlikons removed prior to transfer to USSR.
Total close-range weapons at end of war: Twenty-four 2-pounder (2 × 8 + 2 × 4); forty-two 20-mm (16 × 2 + 10 × 1).

Resolution
September 1941 (after refit in USA):
Nine 20-mm Oerlikons single mountings fitted; two 0.5-inch machine-gun quadruple mountings removed.
1942: One single 20-mm added; two pom-pom quadruple mountings Mk VII added (one on 'B' turret, one on quarter-deck).
Total close-range weapons 1945: Twenty-four 2-pounder (2 × 8 + 2 × 4); ten 20-mm (10 × 1).

Ramillies
1941: Two pom-pom quadruple mountings Mk VII added; ten single 20-mm Oerlikons fitted; two 0.5-inch machine-gun mountings removed.
April 1943 (after one year damage repairs and refit at Durban): Ten single 20-mm Oerlikons added.
1944/45: Three single 20-mm added.
Total close-range armament 1945: Twenty-four 2-pounder (2 × 8 + 2 × 4); twenty-three 20-mm (23 × 1).
(Note: the minor armament of *Ramillies* had been removed by October 1945.)

Revenge
1941: Two 2-pounder pom-pom quadruple mountings Mk VII added; ten single 20-mm fitted.
(This armament remained unchanged until the end of the war.)

Fire-control equipment (1939)
Main armament: Two tripod-type directors, one Dreyer fire-control table Mk IV*.
Secondary armament: Two pedestal-type sights, two Admiralty fire-control clocks Mk IV(S).
High-angle armament: Two high-angle control-systems Mk III* (*Ramillies* two Mk I***), two pom-pom directors (Mk I or Mk II).

Radar
Royal Sovereign
Fitted by 1942: Types '284', '285' (two in number), '273' and '279'.
September 1943: '284' replaced by '284B' and two Type '282' fitted.

Resolution
1941: Types '279' and '285' (two in number) fitted.
1942: Types '284' and '273' fitted.

Ramillies
1941–1943: Unknown.
1943: Types '273', '284B', '279', '285' (two in number) '282' (two in number).
1944: Type '650' guided-missile jamming device fitted for the Normandy landings.
Revenge
1941: Type '279' fitted.
1942: Types '273', '285' (two in number) and '284' fitted.

Armour
This remained generally the same as in 1919, except for the addition of deck armour (as noted in the text) in all ships except *Revenge*, and the removal of the after torpedo-conning tower.

Machinery and fuel
The main machinery received no major modifications during the lifetimes of the ships, but auxiliary machinery was improved. Fuel stowage in 1945 was 3,110 tons of oil fuel and 120 tons of diesel fuel.

Stability
Figures for *Royal Sovereign* after her refit of 1942 to 1943 were as follows:

Condition	GM	Range
Deep	4.15 feet	60°
Average action	3.9 feet	57°
Light	3.61 feet	54°

Below: *Resolution* in 1931. Note the yardarm fitted fore and aft on the mainmast, to carry the MFDF aerials, and the HACS Mk. I director on the fore-top.

Bottom of page: during her refit at Portsmouth in 1933. The aircraft platforms on 'B' and 'X' turret have been removed, as have the two range-clocks on 'X' turret.

of the new ships of the *King George V* class were completed. Nevertheless, they still constituted one third of the battle fleet until 1940 and, as such, merited some improvements. *Royal Oak*, *Royal Sovereign* and *Ramillies* at least, were considered worthy of the expense involved in the fitting of additional deck protection.

Resolution

In December 1929, *Resolution* was fitted with an aircraft catapult on the quarter-deck but no crane was fitted because none was available at the time. In July of the same year, she was taken in hand for refit at Devonport. The refit ended in February 1931; the following alterations and additions having been made.

1. The aircraft catapult was removed. An aircraft crane was fitted at the extreme end of the stern, presumably to test the fixtures; it was then dismantled and placed in store.
2. An experimental 4-inch twin BD mounting was fitted on the starboard side of the shelter-deck, abreast the funnel. The single 4-inch high-angle gun was removed from this position.
3. A HACS Mk I director was fitted in the fore-top.
4. The after submerged torpedo tubes were removed and compartments were sub-divided. (Approval was given in 1930, to remove the after submerged torpedo tubes from the *Queen Elizabeth* and *Royal Sovereign* classes.)
5. The wood offal and cement filling was removed from the upper bulges and the shape of the upper bulge was slightly modified.
6. Water-protection compartments were arranged abreast the magazines.
7. The system of supplying 6-inch ammunition was modified.

Between 1932 and 1933, the aircraft-platforms were removed from 'B' and 'X' turrets and the admiral's bridge (formerly the upper searchlight-platform) was extended forward, and given a curved front. In September 1933, two 0.5-inch machine-gun quadruple mountings were fitted on the conning-tower platform.

Below: three close-up views of *Resolution* at Portsmouth in 1933, with the Admiral's bridge extended and a quadruple 0.5-inch machine-gun mounting added on the C.T. platform.

Right: bow and quarter view of *Resolution* at Devonport in 1938. The rig has been altered, the mainmast made into a tripod, aircraft catapult and crane fitted, bridge modified, two Mk. II HACS added and a twin 4-inch HA/LA mounting fitted.

During a refit at Portsmouth which ended in September 1936, the following work was carried out.

1. An extending-type E III T. aircraft catapult was fitted on the roof of 'X' turret.
2. A seaplane crane was fitted on the port side of the shelter-deck, abreast the mainmast.
3. The after torpedo conning-tower was removed and replaced by an aircraft store.
4. The high-angle control-system Mk I director was removed from the fore-top and replaced by two HACS Mk II directors – one on the fore-top and one on the mainmast. The mainmast was fitted with struts to provide additional support and rigidity for the director.
5. The original searchlight-towers abreast the funnel were removed and a new searchlight-platform carrying four power-operated 36-inch searchlights was fitted.
6. Two multiple pom-poms were fitted on new raised platforms abreast the funnel. Pom-pom directors were fitted on the after corners of the admiral's bridge, and two 24-inch searchlights were removed from this position.
7. The lower searchlight-platform on the bridge was extended aft, to join the searchlight-platforms abreast the funnel. This extension served as a flag-deck and was fitted with signal-lockers, two 24-inch and two 10-inch signalling-searchlights.
8. The torpedo-control position over the chart-house was replaced by an air-defence position containing a 12-foot high-angle range-finder and ALO positions.
9. Bullet-proof plating was added to the compass-platform to protect bridge personnel from strafing attacks by aircraft.

In 1938, the twin BD and single 4-inch high-angle guns were replaced by four 4-inch high-angle/low-angle Mk XIX twin mountings. At the same time, a modified main-top and top-mast rig, incorporating a direction-finder aerial array, was fitted, and the forward submerged torpedo tubes were removed. No further modifications were made to the ship prior to the outbreak of war in 1939.

Revenge

Revenge received few additions during the 1930s and it was not until 1939 that her AA armament was brought up to a reasonable standard. The alterations and additions carried out between 1931 and 1939 were as follows.

Refit of May to November 1931:

1. The wood offal and cement filling in the upper bulge was removed and the shape of the upper bulges was slightly modified.

H.M.S. "RESOLUTION."
1938.

Below: *Revenge* in 1931. Note the aerial frame for the MFDF outfit abaft the spotting top. (The black line running across the illustration is a crack in the original negative).

Bottom of page: *Revenge* in 1937. Note the fitting of a distant-reading thermograph on the top front of the spotting top.

2. Water-protection compartments were fitted abreast the magazines.
3. The after torpedo tubes were removed and the compartment was sub-divided.
4. A new direction-finder aerial was fitted at the rear of the fore-top.
5. One multiple pom-pom Mk V mounting was fitted on the starboard side, abreast the searchlight-tower on the funnel. The foremost starboard tower was modified to accommodate a pom-pom mounting and platform. A pom-pom director-platform was arranged below and abreast the 15-inch director-platform on the fore-mast, and one pom-pom director was fitted on the starboard side.
6. The aircraft platform was removed from 'X' turret.
7. A searchlight-platform, containing two 24-inch signalling-searchlights was fitted on the mainmast.

Circa 1933/1934:
The aircraft platform was removed from 'B' turret. A Type '75' wireless-transmitting set was fitted (aerials were carried on the forward end of the fore-top roof).

Refit at Portsmouth ending August 1939:
1. Four single 4-inch high-angle guns were

Below: close-up of *Revenge* in August 1939, out of Portsmouth after refit. Near the top of the main-topgallant are the crossed yardarms carrying the MFDF aerials.

replaced by four 4-inch high-angle/low-angle Mk XIX twin mountings.
2. A second pom-pom mounting was fitted on the port side, abreast the funnel. The pom-pom director-positions were removed from under the 15-inch director platforms (and probably re-positioned elsewhere).
3. HACS Mk I director was replaced by two HACS Mk III directors, one in the fore-top and one on the torpedo conning-tower aft.
4. Two quadruple 0.5-inch machine-gun mountings were fitted abreast the conning-tower.
5. The direction-finder frame-aerial and office were removed from the foremast and a new direction-finding outfit with fixed aerials was fitted on the main-topgallant-mast.
6. The compass-platform was modified and an air-defence position was constructed over the chart-house.
7. A funnel cap was added.
8. The forward submerged torpedo tubes were removed and the compartment was sub-divided.

In 1936, it was proposed to completely reconstruct *Revenge* on similar lines to the reconstruction of *Warspite*. This was not approved.

Royal Oak

Few alterations were made to *Royal Oak* between 1927 and 1934, but in 1932 a HACS Mk I was fitted on the fore-top. On 29th June 1934, she was transferred to dockyard control for a major two-year refit. No other ship of the class was so extensively modernised, during the 1930s. The following alterations were made.
1. 4-inch non-cemented armour was fitted on the main-deck over the magazines, and 2½-inch non-cemented armour on the main-deck over the engine rooms. The total weight of this additional armour was 900 tons. It was fitted on top of the existing 1-inch plating.
2. The four 4-inch high-angle single mountings were replaced by four 4-inch high-angle/low-angle Mk XIX twin mountings.
3. Two eight-barrel pom-pom Mk VI mountings were fitted on new platforms abreast the base of funnel.

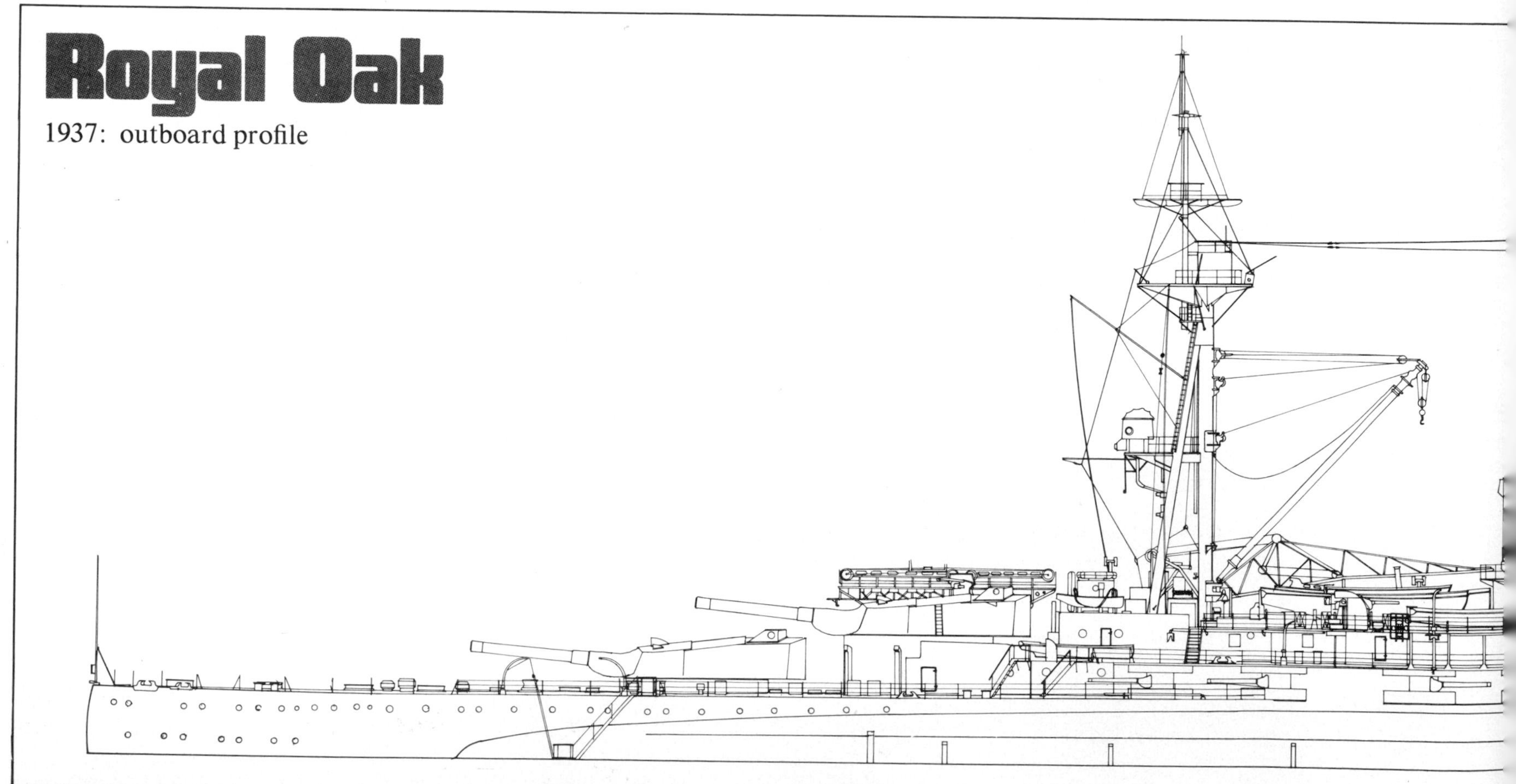

4. Two 0.5-inch machine-gun quadruple Mk II* mountings were fitted abreast the conning-tower.
5. The high-angle control-system Mk I director was replaced by a HACS Mk III director. A second director was fitted on the mainmast which was converted into a tripod to provide a rigid support and absorb additional weight.
6. The secondary armament-directors were removed from the compass-platform and fitted on a new platform below the 15-inch director-position on the foremast.
7. The compass-platform and admiral's bridge were rebuilt and were fitted with wind-deflectors. Two pom-pom directors were fitted abreast the compass-platform. The lower bridge-platform was extended aft to form a new flag-deck.
8. The searchlight-towers abreast the funnels were replaced by a new searchlight structure. Power-operated searchlights were installed.
9. The aircraft-platforms on 'B' and 'X' turrets were removed and a slider catapult Type 'S II T' was fitted on the roof of 'X' turret. An aircraft crane was fitted on the shelter-deck on the port side of the mainmast.
10. A new medium-frequency direction-finding outfit and office was fitted on the mainmast starfish, and fixed aerials were rigged to the main-topmast. A Type '75' short-range wireless-transmitting set was fitted, with the aerials on the forward end of the fore-top roof.
11. The after superstructure and torpedo conning-tower were removed.
12. Four submerged torpedo tubes were removed and the compartments were subdivided. Four fixed, above-water torpedo tubes were fitted on the upper-deck forward, two on each beam.
13. The main-topgallant-mast was replaced by a flagstaff and a stump topmast was added at the rear of the fore-top.

As far as is known, no further substantial modifications were made to *Royal Oak*, and, at the beginning of the war, she was the best ship of her class.

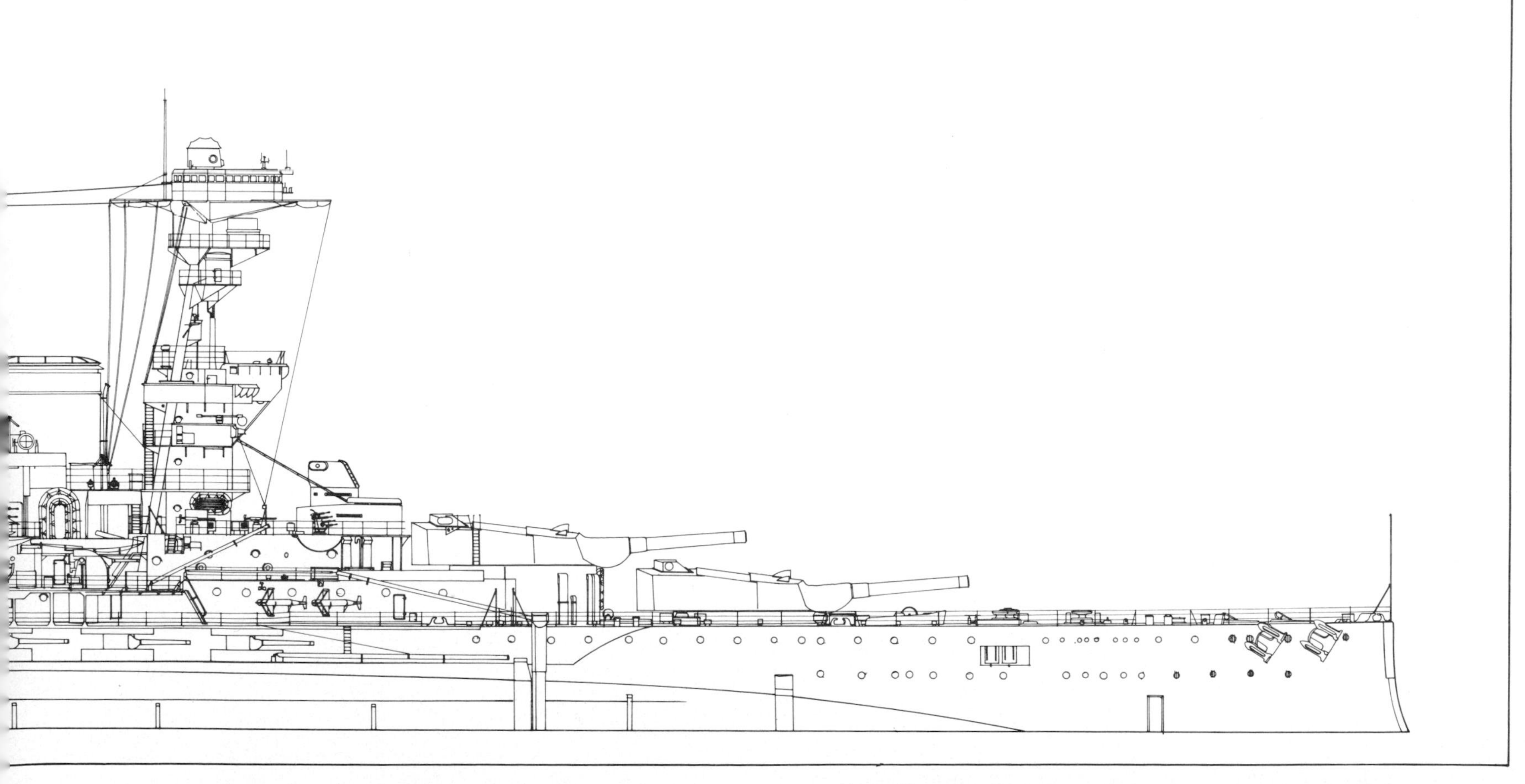

Royal Oak in 1938 after refit.

Below right: *Royal Sovereign*'s bridge and funnel while at Malta in 1932/3; **below left**, the ship leaving Malta in 1934. Note the aircraft catapult and crane on the quarter-deck.

Royal Sovereign
Alterations and additions to *Royal Sovereign* between 1930 and 1939 were as follows.

Circa 1930:
A HACS Mk I director was fitted on the fore-top.

Refit at Portsmouth, January to November 1932:
1. Two multiple pom-pom Mk V mountings were fitted on new platforms abreast the base of the funnel.
2. Two pom-pom directors were fitted on a new platform beneath and abreast the 15-inch director-tower platform.
3. The after submerged torpedo tubes were removed and the compartment was subdivided.
4. The searchlight-towers abreast the funnel were replaced by a new searchlight structure. Power-operated searchlights were fitted.
5. The compass-platform was modified and fitted with bullet-proof sides and roof.
6. The lower bridge-platform was extended aft to provide a new flag-deck.
7. Water-protection compartments were fitted abreast the magazines.

1933:
An aircraft catapult and crane were fitted on the quarter-deck (removed *c* 1936). Two 0.5-inch machine-gun Mk II mountings were fitted abreast the conning-tower.

Circa 1935:
The range-finder hood was removed from the torpedo-control position above the compass-platform and a new platform was added on the roof (possibly an air-defence position).

Refit at Portsmouth, 1937 to 1938:
1. The HACS Mk I director in the fore-top was replaced by a HACS Mk III director. A second Mk III director was fitted aft, on the torpedo conning-tower.
2. Four single 4-inch high-angle guns were replaced by four 4-inch high-angle/low-angle Mk XIX twin mountings.
3. A medium-frequency direction-finder with fixed aerials, was fitted on the main-topmast.
4. The control-position above the compass-platform was replaced by a new air-defence position.
5. The forward submerged torpedo tubes were removed and the compartments were subdivided.

Left and right: bow and quarter views of *Royal Sovereign* after refit, out of Portsmouth in March 1938. She now has two HACS Mk. III, twin 4-inch HA/LA mountings, MFDF aerials on the main-topmast and an air-defence position above the compass-platform.

Abovc: *Ramillies* in 1934. The mainmast has been converted into a tripod, two HACS Mk. I have been added and two multiple pom-poms fitted. An aircraft catapult has been fitted on 'X' turret, with a crane at the base of the mainmast.

Below: *Ramillies* entering Portsmouth harbour in July 1939.

Below: amidships view of *Ramillies* in 1937.

Below right: a close-up of *Ramillies'* bridge and funnel on 22nd August 1941.

Right: *Royal Sovereign*, after her refit at Norfolk Navy Yard, in September 1943.

Ramillies

Ramillies was paid off into dockyard control at Devonport on 10th February 1933 for refit and repairs. The refit ended in August 1934, after the following modifications:

1. Two HACS Mk I directors were fitted, one on the fore-top and one on the mainmast. The mainmast was fitted with struts to accommodate additional weight and provide rigid support for the director.
2. Two multiple pom-pom Mk VI mountings were fitted on new platforms abreast the funnel.
3. Two pom-pom directors were fitted on a new platform beneath and abreast the 15-inch director-platform.
4. A new searchlight structure was fitted abreast the funnel and the searchlights were fitted with power control.
5. Two 0.5-inch machine-gun Mk I multiple mountings were fitted abreast the conning-tower.
6. The aircraft platforms were removed from 'B' and 'X' turrets, and an aircraft catapult Type 'S I T' was fitted on 'X' turret. An aircraft crane was fitted on the shelter-deck on the port side of the mainmast.
7. The after superstructure and torpedo conning-tower were removed.
8. The compass-platform was modified and bullet-proof plating was fitted to the sides and roof.
9. The 6-inch ammunition supply arrangements were modified and improved.
10. The after torpedo tubes were removed and the compartment sub-divided.
11. Provision was made for oiling destroyers at sea.
12. Bulk stowage of aviation-spirit was provided below decks.
13. The lower bridge-platform was extended aft, to provide a new flag-deck.

During this refit, 198.53 tons were added and 65.3 tons were removed from the weights of the ship. Between 1938 and 1939, the four single 4-inch high-angle guns were replaced by four Mk XIX twin mountings, the torpedo-control position above the compass-platform was replaced by an air-defence position, the forward submerged torpedo tubes were removed and the compartment sub-divided, a medium-frequency direction-finder outfit (with fixed aerials on the main-topmast) was fitted, and the aircraft catapult was removed.

Arrangement of bridges

Although, by 1939, there were a number of differences between the bridges of the ships of the class, generally speaking, they had been modified along similar lines. The most marked variations were in the design of the compass-platform which was modified in each ship as a result of sea experience. In 1931, it had been approved to fit bullet-proof plating to the sides and roofs of the raised compass-platforms, in order to protect the bridge personnel from strafing attacks by aircraft. This work was first carried out in *Royal Sovereign*, during her 1932 refit, after which she rejoined the Mediterranean Fleet.

Her commanding officer expressed strong disapproval of the arrangements of the new bridge. He considered that it compared unfavourably to the larger bridge of *Revenge*, being overcrowded with personnel and instruments. He preferred the enclosed bridge rather than the open bridge, but remarked that a sunshine roof was necessary for aerial lookout. As a result of this and other reports, the bridge of *Ramillies* was rearranged in detail, and enlarged to provide more space. The roof of the raised compass-platform was made

Below: aboard *Revenge* in 1940—looking forward on the boat-deck (left) and looking astern (right). Note the camouflage painted on the quarter-deck and the flag-deck.

Below: *Revenge* in 1942, after being fitted with radar and additional close-range armament.

bullet-proof over the central position only, the overhead weather protection being completed by canvas wings.

The new arrangement was considered greatly superior to that in *Royal Sovereign*, but it was pointed out that the bridge still lacked a good all-round and overhead view. The ultimate development was the compass-platform fitted in *Royal Oak* during 1934 to 1936. This was much larger than those of the other ships of the class and no roof was fitted; protection against the weather was provided by wind-scoops and canvas awnings. As for the other two ships, the raised compass-platform of *Revenge* was not substantially modified and that of *Resolution* was fitted with a roof similar to that of *Royal Sovereign*, but probably without the bullet-proof protection.

Proposed reconstruction of *Royal Sovereign* and *Ramillies*

In February 1939, it was proposed to take these two ships in hand, for the fitting of 4-inch and 2½-inch non-cemented armour on the main-deck, as had been fitted in *Royal Oak*. The bulges of the ships however, were of a different form from those of *Royal Oak*, and it was decided to modify the tops of the bulges in order to provide the required stability for the additional top-weight. While these alterations were being made, it was intended to remove the conning-tower and to replace the old bridge with a new structure similar to the one being fitted in *Valiant* at that time. The Director of Naval Construction pointed out, however, that a bridge of this type would be too close to the funnel and that if the funnel were moved farther aft, it would mean a complete rearrangement of the boat stowage. It was decided, subsequently, to modify the bridge on similar lines to that of *Royal Oak* and to modify the 15-inch gun-mountings so as to provide the guns with 30° elevation.

In April 1939, work of a higher priority was brought forward (principally the need for *Rodney* and *Nelson* to be refitted) and it was decided to restrict the modifications to the fitting of the additional deck armour. Shortly after the outbreak of war, the re-armouring was postponed indefinitely.

War modifications

Externally, the alterations made to the class between 1939 and 1945 were almost exclusively related to the addition of close-range anti-aircraft weapons and radar equipment. Apart

Anti-Aircraft Gun Positions
Resolution
A Early 1941: Two 0.5-inch MGs removed.
B September 1941: Nine single 20 mm mounts fitted.
C 1942: One single 20 mm mount added.
D 1942: positions for quadruple pom-pom on roof of 'B' turret, plus one on the quater-deck

Royal Sovereign
E June 1941: Two 0.5-inch MGs removed.
F June 1941: Eight single 20 mm mounts fitted plus two on the quarter-deck.
G Early 1942: Two quadruple pom-poms fitted.
H September 1943: Ten single 20 mm mounts added plus four more on the quarter-deck.
I September 1943: Sixteen twin 20 mm mounts fitted.

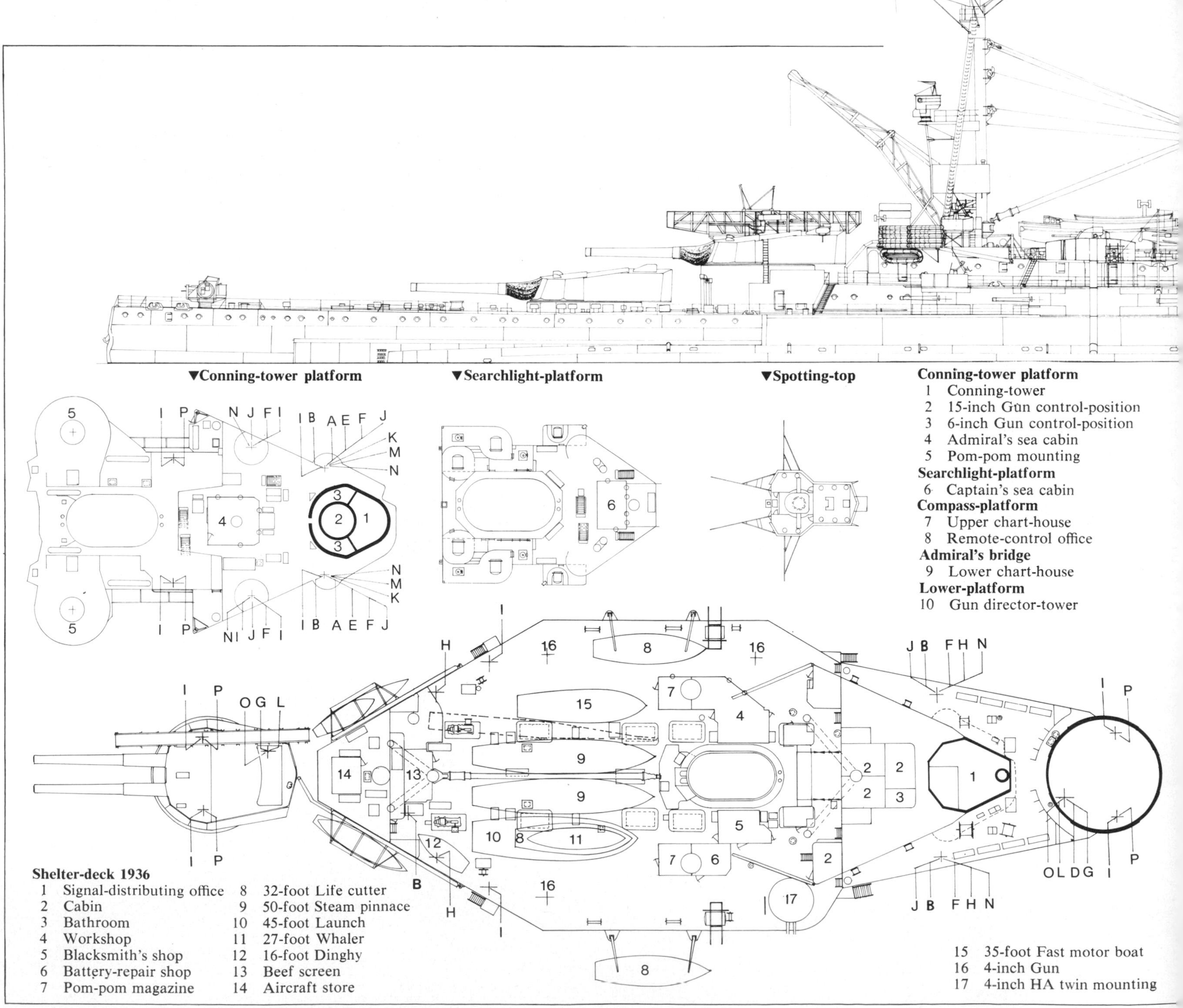

▼Conning-tower platform

▼Searchlight-platform

▼Spotting-top

Conning-tower platform
1 Conning-tower
2 15-inch Gun control-position
3 6-inch Gun control-position
4 Admiral's sea cabin
5 Pom-pom mounting
Searchlight-platform
6 Captain's sea cabin
Compass-platform
7 Upper chart-house
8 Remote-control office
Admiral's bridge
9 Lower chart-house
Lower-platform
10 Gun director-tower

Shelter-deck 1936
1 Signal-distributing office
2 Cabin
3 Bathroom
4 Workshop
5 Blacksmith's shop
6 Battery-repair shop
7 Pom-pom magazine
8 32-foot Life cutter
9 50-foot Steam pinnace
10 45-foot Launch
11 27-foot Whaler
12 16-foot Dinghy
13 Beef screen
14 Aircraft store
15 35-foot Fast motor boat
16 4-inch Gun
17 4-inch HA twin mounting

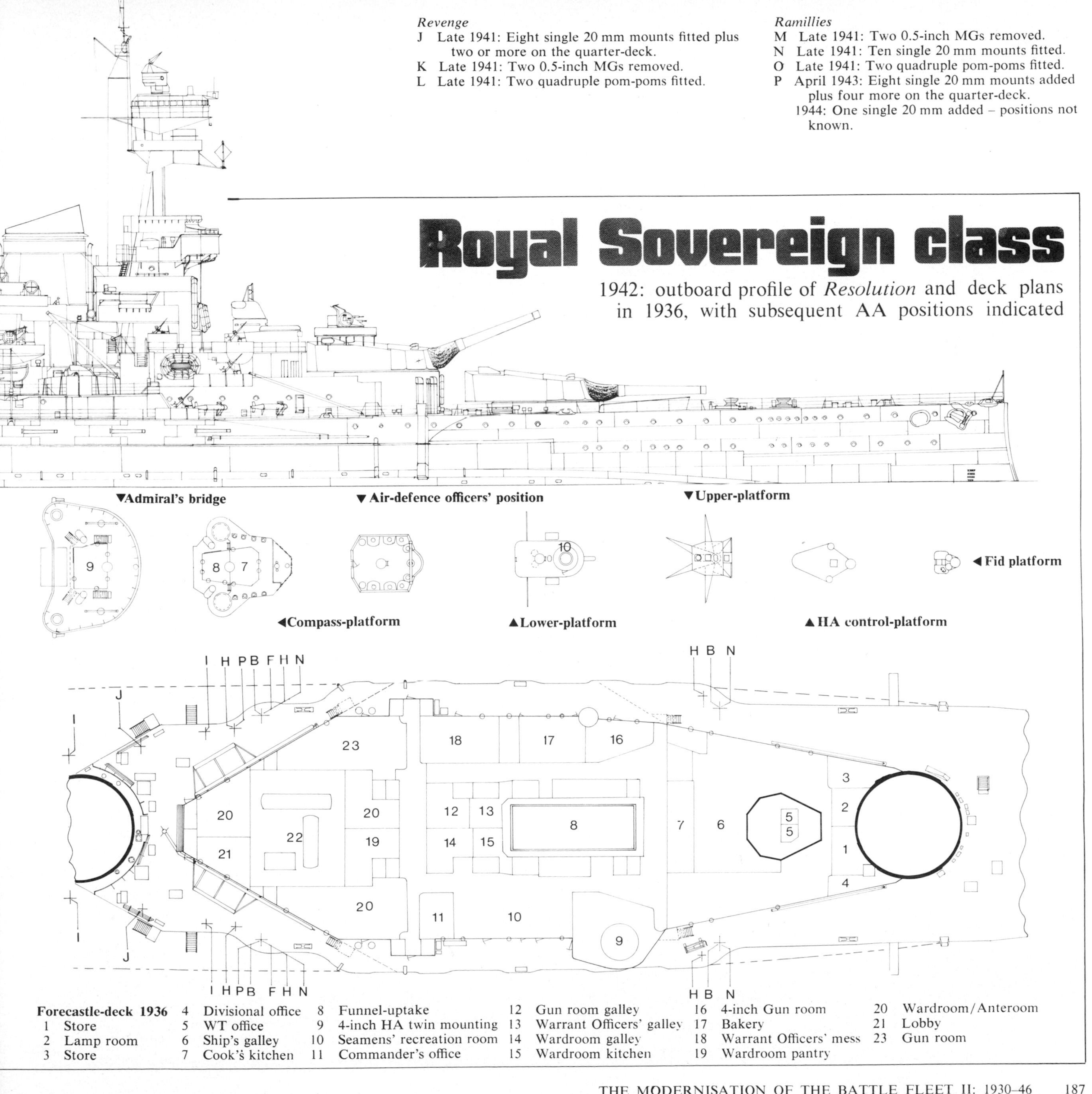
Revenge
J Late 1941: Eight single 20 mm mounts fitted plus two or more on the quarter-deck.
K Late 1941: Two 0.5-inch MGs removed.
L Late 1941: Two quadruple pom-poms fitted.
Ramillies
M Late 1941: Two 0.5-inch MGs removed.
N Late 1941: Ten single 20 mm mounts fitted.
O Late 1941: Two quadruple pom-poms fitted.
P April 1943: Eight single 20 mm mounts added plus four more on the quarter-deck.
1944: One single 20 mm added – positions not known.
Royal Sovereign class
1942: outboard profile of *Resolution* and deck plans in 1936, with subsequent AA positions indicated
▼Admiral's bridge
▼Air-defence officers' position
▼Upper-platform
◀Fid platform
◀Compass-platform
▲Lower-platform
▲HA control-platform
Forecastle-deck 1936
1 Store
2 Lamp room
3 Store
4 Divisional office
5 WT office
6 Ship's galley
7 Cook's kitchen
8 Funnel-uptake
9 4-inch HA twin mounting
10 Seamens' recreation room
11 Commander's office
12 Gun room galley
13 Warrant Officers' galley
14 Wardroom galley
15 Wardroom kitchen
16 4-inch Gun room
17 Bakery
18 Warrant Officers' mess
19 Wardroom pantry
20 Wardroom/Anteroom
21 Lobby
23 Gun room

Below: three views of *Royal Sovereign* on 14th September 1943, out of Philadelphia Navy Yard after extensive refit.

from the fitting of several radar offices, few additions were made to the superstructure. The aircraft catapult was removed from *Royal Sovereign* shortly before the war, but this equipment was retained in *Resolution* until late 1942 or early 1943. Funnel caps were fitted on *Royal Sovereign* between 1939 and 1940, and in *Ramillies*, between 1941 and 1942.

In 1940, proposals were again put forward to increase the deck protection of the *Royal Sovereigns*, but this time it was to be a "rough and ready job with 'flame-cut' armour, supported as well as possible". This scheme was not proceeded with. In October 1940, after *Resolution* had been damaged, off Dakar, consideration was given to fitting additional deck armour and a "super bulge" while the ship was undergoing damage repairs. With these modifications, and increased vertical protection to machinery uptakes and downtakes, the estimated deep displacement was 36,420 tons, with a draught of 32 feet. The speed would have been 20.3 knots with 40,000 shaft horse-power. All these proposals were vetoed, and in December 1940, it was decided to confine the refit to making good the damage and carrying out minor alterations. It had been intended to increase to 30° the elevation of the guns of 'A' and 'B' turrets, but this was not carried out.

In 1941, the question of increased deck protection was raised once more and it was decided to fit 2-inch non-cemented armour on the main-deck over the magazines, when opportunity offered. The additional weight involved was 340 tons. This work was carried out in *Resolution*, *Royal Sovereign* and, partially, in *Ramillies* during 1942.

Considerable problems were encountered during the war due to the overcrowding produced by the increased complements carried by the *Royal Sovereigns* and indeed by all classes of warship. In 1942, approval was given to remove the two foremost 6-inch guns on each side, to provide additional space for sleeping and messing. The work was carried out in 1943, but only two guns were removed from *Resolution*. Between 1943 and 1944, proposals were made for the removal of the entire 6-inch battery which was not watertight, and in view of the increased weight caused by wartime additions, constituted a threat to the safety of the ships. It was also intended to replace the battery armour with 2-inch non-cemented plating in order to reduce top-weight, but these alterations were not made.

Other alterations included the following:

1. Watertight sub-division was improved by fitting access trunks, blanking side scuttles, modifying ventilators etc.
2. Additional distillation plant was installed.
3. The damage-control communications were improved.
4. The 15-inch guns and magazines were rearranged to take the modified 15-inch shell (with improved qualities and supercharge). (The exact extent of this work is not known.)
5. A fighter-direction office was fitted.
6. Blind-fire gear for the main armament was installed.
7. The main engine lubrication system was modernised so as to operate when the ship had 15° of heel.
8. Fire-fighting arrangements were improved.
9. Searchlight arrangements were improved.

HOOD, 1929 to 1941

Despite the fact that *Hood*, almost certainly, offered greater scope for modernisation than ships of a lesser displacement, she remained substantially unaltered between her completion in 1920 and her loss in 1941. Plans were made for her reconstruction, but as she was reasonably well-protected, compared to the older ships of the Fleet, she was not given top priority in this respect. It had been intended to take her in hand for reconstruction after *Queen Elizabeth*, but on the outbreak of war in 1939, this was cancelled. Most of the alterations that were carried out, were directed towards the improvement of her high-angle armament. The modifications made to the ship between 1929 and 1941 were as follows.

Refit at Portsmouth 3rd June 1929 to 28th May 1931:

1. HACS Mk I director was fitted on the after searchlight-platform.
2. Two pom-pom Mk V mountings were fitted on the shelter-deck, abreast the funnels.
3. One pom-pom director was fitted at the after end of the fore-top. Two positions were provided, one each side on the arms of the starfish in preparation for delivery of the second director.
4. An aircraft catapult Type 'F IV H' and a crane were fitted on the quarter-deck. Jettisonable tanks for 300 gallons of aviation-spirit were fitted at the extreme after end of the quarter-deck on the port side, and at the forecastle-deck edge, abreast the mainmast.
5. The 15-inch transmitting-station was made gastight.
6. Auto-synchronous transmission gear was fitted to the director-firing system.
7. The secondary armament was fitted with experimental fire-control for long-range barrage-fire against aircraft.
8. A Type '31' fire-control wireless-transmitting set with office was fitted on the platform-deck adjacent to the transmitting-station and an aerial was rigged between the signal-deck and the fore-top. Short-range Type '71' wireless-transmitter fitted, with aerials rigged abaft the second funnel. Type '363' wireless-transmitter fitted.
9. Extensive repairs carried out to hull, machinery and electrical equipment.
10. Oil-fuel stowage was increased from 3,895 tons to 4,615 tons (95 per cent capacity including diesel fuel).
11. Signalman's shelters were fitted at the fore end of the signal-deck, abreast the conning-tower.
12. The torpedo-control position above the compass-platform was fitted with a roof and windows.
13. The aircraft platform was removed from 'X' turret.

Below and **right:** views of *Hood* in late 1931.

After this refit, *Hood* was inclined; the results showed an increase in displacement and a reduction in stability, since her original inclining in 1920:

Half-oil condition (fully equipped with 2,307 tons of oil fuel (47.5 per cent) and reserve feed tanks full):
Displacement, 45,693 tons.
Mean draught, 31 feet 5 inches.
GM, 2.9 feet.
Angle of maximum stability, 35°.
Range, 65°.

Deep condition (fully equipped with 4,615 tons of oil fuel (95 per cent) 58 tons of coal and reserve feed tanks full):
Displacement, 48,000 tons.
Mean draught, 33 feet.
GM, 3.1 feet.
Angle of maximum stability, 35°.
Range, 68°.

Light condition:
Displacement, 42,037 tons.
Mean draught, 28 feet 10½ inches.
GM, 3.1 feet.
Angle of maximum stability, 35°.
Range, 64°.

The aircraft catapult on the quarter-deck proved unsatisfactory during trials. Apart from restricting the fire of the after turrets, the catapult was vulnerable to gun-blast and weather, and was subject to heavy vibration when the ship was moving at high speed. It was also very difficult to operate the catapult and handle the aircraft in anything but calm weather. Between 21st March and 25th June 1932, the catapult and crane were removed. The crane was subsequently modified (the jib was lengthened) and fitted in *Ramillies*. At the same time as this work was being carried out, the 5.5-inch gun range-finder towers were removed from the fore-top (and were subsequently refitted in a different position during the 1934 refit).

Refit at Portsmouth, 31st March to 10th May 1932:
1. Two 0.5-inch machine-gun Mk I quadruple mountings were fitted on raised platforms, abreast the conning-tower at the fore end of the signal platform.
2. The aircraft platform was removed from 'B' turret.

Refit, 1st August to 5th September 1934:
1. 5.5-inch gun range-finder towers were fitted on the signal-deck.
2. As a result of problems caused by funnel gases, the pom-pom director-positions were moved from the arms of the starfish to the corners of the 5.5-inch spotting-top (this position was formerly occupied by the 5.5-inch gun range-finder towers). A starboard pom-pom director was fitted but the port director was unavailable. It was fitted between 1st April and 13th May 1935.

Refit, 26th June to 10th October 1936:
1. The pom-pom directors were still subject to smoke interference and were moved to new positions at the rear corners of the fore bridge.
2. A Type '75' very-high frequency fire-control wireless-transmitting set was fitted in the Type '31' office, with aerials on the fore-top roof and mainmast starfish. The Type '31' set was removed.
3. The 36-inch searchlight-platform was removed from the foremast.
4. The platform above the compass-platform was fitted with a steel screen, and was converted to an air-defence position.

It had been intended to fit a catapult on 'X' turret during the refit, but the work was not carried out.

Refit at Malta, 8th November to 16th December 1937:
1. One pom-pom Mk VI mounting, on a new bandstand, was fitted on the roof of the after torpedo-control tower. The range-finder hood was removed from the tower.
2. Two 0.5-inch machine-gun Mk III mountings were fitted on raised platforms abreast the after superstructure.

Below: *Hood* in 1934. The aircraft platforms have been removed.

Bottom of page: *Hood* in June 1939, out of Portsmouth, Note the single 4-inch HA gun in place of the shelter-deck 5.5-inch.

Left: *Hood* in dry-dock in 1939. Behind 'X' turret can be seen the 2-pounder pom-pom platform; this was set slightly to starboard because an aircraft crane was fitted on the port after-end of the shelter-deck for a short period of time.

3. The after submerged torpedo tubes were removed and the compartments were sub-divided (this work was only partially completed).
4. Two single 4-inch high-angle Mk IV mountings were fitted on the shelter-deck, amidships.

Refit at Malta, 16th May 1938 to 22nd June 1938:
1. A pom-pom Mk II director (for the after pom-pom) was fitted on the after superstructure, abaft the HACS director.
2. Two 5.5-inch guns on the shelter-deck were replaced by two single 4-inch high-angle Mk IV mountings, making a total of eight single 4-inch high-angle guns.
3. Work connected with the removal of the after submerged torpedo tubes was completed.
4. The wireless-receiving apparatus was modernised.

Refit at Portsmouth, February to June 1939:
1. Four 4-inch high-angle/low-angle Mk XIX twin mountings were fitted on the shelter-deck amidships, two port and two starboard. The two 4-inch single Mk IV amidships were removed, leaving a total of six singles and four twin mountings.
2. Four 44-inch searchlights were fitted, two on a new platform abaft the second funnel, and two on new platforms at the forward corners of the after superstructure.
3. Two high-angle control-system Mk III directors were fitted at the after end of the signal-deck, port and starboard.
4. A 'FH3' high-frequency direction-finder was fitted, with an office on the main-mast starfish and an aerial at the top of the main-topgallant-mast.
5. The signal-deck was extended aft.

Refit, July to August 1939:
1. All the single 4-inch high-angle guns were removed and two 5.5-inch guns replaced at the fore end of the shelter-deck.
2. The after HACS Mk I director was replaced by a Mk III director.
3. The searchlights and searchlight-towers between the funnels were removed.
4. The bridge structure was slightly modified.

Left: *Hood* in August 1939. Note that the 5.5 inch shelter-deck gun has been refitted.

PARTICULARS OF *HOOD*, 1931 to 1941
Except where noted below, the general particulars remained the same as when the ship was completed in 1920.

Displacement	Deep	Light
March, 1931	48,000 tons	42,037 tons
January, 1939	48,650 tons	42,752 tons
May, 1940	48,360 tons	42,462 tons

Secondary armament
Reduced to ten guns 1938 to 1939; removed 1940.

Long-range AA armament
1931 to 1937: four 4-inch Mk V: single high-angle mountings Mk III.
1937: six 4-inch Mk V: single high-angle mountings Mk III and IV.
1938: eight 4-inch Mk V: single high-angle mountings Mk III and IV.
June, 1939: six 4-inch Mk V: single high-angle mountings Mk III and IV; eight 4-inch Mk XVI; high-angle/low-angle twin mountings Mk XIX; (six singles removed by August 1939).
1940 to 1941: fourteen 4-inch Mk XVI: high-angle low-angle twin mountings Mk XIX.

Close-range AA armament (dates fitted)
1931: sixteen 2-pounder Mk VIII: two Mk V mountings.
1932: eight 0.5-inch Mk III: two Mk I mountings.
1937: eight 2-pounder Mk VIII: one Mk VI mounting; eight 0.5-inch Mk III: two Mk III mountings.
1940: five twenty-barrel mountings.
Total, 1941 = twenty-four 2-pounder (3 × 8); sixteen 0.5-inch (4 × 4); one hundred UP (5 × 20).

Ammunition stowage (AA armament)
4-inch (single): 150 rounds per guns; 200 star shell.
4-inch (twins): 250 rounds per gun; 250 star shell.
2-pounder: 720 rounds per gun.
0.5-inch: 2,500 rounds per gun.

Fire-control equipment (1939)
Main armament: two tripod-type directors, one Dreyer table Mk V.

Secondary armament: two pedestal-type sights, two transmitting-clocks Type 'F'.

High-angle armament: three HACS Mk III*, three pom-pom directors.

Fuel and endurance
4,615 tons oil fuel capacity.
Endurance (under trial conditions): 8,500 nautical miles at 14 knots.

The above modifications are divided into two dated groups; in June 1939, *Hood* went to sea for gun trials of the twin 4-inch high-angle/low-angle guns and mountings and so, for a short period, appeared in a partially modified condition.

Refit at Devonport, 29th March to 27th May 1940:
1. All the 5.5-inch guns were removed and the forward gun battery openings were plated over.
2. Three 4-inch Mk XIX twin mountings were fitted on the shelter-deck, one at the extreme after end, and one, on each side abreast the after superstructure.
3. Five UP mountings were fitted, one on 'B' turret, one on each side of the shelter-deck, abreast the fore funnel and one on each side of the shelter-deck, abreast the boats.
4. A de-gaussing coil was fitted externally.

Refit at Rosyth, 16th January to 15th March 1941:
1. A Type '284' gunnery radar set for the main armament was fitted, with aerials on the fore-top director-control tower.
2. The direction-finder office was removed from the mainmast starfish.
3. The fore-topmast was removed.
4. The torpedo look-out was removed from the foremast.

In December 1938, it was proposed to reconstruct *Hood* on the following lines:

1. Provide new main and auxiliary machinery.
2. Replace the 5.5-inch and 4-inch gun armament by eight 5.25-inch twin mountings.
3. Increase the close-range AA armament to six pom-pom mountings, and remove all 0.5-inch machine-gun mountings.
4. Fit a cross-deck catapult DIIIH, aircraft and hangars, arranged on similar lines to that of the *King George V* class.
5. Remove the above-water torpedo tubes.
6. Remove the conning-tower and reconstruct the bridges.

Bottom of page: *Hood* in August 1940.

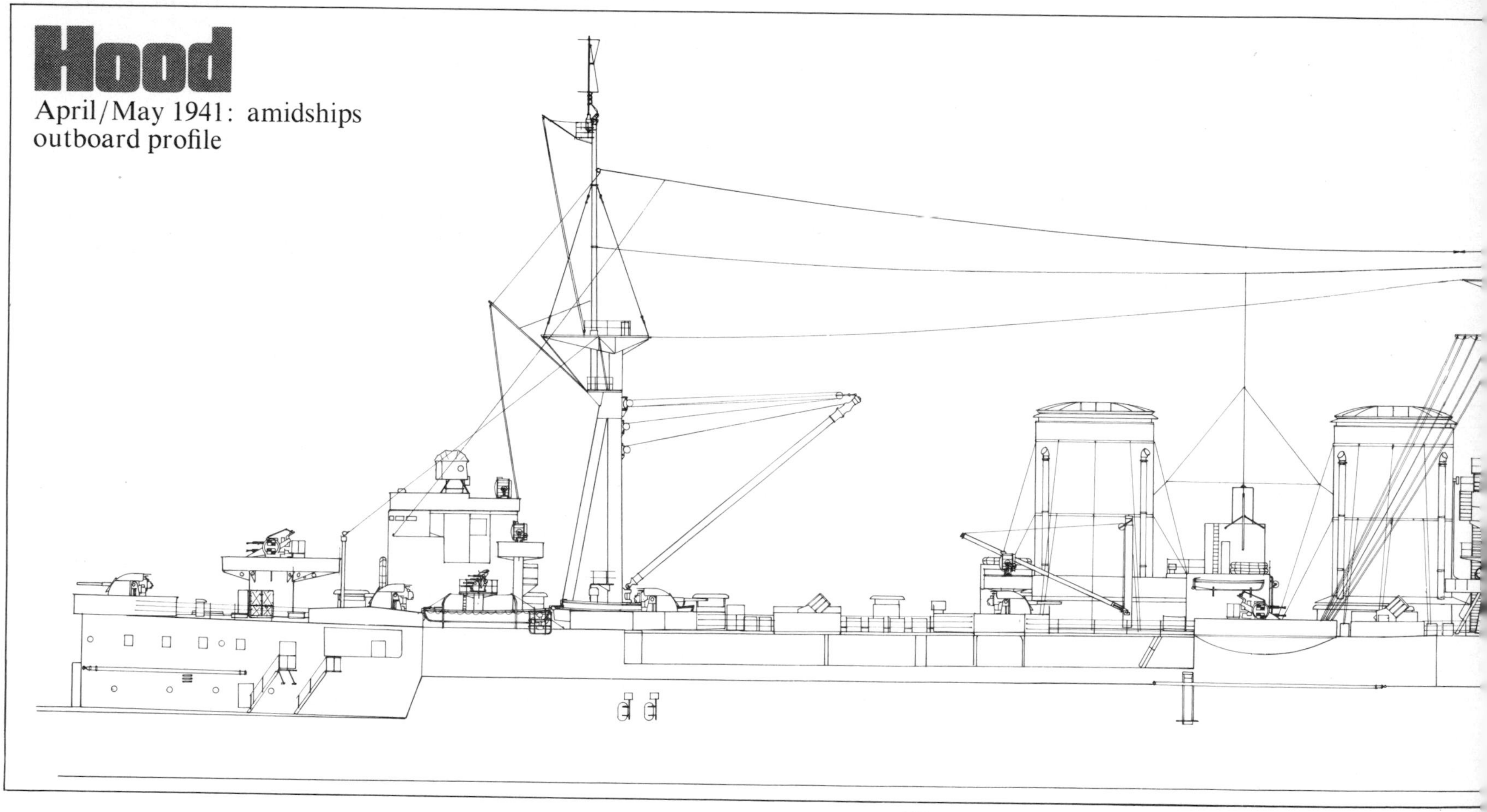

Hood

April/May 1941: amidships outboard profile

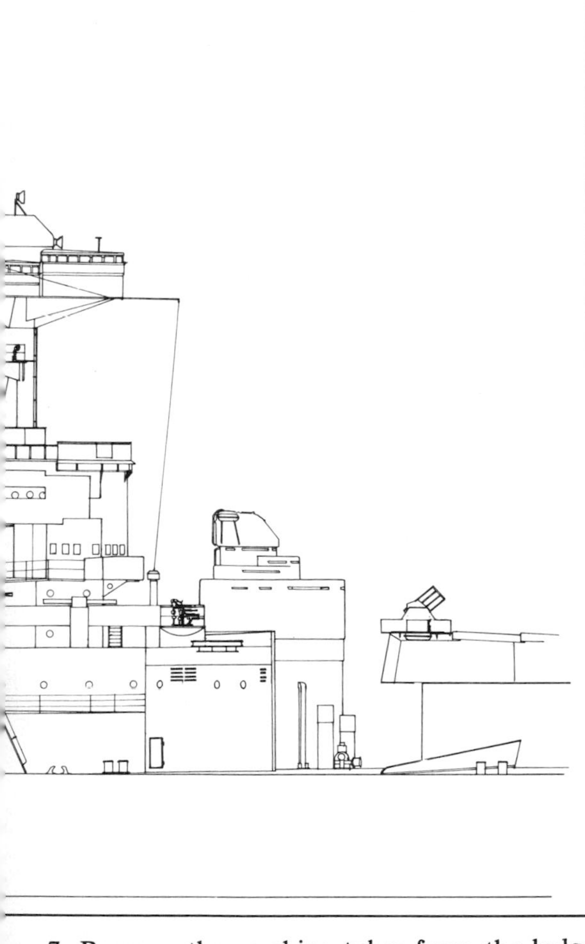

7. Remove the crushing tubes from the bulge protection and fit out buoyancy spaces as oil-fuel tanks.
8. Rearrange the protection by removing the upper 5-inch armour belt, and improving the 2-inch splinter protection on the lower-deck and either (a) extend the 12-inch belt armour to the upper-deck, increasing the thickness of the upper-deck to 2½ inches over the machinery and 4 inches over the magazine, or; (b) leave the 12-inch and 7-inch belts as they were, and increase the thickness of the main-deck to 4 inches over the machinery and 5 inches over the magazines.
9. Modifying the shape of the upper bulge to improve stability.

In 1939, *Hood*'s machinery was twenty years old and showing signs of wear. She needed reboilering and her turbines needed reblading. The likelihood of her being able to steam at high speed for any length of time – as would be required in war – was considered remote. Her displacement was too high, her stability too low and her horizontal protection needed strengthening. At a meeting of the Sea Lords in March 1939, the First Sea Lord said: "If this ship is to last another fifteen years, which is probable, it is evident that the vessel will have to be laid up for large machinery repairs and it will be a matter for eternal regret afterwards that the big thing [complete reconstruction] was not done". The First Sea Lord then said that he would initiate action to have *Hood* taken in hand after *Queen Elizabeth*, for complete reconstruction including new machinery.

BARHAM, 1931 to 1941

Barham was the last ship of the *Queen Elizabeth* class to be bulged, and the first battleship of the fleet to be fitted with deck armour (excluding *Nelson* and *Rodney*). Her bulging refit was carried out at Portsmouth, between January 1931 and January 1934, and included many alterations and additions not made in her sister ships which was reflected in both the longer time required and in the greater cost, £424,000 compared to £195,000 for the bulging refit of *Warspite*. Details of the work carried out are as follows:
1. Bulges were fitted.
2. Water-protection compartments were added abreast the magazines.
3. Additional deck protection was fitted over the magazines.
4. 6-inch gun-bays were enclosed.
5. The system of supplying 6-inch ammunition was improved.
6. Two HACS Mk I directors were fitted in the fore-top and on the mainmast.
7. The mainmast was fitted with struts to provide rigid support for the after high-angle director.
8. Two pom-pom Mk VI mountings were fitted on new platforms, abreast the base of the funnel.
9. Two pom-pom directors were fitted, port and starboard, in a platform abreast and beneath the fore-top.
10. Two 0.5-inch machine-gun Mk I mountings were fitted abreast the conning-tower.
11. The after submerged torpedo tubes were removed and the compartment was sub-divided and converted into store-rooms.
12. The after torpedo-control tower was removed.
13. A new enclosed torpedo-control position with a range-finder hood was fitted above the compass-platform.
14. The aircraft platforms were removed from 'B' and 'X' turrets and an extending aircraft catapult Type 'EIT' was fitted on 'X' turret.
15. An aircraft crane was fitted on the port side of the after shelter-deck.
16. Jettisonable tanks for the stowage of aviation-spirit were provided on each side of the forecastle-deck abreast the mainmast.
17. The bridge-platforms were modified, the lower bridge-platform was extended aft to provide a new flag-deck and the compass-platform was enlarged and fitted with a flared steel screen. The raised compass-platform was fitted with a roof, and this platform and the spotting-top were fitted with bullet-proof plating.
18. The funnels were trunked.
19. The searchlight-towers on the funnel were modified, and the searchlights were fitted with power control.
20. The after superstructure was remodelled and the torpedo range-finder was removed.
21. A medium-frequency direction-finder with rotating-frame aerial was fitted at the rear of the fore-top with an office on the after end of the 15-inch director-platform.
22. A Type '71' wireless-transmitting set was fitted.
23. Echo-sounding gear Type '2752' was fitted.
24. Collective protection was fitted.

Protection

The decision to fit extra deck protection in *Barham* was made in 1931. The 4-inch thick

Bow and quarter views of *Barham* in July 1934, after her 1931/4 refit.

Below: *Barham* in June 1937.

Below: three on-board views of *Barham* in 1937, during the Coronation Review. Note the pom-pom mountings abreast the funnel.

non-cemented armour was fitted on the flat of the middle-deck over the magazines, and for a few feet fore and aft of these compartments. The new armour was fitted on the original 1-inch thick protective plating, but the extra plating that had been added after Jutland was removed. The additional weight amounted to about 500 tons.

Early in 1932, approval was given for enclosing the 6-inch gun-bays, and this alteration was incorporated in *Barham* during her refit. The rear of each casemate was sealed off by a bulkhead of 1½-inch DI plating which, it was considered, would be sufficient to keep out large shell and bomb splinters and fumes. Each bulkhead contained a hinged flap for the supply of shell and cordite, and a hinged scuttle for the return of empty Clarkson's cordite cases. The estimated cost of this alteration was £12,000.

Bridge modifications

Barham was fitted with a fully-enclosed raised compass-platform similar to that in *Royal Sovereign*. Her Captain, G. C. Harrison, expressed "a very strong disapproval of the arrangement". He considered that to cover the compass-platform with a roof was wrong in principle, and that increasing the height of the bullet-proof screen by six inches to 5

Barham

1941: outboard profile and bridge deck plans

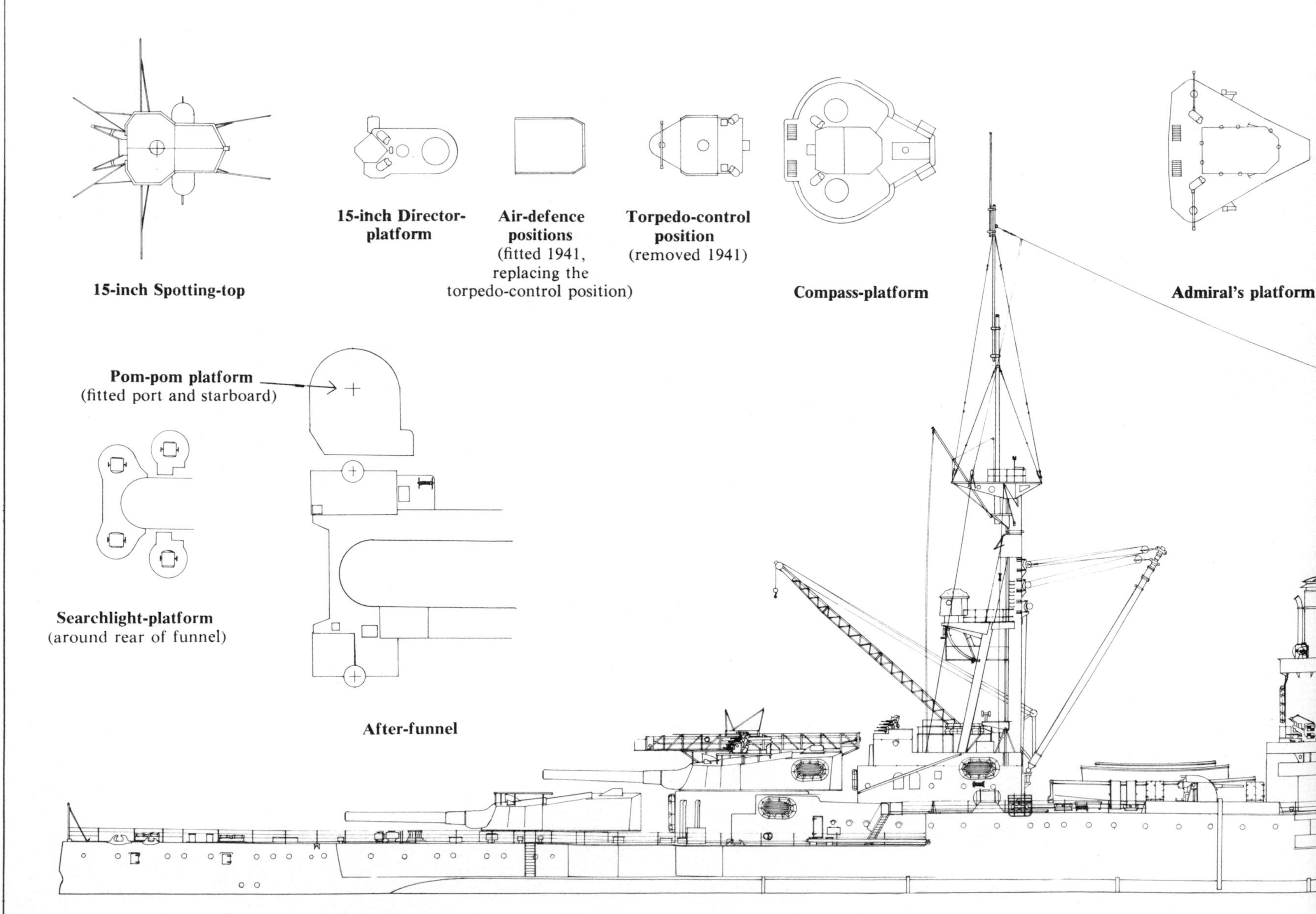

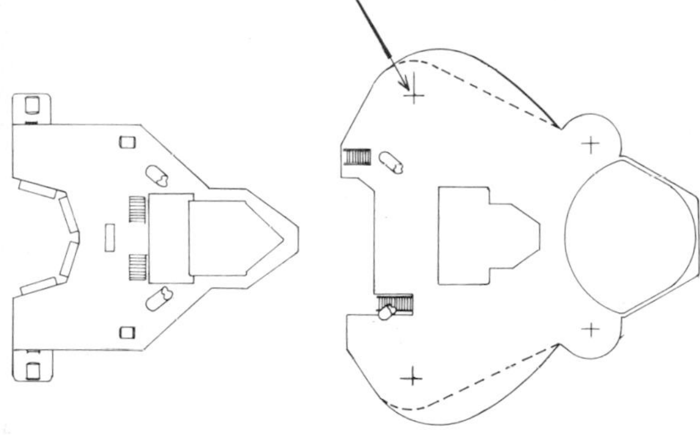

PARTICULARS OF *BARHAM*, 1933 to 1941

Dimensions and details of main and secondary armaments remained the same as they were in 1918.

Displacement (November, 1933)
Deep: 35,970 tons.
Standard: 31,350 tons.
Extra deep (including 815 tons of water in water-protection compartments): 36,785 tons.

Long-range AA armament
1933 to 1938: four 4-inch Mk V: four high-angle single mountings Mk III.
1938 to 1941: eight 4-inch Mk XVI: high-angle/low-angle twin mountings Mk XIX.

Close-range AA armament
1933: sixteen 2-pounder Mk VIII: two Mk VI mountings; eight 0.5-inch Mk III: two Mk I mountings.
1940: one twenty-barrel UP mounting fitted.
1941: two 0.5-inch machine-gun mountings fitted, and UP removed; two 2-pounder Mk VI mountings fitted.

Ammunition Stowage (1938)
15-inch: 100 rounds per gun; 6 shrapnel rounds per gun.
6-inch: 130 rounds per gun.
3-pounder saluting guns: 64 rounds per gun (peacetime only).
4-inch: 250 rounds per gun; 250 star shell for ship.
2-pounder: 720 rounds per gun.
0.5-inch: 2,500 rounds per gun.

Fire-control equipment (1938)
Main armament: two tripod-type directors, one Dreyer table Mk VI*.

Secondary armament: two pedestal-type sights, one Admiralty fire-control clock Mk IV(S) and one Mk IV(M)

High-angle armament: two HACS Mk I (later replaced by Mk III*), two pom-pom directors (one Mk I* and one Mk I**).

Range-finders
Two 30-foot in 'B' and 'X' turrets.
Three 15-foot in 'A' and 'Y' turrets and armoured director-hood.
Two 12-foot, one in each HACS director.
Two 9-foot on admiral's bridge.
One 9-foot in forward torpedo control-position (removed in 1938).

Armour
As in 1918, except for the following:
Middle-deck over magazines, 5 inch (4 inch non-cemented + 1 inch high-tensile).
Screens inboard of 6-inch guns, 1½ inch DI.
Armoured torpedo-control tower removed.

Machinery
Apart from general alterations to auxiliary machinery and fittings, this remained as in 1918.

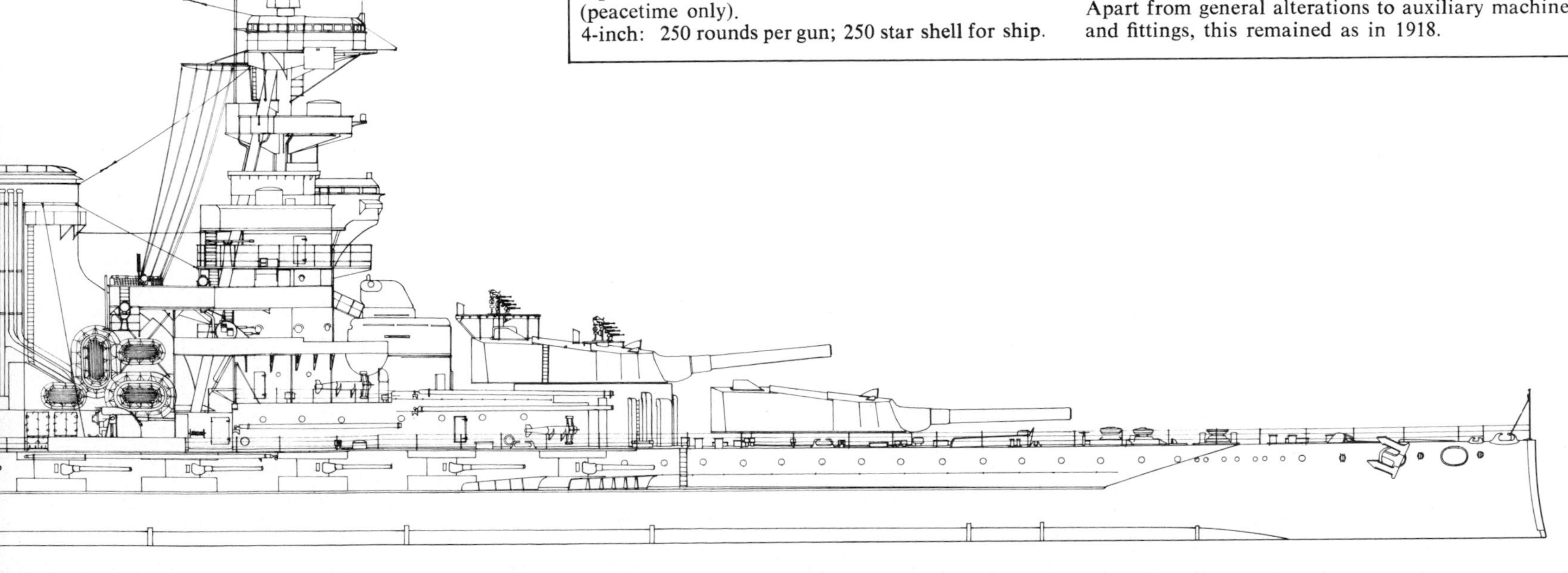

Left: the aircraft crane on *Barham*, 1937.

Below left: *Barham* in February 1938. The large model cockerel on 'B' turret proudly proclaims the ship as 'Cock of the Fleet' after her victory in the Navy's highly-competitive pulling regatta.

Below: an early-1940 view of *Barham*. Note the UP mounting on top of 'B' turret.

feet 8 inches above the floor plating would adequately protect bridge personnel from a short burst of fire from a hostile aircraft. He also made some adverse comments about the bridge windows. These were too low to permit a man of average height – standing on the central raised platform – to see the horizon without stooping. He seems to have been unaware of the problems encountered in *Valiant*, however, and as *Barham*'s bridge did not apparently receive further modification, it would appear that no attention was paid to his criticisms.

The new signal-deck proved most satisfactory, but at high speed, fumes from the funnel came down into the signal-working positions and made conditions there, somewhat uncomfortable.

Steam trials

Steam trials were carried out on 29th November 1933. After working up to full power, which was maintained for two hours, she ran a satisfactory four-hour full-power trial, resulting in a mean speed of 22.5 knots. During the trial, the weather was fine, with a smooth sea, no swell and a wind Force of 1 to 3. The low speed achieved was thought to result from the foul state of the bottom; the ship had been out of dock for seven and a half months. As in *Valiant*, vibration during the trials was minimal, even in the after cabin-flats. The operation of the steering gear was satisfactory throughout the trial, but the Captain, who does not seem to have been entirely satisfied with his new command, refused to use full helm at full speed on the grounds that "this would probably cause a large number of rivets and seams to start".

Catapult trials

On 22nd November, while at sea, five live shots with a dummy Fairy IIIF floatplane and two live shots with the genuine article, were carried out successfully. On the following day, two more live shots were made, while at anchor at Spithead. All these tests proved satisfactory and gave consistent results. During all the live shots there was a slight wind down the catapult, but there was no perceptable drop of the floatplane after launching.

Blast trials were also carried out, to see if the firing of the after 15-inch guns would affect the catapult. The catapult structure and fittings (including the gauge glasses) successfully withstood the heavy blast pressure. The same cannot be said of the ship herself, and a considerable amount of minor damage was done to *Barham*'s structure and fittings.

Alterations and additions, 1934 to 1941

Between the end of her large refit and her loss in 1941, *Barham* received few modifications. She was refitted at Portsmouth between February and July 1938, during which time her four single 4-inch high-angle guns were replaced by four 4-inch high-angle/low-angle Mk XIX twin mountings, the torpedo-control position above the chart-house was replaced by an air-defence position, the forward submerged torpedo tubes were removed and the catapult was arranged to take a Swordfish floatplane instead of a Fairy IIIF.

After being torpedoed in December 1939, she was repaired and refitted at Liverpool. During this time (December 1938 to March 1940), she was fitted with a UP mounting on 'B' turret, two high-angle control-systems Mk III in place of the two Mk Is, the admiral's bridge was extended forward and the conning-tower platform was widened. Early in 1941, the UP mounting was removed, two 0.5-inch machine-gun mountings were fitted, one on 'B' turret and one on the after superstructure, and two eight-barrel pom-poms were fitted on the conning-tower platform. There is no evidence to suggest that any further additions were made to the close-range anti-aircraft armament, or that she was ever fitted with any radar equipment.

Below: *Repulse* in dry-dock, undergoing refit in 1935.

REPULSE, 1933 to 1941

Between April 1933 and May 1936, *Repulse* was reconstructed at Portsmouth. The work carried out was more extensive than that in earlier modernisations, and included additional deck armour over the engine rooms, a cross-deck catapult and aircraft hangars. Similar work was carried out in *Malaya* which was taken in hand a year after *Repulse*, and these two ships represent the half-way point between the partial modernisation of such ships as *Barham* and *Royal Oak* and the complete reconstruction of *Warspite*, *Renown*, *Queen Elizabeth* and *Valiant*. Details of the work carried out on *Repulse* are given below:

Protection

As a result of the *Emperor of India* and *Marlborough* trials, it was decided to fit non-cemented armour over the magazines and engine rooms, but not over the boiler rooms as this would have substantially increased the top-weight, and reduced the stability. It was considered that the risk to the boiler rooms could be accepted, in view of their greater watertight sub-division, and the fact that a ship could still steam, even if her boiler power was considerably reduced.

The existing protective plating on the flat of the main-deck, over the magazines, consisted of three thicknesses of 1-inch high-tensile plating. The upper thickness was replaced by 3¾-inch thick non-cemented armour between the centre of 'A' barbette and the foremost boiler-room bulkhead forward, and between the aftermost engine-room bulkhead and 'Y' barbette aft. For a distance of about twenty feet abaft 'Y' barbette, 3½-inch armour was fitted over the main-deck, on top of the original ¾-inch plating across the full width of the ship, and the existing upper thickness of 1-inch high-tensile plating was removed. The plating on the flat of the main-deck over the engine rooms also consisted of three 1-inch thicknesses of high-tensile plating. The upper two of these were replaced by 2½-inch non-cemented armour. In addition, 3½-

Below: 'A' and 'B' turrets on *Repulse* in 1939.

Bottom of page: broadside view of *Repulse* in 1936, after the completion of her reconstruction.

inch non-cemented armour was fitted horizontally, between the top of the slope of the main-deck and the ship's side abreast the engine rooms. On the lower-deck forward, over the 4-inch and torpedo-head magazines, the 1¾-inch thickness of high-tensile plating was replaced by 3½-inch non-cemented armour, the original ¾-inch plating being retained.

No other modifications were made to the armour protection of the ship, apart from the removal of the torpedo conning-tower from the after superstructure.

To reduce the displacement of the ship, the crushing-tubes were removed from the upper and lower bulge compartments. The upper bulges were strengthened, and the forward and after ends were reconstructed.

Aircraft equipment

A fixed cross-deck aircraft catapult was fitted on the forecastle-deck, between the after funnel and the mainmast. *Repulse* was the first ship to be equipped with a catapult of this type, which superseded all the earlier revolving types. She was also the first capital ship to be fitted with modern aircraft hangars, two of which, each capable of accommodating one aircraft, were constructed abreast the after funnel. Four aircraft could be carried, if two were stowed on the catapult. A crane for handling the aircraft was fitted on the outboard edge of each hangar roof.

Stowage for the aviation-spirit was provided in the hold, and on the platform-deck, right forward. Although these tanks represented a fire risk (which in the past had been allowed for by providing tanks that could be jettisoned if the ship was about to go into action), their position, below the waterline, in an extremity of the ship, made them reasonably safe.

Armament

The midships 4-inch triple mounting was removed, and the four single 4-inch high-angle guns were redisposed, two being fitted on extensions to the hangar roofs, abreast the after funnel, and two at the forecastle-deck edge, abreast the fore funnel. Four 4-inch Mk XV guns in two between-decks high-angle/low-

Left and below: three close-ups of *Repulse* during 1939.

angle Mk XVIII twin mountings were fitted abreast the mainmast, in extensions to the after shelter-deck. Two Mk VI pom-pom mountings were fitted abreast the fore funnel, on extensions to the conning-tower platform and inboard of these, two 0.5-inch machine-gun Mk II* mountings were fitted on raised platforms adjoining the flag-deck.

Repulse was fitted with one Mk I* and one Mk II HACSs. The Mk II director was on the fore-top and the Mk I* director on a pedestal above the after superstructure. A pom-pom director was fitted on each side of the fore-top roof.

The submerged torpedo tubes were removed and the compartments were sub-divided and converted into store-rooms.

Bridge and superstructure modifications

The basic alterations to the superstructure and fittings were:

1. The spotting-top and director-positions on the fore-mast were very slightly altered. The spotting-top roof – apart from accommodating the high-angle control-system and pom-pom directors – was fitted for use as an air-defence position.
2. The compass-platform remained basically as before, but the area of the raised compass-platform was increased and an Evershed bearing-sight was fitted on each side. The instruments on the compass-platform (or upper bridge) were replaced by two 12-foot range-finders (the original 9-foot instruments were moved down to the lower bridge) and two searchlight bearing-sights and one star shell bearing-sight on each side.
3. The lower bridge was enlarged, remodelled and fitted with wings. The 9-foot range-finders from the compass-platforms were fitted in the wings, and a 36-inch searchlight was fitted each side, at the forward end of the platform.

Below: looking down from the bridge, over the bows of *Repulse* in May 1939.

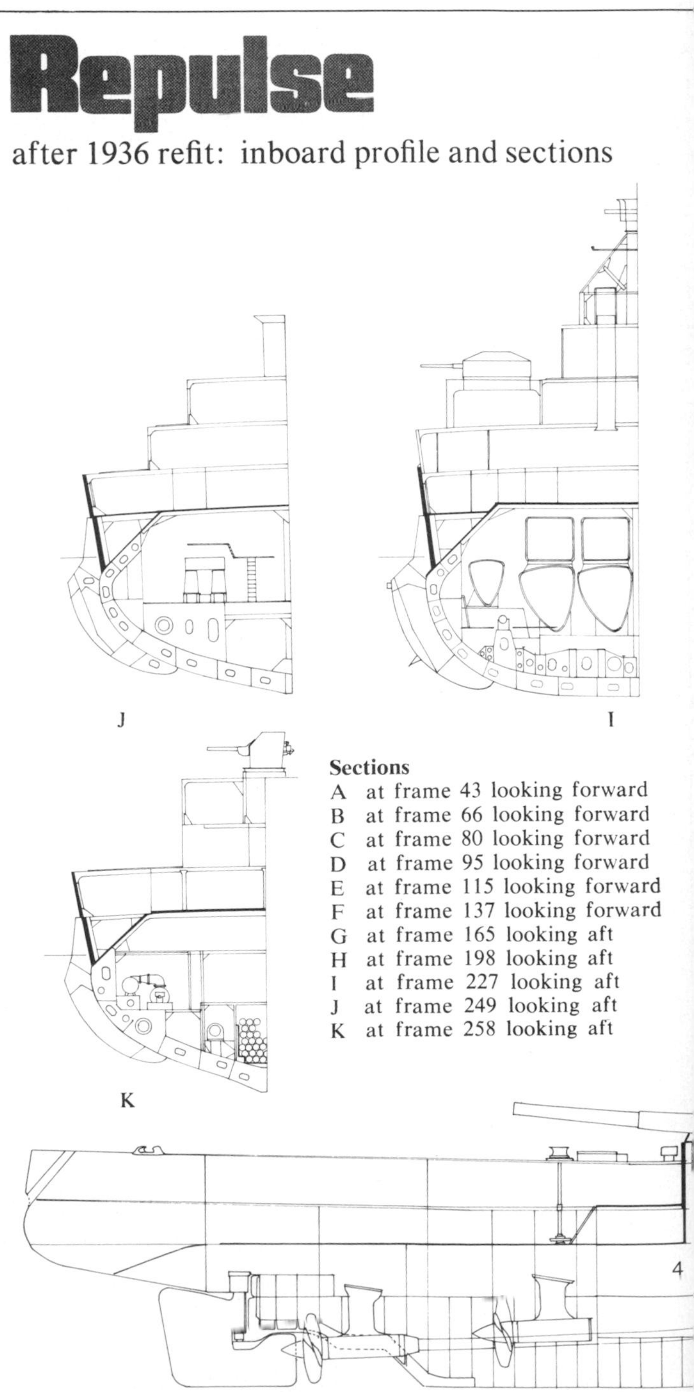

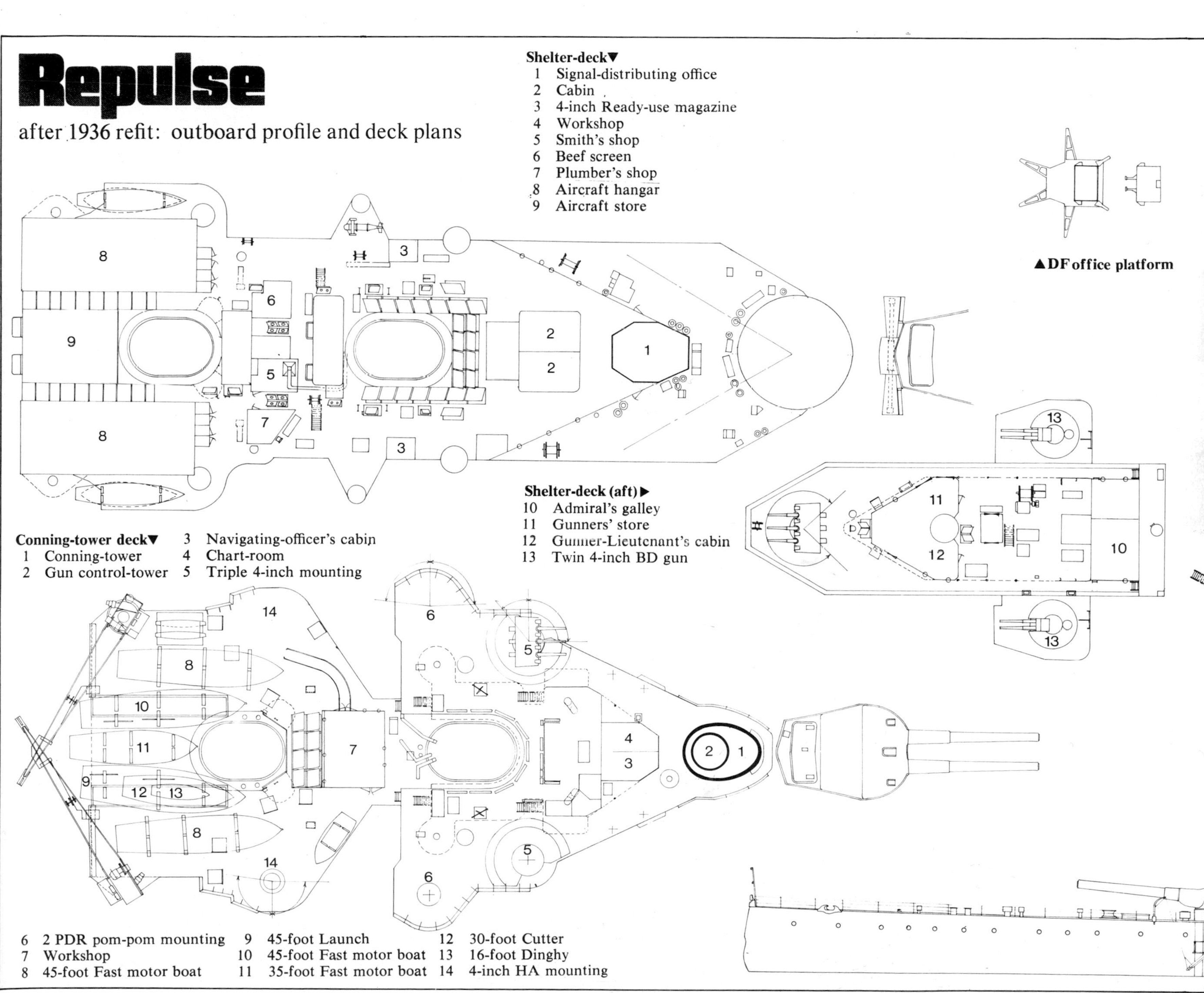

Repulse
after 1936 refit: outboard profile and deck plans
Shelter-deck▼
1 Signal-distributing office
2 Cabin
3 4-inch Ready-use magazine
4 Workshop
5 Smith's shop
6 Beef screen
7 Plumber's shop
8 Aircraft hangar
9 Aircraft store
▲DF office platform
Shelter-deck (aft)▶
10 Admiral's galley
11 Gunners' store
12 Gunner-Lieutenant's cabin
13 Twin 4-inch BD gun
Conning-tower deck▼
1 Conning-tower
2 Gun control-tower
3 Navigating-officer's cabin
4 Chart-room
5 Triple 4-inch mounting
6 2 PDR pom-pom mounting
7 Workshop
8 45-foot Fast motor boat
9 45-foot Launch
10 45-foot Fast motor boat
11 35-foot Fast motor boat
12 30-foot Cutter
13 16-foot Dinghy
14 4-inch HA mounting

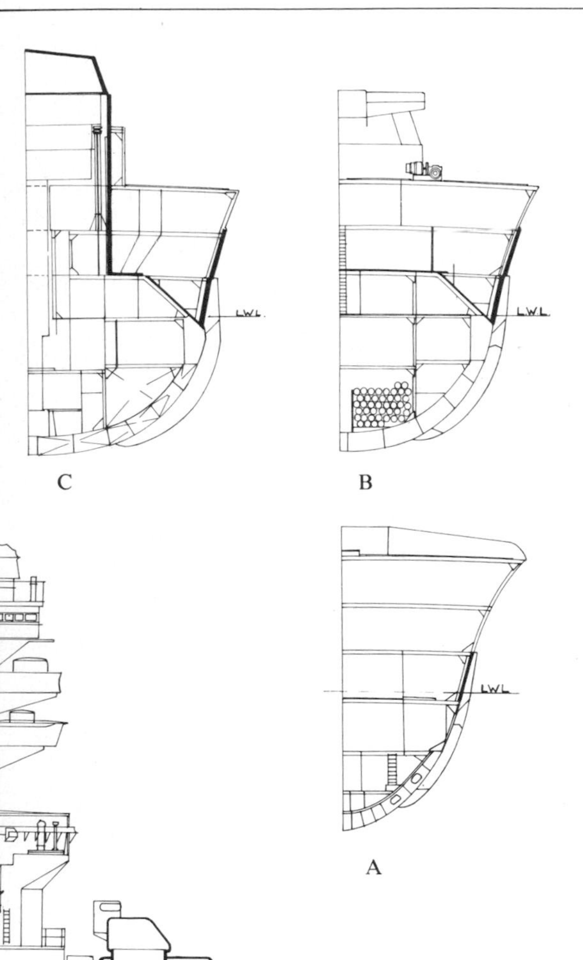

PARTICULARS OF *REPULSE*, 1933 to 1941

Except where noted below, the particulars of this ship remained generally as in 1921.

Displacement

1933 before reconstruction: deep, 38,100 tons; legend, 34,800 tons; light, 32,130 tons (with 1,033 tons of ammunition).
Deep displacement after reconstruction: 38,300 tons.

Armament (1936)

Six 15-inch Mk I: twin mounting Mk I.
Twelve 4-inch Mk IX*: triple mountings Mk I, II.
Four 4-inch Mk XV: between-decks twin mountings Mk XVIII (replaced in 1939 by two 4-inch Mk V: high-angle single mountings Mk IV).
Four 4-inch Mk V: single mountings Mk III.
Sixteen pom-poms Mk VIII: two mountings Mk VI.
Eight 0.5-inch machine-guns Mk III: two mountings Mk II*.
Four 3-pounder Hotchkiss saluting guns Mk I.

Additions to close-range AA armament 1939 to 1941

1939: two 0.5-inch machine-guns: quadruple mountings.
1940: one eight-barrel pom-pom mounting.
1941: eight single 20-mm Oerlikons.

Ammunition stowage (1936)

15-inch: 120 rounds per gun; 6 shrapnel rounds per gun.
4-inch Mk IX*: 200 rounds per gun; 100 star shell per ship.
4-inch Mk V and Mk XV: 340 rounds per gun; 200 star shell per ship.
2-pounder: 720 rounds per gun.
0.5-inch: 2,500 rounds per gun.
3-pounder (saluting): 64 rounds per gun.

Fire-control equipment (1936)

Main armament: two tripod-type directors, one Dreyer table Mk IV*.

Secondary armament: two pedestal-type sights, two transmitting-clocks, Type 'E'.

High-angle armament: one HACS Mk I*, one HACS Mk II, two pom-pom directors Mk I**

Range-finders

Three 30-foot in 'A' and 'Y' turrets and in armoured director-hood.
Three 15-foot in 'A' and 'B' turrets and in armoured director-hood.
Four 12-foot, two in HACS directors and two on bridge.
Two 9-foot on bridge.

Armour

Main-deck:
5¾ inch over magazines (3¾ inch NC + 1 inch HT + 1 inch HT).
4¼ inch abaft 'Y' barbette (3½ inch NC + ¾ inch HT).
3½ inch over engine rooms (2½ inch on 1 inch HT amidships and 3½ inch NC at sides).

Inboard profile

1 4-inch Magazine
2 4-inch Handling room
3 15-inch Shell room
4 15-inch Magazine
5 Boiler room
6 Engine room
7 Boiler room uptake
8 4-inch Shell room
9 Lower conning-tower

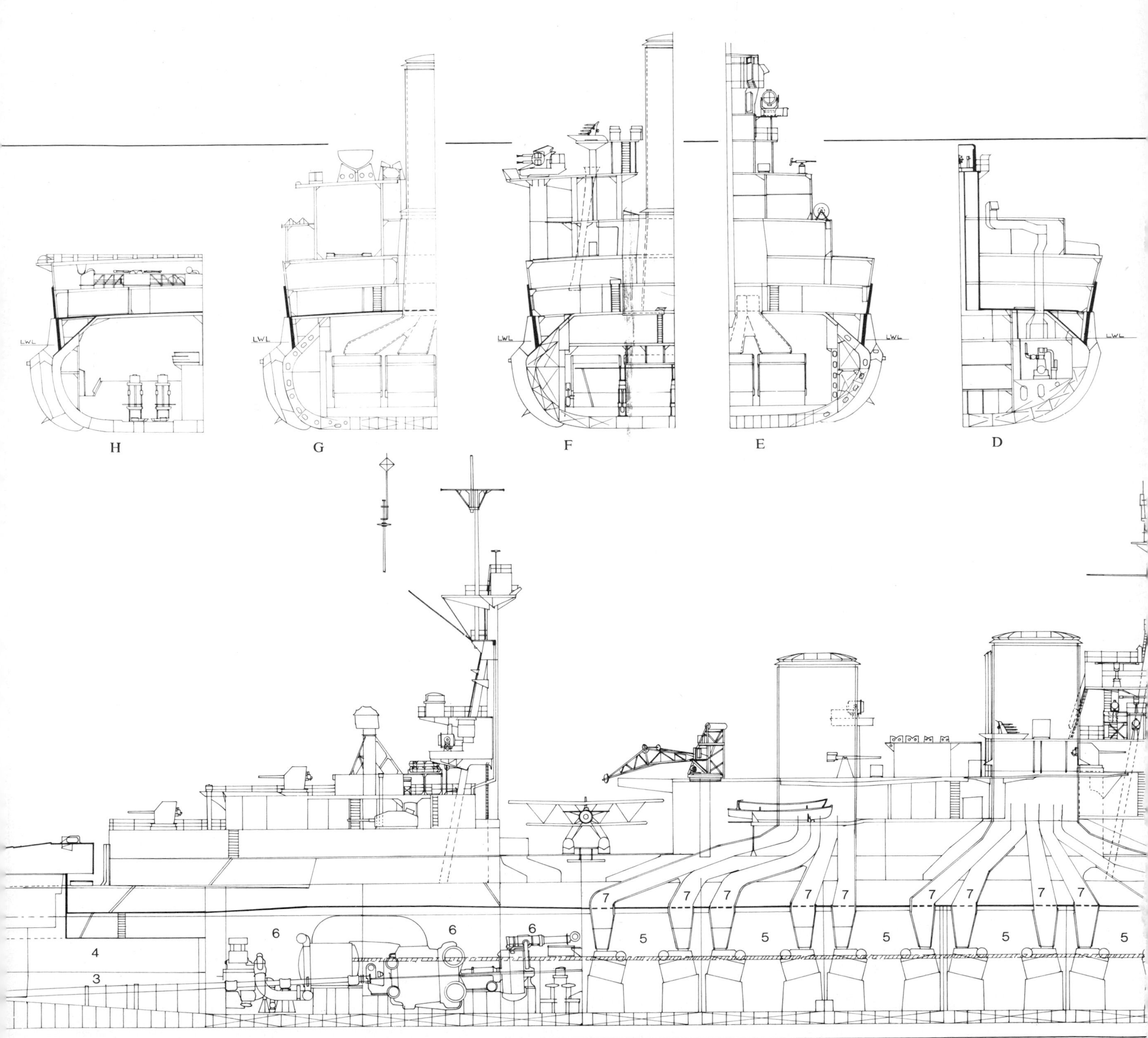
LWL
H
LWL
G
LWL
F
LWL
E
LWL
D
7
7
7
7
7
7
7
7
7
6
6
6
5
5
5
5
5
4
3

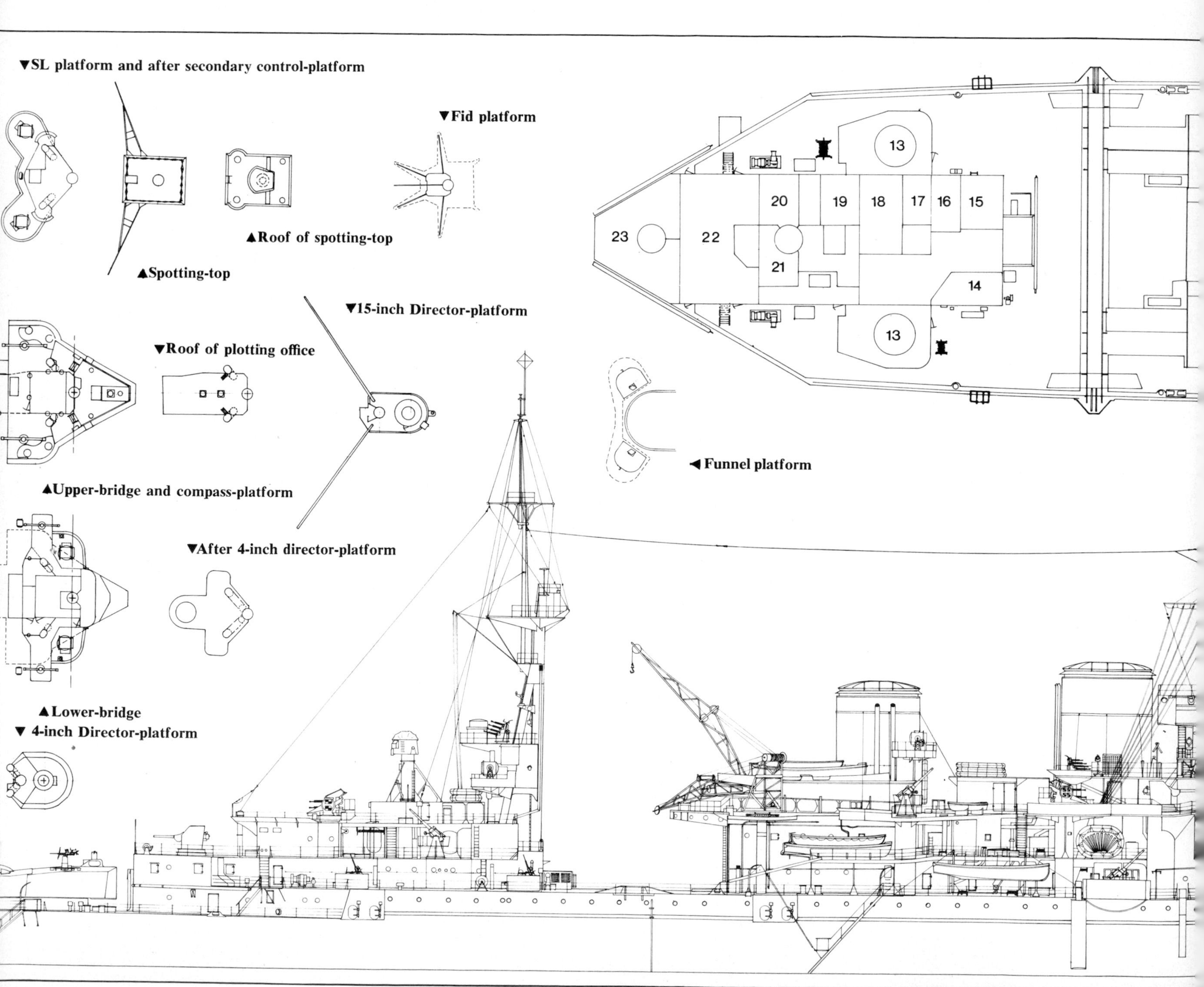
▼SL platform and after secondary control-platform
▼Fid platform
▲Roof of spotting-top
▲Spotting-top
▼15-inch Director-platform
▼Roof of plotting office
▲Upper-bridge and compass-platform
▼After 4-inch director-platform
▲Lower-bridge
▼ 4-inch Director-platform
◄ Funnel platform
13
20
19
18
17
16
15
23
22
21
14
13

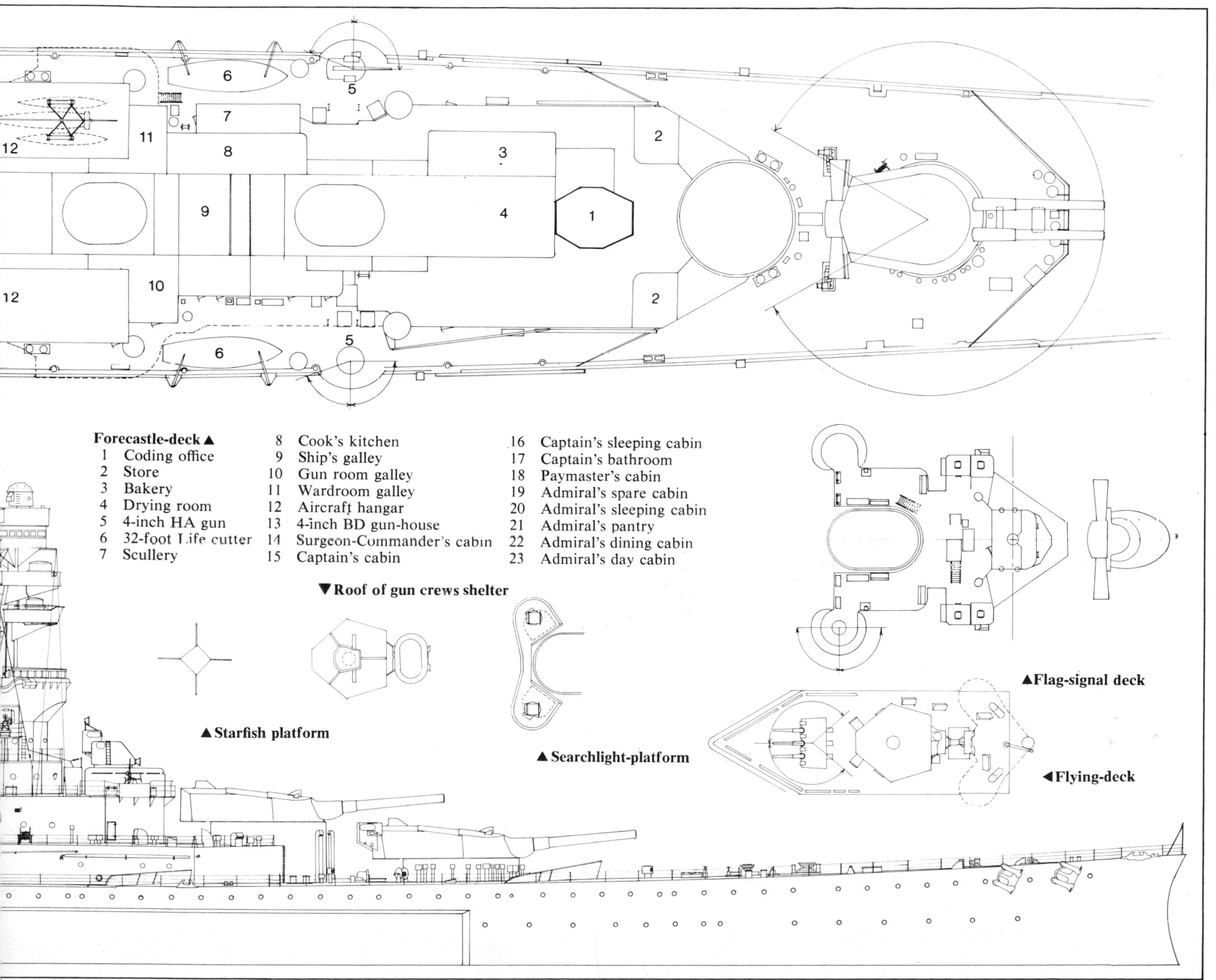
6
5
7
11
12
8
3
2
9
4
1
12
10
2
5
6
Forecastle-deck ▲
1 Coding office
2 Store
3 Bakery
4 Drying room
5 4-inch HA gun
6 32-foot Life cutter
7 Scullery
8 Cook's kitchen
9 Ship's galley
10 Gun room galley
11 Wardroom galley
12 Aircraft hangar
13 4-inch BD gun-house
14 Surgeon-Commander's cabin
15 Captain's cabin
16 Captain's sleeping cabin
17 Captain's bathroom
18 Paymaster's cabin
19 Admiral's spare cabin
20 Admiral's sleeping cabin
21 Admiral's pantry
22 Admiral's dining cabin
23 Admiral's day cabin
▼Roof of gun crews shelter
▲Starfish platform
▲Searchlight-platform
▲Flag-signal deck
◀Flying-deck

Above: the starboard quarter of *Repulse*; **below**, leaving Portsmouth harbour in 1939.

4. The flag-deck remained practically unaltered although two extensions were added aft for the 0.5-inch machine-gun mountings. The 36-inch searchlights were moved up to the lower bridge-platform, (see 3, above) and the 24-inch signalling-projectors were removed. Four 18-inch signalling-searchlights were fitted, two of which were mounted on raised platforms.
5. The conning-tower platform was extended aft to accommodate the pom-pom mountings, and the hangar roof was extended forward to meet it and to provide a platform between the funnels. This carried the boat workshop and the boiler-room vent-openings. Spare floats for the aircraft were stowed in the boat workshop roof.
6. The searchlight-towers were removed from the second funnel and two new 36-inch searchlight-platforms, with their control-positions underneath, were erected on the forward sides of the funnel.
7. The shelter-deck between the mainmast and the second funnel was taken out to make room for the catapult and hangars.
8. The after superstructure was not greatly modified. The flying-deck was extended forward to the base of the mainmast, the torpedo conning-tower was removed, the 36-inch searchlight-platforms were modified, wings were added to the shelter-deck for the between-deck gun-mountings and the anti-aircraft range-finder on the 4-inch director-platform was removed.
9. The boats, which were originally accommodated along the sides of the forecastle-deck, amidships, were stowed on the hangar roofs. The larger boats were replaced by modern motor boats. The main derrick was removed from the mainmast; the boats in their new position being handled by the aircraft cranes.

Trials

Repulse carried out preliminary sea trials on 31st January 1936. The results were generally satisfactory except for the arrangement of the compass-platform which, in order to provide an open platform with a clear view in

Table 55: Royal accommodation aboard HMS *Repulse*

Re-allocation	Displaced	Work to be carried out:
HM the King's apartments	Admiral (forecastle-deck)	4-inch triple mounting on shelter-deck, station '258', to be taken out and forecastle to shelter support removed; openings to be blanked. This mounting to be replaced.
HM the Queen's apartments	Admiral, paymaster, and the after portion of 4-inch port between-decks gun-house (forecastle-deck)	4-inch between-decks mounting port to be taken out and openings blanked. 4-inch between-decks gun-house to be sub-divided as shown; the existing lobby to the existing captain's bathroom and WC being extended to the outer bulkhead of port between-decks gun-house and door fitted to give access on to forecastle-deck port. The 4-inch port and starboard between-decks mountings will not be replaced. 4-inch high-angle single mountings may be mounted in lieu. Additional doors to be fitted as shown. Paymaster's cabin to be sub-divided and an enclosed WC to be built. Square ports to be cut in gun-house. Stiffeners in gun-house to be cut back to about 3 inches, and lining to be fitted to bulkheads at side.
Sun-deck for royal party	Shelter-deck, aft	Light steel screens to be built on shelter-deck, from after island to shelter-deck edge at station '243' port and starboard, and canopy to be erected over shelter-deck in position shown. Glass side screens to be built from the transverse screens to about the after end of the canopy; ladders to be modified if necessary.
Two ladies-in-waiting	Captain, and forward portion of port between-decks gun-house (forecastle-deck)	Side lights to be fitted in gun-house. Doors to be fitted where shown. Lining to be fitted to bulkheads of gun-house.
HM the King's secretary	After portion of 4-inch starboard between-decks gun-house	4-inch starboard between-decks mounting to be taken out and openings to be blanked. Stiffeners to be cut back to about 3 inches, and lining to be fitted.
One gentleman-in-waiting	Forward portion of 4-inch starboard between-decks gun-house (forecastle-deck)	4-inch starboard between-decks gun-house to be sub-divided as shown. Side lights and doors to be fitted as shown. See above re replacing the 4-inch between-decks mounting.
Six gentlemen-in-waiting	Commander, engineer-commander, marine officer, chaplain, navigating officer and senior engineer	Wardroom to be made available to King's secretary and gentlemen-in-waiting, as may be required.
HM the King's store HM the Queen's store	Torpedo-parting space (upper deck)	Bulkheads to be built up and compartment sub-divided as shown.
Four ladies' maids	Gunnery lieutenant, gunners' accoutrement store (shelter-deck)	Bathroom and WC to be erected on forward side of sleeping cabin in most suitable position. Side screens or other arrangements to be made to give protected access to the royal apartments in bad weather.
Ten valets	Captain and wardroom stewards' and cooks' mess, and torpedo office (upper-deck)	Divisional bulkhead to be removed. Bunks to be fitted. Washplace and lavatory to be arranged.
Admiral	Temporary cabin and surgeon-commander (forecastle-deck)	Build temporary cabin and bathroom in position shown. Final arrangements to suit conditions in the ship.

Displaced officers:		
Captain Commander Engineer-commander Surgeon-commander Marine officer Chaplain Navigating officer Senior engineer Gunnery lieutenant	To be accommodated in existing cabins. Temporary cabins on upper-deck and main-deck may be built as necessary to accommodate the displaced personnel. Cabins allocated to HM the King's secretary and gentlemen-in-waiting will be available for ships' officers when Their Majesties are not on board.	Gun-room can be reduced in size and midshipmen's study utilised as necessary.

One seaplane to be landed and hangar thus vacated to be used to accommodate the royal party's baggage and to provide accommodation of displaced personnel as required. A temporary deck and scuttles may be fitted if necessary.
The royal barge is to be stowed. Position to be selected.
Possibilities are: (1) in hangar, on a trolley.
(2) in lieu of one 45-foot fast motor boat; a 35-foot fast motor boat could possibly be carried by one of the cruisers.
Access from royal apartments to the bridge to be modified to make it as convenient as possible.
Ammunition lobby on shelter-deck to be fitted so that it can be used for making and serving tea on the sun-deck.
Portion of paymaster's cabin, as shown, to be made into a valets' and maids' lobby and store.

all directions, had been designed without a roof. To ensure a free flow of air over the compass-platform, all the structure above the roof of the plotting-office had been removed, and the latest type of wind-scoops were fitted to the front and side screens. A canvas awning could be rigged, and windows fitted if required, but these were not carried at the time of the trial which was held in conditions of fog, mist, drizzle and strong winds. Despite the precautions to eliminate down-draughts in the navigating-position, it was found that when proceeding head to wind at speeds over 15 knots, the 4-inch director-platform caused sufficient down-draught to affect the air-flow over the bridge. Consequently, the platform was filled with strong eddying air currents which considerably impaired the navigating and conning of the ship. This, together with the rain and the noise of air flowing past the mast and its fittings, created conditions in which it was impossible for the bridge personnel to maintain efficiency for more than short periods of time. It was found also, that a following wind caused thick funnel smoke to envelope the compass-platform.

Between 1929 and 1932, the raised compass-platform of *Repulse* had been enclosed by a wooden roof, sides, windows and doors. This modification had been carried out by the ship's staff and was satisfactory in almost all respects. It was proposed that this arrangement be re-adopted, but with a bullet-proof roof in place of the wooden one. The alteration was included in the final stages of the modernisation, and when *Repulse* carried out her full-power trials, in March 1936, the enclosed platform proved almost completely free of draughts and funnel gases. It was considered to be generally comfortable, but rather crowded. No objections were raised to the limited overhead view.

On steam trials, she made 28.36 knots with 112,400 shaft horse-power.

Subsequent modifications, 1936 to 1941

In 1938, *Repulse* was taken in hand at Portsmouth, for temporary and some permanent modifications, to make her ready to take the King and Queen to Canada for a royal tour. Most of the alterations involved the re-arranging and redecorating of the senior officers' quarters to accommodate the royal party. The displaced officers were quartered in other parts of the ship, and although their new cabins were probably greatly inferior in size and comfort, the honour of carrying their Majesties no doubt compensated the inconvenience. Table 55 shows how the accommodation was to be re-arranged.

The international situation, however, was steadily worsening, and war seemed imminent. While *Repulse* was still under refit, it was decided that it would be unwise to employ her as a royal yacht, and the liner *Empress of Australia* was substituted. Some alterations and additions were made to the armament before *Repulse* completed her refit in April 1939. The 4-inch between-decks twin mountings aft were replaced by two single 4-inch high-angle guns (this alteration was one of those intended for the royal tour) and two 0.5-inch machine-gun quadruple mountings were fitted on the after 4-inch director-platform. The aftermost 4-inch triple mounting was to have been removed so that a sun-deck could have been provided for the royal party, but this alteration was not made.

Few modifications were made to the ship between the start of the war, and her loss in December 1941. Early in the war, the 4-inch triple mounting on the flying-deck aft, was replaced by a third eight-barrel pom-pom mounting, and in mid-1941, she was fitted with eight 20-mm Oerlikons, and a Type '284' main gunnery radar set.

MALAYA, 1934 to 1946

The original proposals for the modernisation of *Malaya* were directed towards bringing her into line with *Barham*. It had been intended to fit her with additional armour over the magazines, a turret catapult and improved high-angle armament. In 1933, as a result of the *Emperor of India* and *Marlborough* trials, it was decided also that additional deck protection should be fitted over the engine rooms, and later, it was decided to fit a cross-deck catapult and aircraft hangars amidships instead of a turret catapult. This latter modification resulted in *Malaya* having a markedly different profile from that of *Barham*. The difference between the refits of these two ships, however, was not so drastic as their appearance suggested. The reconstruction of *Malaya* was carried out between October 1934 and December 1936.

Armour

The new non-cemented deck armour was fitted on the middle-deck, over the original 1-inch plating. The extra plating over the magazines, that had been added after Jutland,

Left: *Malaya* in 1931, before her 1934/6 refit.

Below left: in December 1936, after her large refit. She now features a rebuilt superstructure, two HACS Mk. III, a fixed cross-deck catapult and aircraft hangers.

was removed. Plates, 4-inches thick, were provided over the magazines, and 2½ inches thick, over the engine rooms. Some additional armour was fitted on the lower-deck over the forward 4-inch magazine. In 1934, it was suggested that the extra protection over the engine rooms might not be so advantageous as had been anticipated, because of the 260 tons of additional top-weight involved. There was also the weight of the new aircraft equipment to be considered, and, of course, the magazine armour, all of which would have a detrimental effect on the ship's stability. It was anticipated that the ship's draught would be some 5½ inches deeper than that of *Barham*, and that her speed would be correspondingly reduced. The engine-room protection was retained, but some compensation was effected by replacing the heavy armoured conning-tower by a smaller conning-tower incorporating the original revolving director-hood and support. This modification saved 220 tons, and almost completely compensated the 240 tons of additional aircraft equipment. The after torpedo conning-tower was also removed, and the after superstructure was raised one deck.

Armament

The single 4-inch high-angle guns were replaced by four of the new 4-inch Mk XIX twin mountings. Two HACS Mk III provided the necessary high-angle/low-angle control, the directors being fitted on the foretop and the after superstructure. The close-range armament consisted of two pom-pom mountings (one Mk V and one Mk VI) which were fitted abreast the funnel, on extensions to the hangar roof, and four 0.5-inch machine-gun Mk II mountings, two of which were fitted in the usual position abreast the conning-tower, and two on the roof of 'X' turret. A pom-pom director was fitted on each side of the compass-platform, and the 6-inch director-towers, that originally were carried on this platform, were re-positioned on after end extensions of the 15-inch director-platform, below the fore- top.

In 1934, a proposal was made to fit eight 21-inch above-water torpedo tubes in *Malaya*

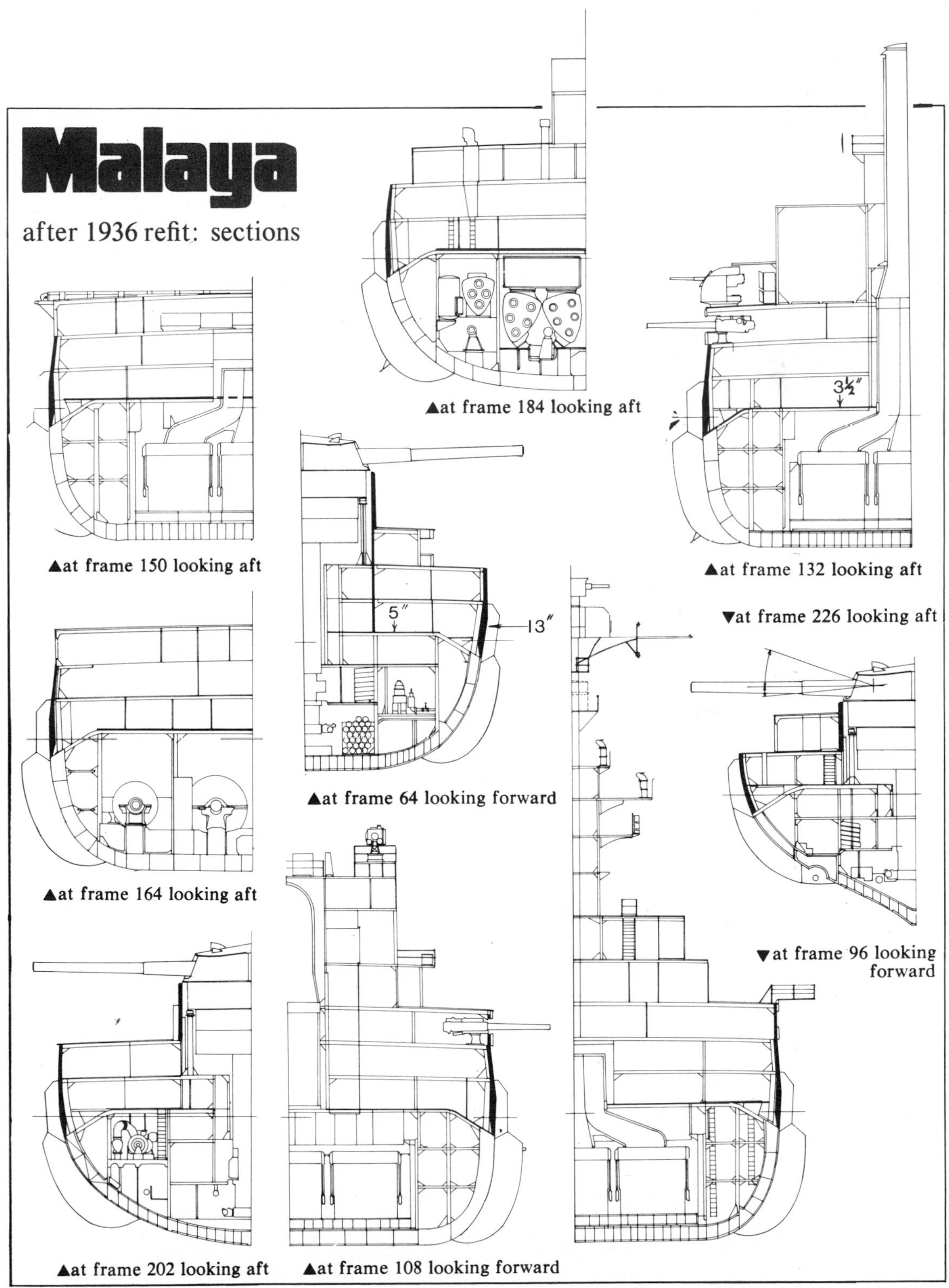

Below: port view of the after part of *Malaya* in January 1937.

and *Warspite*, but as this involved an additional seventy-five tons of top-weight, and would have cost £58,000, it was not approved. The after submerged torpedo tubes had been removed from *Malaya* in 1931, and during her reconstruction, the forward submerged torpedo tubes were also removed.

Aircraft equipment

A Type 'D II H' fixed cross-deck aircraft catapult was fitted athwartships on the forecastle-deck, between the funnel and the mainmast. An aircraft hangar capable of accommodating one aircraft, was constructed on each side of the funnel, and an electrically-powered crane, for handling the aircraft and the ship's heavy boats, was fitted on the outboard side of each hangar. If more than two aircraft were carried, the additional units were stowed on the catapult. The aviation-spirit tanks were fitted right forward, on the platform-deck and in the hold.

Bridge modifications

The original bridge-platforms and offices were generally remodelled and enlarged. The following alterations were made.

1. The torpedo-control position was replaced by an open air-defence position.
2. The raised compass-platform was increased in area and was fitted wih a half-roof, the forward section being left open to give a clear overhead view. The platform was also fitted with bullet-proof screens, wind-scoops and windows.
3. The compass-platform (renamed the upper bridge) was enlarged, fitted with a steel screen and with wind-scoops at its forward end.
4. The admiral's bridge was renamed the lower bridge, and apart from some minor alteration to the offices, was unchanged.
5. The lower searchlight-platform was extended aft around the fore side of the funnel to form a new signal-bridge. Apart from the flag-lockers, this platform also carried four 24-inch searchlight-projectors, four 10-inch signalling-projectors and four semaphore-positions.
6. The conning-tower platform and the forward shelter-deck remained practically unaltered, though some alterations were made to the equipment they carried e.g. the flag-lockers, were moved to the new signal-platform and the conning-tower was replaced by a smaller structure.

General modifications

The ship had three wireless-transmitter offices. The main office was on the main-deck below the after superstructure, the second office was on the main-deck below the bridge and there was an auxiliary office on the middle-deck below the forward turrets. The arrangement of the aerials for these sets was as follows.

Main Aerials: Six wires (three receiving, three transmitting) rigged between the fore-top and the wireless-transmitter yard on the main-topmast.

Auxiliary aerials (for fleet intercommunication): Separated transmitting and receiving aerials were rigged at the front of bridge.

Type '50' set: The aerial was rigged between the fore and main starfish. A receiving aerial was rigged between the main starfish and the after superstructure.

Type '43' set: The aerial was rigged between the after superstructure and the main wireless-transmitter yard.

Type '75' set (Short range, for gunnery): Transmitting and receiving whip-aerials were fitted on the forward end of the fore-top roof and on the main starfish.

Medium-frequency direction-finder: Aerials were rigged to the main-topmast and an office was fitted on top of the after superstructure.

Malaya's heavy boats were replaced by modern motor boats and launches, and as the original boat-stowage area had been occupied by the catapult, these were accommodated on the hangar roofs. The main derrick on the mainmast was removed because the boats, in their new positions, could be served by the aircraft cranes. The smaller, pulling boats were stowed abreast the after superstructure.

Below: four photographs showing the damage sustained by *Barham* early in 1937, when she was in collision with a merchant ship. Note how part of the bulge has been torn away and the forward twin 4-inch twin mounting has been demolished.

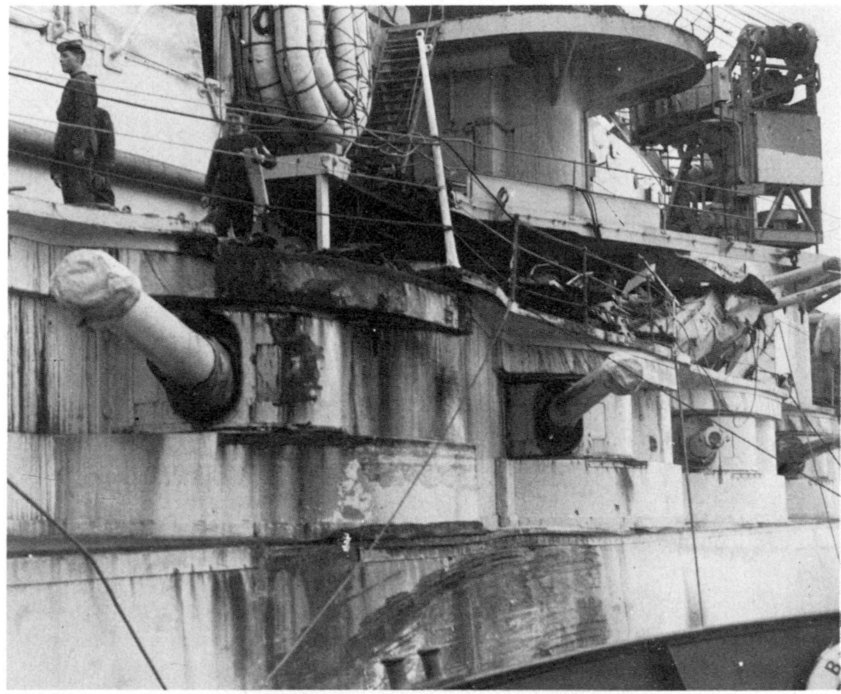

Anti-aircraft gun positions
July 1941:
A Four 0.5-inch MGs removed.
B Eleven single 20 mm mounts fitted.
September 1941:
C Four single 20 mm mounts added.
December 1942:
D Two single 20 mm mounts moved to positions E.
E Two single 20 mm mounts from positions D.
F Two single 20 mm mounts added.
G Two octuple pom-poms fitted.
H Two twin 4-inch guns added.
December 1943: Twenty single 20 mm mounts added, positions not known.
March 1944: Eight single 20 mm mounts added, positions not known.

Malaya

January 1943: outboard profile and deck plans, with subsequent AA positions indicated

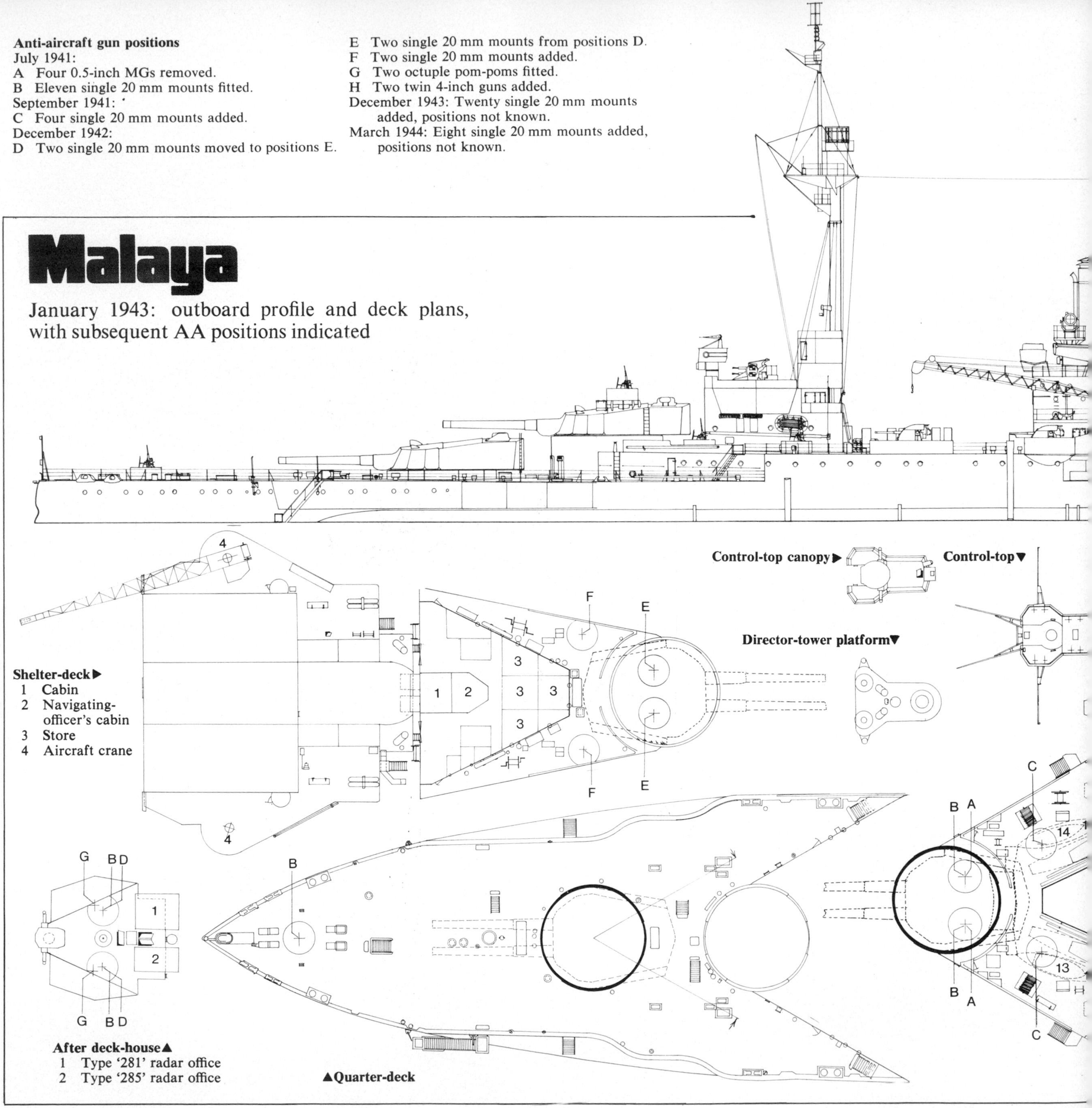

Control-top canopy▶
Control-top▼
Director-tower platform▼
Shelter-deck▶
1 Cabin
2 Navigating-officer's cabin
3 Store
4 Aircraft crane
After deck-house▲
1 Type '281' radar office
2 Type '285' radar office
▲Quarter-deck

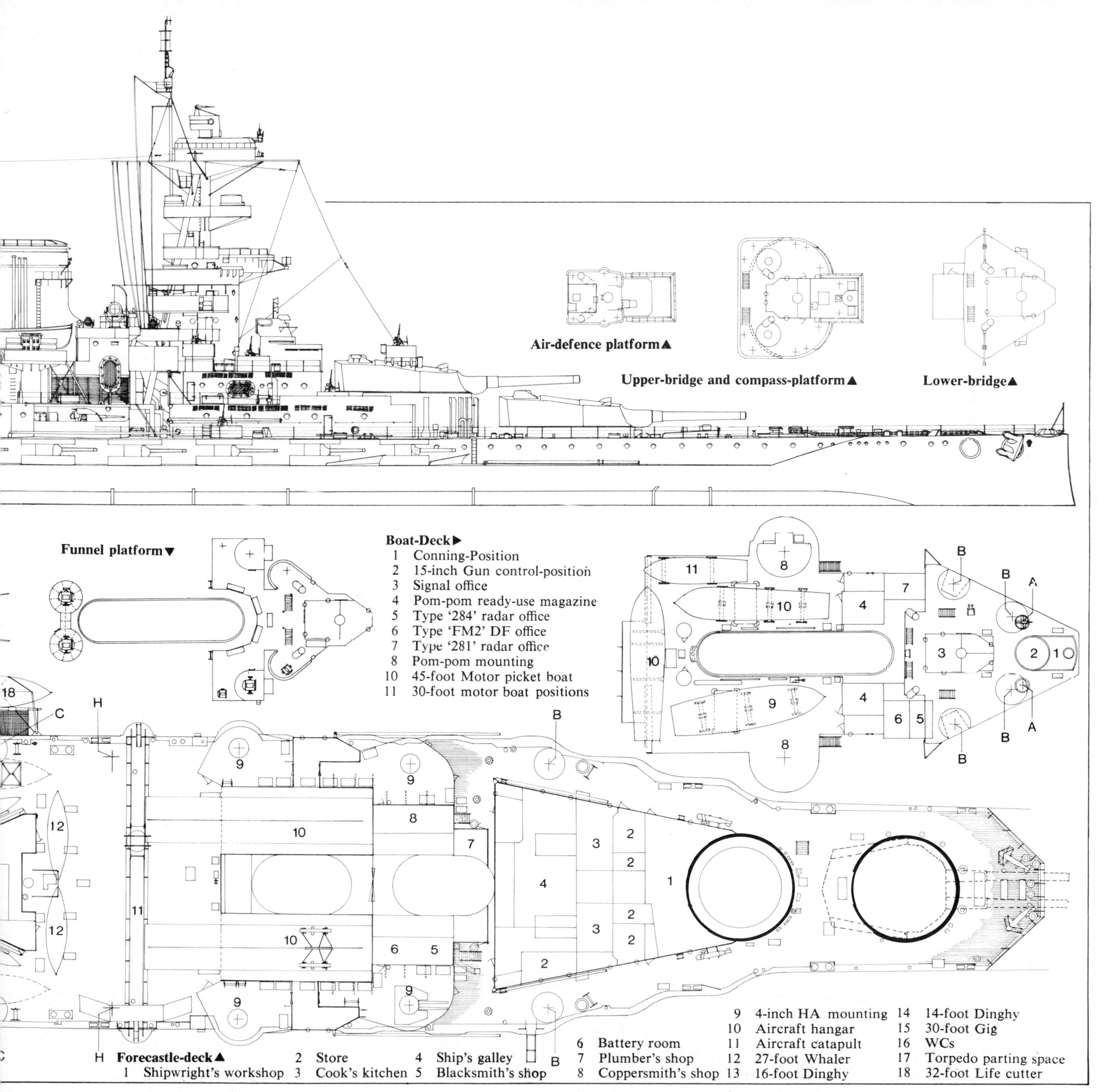
Air-defence platform▲
Upper-bridge and compass-platform▲
Lower-bridge▲
Funnel platform▼
Boat-Deck▶
1 Conning-Position
2 15-inch Gun control-position
3 Signal office
4 Pom-pom ready-use magazine
5 Type '284' radar office
6 Type 'FM2' DF office
7 Type '281' radar office
8 Pom-pom mounting
10 45-foot Motor picket boat
11 30-foot motor boat positions
Forecastle-deck▲
1 Shipwright's workshop
2 Store
3 Cook's kitchen
4 Ship's galley
5 Blacksmith's shop
6 Battery room
7 Plumber's shop
8 Coppersmith's shop
9 4-inch HA mounting
10 Aircraft hangar
11 Aircraft catapult
12 27-foot Whaler
13 16-foot Dinghy
14 14-foot Dinghy
15 30-foot Gig
16 WCs
17 Torpedo parting space
18 32-foot Life cutter

Below: *Malaya* returning to Britain after her refit in the USA in 1941; this was before the installation of radar and 20-mm mountings.

PARTICULARS OF *MALAYA*, 1937 to 1946

Displacement
1937: 31,465 tons standard, 35,380 tons deep.
1945: 32,980 tons standard, 37,710 tons deep (including 815 tons of water in water-protection compartments).

Dimensions
Length and beam remained unchanged.
Deep draught (1945): 34 feet 7 inches forward, 33 feet 4 inches aft.

Armament (1937)
Main and secondary armaments remained as before.
Eight 4-inch Mk XVI: four high-angle/low-angle twin mountings Mk XIX.
Sixteen 2-pounder Mk VIII: one Mk V mounting and one Mk VI mounting.
Sixteen 0.5-inch Mk III: four mountings Mk III.
Four 3-pounder saluting guns.

Ammunition stowage (1937)
15-inch: 100 rounds per gun; 6 shrapnel rounds per gun.
6-inch: 130 rounds per gun.
4-inch: 280 rounds per gun; 250 star shell per ship.
2-pounder: 720 rounds per gun.
0.5-inch: 2,500 rounds per gun.
3-pounder (saluting): 64 rounds per gun.

Fire-control equipment (1937)
Main armament: two tripod-type directors, one Dreyer table Mk IV*.
Secondary armament: two pedestal-type sights, two Admiralty fire-control clocks Mk IV.
High-angle/low-angle armament: two HACS Mk III.
Close-range AA armament: two pom-pom directors Mk I**.

Range-finders
Two 30-foot in 'B' and 'X' turrets.
Three 15-foot in 'A' and 'Y' turrets and armoured director-hood.
Two 15-foot in HACS directors.
Two 9-foot on lower bridge-platform.

Armour
As in 1918 except for the following:
Middle-deck: 5 inch (4 inch NC + 1 inch HT) over magazines, $3\frac{1}{2}$ inch ($2\frac{1}{2}$ inch NC + 1 inch HT) over engine rooms.
Conning-tower: original removed and replaced by small conning-tower built on to front of original armoured director-hood support, with walls approximately 5 inches thick. After torpedo-control tower removed.

Machinery
The main machinery remained as fitted in the ship on completion. Oil-fuel stowage in 1945 was 3,298 tons plus 119 tons of Diesel fuel.

The original searchlight-towers were removed, and the four 36-inch searchlights were re-disposed. Two were fitted on a new platform at the rear of the funnel, and two were mounted on raised platforms on the new signal-platform.

Trials

Malaya was taken to sea for trials in November 1936, before her refit was fully complete, and without her 0.5-inch machine-guns, high-angle directors and port-side 4-inch guns. She left Cawsand Bay for full-power trials at 08.30 hours on 4th November, with a slight list to starboard and a displacement of 31,650 tons. The trials were carried out on the Polperro mile, in calm but overcast and misty weather. A Force 2 wind was blowing from the north-east. A series of runs was made at definite speeds to calibrate the pitometer-log and then, after two runs at 15 knots, the ship spent two hours working up to full power. Two runs on the measured mile resulted in a mean speed of 23.7 knots at about 75,000 shaft horse-power. Forty minutes were spent reducing the ship's speed, and then a series of runs

was made at 21, 18, 12 and 9 knots, before the ship returned to Cawsand Bay at 18.00 hours.

During the trials, opportunity was taken to examine other aspects of the modifications, and the following items were noted. The flow of air over the raised compass-platform, came in under the partial roof and caused some back-draught over the floor, at speeds above 15 knots, but the bridge windows had not yet been fitted, and a canvas awning that had been provided to cover the forward part of the platform, was not rigged. During the refit, 1½-inch thick 'D' steel plates had been fitted below the ventilator openings in the engine room, to protect the engines from splinters. It was found that this tended to diffuse the air supply and generally had a detrimental effect on the ventilation system. It was concluded that the plates were too close to the openings and later, the arrangement of the plates and the direction of the ventilators were modified. Vibration during the full-power trial was no more than expected. The worst position was on the main-deck aft, where the amplitude was about ½-inch. It seems that, originally, it had been intended to fit two of the 0.5-inch machine-gun mountings on 'B' turret, because the gunnery officer said he did not like the intended positions for the mountings on 'B' and 'X' turrets.

War modifications

Damage refit in USA, April to July 1941:
1. The air-defence position was replaced by an office for Type '285' radar. The upper bridge was extended aft and fitted with ALO sights.
2. A double Type '282' radar office was fitted at the rear of the lower bridge-platform. Offices for Type '284' radar and an FM2 direction-finding outfit were fitted on the starboard side at the rear of the conning-tower platform.
3. An office for a Type '281' radar transmitting-set was fitted on the port side, at the rear of the conning-tower platform. An office for a Type '281' radar receiving-set was fitted on the port side of the after superstructure.
4. The direction-finder office on the starboard side of the after superstructure was replaced by an office for a Type '285' radar set.
5. A submarine-look-out hut was fitted on each side of the conning-tower platform. The rig was altered, and positions were prepared for the radar and direction-finder aerials. Steel screens were fitted on the outboard side of the 4-inch twin gun-mountings.

These alterations consisted mainly of preparatory work, and the actual radar sets and aerials were not fitted in the ship until her return to the United Kingdom.

July 1941:
1. The 0.5-inch machine-gun mountings were removed.
2. Eleven single 20-mm Oerlikons were fitted.
3. The direction-finder aerials were removed from the main-topmast.
4. An 'FM2' direction-finder fixed-frame aerial was fitted on the front of the compass-platform.
5. Type '281' radar aerials were fitted on main-(receiver) and fore-(transmitter) top-masts.
6. Type '285' radar aerials were fitted on the HACS directors.
7. Type '284' radar aerials were fitted on the armoured director-hood.
8. Type '282' radar aerials were fitted on the pom-pom directors.

September 1941:
Four single 20-mm Oerlikons were added.

Refit at Rosyth, October to December 1942:
1. The aircraft catapult was removed and the hangars were converted to other uses.
2. An additional 4-inch Mk XIX twin mounting was fitted on each side of the forecastle-deck, abreast the catapult position.
3. Two eight-barrelled pom-pom mountings were fitted on the after superstructure. Sponsons were built out on each side, to provide the necessary space.
4. Two single 20-mm Oerlikons were added.
5. Type '273' radar was fitted, with aerial and office on mainmast starfish.
6. The pom-pom directors on the upper bridge were fitted higher up, in pedestal-mounted bucket-platforms.

January 1943:
Two 20-mm Oerlikons were fitted on 'B' turret.

September 1943:
1. All the 6-inch gun and battery armour was removed, and the gun-ports were plated over with 2-inch non-cemented plating. This alteration was intended to reduce the draught, and improve the stability and watertightness that had been adversely affected by the considerable additional top-weight of wartime fittings. It also provided additional mess space for the larger wartime complement.
2. The secondary armament-directors were removed.
3. Twenty single 20-mm Oerlikons were added.

March 1944:
1. Eight single 20-mm Oerlikons were added.
2. Radar Type '281' was replaced by '281B' and 'Type 273', by '277SQ'.
3. A Type '650' guided-missile jamming-device was fitted.

(Note: In July 1943, *Malaya* was placed in care and maintenance, off Faslane, in order to release her crew for more important duties (principally in *Valiant*). *Malaya* was kept at three months' notice. She was recommissioned for the Normandy landings, but otherwise, stayed in reserve for the remainder of the war. In 1945, most of her armament was removed and she joined *Ramillies* to become the training-ship, *Vernon II*.)

Total AA armament at the end of 1944:
Twelve 4-inch (6 x 2), thirty-two 2-pounder (4 x 8), forty-five 20-mm (45 x 1).

WARSPITE, 1930 to 1946

In 1931 *Warspite* was fitted with a high-angle control system Mk I, and the after submerged torpedo tubes were removed. These were the only substantial modifications made to the

Below: *Warspite* in 1931; and, right, the contrast in her appearance after reconstruction.

ship, between the end of her bulging refit in 1926, and the beginning of her reconstruction in 1934.

Reconstruction, 1934 to 1937

Warspite was the first of the capital ships to be fully reconstructed. This work was carried out at Portsmouth, between March 1934 and March 1937. Although, as modernised, she was by no means so valuable as a new ship, she was certainly a good substitute, and the result fully justified the £2,362,000 spent. The principal feature of the modernisation was the replacement of her original machinery plant, by new turbines and boilers. The weight and space thus saved, was utilised for such items as deck armour over the boiler rooms, and a substantial increase in watertight sub-division.

Table 56: Estimated weights before and after reconstruction (tons)

	Before reconstruction	After reconstruction
Armament	4,970	5,264
Machinery	3,691	2,300
Equipment	1,287	1,420
Hull and protective plating	16,250	17,130
Armour	5,431	5,980
Oil fuel	3,431	3,735
Reserve feed-water	497	267
Ordinary deep displacement:	35,557	36,096

Armament

While the ship was under reconstruction, the 15-inch turrets were lifted out of the ship, and transported to the Vickers Armstrong ordnance works at Elswick. Here, they were so modified as to increase the elevation of the guns from 20° to 30° and to make the shell-loading arrangements suitable for a modified design of 15-inch projectile. This alteration increased the maximum range of the guns from 23,400 yards to 29,000 yards with the old-type projectile, or 32,200 yards with the modified type. The modified mountings were designated Mk I (N), and had a revolving weight of 815 tons compared to 785 tons before alteration. The modified 15-inch shells had a more streamlined ballistic cap (6 crh instead of 4 crh) which reduced their air resistance and therefore increased their range. They weighed 1,938 pounds compared to 1,920 pounds for the 4 crh projectile. A new director-control tower was fitted on the upper bridge to control the main armament, and the original

Warspite

after second reconstruction:
amidships inboard profile

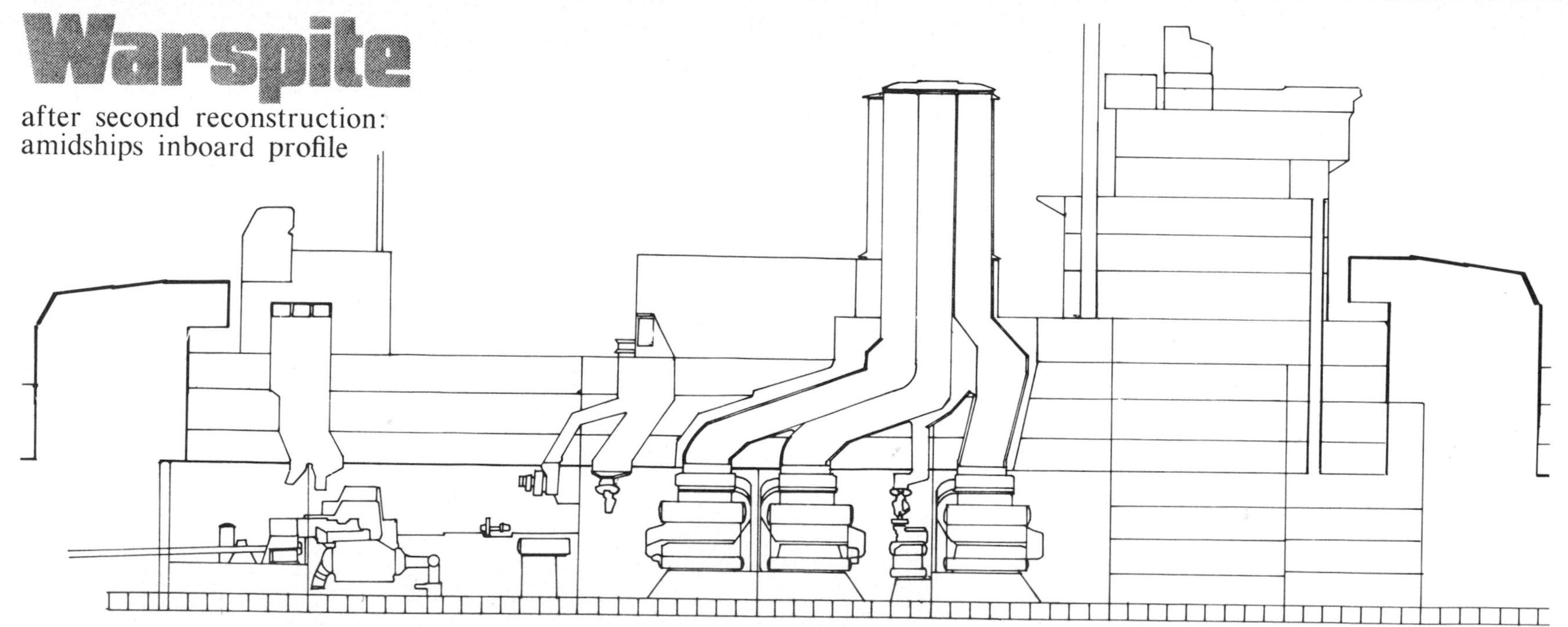

Left: *Warspite* in July 1937, after reconstruction.

Table 57: Estimated armament weights (tons)

	Before reconstruction	After reconstruction
Revolving weight of main armament	3,140	3,260
Fixed weight of main armament	281	281
15-inch shell and cordite	1,075	1,059
6-inch guns and mountings	192	129
6-inch shell and cordite	114	74
4-inch guns and mountings	27	55
4-inch shell and cordite	29	95
Pom-pom mountings	0	67
Pom-pom ammunition	0	126
0·5-inch mountings } 0·5-inch ammunition }	0	5
Catapult	0	24
Aircraft }	57	16
Aircraft torpedoes }		2
Bombs and pyrotechnics	0	22
Paravanes	2	2
Small arms and saluting guns and ammunition	28	40
S.A.S.O. stores	25	7
Total:	4,970	5,264

Table 58: Estimated armour weights (tons)

	Before reconstruction	After reconstruction
13-inch belt	1,909	1,909
6-inch belt (main-deck to upper-deck)	484	484
6-inch belt (below main-deck)	319	319
4-inch belt (below main-deck)	138	138
Bulkheads	315	315
Barbettes	1,166	1,166
Backing	100	100
Bolts	45	45
Battery protection (upper-deck)	447	105
Battery protection (main-deck)	123	123
Conning-tower	339	102
Deck armour over forward magazines		206
Deck armour over after magazines		189
Deck armour over engine rooms		253
Deck armour over boiler rooms		456
2-inch plating around 6-inch ammunition-hoists		16
Torpedo-control tower (aft) and 6-inch gun sighting-hoods	46	
Total:	5,431	5,980

armoured director-hood and its support, was fitted on the after superstructure.

The foremost and aftermost 6-inch guns were removed from each side which reduced the secondary battery to four guns on each beam. This allowed the forecastle-deck to be widened, which reduced the embrassure on each side, and therefore the possibility of the remaining 6-inch guns being adversely affected in a seaway. All the battery armour except the centre-line bulkhead was removed, and the protection of the reduced battery was re-arranged; the sides, bulkheads and partition screens were constructed of 2-inch thick non-cemented armour. The gun-bays were not enclosed on the inboard side. These modifications produced a total saving in weight of 445 tons. The original 6-inch directors were retained, and one was fitted on each side of the admiral's bridge.

The AA armament was similar to that provided in *Malaya,* but included two more pom-pom mountings. The 4-inch twin mountings were fitted on the forecastle-deck, the four pom-pom mountings were grouped around the funnel, and the four 0.5-inch machine-gun mountings were fitted on 'B' and 'X' turrets. She was fitted with two HACS Mk III, the directors being fitted on the admiral's bridge.

The four pom-pom directors Mk I** were fitted on the bridge and the after superstructure. The forward submerged torpedo tubes were removed and the compartments were sub-divided.

Protection

The fitting of non-cemented armour on the middle-deck, followed the pattern set in *Malaya* except that the 2½-inch thickness was extended to cover the boiler rooms. The armoured conning-tower was removed and, as already mentioned, the 6-inch gun battery protection was rebuilt, but apart from these alterations, the arrangement of the armour and protective plating remained substantially unaltered. The 6-inch armour on the main-deck aft – originally provided to protect the after 6-inch guns – was retained as it gave additional protection to the after magazines. The embrassures, however, were plated over and only a small portion of this armour remained visible externally.

Machinery

The twenty-four Yarrow large-tube boilers were replaced by six Admiralty three-drum small-tube high-power boilers. The new installation was capable of producing 80,000 shaft horse-power compared to 75,000 shaft horse-power for the original system. Each new boiler was provided with its own boiler room, by fitting a longitudinal centre-line bulkhead in the three aftermost boiler rooms. The forward boiler-room was no longer required, and this compartment was extensively sub-divided by the addition of decks and bulkheads. The original hydraulic-pumps, together with a number of other auxiliary engines were retained, and this limited the steam pressure to that in use before the reconstruction.

The direct-drive turbines were replaced by Parsons single-reduction geared turbines, and the shaft horse-power on each shaft was 20,000 at 300 revolutions. The new propellers were

Table 59: Comparison of machinery before and after reconstruction

	Before reconstruction	After reconstruction
SHP at full power	75,000	80,000
rpm at full power	300	300
Fuel consumption at full speed (lb/SHP/hour)	1·22	0·75
Fuel consumption at full speed (tons per hour)	41	26·8
Endurance at 10 knots (trial conditions)	8,400 n. miles	14,300 n. miles
Reserve feed-water (tons)	497	267
Fuel capacity (tons)	3,425	3,735
Estimated weights (tons):		
Engine room weights	1,737	967
Boiler room weights	1,461	900
Propellers and shafting	184	184
Workshop machinery	24	24
Distillation plant	29	29
Steering machinery	28	28
Air-compressors	30	19
Diesel generators	60	30
Steam generators	45	45
CO_2 plant	49	30
Lubricating oil	44	44
Total:	3,691	2,300

34

Left: an aerial view of *Warspite* under refit and repair at Puget Sound Navy Yard in 1942.

twelve feet in diameter, with a pitch of 10 feet 7 inches, and the estimated speed in deep condition (36,096 tons) with a clean bottom, was 23.3 knots.

The original three engine-room compartments were sub-divided by a longitudinal centre-line and a transverse bulkhead to provide four engine rooms and four gearing rooms. This additional sub-division of engine and boiler rooms, considerably enhanced the ships watertight integrity and added substantially to the strength of the hull. As Table 59 overleaf shows , the new machinery provided an enormous saving in weight and a marked increase in efficiency.

Aircraft equipment

The aircraft arrangements were practically the same as those fitted in *Malaya.* A 'D II H' catapult was fitted on the forecastle-deck and provision was made to carry four aircraft, two on the catapult and one in each hangar. The new funnel was smaller and farther forward than the original, and this allowed the hangars to be placed side by side abaft, instead of abreast the funnel. When completed, she was equipped with Blackburn Shark TSR seaplanes, but, before the war, these were replaced by the Swordfish seaplane, and in 1940 these were in turn replaced by Walrus amphibian aircraft.

Bridge and superstructure

With the exception of the forward shelter-deck, all the superstructure above the forecastle-deck was replaced by a new structure, the most marked feature of which, was the tower-type bridge. This latter followed the pattern set in *Nelson* and *Rodney*, and provided a solid supporting structure for the directors and other fire-control gear, and more space and shelter for bridge personnel and equipment. A conning-position, protected by 3-inch and 2-inch non-cemented armour, was provided at the forward end of the signalling-platform, with a communication tube that followed the route of the original to the lower conning-position on the lower-deck.

The after superstructure was similar to the original, but was reduced in length in order to clear the catapult. The hangars and structure amidships provided positions for the aircraft crane, pom-pom mountings and ship's boats.

General modifications

The main wireless-receiving office was on the main-deck below the after superstructure, and the transmitting office was on the main-deck below the bridge. The second wireless-transmitting office on the platform-deck below the bridge contained the second and auxiliary wireless sets. The main aerials were rigged between the foremast and mainmast, the secondary aerials between the rear of the bridge and the fore wireless-transmitting yard, and the auxiliary wireless-transmitting aerials, between the sides of the bridge and the fore signal-yard. The aerials for a Type '75' set were fitted on the fore starfish, and those for a Type '7R' set, on the pom-pom director-platform, on the after superstructure. Both '75' and '7R' were short-range sets with combined transmitting and receiving units and small whip-aerials.

A medium-frequency direction-finder was fitted in an office in the after superstructure, with its aerials rigged on the main-topmast. The ship was also provided with an FH3 high-frequency direction-finder outfit, with an office on the signal-platform, and the fixed diamond-frame aerial, on the fore-topgallant-masthead.

Despite the considerable re-arrangement of the ship's structure, the stability was not greatly affected. The calculated metacentric height was slightly reduced to 5.24 feet in the standard and 6.63 feet in the ordinary deep condition.

Trials

Warspite carried out steam trials in March 1937. The performance of the machinery was considered very satisfactory, and during her full-power trial on 15th March, she achieved a mean speed of 23.84 knots with 80,250 shaft horse-power.

Warspite

after 1937 reconstruction: outboard profile early 1943 and deck plans, with subsequent AA positions indicated

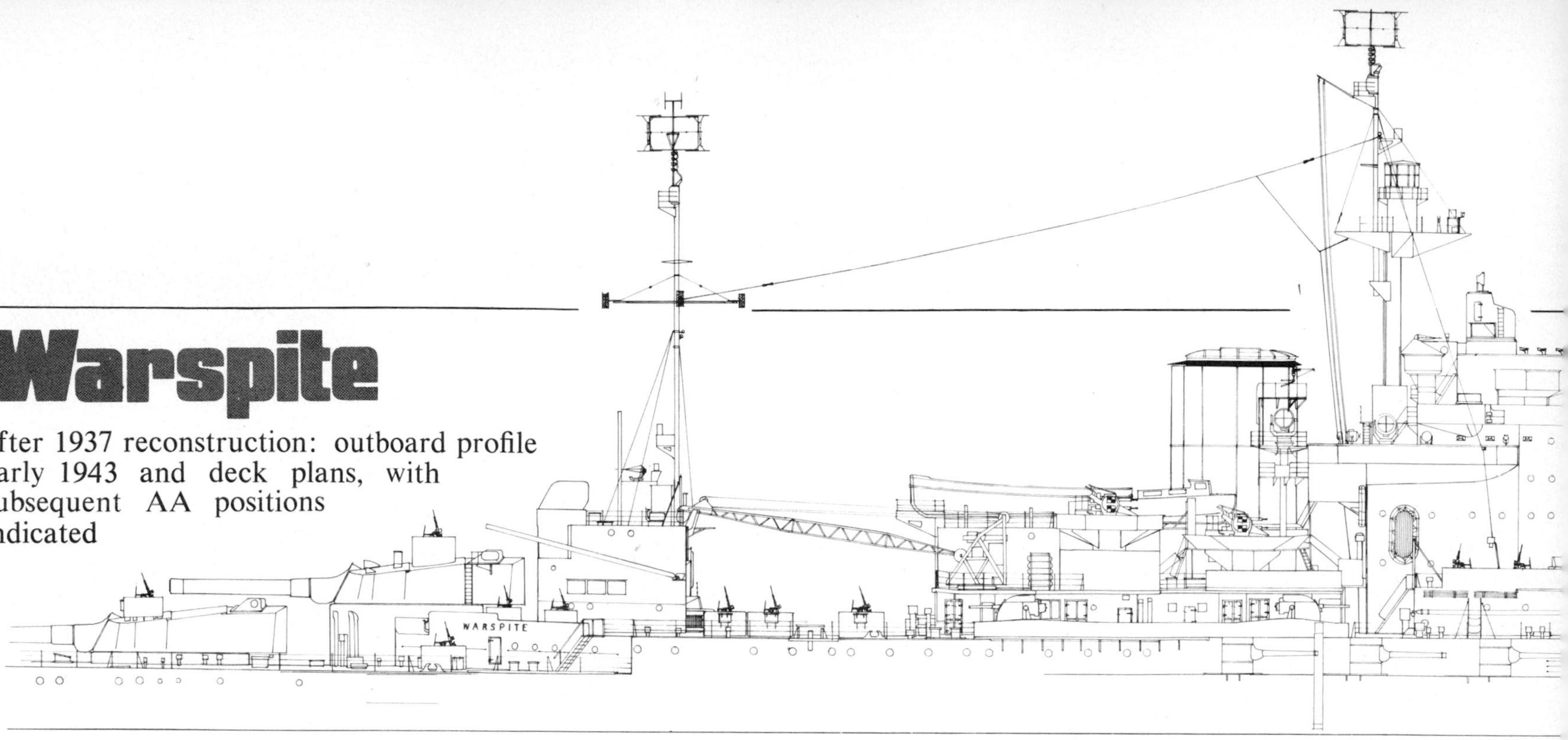

Anti-aircraft gun positions
December 1941:
A Thirteen single 20 mm mounts fitted, including three on the quarterdeck.
B Four 0.5-inch MGs removed.
Autumn 1942:
C Two single 20 mm mounts added.
June 1943:
D Sixteen single 20 mm mounts added, including two on the roof of 'Y' turret and two on the quarter-deck.
June 1944:
E Four twin 20 mm mounts fitted, but only two positions located.
Four single 20 mm mounts removed, from which positions it is not definitely known, but may have been those on the roofs of 'A' and 'Y' turrets.

Shelter-deck▶
1 Store
2 General reading room
3 Beef screen
4 Disinfector compartment
5 Incinerator compartment
6 Pom-pom ready use magazine
7 10-ton Seaplane crane
8 Radar office
9 WCs
10 Store

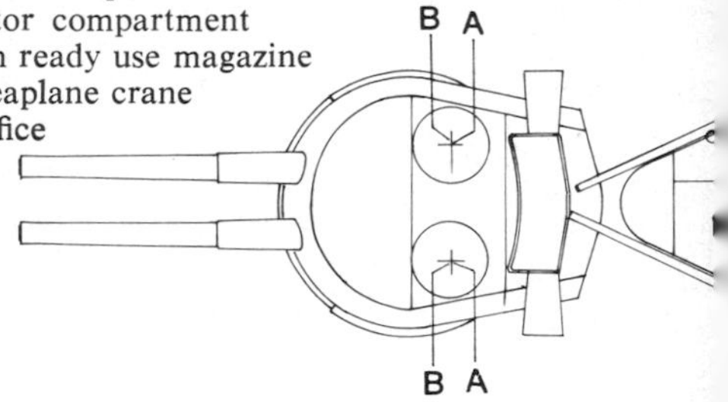

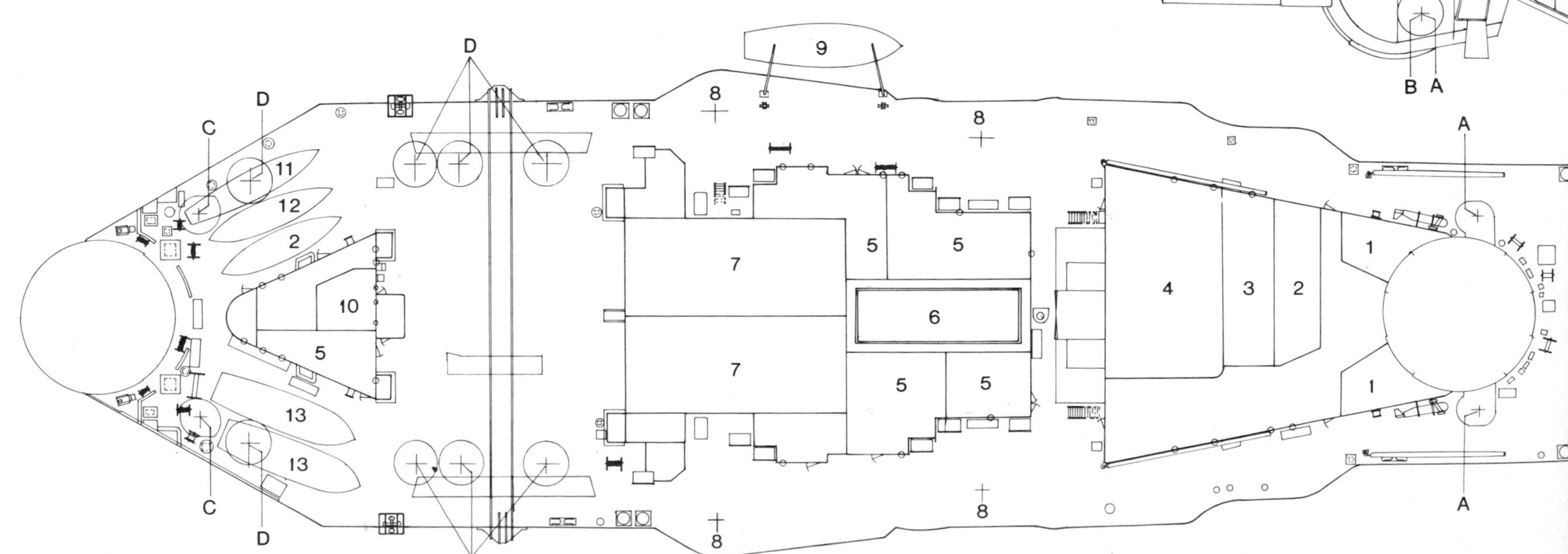

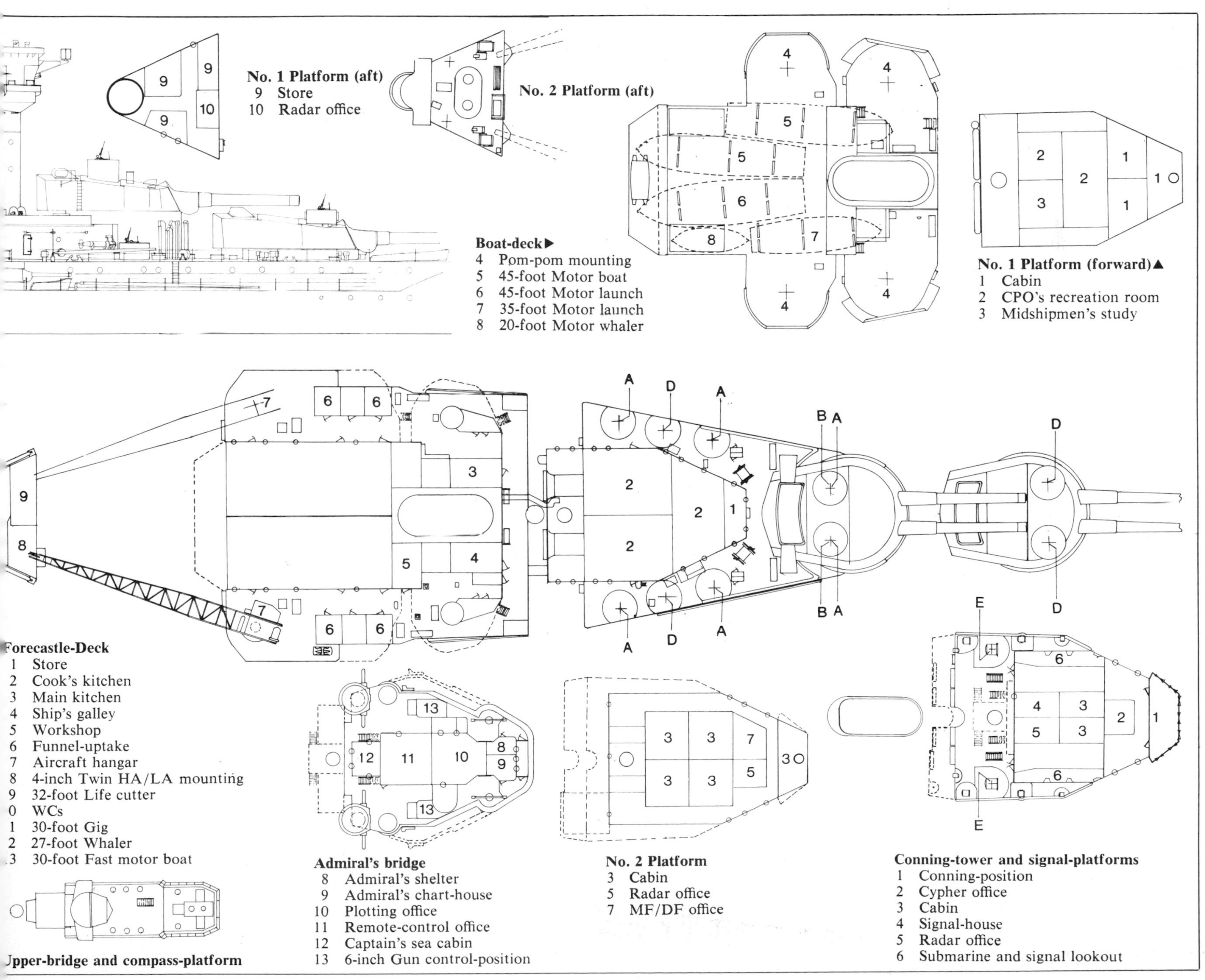

No. 1 Platform (aft)
9 Store
10 Radar office
No. 2 Platform (aft)
Boat-deck▶
4 Pom-pom mounting
5 45-foot Motor boat
6 45-foot Motor launch
7 35-foot Motor launch
8 20-foot Motor whaler
No. 1 Platform (forward)▲
1 Cabin
2 CPO's recreation room
3 Midshipmen's study
Forecastle-Deck
1 Store
2 Cook's kitchen
3 Main kitchen
4 Ship's galley
5 Workshop
6 Funnel-uptake
7 Aircraft hangar
8 4-inch Twin HA/LA mounting
9 32-foot Life cutter
0 WCs
1 30-foot Gig
2 27-foot Whaler
3 30-foot Fast motor boat
Upper-bridge and compass-platform
Admiral's bridge
8 Admiral's shelter
9 Admiral's chart-house
10 Plotting office
11 Remote-control office
12 Captain's sea cabin
13 6-inch Gun control-position
No. 2 Platform
3 Cabin
5 Radar office
7 MF/DF office
Conning-tower and signal-platforms
1 Conning-position
2 Cypher office
3 Cabin
4 Signal-house
5 Radar office
6 Submarine and signal lookout

During the preliminary full-power steering trials, trouble was experienced with the new electro-hydraulic steering gear "in that the rudders were overbalanced and the power required to bring them back from hard-over was found to be much in excess of that provided". As a result, the helm jammed hard-a-starboard which caused the ship to steam in circles, until speed could be sufficiently reduced to enable the rudder to be returned to its fore and aft position. As the original rudders had been retained, it was decided that the only explanation for this behaviour was that the original steam steering gear had developed a much higher power than that for which it was designed. In order to improve the balance of the rudders, their length, forward of the axis, was reduced by eighteen inches, but this did not entirely solve the problem and it was eventually overcome by increasing the relief pressure on the steering gear from 2,000 to 2,400 pounds per square inch. While this work was being carried out, an examination was made of the turbine gearing and propeller shafts. This revealed that the high- and low-pressure couplings on the inner shafts were abnormally worn, while the corresponding couplings on the outer shafts were in reasonably good condition. The cause was eventually traced to interaction of the inner and outer propellers when the ship was turning causing considerable vibration of the inner shaft, on the outside of the turn. (When the ship was turning, the stream of disturbed water from the outer propeller on the outside of the turn passed through the area occupied by the inner propeller on the outside of the turn.) While this problem was being investigated, the use of the rudder at angles over 5° and at a propeller speed above 200 rpm was to be accompanied by a slowing-down of the outer shaft on the outside of the turn. Special instruments, controlled from the bridge, were installed in the outer turbine rooms, to give effect to these instructions, but this problem was never completely solved and the restrictions remained in force, although they could, naturally, be ignored in an emergency.

The gun trials were carried out, off Spithead, on 22nd, 23rd and 24th March. They were generally satisfactory, and the following points came to light:

1. All turrets could be fired on their war arcs, at 30° of elevation, without causing important structural damage to the ship. (These arcs were measured from ahead. When the turrets faced directly forward, they were on 0° angle of bearing; facing directly aft, their angle of bearing was 180°.) The war arc for 'A' and 'B' turrets was 140°, that for 'X' and 'Y' turrets was 40°.

2. The control-positions on the bridge (for the

PARTICULARS OF *WARSPITE*, 1930 to 1946

Displacement

	Standard	Deep
1933	31,446 tons	36,372 tons*
1937	31,315 tons	36,450 tons*

*Including 815 tons of water in water-protection compartments.

Dimensions
Length and beam remained unchanged.
Draught (1937): deep 33 feet 10 inches (forward), 32 feet 4 inches (aft); standard 29 feet 1 inch (forward), 28 feet 6 inches (aft).

Armament (1937 to 1946)
Eight 15-inch Mk I: four twin mountings Mk I (N).
Eight 6-inch Mk XII: single mountings P IX (removed 1944).
Eight 4-inch Mk XVI: four high-angle/low-angle twin mountings Mk XIX.
Thirty-two 2-pounder Mk VIII: four mountings Mk VI.
Sixteen 0.5-inch machine-guns Mk III: four mountings Mk II (removed 1941).
Eleven 20-mm single Oerlikons added 1941.
Four 20-mm single Oerlikons added 1942.
Sixteen 20-mm single Oerlikons added 1943.
Four 20-mm single Oerlikons removed 1944.
Four 20-mm twin Oerlikons added 1944.
Total: 20-mm Oerlikon armament in 1945 = thirty-five (27 × 1, 4 × 2).
Four 3-pounder saluting guns Mk I (removed 1939).

Ammunition stowage
15-inch: 100 rounds per gun; 6 shrapnel rounds per gun.
6-inch: 150 rounds per gun.
4-inch: 250 rounds per gun; 250 star shell per ship.
2-pounder: 750 rounds per gun.
0.5-inch: 2,500 rounds per gun.
3-pounder (saluting): 64 rounds per gun.

Fire-control equipment (1937)
Main armament: one director-control tower, one tripod-type director, one Admiralty fire-control table Mk VII.
Secondary armament: two pedestal-type sights, two Admiralty fire-control clocks Mk VI.
High-angle/low-angle armament: two HACS Mk III.
Close-range AA armament: four pom-pom directors Mk I**

Range-finders
Two 30-foot in 'B' and 'X' turrets.
Six 15-foot in main director-control tower armoured director-hood (aft), HACS directors and 'A' and 'Y' turrets.
Two 9-foot on admiral's bridge.

Searchlights and signalling-projectors
Two 44-inch on funnel; two 36-inch (removed 1944); four 18-inch, four 10-inch on signal-bridge.

Armour (1937)
As in 1918, except for the following.
Middle-deck: 5 inch (4 inch NC + 1 inch HT) over magazines, 3½ inch (2½ inch NC + 1 inch HT) over machinery.
Main-deck (forward): 3⅛ inch (1⅞ inch + 1¼ inch).
6-inch gun-battery: 2 inch NC.
Conning-tower: 3 inch sides and front, 2 inch back NC.
Communication tube: 4 inch and 3 inch NC.
After director-hood: 4 inch.
After director-hood support: 6 inch and 2 inch.

Machinery
Parsons single-reduction geared turbines, four shafts. 30,000 SHP = 23.5 knots at 300 rpm.
Maximum sea-going speed, 72,000 SHP = 22.5 knots.
Six Admiralty three-drum small-tube boilers.

Fuel and endurance
3,501 tons oil fuel, 208 tons diesel fuel.

*Endurance	Speed	SHP	Fuel consumption	Range
With clean bottom	12 knots	7,400	5 tons/hour	7,579 n.miles
6 months out of dock	12 knots	9,900	6.5 tons/hour	5,830 n.miles

*Estimated 1936. The above figures were based on the assumption of starting in the ordinary deep condition with 95 per cent of the oil fuel capacity (3,509 tons) and allowing 5 per cent for residue, and a further 5 per cent for bad weather, leaving 3,158 tons of oil available.

secondary and high-angle armaments, and the 9-foot range-finders) would have to be abandoned when 'B' turret was firing at 30° elevation, and angles of training beyond 115°.
3. To avoid damaging an aircraft on the catapult, the limit on turret training was 130° for 'B' turret, and 80° for 'X' turret. The limit, when an aircraft was in the hangar, was 70° for 'X' turret only.

The extreme bearing and elevation on which 'B' turret was fired during the trials were 135° and 25°. Only the right gun was fired and this destroyed the reflector-lens and the front glass of the starboard 36-inch searchlight on the bridge. All the firings prior to this, caused only minor damage such as breaking welds on vent-trunks and breaking electric-light fittings.

During the trials, trouble was also experienced with funnel smoke being drawn down into the boiler-uptakes.

War modifications

Warspite received no major alterations between the end of her reconstruction and her damage repairs, after the battle for Crete in 1941. During these repairs, which were carried out in the USA, between June and December 1941, the following alterations and additions were carried out:

1. Armament: Four 0.5-inch machine-gun mountings were removed and eleven single 20-mm Oerlikons were fitted.
2. Radar: Type '281' was fitted, with a transmitting office on the starboard side abaft No. 2 bridge-platform, and a receiving office in the after superstructure. Aerials were fitted on the fore- and mainmast-heads. Type '284' office was fitted in the high-frequency direction-finder office on the signalling-platform and aerials on the main director-control tower. Type '271' was fitted, with an aerial on the foremast starfish. Type '285' (two sets) was fitted, with offices at the rear of the admiral's bridge, port and starboard, and aerials were fitted on the HACS directors. Types '282' (four sets) were fitted on the pom-pom directors.
3. Type 'FM2' medium-frequency direction-finder outfit was fitted with an office on No. 2 bridge-platform, and a fixed-frame aerial on the front of the compass-platform.
4. Bridge Modifications: The signal-platform was extended aft by seven feet. The admiral's bridge was increased in width and the forward end was enclosed and fitted with windows.
5. Surface look-out huts were fitted abreast the funnels.
6. Steel screens were fitted on the outboard edges of the forecastle-deck, abreast the 4-inch twin mountings.

While she was serving in the Eastern Fleet, during 1942, a further four single 20-mm Oerlikons were added, and the Type '271' radar set was replaced by Type '273'. In March 1943, she returned home, and between May and June was refitted in preparation for her return to the Mediterranean. Sixteen single 20-mm Oerlikons were added, bringing the total to thirty-one, and her aircraft and catapult equipment were removed. The starboard aircraft hangar was converted to a cinema.

In September 1943, *Warspite* was heavily damaged by a glider-bomb off Salerno. Damage repairs were carried out at Malta, Gibraltar and Rosyth and, probably at the latter dockyard, she was fitted out for use as a bombardment-ship for Operation Overlord. The following alterations and additions were carried out:

1. Four 20-mm Oerlikon twin mountings were fitted and four singles removed.
2. Radar Type '284' was replaced by '274'. Two barrage-directors with '283' radar were fitted on the after superstructure.
3. A Type '650' guided-missile jamming device was fitted.
4. The 6-inch guns were removed and the gun-ports were plated over in order to reduce weight, improve reserve of buoyancy and to provide more space for mess-decks and ablutions.
5. The two 36-inch searchlights were removed from the signal-bridge (they were replaced by two of the 20-mm twin mountings).

Early in 1945, *Warspite* was reduced to category 'C' reserve.

Below: *Warspite* in late 1942.

Below: a broadside view of *Queen Elizabeth,* showing her appearance prior to being taken in hand for reconstruction. The dark mounds visible on the after superstructure are 0.5-inch machine-gun mountings.

Right: *Valiant,* after reconstruction, late in 1939.

Below right: *Queen Elizabeth* in dry-dock at Rosyth, in January 1941, for final fitting out. In the next dock is *Prince of Wales.*

QUEEN ELIZABETH AND VALIANT, 1930 to 1946

Between the end of their bulging refit and 1937, when both were taken in hand for reconstruction, these two ships received few modifications. The alterations that were made are as follows:

Queen Elizabeth
1930: A high-angle control-system Mk I was fitted with a director on the fore-top; two after submerged torpedo tubes were removed and the compartment was sub-divided; the medium-frequency direction-finder was replaced by a new set and a new aerial, both fitted in the same positions as the previous equipment.
1934: The aircraft-platform was removed from 'B' turret.
1936: Two pom-pom Mk VI mountings were fitted on the conning-tower platform; two pom-pom directors were fitted on the new platform, beneath and abreast the fore-top; two 0.5-inch machine-gun mountings, one Mk II and one Mk II*, were fitted on the after superstructure.

Valiant
Circa 1932/33: A second pom-pom Mk V mounting was fitted on the port side of the conning-tower platform; a second pom-pom director was fitted.
1933: The aircraft-platform was removed from 'B' turret.
1936: Two 0.5-inch machine-gun Mk II* mountings were fitted.

Reconstruction, 1937 to 1941

The reconstruction of *Queen Elizabeth* and *Valiant* was generally similar to that of *Warspite,* but included several new features. Principal among these, was a different arrangement for the machinery and the substitution of the 4.5-inch between-decks twin mounting for the original secondary armament. Both these features followed the pattern set in *Renown*, but, as *Queen Elizabeth* was shorter, it also involved greater difficulties in finding sufficient space for the 4.5-inch magazines.

Valiant was taken in hand at Devonport on 1st March 1937, and *Queen Elizabeth,* at Portsmouth on 11th August in the same year.

Armament

As in *Warspite,* the 15-inch mountings were taken out and altered to accept the modified 15-inch shell, and to provide 30° elevation for the guns.

Table 60: Estimated weights before and after reconstruction (*Queen Elizabeth*)

	Before reconstruction:		After reconstruction:	
	Deep displacement	Standard displacement	Deep displacement	Standard displacement
Armament	5,107·6	5,107·6	5,704	5,704
Machinery	3,765	3,765	2,280	2,280
Equipment	1,256·7	944·1	1,343	1,057
Armour	5,400	5,400	6,017	6,017
Hull and protective plating	16,578	16,578	17,124	17,124
Oil fuel	3,417		3,581	
Reserve feed-water	492		316	
Total (tons):	36,006·3	31,794·7	36,365	32,182

The entire 6-inch gun armament, its equipment and protection were removed, and the embrasures on each side were plated over. This naturally improved the watertightness of the ship above the upper-deck, and increased the reserve of buoyancy. In its place ten 4.5-inch high-angle/low-angle twin mountings were fitted in a four-cornered arrangement, similar to that of *Renown.* Three were mounted on each side of the forecastle-deck forward, and two, on each side of the upper-deck aft. The forecastle-deck was cut back on each side to accommodate the after mountings, in order to keep them clear of the aircraft catapult and the blast of 'X' and 'Y' turrets.

The removal of the 6-inch gun armament was not undertaken without some misgivings. Although of limited use against aircraft, its effectiveness against surface targets was considered much superior to the 4.5-inch gun, because of the greater stopping power of its heavier projectile. It was considered, however, that this disadvantage could be accepted in

Table 61: Estimated armament weights (*Queen Elizabeth*)

	Before reconstruction	After reconstruction
Revolving weight of main armament	3,200·5	3,260
Fixed weight of main armament	275·4	260
15-inch shell and cordite	1,086	1,056
6-inch guns and mountings	192	
6-inch shell and cordite	112	
4·5-inch guns and mountings		418
4.5-inch ammunition (including RU)		375
4-inch guns and mountings	26·8	
4-inch ammunition	29·3	
2-pounder pom-pom guns and mountings	31·3	64
2-pounder pom-pom main ammunition	48	115
2-pounder pom-pom RU ammunition		18
0·5-inch machine-guns	2·3	6
0·5-inch ammunition	2	4
Catapult		34
Aircraft		21
Torpedoes	59	3
Bombs and pyrotechnics		17
Depth-charges		4
Paravanes	3	2
Small arms	23·9	37
Fuses, miscellaneous stores and SASO stores	15·1	10
Total weight of armament:	5,107·6	5,704

Table 62: Estimated armour weights (*Queen Elizabeth*)

	Before reconstruction	After reconstruction
13-inch belt	1,909	1,909
6-inch belt	484	484
6-inch belt (below main-deck)	319	319
4-inch belt (below main-deck)	138	138
Bulkheads	315	315
Barbettes	1,166	1,166
Backing	100	100
Bolts	45	45
Battery protection (upper-deck)	445	
Battery protection (main-deck)	123	114
After tower and 6-inch hoods	17	
Conning-tower	339	52
Main-deck over soft end, forward		108
Middle-deck over magazines, forward		259
Middle-deck over machinery		624
Middle-deck over magazines, aft		312
Armour support to director-control tower, aft		17
15-inch director-control tower, aft (ex forward conning-tower)		55
Total (tons):	5,400	6,017

view of the importance of anti-aircraft defence, and the great improvement in this respect that would be achieved by the fitting of the 4.5-inch armament. The forward 6-inch magazines were converted to accommodate the ammunition for the forward 4.5-inch guns. The magazines for the after 4.5-inch mounting were built into the after part of the original engine rooms, at lower-deck level.

The close-range armament was the same as that fitted in *Warspite*, with four pom-pom Mk VI mountings grouped around the funnel, and four 0.5-inch machine-gun Mk III mountings, two on 'B' and two on 'X' turrets. The fire-control equipment was similar to that in *Renown*, but the port and starboard high-angle/low-angle directors were mounted closer together, by fitting them at staggered heights, and allowing their range-finders to overlap. Both forward and aft, the port-side director was lower than that to starboard.

The forward submerged torpedo tubes were removed and the compartments were sub-divided. The aircraft equipment was the same as that provided in *Renown*.

Armour

The approved deck protection was the same as that fitted in *Warspite*, that is, 4-inch non-cemented over the magazines and 2½-inch non-cemented over the machinery. Consideration, however, was given to re-arranging the protection, in order to eliminate the following weak points:

"(1) Plunging shell may strike the middle deck between the side armour and the added [deck] protection.

(2) Bombs could penetrate to below the middle deck and explode in the wing compartments without passing through any horizontal protection except the ordinary structural steel decks.

(3) A shell could penetrate the base of the barbette after passing through only 4 inches of turret [sic] armour."

The alternative proposals for deck protection were:

1. Fit the same armour thickness on the main-deck, instead of on the middle-deck.

2. Extend the armoured-deck five feet outboard of the torpedo bulkhead on each side. Reduce the thickness of the middle-deck over the magazines from 4 to 2½ inches, and fit 5-inch armour on the full width of the upper-deck, over the magazines.

3. Leave the armour on the middle-deck over the machinery at 2½ inches, as approved. Fit 1½-inch armour on the middle-deck over the magazines extending five feet outboard of the torpedo bulkhead, and fit 4-inch armour on the upper-deck, over the magazines.

None of these proposals, however, were adopted presumably because of the increased top-weight and reduced stability they would entail. The armour arrangement of *Warspite* was repeated, therefore, with the addition of 2-inch – 1½-inch armour, over the soft forward end on the main-deck, between the foremost armoured bulkhead and 'A' barbette.

Machinery

The machinery and general internal layout was developed from a proposal by the Engineer-in-Chief to fit eight boilers instead of six as in *Warspite*. All four of the original boiler rooms were used, but these were reduced in width from 56 feet to 32½ feet by the fitting of new wing bulkheads. The wing compartments thus formed, were further sub-divided by the addition of platform-decks, thereby increasing the number of watertight compartments per boiler room, from one to five. No centre-line longitudinal bulkhead was fitted, as in *Warspite*, and each of the boiler rooms, therefore, contained two instead of one boiler. The wing compartments were used for reserve-feed water tanks, turbo- and diesel-generator compartments, and air-compressor compartments.

Parsons geared-turbines replaced the direct-drive turbines as in *Warspite*, but the machinery arrangements was recast. The original engine rooms were divided into three groups, by the addition of two transverse bulkheads, and these were further sub-divided by the inclusion of a longitudinal centre-line bulkhead. The foremost group contained the

Below: *Queen Elizabeth* just out of Rosyth, in February 1941, before beginning trials.

four turbine rooms, the centre group contained the four gearing rooms, and the after group contained the 4.5-inch magazines, auxiliary-machinery compartments, oil-fuel tanks and shaft passages.

The auxiliary machinery was generally similar to that fitted in *Renown*.

Bridge and superstructure

The superstructure above the forecastle-deck was completely rebuilt, following the practice adopted in the earlier reconstructions. The bridge was arranged on very similar lines to that of *Renown*, but differed in detail and was slightly larger. In order to reduce the likelihood of smoke being drawn into the bridge, boiler-uptakes and after structure, the funnel was sited farther away from the bridge and was higher than that fitted in *Warspite*. In addition, the funnels were fitted with "funnel air jets" designed to blow the funnel gases vertically upwards as far as possible before they began their horizontal and, usually, downward trend. It is assumed that the air-jets were supplied by the air-compressor machinery, as there are no outwardly visible signs of a natural supply of this type, which would in any case have been somewhat unreliable.

As the funnel was farther aft, the hangars were placed abreast instead of behind it, as in *Warspite,* and this allowed the catapult to be placed farther forward, and the after superstructure to be enlarged. *Queen Elizabeth* was fitted with tripod fore and mainmasts, and *Valiant* was fitted with a tripod foremast and a pole mainmast.

Completion and trials

Valiant's reconstruction was completed on 25th November 1939, and in December, she carried out her sea trials. The preliminary two-hour full-power trial on the 11th, produced the following results:

Displacement, 36,000 tons.
Draught, 32 feet (forward) 32¾ feet (aft).
Mean rpm, 296.
Mean shaft horse-power, 80,620.
Oil fuel consumption, 28.2 tons/hour= 0.789 lb/SHP/hour.
Number of runs, six.
Best run, 298 rpm with 80,870 shaft horse-power.
Conditions, Wind Force 4, Sea 2 – 3.

No speed could be recorded, because war conditions required the ship to steam a zigzag course without streaming a log. In addition, the ship had a dirty bottom, having been out of dock for three months, and she had her paravanes streamed. During a later trial, she developed 80,314 shaft horse-power.

The funnel air jets were also tried out on 11th December, under the supervision of one of the assistant constructors, Mr. Purvis, who rendered the following report:

"Steaming out the wind was astern and it had been arranged with CO, who was very helpful in arranging trials, to turn ship into the wind at 1300.

At 1300 a message was received ordering the ship to Portland and the CO decided he could not proceed with the trials. I did however try out the jets when the relative wind was 40–60 ft. per second and 30° off the bow. When jets were not in use, the funnel gas burbled [sic] over the funnel top on windward side along the front half of funnel and was then swept aft along funnel top.

On reaching aft end of funnel, this stray stream was sucked down a few feet but rejoined the main smoke stream. With funnel jets in use, this did not occur, the funnel gas stream coming straight out of the funnel, their being no trace of any smoke leaving main smoke stream.

The main smoke stream reached sea level at a greater distance from the ship than before.

In both above cases, the hangar doors were closed . . .

For a short period just before 1300 ship was head to wind and making smoke but no smoke left main stream to percolate down to

Below: the bow of *Valiant,* after her refit, on 5th May 1943. Note the staggered heights of the HACS directors.

boiler intakes as in the case of *Warspite* and the smoke cleared the ship aft.

From the very short observation it does appear that any trouble on *Valiant* (without jets) would have been on a much smaller scale than that in *Warspite,* presumably due to increased funnel height and better relative position of funnel and bridge in *Valiant.*"

Steering trials revealed that the rudders, modified after the experience in *Warspite,* were still slightly-overbalanced. Trouble was also encountered with interaction of the inner and outer propellers, and, as with *Warspite,* restrictions were placed on the use of the helm at high speeds. (This trouble was also encountered in *Queen Elizabeth.*)

In almost all other respects, the ship was found to be entirely satisfactory. No serious damage was caused by blast during the gun trials, the bridge was almost completely free of vibration and unpleasant draughts, and the ship, as a whole, was not greatly affected by vibration even at the after end.

After her trials, *Valiant* sailed for the West Indies, to work up before returning home to join the Home Fleet, in February 1940.

On the outbreak of war in September 1939, the completion of reconstructions was given high priority and in the case of *Queen Elizabeth,* equipment was diverted from other ships in order to expedite her completion. She did however, take much longer to reconstruct, than her sister ship. Late in 1940, it was decided to move her from Portsmouth dockyard which was suffering heavy air raids. She sailed on 12th December 1940, and three days later, arrived at Rosyth dockyard where the reconstruction was completed on 31st January 1941.

Queen Elizabeth's full-power trial was due to take place on 25th February. The weather was fine and the wind, Force 4. After a preliminary steering trial, the full-power trial was started but it was abandoned soon after because of heavy vibration in 'X' turbine, and – to a lesser extent – in 'Y' turbine. During the following few days, the turbines were opened up and damage was found to have been caused by a nut or piece of a broken file that had been left in the casing of 'X' turbine. The trouble was not serious, however, and she later produced 80,301 shaft horsepower on full-power trials.

As in *Valiant,* no serious trouble was encountered with funnel smoke, gun-blast, draughts or vibration, her Captain and officers were generally very pleased with the ship.

Below: an aerial view of *Valiant* on 26th May 1943. Note the extra length of the lower fore-yard.

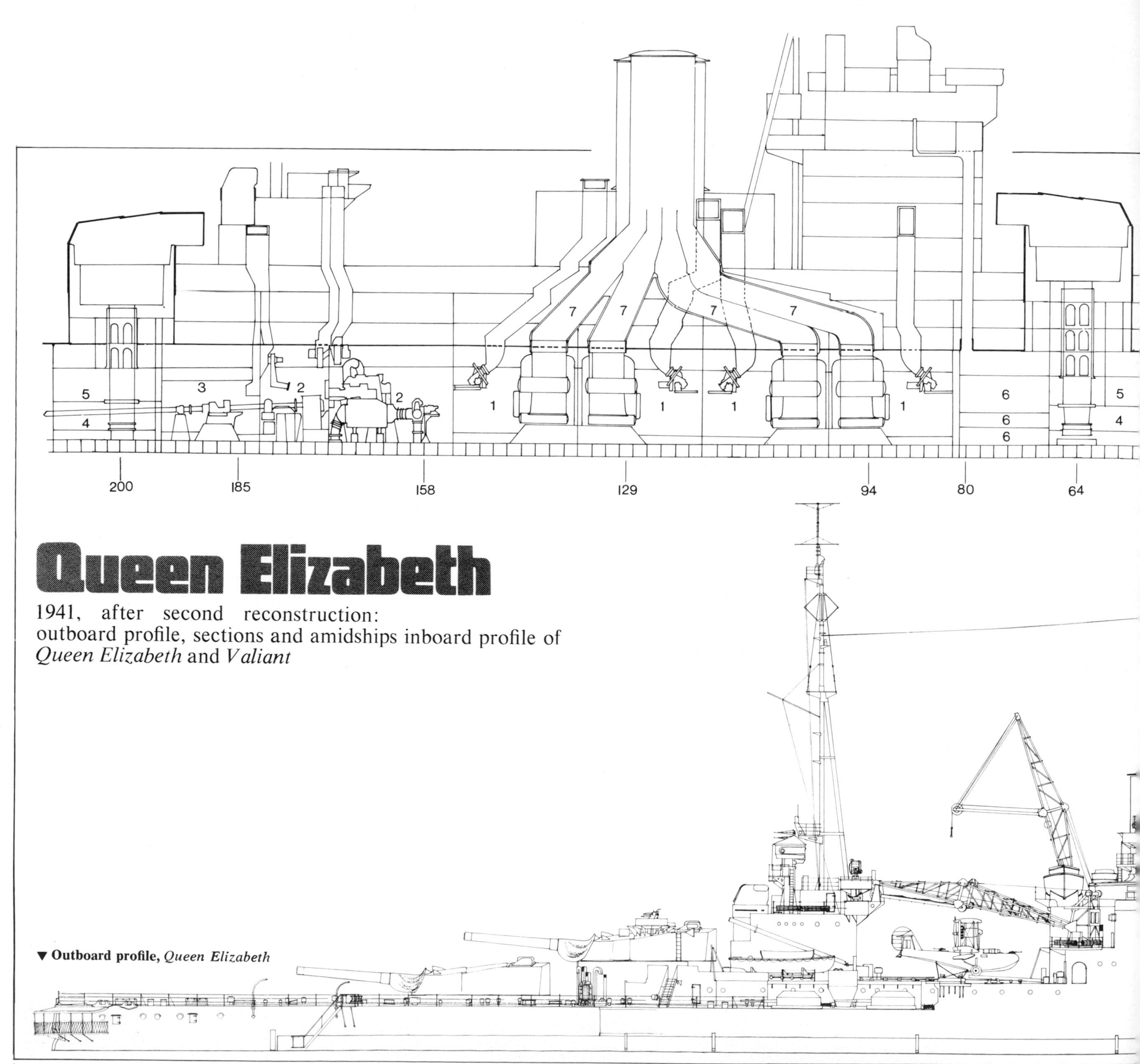

Queen Elizabeth

1941, after second reconstruction:
outboard profile, sections and amidships inboard profile of *Queen Elizabeth* and *Valiant*

▼ **Outboard profile,** *Queen Elizabeth*

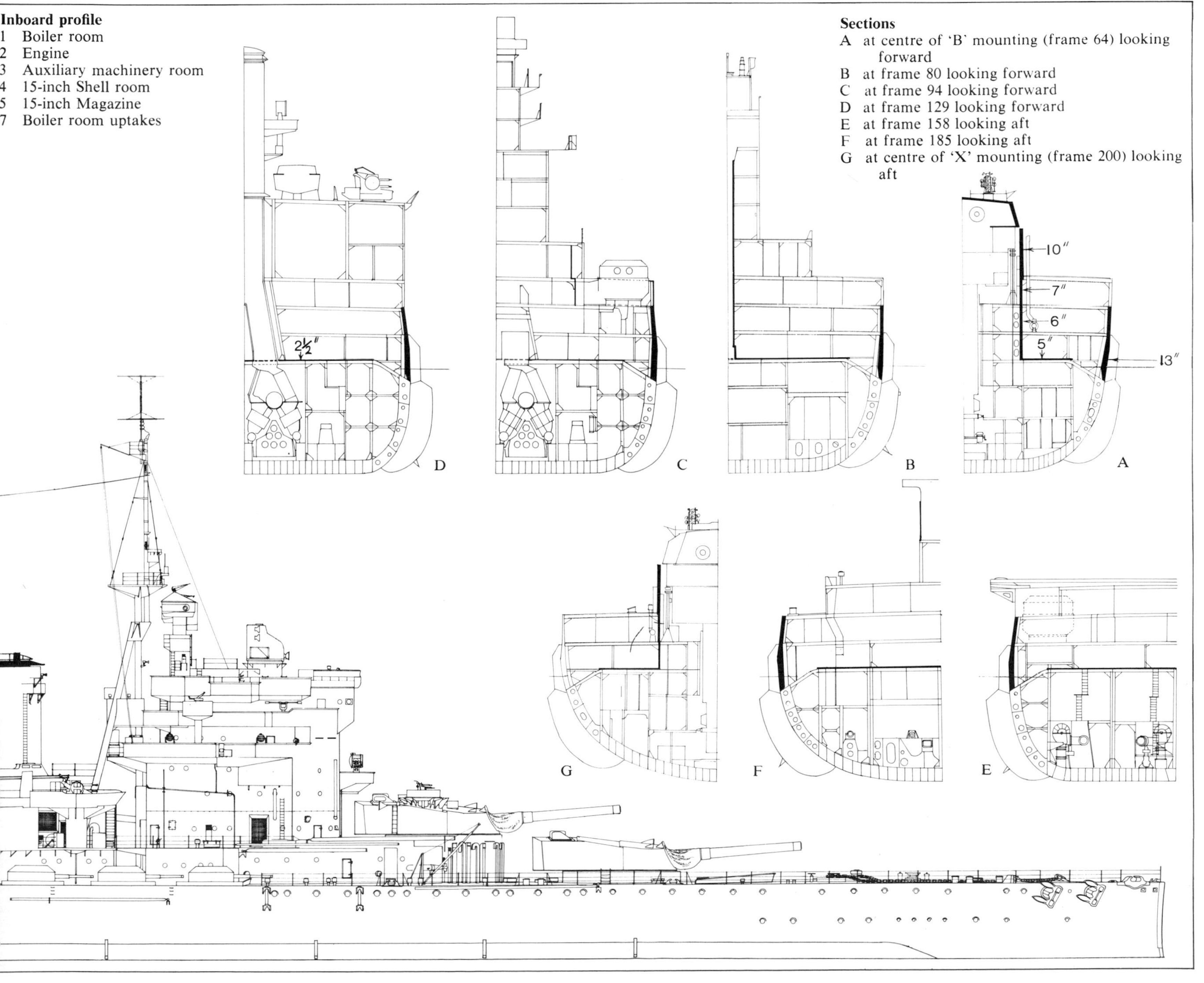

Inboard profile
1 Boiler room
2 Engine
3 Auxiliary machinery room
4 15-inch Shell room
5 15-inch Magazine
7 Boiler room uptakes
Sections
A at centre of 'B' mounting (frame 64) looking forward
B at frame 80 looking forward
C at frame 94 looking forward
D at frame 129 looking forward
E at frame 158 looking aft
F at frame 185 looking aft
G at centre of 'X' mounting (frame 200) looking aft
2½″
10″
7″
6″
5″
13″
D
C
B
A
G
F
E

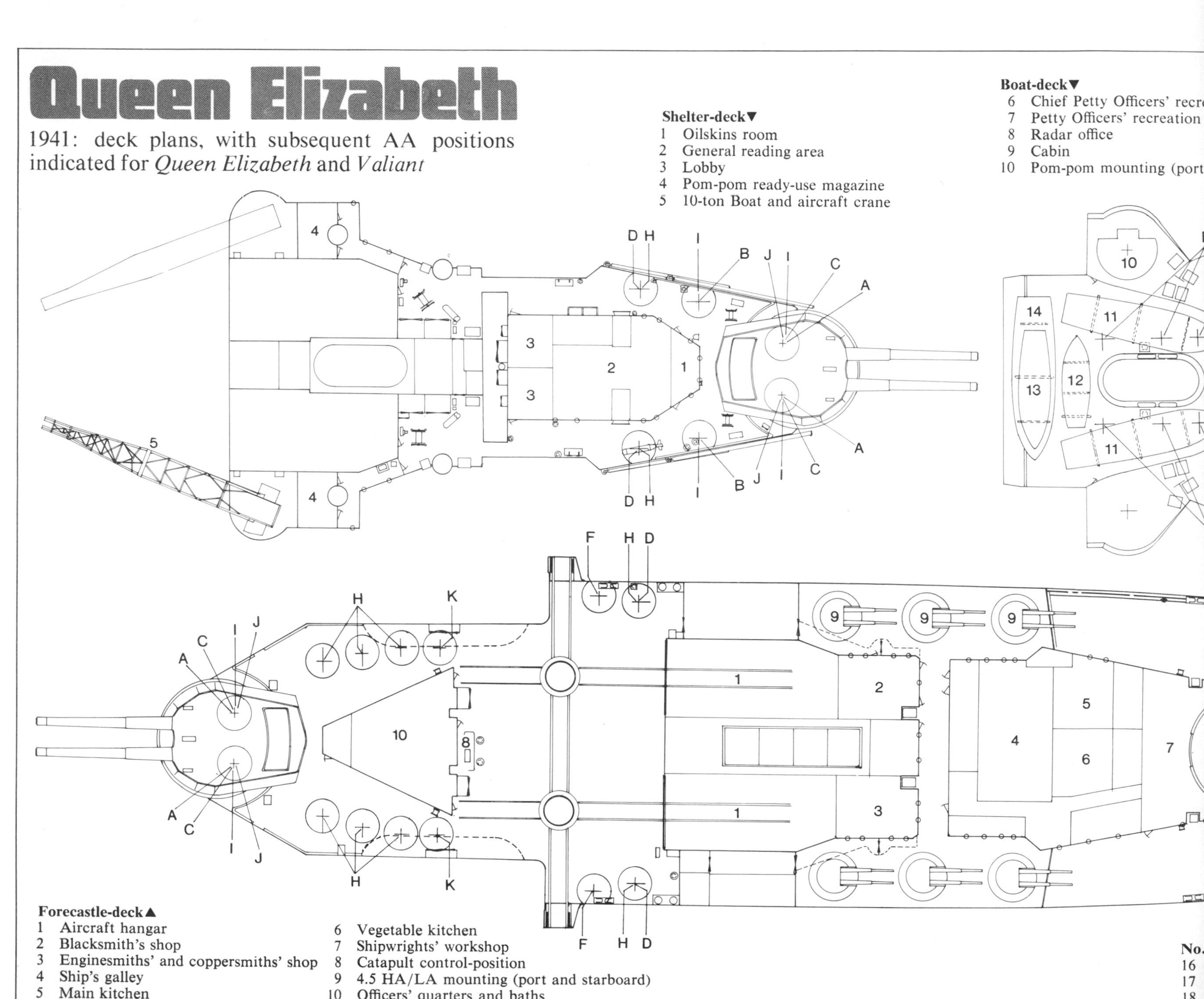
Queen Elizabeth
1941: deck plans, with subsequent AA positions indicated for *Queen Elizabeth* and *Valiant*
Shelter-deck▼
1 Oilskins room
2 General reading area
3 Lobby
4 Pom-pom ready-use magazine
5 10-ton Boat and aircraft crane
Boat-deck▼
6 Chief Petty Officers' recre
7 Petty Officers' recreation
8 Radar office
9 Cabin
10 Pom-pom mounting (port
Forecastle-deck▲
1 Aircraft hangar
2 Blacksmith's shop
3 Enginesmiths' and coppersmiths' shop
4 Ship's galley
5 Main kitchen
6 Vegetable kitchen
7 Shipwrights' workshop
8 Catapult control-position
9 4.5 HA/LA mounting (port and starboard)
10 Officers' quarters and baths
No.
16
17
18

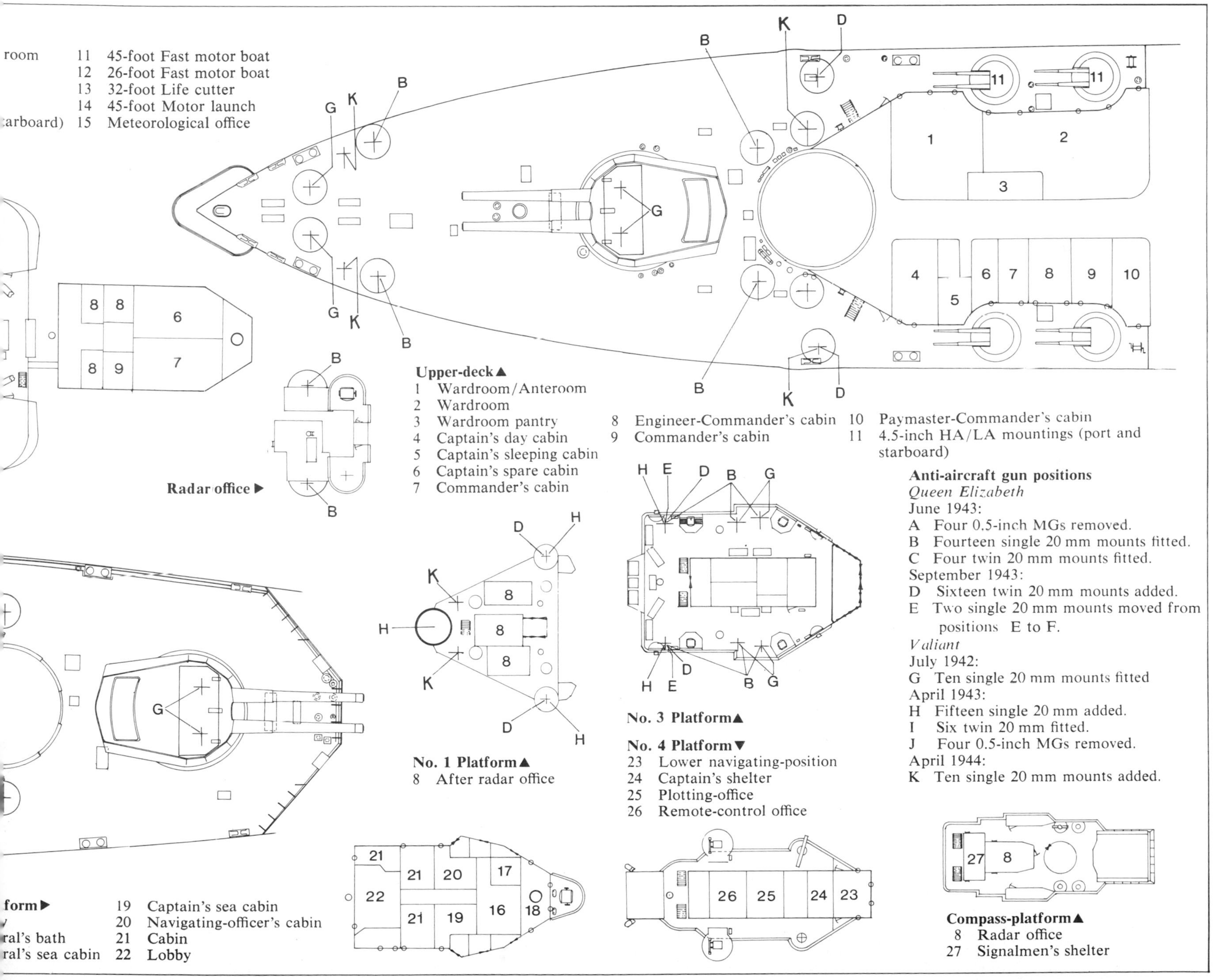

Anti-aircraft gun positions

Queen Elizabeth

June 1943:

A Four 0.5-inch MGs removed.
B Fourteen single 20 mm mounts fitted.
C Four twin 20 mm mounts fitted.

September 1943:

D Sixteen twin 20 mm mounts added.
E Two single 20 mm mounts moved from positions E to F.

Valiant

July 1942:

G Ten single 20 mm mounts fitted

April 1943:

H Fifteen single 20 mm added.
I Six twin 20 mm fitted.
J Four 0.5-inch MGs removed.

April 1944:

K Ten single 20 mm mounts added.

Below: *Queen Elizabeth* in September 1943, after a short refit.

War modifications to *Valiant*

December 1939:
Type '279' radar was fitted, with a transmitting office at the after end of the lower bridge, between the legs of the fore tripod mast, and a receiving office on the after superstructure.

Refit at Durban, 15th April 1942 to 7th July 1942:
Ten single 20-mm Oerlikons were fitted (it is possible that some of these were fitted prior to the refit). Radar Types '284', '273', '285' (four sets) and '282' (four sets) were fitted. Type '279' was replaced by Type '281'.

Refit at Devonport, 4th March 1943 to 28th April 1943:
Fifteen single and six twin 20-mm Oerlikon mountings were fitted, and four 0.5-inch machine-gun mountings were removed.
Catapult and aircraft equipment were removed, and boat stowage was re-arranged.
Two pom-pom directors on the after superstructure re-positioned on the hangar roofs. Type '284' radar was replaced by Type '274'.

Mid-1943 to mid-1944:
Ten single 20-mm Oerlikons were added, making a total of 35 singles and six twins.
Four Type '285' radar sets were replaced by Type '275'.
Four barrage-directors with Type '283' radar were fitted.

In August 1944, *Valiant* was being refitted at Trincomalee, in the floating dock, AFD 28. On 8th August, this dock suddenly collapsed causing extensive damage to the ship. She was temporarily repaired and sent back to the UK where she underwent repairs and refit at Devonport, between 7th February 1945 and 18th April 1946. During this period, she was fitted with a tripod mainmast, struts to the fore-topmast, a new deck-house over the catapult-deck, on which the boats were stowed, and her 44-inch searchlights and their platforms and equipment were removed. Shortly after the completion of this refit, she became part of the stokers' training-ship *Impérieuse* at Devonport.

Her close-range AA armament at the end of the war, is something of a mystery. The armament listed for the ship in October 1945 (when she was being refitted at Devonport) was:
Sixty-eight 2-pounder pom-poms (6 x 8 + 5 x 4).
Ten 40-mm single Bofors.
Six 40-mm single Boffins.
Sixteen 20-mm (7 x 2 hand-operated, + 2 x 1).

This considerable increase in the close-range AA fire power is of the order that might be expected to be fitted, as defence against Kamikaze attacks. It is not known, however, if the increases were made prior to August 1944, or were being fitted at Trincomalee when the dock collapsed, or were going to be fitted during her refit at Devonport. In April 1946, when her refit ended, the ship carried six eight-barrel and two four-barrel pom-poms, twelve 40-mm singles, seven hand-operated 20-mm twins, and two 20-mm singles. The positions of the 40-mm and 20-mm weapons are not known, but the two additional eight-barrelled pom-poms were fitted abreast the funnel, and the four-barrelled pom-poms, on 'B' and 'X' turrets.

War modifications to *Queen Elizabeth*

January 1941:
On the completion of her reconstruction, she carried radar Types '279', '284' and '285' (four sets).

Damage repairs and refit at Norfolk Navy Yard USA, 6th September 1942 to 1st June 1943:
Fourteen single, and four twin 20-mm Oerlikons were fitted and four 0.5-inch machine-gun mountings were removed.
Radar Types '273', '282' (four sets) and '283' (four sets) were fitted.
August to September 1943:
Sixteen twin 20-mm Oerlikon mountings were added.
Aircraft catapult and equipment were removed and boat stowage was re-arranged.
A direction-finder outfit was fitted on the quarter-deck.
The pom-pom directors on the after superstructure were moved to the hangar roofs.

Very little information, photographic or othewise, is available about the modifications made to *Queen Elizabeth* during 1944 to 1945. She was refitted at Durban, between 6th October and 17th November 1944, but very few alterations appear to have been made to the ship at that time. It is known that the two 44-inch searchlights on the after superstructure were removed, and it is possible that the AA armament was further increased.

Displacement increases

Like *Renown*, a substantial increase of over 1,000 tons occurred in the displacements of *Queen Elizabeth* and *Valiant* between their leaving Home Waters in 1943, and mid-1944 when they were serving with the Eastern Fleet. The resultant increase in draught was regarded with some concern, because the advantage in stability provided by the bulge was considerably reduced. It was proposed therefore, that no further alterations and additions involving additional weight be made to the ships without equal compensatory weights being surrendered elsewhere. It was also decided that action should be taken to lighten the ships.

PARTICULARS OF *QUEEN ELIZABETH* AND *VALIANT*, 1936 to 1946

Except where noted, details are as on completion of reconstructions.

Displacement	Standard	Deep*
Queen Elizabeth, 1936	31,795 tons	36,821 tons
Valiant, 1939	31,585 tons	36,513 tons
Queen Elizabeth, 1943	32,700 tons	37,385 tons
Queen Elizabeth, 1944	34,000 tons (approx)	38,450 tons

*Includes 815 tons of water protection.

Draught	Standard	Deep
Queen Elizabeth, 1936	29 feet 6 inches (forward) 29 feet 6 inches (aft)	33 feet 3 inches (forward) 33 feet 6 inches (aft)
Valiant, 1939	28 feet 9 inches (mean)	31 feet 8 inches (forward) 34 feet (aft)
Queen Elizabeth, 1943		33 feet 10 inches (forward) 33 feet 6 inches (aft)
Queen Elizabeth, 1944		34 feet 6 inches (mean)

Armament
Eight 15-inch Mk I: four mountings Mk I (N).
Twenty 4.5-inch Mk III: ten high-angle/low angle twin mountings Mk II.
Twenty-four 2-pounder Mk VIII: four mountings Mk VI.
Sixteen 0.5-inch Mk III: four mountings Mk III.

Close-range AA armament, 1944
Queen Elizabeth:
Thirty-two 2-pounder (4 × 8), fifty-four 20-mm (20 × 2 + 14 × 1).
Valiant:
Thirty-two 2-pounder (4 × 8), forty-seven 20-mm (6 × 2 + 35 × 1).

Ammunition stowage
15-inch: 106 rounds per gun.
4.5-inch: 250 high-angle rounds per gun; 150 low-angle rounds per gun.
2-pounder: 1,800 rounds per gun.
0.5-inch: 2,500 rounds per gun.

Fire-control equipment
Main armament: one director-control tower, one tripod-type director in armoured tower aft, one Admiralty fire-control table Mk VII.

Secondary armament: four high-angle/low-angle directors Mk IV, four HACS tables Mk IV, four Admiralty fire-control clocks Mk VII (M).

Pom-poms: four pom-pom directors Mk III*.

Range-finders
Two 30-foot in 'B' and 'X' turrets.
Eight 15-foot in 'A' and 'Y' turrets, main DCT, after DCT, and four high-angle/low-angle directors.
Two 9-foot on lower bridge.

Searchlights
Five 44-inch (two removed *circa* 1944/45); four 20-inch and four 10-inch signalling-projectors.

Armour
Except where noted below, the armour remained as it had been in 1919.
Conning-tower: 3 inch and 2 inch NC.
Conning-tower tube: 4 inch and 3 inch.
After director-control tower: 4 inch hood, 6 inch support.
Box protection to 4.5-inch mountings: 2 inch and 1 inch D steel.
Deck (flat): 5 inch (4 inch NC + 1 inch HT) over main and secondary magazines, $2\frac{1}{2}$ inch ($1\frac{1}{2}$ inch NC + 1 inch HT) over machinery.
Main-deck (forward): $1\frac{7}{8}$ inch.

Machinery
Parsons single-reduction geared turbines, four shafts. 80,000 SHP = 24 knots at 300 rpm.
Maximum sea-going speed 72,000 SHP = 23.5 knots.
Eight Admiralty three-drum small-tube boilers.
Maximum working pressure 400 pounds per square inch.

Fuel
Oil-fuel capacity (max 95% full): 3,393 tons oil fuel, 202 tons Diesel fuel (*Valiant*); 3,366 tons oil fuel, 204 tons Diesel fuel (*Queen Elizabeth*). (95% stowage in 1936 was 3,300 tons oil fuel and 107 tons Diesel fuel.

Three views of *Queen Elizabeth* after her repair and refit in June 1943 in the United States.

Below: *Renown* in 1933. Note the aircraft catapult abaft the after funnel and the crane on the starboard side.

RENOWN, 1930 to 1946

Renown was refitted at Portsmouth, between 1931 and June 1932, during which time the following alterations were carried out:

1. A HACS Mk I was fitted, with a director on the fore-top roof.
2. The conning-tower platform was extended aft, to provide platforms for two pom-pom mountings, and positions for two pom-pom directors were provided on the fore-top roof.
3. One pom-pom Mk V mounting and one director were fitted on the starboard side. Equipment for the port side was not available at the time of the refit.
4. Two after searchlight-towers were removed from the second funnel.

In 1933, an aircraft catapult was fitted amidships, on the shelter-deck, between the after funnel and the mainmast. This addition entailed the removal of the midship 4-inch triple gun-mounting. Some time after this, a second pom-pom Mk V mounting was fitted on the port side, but the director was not fitted. At the same time, she was fitted with two 0.5-inch machine-gun Mk II* quadruple mountings.

Reconstruction, 1936 to 1939

Renown was taken in hand at Portsmouth Dockyard, in September 1936, for a complete reconstruction along similar lines to that carried out in *Warspite*. There were, however, some important differences because the ship was of a different type, and her deck protection had already been substantially increased during her 1923 to 1926 refit. The reconstruction was completed on 2nd September 1939.

Armament

The 15-inch gun turrets were taken out and converted to Mk I (N) standard, with 30° elevation. The 15-inch projectiles were converted from existing shells, and had an improved calibre radius head. As in *Warspite*, a new director-control tower was fitted on the bridge, and the armoured director-hood and support from the original conning-tower was refitted on the after superstructure.

The entire secondary and AA armament was replaced by completely new equipment. The principal feature of this new armament was the provision of twenty 4.5-inch guns, in the new high-angle/low-angle between-decks twin mounting which was considered much superior to the 4-inch Mk XIX twin mounting. They were fitted in the shelter-decks, three on each side forward and two on each side aft, which gave good all round arcs of fire on the beam, but limited capability of tracking across the stern, and practically none of tracking across the bow. These guns, with their high rate of fire, required a considerable amount of new magazine space, but this was made available because the new main machinery occupied much less space than the original installation.

Control of the secondary armament was provided by four high-angle/low-angle Mk IV directors, two, mounted on a raised structure at the rear of the bridge, and two on the after superstructure. They provided a four-cornered arrangement for the four groups of 4.5-inch mountings. High-angle fire was controlled via a HACS Mk IV table, and low-angle fire, via an AFCC Mk VII.

The close-range armament consisted of three pom-pom Mk VI mountings, two, on a raised platform between the funnels, one on the after shelter-deck, and four 0.5-inch machine-gun mountings, two on the forward, and two on the after shelter-deck.

The forward submerged torpedo tubes were removed, and eight above-water tubes were added.

Below: *Renown* in 1939, after completion of her reconstruction.

Protection

The provision of new deck protection was restricted to areas not fitted with non-cemented armour during her 1923 to 1926 refit, and to the decks immediately over the new 4.5-inch magazines. Where new non-cemented armour was fitted, all the existing deck plating was replaced by 'D' steel. On the flat of the main-deck, 4-inch armour was added over the new magazines, and 2-inch armour over the engine rooms. The longitudinal bulkheads, abreast the boiler-uptakes between the main-deck and the upper-deck were removed, and the area between them was fitted with 1½-inch armour, thus making the flat of the main-deck over the boiler rooms, of uniform thickness. Additional protection against end-on fire was provided by fitting 2-inch armour on the main-deck forward, and 3/2½-inch armour on the lower-deck aft.

The sides of 'A' barbette between the main-deck and the upper-deck, and 'B' barbette, between the main-deck and forecastle-deck,

Below: *Renown* on 25th June 1942.

were increased in thickness from four to six inches. Although an improvement, this could hardly be considered sufficient protection for the barbettes above the level of the side armour, but the amount of protection that could be added was limited by the necessity of retaining a high speed.

Machinery

The new machinery produced a saving in weight of approximately 2,800 tons, without any loss in power, and considerably increased endurance, and the standard of watertight sub-division. Eight Admiralty three-drum boilers replaced the original installation, and were accommodated in four of the original six boiler rooms. The width of the boiler rooms was reduced by the addition of longitudinal bulkheads of $\frac{3}{4}$-inch thick 'DI' quality plating supported by 10-inch 'I' girders. The wing compartments thus formed, were employed as oil-fuel and reserve-feed water tanks. This added substantially to the underwater protection, and also eliminated the risk of salt-water contamination of the reserve-feed water that was formerly stowed in the double-bottomed compartments. The boiler rooms were further sub-divided by the addition of a longitudinal centre-line bulkhead. The two funnels were fitted farther aft, in order to keep them as far away from the bridge as possible and, after the problems encountered during the trials of *Warspite*, the funnels were increased in height.

The two original forward boiler rooms were substantially sub-divided to provide an auxiliary boiler room, 4.5-inch magazines, HACP and oil-fuel tanks.

The transverse bulkhead separating the original engine and condenser rooms was taken out, and two new transverse bulkheads were fitted to provide three groups of compartments instead of two. The foremost contained the turbines, the second, the reduction-gears and the third, the after 4.5-inch magazines. The longitudinal bulkheads dividing the wing and centre engine compartments were rebuilt with 'DI' quality plating, and a new longitudinal bulkhead was fitted on the centre-line, which

Below: an aerial view of *Renown* in August 1943.

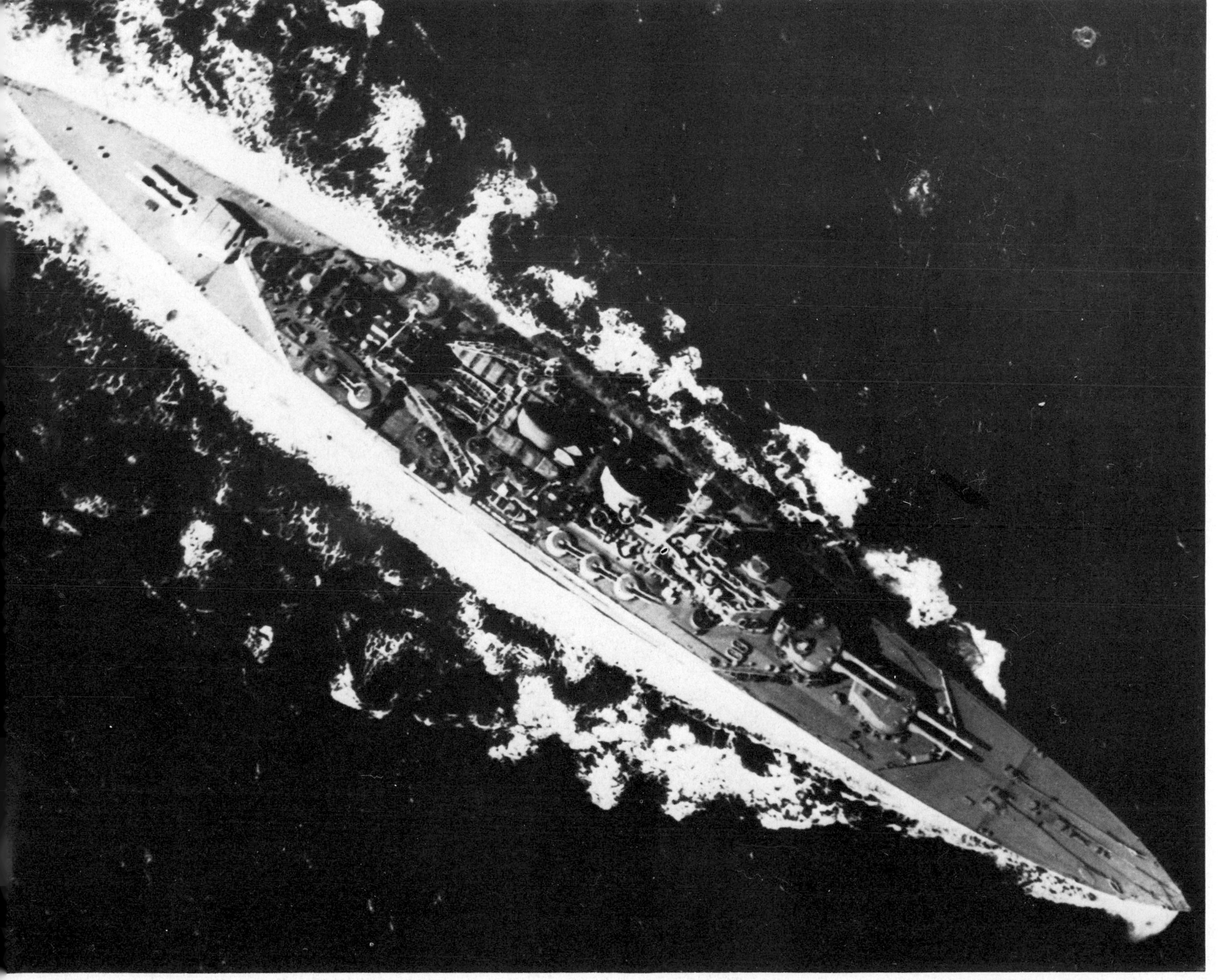

increased the number of turbine and gearing rooms from six to eight.

Auxiliary machinery

Unlike *Warspite*, *Renown* was fitted with entirely new auxiliary machinery which allowed the boiler pressure to be increased from 285 to 400 pounds per square inch. The modifications that were made are listed below, and were generally directed towards increasing the number of electrically-driven auxiliaries and reducing those that were steam-driven.

1. New electro-hydraulic steering gear.
2. New dynamos driven by either diesel-engines or turbines.
3. New hydraulic and air-compressing machinery.
4. Electric capstan machinery was fitted in place of steam capstan engines.
5. Pumping arrangements were improved by fitting seven 350-ton pumps.
6. An electric bakery was installed.

Aircraft equipment

Renown was fitted with a 'D III H' catapult and the hangars were constructed abreast the after funnel, but otherwise the aircraft arrangements were generally similar to those in *Warspite*.

Bridge and superstructure

The original structure above the forecastle-deck, with the exception of the forward barbettes, was stripped off and an entirely new superstructure was built in its place. The new shelter-decks occupied the full width of the ship, and this allowed the secondary armament to be placed one deck higher, where it was less vulnerable in heavy weather. The new bridge was placed close abaft 'B' turret, which still further increased its distance from the funnels. Although based on the bridge fitted in *Warspite*, the general proportions and arrangement of the platforms were somewhat different. Among the more obvious external differences, was the curved front to the compass-platform and lower navigating-position, based on that fitted in the *Liverpool* class

Below: looking aft from the flag-deck on *Renown*.

F at frame 280
looking aft

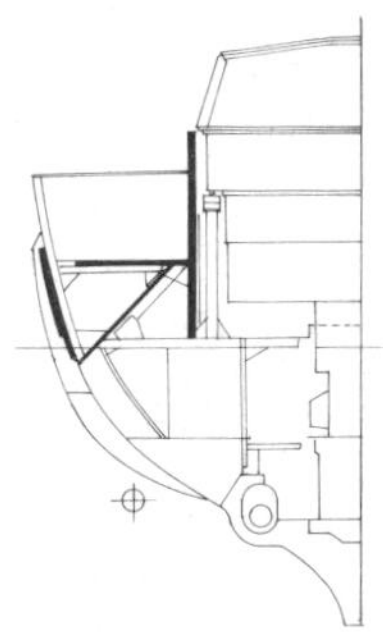

Inboard Profile
1 Boiler room
2 Engine room
3 Boiler room uptake
4 Boiler room vent
5 Engine room vent
6 Conning-position
7 15-inch Director-control tower
8 HACS director
9 After Director-control tower

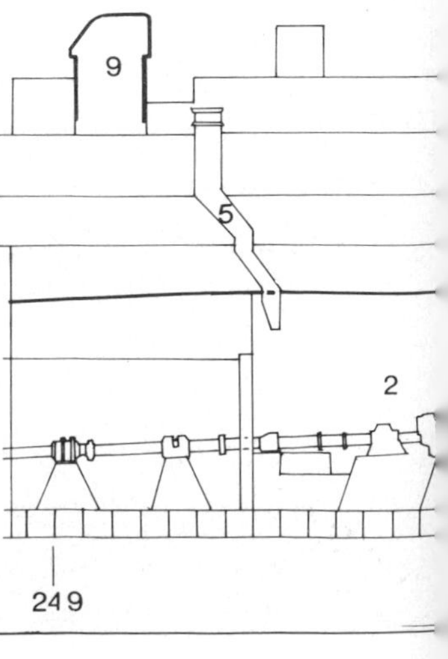

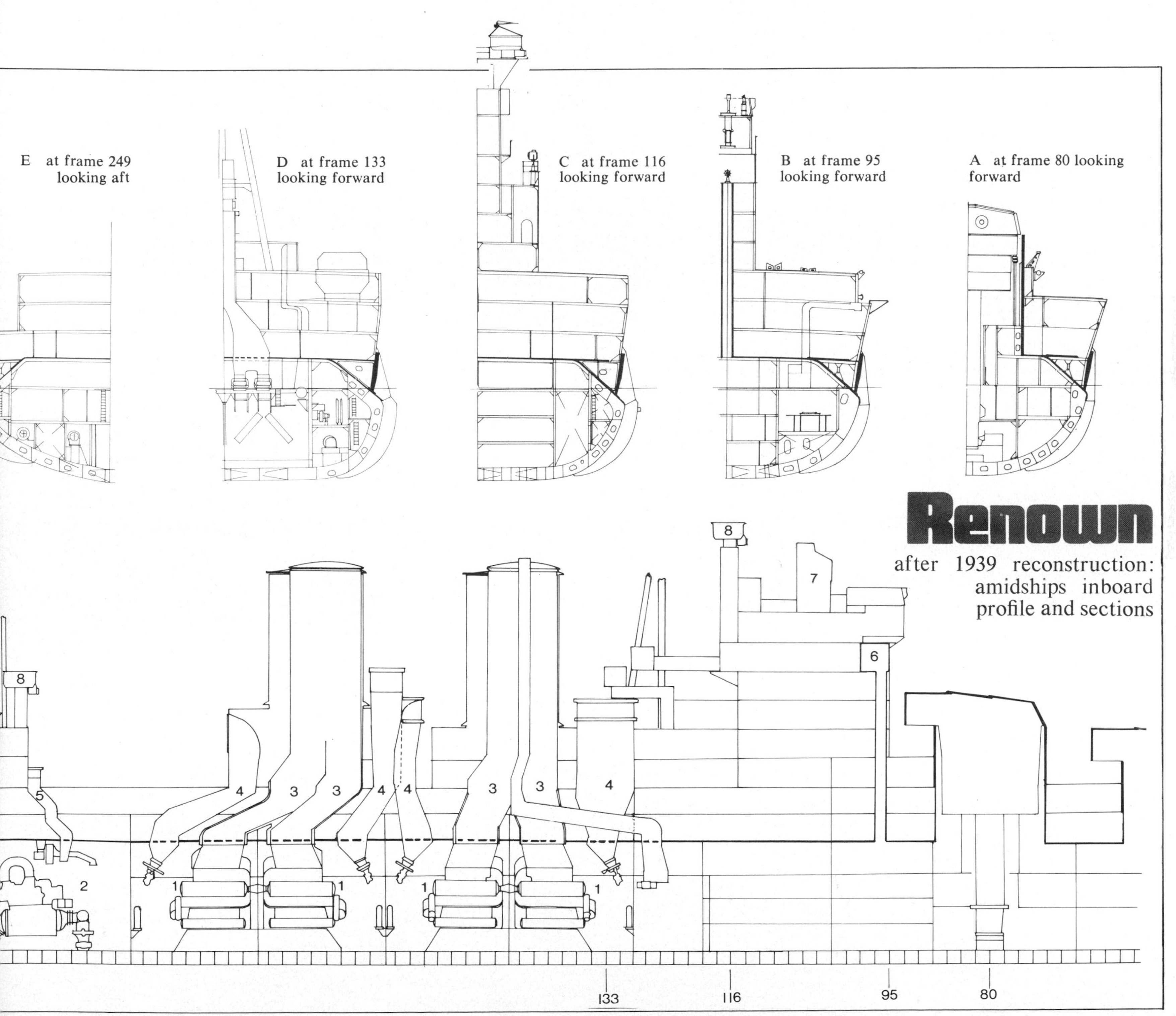
E at frame 249
looking aft
D at frame 133
looking forward
C at frame 116
looking forward
B at frame 95
looking forward
A at frame 80 looking
forward
Renown
after 1939 reconstruction:
amidships inboard
profile and sections
8
7
6
5
4
3
2
1
133
116
95
80

Below: *Renown* at Trincomalee in 1944.

cruisers, and the signal-deck which was extended aft to the tripod foremast.

Stability

In 1936, the estimated deep displacement of *Renown*, as reconstructed, was 38,105 tons. After reconstruction, the actual deep displacement was more than 2,000 tons less than this figure and more than 1,500 tons less than when taken in hand. The ship was inclined on 1st July 1939 and the following figures were established:

Table 63: Stability particulars of *Renown*, 1939

Conditions:	Extreme deep with 4,857 tons of oil fuel and 154 tons of water protection	Average action with 2,506 tons of oil fuel and 154 tons of water protection	Light
Displacement	36,080 tons	33,725 tons	30,025 tons
Mean draught	30 feet 5¼ inches	28 feet 8¼ inches	25 feet 11¼ inches
GM	5·56 feet	4·71 feet	4·58 feet
Range	76·4°	70°	65°
Angle of maximum stability	39·4°		37°

Trials

Renown carried out sea trials on 10th, 11th, 24th and 25th July 1939. During the contractor's measured-mile trial, she made 29.93 knots with 120,560 shaft horse-power at a displacement of 32,800 tons. The trial was run in shallow water, and it was estimated that this resulted in a loss of speed of 0.75 knots. During a later trial, she made 30.1 knots at a displacement of 34,800 tons.

The gun trials were completed without trouble, and the new 4.5-inch gun-mountings proved very satisfactory, having a rate of fire well up to expectations.

The new compass-platform was disappointing in that the conditions at the rear of the compass-platform and in the area of the ADO and searchlight-sights, were uncomfortable because of the back-draught caused by the main director-control tower. There were no problems of funnel smoke being drawn into the bridge, or in the vicinity of the catapult and quarter-deck.

War modifications

The ship was not substantially modified until 1941, when she was taken in hand at Rosyth, between 18th August and 31st October. During this refit, six 20-mm Oerlikons were fitted. At some time between the end of this refit and the autumn of 1942, a further ten 20-mm were added, and the 0.5-inch machine-gun mountings were removed. The following additions were made during the 1941 refit:

1. Two Type '285' radar sets were fitted, with a double office on the signal-platform, and aerials on the HACS.
2. Type '284' radar was fitted, with an office on the signal-platform, and aerials on the main director-control tower.

3. Type '281' radar was fitted, with a transmitting-office at the after end of the signal-platform, between the legs of the tripod mast, a receiving office was fitted on the after superstructure, and aerials were fitted at the mastheads.
4. Two Type '282' radar set were fitted, with a double office abaft No 2 bridge-platform and aerials on the bridge pom-pom directors.
5. Three Type '283' radar sets were fitted, with a double office on No 1 bridge-platform, a single office on the after superstructure, and aerials on the three barrage-directors. (One of the barrage-directors replaced the after pom-pom director, and the remaining two replaced the 9-foot range-finders on the lower bridge.)
6. Type '273' radar was fitted, with an aerial and an office on the foremast starfish.
7. An 'FM2' medium-frequency direction-finder was fitted, with an office on No 2 bridge-platform, and a fixed-frame aerial on the front of the bridge.
8. Struts were fitted to the mainmast.

The ship was again refitted at Rosyth, between 22nd February and 9th June 1943. The aircraft equipment was removed, and its space was utilised to re-arrange the boat stowage, and to provide some of the positions for the close-range anti-aircraft weapons, then being fitted. A total of thirteen twin, and three single 20-mm Oerlikons were added to the existing armament. Because of the increase in top-weight, the stability was considerably reduced. The estimated condition of the ship in June 1943 was as shown in Table 64:

PARTICULARS OF *RENOWN*, 1930 to 1946

Displacement	Deep Load	Light
1933	37,630 tons	31,870 tons
1939	36,080 tons	30,025 tons
1943	37,600 tons	31,230 tons
1944	38,395 tons	32,025 tons

Standard displacement in 1939 was 30,750 tons.

Note: the deep-load figures include 154 tons (320 tons in 1943) of water carried in water-protection compartments abreast the magazines. As much as 1,040 tons of water could be carried for this purpose in special and double-bottomed compartments, but in 1940 it was restricted to the 154 tons in the special compartments, in order to preserve the ship's freeboard.

Weights (1939)

General equipment	700 tons
Machinery	3,200 tons
Armament	4,729 tons
Armour, protective plating and hull	21,396 tons
Light displacement	30,025 tons

Dimensions
Length and beam remained unchanged.

Draught (1939):
26 feet 6 inches (mean) in standard condition;
30 feet 6 inches (mean) in deep condition.

Armament
Up to 1936, the armament remained as it had been in 1926, except that one 4-inch triple mounting was removed and two pom-pom mountings Mk V and two 0.5-inch machine-gun mountings Mk II* were fitted.

1939:
Six 15-inch Mk I: twin mounting Mk I (N).
Twenty 4.5-inch Mk III: ten high-angle/low angle twin mountings Mk I.
Twenty-four 2-pounder Mk VIII: three mountings Mk VI.
Sixteen 0.5-inch Mk III: four mountings Mk III.
Four 3-pounder Hotchkiss saluting guns Mk I.
The close-range AA armament in January 1944 was:
Twenty-eight 2-pounder pom-poms (3 × 8 + 1 × 4).
Sixty-four 20-mm Oerlikons (20 × 2 + 24 × 1).

Ammunition stowage (1939)
15-inch: 120 rounds per gun; 8 practice rounds per gun.
4.5-inch: high-angle 250 rounds per gun; 75 practice rounds per gun.
4.5-inch: low-angle 150 rounds per gun; 25 practice rounds per gun.
2-pounder: 1,800 rounds per gun; 84 practice rounds per gun.
0.5-inch: 2,500 rounds per gun.
Nine 21-inch torpedoes.

Fire-control equipment
1936:
15-inch: two tripod-type directors, one Dreyer table Mk IV*.
4-inch low-angle: two pedestal-type sights, two transmitting-clocks.
4-inch high-angle: high-angle control-system Mk I.
Pom-poms: one pom-pom director.
1939:
15-inch: one director-control tower, one tripod-type director, one Admiralty fire-control table Mk VII.
4.5-inch: four high-angle/low-angle directors Mk IV, HACS tables Mk IV, four Admiralty fire-control clocks Mk VII (M) (for low-angle fire-control).
Pom-poms: three pom-pom directors Mk III*.

Range-finders (1939)
One 30-foot in 'B' turret.
Eight 15-foot in 'A' and 'Y' turrets, 15-inch director-control tower and armoured director-hood and four high-angle/low-angle directors.
Two 9-foot on lower bridge.

Searchlights
In 1939, six 44-inch searchlights were carried; four had been removed by 1945. Four 24-inch and four 10-inch signalling-searchlights were carried on the signal-platform.

Armour
Except where noted below, the armour protection in 1939 was the same as it had been in 1926.
Barbettes: 7 inch, 6 inch and 4 inch.
Conning-tower: 3 inch front, sides; 2 inch rear NC.
Conning-tower tube: 4 inch and 3 inch.
After director-control tower: 6 inch hood, 6 inch support.
Box protection to 4.5-inch mountings: 2 inch and 1 inch D steel.
Box protection to torpedo tubes: 2½ inch, 2 inch and 1½ inch D steel.
Funnel-uptakes: 1 inch D steel.
Main-deck (flat): 5 inch (4 inch NC + 1 inch D) over 4.5-inch magazines.
2½ inch (1½ inch NC + 1 inch D) over boiler rooms amidships, between previously fitted NC armour.
3 inch (2 inch NC + 1 inch D) over engine rooms.
2¾ inch (2 inch NC + ¾ inch D) between 'A' barbette and foremost armoured bulkhead.
Lower-deck: 3¼ inch (2½ inch NC + ¾ inch D) between stations '295' and '300' aft. (The aftermost armoured bulkhead was at station '300').

Machinery (1939)
Parsons single-reduction geared turbines, four shafts.
120,000 SHP = 30.75 knots (designed).
Maximum sea-going speed, 108,000 SHP = 29.5 knots.
Eight Admiralty three-drum small-tube boilers. One small auxiliary boiler forward of 'A' boiler room.

Fuel and endurance
4,613 tons oil fuel and 244 tons Diesel fuel (1939).
4,754 tons oil fuel and 116 tons Diesel fuel (1943).
Endurance: 1,300 nautical miles at 10 knots.

Complement
1939: 1.200; 1945: 1,433.

Table 64: Stability particulars of *Renown*, 1943

Condition:	Extreme deep with 4,871 tons of oil fuel and 320 tons of water protection	Average action with 2,513 tons of oil fuel and 320 tons of water protection	Light
Displacement	37,600 tons	35,240 tons	31,230 tons
Mean draught	31 feet 7¼ inches	29 feet 10¼ inches	26 feet 9¾ inches
GM	4·8 feet	4·4 feet	3·5 feet
Range	73°	67°	62°
Angle of maximum stability	39°		36°

From December 1943 to January 1944, she was once again at Rosyth, being prepared for the Eastern Fleet. A four barrelled pom-pom mounting replaced the Oerlikons on 'B' turret (these latter were re-positioned) and a further seven twin, and five single 20-mm Oerlikons were added. Two of these twin mountings replaced the two 44-inch searchlights on the signal-bridge.

She was refitted in Durban, between 21st December 1944 and 21st February 1945, during which – as far as is known – no major alterations and additions were carried out. The two 44-inch searchlights on the after superstructure were replaced by two single Oerlikons; the '284' radar set was replaced by 'Type 285', and it is possible that some of the remaining close-range armament was re-arranged or augmented. The 21-inch torpedo tubes were removed in April 1945.

Weight increases and reconstruction

Renown's main belt armour was 8 feet 8 inches deep and, in 1939, 4 feet 5 inches of this depth was above the waterline, when in the deep condition. By 1944, it was estimated from the recorded draughts of the ship, that 2,315 tons had been added to her displacement, and of this weight, only 694 tons could be ascribed to the known weights of alterations, additions, ammunition and stores. As a result, the main belt was only 2 feet 8 inches, and the armoured deck, only 8 inches above the deep waterline. The Director of Naval Construction considered that "of this 1,621 tons of added weight which cannot be accounted for, there is no doubt that a large proportion is due to the carrying of stores, spare gear and equipment which the officers may consider will be necessary in an emergency or when the ship is far from base. For example between January 1944 when the ship left Rosyth and May 1944 when she was with the Eastern Fleet the displacement increased over 400 tons without the ship having been in dockyard hands at all".

The drawings of the ship were examined, but revealed very little that could be removed. Landing the 44-inch searchlights and their associate equipment, the torpedo tubes and their fittings, the aviation-spirit and motor boat fuel tanks, and the fittings for working the petrol, would have produced a grand saving of 60 tons. It was concluded that more drastic methods were necessary, and it was decided to inform the Commander-in-Chief, Eastern Fleet, that "considerations of protection, stability and strength demand that the draught of the *Renown* should not exceed a mean of 32 feet which is approximately the condition in which the ship left Rosyth". This meant, removing some 425 tons, and how this was to be achieved (by reducing oil fuel, water, stores or ammunition) was left to the discretion of the commanding officer, and depended on the ship's operational requirements.

The saving in weight was all the more important because of proposals then being made (1944) for the refit and reconstruction of *Renown* in 1945. Unfortunately, no details of this reconstruction are available but it is known that the proposed alterations would have resulted in an increase of 3 inches in the draught (equal to approximately 350 tons) and a reduction in the GM to 4.5 feet. The 6-month refit and reconstruction was scheduled to begin in October 1945, but in September 1945 it was cancelled.

Below: *Renown* in home waters, late 1945. Note that her three forward 4.5-inch HA/LA mountings have been removed.

Renown

1942: outboard profile and deck plans, with AA positions indicated

Anti-aircraft gun positions

A October 1941: Six single 20 mm mounts fitted.
B Early 1942: One single 20 mm mount added.
C by mid 1942: One single 20 mm mount added.
D by late 1942: Four 0.5-inch MGs removed.
E by late 1942: Eight single 20 mm mounts added.
June 1943:
F Seven single 20 mm mounts removed and repositioned.
G Three single 20 mm added, plus seven mounts from positions F.
H Thirteen twin 20 mm mounts fitted.
January 1944:
I Nine single 20 mm mounts removed and repositioned.
J Five single 20 mm mounts added, plus nine from positions I.
K Three twin 20 mm mounts removed and repositioned.
L Seven twin 20 mm mounts added plus three from positions K.
M One quadruple pom-pom fitted.

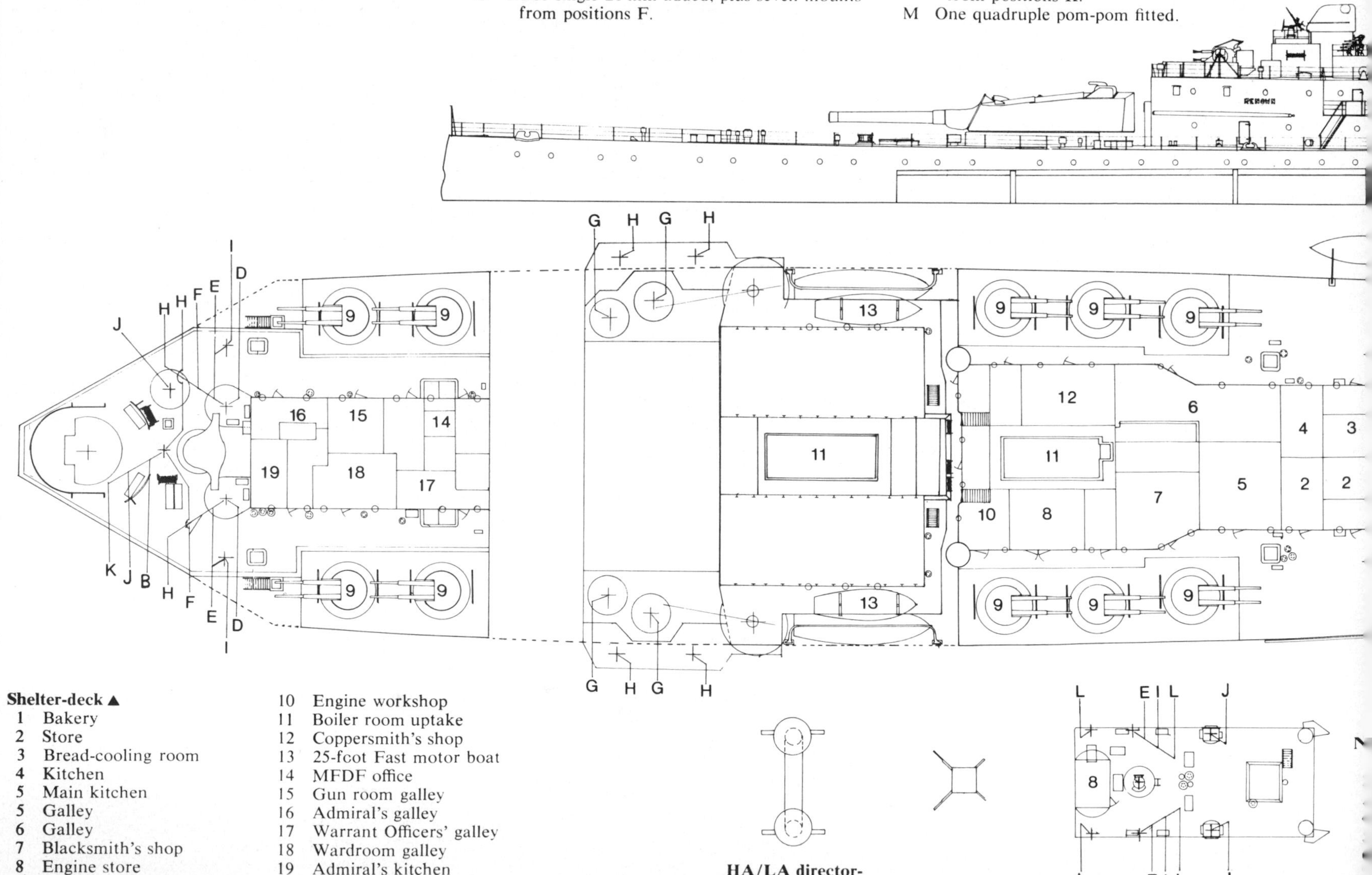

Shelter-deck ▲

1 Bakery
2 Store
3 Bread-cooling room
4 Kitchen
5 Main kitchen
5 Galley
6 Galley
7 Blacksmith's shop
8 Engine store
9 4.5-inch BD twin mounting
10 Engine workshop
11 Boiler room uptake
12 Coppersmith's shop
13 25-foot Fast motor boat
14 MFDF office
15 Gun room galley
16 Admiral's galley
17 Warrant Officers' galley
18 Wardroom galley
19 Admiral's kitchen
20 27-foot Whaler

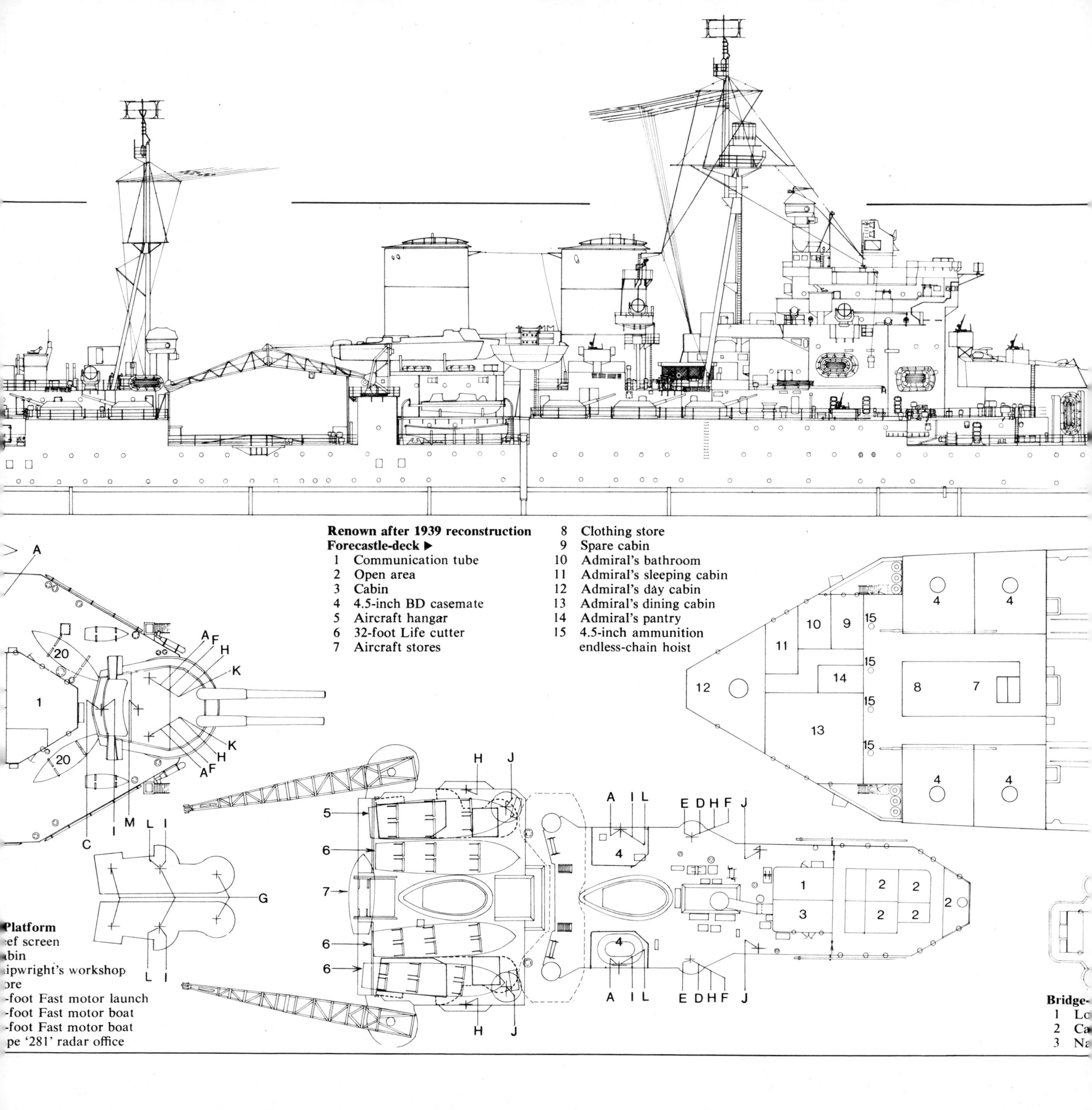

Renown after 1939 reconstruction
Forecastle-deck ▶
1 Communication tube
2 Open area
3 Cabin
4 4.5-inch BD casemate
5 Aircraft hangar
6 32-foot Life cutter
7 Aircraft stores
8 Clothing store
9 Spare cabin
10 Admiral's bathroom
11 Admiral's sleeping cabin
12 Admiral's day cabin
13 Admiral's dining cabin
14 Admiral's pantry
15 4.5-inch ammunition endless-chain hoist
Platform
ef screen
bin
ipwright's workshop
ore
-foot Fast motor launch
-foot Fast motor boat
-foot Fast motor boat
pe '281' radar office
Bridge-
1 Lo
2 Ca
3 Na

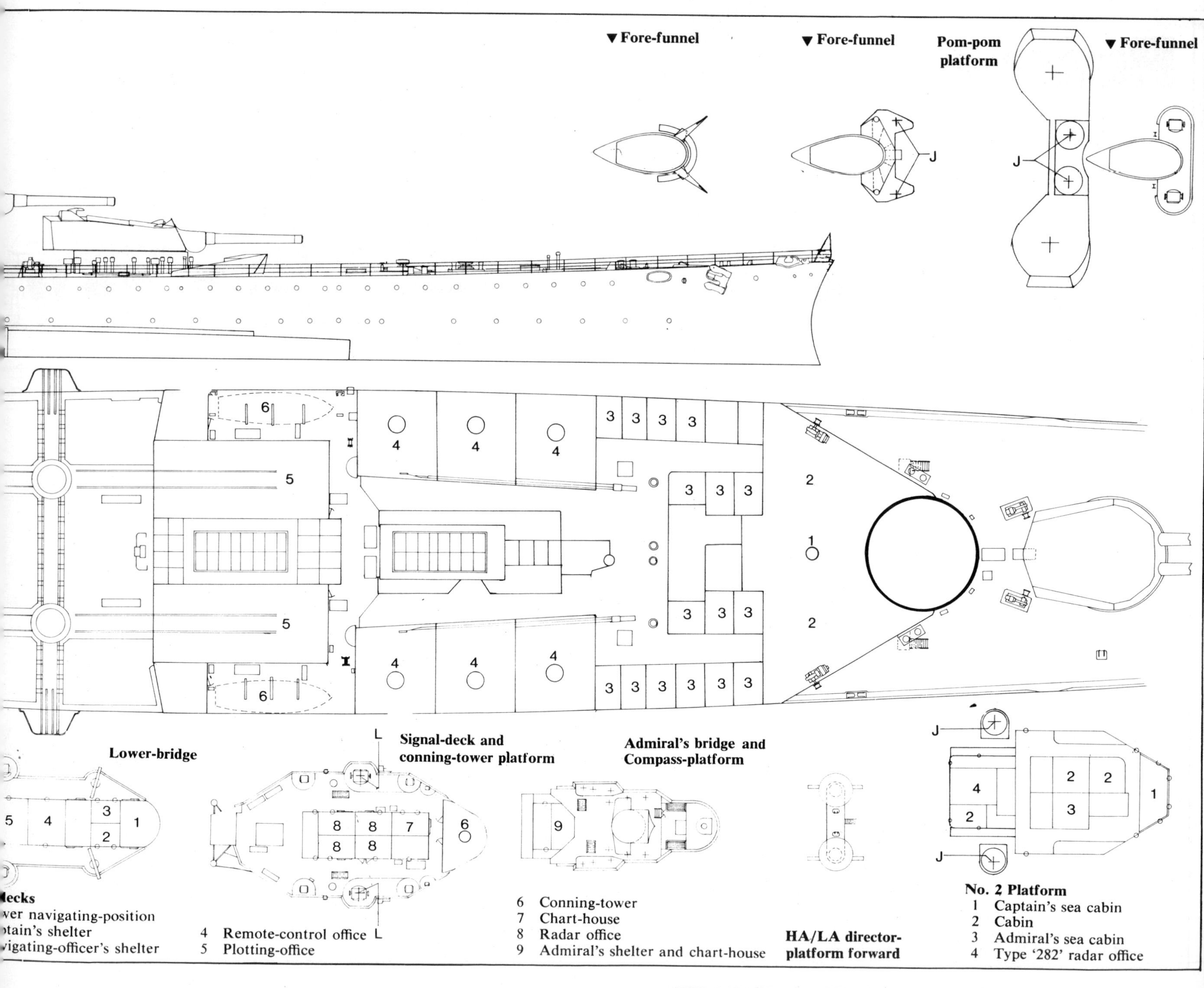
▼ Fore-funnel
▼ Fore-funnel
Pom-pom platform
▼ Fore-funnel
J
J
Lower-bridge
Signal-deck and conning-tower platform
Admiral's bridge and Compass-platform
HA/LA director-platform forward
No. 2 Platform
1 Captain's sea cabin
2 Cabin
3 Admiral's sea cabin
4 Type '282' radar office
lecks
ver navigating-position
tain's shelter
vigating-officer's shelter
4 Remote-control office
5 Plotting-office
6 Conning-tower
7 Chart-house
8 Radar office
9 Admiral's shelter and chart-house

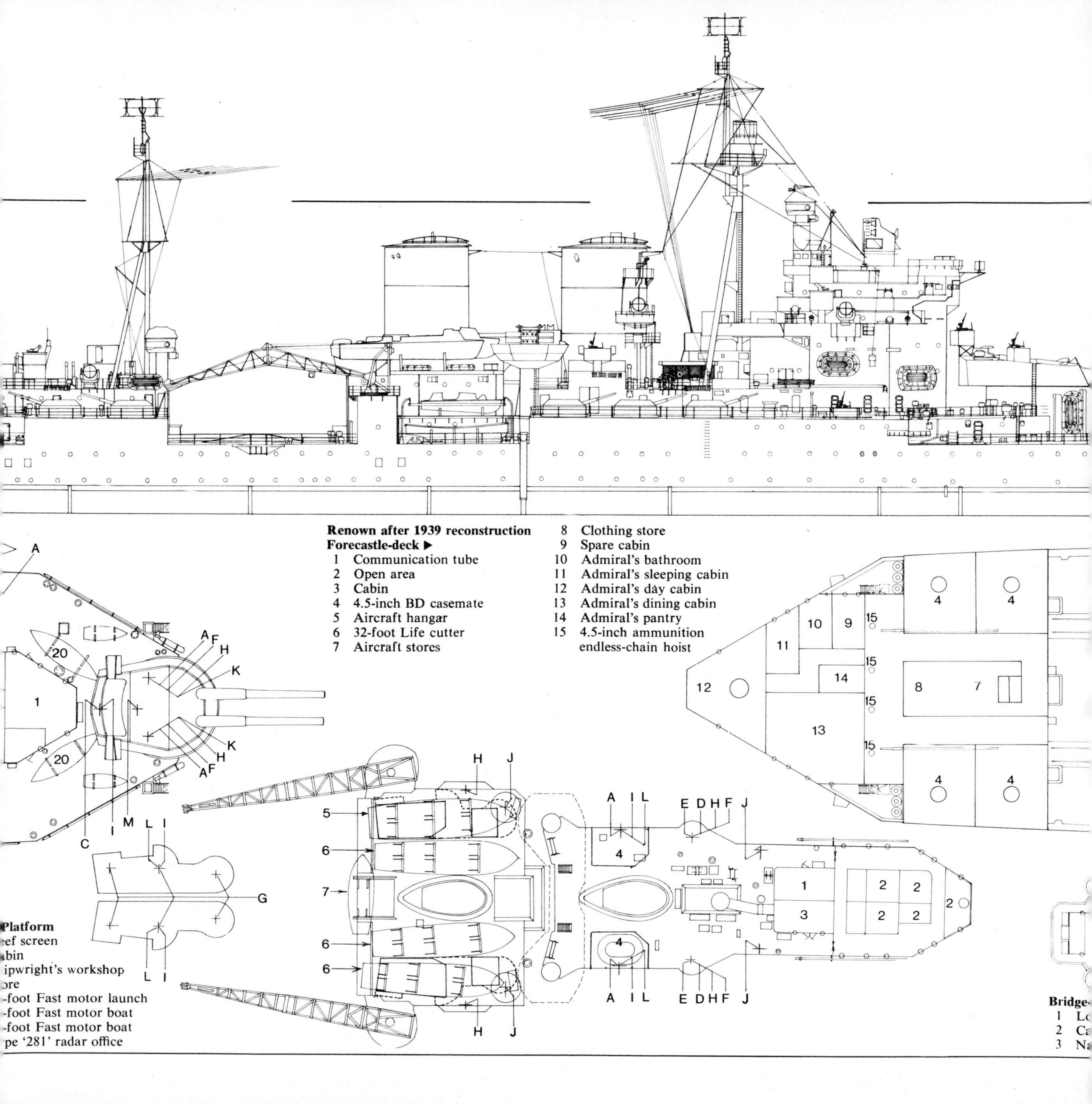

Renown after 1939 reconstruction
Forecastle-deck ▶

1 Communication tube
2 Open area
3 Cabin
4 4.5-inch BD casemate
5 Aircraft hangar
6 32-foot Life cutter
7 Aircraft stores
8 Clothing store
9 Spare cabin
10 Admiral's bathroom
11 Admiral's sleeping cabin
12 Admiral's day cabin
13 Admiral's dining cabin
14 Admiral's pantry
15 4.5-inch ammunition endless-chain hoist

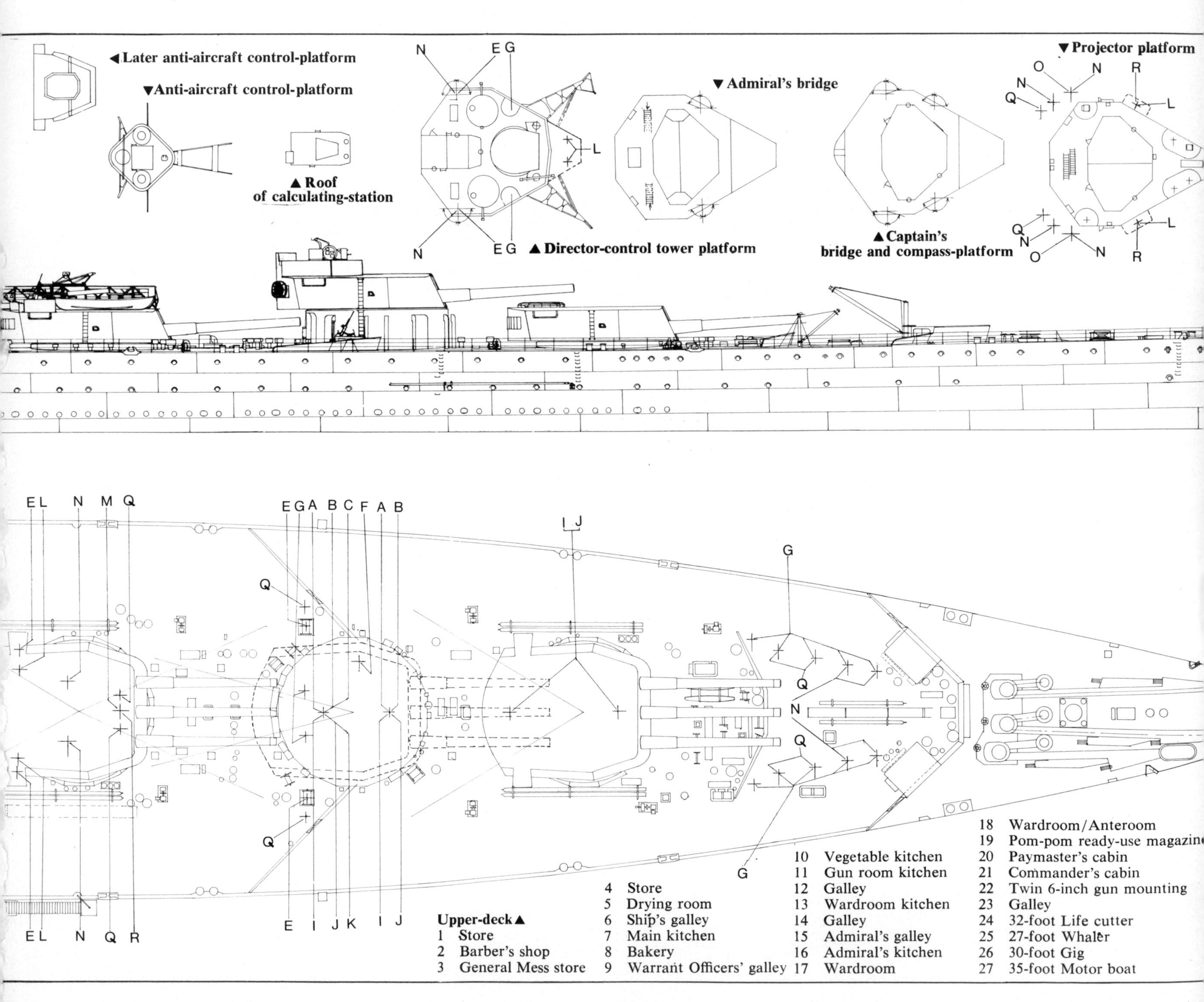

Later anti-aircraft control-platform
Anti-aircraft control-platform
Roof of calculating-station
Director-control tower platform
Admiral's bridge
Captain's bridge and compass-platform
Projector platform
Upper-deck
1 Store
2 Barber's shop
3 General Mess store
4 Store
5 Drying room
6 Ship's galley
7 Main kitchen
8 Bakery
9 Warrant Officers' galley
10 Vegetable kitchen
11 Gun room kitchen
12 Galley
13 Wardroom kitchen
14 Galley
15 Admiral's galley
16 Admiral's kitchen
17 Wardroom
18 Wardroom/Anteroom
19 Pom-pom ready-use magazine
20 Paymaster's cabin
21 Commander's cabin
22 Twin 6-inch gun mounting
23 Galley
24 32-foot Life cutter
25 27-foot Whaler
26 30-foot Gig
27 35-foot Motor boat

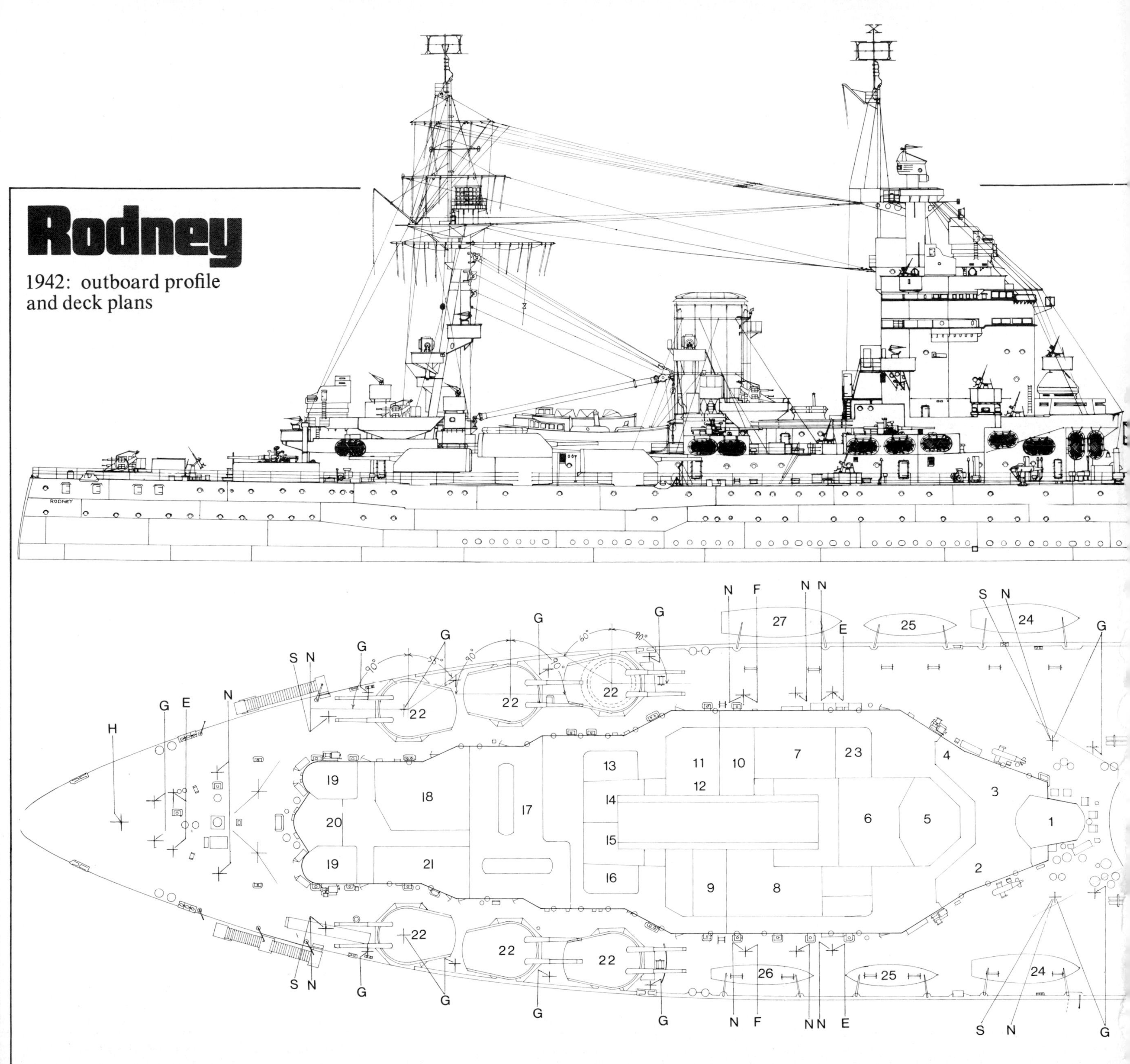

Rodney

1942: outboard profile and deck plans

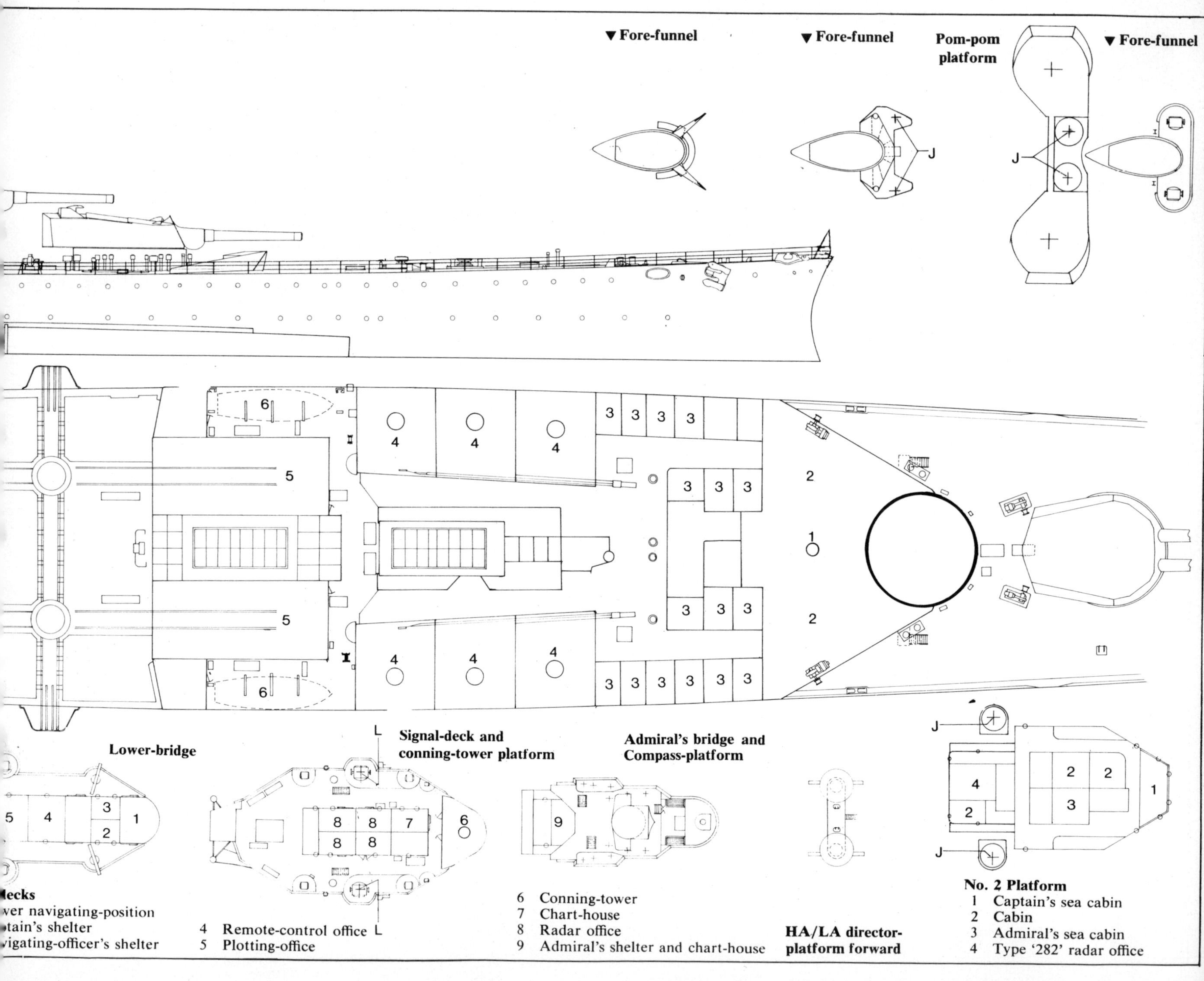
▼ Fore-funnel
▼ Fore-funnel
Pom-pom platform
▼ Fore-funnel
J
J
Lower-bridge
Signal-deck and conning-tower platform
Admiral's bridge and Compass-platform
HA/LA director-platform forward
No. 2 Platform
1 Captain's sea cabin
2 Cabin
3 Admiral's sea cabin
4 Type '282' radar office
lecks
ver navigating-position
tain's shelter
vigating-officer's shelter
4 Remote-control office
5 Plotting-office
6 Conning-tower
7 Chart-house
8 Radar office
9 Admiral's shelter and chart-house

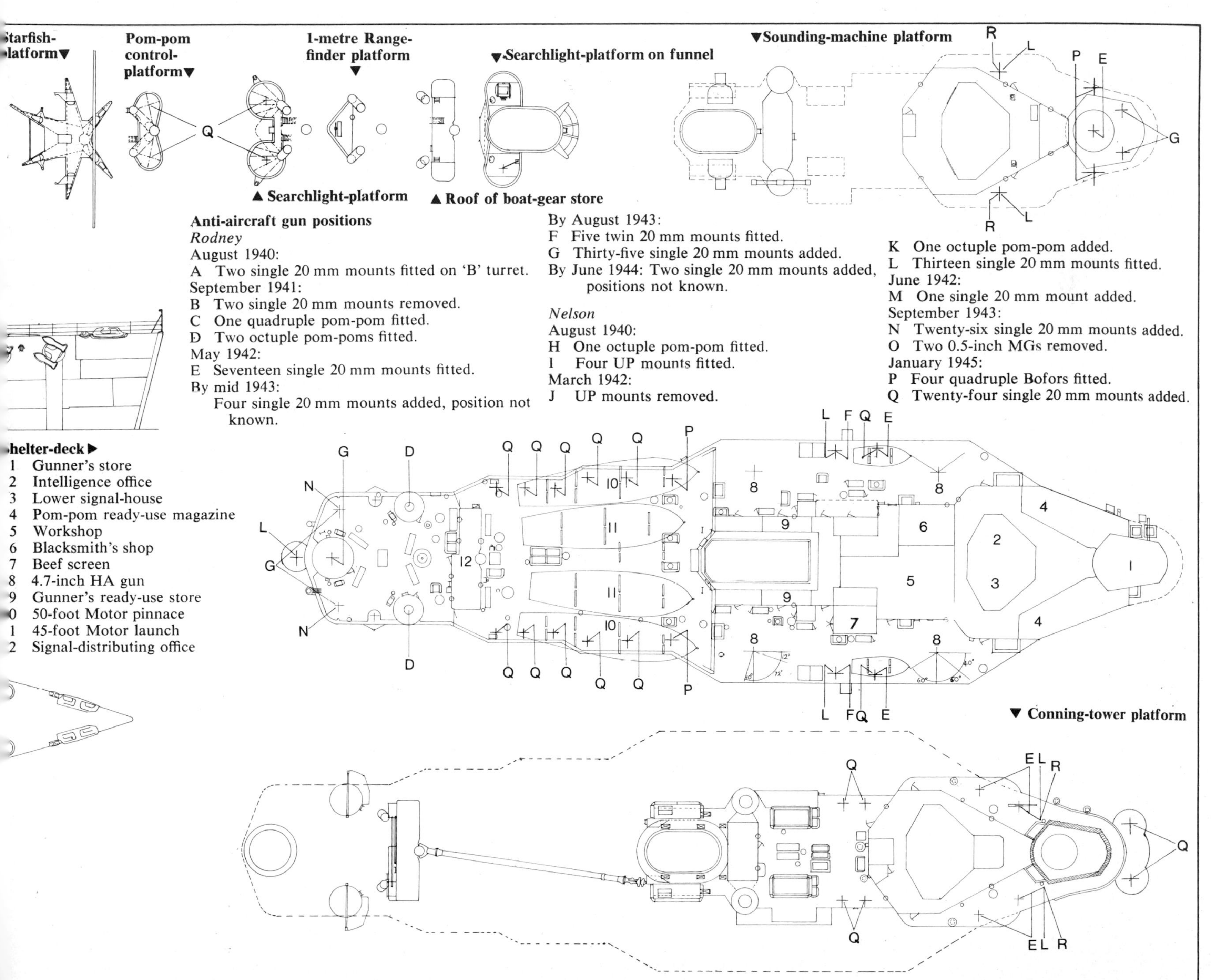
Starfish-platform ▼
Pom-pom control-platform ▼
1-metre Range-finder platform ▼
▼ Searchlight-platform on funnel
▼ Sounding-machine platform
▲ Searchlight-platform
▲ Roof of boat-gear store
Anti-aircraft gun positions
Rodney
August 1940:
A Two single 20 mm mounts fitted on 'B' turret.
September 1941:
B Two single 20 mm mounts removed.
C One quadruple pom-pom fitted.
D Two octuple pom-poms fitted.
May 1942:
E Seventeen single 20 mm mounts fitted.
By mid 1943:
Four single 20 mm mounts added, position not known.
By August 1943:
F Five twin 20 mm mounts fitted.
G Thirty-five single 20 mm mounts added.
By June 1944: Two single 20 mm mounts added, positions not known.
Nelson
August 1940:
H One octuple pom-pom fitted.
I Four UP mounts fitted.
March 1942:
J UP mounts removed.
K One octuple pom-pom added.
L Thirteen single 20 mm mounts fitted.
June 1942:
M One single 20 mm mount added.
September 1943:
N Twenty-six single 20 mm mounts added.
O Two 0.5-inch MGs removed.
January 1945:
P Four quadruple Bofors fitted.
Q Twenty-four single 20 mm mounts added.
Shelter-deck ▶
1 Gunner's store
2 Intelligence office
3 Lower signal-house
4 Pom-pom ready-use magazine
5 Workshop
6 Blacksmith's shop
7 Beef screen
8 4.7-inch HA gun
9 Gunner's ready-use store
10 50-foot Motor pinnace
11 45-foot Motor launch
12 Signal-distributing office
▼ Conning-tower platform

NELSON AND RODNEY, 1930 to 1946

The modifications made to *Nelson* and *Rodney* between 1930 and 1935, were virtually the same for both ships.

1930 to 1931: A high-angle control-system Mk I was fitted. The high-angle control-platform was replaced by a new platform to accommodate the high-angle director.
1931 to 1932: A 9-foot range-finder was fitted on the bridge, on the roof of the high-angle control-position in *Rodney* only. The Type '71' wireless set was removed, and a Type '75' set was installed.
1932 to 1933: A new enclosed compass-platform was built above the original, at the level of the admiral's bridge and a new platform was built across the front of the main director-control tower on the bridge, in *Nelson* only.
1933 to 1934: A direction-finder outfit was fitted in *Nelson*, with a fixed-frame aerial on the main-topgallant-masthead. Two pom-pom Mk V mountings were fitted abreast the funnel, and the torpedo range-finder towers were removed. Pom-pom directors Mk I* were fitted on the director-control tower platform.
1934 to 1935: Two multiple machine-gun mountings were fitted on the after corners of the bridge structure, at the level of the projector-platform; Two Mk. I* mountings in *Nelson* and two Mk II*, in *Rodney*.

During the firing trials against *Emperor of India* in 1931, one shell burst under her armour belt at the moment of contact with the skin plating, and caused a considerable amount of damage. This emphasised the desirability of a deep belt which *Nelson* and *Rodney* did not possess. In 1936, therefore, it was proposed to deepen the side armour by adding a strip of armour below the existing belt, as shown in the diagram. It was also proposed, to protect the soft forward end, by the addition of armour on the lower-deck forward, and to reconstruct the ships generally in one of the following ways:

Section of *Nelson* class, showing proposed deepening of the side armour

1. Remove the 6-inch armament and fit four 5.25-inch high-angle/low-angle twin mountings on each side. Add two more pom-pom mountings. Fit an aircraft catapult on 'X' turret.
2. Remove the 6-inch armament and fit five 4.5-inch high-angle/low-angle twin mountings on each side. Add two more pom-pom mountings. Fit an aircraft catapult and hangars on the shelter-deck.
3. Remove the 6-inch armament and fit three 5.25-inch high-angle/low-angle twin mountings on each side. Add two more pom-pom mountings. Fit a catapult on 'X' turret.

The ships could not be taken in hand for reconstruction until 1940 at the earliest, and as both were due for a large refit and repair during 1937 to 1938, it was approved to fit the additional armour during these refits. The total cost would have been £330,000 per ship, but the dockyard programme was such that it could not cope with the additional work.

In December 1937, it was decided to defer the fitting of the additional protection in *Rodney* and it was never actually fitted. *Nelson* was fitted with the deck armour forward, but not the side protection. The work carried out on the two ships during 1936 to 1939 was as follows.

Rodney, 1936:
1. An aircraft catapult was fitted on 'X' turret.
2. A crane was fitted on the forecastle-deck, on the port side abreast the bridge.
3. An open compass-platform was built above the original enclosed compass-platform.
4. A sponson was built out on the starboard side of the conning-tower platform, and the bridge was recessed behind it. This modification has no apparent value, but it seems likely that a pom-pom mounting had been proposed for this position. No such mounting, however, was fitted.

Rodney, 1938:
1. A pom-pom Mk VI mounting was fitted on the quarter-deck.
2. Radar Type '79Y' was fitted. *Rodney* was the first battleship to be fitted with radar.

Nelson, refit at Portsmouth, 1937 to January 1938:
1. Fitted with $2\frac{3}{4}$-inch and 3-inch non-cemented armour on the lower-deck forward, 4-inch armour on the platform-deck, between stations '80' and '84', and a 4-inch bulkhead at station '80' from the hold to the platform-deck.
2. The HACS Mk I and the high-angle calculating-position were removed from the director-control tower platform and two high-angle control-systems Mk III* were fitted. Directors were fitted on the tower and platform built up from the director-control tower platform and new HACP's fitted below the armoured-deck.
3. A crane was fitted on the port side of the forecastle-deck, abreast the bridge.
4. The director-control tower platform was extended forward, and made flush with the platform below.
5. A new outfit of fast motor boats was provided.

War modifications to *Rodney*

Rodney was one of the ships from which the war extracted a heavy toll and caused her early retirement from active service. She was in need of a refit when the war started, and it is not surprising that her troubles began early.

In November 1939, while operating with the Home Fleet in the North Sea, she developed serious rudder defects and was ordered to return to the Clyde. She was repaired at Liverpool, where additional stiffening was fitted to the fore part of her rudder. (This was a modification that was also carried out in *Nelson*.)

Left: *Rodney*'s funnel and mainmast, with one of her Mk. VI pom-pom mountings in the foreground.
Centre left: *Nelson* in 1934, with modified bridge, HACS Mk. I and pom-pom mountings added on the superstructure.
Below left: *Rodney* in September 1937. Note the range-finder on the roof of the HA control-position (at the rear of the director control-tower platform), and the mysterious sponson and recess on the starboard side of the bridge.

Early in 1940, trouble was experienced with panting of the ship's side, which caused a certain amount of leakage, forward. The effect was greatest in the watertight compartments below the lower-deck, between the two foremost watertight bulkheads at stations '9' and '16'. The ship's staff welded one beam from frame to frame across the ship, in this area, but the compartment remained leaky because of defective riveting. No permanent-repairs were made, however, even after the trouble was increased by the effect of two near misses by German bombs in April 1940.

During the 6th and 8th December 1940, the ship encountered particularly heavy weather in the North Atlantic. She rode out the gale at a speed of 7.5 knots with her head to the wind and although she rolled little, the pitching motion was exceptionally heavy. The panting of the ship's side caused the beam that had been fitted by the ship's staff to be torn away, and leakage increased to the extent where the two water-tight (sic) compartments between bulkheads '9' and '16' were flooded. The inflammable store on the platform-deck also became flooded through a $\frac{5}{8}$-inch diameter hole in No '16' bulkhead. This hole, which was fitted with an adaptor for a hose, had been made in the bulkhead by a former officer of the ship, and was intended to provide a connection for a portable pump, because the compartments forward of No. '16' bulkhead were formerly inaccessible for pumping purposes. The hole, of course, destroyed the watertightness of the bulkhead.

Also during this gale, the covers of the navel pipes – through which the anchor cables were led below – were torn off by the sea, and water entered the cable-lockers. These began to flood more quickly than the drain-pipes could carry the water away, and attempts to pump out the lockers met with little initial success, as the nearest 50-ton pump was under water, and No. 1 350-ton pump was out of action because of an electrical fault and a damaged starter. The Engineer Commander inspected the drain-pipes and, finding them

Below and **right:** aboard *Rodney* in 1940. Note the two single 20 mm mountings on 'B' turret (right).

at Devonport in the autumn of 1943, but it was later decided that the work should be carried out concurrently with the modernisation. Despite a warning of the progressively worsening situation that would deteriorate with increasing rapidity, the complete repairs and modernisation were never carried out. (Detailed drawings for the modernisation of *Rodney* were prepared in 1944.) *Rodney*'s operational life came to an end in November 1944, when she became a virtually static flagship for the Commander-in-Chief, Home Fleet, at Scapa Flow.

The more detailed alterations and additions made to the ship during 1939 to 1945 are as follows:

By August 1940:
Two 20-mm Oerlikons had been fitted on 'B' turret. The Type '79Y' radar set had been converted to Type '279'.

September 1941 (after refit at Boston):
1. The after secondary director-control towers were removed and two pom-pom Mk VI mountings were fitted in their place.
2. One (four-barrelled) pom-pom Mk VII mounting was fitted on 'B' turret. (The Oerlikons were removed).
3. Type '279' radar was replaced by Type '281', with a receiving office abaft the bridge, and a transmitting office abaft the mainmast.
4. Type '271' radar was fitted, with an office and aerial on the starfish.
5. Type '284' radar was fitted.
6. A 'FM2' direction-finder outfit was fitted, with an office on the roof of the '281' receiving office, and an aerial on the front of the bridge.
7. The sponson on the starboard side of the conning-tower was removed. Submarine lookout positions were built on each side of the conning-tower platform. The bridge was slightly modified.

By May 1942:
1. The 0.5-inch machine-gun mountings were removed, the platforms were rebuilt and fitted with two pom-pom Mk III directors (the original directors were removed).

2. Three pom-pom Mk III directors were fitted aft, two on the mainmast and one at the after end of the shelter-deck.
3. All five pom-pom directors were fitted with Type '282' radar.
4. Four barrage-directors with Type '283' radar were fitted abreast and abaft the mainmast.
5. Type '271' radar was replaced by Type '273'.
6. The high-angle control-system director-platform was enlarged and the director was positioned on a higher pedestal.
7. A Type '285' radar was fitted, with aerials on the high-angle control-system director and an office was fitted on the roof of the high-angle control-position at rear of the director-control tower platform.
8. Seventeen single 20-mm Oerlikons were added.

Circa mid-1942:
Four 20-mm Oerlikons were added.

By August 1943:
1. Thirty-five single 20-mm Oerlikons were added, making a total of fifty-six.
2. Five 20-mm Oerlikon twin mountings were added.
3. The aircraft catapult was removed.
4. The 4.7-inch guns were fitted with shields.

By June 1944:
1. Two single 20-mm Oerlikons were added.
2. Type '650' missile-jamming gear was fitted.

War modifications to *Nelson*

Refit at Portsmouth, January to August 1940:
1. One pom-pom Mk V mounting was fitted on the quarter-deck.
2. The after secondary director-control towers were removed and two pom-pom Mk VI mountings were fitted in their place.
3. Type '281' radar was fitted, with a receiving office abaft the bridge, and a transmitting office abaft the mainmast.
4. A 'FM2' direction-finder was fitted, with an office on the roof of the '281' office.
5. Four UP mountings were fitted, two on 'B', and two on 'X' turrets.
6. The 4.7-inch guns were fitted with shields.

Left: *Rodney* in 1941, after her refit at Boston. Note the external de-gaussing coil and the Mk. VII pom-pom on 'B' turret.

Below left: *Rodney* in May 1942, after refit.

Below: an aerial view of *Rodney* on 27th May 1942.

Below right: an aerial view of *Nelson* on 28th June 1941.

Below: the main armament of *Nelson* in the second half of 1940. Note the UP mountings on the turret roofs.

Bottom of page: on 22nd April 1945, after her major refit in the United States.

Repairs Refit of October 1941 to March 1942:
1. Thirteen 20-mm Oerlikons were fitted and the UP mountings were removed.
2. Three new pom-pom Mk III directors were fitted, two on the mainmast and one at the after end of the shelter-deck. The two original directors were replaced by Mk III directors.
3. Four barrage-directors were fitted at the after end of the superstructure, abreast and abaft the mainmast.
4. Radar Types '273', '284', '282' (five sets for pom-pom directors) '283' (four sets for barrage-directors) and '285' (two sets for high-angle control-system directors) were fitted.
5. One pom-pom Mk VI mounting was fitted on 'B' turret.
6. A submarine look-out was fitted on each side of the conning-tower platform.
7. The submerged torpedo tubes were removed, and the compartments were sub-divided.

By September 1943:
1. The 20-mm Oerlikon armament was increased to forty-one singles.
2. The 0.5-inch machine-gun mountings were removed.

1943 to 1944:
Unknown, except that she was fitted with Type '650' jamming equipment for the Normandy landings.

Refit at Philadelphia Navy Yard, USA September 1944 to January 1945:
1. The armoured director-hood was removed.
2. Pom-pom directors were removed to provide positions for additional 20-mm Oerlikons.
3. Four 40-mm Bofors Mk II (USA pattern) quadruple mountings were fitted, two across the front of the bridge, two abreast the boat-deck. Control was provided by four Mk 51 directors.
4. The 20-mm Oerlikon armament was increased to sixty-five mountings.
5. A considerable number of platforms was added for the 20-mm armament. These required, inter alia, the re-arrangement of the boat stowage.

By April 1945:
Four of the 20-mm mountings had been removed.

PARTICULARS OF *NELSON* AND *RODNEY*, 1930 to 1946
Except where noted below, details remained as when the ships were completed in 1927.

Displacement	Standard	Extra Deep
Nelson, 1945	37,000 tons (approximate)	44,054 tons
Rodney, 1942	36,000 tons (approximate)	43,140 tons

Draught (deep)
Nelson, 1945: 34 feet 11 inches (forward), 36 feet 1 inch (aft).
Rodney, 1942: 34 feet 7 inches (forward), 35 feet 4 inches (aft).

Close-range AA armament (1945)
Nelson: Forty-eight 2-pounder pom-poms (6 × 8), sixteen 40-mm Bofors (4 × 4), sixty-one 20-mm (61 × 1).
Rodney: Forty-four 2-pounder pom-poms (5 × 8 + 1 × 4), sixty-eight 20-mm (58 × 1 + 5 × 2).

Fire-control equipment (1939)
Main armament: two director-control towers, one Admiralty fire-control table Mk I.

Secondary armament: four director-control towers, four fire-control clocks Type 'S'.

High-angle armament: two HACS Mk III (*Nelson*), one HACS Mk I (*Rodney*), two pom-pom directors Mk I*

Armour
As before, except for additional armour on lower-deck forward, in *Nelson* only.

12. The Genesis of the King George V Class, 1933 to 1936

The refusal of France and Italy to sign the London Naval Treaty of 1930, and the re-emergence of Germany as a naval power was, by 1935, beginning to upset the balance of capital ship strength that had existed since the Washington Conference. In 1929, Germany had laid down *Deutschland,* the first of three armoured ships, popularly known as 'pocket battleships' having a speed of 26 knots, an armament of six 11-inch guns and a published displacement of 10,000 tons. This was the largest size of vessel that Germany could build under the terms of the Treaty of Versailles, but these ships actually exceeded this displacement by over 2,000 tons. France replied, by laying down the battlecruisers *Dunkerque* in 1931, and *Strasbourg* in 1934. These two ships displaced 26,500 tons, were armed with eight 13-inch guns and had a designed speed of 29.5 knots. Germany, having by this time renounced the terms of the Treaty of Versailles, followed in 1934 by laying down the battlecruisers *Gneisenau* and *Scharnhorst* of 32,000 tons, armed with nine 11-inch guns and capable of a speed of 31.5 knots. In the same year, this European naval race took a step into the big league, when Italy laid down two 35,000-ton battleships, *Littorio* and *Vittorio Veneto,* armed with nine 15-inch guns and capable of a speed of 30 knots. France replied in the following year, by laying down *Richelieu* of 35,000 tons, armed with eight 15-inch guns and with a speed of 30 knots, which was to be followed by two sister ships, and Germany, in 1936, with *Bismarck,* the first of two 42,000-ton battleships, with eight 15-inch guns and a speed of 30 knots.

This new construction was not undertaken without restriction because the ships laid down by Italy and France were allowed to them as replacement tonnage under the terms of the Washington Treaty. The two German battleships were laid down after the signing of the Anglo-German Naval Treaty of 1935, whereby it was agreed that Germany could build up her naval strength to 35 per cent of that of the Royal Navy (excluding submarines) and that Germany would keep within the qualitative limitations of the Washington and London treaties, although she was not a signatory of those agreements.

By 1934, it was becoming clear that unless Britain undertook a programme of new construction, each of the major European powers would, in a few years, possess two new capital ships, unmatched by a corresponding pair in the Royal Navy. It was impossible, however, to begin such a programme until the expiration of the London Naval Treaty on 31st December, 1936, and before which, a second London Naval Conference was to take place. In April 1934, the Admiralty set out its views on the aims to be pursued at this conference, in an Admiralty paper which was submitted to the Cabinet. In this paper, it was "insisted" that the treaty to be negotiated, should not only provide for a return to a safer naval strength for Britain than had been permitted by the 1930 agreement, but also for the replacement of the battle fleet. Under no circumstances was an extension of the break in battleship construction to be contemplated, and it was regarded as of prime importance that Britain be allowed to commence her new construction immediately after the expiration of the 1930 agreement, i.e. on 1st January 1937. The Admiralty, however, was willing to accept a qualitative limitation which, it was considered, was necessary for political and financial reasons. In this respect, they put forward similar proposals to those made for the 1930 Conference, that is, a maximum limit on capital ships of 25,000 tons displacement, with 12-inch guns, or, if this was considered too little by the other powers, 28,000 tons with 12-inch guns. These proposals, of course, were made before the commencement in Italy and France of ships armed with 15-inch guns.

Staff Requirements for the 1937 capital ships

More than a year before the Admiralty made their views known to the Cabinet, detailed discussions had begun, about the general requirements and characteristics of the 1937 capital ships. This early start had been essential, because, if the first replacement ship was to be laid down on 1st January 1937, it was necessary to have a preparatory design ready before the naval conference that was due to take place in 1935. Time would then be available for the commencement of the detailed design before the orders would be placed, in June 1936.

In March 1933, the Controller submitted to the Assistant Chief of Naval Staff a memorandum in which he pointed out the desirability of investigating the main characteristics of the replacement capital ship at an early date. Although a similar investigation had been carried out in 1928, when the 1931 capital ships were under consideration, he felt that circumstances could have altered sufficiently to necessitate a re-drafting of the Staff requirements. The ACNS agreed, and in April, the Director of Training and Staff Duties circulated a memorandum to the Staff, calling for Staff requirements and putting forward the following considerations as being relevant:

"(a) The ship will be in replacement of a battleship, our battlecruisers will not come in for replacement for some years and before this occurs we will know the trend of foreign naval construction. There will therefore be three fast capital ships available during these years, i.e. 20% of our total numbers, capable of dealing with any foreign capital ship at present in construction or proposed so far as is known.

(b) The ship will commission in 1941 and its life will probably extend over a period of at least twenty years. In the first half of her life she will be confronted with 15 inch and 16 inch guns in foreign navies, whatever reduction the disarmament conference may decide upon. Moreover, the treaty reductions may not remain in force over the whole period [of her life] and abrogation of the treaty would probably see a return to the larger calibre [gun]. Protection in particular is very difficult to add to a ship at a later date and this is the present situation in regard to the great majority of the capital ships and all the 8 inch

[gun] cruisers of our fleet at the present time. They are inadequately protected and in the case of the battleships we cannot remedy the situation [sic].
(c) Considerable progress must be expected from various directions during the above period, e.g. attack from the air will probably develop considerably in extent and technique. Attack will be made in low visibility and at night. High level bombing with 2000 lbs bombs and the development of 'B' bombing may be expected. In underwater attack the magnetic pistol will threaten the, at present, unprotected bottoms of ships and the effect of near misses by big bombs will have to be considered. Extreme range gun-fire has already with the aid of aircraft spotting, become accepted policy in the U.S. Fleet. Concealment by smoke is already extensively practised and is likely to develop leading to the pressing home of torpedo attack to short range and the necessity for indirect fire.
The need for economy in construction and the provision of adequate accommodation for war complement will be an important consideration in future designs. A.C.N.S. has called for requirements in one month".
(Initialled D.T.S.D. 4/4/1933.)

The Staff requirements were duly prepared and are summarised below. They took slightly longer than one month to produce, being ready for submission to the Controller early in June 1933.

Main armament. A main armament in not less than four twin turrets, disposed as in the *Queen Elizabeth* class was strongly recommended. If this could not be achieved, because of limited tonnage or difficulty in arranging the necessary protection, the Staff were willing to accept an armament of three triple turrets disposed as in *Nelson* provided that "(a) the loading cycle of each gun in the triple mounting will not be appreciably greater than that of a similar gun mounted in a twin turret. (b) the loading arrangements will be such that guns of the A and B salvos can be loaded and fired entirely independently of each other".

Secondary armament. Surprisingly, the Staff recommended a return to broadside batteries of six 6-inch guns each side, for the secondary armament, and that the elevation of the guns above 30°, which was necessary for AA purposes, should be sacrificed. The advantages of battery guns compared to turret guns were, that they were cheaper, simpler, easier to replace and better protected, but on the other hand, they had smaller arcs of fire, were more difficult to supply with ammunition and were not watertight. Efforts were to be made, however to overcome these disadvantages by grouping the guns at a higher level than in the *Queen Elizabeth* and *Royal Sovereign* classes. The guns were to be capable of 30° elevation, have a rate of fire of eight rounds per minute, be provided with good flash-tight arrangements and protection from gun-blast and medium shell and bomb fragments. It was considered that the secondary armament could be used for long-range AA purposes, against aircraft coming within their fire up to 30° elevation, if a suitable fire-control system became available for this purpose at a future date.

Long-range AA armament. The long-range AA armament was to be mounted in between-decks twin mountings; either three on each side, or two on each side and one amidships. The largest possible arcs of training were to be provided, and elevation of up to 70°. The ship was to be designed so that 4.7-inch or 4-inch high-angle guns could be carried. The preferred calibre could not be decided until later.

Combination of high-angle and low-angle armament. A combination of the secondary and long-range AA requirements in a dual-purpose mounting was not considered practical, if a smaller calibre of gun than 5.1-inch was adopted. As 4.7-inch was the largest calibre of AA gun, then available, the dual-purpose armament was automatically discounted.

Close-range AA armament. The recommendations for the close-range AA armament were taken directly from the 1931 report of the Naval Anti-Aircraft Gunnery Committee, viz. – "it is considered that capital ships should carry four Mk. M pom poms, director controlled, and eight 0.5 inch M.G. fitted so that they are clear of gun blast and so that, as far as possible, two pom poms and four M.G.'s can fire on any one bearing at the same time".

Torpedo armament. The torpedo armament was to consist of one above-water torpedo tube quintuple mounting on each side. The torpedoes were to run on normal air with the maximum possible speed and an explosive warhead limited to 750 pounds. The arguments for fitting a torpedo armament were:

1. The great destructive power of the modern torpedo which would, at the least, require an enemy to reduce speed, if hit.
2. In daylight at long range, the torpedo was of little use, but in long- and close-range actions, in bad visibility or at night, the torpedo could be decisive.
3. The psychological effect on the enemy who knows you possess the capability to launch a torpedo at a fairly long range.
4. Modern 21-inch torpedoes could be provided with a power equal to or greater than the earlier 24.5-inch torpedo. Using normal air, a modern 21-inch torpedo had a range of 19,000 yards at 30 knots, carrying a 750-pound charge.

The arguments against carrying torpedoes were that the warheads and compressed-air vessels were a danger to the ship, and that the weight and space they occupied could be employed more usefully. These points, however, were dismissed on the grounds that experiments in 1920 showed that torpedo warheads were safe if placed above water in carefully selected positions, and that further trials in 1930 had shown that the explosion of air-vessels would not cause more than slight local damage. The weight and space occupied was considered insignificant, but, at the same time, it was stated that torpedoes were not to be carried at the expense of the anti-aircraft armament.

Armour. Provided the displacement were not reduced, the protection was to be the same as that recommended in 1928 for the 1931 capital ships, i.e. against 16-inch shell and 2,000-pound bombs, but the horizontal protection of the machinery spaces was to be against 1,000-pound bombs and dive-bomber attack. If the displacement were reduced, protection was to be provided against 14-inch instead of 16-inch shell.

Underwater protection. This was to be sufficient to withstand a 750-pound torpedo warhead. As in *Nelson*, a 5-foot deep double-bottom was to be provided.

Speed. A maximum speed of 23 knots.

Endurance. Requirements for endurance were summarised as follows, the last being the most severe:
1. "Sufficient to steam for 200 hours at 16 knots with steam for 18 knots, plus 8 hours at full speed, plus 16 hours at 18 knots with steam for full speed, plus 12 hours at 16 knots with steam for full speed. All on the hypothesis of 6 months out of dock."
2. "An addition of about 35% to the above, E in C being consulted in this matter, to allow for abnormal consumption due to weather, damage, oil left in tanks etc."
3. "As much additional fuel as to give 14,000 miles at 10 knots under trial conditions."

Aircraft. To carry six TSR aircraft amidships, two catapults, two cranes.

Bridges. To have bullet-proof protection, protection from wind and weather, clear view from signal-deck, clear arcs for signalling-projectors, semaphores etc., high signal-hoists and night-fighting arrangements as in *Nelson*.

Searchlights. Two to be fitted below the fore bridge, or in that general area, and four on the funnel positions.

Conning-tower. None to be fitted in order to save weight.

Fire-control positions. One main director-control tower, high up forward, and one low down aft. One secondary director-control tower to be fitted on each side forward. One high-angle director forward, and one aft.

On 10th January 1934, a meeting was held under the chairmanship of the First Sea Lord, Admiral Sir A. E. M. Chatfield, to discuss the size of future battleships in the light of the forthcoming naval conference. Among those present were the A.C.N.S. Vice-Admiral J. C. Little, and the Controller, Rear-Admiral C. M. Forbes. (Little had been one of the naval advisers to the British delegation at Washington in 1921 to 1922. Forbes was Commander-in-Chief, Home Fleet between 1939 and 1940.) The main factors governing any proposed limitation of battleship size were considered to be:
1. A proposal made by Britain at Geneva, to reduce the size of battleships to 25,000 tons displacement with 12-inch guns or 22,000 tons with 11-inch guns.
2. A similar proposal by Japan, for a reduction to 25,000 tons with 14-inch guns.
3. The known wish of the USA to retain the existing limitation of 35,000 tons and 16-inch guns.
4. The laying down of the French battlecruiser *Dunkerque* of 26,500 tons armed with 13-inch guns.
5. Germany had expressed a desire to build larger ships than *Deutschland*.

Of these points, the last was the only one likely to prevent a further limitation of battleship tonnage, but it was thought that the USA could be pressurised into agreeing to a ship of 28,000 tons armed with 12-inch guns. The Controller pointed out, however, that an investigation into the design of a 12-inch gun ship, had shown that if the full Staff requirements were to be met, the ship would displace about 32,000 tons. The initial reaction of the meeting was that this was "impossible" but the Assistant Chief of Naval Staff explained that the requirements were exploratory and based upon the ship being able to withstand 16-inch gunfire, attack by 2,000-pound bombs, and torpedoes with 750-pound warheads. It was generally agreed "that these ideas would have to be modified considerably and while the protection against 750 lbs torpedoes should be provided, if possible, deck armour to meet a 1,500 lbs bomb would have to be accepted". The meeting concluded with the decision that the Controller should investigate the design of a battleship of 28,000 tons, armed with eight, nine or ten 12-inch guns.

The Controller duly directed the Director of Naval Construction to prepare sketch designs and legends to meet these requirements, and on 5th April 1934, the DNC submitted the designs shown in Table 66 (overleaf).

In his description of these designs, the DNC pointed out that, although the Staff requirements for the secondary and anti-aircraft armaments had been met, the resulting arrangement was very cramped, especially in '12Q'. Moreover, the several different calibres of gun (6-inch, 4.7-inch, 2-pounder and 0.5-inch) would cause many problems in providing an efficient supply of ammunition. He asked, therefore, if the Staff requirements might be reconsidered, and as a result, it was decided to sacrifice the secondary armament of 6-inch guns and increase the number of 4.7-inch twin mountings. Designs '12N' and '12P' were considered to be the best, and the Director of Naval Construction modified these designs to include twenty-eight (in '12N') and twenty-four (in '12P') 4.7-inch high-angle guns. In the case of '12N', this necessitated the omission of the torpedo tubes. No subsequent design was to carry a secondary battery of 6-inch guns in casemates.

The development of the 12-inch gun designs continued for a short period, but it was eventually abandoned after the Foreign Office had reported that a qualitative reduction of the limits suggested by the Admiralty was unlikely to be achieved. This conclusion was based on preliminary conversations between the Foreign Office and the major naval powers, which revealed that a 25,000- to 28,000-ton, 12-inch gun ship would only be acceptable to France, Italy and Germany. It is not clear how these three powers agreed so readily to these proposals, when they were all preparing to build ships of 35,000 tons armed with 15-inch guns. Japan, moreover, was claiming the right to parity with the USA and Britain and was not prepared to consider any reduction to the existing qualitative limits until this was recognised.

The problem of deciding upon the outline requirements for the 1937 capital ships was further complicated by the need to counter the 15-inch gun capital ships, building or projected by the European naval powers. All these ships possessed a high speed, whereas the Admiralty had generally tended towards the provision of a speed equal to that of the existing battle fleet, i.e. 23 knots. An increase in the speed of the new ships would entail a sacrifice in either armament, or protection, or both. It was clear that the existing 35,000-ton displacement limit, would almost certainly remain in force and that, therefore, the question to be decided was, what percentage of this displacement was to be allotted to the machinery, protection and armament weights, and in what proportions. If too much weight were allotted to the machinery, the protection and or armament would suffer; if too much weight were allotted to the protection, the speed and or armament would suffer, and so on. Achieving the correct balance of offensive and defensive powers to meet the strategic, tactical, political and financial requirements was no easy task.

Table 66: Legends of battleship designs, April 1934

	12N	12O	12P	12Q
Length (pp) feet	570	570	590	590
Length (oa) feet	614	614	634	634
Beam (max) feet	102	102	103½	103½
Draught at lwl (mean) feet	29	29	28½	28½
Standard displacement (tons)	28,500	28,130	28,500	28,500
Deep load draught feet	32¼	32¼	31¾	31¾
SHP	45,000	45,000	45,000	45,000
Speed (at deep displacement) knots	23	23	23¼	23¼
Oil fuel capacity (tons)	3,500	3,500	3,500	3,500
Complement	1,378	1,400	1,425	1,470
Main armament (12-inch gun turrets):	4 twin	3 triple	5 twin	3 triple
Secondary and HA armament:	twelve 6-inch (12×1) twelve 4.7-inch (6×2 BD) HA twenty-four 2-pounder (4×8) thirty-two 0.5-inch (8×4)			
Torpedo armament:	Ten above-water (2×5) 15 torpedoes (22.25-inch)		None	
Aircraft	One	One	None	
Catapult	one on turret		None	
Armour (inches thickness):				
Belt abreast magazines (upper)	12½	12½	12	12
Belt abreast magazines (lower)	9–7	9–7	9–7	9–7
Belt abreast machinery (upper)	11½	11½	11	11
Belt abreast machinery (lower)	8–6	8–6	8–6	8–6
Deck over magazines	5½	5½	5	5
Deck over machinery	3½	3½	3	3½
Deck over steering gear and shafting	3½	3½	3	3½
Bulkheads (forward)	10 & 4	10 & 4	10 & 4	10 & 4
Bulkheads (aft)	10 & 4	10 & 4	10, 4 and 2	10, 4 and 2
Barbettes (maximum)	11½	11½	11½	11½
Turrets (front)	11½	11½	11½	11½
Turrets (side)	8	8	8	8
Turrets (roof)	5½	5½	5	5
Funnel-uptakes	7	7	6	7
Protection to 6-inch battery side	2	2	1	1½
Protection to 6-inch battery deck traverses and rear	1	1	¾	⅞
Protection to 4.7-inch mountings	1	1	½	¾
Torpedo bulkhead	2	2	1½	1½
Depth of double bottom (feet)	7	7	6	6
Weights (tons):				
Equipment	1,100	1,100	1,050	1,050
Armament	4,070	4,200	4,740	5,140
Machinery	1,900	1,900	1,900	1,900
Armour & protective plating	10,030	9,530	9,710	9,310
Hull	11,400	11,400	11,100	11,100
	28,500	28,130	28,500	28,500

Notes. All four designs had four boilers, and four sets of turbines in separate compartments. Belt armour was on the side and not internal as in *Nelson* and *Rodney*.
Protection was provided against 12-inch 950-pound shells, 1,500-pound bombs and 1,000-pound torpedoes.

The 1935 battleship designs

The Admiralty generally referred to the designs with high speeds as battlecruisers, but as they fit more readily into the category of fast battleship, which was to become the standard battleship type among the world's battle fleets, they are, herein, referred to as battleships.

Initially, the Admiralty favoured ships of 23 knots, armed with 14-inch guns (designs '14A' and '14Q'), but when it became known that 30-knot battleships were being built in Europe, the Director of Naval Construction was requested to produce outline designs for ships with this same speed (designs '16A', '15A', '14C', '14D' and '14E'). These designs were examined in detail, and• the question was raised as to whether the loss in protection, entailed in providing a high speed, could be accepted. It was generally agreed that a ship should be sufficiently protected to enable her to close an enemy to a reasonably effective range. At the same time, she would be able to use her high speed to remain at a favourable range and inclination to the enemy. The Battle Instructions specified that, in action, a decisive range of between 12,000 and 16,000 yards should be attempted. Some thought was given to specifying a greater range; 18,000 to 20,000 yards was suggested, which would reduce the weight of protection required to meet the battle requirements. This possibility, however, was dismissed for the following reasons:

"Decisive actions only occur when both sides either wish to fight or when one or other cannot avoid action, in which case fighting power and not speed is the ultimate requirement. The decision at short range may well depend finally on the morale and striking power of our fleet, a range should therefore be chosen which gives morale the greatest opportunity. Where the rate of hitting is high and factor of luck low, where the enemy is least able to avoid punishment and where our ships are not liable to destruction by magazine explosion [caused] by a lucky hit.

When the battle reaches this stage air spotting and the primary control positions, with many

Table 67: Particulars of 1935 battleship designs

	16A	16B	16C	15A	15B	14A	14Q	14C	14D	14E	14F
Length (pp) feet	730							730	730	730	700
Length (oa) feet	770							770	770	770	740
Beam (max) feet	104							104	104	104	104
Draught (mean)	28							28	28	28	28
SHP	112,000			112,000				112,000	112,000	112,000	80,000
Speed (knots)	30	27	27	30	27	23	23	30	30	30	27
Oil fuel capacity (tons)	4,000			4,000				4,000	4,000	4,000	4,000
Main armament:	nine 16-inch (3×3)	eight 16-inch (2×3+ 1×2)	nine 16-inch (3×3)	nine 15-inch (3×3)	nine 15-inch (3×3)	twelve 14-inch (4×3)	twelve 14-inch (3×4)	twelve 14-inch (3×4)	eight 14-inch (1×4+ 2×2)	ten 14-inch (2×4+ 1×2)	twelve 14-inch (3×4)
Armour (inches thickness):											
Belt, abreast magazines	12	14	12½	12½	14	13	13	12	14	12½	13
Belt, abreast machinery	11	13	12½	12½	13	12¼	12¼	11	13	12½	12
Deck, over magazines	5	6	5¼	5¼	6	5	5	5	6¼	5¼	6
Deck, over machinery	3	5¼	4¾	4¼	5½	3½	3½	3½	5	5¼	4
Bulkheads	10							10	10	10	10
Barbettes (maximum)	12							12	13	12	13
Turrets	16, 11, 9							12, 9, 7½	12, 9, 7½	12, 9, 7½	12, 9, 7½
Torpedo bulkhead	1½							1½	1¾	1½	1¾
Weights (tons):											
General equipment	1,200	1,200	1,200	1,200	1,200	1,200	1,200	1,200	1,200	1,200	1,200
Machinery	2,875	2,375	2,375	2,875	2,375	1,950	1,900	2,875	2,875	2,875	2,375
Armament	7,160	6,450	7,160	6,270	6,270	7,150	6,860	7,160	5,770	6,060	6,860
Armour	10,075	11,725	11,015	11,155	11,955	11,325	10,525	10,075	11,955	11,395	11,365
Hull	13,690	13,200	13,250	13,500	13,200	12,375	12,330	13,540	13,200	13,500	13,200
Standard displacement:	35,000	35,000	35,000	35,000	35,000	35,000	35,000	35,000	35,000	35,000	35,000

All these designs had a secondary HA/LA armament of ten twin 4·5-inch BD gun-mountings and carried four aircraft and one D1H catapult. The 1½-inch torpedo bulkhead gave protection against 750-pound warheads and the 1¾-inch torpedo bulkhead gave protection against 1,000-pound warheads.

of the refinements of fire control, may well be out of action having, it is hoped, contributed to gaining an ascendancy during the earlier stages. Although air spotting can give effective hitting and perhaps even a decision at higher ranges, for the final destruction of the enemy we must be prepared to close to a range where direct spotting is possible in the confusion and smoke of battle and when hits can be assured. For these reasons action ranges of 12,000 to 16,000 yards must be provided for in spite of the advance of air spotting and fire control and the design of the modern and reconstructed ships [must] permit them to fight at these approximate ranges against 14 inch [gun] fire."

Some doubt, therefore, having been cast upon the advisability of a 30-knot speed, it was suggested that a 3-knot reduction to 27 knots might be acceptable for the new ships, in view of the improved fighting power that would result. Many arguments were put forward to support this suggestion, some of them not entirely convincing. Omitting the obvious advantages of an increase in protection as a result of the decreased weight of machinery, these arguments can be briefly summarised as follows:

1. In a decisive action, fighting power, not speed, would be the main requirement of a capital ship.
2. Fast capital ships might be required to deal with similar foreign ships, on detached harassing operations, but not so much in a fleet action.
3. Although the fast ships would be suitable for employment against countries with similar ships, they would not necessarily be suitable against other possible enemies, e.g. a fast ship would be of less importance against Japan than against the European powers.
4. Superior speeds have little effect on strategic considerations.
5. The development of air reconnaissance has, to some extent, reduced the value of superior speed for reconnaissance purposes, and would give greater opportunity for gaining a position to ensure interception of an enemy force even if the British fleet were inferior in speed.

In order to establish in greater detail, the gain in fighting power that would result from a reduction in the speed, the Director of Naval Construction produced a number of 27-knot battleship designs ('16B', '16C', '15B' and '14F'). These, together with the earlier 23- and 30-knot designs, were carefully analysed by the Technical Division of the Naval Staff. The result was a detailed and lengthy paper on the armament and protection of the 1937 capital ships from which the following passage is extracted.

"Calibre of Guns

To decide the calibre of gun it is first necessary to investigate the effect of various mountings on protection and speed, if a proper balance between offence and defence is to be reached. Defence is a somewhat misleading term as applied to armour protection against gunfire for in circumstances where it enables our guns to reach the vitals of the enemy before his can reach ours then it is not purely a passive defence as it secures our offensive. It is generally accepted that a capital ship whether battleship or battlecruiser must be sufficiently powerful to contribute effectively in the battleline and to withstand aircraft and torpedo attack as far as possible.

It is assumed that the maximum displacement must be 35,000 tons and the problem is examined below under the following headings:

(a) Comparison of guns
(b) The 30-knot ship
(c) The 27-knot ship
(d) The 23-knot ship
(e) The *Nelson* design

The General Problem

To clear the issue the following general conclusions resulting from the investigations are outlined below:

(1) For a given displacement and speed there appears to be a correct balance of armament and protection and in faster ships it seems that this can generally be achieved by one of two calibres of gun separated by not more than one inch. The extra protection possible with the smaller guns compensates for the superior hitting power of the larger gun.

(2) A slower ship of the same displacement can be so well protected that no additional protection can usefully be added. The problem then, is that of estimating the value of the more numerous smaller gun, as compared with fewer heavier guns, in their shattering effect before the decisive range is reached. (By decisive range, 12,000–16,000 yards is meant, here and throughout this section.)

(3) Unless the ship with the lighter gun be adequately protected against the heavier gun, the advantage she gains by the greater number of guns is outweighed by the vulnerability of her vitals.

(4) It appears that neither nine 16 inch or twelve 14 inch guns can be mounted on a 30 knot ship with sufficient protection.

(5) A well balanced 15 inch gun ship can be designed which is a match for the ship mentioned in (4) and which is better able to stand in the line.

(6) At 27 knots there is no great difference between the 16 inch and 15 inch gun ships and they are both superior to the 14 inch gun ship.

(7) For a 23 knot ship the 16 inch gun seems the best unless twelve 15 inch or twelve 14 inch guns can be mounted. The more numerous guns might tell at medium or long ranges but the 16 inch guns will be superior at decisive ranges. The inclusion of four turrets congests the design.

The Value of Speed as Protection

The superiority of speed if sufficient is of undoubted technical value in certain circumstances to enable an action to be forced or avoided. The statement, however, that speed can afford protection in action is only true to a limited extent in so far as it enables the fighting range to be dictated but this does not apply when the margin of speed is small or in low visibility. It is also said that the fast ship can use her speed to keep her armour at a favourable inclination and thus increase its protective value. It is very open to question whether, in the uncertainties of varying conditions of battle, the fast ship could in fact dictate the inclination of her armour except perhaps when fighting a much slower ship. The value of speed as protection in battle cannot therefore be relied upon.

Comparison of Guns

It is evident that hitting power produced by the striking energy and explosive power of a shell and the chance of hitting, produced by the number of guns per salvo, are the important factors. It is therefore, on this basis that the comparison is made below. Rate of fire, time of flight, etc., are not taken into account.

Hitting Power

The means by which gunfire can reduce the fighting efficiency of an opponent are:

(a) By penetrating the vitals through the armour protection.

(b) By shattering the soft ends, bridges and fire control positions.

For penetrating the vitals it is evident that against a ship with equal protection the larger gun has the advantage. The shattering effect may be of particular importance when fighting at ranges at which neither ship's armour can be pierced. In these circumstances, the smaller more numerous gun should hit more often but this must be weighed against the extra explosive power of a larger shell.

Table 68: Ranges below which side armour is penetrated by AP shell at 90° inclination

Armour thickness	By 14-inch 1,590-lb shell	By 15-inch 1,938-lb shell	By 16-inch 2,375-lb shell
14-inch	13,700 yards	17,200 yards	20,000 yards
13-inch	15,800 yards	19,400 yards	22,000 yards
12-inch	18,000 yards	21,700 yards	24,500 yards
11-inch	20,500 yards	24,500 yards	28,000 yards
10-inch	23,700 yards	28,000 yards	32,000 yards

Ranges above which deck armour is penetrated by AP shells

Armour thickness	14-inch	15-inch	16-inch
6-inch	immune	32,500 yards	31,000 yards
5-inch	32,000 yards	29,500 yards	
4-inch	28,000 yards	26,000 yards	
3-inch	24,000 yards	22,000 yards	
2-inch	20,000 yards	18,000 yards	

Chance of Hitting

It is here assumed that an increase in the number of guns per salvo results in a proportional increase in the hits to be expected. The exact truth of this assumption in practice is perhaps open to doubt, but it is a fact that the chance of hitting is improved by the extra rounds in a salvo and the increased rate of fire may enable the target to be found more easily.

For the number of guns here considered, that is four to six guns per salvo, this assumption may give an unduly unfavourable view of the more numerous gun. The heavy gun is widely favoured in our service but it must be recognised that both size and number of guns are important considerations.

The 30-knot Ship

The following assumptions are made:

(a) Maximum displacement 35,000 tons.
(b) Speed of 30 knots.
(c) Minimum of eight main armament guns.
(d) Only three turrets.
(e) At least one turret must be able to fire aft and therefore the *Nelson* design cannot be accepted.

Designs '14C' and '16A'

These ships are vulnerable to vital damage by 16 inch and 15 inch gun fire through their belts, considerably outside decisive ranges. They are not well protected against 14 inch gun fire and their machinery compartments are unduly open to penetration by plunging shell and bombs, particularly '16A' with her 3 inch deck.

It might appear that '14C' would have some advantage in the shattering effect of her twelve guns upon unprotected parts. She might expect to obtain four hits for every three scored against her by the 16 inch gun ship but this advantage must be balanced against the explosive effect of individual 16 inch hits which is $1\frac{1}{2}$ times greater than that of the 14 inch and against the considerable extra penetrating power of the 16 inch shell.

Both ships are considered to be over gunned for 30 knot ships of 35,000 tons, they are too lightly protected to stand up against other 30 knot designs and they could not contribute effectively in the battle line without grave risk of damage.

Designs '14E' and '15A'

These ships have similar protection except that the machinery deck of '15A' is weaker than that of '14E', by about 3000 yards against 16 inch plunging shell. Neither could stand in the line at decisive range without grave risk but they could contribute usefully at about 19,000 yards against 16 inch and 15 inch gunfire. Against each other '15A' appears to be the better ship, she has greater hitting power, her protection against 14 inch shell is better than that of '14E' against 15 inch shell and her nine guns compare favourably with her opponent's ten. Because of the superior hitting power of her 15 inch guns she is also better for fighting against other ships and for standing in the line.

Design '14D'

Although her protection is good this ship is considered to be under gunned and is not further considered in this analysis.

Comparison between '15A' and '16A'

The 15 inch guns should be able to penetrate the belt of '16A' slightly before that of '15A' becomes vulnerable to 16 inch gunfire. The machinery deck of '16A' is penetrable by 15 inch shell at 21,000 yards while that of '15A' keeps out 16 inch shell up to 25,000 yards. Taking into consideration the extra explosive power of the 16 inch shell there seems little to choose between these ships when fighting against each other but if both ships had to stand in the battle line against 16 inch or 15 inch gunfire, '15A' would have an advantage in protection and this design is considered a better balanced ship.

Design '14E'

This ship with her ten 14 inch guns and similar protection to '15A' does not compare favourably with '16A' whose 16 inch shell can pierce the belt of '14E' at 18,500 yards, i.e. 1,000 yards before her own belt is vulnerable to 14 inch gunfire.

Protection against Bombs

This problem is not here examined in detail but the decks required as defence against plunging shell are comparable with those required for bombs. It would appear that the deck protection should be as in '14D' or '14E' and that '14C' and '16A' have insufficient deck protection.

Table 69: Heights above which deck armour is penetrated by bombs

Armour thickness (inches)	2,000-lb AP bomb	15,000-lb AP bomb	1,000-lb AP bomb	500-lb SAP bomb
7	9,000 ft	13,000 ft	immune	immune
6	7,000 ft	10,600 ft	15,000 ft	immune
5	5,000 ft	7,800 ft	10,500 ft	immune
4	3,000 ft	5,000 ft	7,000 ft	12,000 ft
3	1,000 ft	2,500 ft	4,000 ft	7,000 ft
2	—	—	2,000 ft	3,200 ft

The 30-knot Ship, Conclusions

(a) All ships except '14C' and '16A' can be well protected against 14 inch gunfire except when the armament is greatly reduced as in '14D'. The 15 inch and 16 inch guns can penetrate the protection of the more heavily armed vessels. It appears, therefore, that the 14 inch gun ship should be ruled out unless required by treaty.

(b) 16 inch guns cannot be mounted in a 30 knot ship with adequate protection ('16A').

(c) 15 inch guns can be mounted in a comparatively well protected ship ('15A').

The 30 knot 15 inch gun ship would incur grave risks at decisive ranges but she is able to contribute effectively in the battle line at useful ranges and would be a match for any 30 knot 16 inch or 14 inch gun ship of 35,000 tons. The conclusion therefore, reached is that the 15 inch gun is the best armament for a 30 knot ship of 35,000 tons displacement.

The 27 knot Ship

Comparison is here made on the basis of fighting power in order to assess the gain resulting from a sacrifice of 3 knots in speed. This margin was chosen as that which while enabling an addition to fighting power is insufficient to permit the faster ship to dictate the fighting range with any certainty. The 27 knot ships are compared below with the 30 knot ships '16A' and '15A'.

Comparison of '14F' with '16A' and '15A'

As compared with '16A', '14F' has a valuable superiority in deck protection. She should obtain four 14 inch hits at useful ranges for every three 16 inch hits by her opponent. '16A' will gain an advantage at 18,500 yards by being able to pierce '14F's' belt 1,000 yards before her own belt can be pierced by 14 inch shells. '14F' will be better able to stand in the line than '16A'. Against '15A' similar remarks apply except that '14F' has not in this case so great an advantage in deck protection but she is able to close to a more effective range for bringing her high volume of fire to bear. It would appear that '14F' is as powerful as '16A' or '15A' and she has an asset in her good decks and torpedo bulkhead.

Comparison of '15B' with '16A' and '15A'

Against '16A', '15B' has a 2,500 yard advantage in belt protection and greatly superior deck protection. Against '15A' she is about equal when between the ranges of 27,000 and 17,500 yards when neither ship's vitals are vulnerable. '15B' having better armour is however more able to withstand air attack and to close to decisive ranges.

Comparison of '16C' with '16A' and '15A'

The same method of comparison shows that '16C' is of definite superior fighting power to '16A' or '15A'.

Comparison of '15B' with '16C'

There is little to choose between these two 27 knot ships other than the superior explosive effect of the 16 inch shell against unprotected parts and the somewhat better protection of '15B' against bombs. If both ships were in the line against battleships the armament of '16C' would have a greater shattering effect but the protection of '15B' would enable her to close to 17,000 yards for decisive results, that is 2,000 yards closer than '16C' could close without risk. '16C' would also be slightly more vulnerable to plunging fire and her torpedo bulkhead is lighter. (NOTE. Design '16C' was an estimation only, derived from the weights given for '16B' and '16A'.)

'16B'

This design had two triple and one twin turret which was not considered satisfactory and was not examined in detail.

The 27 knot Ship, Conclusions

A well balanced 27 knot ship can be built with either nine 16 inch, nine 15 inch or twelve 14 inch guns. '16C' is probably the best design but '15B' may be considered the better general service ship as she can contribute to the battle line more effectively than the 16 inch or 14 inch gun ships and she will be a good match for any 30 knot ship.

The 23 knot Ship

From the figures given for the *Nelson*, '14A' and '14Q' it appears that a nine 16 inch gun ship could be designed with one turret aft and full battleship protection as in '15B'. To mount 15 inch guns in this ship would be of little use unless a considerable increase in numbers were possible, and it appears unlikely that twelve 15 inch guns could be included. The protection is already adequate so that the weight saved by mounting nine 15 inch guns would only serve to reduce the displacement. A twelve – 14 inch gun design would gain in the number of hits over a wide and useful zone, but the extra hitting power of the 16 inch gun combined with its penetrative power at decisive range would favour the larger gun.

The *Nelson* Design

The layout of the *Nelson* design is attractive from a material point of view and if adopted might permit each of the 27 knot designs being given an increased speed to 30 knots or better protection. The DNC however points out that although the *Nelson* design provided a saving in weight it is not considered that a similar economy will result in a ship designed to carry the HA/LA armament, aircraft, etc. Further it is unlikely that the machinery of a 27 or 30 knot ship could be satisfactorily accommodated if the three turrets are grouped forward.

General Conclusions

Although the conclusions regarding the effect of guns on armour must be drawn with great caution it is fair to say that the relative performance of guns against belt armour has been estimated correctly. The information on which the performance of deck armour is based is however scanty. There are important factors which cannot be measured in an analysis of this nature. In good visibility and with aircraft spotting great damage can be done at long ranges in which case the ship with a powerful armament and less protection may be at an advantage and the decisive range for which the better protected ship was designed may never be reached. A margin of protection of one ship over another must be entirely outweighed by the conditions of the battle – visibility, inclination, etc. It is dangerous to assume that fighting range can be dictated.

The problem may be considered as that of obtaining the correct balance between armament, protection and speed. '16A' and '14D' are examples of the two extremes of a well adjusted balance. In '16A' too powerful an armament is mounted with the result that this ship is very vulnerable and '14D' is over protected for her armament.

With the present treaty limitations the ideal would appear to be one of the following: —

(a) a 15 inch gun armament for the 30 knot ship.

(b) A 15 inch or 16 inch gun armament for the 27 knot ship. The 15 inch gun may be preferred because she could stand in the line better and has somewhat stronger decks.

(c) A 16 inch or 14 inch gun armament for the 23 knot ship if, as assumed, twelve 15 inch guns cannot be mounted."

The above quoted paper was discussed at a meeting of the Sea Lords on 20th September 1935, and it was concluded that the new ships should be armed with nine 15-inch guns, and have a speed of not less than 29 knots. These ships were intended primarily to counter the ships then being built in Europe, and it was realised that they would be inferior in gun power to the 16-inch gun ships that would probably be constructed by the USA and Japan.

It was necessary, however, to reconsider this decision when, early in October 1935, the Admiralty were informed that the Government of the USA would probably accept a limitation of gun calibre to 14 inches, with a maximum displacement of 35,000 tons. This was regarded as an important concession, provided that Japan would also agree, but unless considerable delay to the completion of the first two ships of the replacement programme were accepted, it would not be possible to await the outcome of the conference before being committed to a final decision. If the ships were to be commissioned in 1940, it would be necessary to order the guns before the end of 1935 and to begin the design of the gun-mountings immediately. Having pressed for a further qualitative reduction in capital ships for so long, it was felt that the American proposal could not be ignored. It was considered important, moreover, that the USA and Japan be prevented, if possible, from building ships armed with 16-inch guns. A 14-inch gun ship, built to counter the European designs, would then be a match also for the ships of USA and Japan, whereas if these nations built 16-inch gun ships, it would be necessary for Britain to build two types of capital ship. On 10th October, therefore, the Sea Lords decided to recommend that the first two ships be of 35,000 tons displacement, armed with twelve 14-inch guns in three quadruple turrets, capable of a speed of 28 knots and have the best protection possible. This recommendation was sanctioned by the Board on 28th November, and by the Cabinet a few days later. Before examining in detail the design of the 1937 capital ships, it is convenient to describe briefly the results of the London Naval Conference which began on 9th December 1935.

The London Naval Conference, 1935/1936

The Treaty which resulted from this conference was probably the most workable of all those produced since 1922. It was also the most short-lived. Its principle advantage over the earlier agreements, was the abandonment of a quantitive limitation that in the past had caused much grievance, particularly in Japan. Nevertheless, Japan refused to sign the Treaty, and withdrew from the Conference, and Italy withheld her agreement until December 1938. Britain, France and the USA signed the London Naval Treaty in March 1936, in which, among other details, it was agreed to limit capital ships to 35,000 tons and 14-inch guns. If Japan failed to agree to this limitation by April 1937, the maximum gun calibre was to revert to 16 inches. The signatories also had the right of escalation, if any nation built ships outside the Treaty limits.

Similar treaties were negotiated between Britain and Germany, and Britain and Russia, during the same period, and were ratified in November 1937. In these two cases, however, the limit on gun calibre was 16 inches.

The 1935/1936 battleship designs

The legend and sketch design of '14L' were submitted to the Controller on 12th November 1935. After this design had been examined, the Director of Naval Construction was instructed to prepare a second design, with the machinery spaces moved farther aft, in order to reduce the length of the propeller shafts,

Table 70: Legend of particulars of Design 14L, November 1935

Length (pp)	700 feet
Length (wl)	740 feet
Length (oa)	745 feet
Beam (extreme)	104 feet
Draught (mean)	28 feet (standard) 31½ feet (deep)
SHP	100,000
Speed in standard condition	28 knots
Oil fuel capacity	4,000 tons
Armament:	Twelve 14-inch guns (3×4) Twenty 4.5-inch HA/LA guns (10×2) Four eight-barrel pom-poms Four four-barrel 0.5-inch machine-guns Four aircraft One DIIH catapult
Armour:	
Belt, abreast magazines	14-inch
Belt, abreast machinery	13-inch
Bulkheads	10-inch
Barbettes	13-inch (maximum)
Turrets	13-inch front, 9-inch side, 7-inch rear, 6-inch roofs
4.5-inch gun positions	2-inch vertical, 1-inch horizontal
Deck, over magazines	6-inch
Deck, over machinery	5-inch
Torpedo bulkheads	1¾-inch
Weights (tons):	
General equipment	1,050
Machinery	2,550
Armament	6,650
Armour & protection	11,800
Hull	12,950
Standard displacement:	35,000 tons

which was vulnerable to underwater attack. The new design, '14N', had the same legend particulars as '14L' and was generally similar in appearance, except that it had one funnel instead of two, so that the ship's angle of inclination would be less easy to estimate. By moving the machinery farther aft, the length of the propeller shafts was reduced by thirty-two feet and this required that the 4.5-inch magazines and mountings be concentrated forward of the machinery spaces.

Designs '14L' and '14N' were examined at a meeting of the Sea Lords, held on 2nd January 1936. Attention was concentrated on '14N' which was favoured by the Assistant Chief of Naval Staff and the Controller. The most important points raised during the discussions were:

1. The designed speed was 28 knots, but in extra deep condition with 2,000 tons of water in the bouyancy spaces and 4,000 tons of oil fuel, the speed would be reduced to 27 knots. The First Sea Lord questioned the desirability of accepting this reduction in speed, and suggested omitting the water protection. The Director of Naval Construction pointed out that this would result in a considerable loss in underwater protection. It was then suggested that oil fuel might be carried in the buoyancy space, instead of water, thereby reducing the weight of liquid carried, from 6,000 to 4,000 tons. It was decided that the DNC should investigate this possibility.

2. A 5.25-inch twin mounting had been proposed for a new design of small anti-aircraft cruisers (the *Dido* class), and the First Sea Lord suggested that eight of these mountings be substituted for the ten 4.5-inch mountings, as this would greatly improve both the low-angle and high-angle fire of the new ships. The Director of Naval Ordnance was called into the meeting, and he explained that the design of the twin 5.25-inch gun had not yet begun, but that he would be able to provide definite information by the end of 1936. The First Sea Lord said that as the ships would not be ready until 1940, there seemed to be ample time in which to decide this point, and the Director of Naval Construction confirmed that such a delay was acceptable.

3. The Assistant Chief of Naval Staff emphasised the importance of raising the belt armour and fitting the armoured deck at main-deck level instead of at middle-deck level, as in '14N'. This would result in improved stability in the damaged condition, and a reduction in the volume of the structure above the armoured-deck vulnerable to damage by semi armour-piercing bombs.

4. The Engineer-in-Chief proposed that the machinery be designed for a higher power, in anticipation of the probable future development of boilers. He estimated that a ½-knot increase could be expected, if an additional 100 tons was allowed for the machinery.

As a result of the above meeting, the DNC prepared a third design, '14Ø', the particulars of which were the same as for '14L' except for the details given in Table 71.

All the suggested improvements, raising the armoured deck, substitution of oil fuel for water in the buoyancy space, and 5.25-inch mountings for the 4.5-inch mountings were included in Design '14Ø'. The re-arrangement of the armour involved a substantial increase in weight, and to compensate for this, it was necessary to reduce the thickness of the deck and upper belt armour. Thus an improved distribution of armour was accompanied by a sacrifice in armoured strength. This sacrifice was viewed with some concern and was the subject of a lengthy Staff memorandum, in which the suitability of Design '14Ø' to meet British requirements, was examined in some detail. It was concluded that there were two main faults in Design '14Ø'. First, her magazines and machinery spaces were insufficiently protected against shell and bomb attack, and second, the distribution of the secondary and light anti-aircraft armament was such, that much interference would be caused by the blast of the 5.25-inch guns. These armaments were also considered to be too concentrated for safety.

The Staff suggested a number of possible improvements to the protection of '14Ø' which involved either the thickening of the existing armour, or the provision of a 2-inch deck below the main armoured-deck, which would isolate any damage and protect the magazines from splinters. In solving one problem, however, the Staff were creating another, in that the weight required to improve the protection would have to be taken from either the armament or the machinery. The following possible courses of action were put forward:

1. Revert to an armoured-deck at middle-deck level as in Design '14N'. This idea was not viewed with much favour in view of the loss in armoured stability, and the resulting increased vulnerability to bomb damage.

2. Reduce the speed of Design '14Ø' by 2 knots, which might save 500 tons. It was pointed out, that a 27-knot ship would be shorter, and it might not be possible to accommodate the aircraft.

3. Reduce the armament to nine 14-inch guns, which would save 1,200 to 1,400 tons. It was

Table 71: Particulars of Design 14Ø

SHP	100,000 (110,000 at designed overload	
Speed (standard)	28.5 knots (29.25 knots at overload)	
Speed (deep)	27.5 knots (28.25 knots at overload)	
Secondary armament:	Sixteen 5.25-inch HA/LA guns (8×2)	
Armour:		
Upper belt, abreast magazines	13-inch	tapering to 6-inch below waterline
Lower belt, abreast magazines	14-inch	
Upper belt, abreast machinery	12-inch	tapering to 5-inch below waterline
Lower belt, abreast machinery	13-inch	
Bulkheads	10-inch and 9-inch	
Deck, over magazines	5½-inch	
Deck, over machinery	4½-inch	
Weights (tons):		
General equipment	1,050	
Machinery	2,635	
Armament	6,650	
Armour and protection	12,050	
Hull	13,065	
Standard displacement:	35,450 tons	

felt that this might also allow for a slight increase in speed and, although in previous discussions a nine 14-inch gun ship was considered undesirable against European 15-inch gun ships, it was thought that the proposed improvement in protection and speed would warrant a reconsideration of this design.

4. Reduce the armament to nine 15-inch guns, which would save about 800 tons. This proposal was thought to have the most merit as Design '15C' was considered by many to be the best of the designs that had been considered in August and September 1935. Unfortunately, Treaty considerations prevented a 15-inch gun being taken into account.

With regard to the problems of the secondary and AA armaments, it was recommended that the 5.25-inch mountings on each side, be separated into two groups as had been originally provided in Design '14L'. This entailed the revision of the earlier decision to concentrate the secondary armament and its magazines in order to shorten the length of the propeller shafting. The magazines for the after group of 5.25-inch guns would have to be placed abaft the engine rooms, which, in turn, would have to be moved forward. The increased vulnerability of the shafting, however, would be compensated, to some extent, by the reduced vulnerability of the 5.25-inch magazines. Their dispersal meant that not all were at risk from a single, underwater explosion.

The Staff paper concluded that, a nine 14-inch gun design, with improved protection and re-arranged secondary armament should be investigated in detail. This resulted in a fourth, and final, design, '14P', but instead of nine guns, the ship was designed to carry ten. This was achieved by substituting a twin mounting for the quadruple mounting in 'B' position. The saving in armament weight was about 770 tons, and some small saving was also made in the hull weight. In February 1936, a meeting was held to discuss the building programme for the two 1936-programme capital ships, in the event of their being armed with two quadruple, and one twin mounting. It was anticipated that the additional work involved in providing a twin mounting would set the design back by two months, and the following provisional programme was therefore decided:

Order gun mountings, April 1936.
Order ships, September 1936.
Lay down ships, February 1937.
Launch ships, January 1939.
First turret shipped, March 1939.
Second turret shipped, May 1939.
Third turret shipped, December, 1939.
Completion of ships, July 1940.

The design of the 14-inch quadruple mounting was begun in October 1935. The twin mounting involved a new design of mounting, re-designing the supports for 'B' turret and re-calculating the ship's trim. The latter meant moving the citadel four to six feet forward to compensate for the reduced weight of the twin mountings.

On 3rd April, the Board met to make their final decision between the ten- and twelve-gun designs. The consensus was, that a twelve-gun ship would be insufficiently protected and that the ten-gun ship must therefore be accepted. It was pointed out by the Controller, however, that this decision would involve a delay of nine months in the completion of the ships, as the design of the 14-inch twin gun-mounting had not yet begun. The preliminary design for the quadruple mounting had been completed in March, and in May 1936, orders were placed for four quadruple and two twin mountings. As the design of the mountings developed, it became clear that the amount of drawing-office work had been underestimated, and that the forecast for the shipment of the mountings, quadruple and twin, could not be maintained. The problem was further complicated by the shortage of skilled labour to work on the construction of gun-mountings. The final anticipated dates of delivery were February 1940 for the first mounting, April 1940 for the second and May 1940 for the third. Compared to the programme set out in February 1936, this amounted to a delay of eleven months in the completion of the quadruple mountings, and six months, in the completion of the twin mountings.

The two ships of the 1936 programme were sanctioned by Parliament on 21st April 1936. The sketch and legend of Design '14P' were approved by the Board on 24th May 1936, and the final design, on 15th October 1936. The ships were ordered on 29th July 1936.

In October 1936, it became necessary to decide upon the design of the three ships of the 1937 programme. Again, the gun-mountings were the controlling factor, because from this time on, any delay in ordering the mountings, would result in an equivalent delay in the completion of the ships. Japan had still not volunteered any information as to what type of gun she would adopt, and it was clear that a decision would have to be made, without knowing the Japanese intentions. The only option – unless a considerable delay were accepted – was to build ships to the still valid treaty limit. The Controller proposed that the three capital ships of the 1937 programme be repeats of the 1936 programme. This was approved by the Board on 16th November 1936.

Table 72: Legend of particulars of Design 14P, September 1936 (Final design for the *King George V* class)

Length (pp)	700 feet
Length (wl)	740 feet
Length (oa)	745 feet
Beam (maximum)	103 feet
Standard displacement	35,000 tons
Mean draught	28 feet (standard) 31½ feet(deep)
SHP	100,000 (110,000 at 10 per cent overload)
Speed in standard condition	28.5 knots (29.25 knots at 10 per cent overload)
Speed in deep condition	27.5 knots (28.25 knots at 10 per cent overload)
Total oil fuel capacity	3,700 tons
Endurance at 10 knots (trial condition)	14,000 nautical miles
Complement (as C in C's flagship in war)	1,645
Armament:	Ten 14-inch guns (2×4+1×2) 80 rpg Sixteen 5.25-inch HA/LA guns (8×2) 200 rpg Four eight-barrel pom-pom Mk VI mountings, 500 rpg Four four-barrel 0.5-inch mountings 2,500 rpg Four aircraft, one DIIIH catapult

13. The King George V Class, 1937 to 1946

The *King George V* class were excellent ships within the limits imposed by treaty restrictions, and it is somewhat unfortunate that other nations did not observe the restrictions so seriously as the Admiralty. Although there was little in the appearance of the ships to suggest a connection, they were descendants of *Nelson* and *Rodney*, via the considerable number of sketch designs produced between 1927 and 1936.

The five ships of the class were divided between two building programmes (two under the 1936 programme and three under the 1937 programme) but only six months separated the laying down of the first and last ships. Not since the First World War had so many capital ships been on the stocks at one time. The long-delayed replacement programme had begun, but not soon enough for even one of the ships to be completed before war descended upon Europe in September 1939. In that month, the capital ship programme was reviewed and the rate of construction of the *King George V* class was accelerated in the hope that the first ship would complete in September 1940, and the remainder, during 1941. The war, however, brought heavy demands on labour and materials, and much of the effort being put into battleship construction had to be transferred to work of a higher priority such as the repair and construction of merchant ships and escorts. This problem had become so acute by May 1940, that it was necessary to suspend the construction of the last two ships, *Anson* and *Howe*. Work recommenced on *Anson* after three months, and on *Howe,* after about six months. The first ship, *King George V*, was completed in December 1940, and each subsequent ship of the class was delayed slightly more than the the one before, until almost two years separated completion of the first and last ships.

Table 73: Construction of *King George V* class

	Laid down	Launched	Completed	Builders
King George V	1st January 1937	21st February 1939	11th December 1940	Vickers Armstrong
Prince of Wales	1st January 1937	3rd May 1939	31st March 1941	Cammell Laird
Duke of York (ex *Anson*)	5th May 1937	28th February 1940	4th November 1941	John Brown
Anson (ex *Jellicoe*)	20th July 1937	24th February 1940	22nd June 1942	Swan, Hunter
Howe (ex *Beatty*)	1st June 1937	9th April 1940	29th August 1942	Fairfield

Main armament

As a result of the problems encountered with the 16-inch Mk I, the high-velocity heavy gun never regained favour with the British Navy. The new 14-inch 45-calibre Mk VII gun fired a 1,590-pound shell, which, with a full charge of 338 pounds of SC cordite, gave the comparatively moderate nominal muzzle velocity of 2,475 feet per second. These figures did not differ widely from those of the 14-inch Mk I guns that were carried by the battleship *Canada* during the First World War, but the

Armour:	
Belt, above waterline	15-inch abreast magazines 14-inch abreast machinery
Belt, below waterline	15-inch and 5½-inch abreast magazines 14-inch and 4½-inch abreast machinery
Bulkheads	10-inch and 12-inch
Barbettes	14-inch
Turrets	13-inch front, 9-inch sides, 7-inch rear, 6-inch roof
Main-deck	6-inch over magazines, 5-inch over machinery
Lower-deck	5-inch to 2½-inch forward, 5-inch to 4½-inch aft
5.25-inch casemates	2-inch and 1-inch vertical, 1-inch horizontal
Bullet-proof plating	1-inch and ½-inch
Torpedo bulkhead	1¾-inch
Weights:	
General equipment	1,050
Machinery	2,685
Armament	6,050
Armour & protection	12,500
Hull	13,215
Total:	35,500 tons*

* This was the estimated standard in September 1936. It was hoped that careful attention to weight saving in all departments would result in the displacement being reduced to 35,000 tons.

Prince of Wales in heavy seas, May 1941.

PARTICULARS OF THE *KING GEORGE V* CLASS, 1940 to 1946

Displacement

	Standard	Deep
King George V (1940)	36,727 tons	42,076 tons
King George V (1945)	39,100 tons (approx)	44,460 tons
Howe (1942)	39,150 tons	44,510 tons
Duke of York (1945)	39,450 tons (approx)	44,794 tons
Anson (1945)	40,000 tons (approx)	45,360 tons

Tons per inch: 122 in standard condition.

Dimensions

Length:	oa	pp
As designed	745 feet	700 feet
Duke of York	745 feet 1⅝ inches	700 feet 1 inch
Howe	744 feet 11½ inches	699 feet 11½ inches
Anson	745 feet 0¼ inches	700 feet 0¼ inches

Beam (maximum):
103 feet (designed); 103 feet 0⅝ inches (*Howe*).

Draught:	Standard	Deep
King George V (1940)	29 feet (mean)	32 feet 6 inches (mean)
Howe (1942)	29 feet 6 inches (forward) 31 feet 7 inches (aft)	34 feet 2 inches (mean)
Anson (1945)	31 feet 3 inches (mean)	34 feet 9 inches (mean)

Armament
Ten 14-inch Mk VII 45-cal breech-loading: two quadruple mountings Mk III and one twin mounting Mk II.
Sixteen 5.25-inch 50-cal quick-firing Mk I: eight high-angle/low-angle twin mountings Mk I.

Close-range AA armament (1945)
King George V: sixty-four 2-pounder pom-poms (8 × 8), ten 40-mm Bofors (2 × 4 + 2 × 1), thirty-six 20-mm Oerlikons (6 × 2 + 24 × 1).

Duke of York: eighty-eight 2-pounder pom-poms (8 × 8 + 6 × 4), eight 40-mm Bofors (2 × 4), fifty-five 20-mm Oerlikons (39 × 1 + 8 × 2).

Anson: eighty-eight 2-pounder pom-poms (8 × 8 + 6 × 4), eight 40-mm Bofors (2 × 4), sixty-five 20-mm Oerlikons (53 × 1 + 6 × 2).

Howe: eighty-eight 2-pounder pom-poms (8 × 8 + 6 × 4), twenty-six 40-mm Bofors (2 × 4 + 18 × 1), eight 20-mm Oerlikons (4 × 2).

Ammunition stowage (as designed)
14-inch: 80 rounds per gun (100 rounds maximum).
5.25-inch: 400 rounds per gun.
2-pounder: 1,800 rounds per barrel.

Fire-control equipment
Main armament: two main director-control towers, one Admiralty fire-control table Mk VII.
High-angle/low-angle armament: four HACS Mk IV. four HACS tables Mk IV for high-angle fire, four Admiralty fire-control clocks Mk VII(M) for low-angle fire; Mk IV directors in *King George V* and *Prince of Wales*, Mk V directors in remainder. (Mk V replaced by Mk VI in *Anson* only.)

Close-range AA armament: six pom-pom directors Mk IV.

Range-finders
Two 41-foot in 'A' and 'Y' turrets.
One 30-foot in 'B' turret.
Six 15-foot in main and high-angle/low-angle directors.
Two 9-foot on admiral's bridge.

Searchlights
Six 44-inch (four removed 1944/45), four 20-inch (signalling).

Armour
Belt abreast magazines (C): 15 inch, 5½ inch at lower edge.
Belt abreast machinery (C): 14 inch, 4½ inch at lower edge.
Belt forward and aft of citadel: 13 inch, 12 inch and 11 inch, all tapering to 5½ inch at lower edge.
Bulkheads (C): 12 inch forward, 10 inch and 4 inch aft.
Barbettes (C): 13 inch sides, 12 inch and 11 inch forward and aft.
Turrets (C): 12¾ inch front, 8.82 inch front side.
Turrets (NC): 6.86 inch rear side and back, 5.88 inch roof.
Main-deck (NC): 6 inch over magazines, 5 inch over machinery.
Lower-deck (NC): 5 inch, 4 inch, 3½ inch and 2½ inch forward, 4½ inch and 5 inch aft.
5.25-inch turrets: 1½ inch front, 1-inch side, rear and crown.
5.25-inch casemates: 2 inch and 1 inch sides, 1 inch roofs.
Conning-tower: 3 inch front and rear, 4½ inch sides, 2 inch roof and floor.
Conning-tower tube: 2 inch.
Protective bulkhead: 1¾ inch.
Splinter protection to magazines: 1½ inch sides and crowns.
Cable-trunks to director-control towers, etc.: 2 inch.
Funnel-uptakes: 1 inch.
Bullet-proof plating to bridges: 1 inch to ½ inch.

Machinery
Parsons single-reduction geared turbines, four shafts.
110,000 SHP = 28 knots at 230 rpm.
Eight Admiralty three-drum small-tube boilers with superheaters.
Maximum working pressure 400 pounds per square inch.

Fuel and endurance
Oil-fuel capacity 3,667 tons (*Howe*).
Diesel-fuel capacity 185 tons (*Howe*).
Coal storage 6 tons, coke 10 tons (*Howe*).

Fuel consumption and endurance:
Economical speed 13 knots giving fuel consumption of 7½ tons per hour.
Fuel consumption at 28 knots = 40 tons per hour.

Performance figures for *Howe*.
Clean bottom in temperate waters:

Speed (knots)	SHP	rpm	Fuel consumption (tons/hour)	Endurance (n. miles)
12		92	7.2	5,850
14		107	8.2	6,000
16	16,150	122	9.4	5,980
18		138	11.9	5,310
20		154	15.0	4,450
22		170	19.1	3,840
24	66,000	190	24.6	3,070
26		210	31.8	2,575
27		220	36.0	2,360

Six months out of dock in temperate waters:

Speed (knots)	SHP	rpm	Fuel consumption (tons/hour)	Endurance (n. miles)
12		94	8	5,270
14		110	9.2	5,350
16		126	10.8	5,250
18	22,000	142	13.3	4,750
20		157	16.6	4,100
22		174	21.0	3,495
24		194	26.8	2,820
26		216	34.3	2,485
28		240	42.0	2,100

Six months out of dock in tropical waters:

Speed (knots)	SHP	rpm	Fuel consumption (tons/hour)	Endurance (n. miles)
12		97	7.9	5,350
14		112	9.0	5,500
16		129	10.5	5,350
18	22,000	146	12.3	5,150
20		161	17.5	3,800
22	44,000	178	22.0	3,360
24	66,000	198	28.5	2,646
26	99,000	222	39.0	2,110
27	114,000	235	45.0	1,890

Complement
Full war complement (1940) 1,422.

Below: view from the forecastle-deck of *King George V*, showing both main and secondary armament. Note the aerials for Type '284' radar on the main director control-tower and the UP mounting on 'B' turret.

new weapon possessed two major advantages over its predecessor. (The 14-inch Mk I gun fired a 1,586-pound shell, at a muzzle velocity of 2,500 feet per second.) First, the gun was of all-steel construction, which, when compared to wire-wound guns, provided a weapon that was stronger, lighter, less liable to droop, more accurate and less subject to wear. The estimated life of the gun was 340 effective full charges, which was longer than that of the 16-inch and 15-inch guns. The bare gun weighed 77 tons 15 cwt, compared to 85 tons for the 14-inch Mk I, but in order to keep the distance between the breech and the trunnions to a minimum, a large balance-weight of 11½ tons was attached to the rear of the gun. This negated much of the possible weight saving that the gun provided, but, at the same time, reduced the amount of clearance required below the breech. Second, the new 14-inch shells were superior to the earlier type, in ballistic performance and armour-penetrating power, because of the considerable improvement in shell design and material that had taken place since the First World War.

The design of the twin and quadruple turrets was based on the highly successful 15-inch and 13.5-inch Vickers twin gun-mountings. Following the practice adopted in *Nelson* and *Rodney*, the magazines were below the shell rooms, which, although giving greater protection against shell fire, introduced a certain amount of complication to the design of the central and gun-loading hoists. A fixed loading-angle was adopted because the advantages of all-angle loading were not considered worth the resultant complications in gear and maintenance. It was difficult, moreover, to provide all-angle loading from a loading-cage in which the shell was above the cordite, and in any case, the design of the mounting was such, that the fixed loading-angle had little effect on the rate of fire, which was two rounds per gun per minute.

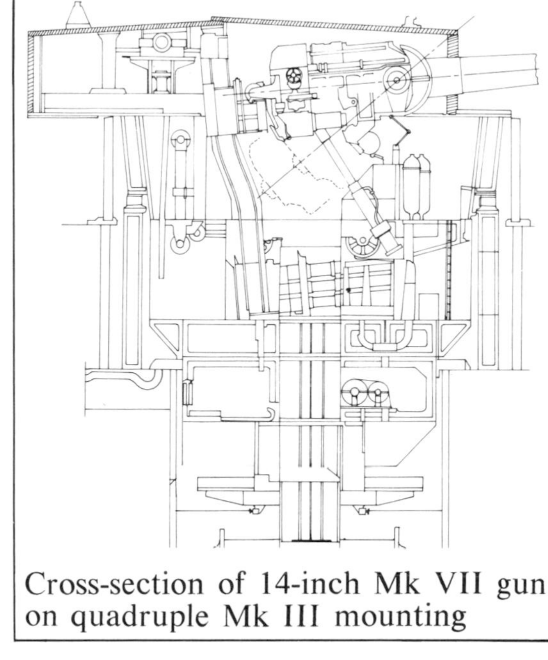

Cross-section of 14-inch Mk VII gun on quadruple Mk III mounting

Projectiles were loaded into the trunk from a large shell ring which held four shells for each gun. This almost completely divorced the shell-room drill from the turret-loading cycle, and therefore avoided a repetition of the problems encountered in this area with *Nelson* and *Rodney*. A considerable amount of attention was paid to making the mountings as flash-tight as possible, but this resulted in greater mechanical complexity and an increased number of interlocks compared to the 15-inch Mk I mounting. The mountings gave some trouble at first, but in 1942, it was stated that "the performance of the mountings in their early life has given good reason to expect that the design will prove to be thoroughly sound and reliable".

The maximum elevation provided by the mountings was 40°, which gave the guns a range of 36,000 yards. The revolving weight of the Mk III quadruple mounting was 1,582 tons, and of the Mk II twin, 915 tons. (These weights exclude the weight of the guns.) These figures exceeded the design weight of each turret by 58 tons.

Secondary armament
The secondary armament consisted of sixteen 5.25-inch guns, mounted in eight high-angle/low-angle turrets, arranged in four groups. The Mk I 50-calibre quick-firing gun fired an 82-pound shell at a muzzle velocity of 2,600 feet per second, giving a maximum surface range of 23,400 yards. The high-angle/low-angle Mk I mountings were self-contained, each having its own electric motor to drive a hydraulic pump which supplied power for elevating, training, ramming and working the ammunition hoists. The guns were fitted in separate cradles and could elevate independently up to a maximum of 70°. The 5.25-inch calibre, with separate ammunition, was chosen because it was considered that it would provide the maximum weight of shell that could be loaded by an average gun-crew, for sustained periods, at all angles of elevation. The mounting was designed for a rate of fire of ten to twelve rounds per minute, but, in fact, the crews could not transfer shell and cordite from the hoists to the loading-trays at this speed, and the more usual rate of fire was seven to eight rounds per minute. In general, the mountings were not liked because they were complex and difficult to maintain. Their high-angle fire, moreover, was not up to expectations because, apart from the reduced rate of fire, their training speed of 10° to 11° per second was not considered adequate.

Close-range AA armament
The original design provided for four pom-pom Mk VI mountings; one on 'B' turret, two abreast the fore funnel (on the hangar roofs) and one on 'Y' turret. Before December 1939, it was approved to increase the

Left: *King George V* in dry-dock at Rosyth, shortly after completion.

Below: two views of the ship late in 1940.

number of pom-pom mountings to six, the two additional mountings being fitted abreast the foremast on the hangar roofs. The necessary weapons, however, were not available at the time of the completion of the first two ships which, initially, did not carry pom-poms on the turret roofs. None of the class was ever fitted with the four 0.5-inch machine-gun mountings that were specified in the original design. The close-range anti-aircraft armament of the completed ships, and the additions made thereto during the war, are listed below:

King George V
As completed, December 1940: Four pom-poms Mk VI, four UP mountings (one on 'B' turret, two on 'Y' turret and one on the quarter-deck).
December 1941: UP mountings removed, one pom-pom Mk VII fitted on 'Y' turret, one pom-pom Mk VI fitted on 'B' turret, eighteen single 20-mm Oerlikons fitted.
By end of 1943: Number of 20-mm Oerlikons increased to thirty-eight.
February to July 1944 (refit at Liverpool): Pom-pom Mk VII on 'Y' turret replaced by pom-pom Mk VI mounting, two pom-pom Mk VI mountings fitted on the after superstructure, two Bofors Mk II (US) quadruple mountings fitted on the after superstructure, six 20-mm Oerlikons Mk V twin mountings fitted; the number of single 20-mm Oerlikons reduced to twenty-six.
By September 1945: Two single 40-mm Bofors fitted and the number of single 20-mm reduced to twenty-four.

Prince of Wales
As completed, March 1941: Four pom-pom Mk VI mountings, three UP mountings (one on 'B' turret, two on 'Y' turret), one 40-mm Mk III mounting on quarter-deck.
Refit at Rosyth, June to July 1941: UP mountings removed and two pom-pom Mk VI mountings fitted, one on 'B' turret and one on 'Y' turret.

Duke of York
As completed, November 1941: Six pom-pom

Prince of Wales in May 1941.
Left: The port side of the upper-bridge, showing one of her star-shell sights and the three port-side air lookouts.
Below left: leaving Scapa Flow on 8th.
Below: the foremast and rear of the bridge.

Bottom of page: a partial view from the air.
Below right: the after superstructure. The after main director control-tower is to the right, the DF office with pom-pom director-position is in the centre, and the port after HACS director Mk. IV can be seen to the left.

Below and right: *Prince of Wales* at Scapa Flow on 28th August 1941, after repairs following the Bismarck action.

Mk VI mountings, six single 20-mm Oerlikons.
By April 1942: Eight single 20-mm Oerlikons added.
Refit at Rosyth, December 1942 to March 1943: Fourteen 20-mm Oerlikons added.
By mid-1944: Two 20-mm Mk V twin mountings fitted, two single 20-mm mountings removed.
Refit at Liverpool, September 1944 to April 1945: Two pom-pom Mk VI mountings fitted on the after superstructure, two 40-mm Bofors Mk II quadruple mountings fitted on the after superstructure, six pom-pom Mk VII mountings fitted, two on the signal-deck, two abreast 'B' turret and two on the quarter-deck, six 20-mm Mk V twin mountings fitted, fifteen single 20-mm mountings fitted.
1946: Four pom-pom Mk VII mountings removed. Single 20-mm mountings reduced in number to fourteen. Four 3-pounder saluting guns fitted.

Anson
As completed, June 1942: Six pom-pom Mk VI mountings, eighteen single 20-mm Oerlikons.
By mid-1943: Twenty-two single 20-mm Oerlikons added.
Refit at Devonport, July 1944 to March 1945: Two pom-pom Mk VI mountings fitted on the after superstructure, two Bofors Mk II (US) quadruple mountings were fitted on the after superstructure, four pom-pom Mk VII

mountings fitted two abreast 'B' barbette and two on the quarter-deck, sponson-positions provided on each side of the signal-deck for two pom-pom Mk VII mountings, but 20-mm Mk V twin mountings fitted in lieu; twin 20-mm later removed and replaced by pom-pom Mk VII mountings; excluding the above, six twin Oerlikons Mk V fitted; thirteen single 20-mm Oerlikons added.
1946: Four pom-pom Mk VII mountings removed, two pom-pom Mk VI mountings removed.

Howe
As completed, August 1942: Six pom-pom Mk VI mountings, eighteen single 20-mm Oerlikons Mk IIIA mountings.
By mid-1943: Twenty-two single 20-mm Oerlikons added.
Refit at Devonport, December 1943 to May 1944: Two pom-pom Mk VI mountings fitted on the after superstructure, two 40-mm Bofors Mk II (US) quadruple mountings fitted on the after superstructure, four 20-mm Mk V twin mountings fitted, and the number of 20-mm singles reduced to thirty-four.
Refit at Durban, 29th June to September 1945: Six pom-pom Mk VII mountings were fitted, eighteen single Bofors Mk III were fitted, all single Oerlikons removed.
By the end of 1945: Six of the single 40-mm mountings had been removed.
Refit at Portsmouth, 21st January to 14th March 1946: Six pom-pom Mk VII removed, eight single Bofors removed, four saluting guns fitted.
Refit at Devonport, 24th May 1948 to 21st June 1949: Two 40-mm quadruple mountings were removed.

(Note: It is possible that during 1945, the ships received temporary additions to the close-range armament, to deal with Kamikaze attacks. The best example of this type of addition is given above for *Howe* (refit at Durban, June to September 1945) which is the only ship of the class for which definite photographic and written information on this point is available.)

Fire-control equipment
As designed, the ships were intended to carry two main director-control towers, one on the bridge and one on the after superstructure; four HACS Mk III, with the directors arranged on the bridge and after superstructure, in a four-cornered arrangement to match the four groups of 5.25-inch guns, and six pom-pom directors, two on each side of the bridge, to control the four mountings on the hangar roofs, one between the HACS directors above the bridge, to control the mounting on 'B' turret, and one between the HACS directors aft, to control the mounting on 'Y' turret. Apart from the main directors, this arrangement was not strictly followed in the completed ships, which varied from the original design, and from each other, in a number of ways.

The first two ships to be completed, *King George V* and *Prince of Wales*, carried four HACSs Mk IV, with fully stabilized high-angle/low-angle Mk IV directors. These could control the 5.25-inch armament through a HACS Mk IV table for high-angle fire, or through an Admiralty fire-control clock Mk VII*(M) for low-angle fire. The same system was installed in *Duke of York*, *Anson* and *Howe*, but high-angle/low-angle Mk V directors were substituted for the Mk IV directors. This new model was introduced because the Mk IV had become cramped as a result of the addition of new equipment, such as radar. *Anson* was further modified during her 1944 to 1945 refit at Devonport, when her Mk V directors were replaced by Mk VI directors. *Anson* was the only capital ship to carry this model, which was entirely new and not based on earlier directors.

On completion, *King George V* and *Prince of Wales* carried two UP directors in place of the two centre-line pom-pom directors, but they were replaced by the intended equipment, when the UP mountings were removed. With these exceptions, all the ships were initially fitted with six pom-pom Mk IV directors, although the one between the forward high-angle control-system directors was eventually

Left: *Duke of York* leaving John Brown's fitting-out yard on 4th September 1941. Her 20 mm armament has not yet been fitted, although the positions have been prepared.

Below: *Duke of York* during trials.

removed. Two additional Mk IV directors were fitted later, to control the two pom-pom mountings fitted on the after superstructure between 1944 and 1945. At the same time, two US pattern Mk 51 directors were fitted, to control the 40-mm quadruple mountings.

Protection

As with *Nelson* and *Rodney*, the 'all-or-nothing' scheme of protection was adopted, but as more weight was allotted for this purpose, the general distribution of the armour was much improved. The detailed arrangement was based on the results of a considerable number of experiments that had been conducted during a period of several years, to ascertain the best system of protection against bombs, shells and torpedoes. These experiments had culminated in 1936, with trials against a target, known as 'Job 74' which was a full size reproduction of the midship section of the new ships. The main improvements over *Nelson* and *Rodney* were (a) protection for the soft ends (b) greater armoured reserve of buoyancy, in both height and width (c) improved protection against diving shell and (d) reduction in the size of the unarmoured structure above the citadel.

The belt armour extended from 8½ feet below the designed standard waterline, to the main-deck. The total depth of the belt was 23½ feet, and it was arranged in three tiers of about equal depth. Each tier was tongued and grooved to the adjacent tiers and each plate, in the same tier, was keyed at the butts. The two upper tiers were fifteen inches thick abreast the magazines, and fourteen inches thick, abreast the machinery. The lower tier was fifteen inches and fourteen inches thick at the upper edge, and this tapered to 5½ inches and 4½ inches respectively, at the lower edge.

An improved type of armour had been developed during the 1930s and this was fitted in the *King George V* class. Little is known about it, as yet, but it was probably a nickel-chrome-molybdenum steel alloy, produced and treated by an improved process. Early in 1936, before plate trials with the new armour had been carried out, it was assumed that it would give an improvement to the resistance of armour-piercing shells, equivalent to about 1,500 yards. On this basis, it was estimated that the belt armour of the *King George V* class would withstand 15-inch shells at a range of about 13,500 yards (15-inch armour) and 15,600 yards (14-inch armour) at normal inclination. The results of the plate trials are not known.

Experiments had demonstrated that the *Nelson* system for venting underwater explosions outboard, by providing internal armour and vent-plates in the ship's sides, was not so great an improvement as had originally been thought. The vent-plates were shown to be ineffective at the time of maximum pressure, and it was found that explosions, vented inboard of the citadel, caused little more damage than those venting outboard. The belt armour of the *King George V* class, therefore, was positioned vertically on the ship's side which was the ideal arrangement for protecting the reserve of buoyancy and withstanding diving shell. It did, however, entail abandoning the increase in relative thickness provided by sloping armour, but the advantages of the arrangement were considered to outweigh this consideration, particularly as the sloping armour tended to deflect shells downward into the bulge compartments.

The main-deck was armoured over the full length of the citadel, from just forward of 'A' barbette to just abaft 'Y' barbette. The magazines were protected by armour six inches thick, that could withstand 15-inch plunging shells from ranges up to 33,500 yards, and 1,000-pound bombs from up to 15,000 feet. The machinery was protected by a 5-inch deck which could withstand 15-inch plunging shells from up to 29,500 yards, and 1,000-pound bombs from up to 10,500 feet. The citadel was completed by a 12-inch bulkhead forward, and a 10-inch bulkhead aft.

The lower tier of the armour belt was continued forward and aft of the citadel for about forty feet, to protect the magazines from raking gunfire. The lower-deck forward, from the citadel to the foremost watertight bulkhead, was fitted with armour, reducing in thickness towards the stem, from 5 inches to 2½ inches. The lower-deck aft was fitted with 4½-inch and 5-inch armour, the latter being

over the steering compartment. The after end of the steering compartment was closed by an armoured bulkhead, 4 inches thick.

The arrangement of the turret and barbette armour followed conventional practice, but the very square design of the turrets, was unusual in a British ship. This shape had advantages, in that it simplified the manufacture of the armour plates, and reduced the likelihood of the front plate, which was vertical, being struck by a shell at normal impact. As in *Nelson* and *Rodney*, the turret back plates were perforated by several explosion vent-holes which were hidden, externally, by light plate covers.

The barbette armour rested on heavy chock castings, fixed rigidly to the main-(armoured) deck. The thickness of the armour on all three barbettes was reduced on the forward and after sides, despite the fact that the raising of the armoured-deck and the omission of a forecastle-deck had greatly reduced the height and, therefore, the weight of these structures. 'A' and 'Y' barbettes were ten feet high, and had an internal diameter of thirty-nine feet. 'B' barbette was twenty feet high, and had an internal diameter of twenty-nine feet.

The remainder of the protection consisted of bullet-proof and splinter plating on the secondary armament, bridges and control-positions. During the construction of the ships, several additions to this protection were approved. The most important was the fitting of splinter plating to the crowns and sides of the main and secondary magazines. Savings in the weight of the main armour protection more than compensated for these additions.

Underwater protection

The underwater side-protection system was designed to withstand the explosion of a 1,000-pound torpedo warhead, in contact with the skin plating. The arrangement consisted of three longitudinal groups of compartments, forming an air-liquid-air sandwich bounded on the inboard side by the protective bulkhead. The outboard air space served to dissipate the initial force of the explosion, and the

Table 74: Approved additions to armour and protection after the completion of design calculations

Addition	Weight
Splinter protection to magazines	220 tons
Protection to RU pom-pom magazines	9 tons
Screens for pom-poms	2 tons
Protection for after director-control tower	19 tons
Protection for DCT cable-trunks	12 tons
Protection for DCT casemates	60 tons
Conning-tower tube, roof to compass-platform	}
Conning-tower, emergency conning-position	} 371 tons
searchlight-platform on fore funnel, additional bridge protection, protection to after island.	}
Total:	693 tons

Table 75: Armour weights as finally designed and as completed (for *King George V*)

Armour	As designed (tons)	As completed (tons)	Weight saving or addition
Side armour	4,755	4,650	−105
Bulkheads	485	464	−21
Barbettes: 'A'	296	336	}
'B'	434	345	} −11
'Y'	301	339	}
Deck armour (including chocks)	4,410	4,255	−155
Conning-tower	28	29	+1
Director-control tower (aft)	0	9	+9
Conning-tower tube	7	10	+3
Total:	10,716	10,427	−289
Protective plating:			
Protective bulkhead	865	846	−19
Oil jackets	255	268	+13
Funnel protection	120*	52	−68
Protection to barbettes	147	148	+1
Armour gratings & protective plating	73	117	+44
Splinter protection to magazines	0	215	+215
Casemate protection	230	259	+29
Cable-trunks	22	44	+22
Total:	1,712	1,949	+237
Backing behind armour:			
Protection other than armour & protective plating	61	37	−24
Grand total:	12,489	12,413	−76

* Based on heavier plating and larger uptakes than finally adopted.

King George

1940: profiles and sections

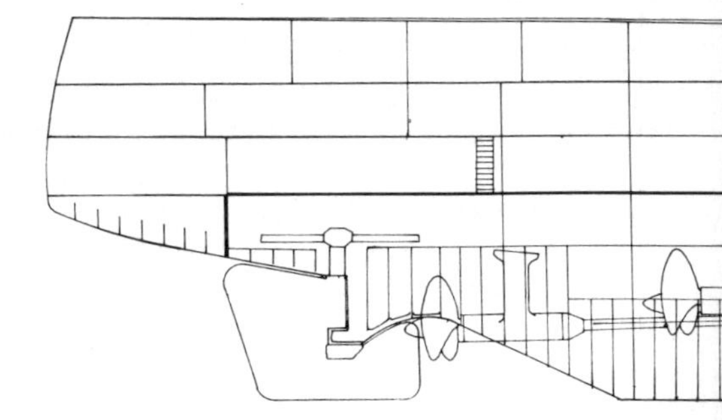

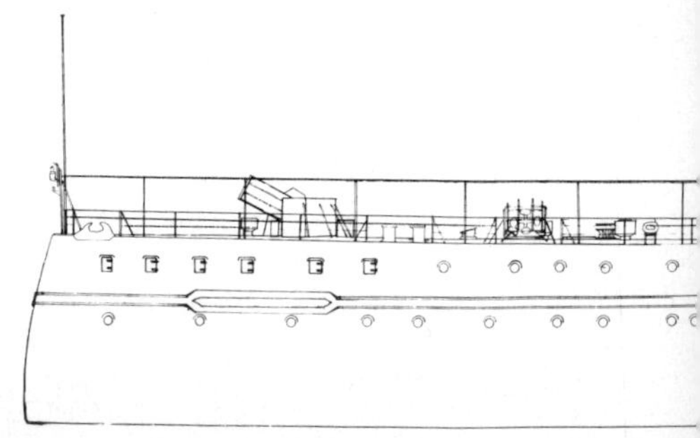

Anti-aircraft gun positions, up to 1944/45 refit

King George V

December 1941:

A Four UP mounts removed.

B Eighteen single 20 mm mounts fitted.

C One quadruple pom-pom fitted.

D One octuple pom-pom fitted.

Late 1943:

E Eighteen single 20 mm added.

AA returns list of thirty-eight single 20 mm mounts at this time, but positions can only be located for thirty-six.

Duke of York

Late 1941:

F Six single 20 mm mounts fitted.

April 1942:

G Eight single 20 mm mounts added.

Mid-1943:

Five single 20 mm mounts behind breakwater removed and distributed among positions H.

H Twelve single 20 mm mounts added, plus five more from behind breakwater.

Mid-1944:

I Two single 20 mm mounts removed and replaced by two twin 20 mm mounts.

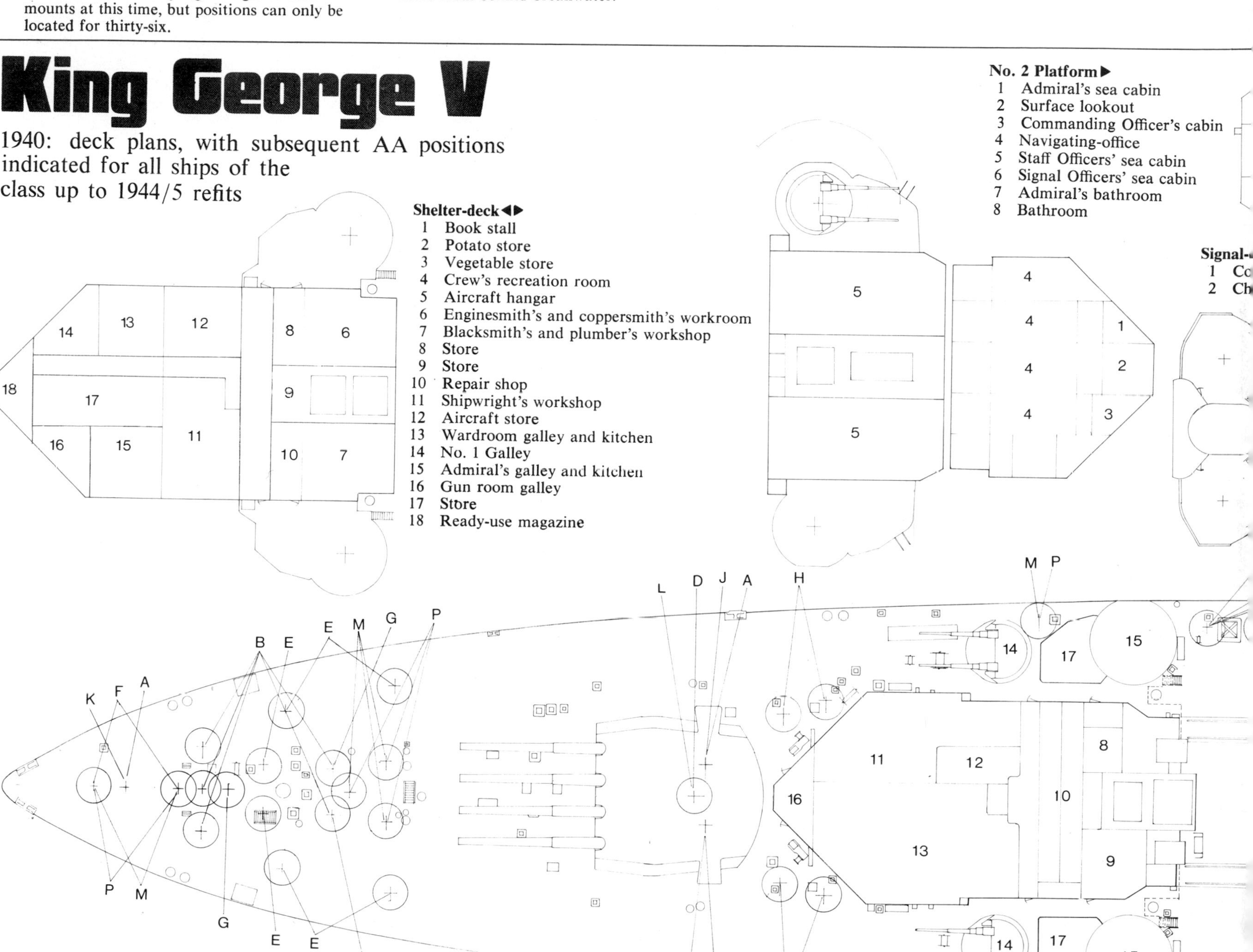

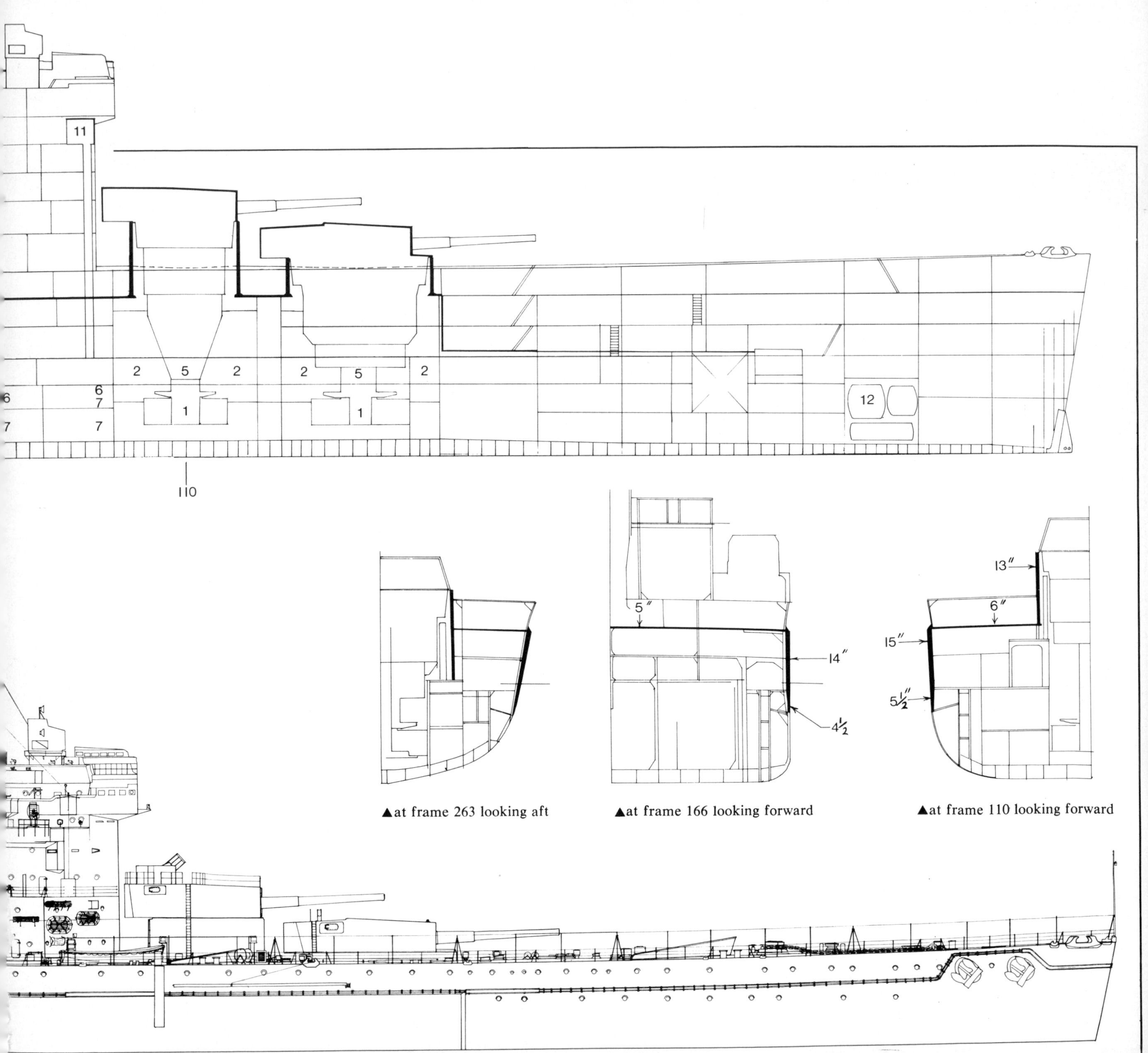

▲at frame 263 looking aft

▲at frame 166 looking forward

▲at frame 110 looking forward

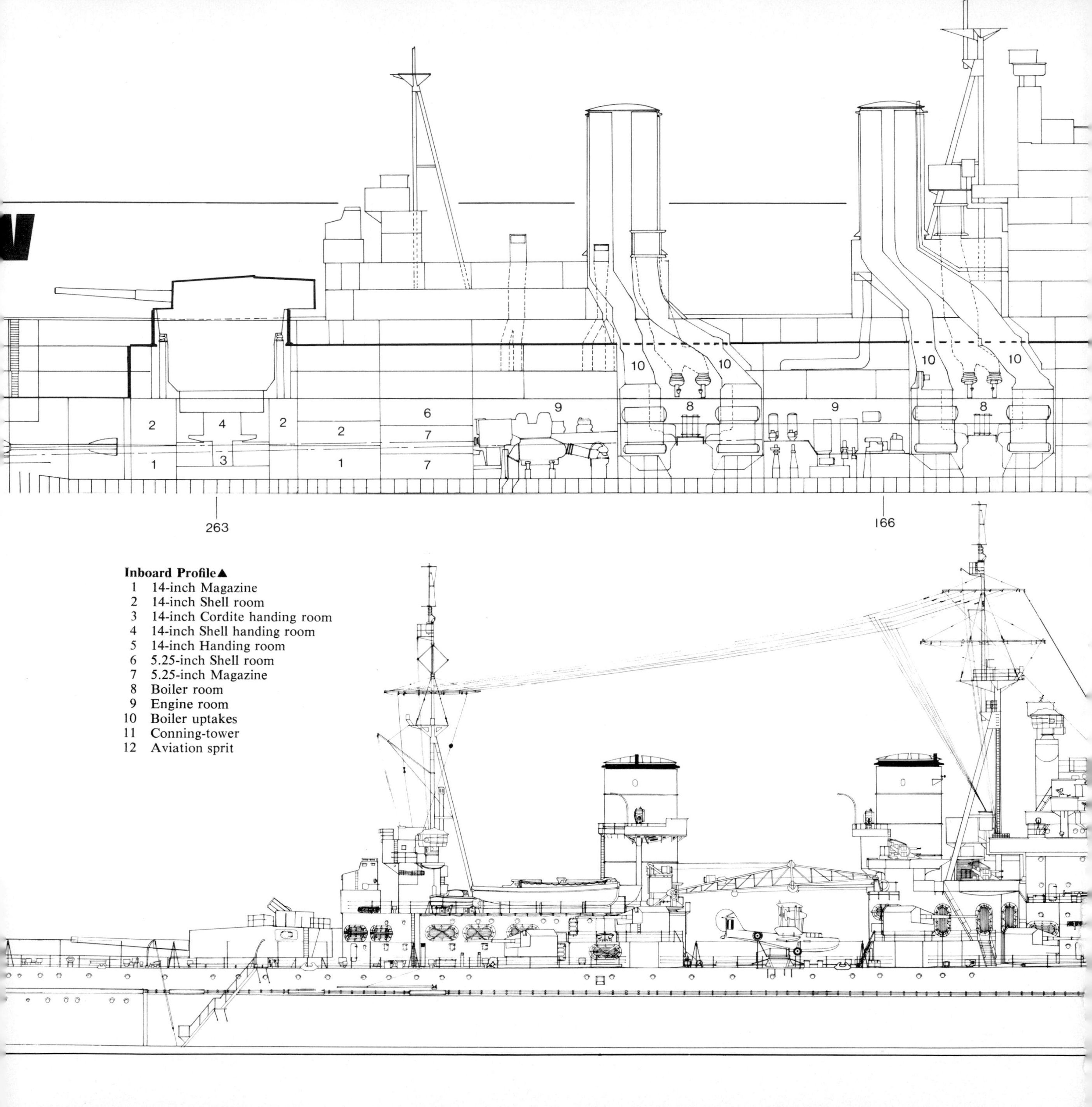

Inboard Profile▲

1 14-inch Magazine
2 14-inch Shell room
3 14-inch Cordite handing room
4 14-inch Shell handing room
5 14-inch Handing room
6 5.25-inch Shell room
7 5.25-inch Magazine
8 Boiler room
9 Engine room
10 Boiler uptakes
11 Conning-tower
12 Aviation sprit

Prince of Wales
May 1941:
J Three UP mounts fitted.
K One single Bofors fitted.
August 1941:
L UP mounts in positions J removed and replaced by two octuple pom-poms.

Anson
June 1942:
M Eighteen single 20 mm mounts fitted.
Mid-1943:
O Eighteen single 20 mm mounts added.
AA returns list twenty-two single 20 mm mounts added in mid-1943, but positions can only be located for eighteen; it is possible that the missing four positions were located on the quarter-deck.

Howe
August 1942:
P Eighteen single 20 mm mounts fitted.
Mid-1943:
Q Eighteen single 20 mm mounts added.
AA returns list forty single 20 mm mounts added in mid-1943, but positions can only be located for eighteen.

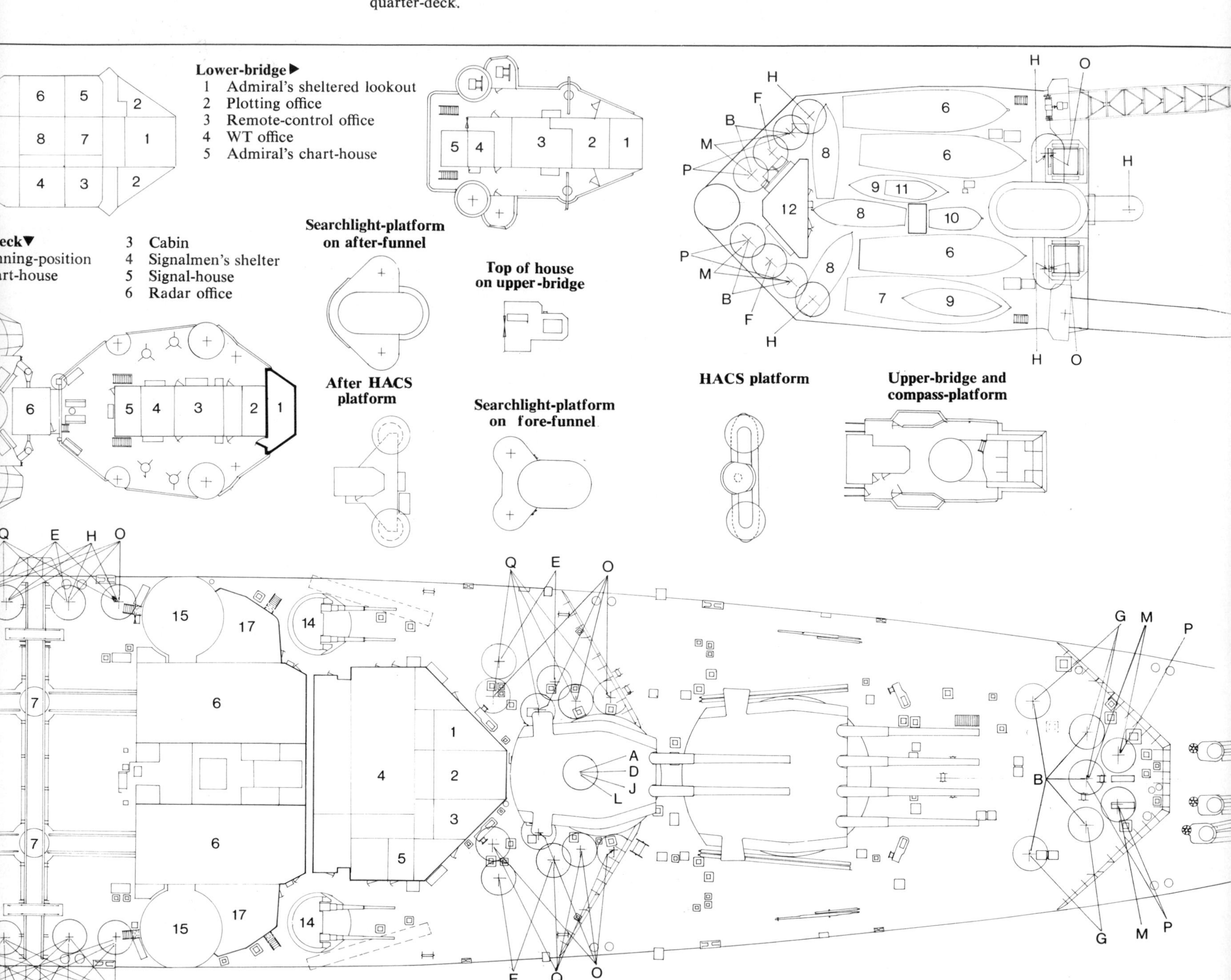

Overleaf: *Duke of York* about to leave dry-dock at Rosyth in early 1943. In the background are the cruisers *Berwick* and *Liverpool.*

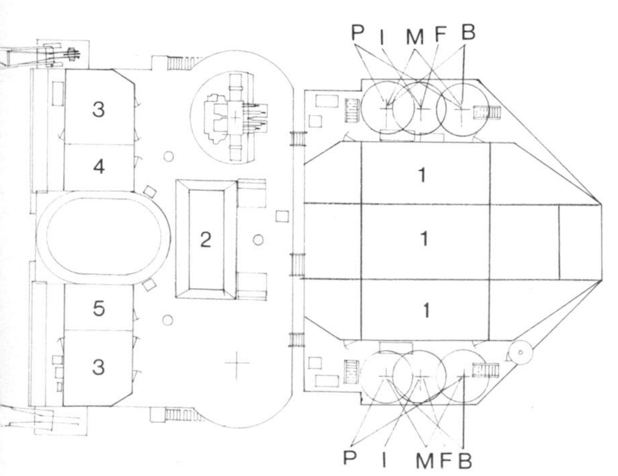

Boat-deck▲
1 CPO's and PO's reading room
2 Boiler room vent
3 Pom-pom ready-use magazine
4 Batter repair room
5 Pom-pom ready-use store and workshop
6 45-foot Fast motor boat
7 45-foot Motor launch
8 25-foot Fast motor boat
9 27-foot Whaler
10 16-foot Fast motor dinghy
11 14-foot Sailing dinghy
12 Aircraft workshop

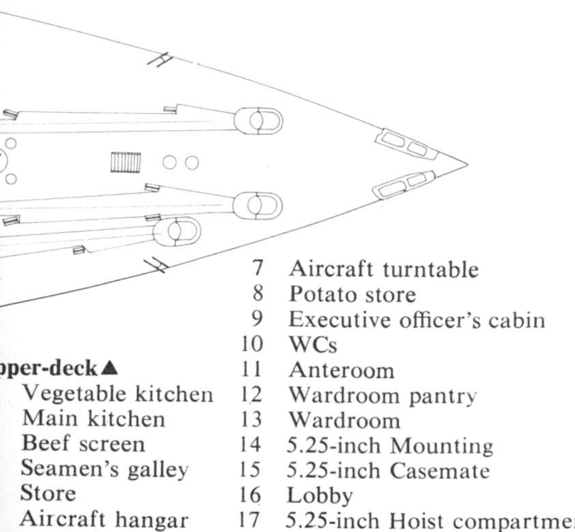

centre, liquid-filled compartment helped to distribute the pressure over a large area of the internal structure and reduce the momentum of small pieces of outer bottom plating that might otherwise have penetrated the protective bulkhead. The inner air space was a new feature, that prevented a pressure wave set up in the centre compartment from being transmitted directly to, and distorting, the protective bulkhead. The wing compartments, inboard of the protective system, prevented any water that might have passed through strained seams and rivet holes in the protective bulkhead, from flooding the main magazine and machinery compartments. No such wing compartments were provided abreast the forward engine rooms. These contained the machinery for driving the wing shafts and were, therefore, farther outboard than the other machinery spaces. Special wing bulkheads, however, were provided abreast these compartments, approximately three feet inboard of the protective bulkhead, to limit any flooding.

The central compartments were filled to within two feet of the crown, and this enabled any pressure within them to be partially relieved by upward movement of their liquid content. The compartments normally contained oil fuel which, when required for the boilers, was transferred to the double-bottom tanks by admitting sea water into the bottom of the compartment. The water displaced the oil which was forced out through a non-return valve at the top of the tanks, thus ensuring that they were always full of liquid, either oil or water, or both. This was only made possible by the fact that oil floats on water and is immiscible, but even so, there was no distinct line of separation between the oil and the water. The zone between the two liquids, known as 'strippings', contained both oil and water and, when necessary, this was drawn off through a special valve and passed to a sullage and recovery tank. The two liquids were then separated by adding a detergent known as 'Teepol' and heating the mixture. If additional oil-fuel stowage was required, the upper compartments of the outer air space between the armour shelf and the lower-deck could be used, but it was required that these be emptied as soon as the necessary space in the double bottom became available.

For counter-flooding, in the event of damage, both the inner and outer air spaces were fitted with arrangements for rapid flooding. The outer compartments provided the greater righting-moment when flooded, and in this condition, only slightly reduced the protective value of the sandwich. Its value, however, was seriously reduced if the inner air space became flooded, and it was specified that this was to be resorted to, only if absolutely necessary.

The protective system described above, extended from the forward end of the citadel, to the watertight bulkhead on the forward side of 'Y' barbette. From this bulkhead to the after end of the citadel, special water-protection compartments were provided. Their capacity, when filled to within two feet of the crowns, was 55 tons of water.

Like *Nelson* and *Rodney*, the *King George V* class had a double bottom, five feet deep, with arrangements for keeping the compartments under the citadel partially flooded with oil or water. Prior to 1936, consideration had been given to providing a deeper double bottom, but 'B'-bomb trials under Job 74, with a seven foot double bottom, demonstrated that no great improvement would result. ('B' bombs were designed to explode under the water.)

Machinery

The arrangement of the main machinery followed the unit system already adopted in many cruisers. There were four boiler rooms, each containing two boilers, and four engine rooms each containing one set of turbines. Each boiler room supplied steam to one set of turbines and their associate auxiliaries, to form a self-contained unit. The services for each unit (feed water, fuel, lubricating oil) could be isolated so that any damage to one unit by flooding or explosion did not affect

Nº4

Duke of York leaving dry-dock at Rosyth in early 1943: three more photographs from the series begun on the previous page. The five 20 mm Oerlikons abaft the breakwater were removed and repositioned shortly afterwards.

Below: an aerial view of *Anson,* July 1942.

Bottom of page: on 5th August 1942.

another. Restricting the effect of damage was also facilitated by staggering the boiler and engine room compartments, although this necessitated longer shafts for the wing propellers. The boilers of one unit could be cross-connected to the engines of another unit if required for harbour service, preparing the engines for steaming, or for economy and convenience in peacetime. This capability was also useful if the engines of one unit and the boilers of another suffered damage, in which case the undamaged portions could be cross-connected to form a new unit.

Each set of turbines consisted of one low-pressure and one high-pressure turbine, driving one shaft through single-reduction gearing. An astern turbine was incorporated into the casing of the low-pressure turbine, and a separate cruising turbine was geared to the fore end of the high-pressure turbine. Steam was supplied to the engines at a maximum pressure of 350 pounds per square inch.

Each of the Admiralty small-tube three-drum boilers had two superheaters and nine sprayers, each capable of supplying 1,500 pounds of oil fuel per hour. The maximum working pressure of the boilers was 400 pounds per square inch.

The machinery was designed to provide 25,000 shaft horse-power on each shaft, at 230 revolutions, but with the capability of

Below and **bottom of page:** *King George V* in late 1943.

Below right: an ecclesiastic visit to the ship in 1944. This snapshot illustrates the extension to the rear of the bridge.

Table 76: Particulars of steam trials of HMS *Howe*

Type of trial	Date	Mean SHP	Mean speed (knots)	Mean rpm	Displacement (tons)	Mean draught	State of sea and wind	Place of trial	Depth of water	State of bottom	When last undocked
Contractors' one-hour full-power preliminary	27th August 1942	112,105	27 (by log)	230.6	42,630	32 ft 1 in	Calm sea wind force 1 to 5 ahead	North Sea	48 fathoms	clean	9th August 1942
Contractors' four hours at maximum cruising power	27th August 1942	29,659	19.7 (by log)	155.3	42,770	33 ft	Calm sea wind force 1 to 5 ahead	North Sea	50 fathoms	clean	9th August 1942
Contractors' four-hour full-power	29th August 1942	113,457	27.7 (by log)	231.9	42,530	32 ft $10\frac{1}{2}$ in	Sea 32 wind force 4	North Sea	35 fathoms	clean	9th August 1942
Two-hour full-power	6th May 1943	110,500	27.1 (by land fixes)	227.9	43,500	33 ft 6 in	Sea 43 wind 15 to 20 knots	West of Orkney	40–50 fathoms	dirty	9th August 1942
Two-hour full-power	11th April 1944	110,530	27.5 (by log and land fixes)	231.6	?	?	Sea 11–10 wind 3 to 2	North Channel	60–100 fathoms	clean	6th March 1944
Two-hour full-power	26th November 1944	114,350	27 (by log and land fixes)	226.5	44,850	34 ft 5 in	Sea 22 wind 2	On passage 8°N 82°E	over 1,000 fathoms	Moderately foul	6th March 1944

Left and **below:** *Howe* in May 1944 after her 1944 refit.

accepting a 10% overload, in anticipation of improvements in boiler design. This proved to be most beneficial as 110,000 shaft horsepower was easily developed in service, and compensated for the loss in speed that would have occurred if the ships exceeded their designed displacement.

The four propellers were three-bladed, with a diameter of 14 feet 6 inches and a pitch of 14 feet 9 inches (outer) and 15 feet (inner).

Auxiliary machinery

Electric power was supplied by eight dynamos (two diesel-driven and six turbine-driven) capable of supplying 350 kilowatts each. Four turbo-driven hydraulic pumping-engines supplied the power for working the main armament. A harbour machinery room was provided between the two forward engine rooms. This compartment contained two of the turbine-driven dynamos and other auxiliaries to provide services when in harbour. The remaining auxiliary machinery was accommodated in the wing compartments abreast the main machinery compartments.

Stability and weights

The armoured reserve of buoyancy, being of much greater volume than in *Nelson* and *Rodney*, allowed for a reduction in the metacentric height compared to those ships. The

Anti-aircraft gun positions, 1944/45 period

King George V

1944 refit:

A Twenty-six single 20 mm mounts fitted.
B Quadruple pom-pom removed and replaced by an octuple pom-pom, plus two more in positions D.
C Six twin 20 mm mounts fitted.
D Two octuple pom-poms fitted.
E Two quadruple Bofors fitted.

Duke of York

1944/45 refit:

F Two octuple pom-poms fitted.
G Eight twin 20 mm mounts fitted.
H Two quadruple Bofors fitted.
I Six quadruple pom-poms fitted.
J AA returns list thirty-nine single 20 mm mounts fitted, but positions not known.

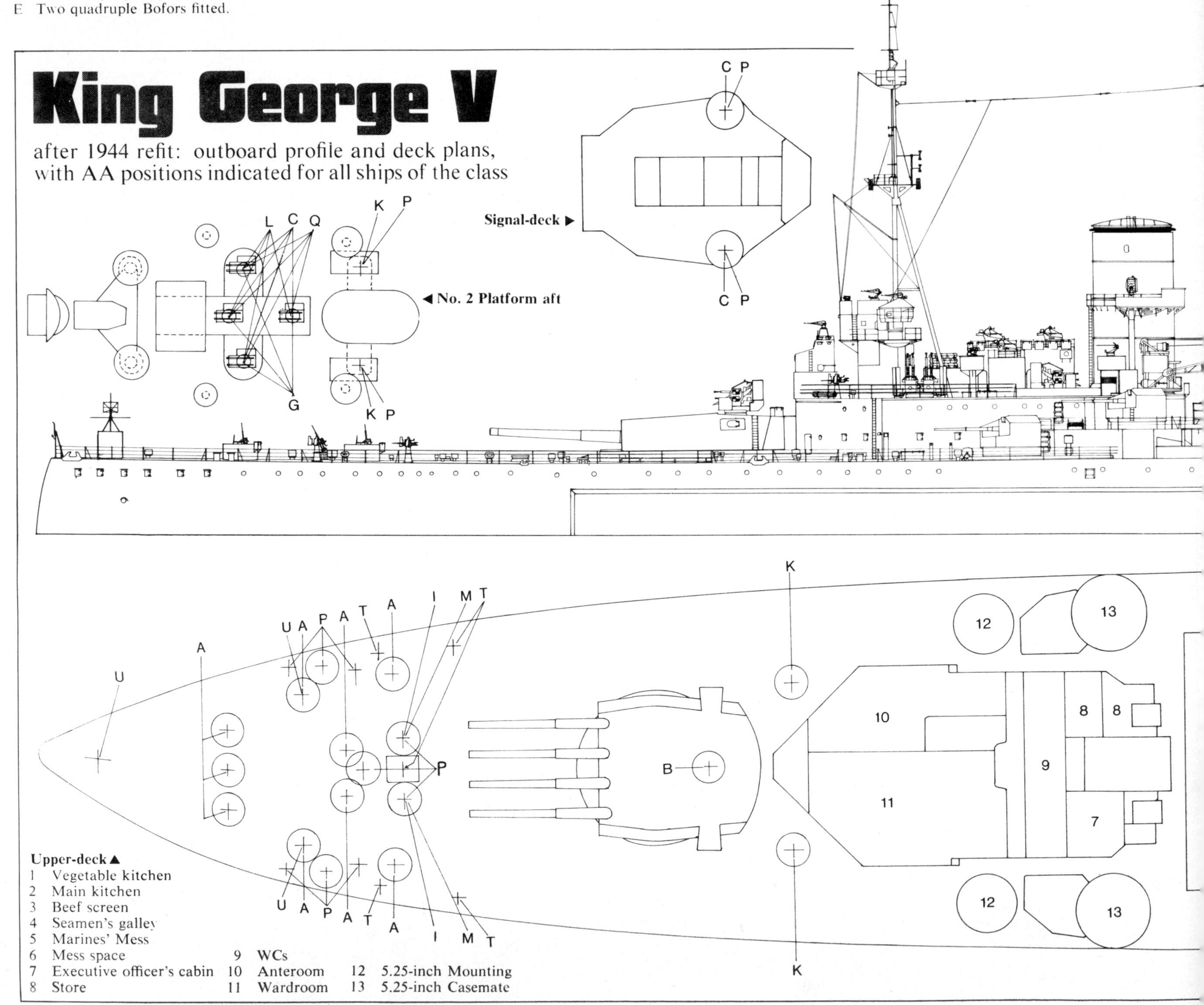

Bottom of page: *Howe* in May 1944.

Howe

1945: outboard profile

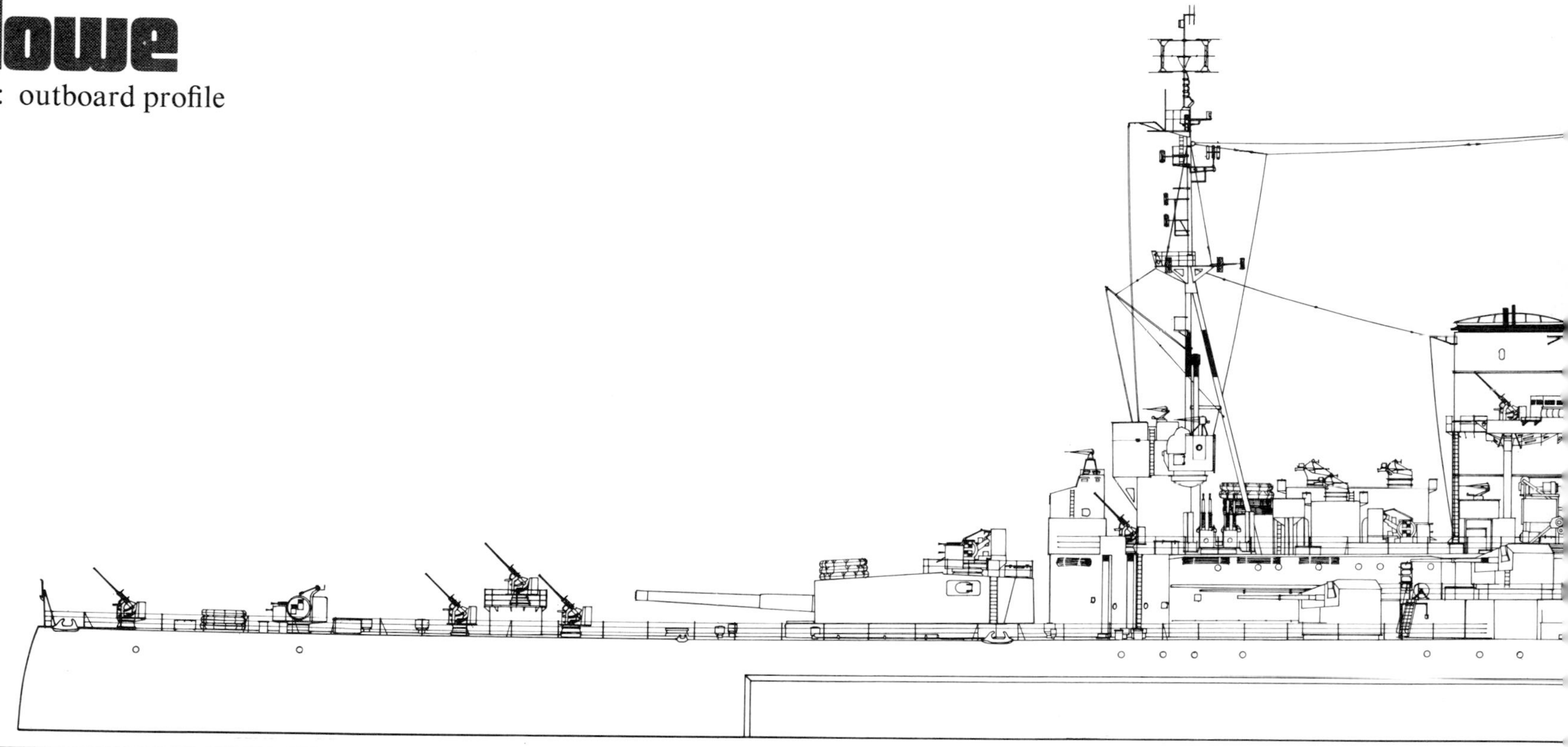

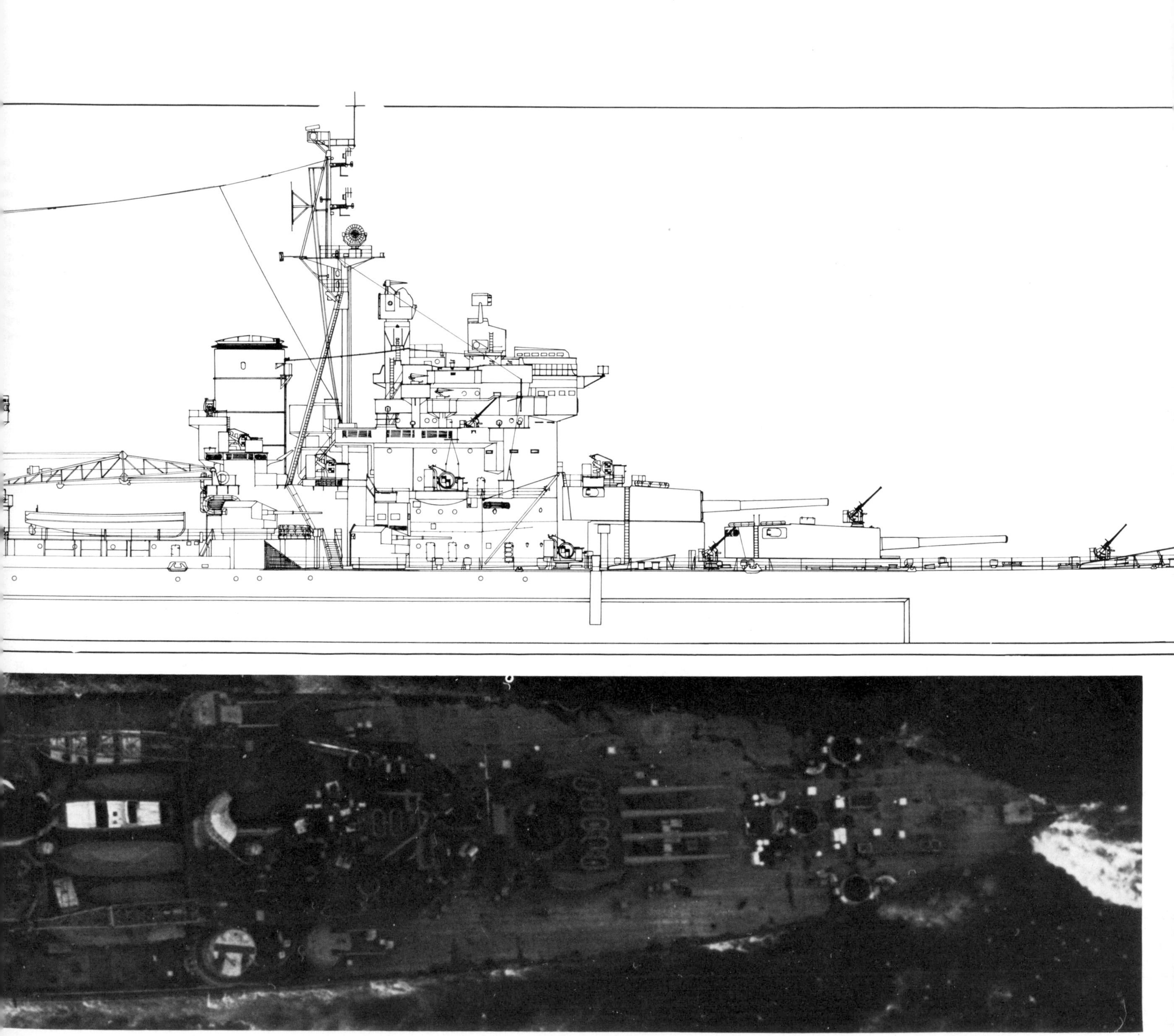

Bottom of page: *Howe* in May 1944.

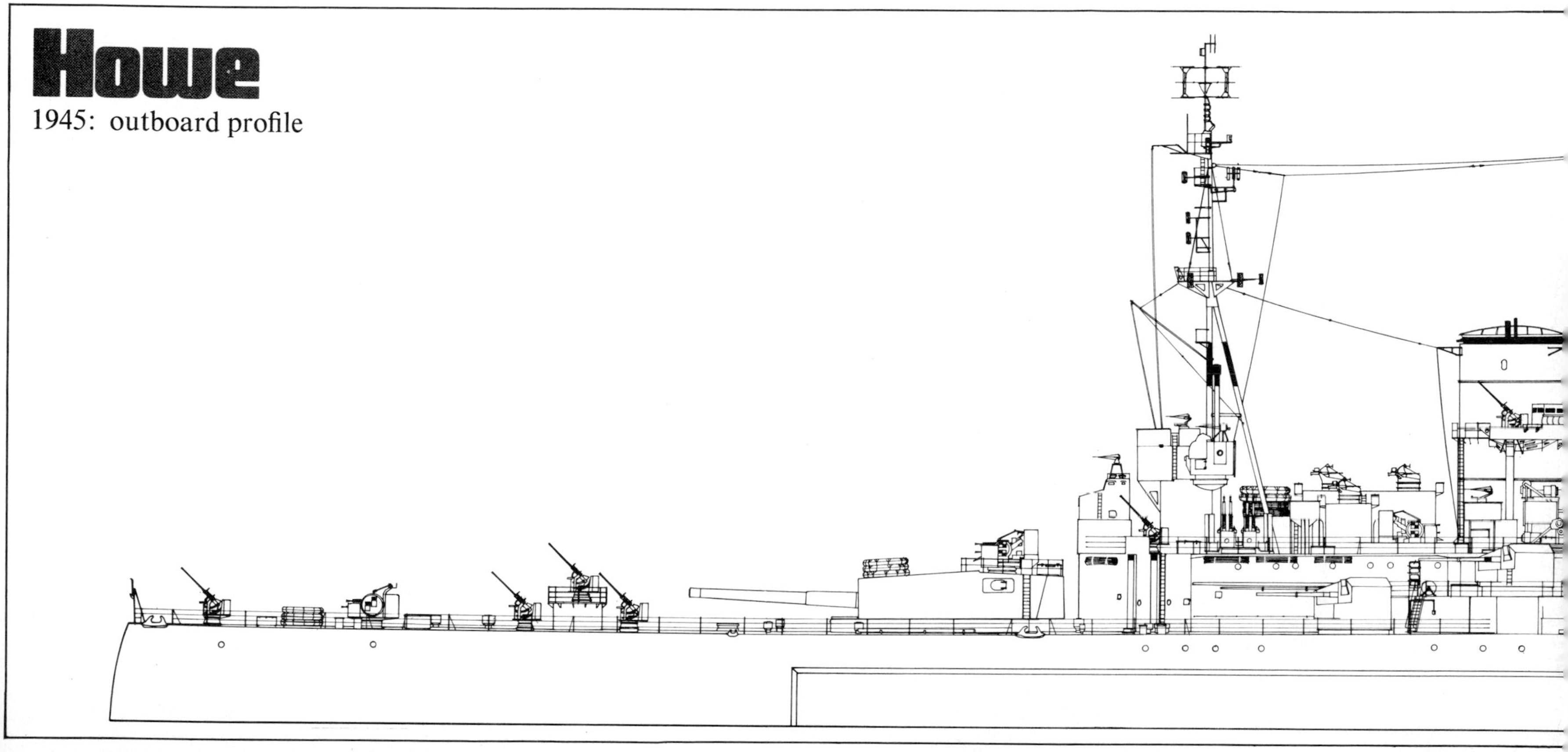

Howe

1945: outboard profile

September 1945:
All single 20 mm mounts removed.
T Eighteen single Bofors fitted.
U Six quadruple pom-poms added.
Note: Two pom-poms on the lower-bridge platform were removed by the end of September 1945, as well as twelve single Bofors.

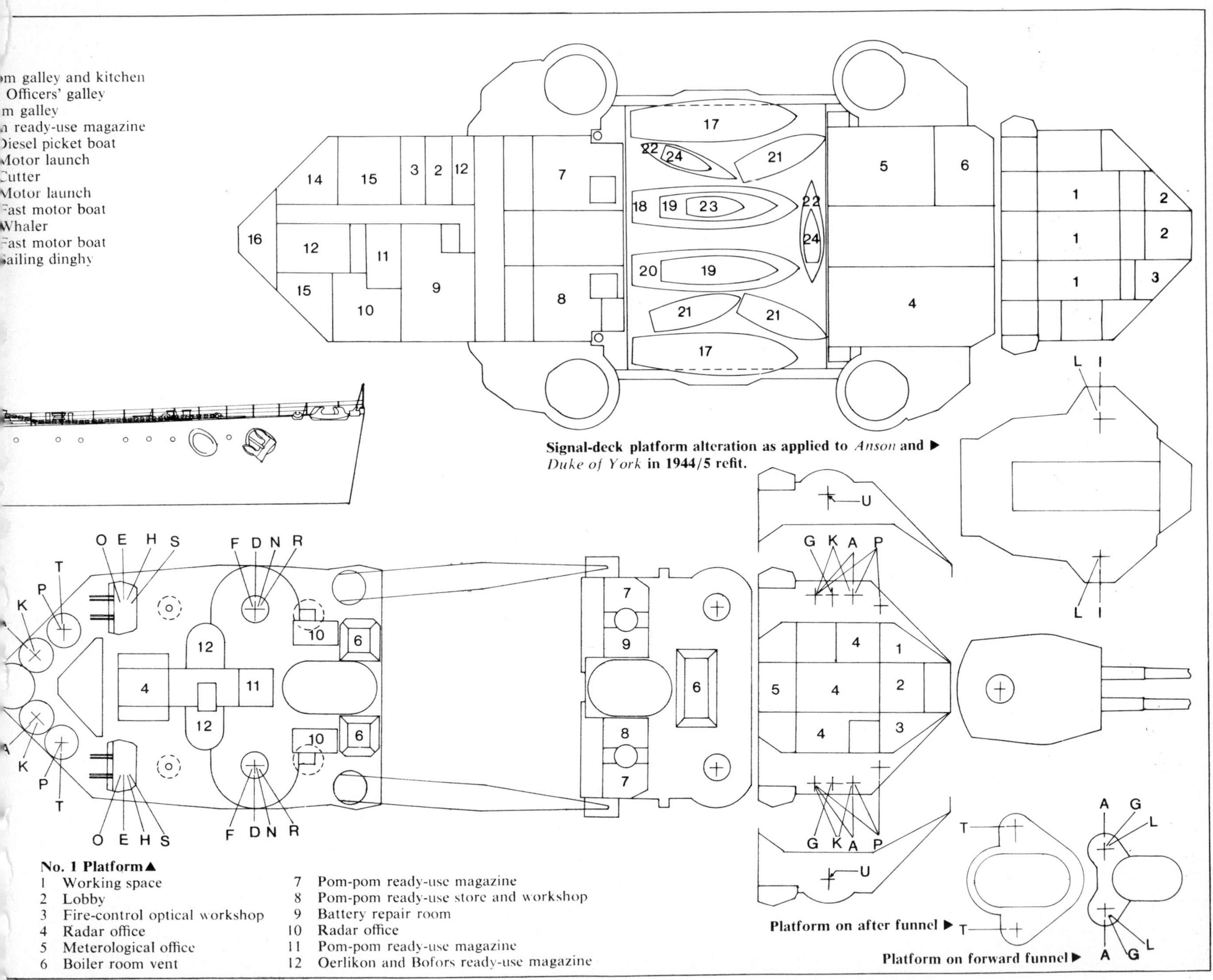

Signal-deck platform alteration as applied to *Anson* and *Duke of York* in 1944/5 refit. ▶

No. 1 Platform ▲

1 Working space
2 Lobby
3 Fire-control optical workshop
4 Radar office
5 Meterological office
6 Boiler room vent
7 Pom-pom ready-use magazine
8 Pom-pom ready-use store and workshop
9 Battery repair room
10 Radar office
11 Pom-pom ready-use magazine
12 Oerlikon and Bofors ready-use magazine

Platform on after funnel ▶

Platform on forward funnel ▶

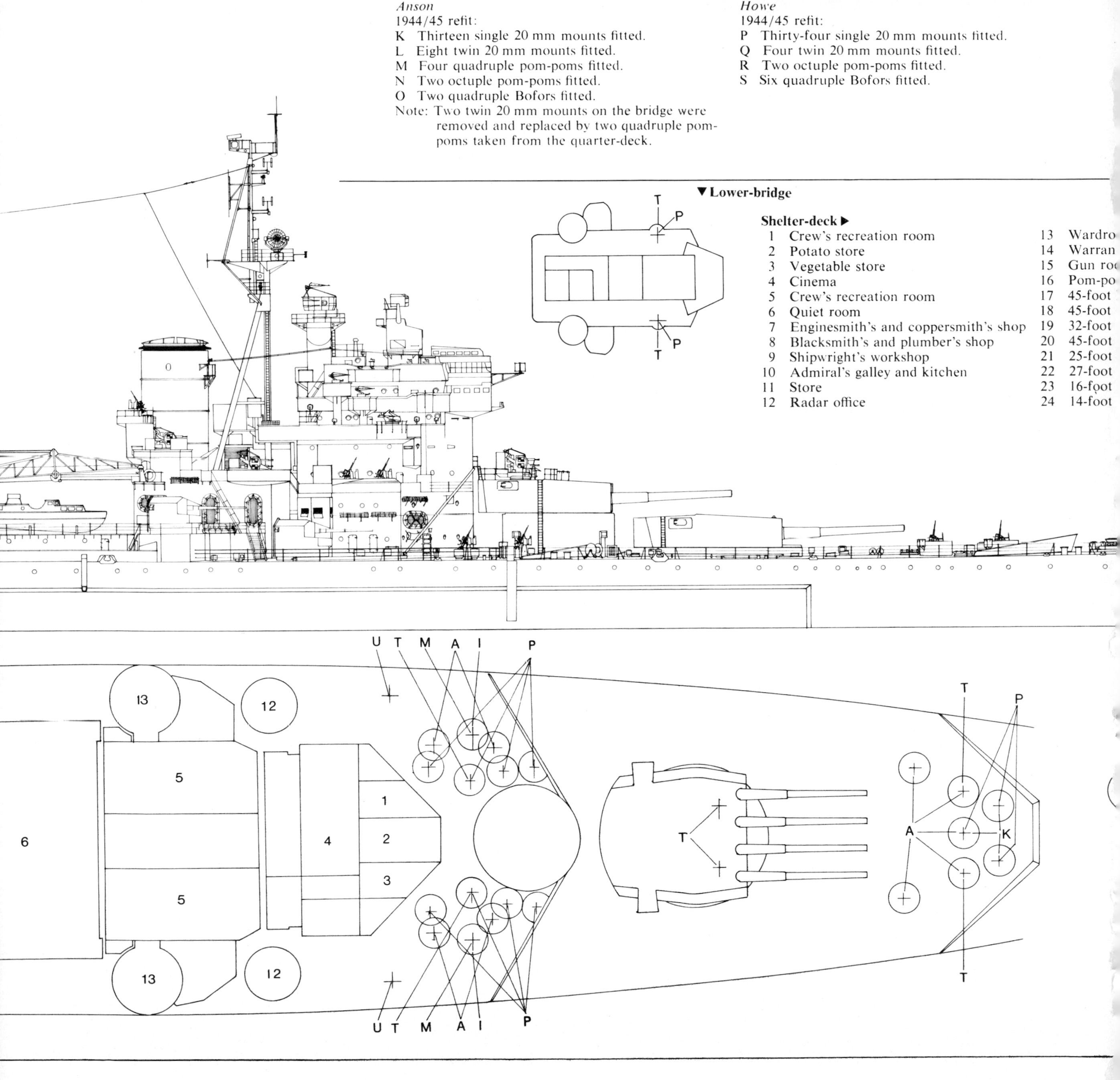
Anson
1944/45 refit:
K Thirteen single 20 mm mounts fitted.
L Eight twin 20 mm mounts fitted.
M Four quadruple pom-poms fitted.
N Two octuple pom-poms fitted.
O Two quadruple Bofors fitted.
Note: Two twin 20 mm mounts on the bridge were removed and replaced by two quadruple pom-poms taken from the quarter-deck.
Howe
1944/45 refit:
P Thirty-four single 20 mm mounts fitted.
Q Four twin 20 mm mounts fitted.
R Two octuple pom-poms fitted.
S Six quadruple Bofors fitted.
▼Lower-bridge
Shelter-deck ▶
1 Crew's recreation room
2 Potato store
3 Vegetable store
4 Cinema
5 Crew's recreation room
6 Quiet room
7 Enginesmith's and coppersmith's shop
8 Blacksmith's and plumber's shop
9 Shipwright's workshop
10 Admiral's galley and kitchen
11 Store
12 Radar office
13 Wardro
14 Warran
15 Gun ro
16 Pom-po
17 45-foot
18 45-foot
19 32-foot
20 45-foot
21 25-foot
22 27-foot
23 16-foot
24 14-foot
T
P
U T M A I P
T P A K
U T M A I P

Below: *Howe*, berthing at Auckland in 1945.

Bottom of page: on 15th September 1945, about to enter Duncan Dock, Cape Town. Note the single Bofors mountings on the forecastle, on 'A' turret, abreast 'B' turret and on the after funnel and after superstructure.

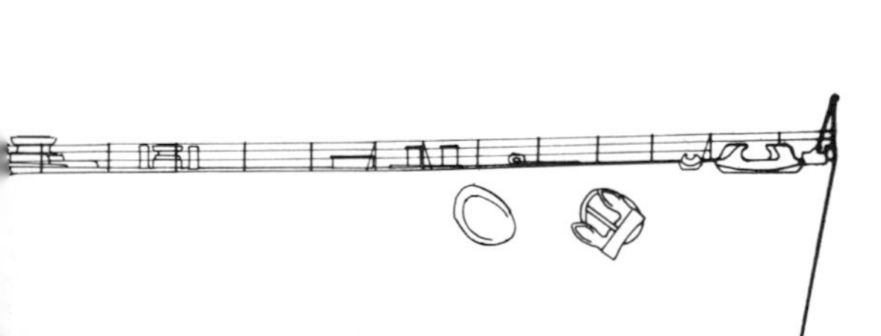

Below: *Prince of Wales'* 'Walrus' aircraft being hoisted aboard the ship.

designed GM was 8.1 feet in the deep condition and 6.1 feet in the light condition; higher than any previous British dreadnought with the exception of *Nelson* and *Rodney*. These figures, however, were reduced by subsequent additions to the weights of the ships. The actual weight of *King George V*, as completed, compared to the final design figure, and the stability particulars of *Howe*, the last ship of the class to complete, are shown in Tables 77 and 78.

Table 77: Comparison of weights of *King George V* with final design

	Design	As completed
Standard condition:		
Equipment	1,150	1,149
Machinery	2,700	2,768
Armament	6,050	6,567
Armour and protective plating	12,500	12,413
Hull	13,500	13,830
Standard displacement:	35,900 tons	36,727 tons
Deep condition:		
Equipment	1,465	1,619*
Main machinery	2,292	2,366**
Auxiliary machinery	411	402
Armament	6,765	7,401***
Armour & protection	12,500	12,413
Hull	13,500	13,830****
Reserve feed-water	300	255
Oil fuel	3,700	3,730
Lubricating oil	30	30
Petrol	30	30
Deep displacement:	40,990 tons	42,076 tons

* Increased equipment weight due to larger fresh-water tanks and more stores than allowed for in design estimate.
** Increase in machinery weight partly due to 11 tons added for increased height of funnels.
*** Increase in armament weight included 175 tons extra for the revolving weight of the 14-inch turrets, 42 tons extra for the 5·25-inch armament, 17 tons extra for the catapult. In addition the weight of the shell room machinery had doubled and that of the magazine handing room trebled.
**** Increase in hull weight included 167 tons extra for lighting and power circuits and 35 tons for de-gaussing coil.

Table 78: Details of the stability of *Howe* based on an inclining experiment of August 1942

A. Average action condition, fully equipped with 2,775 tons oil fuel, 55 tons of water protection and all reserve feed-water tanks full:

Displacement	43,254 tons
Mean draught	33 feet 4 inches
GM	6.45 feet
Angle of maximum stability	34°
Range	62½°

B. Extreme deep condition, fully equipped, with 4,031 tons oil fuel, 55 tons of water protection and all reserve feed-water tanks full:

Displacement	44,510 tons
Mean draught	34 feet 2¼ inches
GM	7.25 feet
Angle of maximum stability	34°
Range	65½°

C. Light condition, with boilers and feed-tanks filled to working height, condensers full, half central stores consumed, no fuel, water provisions, officers' or canteen stores on board:

Displacement	38,850 tons
Mean draught	30 feet 4 inches
GM	4.97 feet
Angle of maximum stability	33°
Range	58½°

Aircraft

As completed, the ships carried a 'DIIIH' fixed, cross-deck catapult amidships, capable of launching a 12,000-pound aircraft with a wing span of 50 feet. (Albacore on floats.) Four aircraft could be carried, two in the hangars and two on the catapult, but the latter pair were never carried. This equipment was eventually removed from all the ships of the class – with the exception of *Prince of Wales*, lost in December 1941 – as follows:

King George V during refit at Liverpool, February to July 1944.
Duke of York during refit at Liverpool, September 1944 to April 1945.
Anson during refit at Devonport, July 1944 to March 1945.
Howe during refit at Devonport, December 1943 to May 1944.

A new deck was built over the space vacated by the catapult to provide stowage space for the ship's boats. This allowed additional anti-aircraft weapons to be fitted on the area of the after superstructure, formerly occupied by the ship's boats.

U.S.S. Duke of York?

On 13th February 1941, the Prime Minister asked the First Sea Lord if he would like to exchange *Duke of York* for eight US 8-inch gun cruisers. On the following day, the Director of Plans was asked to look into the

Below: two views of *Anson* in March 1945, after her 1944/5 refit. Note the Mk. VI directors, the VHF/DF outfit on the quarter-deck and the additional pom-pom mountings on the quarter- and forecastle-decks.

matter and give an opinion. He reported that the eight cruisers would provide a marked increase in the ability of the Fleet to deal with raiders, as it would mean four hunting groups in exchange for one. Assuming the USA would send the ship to the Pacific, the reduction in capital ship strength was just acceptable. There was, however, the problem of finding the necessary crews. The eight cruisers could be manned over a staggered period, ending in 1942 or 1943, and two could be taken on at any time, by paying off three of the old 'C' or 'D' class cruisers into dockyard control. The First Sea Lord sent the following note to the Prime Minister on 28th February: "If we could obtain eight US cruisers in exchange for *Duke of York* I think that at the present time we would be wise to do so. It is clear, however . . . that the best we could do would be to man two 8-inch cruisers in the summer of 1941 and the remainder would have to wait and it could even involve paying off the 'C' and 'D' class cruisers. On this basis I do not consider the exchange worthwhile."

No more was heard of the matter. What prompted the Prime Minister's suggestion is at present unknown – it may have been his own idea; however, it is probable that the Americans knew of the idea, and may even have suggested it. (When the authors were researching for photographs of British ships in the United States Archives one of the lists received contained numbers for photographs of the battleship *Duke of New York*!)

Wireless-transmitting arrangements and radar
All the main wireless-transmitting offices were below the armoured-deck, although there were a number of minor offices situated in the bridge and after superstructure. Transmission was arranged from the foremast and reception from the mainmast. The main transmitting-room was on the lower-deck below the bridge, and the second transmitting-room was on the middle-deck below the bridge. The main receiving office was on the lower-deck below the mainmast.

Below: *Anson* arriving in Sydney harbour on 18th January 1946.

The radar and direction-finder outfits, carried on completion and the subsequent alterations and additions thereto, were:

King George V
As completed, December 1940: Types '279' and '284' Radar; FC2 high-frequency direction-finder with fixed diamond aerial at centre of main topmast and office on after HACS platform.

1941 (early): Type '271' radar fitted; aerial in 'lantern' between forward HACS directors.
1941 (late): Type '271' removed and Type '273' fitted, with 'lantern' on foremost starfish; five Type '282' sets fitted, with aerials on pom-pom directors.
By mid-1942: Four Type '285' sets fitted, with aerials on HACS directors; FM2 medium-frequency direction-finder fitted, with aerial on bridge front.

Refit, February to July 1944: Type '279' removed and Type '279B' transceiver fitted, with aerial on main-topmast; Type '284' replaced by Type '274'; Type '273' removed; Type '293' fitted, with aerial on fore-topmasthead; Type '277' fitted, with aerial on fore starfish; two Type '282' sets fitted, for new pom-pom directors, on after superstructure. Additional Type '285' set fitted, with aerials fitted on after main director-control tower. (Type '285'

fitted because of shortage of Type '274'.) High-frequency direction-finder removed, and RH2 direction-finder set fitted, offce and aerial on quarter-deck.

Prince of Wales
As completed, March 1941: Types '279' and '284' radar; FC2 high-frequency direction-finder as *King George V*.
By May 1941: Type '285' (four sets) and '282' (four sets) radar fitted.
July 1941: Type '271' radar fitted between forward high-angle control-system directors as in *King George V*.

Duke of York
As completed, November 1941: Radar Types '281', '282' (six sets); '285' (four sets); '273' and '284' (the pom-pom director between the forward high-angle control-system directors and its '282' set were later removed, date not known); 'FM2' medium-frequency direction-finder.
Refit, September 1944 to April 1945: Type '281' replaced by Type '281B', aerial on main-topmast; two '282' sets fitted for new pom-pom directors on after superstructure; Type '284' replaced by '274' (two sets), aerials fitted, one on each director-control tower; Type '273' removed; Type '293' and '277' fitted; 'RH2' VHF direction-finder fitted on quarter- deck.

Anson
As completed, June 1942: Radar Types '281', '282' (six sets) '284'; '285' (four sets) and '273' (one '282' set later removed); 'FM2' medium-frequency direction-finder.
Refit, July 1944 to March 1945: Type '281' replaced by '281B'; two '262' sets fitted for new pom-pom directors on after superstructure; five existing '282' sets replaced by '262'; Type '284' replaced by '274' (two sets), aerials on fore and aft director-control towers; Type '273' removed; Type '293' and '277' fitted; four Type '285' sets replaced by Type '275' sets, aerial on new Mk VI directors; 'RH2' direction-finder set fitted, office and aerial on quarter-deck; Type '651' missile jamming gear fitted.

Howe
As for *Anson*, except refit, December 1943 to May 1944: no Type '651' fitted; Type '285' set with aerials on after director-control tower instead of Type '274'; original '285' sets retained.

Alterations and additions
The following modifications, arising directly or indirectly from war experience, were approved generally for the class, by April 1942:

1. Additional equipment fitted or approved to be fitted:
1. De-gaussing coil. In *King George V* this was originally fitted externally; in the remainder of the class, it was fitted internally in all ships at time of completion.
2. Asdic gear. (*Howe* carried a Type '132').
3. Radar outfits, test room and store, eight offices.
4. 'RP 10' remote power-control for pom-pom mountings.
5. Additional surface look-out positions at shelter-deck level.
6. Crow's-nest.
7. Position of No. '3' air look-out altered.
8. Additional oil-fuel tanks forward and provision for existing tanks to be fitted in excess of 95 per cent capacity.
9. Aircraft-plotting arrangements and fighter-direction officers' position.
10. Teleprinter and shore telephone rooms.
11. Shaft-holding gear.

2. Additional protective plating:
1. Protection to radar offices.
2. Protection to emergency conning-position on after funnel, and leads thereto.
3. Protection to cable roots of 5.25-inch mountings.

3. Additional watertight sub-division and improvements thereto:
1. Additional watertight bulkheads on lower-deck aft.
2. Additional watertight bulkheads on lower-deck – ships' companies' wash-places.
3. Trunked access to, and escape from compartments below middle-deck.
4. Blanking of certain watertight doors, side scuttles, skylights and ventilator openings.
5. Stiffening watertight ventilation trunks and valves and fitting of additional valves.

4. Alterations to damage-control arrangements:
1. Extension of pumping system of 350-ton pumps.
2. Additional portable pumps and connections thereof.
3. Larger strainers to pump suctions.
4. Additional stores for action repairs (cement, shores, steel boxes, etc.)
5. Ship's side lining removed near waterline to make side more accessible for damage repairs.
6. Additional isolation valves in fire-main.
7. Additional valves in steering gear installation.
8. Extension of spindles to main steam valves in 'A' and 'B' engine rooms.
9. Emergency evaporators and distillers provided.
10. Battery feed to emergency lighting instead of oil.
11. Electrical apparatus fitted higher above decks.
12. Shock-proof mountings for machinery and fittings.
13. Duplicate power-leads for 5.25-inch mountings.

5. Alterations to assist escape of personnel:
1. Increased provision of life belts, life floats and float nets.
2. Sleeping accommodation below waterline moved to positions above middle-deck.
3. Alterations to heads and heels of sloping ladders and provision of jumping-ladders.
4. Heavy hatches fitted with springs instead of balance weights.

6. Alterations to fire-fighting gear and reduction of fire risks:
1. Increased number of fire-extinguishers and other fire-fighting apparatus.

Below: *Duke of York* on 12th December 1946, after drastic reduction of her close-range armament.

Bottom of page: *King George V*, leaving Portsmouth in December 1948. Note the Type '284' radar aerials, and the Type '285' aerials, on the forward and after director control-tower respectively.

2. Provision of diesel-driven fire-pumps (not fitted by April 1942).
3. Substitution of diesel-engined for petrol-engined motor boats.
4. Removal of ready-use oil tanks for galleys.
5. Quick-closing hangar exhausts, 'Fearnought' curtains and grouping of hangar door and ventilator controls.
6. Additional gauges on service lines.

7. Improvements to meet severe weather conditions:
1. Lagging and heating-coils for exposed fresh-water tanks.
2. Modifications to weather-deck ventilators and fittings, and valves below.
3. Stiffening of rudder and means of preventing rudder lifting.
4. Modifications to paravane arrangement.
5. Improved watertightness of mantles of 14-inch and 5.25-inch mountings.

8. Miscellaneous alterations:
1. Separate receiving-aerial for each wireless-transmitter-room.
2. Extension to and re-arrangement of admiral's bridge.
3. Additional first-aid station.
4. Provision room aft (in case all those concentrated forward were damaged).
5. Louvres fitted to mushroom-top ventilators to give protection from gun-blast.

The majority of the alterations listed above under sections '3' and '4', were, in whole or in part, a result of the lessons learnt from the loss of *Prince of Wales*.

In reference to section '7' it should be mentioned, that the ships were designed with a comparatively small sheer forward, in order to give unobstructed fire ahead to the forward 14-inch guns. The designed freeboard was 23 feet at the side, amidships, and 29 feet at the stem, but these figures were considerably reduced by the subsequent increases in the ships' displacements. As a result, they tended, in heavy weather, to suffer from seas breaking over the forecastle, and they were generally very wet forward.

14. The Lion Class, 1937 to 1944

In April 1937, the Japanese having failed to agree to the terms of the Second London Naval Treaty, the Treaty limit on gun calibre reverted to 16 inches. Shortly afterwards, the Admiralty began preliminary design work on 35,000-ton ships armed with 16-inch guns, but with no great enthusiasm, because it was thought that a well-balanced 16-inch ship could not be produced on this displacement. Early investigations indicated that a reasonable compromise would be a ship, armed with one twin and two triple 16-inch gun-mountings, and twelve 5.25-inch guns; with protection as in *King George V*, and a speed of 28 knots. Weight saving was thus effected, by allowing for the minimum practical number of guns for the main armament, reducing the secondary armament by two turrets – compared to *King George V* – and providing good protection against 15-inch rather than 16-inch, gunfire. At a meeting of the Sea Lords in October 1937, it was decided that the Director of Naval Construction should investigate this design in greater detail, make provision for aircraft if possible, and also provide one or two alternatives.

Shortly after this, it was realised that the design of the two types of 16-inch mounting (triple and twin) would take too long to produce, and that if the ships were to be ordered in 1938, the gun mountings would not be ready, and consequently, there would be a considerable delay to the ship's completion. It was decided, therefore, to concentrate on the design of one type of mounting, the triple, and to substitute one of these for the twin, thereby increasing the armament from eight to nine guns. Preliminary calculations revealed, that a nine 16-inch gun ship, meeting the requirements given above, but without aircraft, would have a standard displacement of 36,150 tons. It became necessary, therefore, to consider methods of reducing the displacement to 35,500 tons, and it was decided to make the following economies in weight. (It was anticipated that weight saving during construction would reduce the displacement from 35,500 tons to within the Treaty limitation. It was thought that not more than 500 tons could be allowed for, in this respect.)

1. Reduce the length of the main magazines, which would save 160 tons. This would reduce the maximum ammunition stowage to 85 rounds per gun for the after turret but the stowage for the forward turrets would remain at 100 rounds per gun.
2. Lower the top of the armour belt by six inches, and raise the lower edge by one foot, which would save 180 tons. This would involve accepting reduced deck heights for the middle-deck and lower-deck and increased vulnerability to diving shell.
3. Reduce the ammunition allowance to 60 rounds per gun in the standard condition, which would save 270 tons. (This would not affect the maximum ammunition stowage. Lowering the armoured-deck was also suggested, but was ruled out on the grounds that the last bombing trial on Job 74, "in October 1937, confirmed the desirability of retaining the main deck at the armoured deck".)

These modifications brought the displacement down to 35,540 tons, and were incorporated in the first detailed legend and sketch design – '16A/38' – in which it was found possible to include aircraft. A second design, '16B/38', was prepared, after a request by the Engineer-in-Chief to include the same turbines as in the *King George V* class, in order to reduce design and production requirements for the machinery.

This involved lengthening the citadel, which increased the displacement by 100 tons. On the instructions of the Controller, a third design, armed with twelve 14-inch guns in three quadruple turrets, was also prepared. In order to allow for the increased main armament weights, compared to *King George V*, the weight of protection and the number of 5.25-inch mountings was reduced, and the aircraft were omitted.

The development of these designs continued until about March 1938, during which time, various methods were considered of squeezing the maximum number of desirable features into the limited displacement available. Events however, were about to release the Admiralty from the unenviable straight-jacket situation of trying to get a large ship into a comparatively small hull.

After their withdrawal from the London Naval Conference, the Japanese became extremely secretive about their intended programme of new construction, and resisted all attempts by the USA and Britain to obtain information, on an exchange or any other basis. This, needless to say, caused a considerable amount of concern, because although the Admiralty felt that if the Japanese exceeded the 16-inch gun calibre they would be faced with "grave technical difficulties", secret sources had indicated that there was a possibility of the new ships being armed with 18-

Table 79: Legend particulars of Designs 16A/38, 16B/38 and 14A/38, December 1937

Length	700 feet (pp) 740 feet (wl)
Beam (maximum)	103 feet
Standard displacement	35,000 tons
Mean draught (standard)	28 feet
Mean draught (deep)	31 feet 9 inches. (16B 31 feet 10 inches)
SHP	100,000
Speed (standard)	28.5 to 29.25 knots
Speed (deep)	27.5 to 28.25 knots
Oil fuel capacity	3,700 tons
Endurance at 10 knots (trial conditions)	14,000 nautical miles
Armament:	Nine 16-inch (14A, twelve 14-inch) Twelve 5.25-inch Four multiple pom-poms Four multiple machine-guns (0.5-inch or 0.661-inch calibre) No torpedo tubes One D111H catapult and four aircraft (no aircraft arrangements in 14A)

Armour (thicknesses as in *King George V* class):

Weights (tons):	16A	16B	14A
General equipment	1,050	1,050	1,050
Machinery	2,550	2,650	2,650
Armament	6,560	6,560	6,450
Armour and protective plating	12,160	12,160	12,180
Hull	13,540	13,220	13,220
Standard displacement:	35,540	35,640	35,530

inch guns. This was considered "likely when remembering the Japanese tendency to over-gun". Other intelligence reports had indicated that the Japanese ships would be of about 42,000 to 43,000 tons, and armed with 16-inch guns, and that there were also three large cruisers, mounting 12-inch guns, under construction. The Admiralty decided that "the only possible method of influencing Japan to restrict the size of capital ships would be by informing her that if she did not accept treaty standards or inform us of her intentions we would invoke the escalation clause and use our greater building capacity and money to outstrip Japanese naval strength". This view was endorsed by the Committee of Imperial Defence on 13th January 1938, and, in due course, was put to the Japanese; the USA probably made a similar representation. The reply was unsatisfactory and on 31st March, Britain, the USA and France invoked the escalation clause to raise the maximum displacement limit.

The Admiralty favoured raising the limit to 40,000 tons, and sent a memorandum to this effect to the USA. The US Government replied that the lowest level they could accept was 45,000 tons. On 26th May, the First Sea Lord, the Controller, the Deputy Chief of Naval Staff, the Assistant Chief of Naval Staff and Sir R. Backhouse, who was about to succeed Chatfield as First Sea Lord, met to consider the proposals that should be made for the two capital ships of the 1938 programme. Agreement was unanimous that Britain should build 16-inch gun ships, but the construction of what were described as "mammoth" ships was strongly opposed. A 45,000 ton ship would be very expensive, and would involve great difficulties in construction and docking. After full consideration, it was decided to confirm the Admiralty's previously held views, and to recommend that the new ships be of 40,000 tons and armed with nine 16-inch guns. The meeting concluded that "although these ships will have nine guns as opposed to the twelve guns which foreign countries would probably instal in any 45,000 ton battleship we feel the design we propose can be perfectly well defended as the most suitable for our requirements, possessing as it will good offensive power, adequate speed and extremely good protection. Able in fact to stand up to any ship it would have to meet". On 27th May, the day after this meeting, the First Lord sent to the Cabinet a memorandum containing the following proposals:

"(a) To accept as the Treaty limit an upper limit of 45,000 tons and of course the already established gun limit of 16 inch. It must be borne in mind that if we do not accept the American limit by the end of June there will be no limit at all. This state of affairs which, although highly acceptable to the United States, would be most detrimental to our interests.

(b) To notify the European naval powers that we do not intend for the present to build capital ships beyond the limit of 40,000 tons."

Table 80: Legend of particulars of Designs 16E/38, 16F/38, 16G/38 and 14B/38

	16E/38	16F/38	16G/38	14B/38
Length (pp) feet	850	730	790	820
Length (oa) feet		770	820	
Beam (max) feet	110	105	106	106
Standard displacement (tons)	48,500	39,500	43,000	42,750
Deep displacement (tons)	55,000	45,200	49,000	48,500
Mean draught (ft)		30	31	
SHP	110,000	115,000	150,000	150,000
Speed (knots) standard	27	29.25	31	31
Speed (knots) deep	26	28.25	30	30
Oil fuel (tons)		4,000	4,400	
Armament:	12 16-in 16 5.25-inch	9 16-in 12 5.25-inch	9 16-in* 16 5.25-inch	12 14-in 16 5.25-inch
	4 multiple pom-poms 2 multiple machine-guns			All designs
Aircraft	four	four	none	four
torpedo tubes	?	none	4 21-in	?
Armour**	As *King George V* class.			
Weights (tons):				
General equipment	—	1,050	1,300	—
Machinery	—	2,685	3,550	—
Armament	—	6,050	7,200	—
Armour & protection	—	12,500	15,050	—
Hull	—	13,215	15,900	—
Total:	48,500	39,500	43,000	42,750
Estimated cost (millions£)	£11	£8.85	£9.75	£9.3

* 16G also carried four 4-inch guns for starshell.
** Barbettes and turret fronts of 16F and 16G, 15-inch.

The Cabinet approved the Admiralty's proposals and, on 30th June, the USA, Britain and France signed a protocol, raising the maximum displacement limit of capital ships to 45,000 tons. Similar protocols were later signed by Russia, Germany and Italy. Britain also announced her intention not to exceed a displacement of 40,000 tons in her new ships, and expressed the hope that the other European powers would abide by this voluntary limit.

One wonders what the reaction would have been had it become known that Japan was in fact building 64,000-ton ships armed with 18-inch guns. Unless the evidence had been substantial, it is probable that the Admiralty would not have believed it, and even if they had, it is unlikely that they would have followed the Japanese lead. The most likely course of action for Britain would have been the continued building of 16-inch gun ships, but with increased allowance for armour to provide them with protection against 18-inch gunfire, and possibly an increase in the number of guns to twelve.

The 1938 sketch designs

These designs were worked out by the DNC between February and March 1938. It appears that '16E', '16G' and '14B' were drawn up on the assumption that there would be no upper displacement limit. Design '16F' was prepared – on the instructions of the Controller – on the assumption that her standard displacement would not exceed 40,000 tons. Designs '16G' and '16F' were examined at the previously mentioned meeting of the Sea Lords on 26th May, after which, the First Sea Lord gave instructions that work should proceed on the development of Design '16F', but with the displacement increased to 40,000 tons. The additional 500 tons was to be used to provide a 15-inch main belt, abreast the machinery, instead of 14-inch, and, if possible, to increase the number of 5.25-inch gun-mountings from six to eight. The resulting Design '16F/38' (modified) was completed on 30th June 1938, and approval for the detailed design to proceed was given by the Board on 25th July. The particulars were the same as those of the original design except for those listed in Table 81.

Table 81: Particulars of Design 16F/38 modified, 30th June 1938

Length	740 feet (pp) 780 feet (oa)
Displacement	40,750 tons standard*
SHP	120,000, 130,000 with higher boiler forcing
Speed	29.25 knots (28.25 knots deep) 30 knots (28.75 knots deep) at 130,000 SHP
Secondary armament	Sixteen 5.25-inch
Aircraft	Four (one D111H catapult)
Belt armour	15-inch abreast magazines and machinery
Weights (tons):	
General equipment	1,100
Armament	6,940
Machinery	3,060
Armour and protection	14,600
Hull	15,050
Standard displacement:	40,750 tons

* Based on the assumption that weight savings during construction would bring the displacement within the 40,000-ton limit.

On 15th December 1938, the Board gave its approval to the final legend and preliminary design drawings for the two battleships of the 1938 programme. The first of these ships, *Temeraire*, was laid down by Cammell Laird on 1st June 1939 and the second, *Lion*, by Vickers Armstrong on 4th July 1939. They were due to complete in July and September 1942, respectively. Two sister ships, *Conqueror* and *Thunderer*, were included in the 1939 programme. The former was due to be ordered from John Brown on 15th August and the latter, from Fairfields on 15th November 1939 and were expected to complete by March 1944. (Britain's capacity for the construction of heavy guns, gun-mountings and armour plate was such, that no more than two capital ships could be included in each year's programme.) Neither of these, in fact, was ever laid down, and it is probable that *Thunderer* was never ordered. Two more ships were to have been included in the 1940 building programme.

On 28th September 1939, after the outbreak of war, the Board met to consider what work should be done on the four ships of the *Lion* class, it having become apparent that the main German naval campaign would be directed against British seaborne trade by the use of submarines and mines. To counteract this threat, the most urgent need was of convoy escorts and anti-submarine vessels, and if the construction of the four battleships were retarded, the labour and materials released could be employed in the construction of eight intermediate-type destroyers. The First Lord felt that, in view of the potential building capacity of Germany and Japan, it would be unwise to delay work on the capital ship programme, but the Controller pointed out that because of the time required to produce the 16-inch gun-mountings, the new ships would, in any case, be late in completion. It was generally agreed that the construction of the *Lion* class be suspended for one year, but that work on the gun-mountings and any other equipment where delay might be expected, should proceed. Thus, bearing in mind that the gun-mountings would be a year late, in any case, the suspension of the ships themselves, did not materially affect the expected completion dates.

In October 1939, the Plans Division suggested completing *Lion* as a six 15-inch gun ship, using three of the four spare 15-inch Mk I twin gun-turrets, that were in store, suitably modernised to Mk I (N) standard. It was also suggested that it might be possible to replace the three 15-inch twin turrets by three 16-inch triple turrets, after the ship had been completed. In November, the Director of Naval Construction submitted his comments on these suggestions. He thought the scheme was practical, but pointed out that the labour for starting work on *Lion* and, more especially, for modernising the 15-inch gun-mountings, was not then available. It was estimated that the ship with six 15-inch guns could be completed about six months before the scheduled completion date, and the Director of Naval Construction asked would it not be better to have "a nine 16-inch gun ship in 1944, rather than a six 15-inch gun ship, six months before that date". The suggestion was later rejected, and so far as is known, the matter was not raised again.

As the war progressed, increasingly heavy demands on labour and materials were made. Escorts, aircraft carriers, merchant ships, tanks and aircraft, repairs to warships and merchant ships, all had higher priorities. Work on the capital ships was continuously postponed, despite the Admiralty's view that they were badly needed. This view was strengthened by the loss of France as an ally, the entry of Italy and Japan into the war and the neutralisation of the USA's battle fleet, at Pearl Harbor. All these events emphasised the need for greater capital-ship strength, but always there were stronger threats from other quarters, requiring more immediate attention. The keel plates of *Lion* and *Temeraire* were eventually broken up on the slips, and all four ships were cancelled in 1944.

General features

No detailed description of the features of the *Lion* class is included here as the general arrangement and distribution of the armament, armour and machinery was basically the same as that of the *King George V* class. The main armament for example, although consisting of 16-inch and not 14-inch guns and mountings, was designed on the same principles, and differed only in weights and dimensions. Similarly, the description of the armour belt of *King George V* could be applied equally well to *Lion*, with the one exception that the thickness abreast the machinery in the latter ship was fifteen and not fourteen inches. What differences there are, can easily be traced by referring to the drawings and list of particulars.

During the early part of the war, it was decided that the design of the *Lion* class should be examined by the Naval Staff and by sea officers who had recently gained experience. As a result, it was decided that modification of the original design was essential. No details of this modification are known, but it was planned to greatly increase the size of the ships. A new body plan was prepared for *Lion*, giving her a displacement of 56,500 tons full load, and dimensions of 810 feet length x 115 feet (maximum) beam x 34 feet 3 inches (mean) deep draught. This would have given the ship a standard displacement of about 49,000 tons.

PARTICULARS OF *LION* CLASS AS DESIGNED, 1938

Displacement 40,550 tons standard.

Weights

General equipment	1,100 tons
Armour and protection	14,180 tons
Armament	7,100 tons
Machinery	3,160 tons
Hull	15,010 tons
Standard displacement:	40,550 tons

Dimensions
Length: 740 feet (pp); 780 feet (wl); 785 feet (oa).

Beam: 104 feet.

Draught (mean): 30 feet (standard); 33 feet 6 inches (deep).

Armament
Nine 16-inch 45-cal Mk II: three triple mountings.
Sixteen 5.25-inch Mk I: eight twin mountings Mk I.
Six pom-pom mountings Mk VI.

Ammunition stowage

	Normal	Maximum
16-inch:	60 rounds per gun	100 rounds per gun
5.25-inch:	150 rounds per gun	400 rounds per gun
2-pounder:	500 rounds per gun	1,800 rounds per gun

Armour
Belt: 15 inch, 5½ inch at lower edge.
Belt forwards and aft of citadel: 13 inch, 12 inch and 11 inch all tapering to 5½ inch at lower edge.
Bulkheads: 12 inch at sides, reducing to 11 inch and 10 inch at centre-line, 4 inch abaft steering gear.
Barbette 'A': 15 inch sides, reducing to 13½ inch and 12½ inch on forward side, 13 inch and 12 inch on after side.
Barbettes 'B' and 'Y': 15 inch sides, reducing to 13½ inch and 12 inch on fore side, and 13 inch and 12 inch on after side; 2 inch below main-deck.
Turrets: 15 inch front, 10 inch forward side, 7 inch after side and back, 6 inch roof.
Main-deck: 6 inch over magazines, 5 inch over machinery.
Lower-deck (forward): 5 inch, 4 inch, 3½ inch, 3 inch and 2½ inch.
Lower-deck (aft): 5 inch and 4½ inch.
5.25-inch casemates: 2 inch and 1½ inch sides, 1 inch roofs.
Conning-tower: 4½ inch sides, 3 inch front and rear, 2 inch floor and roof.
Conning-tower tube: 2 inch.
Protective bulkheads: 1¾ inch.
Splinter protection to magazines: 1½ inch walls and crowns, 2 inch bulkheads below main armour bulkheads forward and aft of citadel.
Cable-trunks to director-control tower: 2 inch.
Bullet-proof plating on bridge: ¾ inch, ½ inch and ⅜ inch.

Machinery
Parsons single-reduction geared turbines, four shafts.
130,000 SHP = 30 knots.
Eight Admiralty three-drum boilers.
Oil-fuel capacity 3,720 tons.
Eudurance at 10 knots = 14,000 miles in trial condition.

Complement 1,680 as fleet flagship.

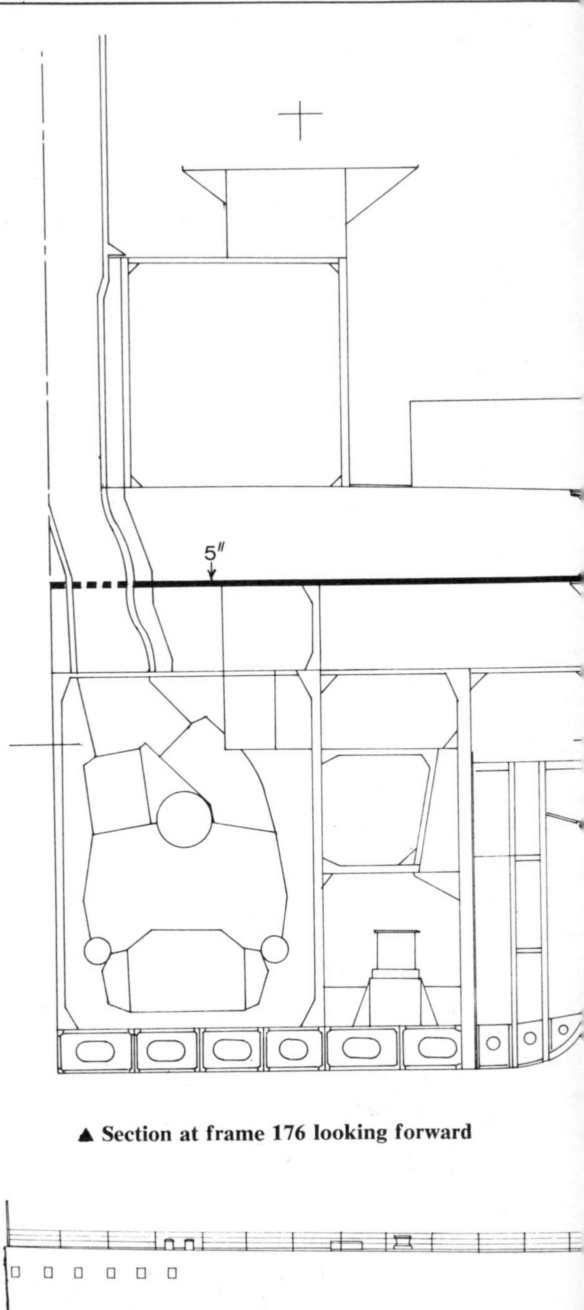

▲ Section at frame 176 looking forward

Vanguard in June 1953.

Vanguard in June 1953.

Lion class

outboard profile and deck plans

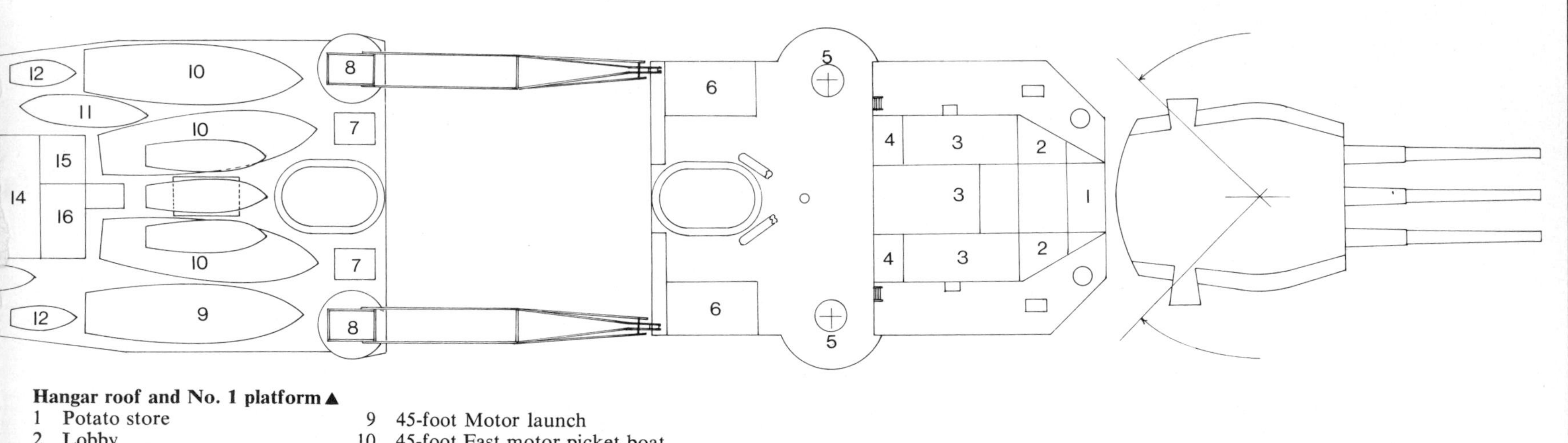

Hangar roof and No. 1 platform ▲

1 Potato store
2 Lobby
3 CPOs' and POs' reading room
4 Boiler room downtake
5 Pom-pom
6 Pom-pom ready-use magazine
7 Downtake
8 Aircraft and boat crane
9 45-foot Motor launch
10 45-foot Fast motor picket boat
11 27-foot Whaler
12 14-foot Sailing dinghy
13 16-foot Motor dinghy
14 Spare AC engine store
15 Motor boat engine workshop
16 Motor boat engine store

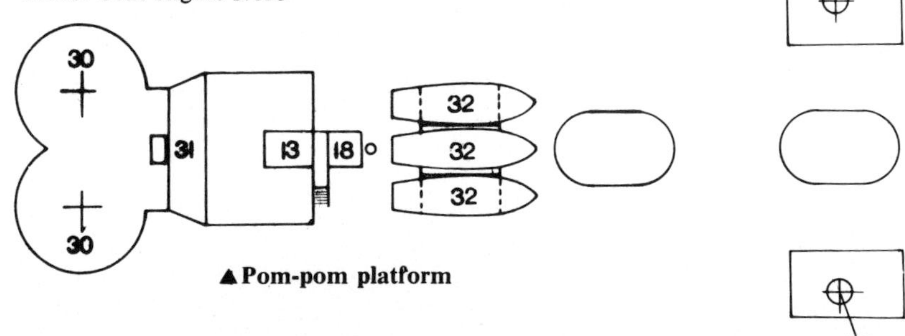

▲ Pom-pom platform

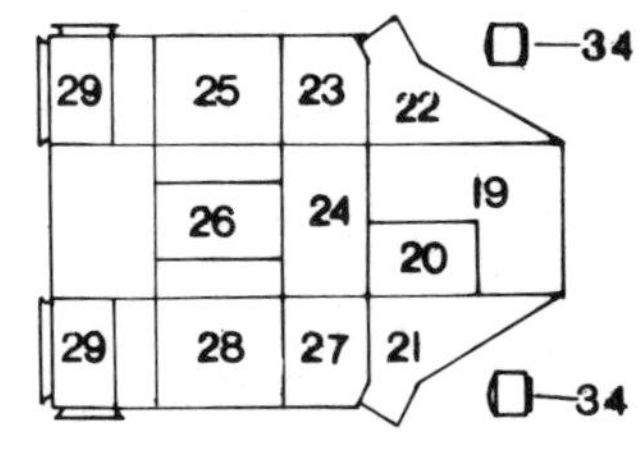

▲ No. 2 Platform

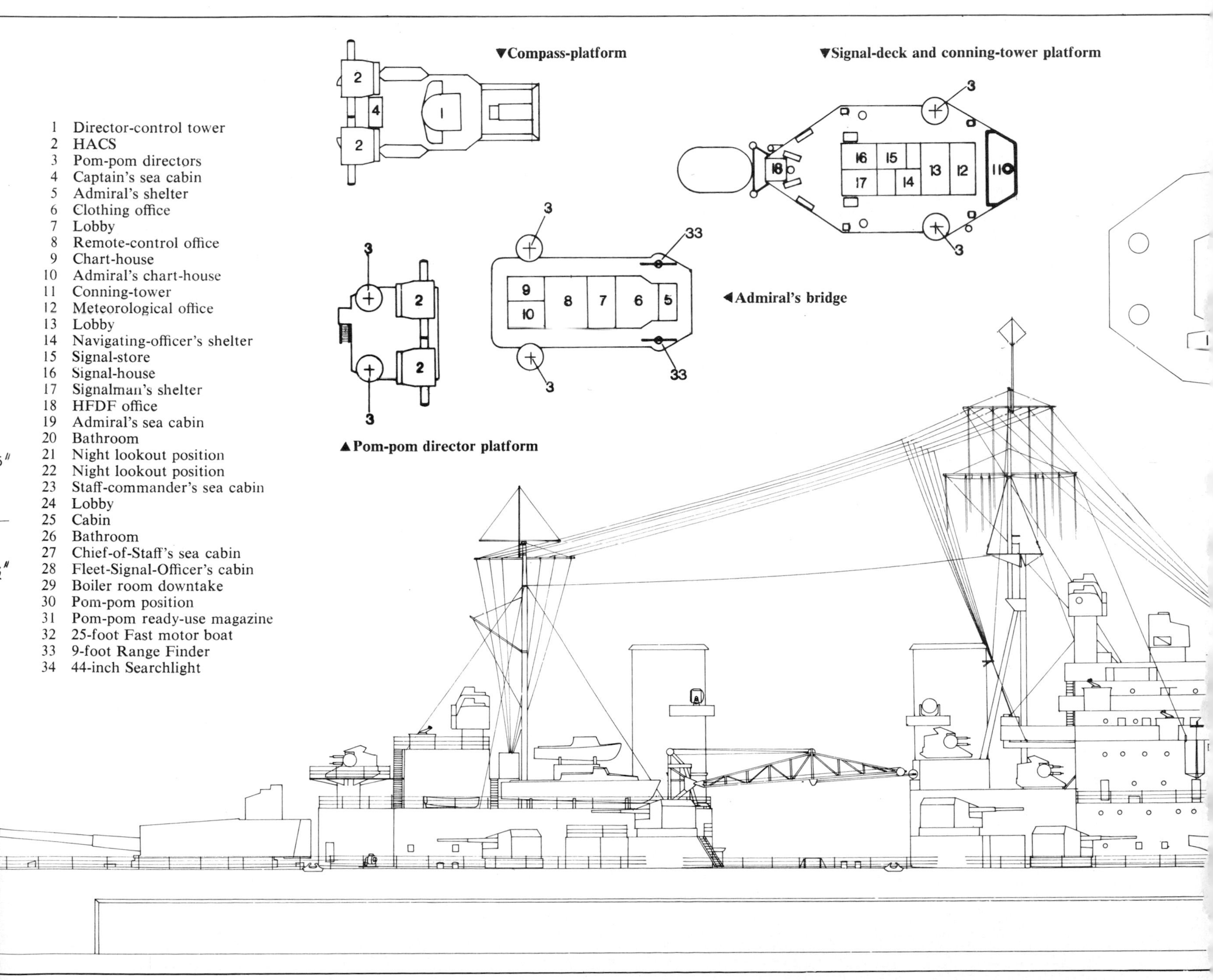

1 Director-control tower
2 HACS
3 Pom-pom directors
4 Captain's sea cabin
5 Admiral's shelter
6 Clothing office
7 Lobby
8 Remote-control office
9 Chart-house
10 Admiral's chart-house
11 Conning-tower
12 Meteorological office
13 Lobby
14 Navigating-officer's shelter
15 Signal-store
16 Signal-house
17 Signalman's shelter
18 HFDF office
19 Admiral's sea cabin
20 Bathroom
21 Night lookout position
22 Night lookout position
23 Staff-commander's sea cabin
24 Lobby
25 Cabin
26 Bathroom
27 Chief-of-Staff's sea cabin
28 Fleet-Signal-Officer's cabin
29 Boiler room downtake
30 Pom-pom position
31 Pom-pom ready-use magazine
32 25-foot Fast motor boat
33 9-foot Range Finder
34 44-inch Searchlight
▼Compass-platform
▼Signal-deck and conning-tower platform
◀Admiral's bridge
▲Pom-pom director platform

15. Vanguard, 1939 to 1946

Vanguard was the last, and largest, British dreadnought battleship, and, as such, holds a special place in the history of the Royal Navy. She was probably the best example of her type ever built in a British yard, and, on the displacement, compared well with any of the world's fast battleships. Although conceived before the Second World War, she was not completed until after it had ended and she was the only British dreadnought that never fired her guns against an enemy. Strangely enough, she carried the same main armament as the ships described in the first chapter of this book, the *Queen Elizabeth* class, and it was from this armament that the original design was evolved.

On 14th February 1915, four 15-inch Mk I twin gun-mountings were ordered for the two light battlecruisers *Courageous* and *Glorious*. These two ships, each carrying two of the 15-inch mountings, were completed early in 1916. Between 1924 and 1930, they were converted to aircraft carriers, and the four gun-mountings were removed and placed in store, as spares for the 15-inch gun battleships of the *Queen Elizabeth* and the *Royal Sovereign* classes.

Early in 1939, it was suggested that these four mountings, suitably modernised, could be employed as the main armament of a new ship. This suggestion was examined by the Plans Division and became the subject of the following memorandum, dated 3rd March 1939, that was circulated among the Naval Staff between March and May 1939.

"Japanese new construction of capital ships remains uncertain but from what evidence is available it is clear that we shall, for many years, have to be prepared to face a Japanese fleet in the Far East with an inferior British Fleet in numbers of capital ships. Although this inferiority will be considerable during the next two or three years it does not become most marked until Germany has completed her full quota of capital ship construction under the Anglo-German Treaty, i.e. until the portion of our fleet in Home waters reaches the maximum. It is estimated that this will occur about the end of 1943, say March 1944, at which date, in the event of a simultaneous war against Germany and Japan, [the situation] is likely to be roughly as follows:

British Fleet in Home Waters	Germany
2 1939 programme	5 new capital ships
5 *King George Vs*	2 *Scharnhorsts*
3 battlecruisers	3 *Deutschlands*
Total – 10	7+3
British Fleet in Far East	**Japan**
2 *Lions*	4 new capital ships
2 *Nelsons*	2 *Nagatos*
3 *Warspites*	4 *Fusos*
2 *Barhams*	4 *Kongos*
3 *Royal Sovereigns*	2 battlecruisers
Total – 12	16 ?

Notes:
1. Since Germany will now possess five 8-inch gun cruisers to the six we shall have in Home Waters and the Atlantic, reliance can no longer be placed on [our] 8-inch gun cruisers to counter the *Deutschlands*.
2. Japanese strength is uncertain but it is unlikely to be less than shown and may be stronger.
3. It is probable that one or two of our capital ships will be undergoing large repairs. This will result in a reduction of our Far Eastern Fleet, the margin at Home being the same.

When it is appreciated that we must also expect the Japanese fleet to be substantially stronger than ours in aircraft carriers and to have a superiority of no less than five 8-inch gun cruisers, two points stand out clearly:
(a) It is urgently necessary either to add to our strength or to replace the *Royal Sovereign* class ships in our Far Eastern Fleet by new ships so as to make up in quality what we lack in quantity.
(b) Our battlecruisers being required at Home, the Far Eastern Fleet will have no ships capable of bringing to action the heavy cruisers that Japan is now reported to be building, they are believed to mount 12 inch guns." (The Japanese were planning to construct two 32,000-ton battlecruisers armed with nine 12.2-inch guns and capable of a speed of 33 knots. They were cancelled in 1942.)

"It is understood that if our next two capital ships of the 1940/1941 programme are of the 16-inch gun design they cannot be completed until late 1944 or early in 1945. The controlling factor being the time necessary to produce the gun mountings. Unless the disadvantages in cost and berthing and docking facilities of building up to the full treaty limit of 45,000 tons are accepted such ships cannot, moreover, be given speeds in access of about 28 knots without sacrificing protection. We have, however, four 15-inch twin turrets in store which, it is understood, could be completely modernised for a further twenty-five years service in much less time than it takes to build the hull of a brand new battleship.

A ship mounting these eight 15-inch guns on a displacement of about 40,000 tons could probably be given a speed of about 30 knots without making any substantial sacrifice in protection and although not quite so powerful as our 16-inch gun ships when lying in the battle-line, she would be of inestimable value as a fully armoured battlecruiser:
(a) To detach in pursuit of Japanese 12-inch gun cruisers raiding our Eastern Trade routes.
(b) To counter Japanese 8-inch gun cruisers in battle.
(c) To operate in Indian and Australian waters before the arrival of our Fleet in the Far East, such a ship would be very appropriate for the Royal Australian Navy to take over.

Since further 15-inch gun turrets will become available when the first of the *Royal Sovereign* class battleships is scrapped, early in 1942, it will be possible, if desired, to build a sister ship later. It does not however appear altogether sound to embark on a further ship of this type until it is quite certain that further turrets will be available. In any case the construction of more than one of these ships at this stage would, presumably, delay our 16-inch gun ship programme.

With reference to the design of this ship it is understood that an appreciable saving in initial cost could be made by accepting either a reduced armament of six instead of eight 15-inch guns or reduced speed of 28 knots or so. In D of P's view, however, this ship would incorporate the maximum armament and speed that can be provided on a displacement of 40,000 tons, regardless of cost, because it is necessary that she should (a) stand up against 16-inch gun ships, (b) make contact with heavy cruisers, (c) avoid action with superior numbers of foreign capital ships."

(Signed: Director of Plans, 3/3/1939).
(ADM1/10141 Design of 15-inch gun battleship. 1939. Public Records Office.)

This paper received the general approval of the Naval Staff, and in order to examine the possibilities in greater detail, the DNC was instructed to prepare a sketch design and legend for a battleship of 40,000 tons, armed with eight 15-inch guns, and capable of a speed of 30 knots. This design, '15B', was, in fact, the second produced by the DNC; an earlier design, '15A', had been drawn up at the verbal request of the Controller, and on the assumption that the ship's speed would be equal to that of the *King George V* class. A third design, '15C', was prepared, following a request by the Engineer-in-Chief to repeat the machinery of the *Lion* class, in order to

Right: *Vanguard* in February 1952.

Below right: in September 1948.

ensure the expeditious completion of the ship. The reason for this was, that much of the detailed design work on the machinery of the *Lion* class was already completed, whereas the provision of a new machinery layout would involve more drawing-office and production work, and could well have involved some delay to the completion of the ship.

Table 82: Particulars of Designs 15A, 15B, and 15C

	15A	15B	15C
Length (pp) feet	730	760	760
Length (wl) feet	770	800	800
Length (oa) feet	775	805	805
Beam (max) feet	104	105	105
Mean draught feet	29	29¾	29¾
SHP (normal)	100,000	130,000	120,000
SHP (overload)	110,000	143,000	130,000
Speed (knots)	28.5–29.25	30.25–31	29.25–30
Oil fuel (tons)		3,800	

Armament:	Eight 15-inch 80 rpg Sixteen 5.25-inch 200 rpg Six 2-pounder pom-pom Mk VI mountings 500 rpg	15A, 15B and 15C
Armour:		
Side	15-inch abreast magazines, 14-inch abreast machinery	
Bulkheads	12-inch and 10-inch	
Barbettes (max)	13-inch	
Turrets	13-in face, 9-in sides, 7-in rear, 6-in roof	
Main-deck	6-in over magazines, 5-in over machinery	
Lower-deck	5-in to 2½-in forward, 5-in to 4½-in aft	
Torpedo bulkheads	1¾-inch	
Splinter protection and bullet-proof plating	2-in, 1¼-in, 1½-in and 1-inch	

Weight (tons):			
General equipment	1,100	1,100	1,100
Machinery	2,750	3,450	3,200
Armament	5,900	5,900	5,900
Armour and protection	14,000	14,450	14,300
Hull	14,300	15,500	15,500
Standard displacement	38,050	40,400	40,000

These three designs were submitted to the Board on 17th July 1939. Design '15B' was preferred by the Controller, ACNS and DCNS, and was generally regarded as the best of the three. It was decided to choose Design '15C', however, because of the delay that might have been caused by the necessity to design and manufacture the machinery for '15B'. The DNC was therefore instructed to work this design out in greater detail. This work proceeded for a short period, but was stopped, pending future developments, on 11th September, eight days after the outbreak of war.

The project remained dormant until early in December 1939, when the new First Lord, Winston Churchill, expressed an interest in the design. He, no doubt, had been informed of the earlier work, and the idea of completing a new battleship at an early date must have appealed to him, for he particularly asked to see the legend and sketch design. On 19th February 1940, the DNC was instructed to continue with the design.

On 27th February a Staff meeting was held under the chairmanship of the First Lord, when it was decided that the following modifications should be included in the design:

1. The provision of splinter protection to the ship's side, forward and aft of the main belt, between the lower-deck and the middle-deck.
2. An increase in the protection of the 5.25-inch casemates, sufficient to withstand 500-pound semi armour-piercing bombs.
3. The provision of a small armoured conning-position, aft.
4. The addition of four unrotated-projectile mountings to the anti-aircraft armament.

A revised design, '15D' incorporating these modifications, was prepared. The particulars were the same as those for '15C' with the exception of the following:

Table 83: Particulars of Design 15D

Length	809 feet*
Beam (maximum)	105 feet 6 inches
Standard displacement	41,200 tons
Draught (standard)	30 feet (mean)
Draught (deep)	33 feet 6 inches (mean)
Speed	29.5 to 30.25 knots
Oil fuel capacity	3,800 tons
Armament:	As 15C but including four UP mountings
Armour:	As 15C except: Splinter belt forward and aft of main belt, 3-inch and 2-inch 5.25-inch casemates, 2½-inch roof, 2½-inch and 1½-inch sides
Weights:	
General equipment	1,100 tons
Machinery	3,250 tons
Armament	5,750 tons
Armour and protection	15,500 tons
Hull	15,600 tons
Total:	41,200 tons

The Controller was not completely satisfied with the protection provided for the 5.25-inch casemates and this was subsequently increased to 3-inch and 2-inch on the sides, with a 2½-inch roof. The weight for this was obtained, by reducing the thickness of the splinter belt, fore and aft, from 3 inches and 2 inches to 2½ inches and 2 inches. It was decided, later, that the casemate protection should be of a uniform thickness of 2½ inches.

Design '15D' was approved on 20th May 1940, but work was suspended between June and October 1940, because of more pressing commitments. As the work progressed, various alterations, prompted by war experience, were incorporated in the design. These included increasing the weights for oil fuel, armament and protection, and improving the watertight integrity. In order to compensate these additions, and to reduce the draught, the beam was increased to 108 feet (which meant the ship would not be able to dock at Portsmouth or Rosyth) and the side armour was reduced in thickness. These modifications were included in a revised design, '15E', which was approved by the Board on 17th April 1941.

The final order for the ship was placed with John Brown on 14th March 1941, and the drawings were handed to the builders, ten days later. The ship was laid down at Clydebank on 2nd October 1941, and, on 3rd November, the builders were informed that the ship was to be named *Vanguard*. When war broke out in the Pacific and Far East in

Right: *Vanguard*, 1952.

Table 84: Particulars of Design 15E

Length	760 feet (pp) 800 feet (wl) 809 feet (oa)
Beam (maximum)	108 feet
Standard displacement	41,600 tons
Draught (mean)	29 feet 6 inches (standard) 33 feet (deep)
SHP	120,000 (130,000 at overload)
Speed in standard condition	29.5 knots (30.25 knots at overload)
Speed in deep condition	28.5 knots (29 knots at overload)
Oil fuel capacity	4,100 tons (+300 tons emergency stowage)
Endurance	1,400 miles at 10 knots, 6,000 miles at 20 knots
Complement as squadron flagship	1,600
Armament:	Eight 15-inch, 80 rpg Sixteen 5.25-inch, 200 rpg Six Mk VI pom-pom mountings, 500 rpg Four UP mountings One D111H catapult, two aircraft
Armour and protection:	
Main belt	14-inch (4½-inch at lower edge) abreast magazines 13-inch (4½-inch at lower edge) abreast machinery
Splinter belt (forward and aft)	2½-inch and 2-inch
Bulkheads	12-inch and 10-inch
Barbettes	13-inch
Turrets	13-inch front, 9-inch side, 7-inch rear, 6-inch roof
5.25-inch turrets	2½-inch shields, 1½-inch roofs
5.25-inch casemates	2½-inch sides, 1½-inch roofs
Main-deck	6-inch over magazines, 5-inch over machinery
Lower-deck	5-inch to 2½-inch forward, 5-inch and 4½-inch aft
Protective plating	1-inch to ½-inch
Splinter protection to magazines	1½-inch
Protective bulkhead	1¾-inch
Weights:	
General equipment	1,100 tons
Machinery	3,250 tons
Armament	5,950 tons
Armour and protection	15,200 tons
Hull	16,100 tons
Standard displacement:	41,600 tons

December 1941, she was given 'A1' priority, and, in order to proceed with her as quickly as possible, the cruiser *Bellerophon* – also building at John Brown – was suspended and some merchant ship construction was stopped. It was hoped that these measures would provide enough additional labour to enable *Vanguard* to be completed by the end of 1944. This, however, proved virtually impossible. Although a large amount of labour was made available, the percentage of this labour that was skilled was insufficient to materially increase the ship's rate of construction. It was difficult, moreover, to exercise maximum effort on *Vanguard* without seriously affecting the production of other equipment that had also been given high priority. (The average number of men and women employed at John Brown on the construction of *Vanguard* was 3,500, and this of course takes no account of the labour employed on sub-contract work.)

In 1942, consideration was given to the possibility of converting the ship to an aircraft carrier. The DNC said that this would present no fundamental difficulties, and that the general design of the 1942 carriers (the *Ark Royal* class) could be followed, and that it would take six months to complete the re-design. The proposal was discussed in detail and rejected on 15th July 1942.

The design was again revised in 1942, as a result of the loss of *Prince of Wales* and in the light of other war experience. The new legend and drawings were approved in September 1942. The principal modifications were a further increase in the freeboard forward, additional oil-fuel stowage, increased AA armament and the omission of aircraft and catapult. A number of other improvements were made, and these are detailed later in the text. The particulars of the September 1942 design were the same as those of '15E' except for the details shown in Table 85.

This was, basically, the final design, although a number of other improvements were incorporated in the ship as her construction progressed. She was launched at Clydebank, by HRH Princess Elizabeth on 30th November 1944. Eighteen months later, on 25th April 1946, she was commissioned for contractor's trials under the command of Captain W. G. Agnew, CB, CVO, DSO.

Table 85: Particulars of *Vanguard*, September 1942

Length (oa)	813 feet
Standard displacement	42,300 tons
Draught (mean)	29 feet 10 inches (standard) 33 feet 10 inches (deep)
Oil fuel capacity	4,850 tons
AA armament:	Nine Mk VI pom-pom mountings, 500 rpg One Mk VII pom-pom mounting, 500 rpg Twelve 20-mm Oerlikons, 1,800 rpg

Armament

For gunnery efficiency, the Naval Staff had always regarded four twin turrets, disposed fore and aft, as in the *Queen Elizabeth* class, as the ideal main armament arrangement. Three turrets had been adopted in new designs, however, because the additional turret would have required a longer ship and more weight. The use of the four existing 15-inch twin mountings in *Vanguard* meant that these disadvantages had to be accepted, but it cannot be said that this detracted from the quality of the completed ship. Although the mountings were of First World War vintage, they suffered little in comparison with modern weapons, once they had been modernised. To make them suitable for fitting in a modern ship, the following alterations were made:

1. The 9-inch armour plates on the front of the gun-house, were replaced by armour 13 inches thick.
2. The elevation of the guns was increased to 30°, which meant cutting into the roof plates and providing armoured hoods over the gun-ports.
3. The 4¼-inch armour roof plates were replaced by non-cemented armour plates, 6 inches thick.
4. The 2-inch armour under the gun-house floor, where it overhung the barbette, was replaced by 3-inch armour. This was not particularly important for protective purposes, but did help to balance the additional weight of the front plates.
5. Improved flash-tightness.
6. Fitting of remote power-control for training only. (*Vanguard* was the only British battleship to have remote power-control for the main and secondary armaments.)
7. 15-foot range-finders were replaced by 30-foot range-finders in all except 'A' turret.
8. De-humidifying equipment and lagging was fitted, to improve the habitability of the gun-house.

Table 86: Main armament weights (tons)
(Detailed calculation for Design 15E, 1942)

Standard condition:	
Revolving weight of 15-inch turrets	3,340
15-inch shell (80 rpg)	554
15-inch cordite (80 rpg)	238
Shell room machinery	120
Magazine handing room machinery	40
Hydraulic machinery	120
Hydraulic pipes, valves, etc.	40
Training racks, lower roller-paths and half of roller-rings.	70
Spare gear	20
Forward 15-inch director-control tower	30
After 15-inch director-control tower	33
Total:	4,605 tons
Additional for extra deep condition:	
15-inch shell (34 rpg)	236
15-inch cordite (31 rpg)	92
15-inch drill shells and charges (14)	14
Hydraulic fluid	80
Total:	422 tons
Grand total: 4,605+422=5,027 tons.	

Following what had become by now, standard practice, the magazines were positioned below the shell rooms, but this presented one of the most difficult problems in the modernisation of the mountings, because the ammunition hoists had been designed to accept the opposite arrangement. It was finally decided to leave the turret-trunk and hoist arrangements as they were, and to fit the cordite-handing rooms above the shell rooms. Hoists were provided in the fixed structure, to transport the cordite from the magazines in the hold, to the cordite-handing rooms on the lower-deck. This system had a disadvantage, in that the cordite-handing room was more vulnerable to shellfire, but the risks involved, were greatly reduced, by extending the 2-inch protection of the barbette ring-bulkhead, armouring the fixed cordite-hoists and fitting them with flash-tight doors at top and bottom, and transporting the charges in box-cloth wrappers.

The mountings were arranged to take the new 1,938-pound 15-inch projectile, and the turret supports were designed to withstand supercharge firings, but, in fact, supercharges were never actually carried by the ship. As completed, the total revolving weights of all four turrets was 3,420 tons, which was 80 tons more than the design figure. Other weight increases for the main armament, included the main director-control towers, from 63 to 70 tons, the hydraulic machinery, from 63 to 70 tons, the hydraulic fluid, from 80 to 91 tons, and the addition of 20 tons for corrosion-inhibiting oil, which was not included in the original design.

The secondary armament, and its distribution, was the same as in the *King George V* class except: (a) the 5.25-inch gun-mountings were Mk 1* with a re-designed gun-house, and (b) the mountings were provided with 'RP10' remote power-control, for both elevating and training. The total weight of the 5.25-inch mountings, guns, remote power-control machinery, pumps and spares, was 854 tons, 29 tons more than had been allowed for in the design calculations.

Although more on paper than in fact, the *Vanguard*'s close-range AA armament developed progressively with the war, as new mountings and control-systems became available. By the end of 1941, it was clear that the six Mk VI pom-pom mountings of Design '15E' were totally inadequate, but it was

Vanguard in September 1948.

almost impossible to find positions for additional mountings, clear of blast from the main and secondary armaments. It was decided therefore, somewhat reluctantly, to omit the aircraft arrangements in order to provide the necessary space. The after funnel was moved forward, and a new structure was fitted amidships on which boat stowage and two additional pom-pom mountings could be provided. This cleared the after superstructure, and allowed the two mountings, thereon, to be moved farther forward and clear of the blast from the after turrets. It was also decided to fit a Mk VII pom-pom on 'B' turret, and another Mk VI pom-pom on the quarter-deck, making a total of nine eight-barrel mountings and one four-barrel mounting.

In June 1943, the DNO reported that a mock-up of a new weapon, the six-barrel 40-mm Bofors, Mk VI, had been inspected, and it seemed likely that it would be in production in time for fitting in *Vanguard*. It was subsequently decided to replace the nine Mk VI pom-poms by these mountings and, at the same time, to replace the Mk VII pom-pom on 'B' turret by a twin 40-mm 'Buster' mounting. By 1945, the intended close-range anti-aircraft outfit was:

Ten 40-mm Bofors Mk VI mountings, four on the forward superstructure, five on the after superstructure and one on the quarter-deck.
One 40-mm 'Buster' twin mounting on 'B' turret.
Six 20-mm Oerlikon Mk XIV quadruple mountings on the superstructure.
Fourteen hand-worked 20-mm Oerlikon Mk XII twin mountings on the upper-deck.

In April 1945, consideration was given to fitting additional 40-mm single and twin mountings, and omitting some or all of the 20-mm twin mountings. It also became necessary to replace the 20-mm quadruple mountings when approval was given to suspend the manufacture of this new weapon in order to increase the rate of production of the power-operated 40-mm Mk VII single mounting. Various alternatives were discussed and the final proposals were:

1. To retain seven of the 20-mm Mk XII twin mountings in their existing positions, and to replace the remaining seven by 40-mm Bofors Mk III single mountings.
2. To fit two 20-mm Mk XII or Mk V Oerlikons and four 40-mm Bofors Mk VII in lieu of the six 20-mm quadruple mountings.
3. To fit two twin 20-mm Oerlikons Mk XII temporarily in the forward medium-range system Mk I director-positions until the latter equipment was available for fitting in the ship.

In addition, a twin stabilised tachymetric 40-mm Mk II anti-aircraft gun (STAAG) was substituted for the 'Buster' on 'B' turret, and, as the ship's completion had to be put back to April 1946, the seven hand-worked 40-mm Mk III were replaced by power-operated 40-mm Mk VII. None of the 20-mm mountings was fitted in the completed ship and the final close-range anti-aircraft armament was:

Ten 40-mm Mk VI mountings.
One 40-mm STAAG Mk II mounting.
Eleven 40-mm Mk VII mountings.

A large increase in magazine space was required for the 40-mm armament, which totalled 73 barrels, and it was necessary to re-arrange the existing stowage and to convert additional spaces. Even so, it was impossible to provide the standard allowance of 1,564 rounds per gun. The total available stowage, including ready-use, was 92,637 rounds, which provided an average of 1,269 rounds per gun. The total weight of the ten Mk VI mountings, one STAAG mounting, 40-mm ammunition and close-range barrage-fire directors was 599 tons.

Fire-control equipment

The main armament could be controlled either from the forward or the after main director-control towers through the transmitting-station. Secondary control was provided by 'B' turret controlling 'A' and 'X' turrets, and 'Y' turret being controlled via 'X' turret. Divided control was achieved with the forward director-control tower controlling 'A' and 'B' turrets through the transmitting-station, and the after director-control tower controlling 'X' and 'Y' turrets, using direct telephone communication. Two Type '274' radar sets were provided for controlling the main armament, one forward and one aft, with the aerials on the main director-control tower. There was only one '274' display in the transmitting-station and this could be fed forward or aft, through a change-over switch in the transmitting-station.

Shortly before the war, work had begun on a tachymetric system of high-angle control which was to supersede the existing HACS. Known as TS1, it was intended that this equipment be fitted in the *Lion* class ships, in *Vanguard*, *Indefatigable* and in later carriers and new cruisers. The production of this complex new equipment in wartime, however, would have placed an excessive strain on British fire-control manufacturers and it was decided not to proceed with TS1 except for the production of a pilot model. Fortunately, the US Navy had already produced and taken to sea, a tachymetric HACS and the Admiralty was able to obtain a number of these systems for RN warships, including *Vanguard*.

The US system consisted of a Mk 37 director, a fire-control computer and a gyro stabilising unit. *Vanguard* carried four such systems in a diamond arrangement, instead of the more usual four-cornered arrangement, to control various combinations of the eight 5.25-inch gun-mountings. Generally, the directors were of standard US pattern, except that they were fitted with British Type '275' stabilised radar. The total weight of the four directors was 64 tons. (When TS1 was suspended, four HACS Mk III were initially substituted, and these were included in the design weight calculations, at 44 tons.)

Four of the 5.25-inch gun-mountings could be controlled, for star shell, by the combined sights in the air-defence positions.

Each of the Bofors Mk VI mountings was provided with a close-range barrage-fire director, with '262' radar. Although they were available, the ship seems never to have carried the complete outfit of ten directors, those not on the ship being stored ashore. The STAAG mounting on 'B' turret was a self-contained weapon with its own on-mounting fire-control equipment and '262' radar. The single Bofors Mk VII were fitted for local control.

Action information centre

An action information centre, consisting of an operations-room, radar-display rooms and an aircraft-direction room with all the necessary target-indicating units and radar displays, was fitted in one block around the lower conning-position, below the armoured-deck. It was introduced after the ship had been laid down, and the available space was rather less than was desirable. In order to ensure the most efficient layout, a full-sized mock-up was built, and the proposed arrangement was agreed. The general layout was approved in September 1943, but it was not possible to settle the detailed internal layout until the ship was nearing completion.

Protection

The arrangement of armour protection was generally similar to that of the *King George V* class except that a thinner belt was provided and the splinter protection was more extensive. The 14-inch belt armour, abreast the magazines, was capable of withstanding 15-inch armour-piercing shell at up to 15,000 yards. (This figure is presumably based on actual proof trials – see Table 68 on page 278 and figures estimated for *King George V* on page 293. It is possible, but very unlikely, that *Vanguard*'s armour was slightly different from that of the *King George V* class.) Two major additions were made to the splinter protection. The first resulted from the action between *Prince of Wales* and *Bismarck*, during which a diving shell penetrated the British ship's side below the belt, but fortunately, did not explode. In order to prevent splinters, from such a hit, penetrating the magazines, it was approved, on 15th August 1941, to fit 1½-inch non-cemented armour to the longitudinal bulkheads of the main and secondary magazines, in *Vanguard*, *Duke of York*, *Anson* and *Howe*. This involved an increase in weight of about 80 tons.

The second was intended to prevent loss of buoyancy and water-plane area, forward and aft of the citadel, as a result of splinter damage. This was achieved, by fitting 2½-inch and 2-inch non-cemented armour to the ship's side, between the lower-deck and the middle-deck, forward and aft of the main belt extensions, and 1-inch bulkheads, within this area. This gave protection against bombs or shells exploding on the armoured-deck, and rupture of the ship's unarmoured structure above, by blast and splinters. It also prevented the ship's side, at the waterline, from being peppered by splinters from near-miss bombs and shells, exploding in the sea. The belt gave full protection against projectiles of medium and light calibre, as shown in Table 88.

Table 87: Armour weights (detailed calculation for Design 15E, 1942) (tons)

Item	Tons
Belt including extensions forward and aft of citadel	4,666
Bulkheads	516
Barbettes	1,500
Main-deck, including barbette chocks	4,153
Lower-deck (forward)	362
Lower-deck (aft)	578
Additional for bulkheads	75
Conning-tower	44
After emergency conning-position and communication tubes	57
Protection to director-control towers, etc.	31
Splinter belt at ends	218
Protective bulkheads and oil-jacket bulkheads	1,375
Splinter protection to cordite handing rooms	626
Funnel protection	52
Splinter protection to bulkheads between lower-deck and middle-deck, forward and aft	33
5·25-inch casemate protection	443
Protection rings to ring bulkheads	80
Armour gratings	24
Bullet-proof protection to bridges, etc.	110
Protection to 5·25-inch turrets	17
Armour backing	40
Total:	15,000

Table 88: Ranges below which, 2½-inch NC armour is penetrated at normal impact

Shell calibre (inches)	Shell weight (pounds)	Range (yards)
6	112	18,000
5·9 (German)		20,000
5·25	82	13,000
4·7	62	11,500
4·7	50	6,500
4·5	55	10,500

Underwater protection

The system of underwater protection was the same as that provided in *King George V*, but as a result of the loss of *Prince of Wales*, it was decided to increase the height of the longitudinal bulkheads that formed the three groups of compartments outboard of the protective bulkhead. Thus, instead of terminating at lower-deck level, they were extended up to the middle-deck, and provided greatly improved sub-division behind the armour near

Table 89: Protective value of internal bulge system

Station of bulkhead and position	Maximum depth of bulge Feet	Inches	Thickness of protective bulkhead Inches	Protective value (pounds of TNT)
'74'–Fore end 'A' magazine	8	7	1¾	470
'92'–Between 'A' and 'B' magazines	11	9	1¾	870
'110'–Aft end 'B' magazine	13	7	1¾	1,200
'134'–Fore end forward BRs	13	5	1½	980
'156'–Between forward ERs and BRs	14	1	1½	1,100
'178'–Fore end after BRs	15	0	1½	1,300
'200'–Between after ERs and BRs	14	1	1½	1,100
'222'–Aft end after BRs	14	2	1½	1,300
'236'–Aft end after 5.25-inch magazines	13	0	1¾	1,080
'247'–Fore end 'X' magazine	11	10	1¾	900
'283'–Aft end 'X' magazine	9	9	1¾	600

Below: a close-up of *Vanguard's* superstructure.

the waterline. The crew's wash-places, that formerly occupied this space, were moved to positions on the middle-deck. The maximum protection given by the underwater compartments, at various points along the hull, is shown in Table 89.

Machinery

The main machinery was arranged in four boiler rooms and four engine rooms, on the unit system as in the *King George V* class. Each engine room contained one high-pressure and one low-pressure turbine, driving a single shaft through double-helical gears. An astern turbine was incorporated in the casing of each low-pressure turbine. Steam was supplied to the turbines at a maximum working pressure of 350 pounds per square inch, and at a temperature of 700° F. The designed normal maximum output of each shaft was 30,000 shaft horse-power at 245 revolutions, but it was also specified that the turbines be capable of accepting an overload to 32,500 shaft horse-power at 250 revolutions. In September 1942, the estimated speed with 130,000 shaft horse-power was 30 knots at the standard displacement of 42,300 tons, and 28.75 knots at the deep displacement of 49,100 tons. Each boiler room contained two Admiralty three-drum boilers, with a maximum working pressure of 400 pounds per square inch, at a temperature of 750° F superheat. Early alterations to the machinery arrangements included:

1. A cruising turbine was originally geared to each high-pressure turbine, but in September 1942, it was approved to omit these in order to save weight. Although a saving of 100 tons was envisaged, this was not realised, and the machinery weight remained at 3,250 tons in the completed ship.
2. In March 1942, it was decided to increase the fore and aft separation of the inner and outer propellers, from 33½ feet to 51½ feet, in order to reduce the likelihood of both propellers being put out of action by a single torpedo hit.

The machinery more than realised its designed power, and despite the fact that the ship exceeded her designed displacement by over 2,000 tons, she achieved speeds, on trial, in excess of the designed figures. In July 1946,

Below: *Vanguard* in one of her peace-time roles. A photograph taken from the forecastle, at Plymouth's Navy Day in 1955.

Vanguard

1946: outboard profile and deck plans

Shelter-deck▼

1 CPO's and PO's Mess
2 Bathroom
3 WCs
4 5.25-inch Mounting
5 Cabins
6 CPOs and POs servery
7 Chief Petty Officers' Mess
8 Petty Officers' Mess
9 Funn
10 Staff
11 Adm
12 Adm

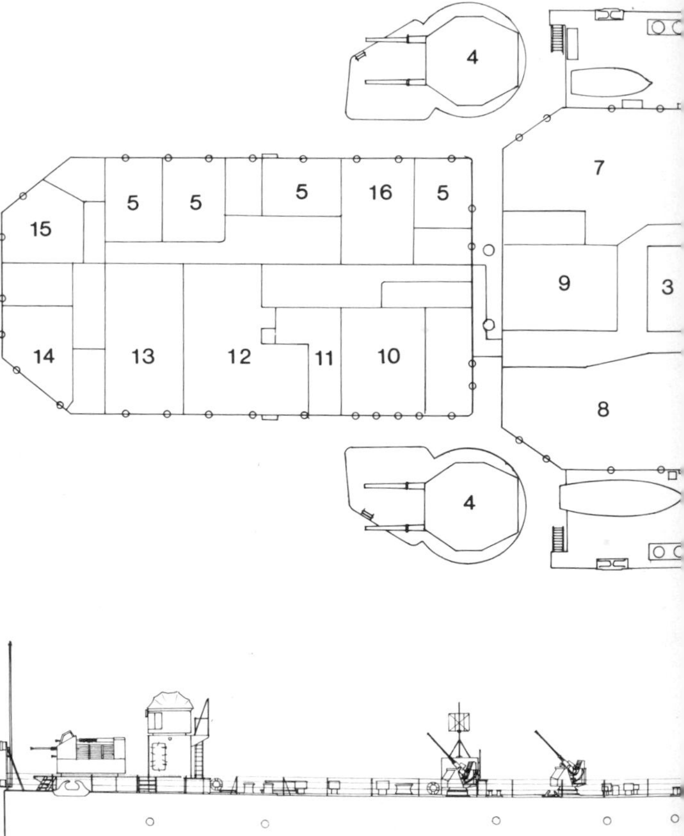

Vanguard

1946: inboard profile and sections

Inboard profile▼

1 Boiler room
2 Engine room
3 15-inch Magazine
4 15-inch Shell room
5 15-inch Shell handing room
6 15-inch Cordite handing room
7 5.25-inch Magazine
8 5.25-inch Shell room
9 Bofors magazine
10 Transmitting station
11 Air-plotting room/LP room
12 Operations room
13 Radar display room/lower steering-position
14 Computer room
15 LP room
16 Boiler room uptakes
17 Mk 37 secondary director
18 15-inch director control-tower
19 Close-range barrage director
20 VHFDF
21 Boiler room vent
22 Engine room vent

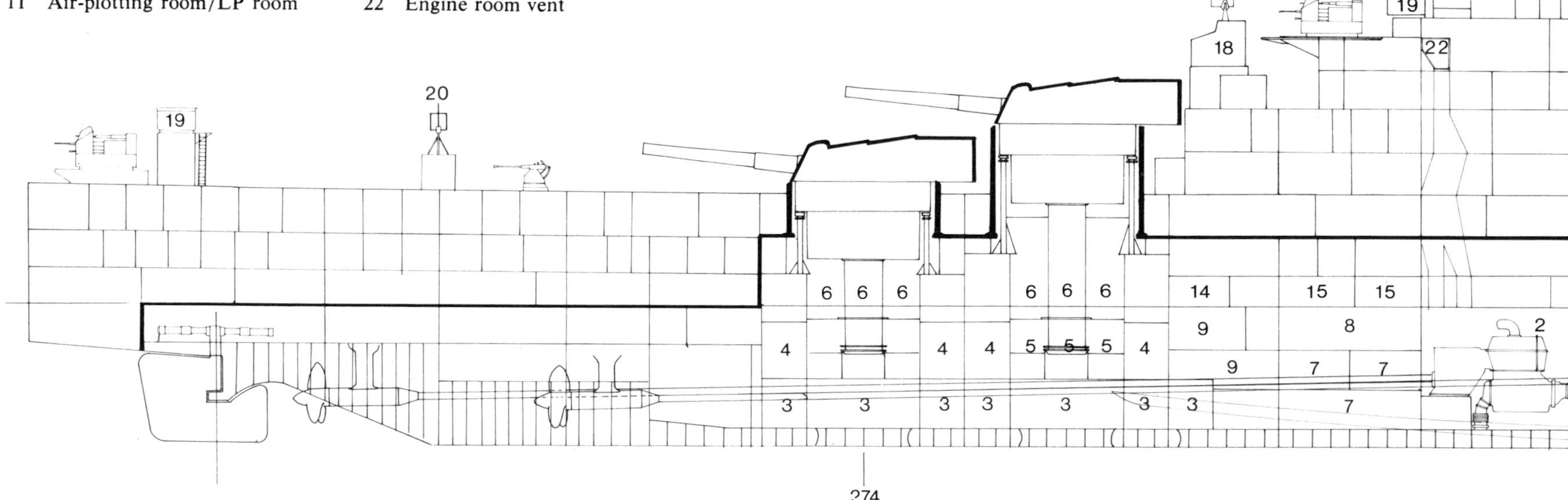

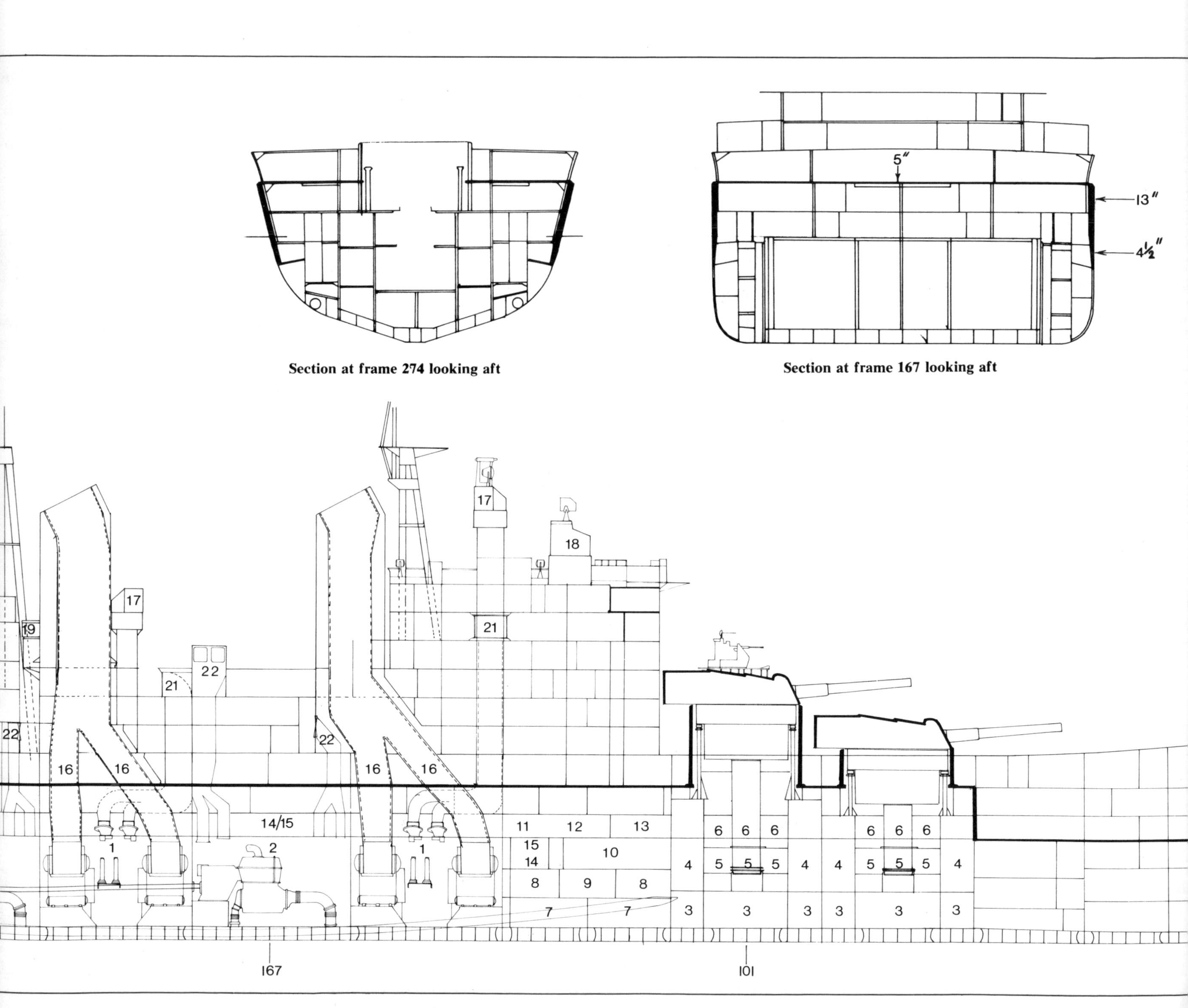

Section at frame 274 looking aft

Section at frame 167 looking aft

Vanguard

1946: inboard profile and sections

Inboard profile▼

1 Boiler room
2 Engine room
3 15-inch Magazine
4 15-inch Shell room
5 15-inch Shell handing room
6 15-inch Cordite handing room
7 5.25-inch Magazine
8 5.25-inch Shell room
9 Bofors magazine
10 Transmitting station
11 Air-plotting room/LP room
12 Operations room
13 Radar display room/lower steering-position
14 Computer room
15 LP room
16 Boiler room uptakes
17 Mk 37 secondary director
18 15-inch director control-tower
19 Close-range barrage director
20 VHFDF
21 Boiler room vent
22 Engine room vent

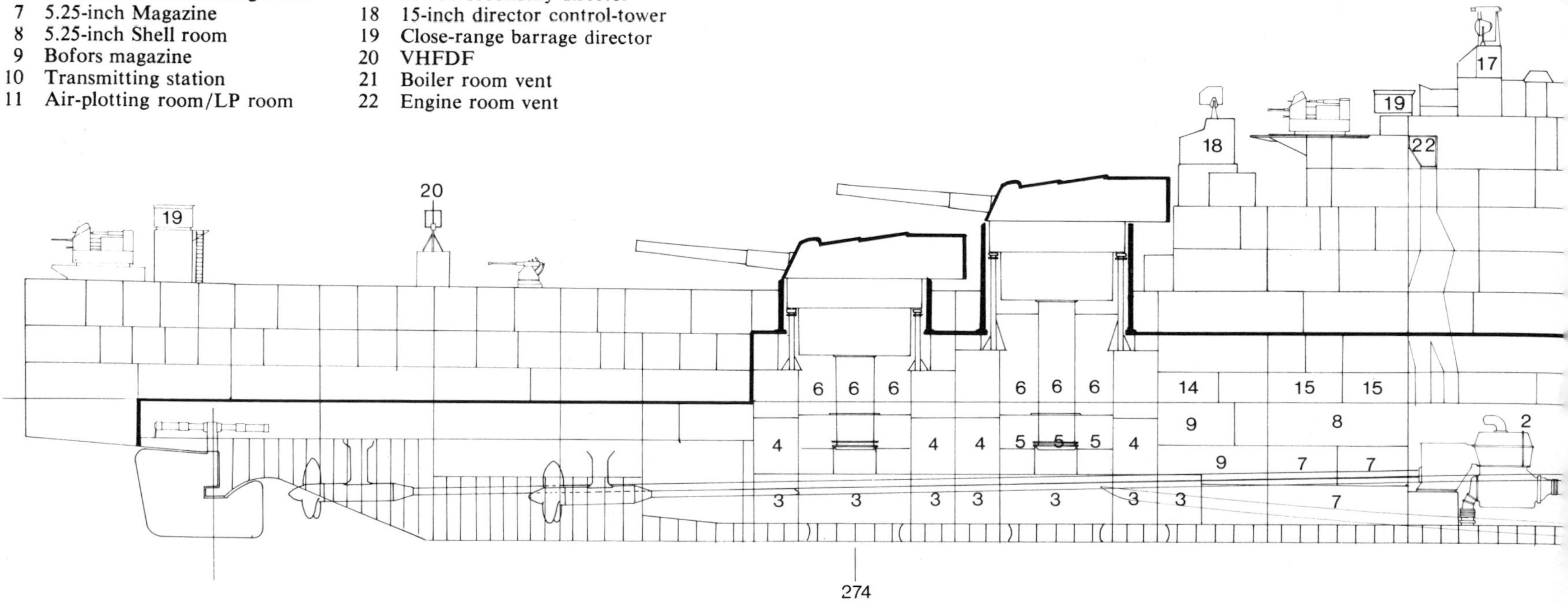

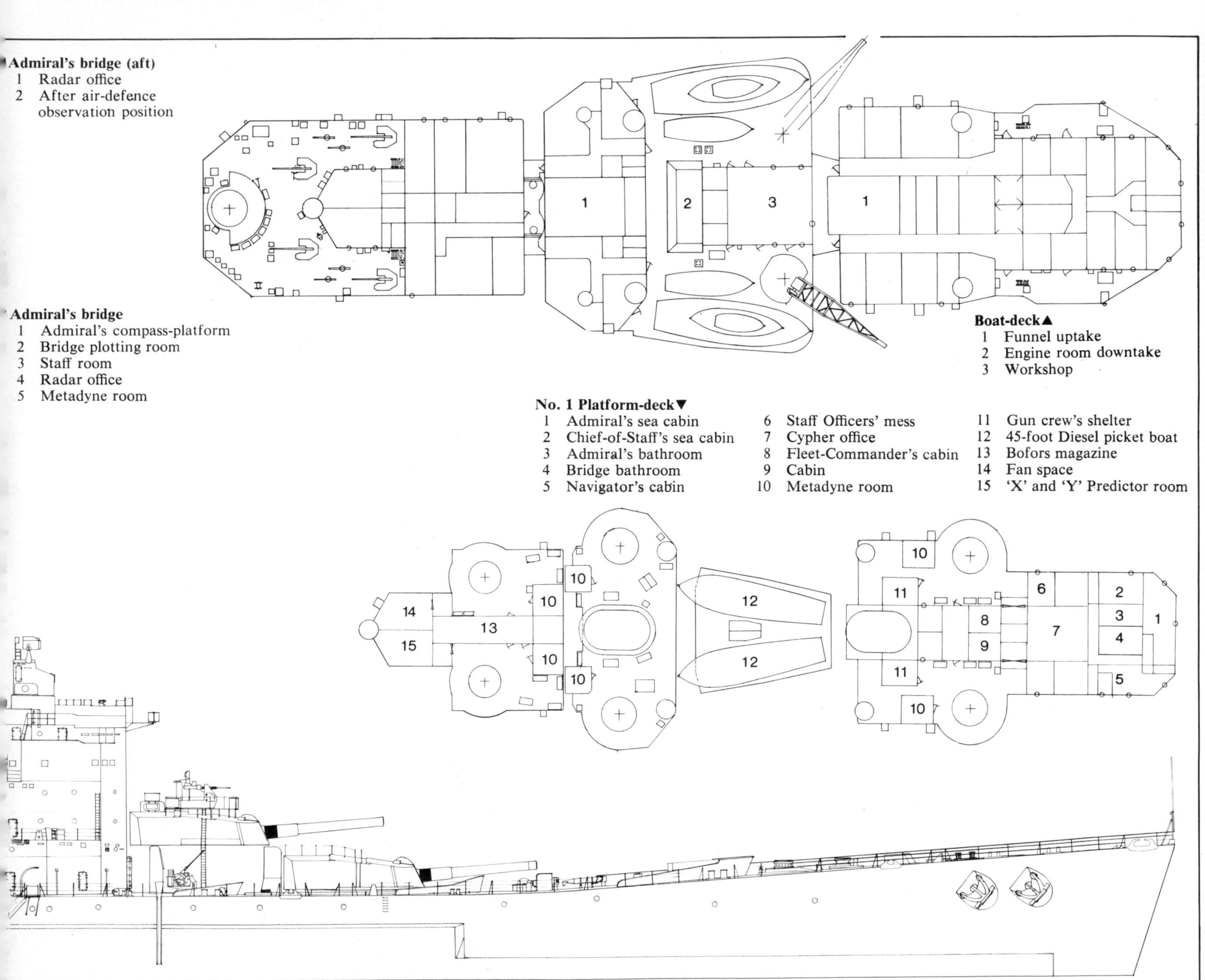
Admiral's bridge (aft)
1 Radar office
2 After air-defence observation position
Admiral's bridge
1 Admiral's compass-platform
2 Bridge plotting room
3 Staff room
4 Radar office
5 Metadyne room
Boat-deck▲
1 Funnel uptake
2 Engine room downtake
3 Workshop
No. 1 Platform-deck▼
1 Admiral's sea cabin
2 Chief-of-Staff's sea cabin
3 Admiral's bathroom
4 Bridge bathroom
5 Navigator's cabin
6 Staff Officers' mess
7 Cypher office
8 Fleet-Commander's cabin
9 Cabin
10 Metadyne room
11 Gun crew's shelter
12 45-foot Diesel picket boat
13 Bofors magazine
14 Fan space
15 'X' and 'Y' Predictor room

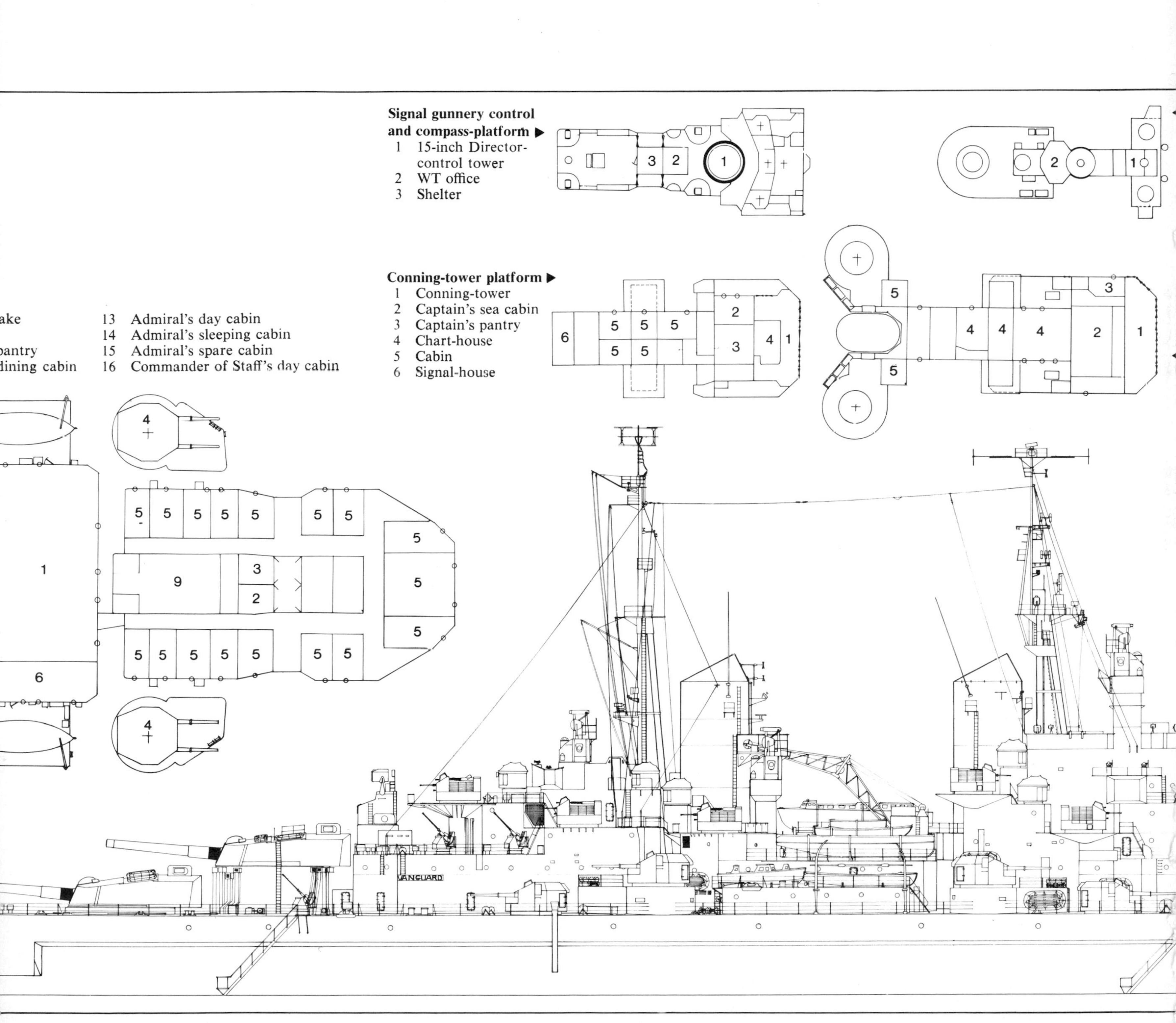
Signal gunnery control and compass-platform ▶
1 15-inch Director-control tower
2 WT office
3 Shelter
Conning-tower platform ▶
1 Conning-tower
2 Captain's sea cabin
3 Captain's pantry
4 Chart-house
5 Cabin
6 Signal-house
ake
pantry
dining cabin
13 Admiral's day cabin
14 Admiral's sleeping cabin
15 Admiral's spare cabin
16 Commander of Staff's day cabin
VANGUARD

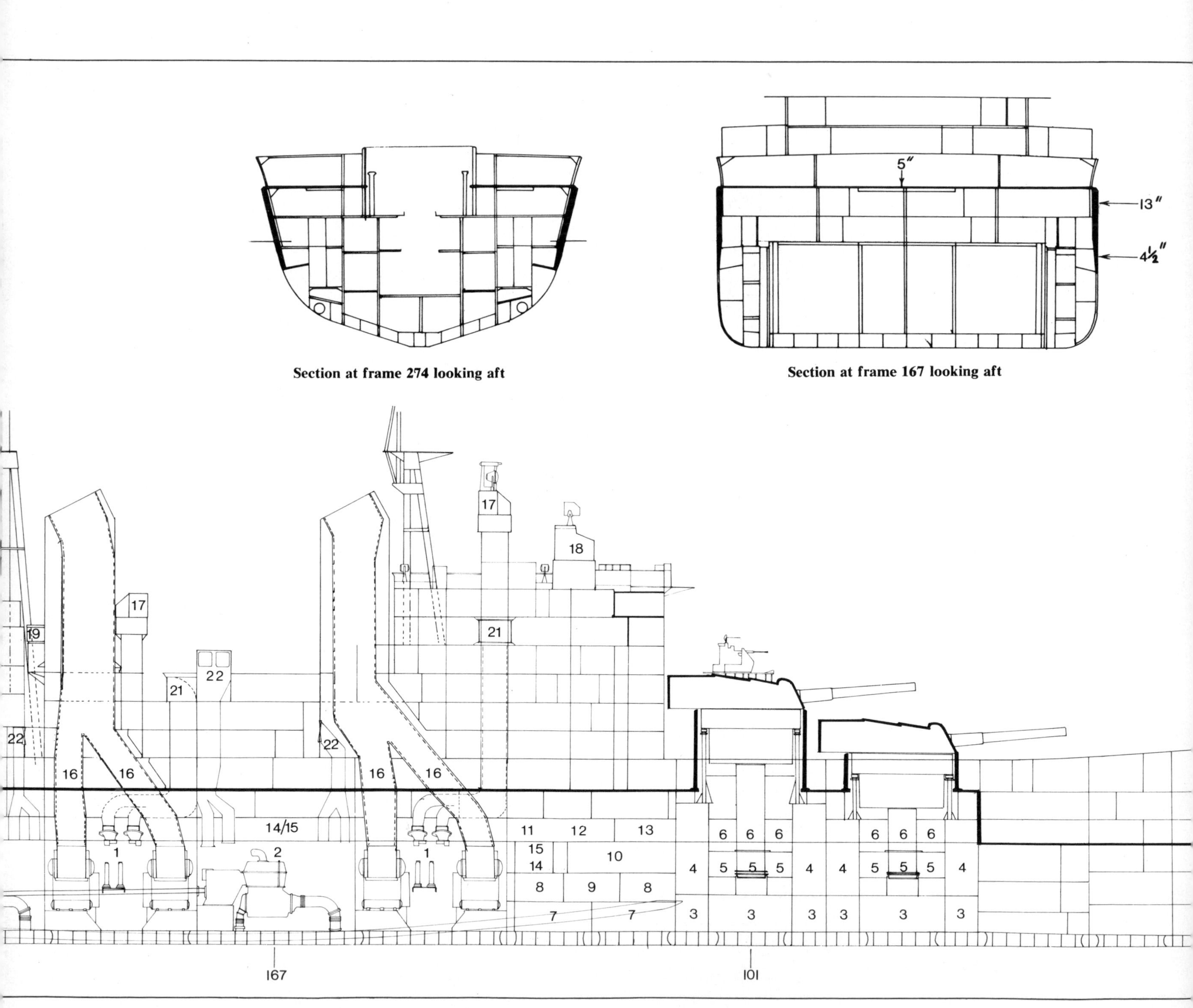

Section at frame 274 looking aft

Section at frame 167 looking aft

Below: on board *Vanguard*. On the lower part of the mainmast, below the level of the funnel, can be seen the platform on which the aerial for Type '268' radar was carried when the ship was completed. However, the aerials shown in this, later, illustration are for receiving television programmes.

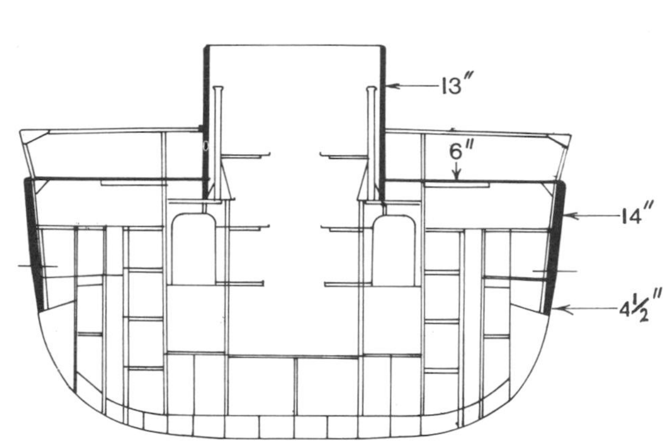

Section at frame 101 looking forward

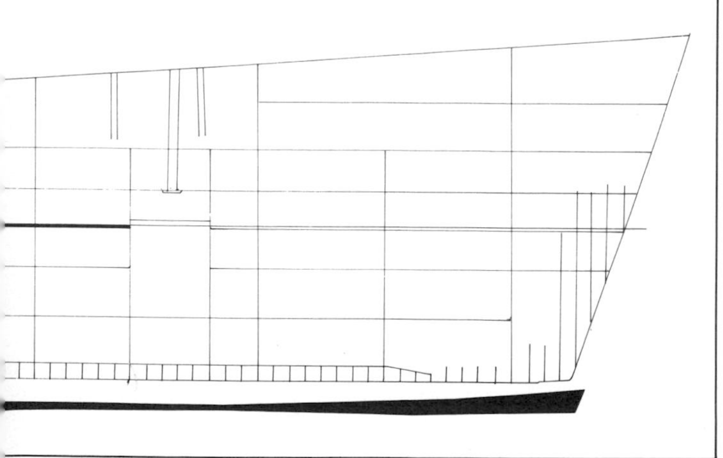

on the measured mile at Arran, she attained a speed of 31.57 knots on a displacement of 45,720 tons, with 136,000 shaft horse-power. Trials at deep displacement, produced the results shown in Table 90.

Table 90: Measured-Mile trials at deep load, Arran, July 1946

Speed (mean, knots)	rpm (mean)	SHP (mean)	Displacement (tons)
11·86	91·8	6,130	51,050
15·266	118	20,640	51,000
18·963	114·6	24,110	50,170
20·557	159·5	31,360	50,940
21·873	170·3	38,240	51,300
25·477	200·16	64,960	51,260
26·285	210·8	75,120	51,220
28·160	230·9	120,240	51,160
30·379	250·6	132,950	51,070

Little vibration was experienced during the trials, except at 24 knots with 200 revolutions, when the bridge and the engine room were affected. This vibration was eased, however, by running the inner shafts at 222 revolutions and the outer shafts at 174 revolutions, which gave the same speed of 24 knots.

Endurance

During the *Bismarck* action in 1941, shortage of fuel in *King George V* and *Rodney*, almost resulted in their abandoning the pursuit, and caused their early retirement from the scene of action (not, however, before *Bismarck* had been completely neutralised). As a result of this experience, the Naval Staff reviewed the endurance requirement for *Vanguard*, and in March 1942, specified that this figure be increased from 14,000 miles at 10 knots, to 6,000 miles or more, at 24 knots. This was to be achieved with the ship six months out of dock, in action conditions, and with steam at a half-hour's notice for full speed. The fuel stowage was raised to 4,850 tons, by increasing the width of the wing tanks from 3 feet 10 inches to 6 feet 1 inch. This gave an endurance of 6,000 miles at 20 knots, or 4,200 miles under the conditions specified by the Naval Staff. The DNC pointed out that to meet the requirements of 6,000 miles at 24 knots, an oil-fuel capacity of 6,900 tons would be required, which would be difficult to achieve without seriously affecting the balance of the design. The fuel stowage was therefore accepted at 4,850 tons (including 427 tons of diesel fuel) which gave the ship the endurance figures shown in Table 91.

Table 91: *Vanguard*, endurance (nautical miles)

Speed (knots)	With clean bottom	6 months out of dock: In temperate waters	In tropical waters
Economic*	8,414	7,413	6,100
15	8,250	7,150	5,700
20	6,950	5,800	4,500
25	5,350	4,400	3,350
29·5	3,600	3,350	2,900

* Economic speeds were: 14 knots (with clean bottom), 13 knots (6 months out of dock, temperate waters), 11·5 knots (6 months out of dock, tropical waters).

Auxiliary machinery

The main auxiliary machinery was fitted in two harbour machinery rooms and ten action machinery rooms. The former compartments were positioned between the forward engine rooms, and the latter, in wing compartments abreast the machinery spaces and secondary magazines.

In the original design, electric power was provided by six turbo-generators and two diesel generators, each capable of supplying 400 kilowatts into a common ring main at 220 volts direct current. This arrangement was later modified as a result of the damage to the cruiser *Belfast* in 1939, and later experience, such as the loss of *Ark Royal* and *Prince of Wales*, which emphasised the need for an increased proportion of diesel generators that were independent of a steam supply from the main machinery. In the case of *Belfast*, the explosion of a magnetic mine under the ship, caused the total loss of steam, and, therefore, of motive power and electric power from the turbo-generators.

The final arrangement for *Vanguard* consisted of four 450-kilowatt diesel generators and four 480-kilowatt turbo-generators each supplying a common ring main at 240 volts direct current. There was also a low-power 22-volt supply, and both this and the high-power supply were distributed throughout the ship via eighteen contact-breaker rooms, arranged along each side of the ship at lower-deck level. The diesel generators were fitted in numbers '1', '2', '7' and '8' action machinery rooms, the former pair being abreast the forward 5.25-inch magazines, and the latter pair, abreast the after engine rooms. The turbo-generators were fitted in numbers '3' and '4' action machinery rooms, abreast the forward boiler rooms and one was fitted in each harbour machinery room.

Other auxiliary machinery included:

1. Four turbine-driven hydraulic-pumps to supply power for working the main armament. Positioned in four separate action machinery rooms, each was capable of supplying 95 cubic feet of hydraulic-fluid per minute, at a pressure of 1,000 pounds per square inch.
2. Four distilling plants, three of which were capable of producing 100 tons of fresh water per day, and one, 200 tons per day. The 200-ton plant was in the starboard harbour machinery room, and the remaining three in numbers '9' and '10' action machinery rooms, and in the port harbour machinery room. The last named 100-ton plant was of a special type, that proved unsatisfactory in service and was later replaced by a second 200-ton plant.
3. Four motor-driven air-compressors of 95 horse-power each capable of supplying 128 cubic feet of free air per minute at a pressure of 400 pounds per square inch. This was the high-pressure supply for the armament, diesel starters, etc.
4. Two motor-driven air-compressors of 26 horse-power, each capable of supplying 75 cubic feet of free air per minute at a pressure of 120 pounds per square inch for the low-pressure supply.

The ship's fresh-water stowage capacity was 390 tons, but this was increased by 100 tons for the Royal tour to South Africa in 1947, and was again increased, to a total of 590 tons, in 1948.

Table 92: Stability of *Vanguard*, as designed, 1941; and as completed, 1946

	1941	1946
Light condition:		
Displacement (tons)	42,220	45,116
GM (feet)	7·91	5·89
Angle of maximum stability	36°	35°
Range	66·8°	60·7°
Standard condition:		
Displacement (tons)	41,730	44,500
GM (feet)	7·84	5·79
Angle of maximum stability	36°	35°
Range	66·8°	60·5°
Average action condition:		
Displacement (tons)	46,810	50,145
GM (feet)	9·19	7·48
Angle of maximum stability	37·3°	34·4°
Range	72·3°	65·3°
Deep condition:		
Displacement (tons)	48,140	51,420
GM (feet)	9·9	8·2
Angle of maximum stability	38°	35°
Range	75·5°	68°

Table 93: Stability of *Vanguard* in riddled condition, with ship open to the sea above the armoured decks

	1941	1946
Deep condition:		
Displacement (tons)	48,140	51,420
GM (feet)	8·07	6·2
Angle of maximum stability	14°	10°
Range	30°	18°
Light condition:		
Displacement (tons)	42,220	45,116
GM (feet)	5·5	3·62
Angle of maximum stability	20°	14°
Range	36°	25°

Table 94: Weights for Design 15E (tons)

Condition	Standard	Light	Deep	Average action
Equipment	1,120	770	1,650	1,650
Machinery	3,250	3,250	3,250	3,250
Armament	6,000	6,840	6,840	6,840
Armour and protective plating	15,000	15,000	15,000	15,000
Hull	16,360	16,360	16,360	16,360
Oil fuel			4,440	3,110
Reserve feed-water			370	370
Lubricating oil			30	30
Petrol			20	20
Water protection abreast 'Y' turret			110	110
Water protection around petrol			70	70
Displacement:	41,730	42,220	48,140	46,810

Weights and dimensions

The detailed weight calculations for Design '15E' produced the figures shown in Table 94. When the design was revised in September 1942, the estimated deep displacement was increased to 49,200 tons and the Director of Naval Construction pointed out that, for strength reasons, no further additions should be made to this weight. It was impossible to keep within this limitation, however, because of the need of additional equipment resulting from wartime developments in radar, anti-aircraft weapons, communications, etc. There was also a large increase in weight brought about by wartime shortages of materials and labour, which militated against the careful attention to detail required if economies in weight were to be achieved. The actual increases in weight between September 1942 and completion in 1946 were accounted for as follows.

Increase in equipment weight, resulting from the increased complement requiring larger mess, canteen, victualling and naval stores. Some increases resulted from the increased size of the anchor cables, and the heavier rig needed for radar equipment:	150 tons
Increase in electric light and power circuits:	500 tons
Additional radar aerials and equipment:	30 tons
Improvements in ventilation and the fitting of air-conditioning for use in tropical conditions:	200 tons
Increases in pumping-, flooding- and draining-systems, as a result of war experience:	170 tons
Additional navigation equipment:	20 tons
Lagging, arctic-isation and steam-heating equipment, etc.:	90 tons
Action information centre:	50 tons
Structural increases resulting from the fitting of cofferdams, trunked access to compartments, increase in scantlings, platforms in hold, etc.:	250 tons
Additions to the upper-deck structure to meet higher stresses as a result of anticipated displacement increase:	770 tons
Increases brought about by wartime shortages of material, demanding use of heavier materials, i.e., sheet steel instead of aluminium, lead paint instead of aluminium paint, etc.:	150 tons
Increases in fuel weight resulting from larger oil-fuel and lubricating-oil stowage:	100 tons
Increases in armament weights resulting from larger ammunition stowage, increased anti-aircraft armament, increased fire-control gear, duplication of ammunition-hoists, additional auxiliary machinery:	420 tons
Total weight increase:	2,900 tons

Fortunately, the armour and protection showed a decrease in weight on the September 1942 estimate, which helped to compensate these increases.

Having exceeded the September 1942 deep-displacement estimate by 2,220 tons, it was decided to impose a restriction on all further additions to the ship. All proposals for increasing the load were to be accompanied by proposals for the removal of an equivalent weight. Limitations of this type were not unusual, and similar restrictions had been placed on other British and US battleships as a result of the considerable weight increases resulting from wartime additions. Despite this restriction, and despite the removal of various items, such as

Table 95: *Vanguard*, weights (tons)

	1946	September 1942
Standard condition:		
Hull	18,657	16,500
Equipment	1,247	1,200
Armament	6,718	6,100
Armour and protection	14,741	15,350
Machinery	3,251	3,150
Standard displacement:	44,614	42,300
Deep condition:		
Hull	18,657	16,500
Equipment	1,847	1,700
Armament	7,606	7,140
Armour and protection	14,741	15,350
Machinery	3,251	3,150
Oil fuel	4,925	4,850
Reserve feed-water	358	370
Lubricating oil	52	30
Water protection	100	110
Deep displacement:	51,537	49,200

Note. When the ship was inclined in June 1946, the accepted displacements were: 44,500 tons (standard), 51,420 tons (deep).

AA guns and their equipment, the displacement increased and by 1954, amounted to 51,915 tons, deep. To bring the displacement down, it was decided to reduce the endurance to 5,000 miles at 20 knots (the same as that of the *King George V* class), which reduced the fuel weight by 907 tons, and to temporarily reduce the 15-inch ammunition stowage by 25 per cent, saving 245 tons. This gave a margin, over the weight required, of 657 tons – to allow for future additions – and reduced the deep displacement to 50,760 tons.

The beam of *Vanguard* was so wide that she could not be docked at Rosyth or Portsmouth. She could, however, be accommodated in the following docks.

Naval docks in Home Waters: Devonport, No. 10 dock.

Private docks in Home Waters: Liverpool, Gladstone dock; Southampton, KGV dock.

Empire docks: Gibraltar, No. 1 dock; Singapore, KGV dock; Durban (in emergency only); Cape Town; Sydney; Esquimalt, British Columbia; Quebec; New Brunswick.

The maximum draught that could be accommodated in the Panama Canal was 34 feet 9 inches, which was equal to 33 feet 9 inches in sea water. *Vanguard*'s displacement at this draught was 49,180 tons. For passage through the canal, it was necessary to remove all outboard fittings such as ladders, refuse-chutes, etc.

Vanguard was the only British battleship to be completed with a transom stern, which provided a saving in weight and length. Experiments at Haslar had shown that this type of stern, when carried below the waterline, would give an increase in speed of approximately ⅓ knot.

Handling and sea trials

In September 1942, following the discovery that the *King George V* class were very wet in heavy weather, it was decided to increase the sheer of *Vanguard*, forward of 'A' turret. At the same time, it was decided to provide a modified anchor-recess in order to reduce the spray thrown up by a projecting anchor, and to increase the number of breakwaters forward of 'A' turret. The increased freeboard meant sacrificing the requirement that 'A' turret be capable of firing directly ahead, at low angles of elevation. The freeboard, in fact, had already been increased in early designs, and was increased again before the ship was completed.

Table 96: Freeboard of battleship designs, 1937 to 1942

Freeboard	*King George V* class as designed, 15A, B and C	*Lion* class	15D	15E	*Vanguard* September 1942	1946
Forward	27 ft 9 in	28 ft	32 ft 6 in	32 ft 6 in	36 ft 8 in	37 ft
Amidships	22 ft 9 in	22 ft 6 in	22 ft 6 in	23 ft	22 ft 8 in	23 ft
Aft	23 ft 9 in	24 ft 6 in	24 ft 6 in	25 ft	24 ft 8 in	25 ft 6 in

Vanguard proved to be the most weatherly capital ship ever built in a British yard, and possibly in the world. During sea trials, she produced a period of roll of 14.25 seconds, which was about equal to that of the *King George V* and *Nelson* classes whose average rolling period was about 14 seconds. The pitching period was 6.7 seconds.

Early in 1942, consideration was given to the fitting of an auxiliary retractable bow rudder in order to provide a secondary control if the main rudder were damaged. This proposal arose from a study of the torpedo damage that had been inflicted on *Bismarck* and *Prince of Wales* before they sank. Both ships had been partially immobilised because their rudders jammed. In February 1942, however, the Director of Naval Construction stated that the ship was too far advanced for a bow rudder to be fitted and the idea was dropped.

During high-speed turning trials, at 30.8 knots with full 35-degree rudder, the ship turned through 360° in 4 minutes 55 seconds. The turning-circle of the ship, on this occasion, was 1,025 yards and the maximum angle of heel recorded during the turn was 4°. The rudder could be put over from the centre-line to 35° in 15 seconds, and while steaming at high speed, the rudder was turned hard a-port and then hard a-starboard, producing a maximum angle of heel of 7½°. The ship could be brought to rest from full speed in 4 minutes 46 seconds, by putting the turbines to full-astern.

A certain amount of vibration was experienced in the ship when manoeuvring at speeds of more than 180 revolutions per minute (about 22 knots), and it was found that the inner shafts suffered from severe axial vibration when turning. The cause of this was traced to the interaction of the inner and outer propellers, and restrictions were imposed on the speed of the outer shaft, on the outside of the turn, at speeds of more than 180 revolutions per minute. Five-bladed propellers were later fitted to the inner shafts, to obtain smoother operation at high speeds, but it was still necessary to impose some restrictions on the use of the helm.

Radar and communications

The ship's radar was naturally updated as new sets were introduced, and, as completed, she carried the following:

Type '960': *Vanguard* was the first ship to be fitted with this set, which was a combined air/sea warning type, capable of picking up a target at great range and height to give advance warning of the approach of aircraft or ships. The aerial was positioned at the head of the mainmast.

Type '277': Low air and sea warning. Aerial on fore starfish.

Type '268': Navigation and surface warning. Aerial on mainmast.

Type '293': Combined air/sea target indicating set, aerial on head of the foremast.

Type '274': (Two) main armament gunnery sets – aerials on forward and after main director-control towers.

Type '275': (Four) secondary armament gunnery sets – aerials on Mk 37 directors.

Type '262': (Eleven) anti-aircraft armament

sets. Aerials on the close-range barrage-fire directors and stabilised tachymetric anti-aircraft gun-mounting.
Type '242' M & P: Interrogator (Identification Friend or Foe transmitter) sets for radar Types '277' and '293'.
Type '253': (Two) IFF (Identification Friend or Foe) receivers for '242' M & P.
Type '930': General navigation. (The authors have been unable to confirm the exact function of Type '930'.)

Types '930', '277', '268', '293', '274', '275' and '262' had stabilised aerials, and it was considered that all except Types '930' and '274' would be capable of operating within any roll likely to be experienced. The Type '960' set suffered from serious interference from the '275' sets and from most of the W/T and R/T sets. TBS ('Talk between ships') interfered with the Type '242' sets, and the DS 10 interfered with Types '275', '277' and '293'. The Type '268' set was found to be practically useless, because, on

Vanguard, from her port quarter.

Below: *Vanguard*'s impressive bridge.

all bearings, the aerial was blanketed by the mainmast, funnel and after Mk 37 director. The Type '277' aerial was badly wooded on after bearings. In practically all other respects, the radar outfit was satisfactory.

As a result of war experience, the wireless-transmission arrangements were re-worked, to provide a bridge receiving-office and a transmitting-room in the after superstructure. W/T and R/T sets included Types '57 DMR', '59D' and TBS Types '86', '87' and '91'. Direction-finder sets included a very high-frequency direction-finder set with aerial and an office on the quarter-deck, RM1 with the aerial on the fore starfish, RM4 with aerials on the sides of the fore funnel, and a medium-frequency direction-finder set with the aerial on the front of the bridge. Two 30-foot whip aerials were fitted on each funnel, for emergency use. The ship also carried two 'Headache' sets, for listening to enemy 'talk between ships' transmissions, radar reflectors, radar direction-finders and radar jamming gear. At a later date, several ultra high-frequency direction-finder sets were fitted, with aerials at the end of the yard-arms.

Internal communication-systems included sound-powered telephones, command intercom and pneumatic transmission arrangements.

General features

The very large bridge structure was given exceptionally careful consideration to ensure that all important positions were as free from excessive draughts as possible. Various arrangements of bridge were subjected to wind-tunnel experiments, and the layout of bridge instruments was rigged-up on a full-scale model, before the final arrangement was decided. The result was generally satisfactory, but it was still found to be too draughty for efficiency. The ship carried no magnetic compass, but was equipped with three separate gyro-compasses.

The ship was divided by transverse bulkheads into twenty-seven main compartments, each of which was substantially sub-divided.

Below the main-deck, there were 1,059 watertight compartments. Trunked access was provided for all compartments occupied during action, both inside and outside the citadel, as a result of the loss of *Prince of Wales*. Ten bulkheads were fitted on the middle-deck, to restrict the flow of free water should that deck become flooded.

The pumping, flooding and fire-fighting arrangements were extensive, and were based on war experience. In addition to the main and secondary damage-control head-quarters, the ship was divided into six sections, each with its own damage-control base.

The complement envisaged for the original designs was 76 officers and 1,412 men when the ship was acting as a squadron flagship. It was necessary to revise this figure, because of the increase in close-range armament and radar, the introduction of the action information centre and the decision to fit the ship as a fleet flagship. As a result, many of the compartments in the ship, particularly the action information centre, were congested and in August 1947, the DNC stated that the full war complement, as a fleet flagship, should not exceed 115 officers and 1,860 men, or serious overcrowding would be caused.

The ship was fitted out for service in tropical or arctic conditions, with asbestos insulation fitted to the ship's sides, decks and bulkheads, where exposed. For arctic conditions, steam-heating was provided for many of the ship's fittings, armament, navigation instruments, look-out positions, ventilation to accommodation, and sea-cocks. Air-conditioning was provided for the following compartments: air-direction room, radar-display room, lower steering-position, computer rooms, transmitting-station, secondary armament magazines near boiler rooms, damage-control head-quarters, lower sick-bay, electronics-maintenance room, lower receiving-room and lower transmitting-room.

The total cost of the ship was £11,530,503, which included £3,186,868 for the armament. (The original cost of the main armament was not included in this figure.)

PARTICULARS OF *VANGUARD*, 1946

Displacement
44,500 tons standard; 51,420 tons deep.
Tons per inch: 140.9 in standard condition.

Dimensions
Length: 759 feet 11⅝ inches (pp); 799 feet 11⅛ inches (wl); 814 feet 4⅛ inches (oa).

Beam: 108 feet.

Draught: 28 feet 11 inches (forward), 32 feet 8 inches (aft) in standard condition; 34 feet (forward), 36 feet (aft) in deep condition.

Armament
Eight 15-inch 42-cal breech-loading Mk I: four twin mountings Mk I (N).
Sixteen 5.25-inch Mk I: eight twin mountings Mk I*.
Seventy-three 40-mm Bofors: ten sextuple mountings Mk VI, one twin STAAG mounting Mk II and eleven single mountings Mk VII.
Fourteen 0.303-inch Bren guns.
Four 0.303 Vickers machine-guns.
Two 0.303 Lewis machine-guns.
One 3-inch mortar.
One 2-inch mortar.
Four projectors, infantry, anti-tank (PIAT).
Four 3-pounder saluting guns.

Ammunition stowage
15-inch: 100 rounds per gun (95 APC + 5 HE); 9 practice rounds per gun.
5.25-inch: 391 rounds per gun (111 SAP + 280 HE); 25 star shell per gun; 25 low-angle practice rounds per gun; 50 high-angle practice rounds per gun.
40-mm: 1,269 rounds per gun (including 34 practice rounds per gun).

Fire-control equipment
Main armament: two director-control towers, one Admiralty fire-control table Mk 10.
Secondary armament: four Mk 37 directors and four US fire-control systems.
Mk VI Bofors: ten CRBF directors.
STAAG and single Bofors: local control.

Armour
Cemented (C):
Belt abreast magazines: 14 inch, 4½ inch at lower edge.
Belt abreast machinery: 13 inch, 4½ inch at lower edge.
Belt forward and aft of citadel: 13 inch, 12 inch and 11 inch all tapering to 4½ inch at lower edge.
Bulkheads at end of citadel: 12 inch.
Barbettes: 13 inch sides, tapering to 12 inch and 11 inch towards centre-line.
Turrets: 13 inch front, 9 inch fore side, 7 inch rear side, 11 inch back.
Non-cemented (NC):
Main-deck over magazines: 6 inch.
Main-deck over machinery: 5 inch.
Lower-deck forward: 5 inch, 4 inch, 3½ inch, 2½ inch.
Lower-deck aft: 4½ inch and 2½ inch.
Splinter belt forward and aft: 2½ inch and 2 inch.
Bulkhead at after end of steering-gear compartment: 4 inch.
Bulkheads at end of citadel, below lower-deck: 1½ inch.
Turrets: 6 inch roof.
5.25-inch casemates: 2½ inch sides, 1½ inch roof.
5.25-inch turrets: 2½ inch sides, 1½ inch roof.
5.25-inch hoists: 2 inch, 6 inch at main-deck.
Splinter protection to cordite handing room: 1 inch.
Splinter protection to magazines: 1½ inch.
Splinter protection to ring-bulkhead: 2 inch.
Conning-tower: 3 inch front, 2½ inch sides and rear.
Plotting office and communication tube: 2 inch.
Director-control tower supports and after conning-tower: 2 inch.
Cable-trunks: 2 inch at main-deck.

Protective plating
Splinter bulkheads forward and aft: 1 inch DW.
Funnel-uptakes: 1 inch DW.
Cable-trunks: 1½ inch, 1 inch, ½ inch DI.
Splinter protection to superstructure: ½ inch and ⅜ inch DI.
Torpedo bulkheads: 1½ inch and 1¾ inch DI.
Conning-tower roof: 1 inch non-magnetic bullet-proof plating.
Plotting office: 1 inch DI.

Machinery
Parsons geared turbines, four shafts.
130,000 SHP = 30 knots at 250 rpm.
Maximum continuous sea-going speed 29.75 knots.
Eight Admiralty three-drum small-tube boilers with superheaters.
Maximum working pressure 400 pounds per square inch.

Fuel
Oil-fuel capacity 4,423 tons.
Diesel-fuel capacity 427 tons.
Consumpton approximately 0.63 pounds/SHP/hour between 60,000 and 136,000 SHP.

Complement 1,893 (2,000 as fleet flagship).

16. War, 1939 to 1945

Below: *Malaya*, in late 1943 or early 1944.

Many books have described – in varying degrees of thoroughness – the history of general naval operations during the Second World War. The Royal Navy's contribution has been excellently described in S. W. Roskill's official history, *The War at Sea*, and most of the more important operations and actions have received detailed attention in other works. To relate fully, the operational history of British capital ships in this book, would not only involve the repetition of a considerable amount of previously published information, but would result in a book of unrealistic size and cost. This chapter, therefore, has been restricted to a description of the more important capital-ship actions and operations of the war, with emphasis on the technical aspects and with as much new information as we have been able to obtain.

1. HOME WATERS AND THE ATLANTIC, 1939 to 1944

On the outbreak of war, the Home Fleet was based at Scapa Flow, whence it could enforce the blockade of Germany, as the Grand Fleet had done, during the First World War. This blockade performed the dual role of preventing seaborne supplies reaching the enemy and preventing enemy warships and armed merchant raiders from breaking out into the Atlantic. The Fleet was successful in achieving the first, but less so in the latter, and during the first months of the war, many hours were spent steaming back and forth across the North Sea and Northern waters, trying to intercept an elusive enemy. The capital ships of the Home Fleet were mainly concerned with the interception of German heavy units, but, although enemy warships were frequently forced to abandon attempts to break out, it was not until the *Bismarck* action in May 1941, that a successful interception was made. The fleet action, towards which the majority of pre-war planning had been directed, never really came to pass, though the *Bismarck* and *Scharnhorst* actions almost fit the bill. As the war progressed, the duties of the Home Fleet were expanded, initially by the need to protect Atlantic convoys from surface raiders, and later, to protect Russian convoys from German warships, stationed in Norway. At this stage of the war, heavy unit surface actions were practically non-existent, but the mine, torpedo and bomb were all quick to make their mark on the British battle fleet.

The bombing of the Fleet, 1939

On 26th September 1939, *Nelson* (Flag-Admiral Forbes, Commander-in-Chief, Home Fleet) *Rodney* and the aircraft carrier *Ark Royal* were in the North Sea, covering the return home of the damaged submarine *Spearfish*. The battlecruiser squadron, consisting of *Repulse* and *Hood*, was also at sea, but operating separately from the main fleet. At 11.00 hours, a patrol of Swordfish aircraft from *Ark Royal* located three Dornier 18 flying boats that were shadowing the fleet. Two of these were subsequently chased off and the third was shot down by the carrier's Skua fighter-bombers. It was fairly obvious – the position of the fleet being now known to the enemy – that some form of air attack would probably develop. Every confidence, however, was felt in the ability of the fleet's AA fire to deal with such an attack and *Ark Royal*'s aircraft were recalled.

That afternoon, five Heinkel bombers appeared to the south-east, and as soon as they came within range, the guns of the fleet opened fire. The bombers broke formation and all but one eventually turned away. From 6,000 feet the remaining enemy aircraft, dive-bombed *Ark Royal*, which was narrowly missed by a bomb which exploded in the sea about 100 feet off the carrier's port bow. Other attacks followed, but the only ship to be hit was *Hood*; a bomb struck her port bulge aft, and glanced off without exploding. The blow caused minor damage to the bulge plating, and flooded the bulge compartments in the immediate vicinity.

This first air attack on the fleet was something of a non-event, but it served to demonstrate the ineffectiveness of AA fire, except as a deterrent. The enemy's bombing was equally ineffective; both sides had much to learn about air attacks on warships.

Left: two views of *Revenge* engaged in gunnery practice in 1941.

Below: *Royal Oak* as she appeared after the extensive modifications of the 1930s.

The loss of *Royal Oak*

During the night of 13/14th October 1939, the German submarine U47, commanded by Lieutenant Prien, penetrated the defences of Scapa Flow. Most of the fleet was at sea, but the battleship *Royal Oak* was anchored close to the north-east shore. At 00.58 hours, Prien fired three torpedoes from about 4,000 yards range. One scored a hit near the bows of the ship but the detonation was so slight, that those on board the ship believed the cause to be internal. Eighteen minutes later, *Royal Oak* was struck by two more torpedoes and, at 01.29 hours, she rolled over and sank, taking 24 officers and 809 men of her complement with her.

That the ship sank so quickly was largely the result of the minimal level of watertight integrity being exercised at that time. She was in what was, no doubt, regarded as a comparatively safe position, and in the generally relaxed atmosphere of harbour routine, many doors, hatches and ventilators were open, that normally would have been closed. Had there been more time available to take adequate counter-measures, the ship might well have been saved.

The torpedoing of *Barham* 1939

At the end of December 1939, *Barham* and *Repulse*, with a screen of five destroyers were operating off the north-west coast of Scotland. On 28th December, when the force was north of the Hebrides and about ten miles from the Butt of Lewis, *Barham* was torpedoed by the submarine U30. The battleship was travelling at nineteen knots when the torpedo struck her port side, abreast the forward 15-inch shell rooms. These compartments were flooded, together with most of the wing and bulge compartments in the vicinity of the explosion, and the ship quickly heeled 7 degrees to port. The heel was corrected by the transference of oil fuel, and speed was reduced to 10 knots, but ninety minutes later, it was possible to increase speed to sixteen knots.

On 29th December, *Barham* arrived at Liverpool where she remained for three months, undergoing repair. Examination revealed that the bulge structure had been ripped open and distorted, over an area thirty-two feet in length and seventeen feet deep, and the main protective bulkhead had been forced inboard a distance of about six feet. The armament and machinery were undamaged, but the forward turrets were inoperative because their magazines had been flooded. The maximum depth of the underwater protection, at the position where the torpedo struck, was about twelve feet. This incident confirmed that vent-plates in underwater protective systems did not reduce the damage caused by underwater explosions, as had been indicated in pre-war experimental work.

The mining of *Nelson*, 1939

On 4th December 1939, the Home Fleet flagship, *Nelson*, was entering Loch Ewe at thirteen knots, when a magnetic mine detonated beneath the ship's bottom, on the starboard side. The explosion forced the outer bottom plating and framing approximately four feet inboard for a distance of seventy feet, and opened up the ship in several places. Flooding occurred over a distance of 140 feet, and the ship heeled 3 degrees to starboard, with a trim by the bow.

The ship could not leave Loch Ewe until the channel had been swept, and while waiting, the damage was inspected and temporary repairs were carried out. By 14th December, the shoring-up of all damaged compartments had been completed, and by 3rd January, the ship's hull had been fitted with a de-gaussing coil. The mine caused serious shock damage to the loading arrangements for the main armament, but no major shock damage was caused to the main machinery.

On 4th January, after two days intensive mine-sweeping of the channel, by trawlers and drifters, equipped with Oropesa magnetic sweeps, *Nelson* sailed from Loch Ewe and, escorted by the destroyers *Faulknor*, *Foxhound*, *Foresight*, *Fame*, *Isis* and *Impulsive*, set course for Portsmouth, at a speed of fourteen knots. At 10.50 hours on Monday, 8th January 1940, *Nelson* berthed at the

Right: *Resolution* in the North Atlantic early in 1941.

South Railway Jetty, Portsmouth, having travelled approximately 1,000 miles without any appreciable increase in the flooding. Full repairs in the Royal Dockyard were to take about six months, and some modifications were made to the pumping arrangements as a result of this incident.

The bombing of *Rodney*, Norway, 1940

During the afternoon of 9th April 1940, a force consisting of *Rodney* (flag, C in C, Home Fleet), *Valiant* and an escort of cruisers and destroyers was steaming northwards about sixty miles off the western coast of Norway. The weather was exceptionally good, and, as might be expected when operating so close to enemy-held territory, the fleet was subjected to several air attacks, which began at noon and continued until late evening. Again, AA fire proved ineffective, and it was fortunate that most of the enemy sorties consisted of high-level bombing – the least effective form of air attack on ships. During the afternoon, the cruisers *Southampton* and *Glasgow* were damaged, and the destroyer *Gurkha* was sunk.

During a lull in the late afternoon, a single enemy aircraft suddenly appeared and made straight for *Rodney*. Approaching from the starboard bow, through a blind-spot in the flagship's AA defence, the aircraft released its 1,100-pound armour-piercing bomb, with exceptional accuracy. The missile narrowly missed the octopoidal bridge structure and hit the shelter-deck just forward of the funnel. It penetrated the upper-deck and main-deck, but broke up in passing through the 4-inch armour on the middle-deck, where it partially detonated.

Minor damage was inflicted upon the internal structure by blast and splinters, and a fire started in the galley flat, but was quickly extinguished. 'Pl' 6-inch gun-turret was put out of action temporarily, and the ship suffered eighteen minor casualties. "Altogether the ship suffered very little inconvenience from this attack, though it was generally agreed that a later BBC announcement that a heavy bomb had bounced off the ship's deck was on the optimistic side!" (*HMS Rodney at War*, by Kenneth Thompson, p. 22)

Renown in action, Norway, 1940

Early in the morning of 9th April 1940, *Renown* (flag, Vice-Admiral W. J. Whitworth) and nine destroyers were steaming south-eastwards at a speed of twelve knots, in an area approximately eighty miles to the west of the Lofoten Islands. At 03.37 hours, a ship, later identified as the battlecruiser *Gneisenau*, was sighted to the east, and shortly afterwards, a second ship which was identified as a *Hipper* class cruiser but was, in fact, the *Gneisenau*'s sister ship, *Scharnhorst*. *Renown* turned towards the enemy and increased speed to twenty knots to close the range, and at 19,000 yards, turned again to bring her full broadside to bear. At 04.05 hours she opened fire on *Gneisenau*, whose officers had been wondering if she were friend or foe, taking *Scharnhorst* completely by surprise.

Gneisenau replied at 04.11 hours and, with the antagonists steaming on parallel courses, a heavy gun duel developed. Theoretically, *Renown* was in the unenviable position of having engaged with only six 15-inch guns an enemy armed with eighteen 11-inch guns. She did have the advantage of the light, however, and the Germans believed they were engaging a more powerful force, because the British destroyers had opened fire, at a range far beyond the capabilities of their 4.7-inch guns. In poor light, with a gale blowing and a heavy sea running, gunnery conditions were far from ideal, but at 04.17 hours, *Renown* scored the first, and most effective hit, putting *Gneisenau*'s main fire-control position out of action. The German ship turned away, while changing over to her secondary control-position, and *Scharnhorst* covered her retreat by making smoke, and then turned away herself. *Renown* turned in pursuit. All three ships were now steaming into the teeth of the north-easterly gale. Despite the heavy sea, the German ships increased speed to twenty-eight knots. *Renown* struggled to keep pace with the enemy but, with the ship taking solid water over her bows and water being shipped through a hatch on the forecastle-deck and through 'A' turret, it was necessary to reduce speed to twenty knots. Two more hits, however, were scored on *Gneisenau* before she drew out of range. One of these put one of *Gneisenau*'s forward turrets out of action.

Renown had, for a time, steamed at twenty-nine knots, but at this speed it was impossible for her to keep her forward turrets in action, and to continue would almost certainly have caused substantial damage forward. The Germans suffered similarly through forcing their ships into the heavy seas, but apparently, they were willing to accept this, in order to escape. The action had not been entirely one-sided; *Renown* having been hit by two or three 11-inch shells. One shell had passed through the main leg of the forward tripod, (cutting the leads to the RDF, navigation- and signalling-lights, etc.) and had continued on its way without exploding. (It is believed that *Renown* was not, in fact, carrying radar at this time, but some preparatory work may have been carried out. A report on this action mentions the RDF leads having been cut.) The second 11-inch shell passed – without exploding – through the extreme stern of the ship, from starboard to port, between the upper-deck and the main-deck and damaged a fan and a few light-fittings. The casing at the top of the forward funnel was split and bulged, and it was believed that this was caused by a third shell. The fact that the shell did not explode is not entirely significant, because normally, it required a hit on a fairly substantial structure to activate the fuse of an armour-piercing shell. *Renown* spent one month in dockyard hands for repairs to action, weather and blast damage.

The bombing of *Resolution*, Norway, 1940

Early in May 1940, *Resolution* was being employed as a support ship for land-based operations in the vicinity of Narvik. On 16th May, she was anchored at Tjeldsundet, about thirty miles west of Narvik, when she was located and attacked by enemy aircraft. She

Below: two photographs of *Malaya* on 11th February 1942.

was hit by one 250-pound armour-piercing bomb, which struck the starboard side of the upper-deck between 'X' and 'Y' turrets, and penetrated to the slope of the middle-deck before partially exploding. Damage was slight, and some minor fires that had started among clothing and bedding, were quickly extinguished. Temporary repairs were made by the ship's staff and *Resolution* remained operational for one month before permanent repairs were carried out.

The torpedoing of *Malaya*, 1941

On 20th March 1941, *Malaya* was torpedoed by a submarine about 250 miles WNW of the Cape Verde Islands. At the time, the battleship was escorting a convoy from Sierra Leone to the U.K., and was steaming at a speed of seven knots. The torpedo detonated on the port side, abreast the forward bulkhead of the forward boiler room. It destroyed the bulge structure over a length of thirty-five feet, distorted and holed the inner and outer bottom plating over an area twenty-two feet long and ten feet deep, and displaced five armour plates in the main belt. Flooding occurred in the bulge compartments for a length of one hundred feet, in the wing compartment for a length of sixty feet and in the oil-fuel tanks, abreast the forward boiler room. The main protective bulkhead withstood the explosion and no serious damage occurred to the main machinery, armament or electrical equipment. The ship heeled seven degrees to port, but this was corrected to 1½ degrees by counter-flooding. The forward boiler room – although intact – was shut down as a precautionary measure, and speed was restricted to a maximum of fourteen knots. Temporary repairs were carried out in Trinidad, and permanent repairs in the USA, the latter being completed on 9th July 1941.

The *Bismarck* action, 1941

On the evening of 21st May 1941, the newly-completed battleship *Bismarck*, accompanied by the heavy cruiser *Prinz Eugen*, sailed from Korsfiord, near Bergen, Norway, destined for the Atlantic. If this ship could have joined *Scharnhorst* and *Gneisenau* at Brest, the German Navy would have possessed a powerful fleet in the Atlantic which, in theory, could have destroyed any convoy it encountered, together with any escorting battleship. Such a force would also have had the necessary speed to escape from any concentration of forces that the Admiralty would have been likely to deploy. The only capital ships in the British fleet, capable of catching them, were the three battlecruisers but these were all old ships whereas the German vessels were modern. It is not surprising, therefore, that the Admiralty attached great importance to the interception and destruction of *Bismarck*, and that little effort was spared to achieve this end.

At 19.22 hours on 23rd May, the cruiser *Suffolk*, patrolling in Denmark Strait, sighted *Bismarck* and *Prinz Eugen* and, manoeuvring to place herself astern of the enemy, she began shadowing them with her radar; one hour later, she was joined by a sister ship, *Norfolk*.

Patrolling the south-west coast of Iceland, 300 miles to the south, was a force consisting of *Hood* (flag, Vice-Admiral L. E. Holland), *Prince of Wales* and four destroyers. (Six destroyers were originally with this force, but two had been detached earlier, to refuel in Iceland.) At 19.39 hours, this force picked

Below: a deck scene aboard *Hood* in 1941.

Bottom of page: broadside view at Scapa Flow, shortly before she set out on her last sortie.

up one of *Suffolk*'s many sighting reports, and at 19.54 hours, Admiral Holland ordered his ships to increase speed to twenty-seven knots and to steer 295 degrees on an interception course. At 02.05 hours on 24th May, the force altered course to 200 degrees and Admiral Holland ordered *Prince of Wales* to search ahead with her Type '284' gunnery radar set. The battleship's commander, Captain Leach, asked if he might use the Type '281' set because the Type '284' was defective, but permission was refused on the grounds that this set would interfere with *Hood*'s Type '284'. At 03.40 hours, course was altered to 240 degrees to converge with the enemy, and thirteen minutes later, speed was increased to twenty-eight knots. At 05.10 hours, the ships were brought to full action stations, and at 05.37 hours, *Prince of Wales* signalled "enemy in sight, distance seventeen miles" as the ships once more changed course to 280 degrees, in order to close the range.

Hood, with *Prince of Wales* off her starboard quarter, was now approaching the enemy at such an angle that only her forward turrets could be brought to bear. *Prince of Wales* moreover, had a defect in one of her forward guns which was only able to fire in the first salvo. The disadvantages of the end-on approach, however, were justified by the need to close the range as rapidly as possible in order to get within a range where the ill-protected decks of *Hood* were not vulnerable to plunging shell.

At 05.49 hours the British ships both turned 20 degrees to starboard, slightly increasing the angle of approach, and Admiral Holland ordered fire to be concentrated on the left hand ship, which had been erroneously identified as *Bismarck*. In fact, the leading ship was *Prinz Eugen*, and the gunnery officer of *Prince of Wales*, realising this, transferred his attention to the second ship in the enemy line. The mistake was also discovered in the flagship which, a few seconds before fire was opened, hoisted the signal "shift target right", but there is some doubt as to whether this order was received by the gunnery office of *Hood*.

Four views of *Prince of Wales* in May 1941—shortly after her completion and just prior to her action with *Bismarck*.

Below: looking aft from the bridge of *Prince of Wales* in May 1941.

Shortly after 05.52 hours, *Hood* opened fire at a range of 26,500 yards, followed half a minute later by *Prince of Wales.* At 05.55 hours the British ships turned back onto a course of 280 degrees and at that moment the enemy opened fire on *Hood. Bismarck*'s first salvo fell short, the second was over and the third straddled. *Prinz Eugen* scored a hit or hits which started a fire among *Hood*'s ready-use anti-aircraft ammunition on the shelter-deck. At 06.00 hours, with the range down to about 14,500 yards, Admiral Holland ordered his ships to turn 20 degrees to port so as to bring their full broadsides to bear. As this order was being executed, *Bismarck*'s fifth salvo straddled *Hood*, scoring one, or perhaps two hits. A sheet of flame was seen to leap into the air from the vicinity of the flagship's mainmast, followed by a tremendous explosion which broke the ship in two. The after part sank very quickly while the fore part sank in three minutes. There were three survivors from the crew of 1,418 officers and men.

Prince of Wales had to alter course to avoid the wreckage of *Hood*. Up to this time, the battleship had been operating undisturbed, but with the loss of the flagship, she became the target for the concentrated fire of both enemy ships. During the following twelve minutes, *Prince of Wales* was hit by seven 15-inch and 8-inch shells, and at 06.13 hours, it was decided to break off the action and retire. This decision was prompted by the fact that 'A' turret had jammed and was partially flooded, 'Y' turret was out of action and several of the 14-inch guns had jammed in elevation. The loss of 'Y' turret was due to the shell ring in 'Y' shell room having become jammed when a 14-inch shell was accidentally dropped into its training mechanism – it took more than two hours to make this turret fully operational again. *Bismarck* continued on her south-westerly course, shadowed from a respectable distance, by *Norfolk*, *Suffolk* and *Prince of Wales.*

A Court of Inquiry, presided over by Vice-Admiral Sir G. Blake, was set up to investigate the technical aspects of the loss of *Hood.* The following passage is an extract from the Court's report.

" . . . The third salvo from "Bismarck" included at least one hit, which apparently burst on the port side just before the mainmast and caused a cordite fire. Presumably this must have come from the 4 inch ready-use ammunition. There was apparently no large explosion connected with the fire. Captain Phillips, H.M.S. "Norfolk", associated this hit with the starboard upper-deck torpedo tubes and stated that he saw a bright flash in about that position. There is no confirming evidence of this, and had the warheads detonated, the shattering effect would have been apparent. The cordite fire appears to have spread fore and aft from the initial position. Probably the 4 inch, U.P. and pom-pom ready-use ammunition were all involved. It flared high at first, but after spreading appeared lower. The fire was still burning between the after end of the superstructure and the after funnel, when the hit or hits from the fifth salvo occurred which blew the ship up.

It is considered that the fifth salvo, which straddled "Hood" obtained one or more hits. The actual position of the hit was not seen, except by one observer, who stated that it was somewhere near the mainmast. The result was a large explosion, the centre of which appeared to be at the base of the mainmast.

The magnitude of the explosion and the rapidity with which the ship disappeared lead to the conclusion that one or more of the after magazines exploded, causing a large area of the outer bottom plating to be blown out. The position round about the base of the mainmast, where the explosion became visible, has no magazine directly below that point. The nearest magazine is the 4 inch high-angle magazine, 65 feet abaft the mainmast. Should this magazine explode, there is a possibility that it might vent itself through the after engine room to the observed position. At the same time, the explosions of this 4 inch magazine would almost certainly cause adjacent 15 inch magazines to blow up."

In June 1941, the Director of Naval Construction, S. V. Goodall, made the following comments on the Court's report.

"The reason for the ship sinking may be as described by the Court, since it was possible for the 15 inch shells fired from "Bismarck" at the range and inclination stated to reach the after 4 inch magazine and blow it and the adjacent 15 inch magazines up. But a certain amount of mystery attaches to the occurrence. There is a consensus of opinion that the centre of the explosion was at the base of the main-mast 65 feet away from the nearest magazine. If the large quantity of cordite contained in this and the magazine still further from the mainmast had blown up, there is no doubt that the resulting violent explosion would have been observed much further aft than it was actually observed. Is there any other possible explanation that would account for an explosion at the base of the mainmast and the consequent rapid foundering of the ship? The hit or hits from the third salvo entered the ship from starboard and apparently burst on the port side just before the mainmast. The result must have been considerable devastation and probably fire on the forecastle, upper and main decks over the centre engine room. On the weather deck over [head] there was a considerable quantity of ready-use ammunition spread about in lockers. The contents of some of these lockers were probably set on fire by the shell or fragments but generally such a conflagration in the open does not spread to adjacent lockers, and the fact that the fire did spread and apparently all the lockers in the neighbourhood went up could be explained if there was also a fire raging below in the officer's quarters largely furnished with non fire-proofed wood (the practice when "Hood" was built). If one or more shells from the 5th salvo burst in this devastated area where there are eight torpedo heads, four each side, each containing about 500 lbs of TNT at the base of the mainmast, and if one or more of these warheads detonated, the result would be an explosion where it was actually observed. Such an explosion could break the ship's back already weakened in this neighbourhood by the earlier damage. With the force on the after bulkhead of the engine room due to the ship's speed of 28 knots and the low reserve of buoyancy of the after part of the ship, this portion would rapidly sink. The foregoing is an alternative explanation of the occurrence which is as likely as the explanation in the finding of the Court."

Prince of Wales had straddled *Bismarck* with her sixth salvo, despite her defective Type '284' radar and the teething troubles of her gun-mountings. After *Hood* had sunk, she switched on her Type '281' air-warning radar set which she used to determine the range of the enemy, with some considerable success. She straddled *Bismarck* several times before breaking off the action. The problems with the main armament were entirely the result of mechanical breakdowns, and errors in drill, and were not a result of enemy action. (*Prince of Wales* had only recently commissioned and was not fully worked up. Many civilians were still on board making adjustments to the armament when the ship sailed to intercept *Bismarck*.) The damage caused to *Prince of Wales* by *Bismarck* and *Prinz Eugen* is described below:

1. A 15-inch shell passed from starboard to port, through the compass-platform, without exploding. It caused a considerable amount of minor damage in the fore bridge (although the entry and exit holes were clean) and killed or wounded everyone on the bridge except Captain Leach and the Chief Yeoman of Signals. The casualties were probably caused by concussion, and splinters from the bridge structure and instruments in the path of the shell.

2. An 8-inch or 15-inch shell passed through the base of the support of the forward HACS directors without exploding. This hit put the directors out of action.

3. A 15-inch shell hit the base of the after funnel and partially exploded, causing splinter damage to the after funnel, after superstructure and after starboard HACS director. Fumes from the damaged funnel were sucked down the after boiler room ventilation-trunks, and permeated the after boiler rooms.

4. An 8-inch shell penetrated the after superstructure and came to rest on the upper-deck without exploding. It was later thrown overboard.

5. A 15-inch diving shell penetrated the ship's side below the armour belt amidships, failed to explode and came to rest in the wing compartments on the starboard side of the after boiler rooms. The shell was discovered and defused when the ship was docked at Rosyth.

6. An 8-inch shell exploded, with only a mild detonation, on the lower armoured-deck aft.

7. An 8-inch shell struck the ship's side right aft, and exploded with only a mild detonation above the armoured-deck.

The main lessons learnt as a result of the damage received by *Prince of Wales* were:

1. The necessity for the water-tight doors to certain important compartments below the armoured-deck to be blanked off and replaced by trunked access.

2. Portable pumps needed to be splash-proof and their overboard discharge required modification.

3. The ventilation of action machinery rooms and other important compartments was inadequate against excessive rises of temperature.

4. Serious danger to boiler-room personnel was likely to be caused when boiler-room intakes were situated close to a damaged funnel.

5. The number of electricity-supply sockets, provided at the fore and after ends of the ship, was inadequate to meet emergency conditions.

6. In order to transmit orders quickly from the damage-control head-quarters to repair stations, a warning telephone system was required.

7. HACS directors were found to be extremely vulnerable to splinters.

Bismarck did not emerge from this action unscathed. She had been hit three times by 14-inch shells from *Prince of Wales*. One shell had penetrated an oil-fuel tank causing a serious oil leak and contaminating the oil fuel in adjacent tanks. Another had struck the side armour amidships, causing a leak, and subsequent flooding put one dynamo and one boiler out of action, reducing her maximum speed by two knots. The third hit caused only minor damage. As a result, *Bismarck*'s proposed Atlantic sortie was abandoned, and the commander of the German force, Admiral Lütjens, decided to make for St. Nazaire where repairs could be carried out. The undamaged *Prinz Eugen*, however, was to continue with the original plan, and later in the day, separated from her consort and disappeared into the Atlantic.

Three days passed before *Bismarck* was finally brought to action, during which time she was lost to her pursuers and found again, attacked by aircraft from the carriers *Victorious* and *Ark Royal*, and by the destroyers of the Fourth Destroyer Flotilla. There is no room here in which to relate the details of these actions and we must concentrate on the two vessels that finally engaged

Below: *King George V* in mid-1941. Note that Type '271' radar has been fitted between the forward HACS directors.

Bismarck and that form part of the subject of this book, *King George V* (flagship of the C in C, Home Fleet, Admiral Tovey), and *Rodney* (Captain Dalrymple-Hamilton).

On 22nd May, *Rodney*, with four destroyers and the liner *Britannic*, had sailed from the Clyde bound for Halifax. The battleship's ultimate destination was Boston, where she was to be taken in hand for a badly needed refit. When *Bismarck* was sighted in Denmark Strait, *Rodney*, now a day and a half out, was recalled and, leaving the destroyer *Eskimo* to escort *Britannic*, turned back with the remaining three destroyers. The immediate purpose of this move was to provide additional cover should *Bismarck* evade the main units of the Home Fleet. On the morning of 24th May, *Rodney* was more than 500 miles to the south-west of *Bismarck*.

After the loss of *Hood*, *Rodney* steered an interception course, but on the morning of 25th May, all contact with *Bismarck* was lost. Finding himself in a position between the enemy and the French coast, Captain Dalrymple-Hamilton decided to cruise in this area, thus anticipating the Admiralty's order that he should act on the assumption that *Bismarck* was making for Brest. The enemy was located again on 26th May, and *Rodney* returned to an interception course. It should be mentioned that during this period, *Rodney* was steaming at full power for up to twelve hours at a stretch, with machinery that had not received a thorough overhaul since the beginning of the war, hence her intended refit in the USA. Her maximum speed at this time was theoretically about twenty knots, but she is estimated to have reached twenty-two knots during the pursuit of *Bismarck*. This forcing of the machinery, however, was not achieved without cost. One of her boilers broke down and was repaired, in a temperature of 124 degrees F. in four and a half hours. The engine-room vent supply-fans failed, which caused the temperature in these compartments to rise unpleasantly, and numerous other breakdowns exercised the abilities of her engine-room personnel to the maximum.

We must now retrace our steps to the 22nd May, in order to follow the movements of *King George V* during the initial stages of the hunt for *Bismarck*. At 22.45 hours on this day, she had sailed westward from Scapa Flow, in company with the carrier *Victorious*, the cruisers *Aurora*, *Galatea*, *Kenya* and *Hermione*, and seven destroyers. At 07.10 hours on 23rd May, this group of ships was joined by *Repulse* and three destroyers, that had sailed north from the Clyde, and the entire force set a north-easterly course, to patrol an area covering the Iceland–Faroes passage. It was not until 20.32 hours on 23rd May, when one of *Norfolk*'s sighting reports was picked up, that Admiral Tovey learned that *Bismarck* was in the Denmark Strait. No major alteration of his existing position was required, however, because the west-north-westerly course of the fleet was already carrying him towards the enemy.

After the loss of *Hood*, the fleet altered course to bring it onto a direct interception course which was progressively altered as new reports of *Bismarck*'s position were received. On the morning of 24th May, the fleet was on a south-westerly course in a position to the east of *Bismarck*, and it was hoped that contact would be made at about 09.00 hours on the following morning. At 04.00 hours, Admiral Tovey detached *Victorious* and four cruisers, ordering them to close the enemy sufficiently to allow an air strike by the carrier's Swordfish. This later resulted in one torpedo hit on *Bismarck* which did little damage. It did, however, increase the rate of flooding through the existing hull damage.

On the morning of 25th May, when contact with *Bismarck* was lost, Admiral Tovey continued on his south-westerly course and actually crossed ahead of the enemy vessel's course. At 09.06 hours, *Repulse*, which was running low on fuel, separated from the flagship and headed for Newfoundland. At 10.47 hours, *King George V* altered course to the north-east, Admiral Tovey mistakenly thinking that *Bismarck* was breaking back towards the Iceland–Faeroes passage. It was 18.10 hours before the C in C realised his error and turned onto a south-easterly course towards the coast of France. He was now 150 miles behind the enemy and the chances of catching up were beginning to look remote. At 10.30 hours on 26th May, *Bismarck* was re-located, by a Catalina aircraft of Coastal Command, about 130 miles south of *King George V*.

At 18.00 hours on 26th May, *King George V* was joined by *Rodney* which took up a position astern of the flagship. By this time, the fuel situation in the battleships was becoming critical, and it was clear that unless *Bismarck* were slowed down, it was unlikely that she would be brought to action. The one real chance of achieving this lay with the carrier *Ark Royal*, which had sailed north from Gibraltar with Force 'H' and was about to make an airstrike against the enemy before dark. The attack was carried out by fifteen Swordfish aircraft at about 21.00 hours, and two torpedo hits were scored. One struck amidships, causing no serious damage, but the second struck aft and jammed *Bismarck*'s rudders at fifteen degrees to port.

At 21.36 hours, the cruiser *Sheffield*, shadowing *Bismarck*, signalled "Bismarck changing course 340 degrees NNW". This news was received with scepticism by the Commander-in-Chief, for such a course would bring the enemy directly towards his flagship. Nevertheless, at 21.42 hours, he altered course to south and steered towards *Bismarck*'s reported position. Soon afterwards, a signal was received from *Ark Royal* stating that the aircrews from the last strike were claiming at least two hits. Then came a report from a flying boat, saying that the enemy was steering a northerly course, confirming the *Sheffield*'s earlier message. *Bismarck*, now unmanoeuvrable, could not escape and would soon be within range of the guns of *King George V* and *Rodney*. Admiral Tovey did not wish to engage in a night action, however, and reduced speed until dawn, when the final approach would be made.

Early on the morning of 27th May, *King George V* and *Rodney* began to work up speed and headed towards *Bismarck*'s position from the west-north-west. A Force 6 wind was blowing from the north-west, there was a rough sea with a heavy swell from the north-west and the sky was overcast. Visibility was good. Admiral Tovey had decided to approach from the west in order to have the advantage of the conditions of light and the direction of the swell, which would be particularly important during the end-on approach. It was important also, that the British ships should not get to leeward of *Bismarck*, as she might then use a smoke-screen to delay her destruction. Considerations of fuel, U-boat and air attack, moreover, made an early and close action essential. The approach from the west, however, made it very difficult to avoid the effects of smoke interference.

At 07.08 hours, Admiral Tovey ordered *Rodney* to assume open order from the flagship, that is, to say, she was given permission to manoeuvre independently some distance from *King George V*. At 08.20 hours, *Norfolk* was sighted and she reported *Bismarck*'s exact position, which allowed the British battleships to make some final course adjustments. The enemy was sighted by the air-defence officer of *Rodney*, at 08.43 hours, bearing 115 degrees just off the starboard bow, at a range of about 25,000 yards and steering directly towards the British ships. *Rodney* and *King George V* were steering 110 degrees in line abreast, about 1,600 yards apart.

At 08.47 hours, *Rodney* opened fire with 'A' and 'B' turrets at a range of 23,400 yards, and *King George V* opened fire one minute later. *Bismarck* chose *Rodney* as her target, and opened fire will all four guns of her forward turrets at 08.49 hours. The enemy's first salvo was 1,000 yards short, the second, at 08.50 hours, straddled, one shell falling short and the remainder, over; the nearest was twenty yards away, just abaft the bridge. *Bismarck*'s next salvo fell over, and this was followed by one short and then several overs. *Rodney* was manoeuvring to avoid the enemy salvoes, apparently with success.

Rodney straddled *Bismarck* with her third

and fourth salvoes and scored a hit with the former at 08.50 hours. At 08.57 hours, she scored another hit which penetrated the forecastle and put *Bismarck*'s 'A' turret out of action. By 09.00 hours, the enemy's rate of fire had slowed and had become erratic. At 08.59 hours, with the range down to 16,000 yards, *King George V* turned to starboard to bring her after turret into action and, three and a half minutes later, *Rodney* conformed. At 09.02 hours, a 16-inch or 14-inch shell penetrated *Bismarck*'s 'B' turret, detonated inside, and blew the rear plate of the gun-house over the ship's side. At about the same time, a shell destroyed her foretop, together with the central armament-control position, and killed most of the senior officers. At 09.12 hours, the forward fire-control position was destroyed, and six minutes later, the after fire-control position, leaving the ship without a centralised fire-control. At 09.15 hours, *Bismarck* shifted the fire of her after turrets to *King George V*, but shifted back to *Rodney* five minutes later, by which time only 'X' turret of the main armament was still firing.

By this time, *Bismarck* was drawing aft of the British ships and at 09.16 hours, *Rodney* turned 180 degrees to starboard, which brought her onto a northerly course, parallel with the enemy, at a range of about 9,000 yards. At 09.25 hours, *King George V* also turned north, bringing the range down to 12,000 yards, but at the same time, fire from the flagship slackened, for several reasons. First, the target was obscured by smoke and by *Rodney*'s shell splashes, second, her gunnery radar set had temporarily broken down, and third, she had suffered several mechanical breakdowns in her 14-inch turrets, one of which was out of action for half an hour. Meanwhile, *Rodney* had altered course to starboard, to cross ahead of *Bismarck*'s course, and for the next thirty minutes, passed back and forth across the enemy's bow, firing at ranges between 4,000 and 3,000 yards. By 09.40 hours, *Bismarck* was silent, her main and secondary armaments having been put out of action.

At 10.05 hours, *King George V* closed *Bismarck* and fired several salvoes at 3,000 yards range, into what was now a floating hulk. The fuel situation of the battleships had now become critical, and at 10.15 hours, Admiral Tovey ordered *King George V* and *Rodney* to break off the action and steer 027 degrees for home. *Rodney* fired her last salvo at 10.14 hours and *King George V*, at 10.22.

Bismarck, her flag still flying, was very low in the water and on fire, but she showed no signs of sinking. Admiral Tovey ordered any ships in the area that still had torpedoes, to close, and sink her. At 10.25 hours, the cruiser *Dorsetshire* fired two torpedoes into her starboard side, and these exploded below the bridge. At 10.36 hours, she fired another torpedo into her port side, and *Bismarck* heeled to port and began sinking by the stern. At 10.40 hours, she capsized and sank.

The qualities of the battleship *Bismarck*, and the manner in which she was sunk have been widely discussed. She has often been described as 'almost indestructable' and, since the war, many mythical qualities have been ascribed to her. The most usual reason put forward for the sinking of this 'almost unsinkable' ship is that, towards the end of the action, she was scuttled by her crew, who fired explosive charges in the ship's bottom and opened her sea-cocks. This may or may not be true, but it seems unlikely that *Bismarck* could have stayed afloat, for, although an exceptionally well built ship, it cannot be said that she was substantially better than the modern battleships of other navies. In fact, in many ways, her design was of First World War vintage, and therefore, was not so advanced as the new ships of Britain, the USA and other nations. The following points are worthy of note:

1. A ship can sink in one of two ways, by excessive flooding, which causes loss of buoyancy and eventual foundering, or by excessive heel, causing loss of stability and eventual capsizing. The former process can take many hours, and there can be little doubt that *Bismarck* was sinking in this manner before scuttling charges or *Dorsetshire's* torpedoes or some sudden spread of her internal flooding caused her to capsize. When a warship sinks, it is usually through capsizing, because the damage caused in action is generally confined to or concentrated on one side of the ship. In *Bismarck*'s case, the damage appears to have been fairly evenly distributed, which is somewhat unusual.

2. Gunfire is not the most effective way of sinking a heavily-armoured warship, because most of the damage caused, is above the waterline. The torpedo and the mine are by far the most effective weapons in this respect. *Bismarck* was hit by several torpedoes before the action on 27th May, and there may have been as many as three hits, but no more than two of these were made on any one occasion, which allowed sufficient time between attacks for adequate counter-measures to be taken.

3. *Bismarck*'s armour has been much acclaimed, and has been described as representing a 50 per cent improvement in penetration resistance compared to other armour. This is completely untrue, and it is very unlikely that there was much to choose between the qualities of the armour plate being produced by any of the major naval powers at that time. Another popular fallacy is that *Bismarck* had an armour belt made from a special nickel-chrome steel alloy which is generally thought to have been a remarkable new development of the steel age. In fact, nickel-chrome armour had been in general use by the world's battle fleets since the 1890s, and *Bismarck*'s armour was of a nickel-chrome-molybdenum steel alloy, produced – without doubt – by a modern process and in much the same way as the armour plates of every other naval power.

4. Gunfire can reduce the fighting efficiency of an opponent, by penetrating her vitals through the armour, or by shattering the soft ends, bridges and fire-control positions. There can be little doubt that *Bismarck* was defeated by the latter means, and it was partly for this purpose that the *King George V* class were originally designed with twelve 14-inch guns,

Below: *Duke of York* on 13th April 1943.

rather than with a smaller number of larger weapons.

So far as the British were concerned, the object of the exercise had been achieved, and whether *Bismarck* was eventually sunk by scuttling or by torpedoes did not really matter. Finally, it should be said that the above remarks are intended to place *Bismarck*'s situation in perspective, and not to show that she was an inferior design, just a standard one. No ordinary battleship, already in a damaged condition, could expect to survive the attack of two modern adversaries.

Of the two British battleships, only *Rodney* was damaged, and most of her damage was self-inflicted, by the blast of her own main armament (see Appendix 3).

The battle of the North Cape, 1943

On the evening of 25th December 1943, the battlecruiser *Scharnhorst* sailed from Altenfiord, Norway, to attack the eastbound Russian convoy, JW55A. Apart from its local escort, the convoy, together with the homeward bound RA55A, were protected by two covering forces. Force 1, consisted of the cruisers *Belfast* (flagship Vice-Admiral R. L. Burnett), *Sheffield* and *Norfolk*; Force 2, consisted of *Duke of York* (flag of Admiral Sir Bruce Fraser, C in C, Home Fleet), the cruiser *Jamaica* and four destroyers.

News that *Scharnhorst* was at sea reached the C in C at 03.39 hours, on 26th December. Admiral Fraser ordered some preliminary adjustments to the course of the convoy and later, ordered Force 1 to close and support the convoy escort. In the meantime, he increased the speed of his own force from seventeen to twenty-four knots, and, steering slightly north of east, into a steadily rising gale, attempted to gain a position between the enemy and the Norwegian coast.

While attempting to approach the convoy, *Scharnhorst* was twice intercepted and brought to action by Admiral Burnett's cruisers. At 13.00 hours, she abandoned her mission and steered south, for home, with Force 1 shadowing astern. Meanwhile, about 100 miles to the south-west, Force 2 was steering an interception course.

At 16.17 hours, *Duke of York* picked up *Scharnhorst* on radar, at a range of 45,500

yards. She was still steering south, and *Duke of York* was steaming eastwards across her path. At 16.32 hours, *Duke of York* located *Scharnhorst* on her Type '284' gunnery radar set, at a range of 29,700 yards. Eight minutes later, Admiral Fraser ordered *Belfast* to illuminate the target with star shell, and at 16.44 hours, *Duke of York* turned slightly to starboard to bring her full broadside to bear. *Belfast*'s star shell failed to reveal *Scharnhorst* so, at 16.48 hours, the battleship fired a star shell from one of her 5.25-inch guns. This successfully illuminated the target and, at 16.50 hours, *Duke of York* opened fire with her main armament at a range of 12,000 yards. She straddled *Scharnhorst* with her first salvo (one shell putting 'A' turret out of action) and again with her third salvo. At 16.52 hours, *Jamaica*, six cables astern of the flagship, also opened fire at a range of 13,000 yards, and straddled the target with her third salvo, scoring one hit.

Scharnhorst was completely surprised by this sudden attack, from a direction in which she believed there were no enemy forces. (*Scharnhorst* was unable to detect the approach of *Duke of York* on her radar because the aerials of this equipment had been destroyed earlier by the gunfire of *Norfolk*.) She turned north, away from *Duke of York*, but at 16.57 hours, ran into Force 1, and came under fire from *Belfast* and *Norfolk*. At 17.08 hours, she turned onto an easterly course and attempted to use her superior speed to escape. *Duke of York* had conformed to these alterations of course, and was now chasing the battlecruiser from a position off her starboard quarter.

It was clear, however, that unless the enemy was slowed down, she could quite easily escape. At 17.13 hours, Admiral Fraser ordered his four destroyers to carry out a torpedo attack, but first, they had to catch up with their quarry, which was no easy task, in the prevailing weather conditions. By 17.42 hours, only *Duke of York*'s 14-inch guns could reach the enemy, the range having increased to 18,000 yards, but the fire of the British ship was proving very effective. One 14-inch shell damaged the ventilation-trunks to 'B' turret, which rapidly filled with cordite fumes and had to be abandoned. Another shell penetrated *Scharnhorst*'s armour and detonated in No. 1 boiler room, cutting several steam pipes, and reducing the ship's speed to ten knots. The damage, however, was quickly isolated, allowing speed to be increased to twenty knots. *Scharnhorst* ceased fire at 18.20 hours and *Duke of York*, four minutes later, the range having opened out to 21,400 yards. Admiral Fraser, by this time, had altered the course of Force 2 to south-east in the hope of blocking the enemy's escape route southward, but it was soon noticed that *Scharnhorst*'s speed had been reduced, and at 18.38 hours, Fraser once more altered course and steered towards the enemy.

Scharnhorst's reduction in speed, caused by damage to the forward boiler room, had enabled the four destroyers of Force 2 to overtake her. Between 18.40 hours and 19.00 hours, *Scharnhorst* was attacked by these destroyers, at ranges between 3,500 and 1,800 yards. Twenty-eight torpedoes were fired, and four hits were scored, one forward on the starboard side, and one amidships, and one forward and one aft on the port side.

At 19.01 hours, *Duke of York* and *Jamaica* re-opened fire at a range of 10,400 yards. The battlecruiser replied with the guns of her after turret, the only part of her main armament that was still serviceable. By 19.11 hours, *Scharnhorst*'s speed had dropped to ten knots, and about five minutes later, the after turret ceased firing, leaving only a few of her 5.9-inch guns still in action. *Duke of York* ceased firing at 19.30 hours to allow the lighter forces to close the enemy. *Scharnhorst* was subsequently hit by two torpedoes from *Jamaica*, three from the destroyer *Musketeer* and two from the destroyer *Virago*. At 19.45 hours, *Scharnhorst*'s magazines exploded, and she sank. There were thirty-six survivors.

Damage to *Duke of York* was negligible. One 11-inch shell had passed through the mainmast and its port strut, without exploding. About half the sectional area of the mainmast, and slightly more of the strut section, in the path of the shell, were destroyed. One 5.9-inch shell completed the picture by passing through the port strut of the foremast, destroying a little less than half its sectional area.

The battle of North Cape was one of the last capital-ship actions in which aircraft took no part, and as such, it serves well as an example of what a well-handled fleet could do, without such aid. The destruction of *Scharnhorst* was achieved, partly by the cruisers of Force 1, which shadowed the enemy and kept the C in C informed of her position, and partly by the excellent gunnery of *Duke of York*. The accuracy of both of these features, was largely the result of radar. In a night action, with a gale blowing, radar had enabled the cruisers to keep in contact with the enemy, and *Duke of York* to straddle the target continuously. It had also enabled the battleship and the cruisers to fire blind, when the enemy was obscured from view. It is interesting to note, that the accuracy of *Duke of York*'s gunfire deteriorated when, for a short period, her '284' gunnary radar set was put out of action by the shaking-up it had received from the firing of the main armament. Finally, it should be said that it was *Duke of York*'s gunfire that ultimately ensured the defeat of *Scharnhorst*, for it was this that reduced the battlecruiser's speed and prevented her escape eastwards.

2. THE MEDITERRANEAN, 1940 to 1943

The entry of Italy into the war in June 1940, followed by the loss of France, and the neutralisation of the French fleet, produced a situation that appeared to favour the enemy to such an extent, as to seriously threaten the existence of British naval power in the Mediterranean. The Italian battle fleet consisted of four extensively modernised battleships *Conte di Cavour*, *Guilio Cesare*, *Caio Duilio* and *Andrea Doria*, and two modern battleships, *Littorio* and *Vittorio Veneto*.

(There were two sister ships to the modern battleships in the Italian fleet, *Roma* which was not completed until June 1942, and *Impero*, which was later cancelled.) Against these ships, Britain had *Warspite*, *Malaya* and *Royal Sovereign*, based at Alexandria, and *Hood*, *Valiant* and *Resolution*, in the newly formed Force H, at Gibraltar. This gave the opposing forces equality in numbers, but the British ships were less modern and only *Hood* had a speed anywhere near that of the Italian ships. The British forces, moreover, were divided, while the Italians could, at any time, have concentrated their forces in the eastern or western Mediterranean to their considerable advantage.

The Italians also possessed a substantial superiority in practically all other types of naval vessels, particularly submarines, and in air power. Their air force, however, was entirely land based, while Force H had the carrier *Ark Royal* which offered some advantage, at least, in seaborne operations.

Theoretically, Italy should have completely dominated the central Mediterranean and rapidly reduced and occupied the island of Malta which lay across her supply route to North Africa. In fact, she did neither, but considerable effort was expended in an endeavour to prevent supplies reaching the island and in trying to bomb Malta into submission. The Italian battle fleet adopted a defensive role, and seldom sought a fleet action except when defending a convoy threatened by a British force. Italy never subscribed to the doctrine that attack is the best form of defence, and generally looked upon a fleet action as something to be avoided, unless the enemy was greatly inferior. The Italian air force was more inclined towards an offensive policy, and many air attacks were made on British warships and convoys in the central Mediterranean. The Italians favoured precision high-level bombing, which proved comparatively ineffective against ships, although their torpedo-bombers were extremely efficient. It was not until the Luftwaffe's dive-bombers arrived in the Mediterranean and *Illustrious* was damaged, that the British really began to suffer through lack of air superiority.

The first indication of how the Italian fleet would behave in a surface action, came only a few weeks after the entry of Italy into the war. On 9th July 1940, British and Italian forces were at sea, the former covering a convoy to Malta, and the latter, a convoy to North Africa. The British force included *Warspite*, *Malaya* and *Royal Sovereign* and the Italian force, *Giulio Cesare* and *Cavour*. During the afternoon, the two fleets came into action off the coast of Calabria. Fire was opened at 26,000 yards, at which range, only the guns of *Warspite* could reach the enemy. Incredibly, *Warspite* straddled the Italian flagship, *Cesare*, with her first salvo, and scored a hit amidships which caused a substantial amount of superficial damage, and started a fire. The Italian fleet promptly turned away under cover of a smoke-screen, and made off in the direction of its base. After the action, the ships of both sides were subjected to air attacks by Italian aircraft, and the British force retired to the south.

Admiral Cunningham, C in C, Mediterranean Fleet, was disappointed at the ease with which the Italian ships had escaped, and later requested that his fleet be reinforced by a capital ship with a gun-range equal to that of *Warspite*, and a modern aircraft carrier to provide air-strike and air-defence capabilities. (The fleet had the old carrier *Eagle* but she carried only a small complement of aircraft.) The reinforcements subsequently arrived in the shape of *Valiant*, and the carrier *Illustrious*.

Illustrious proved her worth on 11th November 1940, when she delivered an air strike against the Italian fleet's base at Taranto. The attack took the Italians completely by surprise; the battleship *Cavour* was sunk and the battleships *Littorio* and *Duilio* were heavily damaged. Thus, for a while at least, the balance of capital-ship strength in the Mediterranean favoured the British.

After Calabria and Taranto, Italian battleships put to sea on very few occasions, and whenever a fleet action appeared imminent, they invariably turned for home. Only one engagement – the battle of Matapan – in March 1941, saw the British battleships in action against an enemy surface fleet, and even here, it was cruisers with which they engaged and not battleships.

The Battle of Matapan, 1941

The Italian force consisted of *Vittorio Veneto*, eight cruisers and seventeen destroyers, which had sailed to intercept British military convoys, on passage to Greece. The Italians had the mistaken idea that two of the three British battleships at Alexandria had been put out of action by German air attacks. These three ships, *Warspite*, *Barham* and *Valiant*, together with the carrier *Formidable*, were, in fact, at sea, protecting the convoys the Italians intended to attack.

Light forces of the two fleets located each other on the morning of 28th March, and for a short period neither side suspected the presence of battleship(s) in the opposing force. A cruiser action ensued, while the heavy unit(s) of each force closed the scene to give support. *Vittorio Veneto* arrived first, but shortly after opening fire on the British cruisers, she was attacked by torpedo-bombers from *Formidable*. Although no hits were scored, the enemy force promptly retired from action.

The British battleships, under the command of Admiral Cunningham, were still some considerable distance from the Italians who were rapidly making for home. If *Vittorio Veneto* were to be brought to action she must first be slowed down, and the only hope of this lay with *Formidable*'s torpedo-bombers and a few similar aircraft from land bases in Crete and Greece. The carrier's second strike against *Vittorio Veneto* produced one hit, which reduced her speed to sixteen knots and enabled Cunningham's battleships to close the gap, but later, she was able to increase her speed to nineteen knots and escape during the night. The carrier's third strike failed to damage the Italian battleship, but one torpedo stopped the cruiser *Pola.* Two other Italian cruisers, *Zara* and *Fiume*, and four destroyers, were later sent back by the Italian C in C, Admiral Iachino, to assist *Pola.*

At 22.03 hours, on 28th March, *Valiant* detected *Pola* on radar at a range of 16,000 yards. Hoping that this was *Vittorio Veneto*, Cunningham altered course towards the enemy vessel. Shortly afterwards, *Zara* and *Fiume* were sighted ahead of the fleet, which turned to bring the battleships into line ahead with all guns bearing on the enemy. Searchlights lit up *Zara*, *Fiume* and the destroyer *Alfieri*, and at ranges of between 3,000 and 4,000 yards, the battleships opened fire. *Warspite* and *Valiant* rapidly reduced *Fiume* to a floating wreck, and heavily on fire, she turned away and sank about fifty minutes later. *Zara* was fired on by all three British battleships and was left a crippled and burning wreck, together with *Alfieri*, which was fired on by *Barham.* The battleships later withdrew from the scene, and left the destroyers to finish off the Italian ships. *Zara*, *Pola*, *Alfieri* and another destroyer, *Carducci*, were subsequently sunk by British destroyer forces under the command of Captain Philip Mack.

The night action off Matapan could not be claimed as a great British victory, because the forces involved were substantially unequal, but it did serve to demonstrate the efficiency of the British night-fighting arrangements which were only partially aided by radar. The Italians had never developed adequate night-fighting systems, and suffered in consequence.

The Italians used their battle fleet as a 'fleet in being' rather than an offensive weapon during the war in the Mediterranean, and their lack of confidence led them to miss many opportunities of gaining complete command of the central Mediterranean. Their main disadvantages were their lack of aircraft carriers and radar. One wonders how a British fleet would have fared had the roles of the opposing forces been reversed.

Airpower was the key to the Mediterranean, and it was this, more than any other factor, that controlled the fortunes of both sides. It was also the weapon that was to do the greatest damage to the British fleet as a whole, though the battleships were to suffer more from underwater attacks.

The bombing of the Fleet, 1940

On 7th July 1940, *Warspite*, *Malaya* and *Royal Sovereign* sailed from Alexandria, to cover the passage of two convoys from Malta. On the following day, the fleet was subjected to several high-level bombing attacks by Italian aircraft. Only the cruiser *Gloucester* was hit, but both *Warspite* and *Malaya* suffered minor damage from near misses. The damage to *Warspite* was caused by splinters from a 220-pound bomb which exploded in the sea on the port side abreast 'P2' 4-inch gun-mounting. In *Malaya*, a splinter cut one of the multi-core cables to the forward HACS director. This affected the telephones, Evershed, and firing-circuits of the forward 4-inch HA guns. Temporary repairs were made in about thirty minutes.

Crete, 1941

The battle for Crete, during May to June 1941, proved disastrous for the British naval forces in the Eastern Mediterranean. The Germans possessed complete command of the air, and whenever the British fleet was at sea, it was subjected to continuous air attacks during the daylight hours. As a result, a large number of ships were either sunk or damaged, and the strength of the fleet was seriously weakened. Three of the battleships were damaged, but only one, *Warspite*, seriously enough to require withdrawal from the Mediterranean.

In the afternoon of 22nd May 1941, *Warspite* was operating in the Kithera Channel to the north-west of Crete when she was attacked by several groups of enemy aircraft. She received one direct hit from a 550-pound semi armour-piercing bomb, which perforated the forecastle-deck, on the starboard side of the funnel, and exploded on the upper-deck in the starboard 6-inch gun-battery. The forecastle-deck was extensively damaged over an area of 90 feet x 30 feet, and the upper-deck, over an area of 130 feet x 30 feet. There was a hole 8 feet x 6 feet in the upper-deck, and minor fires started, in the vicinity of the explosion. Two of the four 6-inch guns in the starboard battery were extensively damaged and 'S1' 4-inch twin mounting was blown overboard. The fires were quickly extinguished, but smoke and fumes permeated No. 3 boiler room, which had to be abandoned. Thirty-eight members of the crew were killed and thirty-one wounded.

Warspite remained with the fleet, but it was decided that it would be unsafe to fire the main armament, or the two serviceable 6-inch guns on the starboard side, because of the structural weaknesses caused by the explosion. She returned to Alexandria on 24th May, where she was taken in hand for temporary repairs, to fit her for passage to the USA, where permanent repairs could be carried out. She was damaged again on the night of 23rd/24th June, during an air raid on Alexandria. A 1,100-pound bomb, narrowly missed the ship and burst underwater on the starboard side, abreast 'A' turret. The upper and lower bulge plating was damaged over a length of sixty feet, and the lower bulge was flooded over a length of ninety feet. The damage, however, was not sufficiently serious to prevent her putting to sea, and on 25th June, she sailed for the USA. She docked at Bremerton Navy Yard on 11th August, and completed her damage repairs and refit on 28th December.

Valiant was damaged on the same day as *Warspite*, and during the same series of air attacks. She was hit by two 110-pound bombs on the port side of the upper-deck, abreast 'X' turret. These comparatively small bombs caused only minor structural and splinter damage. A third bomb of the same size narrowly missed the port bulge, and exploded in the sea, abreast the funnel, causing minor damage to the upper and lower bulge, and flooding one bulge compartment. The damage was repaired at Alexandria.

Barham was damaged during an air attack on 27th May, while taking part in an opera-

Below: *Barham* in the spring of 1941.

tion against the enemy-held island of Scarpanto. During a dive-bombing attack, she was hit by a 550-pound bomb, which detonated on contact with the roof of 'Y' turret. An 18-inch diameter hole was made in the $4\frac{1}{4}$-inch roof plate, which was distorted and slightly lifted, and the 0.5-inch machine-gun mounting in the roof of 'X' turret was badly damaged. Splinters from the bomb ignited cordite charges in the port gun-loading bay of 'Y' turret, and started a fire which damaged the electric cables in the gun-house. The fire was brought under control twenty minutes later. A second 550-pound bomb, narrowly missed the ship and exploded in the sea on the port side abreast 'A' turret. The lower bulge, which was extensively damaged, was holed and distorted over an area twenty feet x sixteen feet. The flooding caused a heel of $1\frac{1}{2}$ degrees to port, but this was later corrected by the transfer of oil fuel. Repairs, which took two months, were carried out in Alexandria.

The torpedoing of *Nelson*, 1941

Nelson was torpedoed by an aircraft on 27th September 1941, while escorting a convoy to Malta (Operation Halberd). She was steaming at fifteen knots when the torpedo struck forward on the port side, at platform-deck level. A hole, thirty feet long and fifteen feet deep, was blown in the outer bottom, causing extensive flooding. The platform-deck was flooded for a length of seventy-five feet, and the torpedo room was wrecked. Speed was restricted to fifteen knots in order to avoid excessive strain on the damaged structure. The ship remained with the convoy for a short period, and then proceeded independently to Gibraltar, where temporary repairs were carried out. In October, *Nelson* sailed to Rosyth, where permanent repairs were completed in April 1942. As a result of this experience, the fixed and portable pumping-systems of *Nelson* and *Rodney* were modified.

The sinking of *Barham*, 1941

On 24th November 1941, *Queen Elizabeth*, *Barham* and *Valiant*, with an escort of eight destroyers, sailed from Alexandria to cover operations against two enemy convoys reported to be making for Benghazi. On the following day, at 16.25 hours, *Barham* was torpedoed by the German submarine U331, which, undetected, had penetrated the destroyer screen. The submarine fired four torpedoes, three of which detonated on *Barham*'s port side, between the funnel and 'Y' turret. She quickly listed to port and, after a pause of a few seconds, at an angle of 40 degrees, turned onto her beam ends. Four minutes after the torpedoes had struck, the after 15-inch magazines exploded and vented through the upper-deck and the starboard side. The ship was hidden by an enormous cloud of smoke, and when this cleared, she had gone. *Barham*'s Captain, G. C. Cooke, and 861 officers

Below: *Queen Elizabeth* on completion of her damage repairs and refit at Norfolk Navy Yard, USA, in June 1943.

and men were lost with the ship. Vice-Admiral Pridham-Wippell and 395 members of the crew were rescued.

The exact cause of the explosion of the ship's magazines could not be established because of the rapidity with which she had sunk. The Court of Inquiry put forward the theory that a fire might have started in the after port 4-inch magazine, and subsequently, spread to the main magazines. After the torpedoes had struck, the internal lighting and communication systems failed, and no general orders were received because the broadcasting system failed. *Barham* was operating the correct degree of watertight sub-division for cruising, but she listed too quickly for any effective counter-measures to be carried out.

The mining of *Queen Elizabeth* and *Valiant*, 1941

Despite their failings in large-scale operations, the Italians always showed a marked flair in the planning and execution of small-scale operations requiring a high degree of daring and skill. Their most successful operation of this type was carried out during the night of 18th December 1941, when three two-man submarines penetrated the defences of the harbour at Alexandria and deposited their delayed-action charges under *Queen Elizabeth*, *Valiant* and the tanker, *Sagona*. At 06.00 hours the following morning, the first charge detonated under *Sagona* and badly damaged both the tanker and the destroyer *Jervis*, which was moored alongside. The charge under *Valiant* detonated at 06.20 hours, and that under *Queen Elizabeth*, four minutes later. The depth of water was fifty feet and the charges were judged to have weighed between 500 and 1,000 pounds.

Valiant's charge exploded under the port bulge, abreast 'A' turret, and holed and forced upwards the lower bulge over an area of sixty feet x thirty feet. Internal damage extended from the middle-line to the lower bulge compartments and the inner bottom, lower bulge, 'A' shell room and magazine, and the adjacent compartment up to lower-deck level immediately flooded. The main and auxiliary machinery were undamaged, but the revolving trunk of 'A' turret was distorted, and some minor shock damage was done to electrical equipment. The ship had a heavy trim by the bow, but could have proceeded to sea in an emergency. Temporary repairs were made at Alexandria, and eventually she sailed for Durban where permanent repairs were carried out between 15th April and 7th July 1942.

The charge below *Queen Elizabeth* detonated under 'B' boiler room and blew in the double bottom structure in this area, and, to a lesser extent under 'A' and 'X' boiler rooms, upwards into the ship. Damage to the ship's bottom covered an area of one hundred and ninety feet x sixty feet and included both the port and starboard bulges. 'A', 'B' and 'X' boiler rooms, and the forward 4.5-inch magazines flooded immediately, and 'Y' boiler room and several other compartments in the vicinity, flooded slowly up to main-deck level. The boilers, and the auxiliary machinery, together with its electrical equipment were severely damaged by the explosion and subsequent flooding. The armament was undamaged, but

all hydraulic power was lost, and the guns of the main and secondary batteries could have been used only at greatly reduced efficiency. The ship sank to the harbour bottom, but was raised and temporary repairs were carried out in the floating dock at Alexandria. She subsequently proceeded to the USA, where permanent repairs were carried out, between 6th September 1942 and 1st June 1943, at the Norfolk Navy Yard, Virginia. *Queen Elizabeth* was out of action for a total of seventeen and a half months.

3. THE FAR EAST, 1941 to 1942

After the US fleet had been neutralised at Pearl Harbor, and *Prince of Wales* and *Repulse* had been sunk, Japanese naval power, in the Far East and the Pacific Ocean, was almost unchallenged. Britain quickly formed a new fleet, based in the Indian Ocean, but it was largely composed of old ships and could not hope to withstand a full-scale onslaught by the Japanese fleet. Japan made only one such incursion into the Indian Ocean, and this, although causing considerable damage, did not result in a fleet action. Thereafter, in the Pacific, Japan concentrated her efforts against American forces, and the British Far East Fleet was left in comparative peace until it had built up its strength sufficiently to join in the final onslaught against Japan.

The following section largely concerns the sinking of *Prince of Wales* and *Repulse*, probably the most important single event of the war, in its effect on British battleship design. *Prince of Wales* was a brand-new ship, and incorporated practically all the experience of many years of experimental work. Her loss, therefore, was viewed with great concern, and brought about many modifications to the remaining ships of the *King George V* class and to *Vanguard*.

The loss of *Prince of Wales* and *Repulse*, 1941

On 2nd December 1941, *Prince of Wales* (flag) and *Repulse*, under the command of Admiral Sir T. Phillips, arrived at Singapore. These two ships, known collectively as Force Z, were to form the backbone of the Eastern Fleet. Five days later, the Japanese attacked Pearl Harbor and landed troops in Siam and Malaya.

At 17.35 hours on 8th December, *Prince of Wales* and *Repulse*, escorted by the destroyers *Express*, *Electra*, *Vampire* and *Tenedos*, sailed from Singapore to attack a Japanese landing-force at Singora, on the north-west coast of Malaya. Force Z made a wide sweep, well clear of the Malayan coast, but in the evening of the following day, was sighted by enemy aircraft. Having lost the element of surprise, Admiral Phillips decided to cancel the operation. The destroyer *Tenedos*, which was short of fuel, was detached to Singapore at 18.35 hours, but the main force continued on its way, in order to mislead the shadowing enemy aircraft. At 19.00 hours they altered course north-westwards towards Singora, and at 20.15 hours, under cover of darkness, turned south for Singapore. Shortly before midnight, Admiral Phillips received a signal reporting a Japanese landing at Kuantan, 10 miles north of Singapore. At 00.50 hours on 10th December, Force Z altered to a south-westerly course towards Kuantan. They were sighted at 02.20 hours by the Japanese submarine I58, which reported their position and course. The Japanese had already made several air searches for Force Z, and upon receipt of this news organised another, followed by the launching of an air-striking force of thirty bombers and fifty torpedo-bombers.

At 08.00 hours, Force Z arrived off Kuantan, but found no sign of an enemy invasion fleet. Admiral Phillips decided to search to the north-east in case the Japanese force (in fact, it was non-existent) had not yet arrived. Enemy aircraft had been sighted at 06.30 hours that morning, and shortly after Force Z had begun their search, *Tenedos*, still on her way back to Singapore, reported that she was under air attack. With a serious risk of air attack developing, and no sign of the air cover from the mainland that had been promised, Admiral Phillips decided to abandon the search and steer for Singapore.

At 11.00 hours, enemy aircraft were detected by the radar of *Repulse* and *Prince of Wales*. At this time, Force Z was steering 095 degrees at a speed of twenty knots, with the ships at first degree anti-aircraft readiness. The sea was calm, and the visibility was good. Nine high-level bombers soon came into view and approached the ships in a tight line-abreast formation at a height of approximately 10,000 feet. The two capital ships increased speed to twenty-five knots, and at 11.13 hours, the 5.25-inch guns of *Prince of Wales* opened fire, followed shortly afterwards by the 4-inch guns of *Repulse*. The aircraft passed down the starboard side of *Prince of Wales* and attacked *Repulse* from ahead, each dropping one 550-pound bomb simultaneously. At 11.18 hours one bomb hit and passed through the battlecruiser's port hangar and burst on the armoured-deck, below the marine's mess-deck. The explosion started a fire, and fractured several steam pipes, making conditions between decks very difficult for the ship's personnel, but otherwise causing no serious damage. A second bomb narrowly missed the starboard side, abreast 'B' turret, and the remainder fell close to the port side. The enemy's approach from ahead, and their alterations of course, made sustained AA fire difficult and comparatively ineffective, but *Repulse* managed to shoot down one aircraft. By the time the second attack developed, 30 minutes later, the fire in *Repulse* had been brought under control.

At 11.30 hours, *Prince of Wales* detected on her radar, another group of enemy aircraft approaching from starboard. Nine torpedo-bombers, in line-astern formation, crossed ahead of *Prince of Wales* at extreme range, and using cloud on the port beam to hide their movements, made a series of turns and attacked the battleship in waves of two or three. *Prince of Wales* opened fire at 11.41½ hours, and hit two of the aircraft. They crashed into the sea on the starboard side, after having released their torpedoes. Another aircraft, seen making off at sea level, was claimed as possibly damaged. The attack was

Below: *Prince of Wales* on 28th August 1941. *Repulse* is just visible in the background.

exceptionally well executed, the aircraft approached in line abreast, and were in no way deterred by the battleship's anti-aircraft fire. The torpedoes were released at ranges of between 1,000 and 2,000 yards and from a height that was "noticeably greater" than British practice. They ran very straight, and their tracks were easily visible. *Prince of Wales* turned to port, to comb the tracks, and so avoided all the torpedoes except one, which struck the ship (at 11.44½ hours) on the port side abreast 'P4' 5.25-inch gun-turret. The concussion was very heavy, and later it was thought that she might have been hit by two torpedoes, but only one explosion was seen and the idea was rejected for lack of supporting evidence. The damage caused by this one torpedo, which was thought to have carried

a charge of 867 pounds was catastrophic, and as good as guaranteed the ultimate destruction of *Prince of Wales*. She rapidly listed 11½ degrees to port and, with both port propeller shafts stopped, her speed dropped to fifteen knots. The steering gear was also out of action, and the ship was never again under complete control. The explosion seriously damaged the port outer propeller shaft, which was badly distorted and as a result, all the watertight bulkheads in the shaft passage and machinery spaces through which the shaft passed, were open to the sea. (This shaft extended from the port forward engine room ('B' engine room) through the wing compartments abreast the after engine room, boiler room and magazines.) Flooding occurred in the underwater-protection compartments, and in the wing compartments inboard of the protective bulkhead abreast 'Y' engine room. The flooding spread forward into the diesel-generator room abreast 'Y' boiler room, and later into 'Y' boiler room itself, which, when last seen, had eight feet of water in it. It also spread aft into 'P3' and 'P4' 5.25-inch magazines and shell rooms, and then across the ship to 'S3' and 'S4' magazines and shell rooms. The flooding and shock damage put five of the ship's eight dynamos out of action, and electric power failed for all the services fed from the after section of the ring main. The remaining three turbo-generators continued to supply power while steam lasted, except that the power-supply breaker to one of them came off when the first torpedo exploded but the circuit was remade almost immediately. The failure of power and the list of the ship rendered all the 5.25-inch turrets, with the exception of 'S1' and 'S2', inoperative as shown below:

'P1': Training jammed because of mechanical fouling of the mechanism. It was later cleared, but it was still found impossible to train the turret against the list, i.e., up-hill, in power or by hand. The cause was not traced.

'P2': Power failed apparently as the result of an electrical overload. Emergency electric leads were rigged, but power was later restored, and they were not used. The turret, however, could not be trained until the list was reduced, after the second attack on *Prince of Wales*. This turret continued to fire thereafter, until the end, when the electro-hydraulic pump had to be stopped because of a bad oil leak.

'P3' & 'P4': Out of action through power failure, it was found impossible to train the turrets by hand.

'S1': Training jammed but freed itself almost immediately, and the turret remained in action until the end.

'S2': Turret was operative but extremely difficult to train; it was, nevertheless, in action until the end.

'S3' & 'S4': Out of action through power failure. It was found impossible to train the turrets by hand. An emergency power supply was rigged for both turrets, but this failed.

The failure of electric power aft, seriously affected the ship's pumps, steering gear and internal communications. The primary power for the pom-pom mountings amidships, failed, but they were able to switch over to secondary supplies. The depth of the underwater protection at the point where the torpedo struck was, theoretically, sufficient to withstand the explosion and prevent excessive damage or flooding inboard of the protective bulkhead. There are two possible explanations for the failure of the system. (a) That two torpedoes, not one, struck the ship simultaneously in about the same area. (b) That the torpedo struck the ship at the turn of the bilge, where the protective system was more vulnerable, and the force of the explosion damaged and opened up the protective bulkhead at its lower edge.

The Captain of *Prince of Wales* ordered counter-flooding, and while her crew were endeavouring to restore order, the enemy delivered two more attacks against *Repulse*. The first, at 11.56 hours, was carried out by eight or nine torpedo-bombers from the port side. *Repulse* succeeded in combing the tracks of the torpedoes and was not hit. Two minutes later, she was attacked by a formation of high-level bombers, which were fired on by both *Repulse* and *Prince of Wales*, and one aircraft was believed to have been shot down. Again, *Repulse* was not hit, and after the attack was over, she turned back to rejoin the flagship. At 12.10 hours, *Prince of Wales* hoisted the signal "not under control" and ten minutes later, the next attack, by nine torpedo-bombers, began. Three of the aircraft attacked *Repulse* at a moment when she was committed to a turn to starboard. She was hit by one torpedo on the port side amidships, but withstood the damage well, and continued to manoeuvre at twenty-five knots. The remaining aircraft attacked *Prince of Wales* in two waves of three and, after dropping their torpedoes, passed very close to the ship firing machine-guns at the superstructure. One of the aircraft was shot down. The battleship was incapable of taking avoiding action, and was hit by four torpedoes on the starboard side. The first two struck at 12.21 hours, one abreast the forward breakwater, and the second, below 'S4' turret. The third struck half a minute later, abreast 'B' turret and the fourth, at 12.23 hours, in the after cabin-flats. The starboard outer propeller shaft stopped and the ship's speed dropped to eight knots. The flooding of the starboard side reduced the ship's list to three degrees to port. In this state, she had a trim aft, of about twenty feet.

This attack had barely ceased when, at 12.25 hours, nine torpedo-bombers descended on *Repulse* from several directions. A torpedo hit her abreast the gun-room aft on the port side and jammed the rudder. Steaming at twenty knots, and out of control, the ship was hit by three more torpedoes, one aft and one abreast the engine rooms on the port side, and one abreast 'E' boiler room on the starboard side. She turned sharply to starboard, and gradually came to a halt, listing heavily to port. Captain Tennant, the commander of *Repulse*, realised that his ship would soon

Right: an anchor party at work on *Repulse*.

sink, and ordered his crew to prepare to abandon ship. The ship's broadcasting system for the most part, was fully operational, and this, together with Captain Tennant's timely decision, saved most of the crew. The ship rapidly listed to port, and after a pause of about two minutes at approximately sixty-five degrees, she rolled over, at 12.33 hours, and sank two minutes later, in position 3° 45′ N, 104° 24′ E. The destroyers *Electra* and *Vampire* picked up 796 survivors, including Captain Tennant. Before she sank, *Repulse* shot down two of the aircraft that had made the final attack against her.

The final attack on *Prince of Wales*, was carried out at 12.42 hours, by nine high-level bombers approaching the ship from ahead. She was hit near 'S3' turret by one 500-pound bomb, which burst on the main-deck, and there were near misses on both sides aft. The hit did not penetrate the armoured-deck, but the near misses may well have added to her underwater damage. The ship's speed had, by this time, dropped to six knots, and she was steering northwards. At 13.05 hours, the destroyer *Express* came alongside the flagship to disembark wounded and non-essential personnel. By 13.10 hours, *Prince of Wales* was settling rapidly with a heavy list to port. *Express* remained alongside until the last possible moment. At 13.20 hours the battleship listed sharply to port, and then rolled over and sank, one hour and twenty minutes after the first torpedo had struck. A squadron of Buffalo aircraft from Sembawang arrived on the scene while *Express* and *Electra* were picking up survivors.

A certain amount of confusion seems to exist, even in official documents, as to how many torpedoes actually hit *Prince of Wales.* The number varies from one to three hits in the first attack and from three to four in the second. It was stated, however, in a diary kept on the admiral's bridge, that there was definitely only one explosion after the first torpedo attack. It is interesting to note that whatever the correct number may be, there were probably more (perhaps as many as three more) hits on the starboard side, than on the port side, and yet the ship listed to port.

The lessons learnt as a result of the loss of *Prince of Wales* are as follows.

1. The space above the underwater-protection compartments on the lower-deck was employed for crew's wash places, etc., and this was found to diminish the value of the underwater protection and watertight integrity of the ship. In *Vanguard*, the bulkheads of the sandwich protection were carried up to the middle-deck, thus increasing its height and providing a high degree of watertight sub-division behind the side armour. It was also suggested that the deck armour be terminated at the protective bulkhead, to allow an underwater explosion to vent itself upwards and outside of the citadel, proper. This would have also saved weight, but would have resulted in increased vulnerability to bombs.

2. Too much reliance had been placed on electrically-driven auxiliaries. Electricity provided the power for working the secondary and anti-aircraft armaments, steering gear, a large proportion of the ship's pumps, and most of the internal communication system. In addition, the proportion of diesel- and turbo-driven generators was not sufficiently balanced. The two diesel-generators were put out of action by the first explosion, which left only turbo-generators in operation. Although on this occasion, the effect was not serious, these could only operate so long as steam-power lasted. In *Vanguard*, the proportion of diesel/turbo-generators was changed from 2/6 to 4/4, and the proportion of steam-driven auxiliaries was also increased. At first sight, these requirements may appear to conflict with each other, but it was intended to reduce the amount of dependence on any one system.

3. It was necessary to provide trunked-access to important machinery compartments.

4. Air-escape pipes, to tanks, etc., required the fitting of valves so that they could be shut off.

5. Side scuttles, ventilation systems, watertight doors and hatches through which flooding could spread, required to be reduced to a minimum.

6. It was necessary to provide rapid pumping arrangements for the compartments immediately inboard of the protective bulkhead.

7. The number and distribution of portable pumps was inadequate.

8. It was necessary to continue watertight bulkheads as high as possible.

9. The watertightness of the 5.25-inch ammunition supplies required improvement; when 'P3' and 'P4' magazines flooded, the doors at the top of the fixed hoists had been shut, but it was found that they were no longer watertight.

10. Scuppers and drains were not sufficiently watertight and required improvement.

11. The steering gear having failed from loss of electric power, it was decided to review the question of providing steam- or electrically-driven pumps for this equipment.

12. Bulkhead-glands for long propeller shafts required redesign to remain watertight if the shaft became slightly out of true. It was also decided to re-examine the question of the number of plummer-blocks provided on long shafting.

13. The sound-powered telephone system needed to be extended and the essential communication services required duplication and watertightness. The communication system for the damage-control organisation needed to be sound-powered and independent of the main telephone-exchange.

14. The personnel in the damage-control head-quarters required reorganisation and the head-quarters itself, needed to be more easily accessible.

15. The shipwright complement of *Prince of Wales* was too small to be able to deal with the damage.

16. Draught-indicators were necessary.

The torpedoing of *Ramillies*, 1942

On 30th May 1942, *Ramillies* lay at anchor in the inner harbour of Diego Suarez Bay, at the northern end of Madagascar, having taken part earlier that month, in the occupation of

Left: *Ramillies.* The top-left picture shows her in 1941, without radar or 20 mm guns. Zarebas have been fitted around the twin 4-inch guns. The other illustrations show her in mid 1943, after refit.

the island. During the afternoon of that day, two Japanese midget submarines penetrated the harbour and, between 20.00 hours and 21.00 hours, torpedoed *Ramillies* and a tanker. The torpedo aimed at the battleship, exploded against the port bulge just forward of 'A' turret, and holed the bulge and the bottom plating. The hole in the bulge measured thirty feet x thirty feet, and that in the outer bottom twenty feet x sixteen feet. Internal damage extended from the inner bottom to the lower-deck, and as far inboard as the middle-line. The forward 4-inch magazines, 'A' and 'B' 15-inch magazines and shell rooms, the high-angle control-position and other compartments in the vicinity up to the level of the main-deck, were flooded. Extensive damage was caused to the gunnery and electrical equipment in the vicinity of the explosion, and all lighting, power supplies and telephone communications, forward of 'B' turret, failed. Only minor damage occurred outside the fore part of the ship, and the main machinery was undamaged. Temporary repairs were completed on 3rd June, when she proceeded to Durban, where permanent repairs were carried out. *Ramillies* was out of action for a total of twelve months.

4. SHORE SUPPORT, 1940 to 1945

During the Second World War, most of the battleships of the Royal Navy were called upon, at one time or another, to lend the support of their big guns to an amphibious landing. The big gun had several advantages:

1. The heavy guns of battleships and monitors were the only guns that were effective against heavily-protected targets. (Nevertheless, in 1943, it was estimated that an average of 640 rounds of 15-inch shell would have to be fired, to score a direct hit on a single gun in a concrete emplacement.)

2. The longer range of the big gun enabled it to fire much farther inland than smaller weapons, and it could therefore, give a more versatile level of fire support.

3. The big gun had a good morale effect on the troops of the invasion force, and a bad effect on the troops of the defenders.

Of these advantages, the second was probably the most important and often proved of great value. *Rodney*, for example, once fired on a target that was seventeen miles inland, thereby allowing a more rapid advance by the troops in that area, than would otherwise have been possible. Nevertheless, for general bombardment purposes, the cruiser was of greater value. The 6-inch guns of these ships, although smaller, could deliver a much higher rate of fire, and the saturating effect of a large number of small shells on an open target could be much more destructive than a few 15-inch shells. It was estimated that an open battery of four guns, in an area of two hundred x fifteen yards, could be neutralised by a rate of fire of either eleven 15-inch shells per minute, or thirty-eight 6-inch shells per minute. A battleship armed with eight 15-inch guns could just achieve the former; a cruiser armed with nine 6-inch guns could fire seventy rounds per minute.

Dakar, 1940

In September 1940, an unsuccessful attempt was made to land a Free French force at Dakar, on the coast of the Vichy French colony of Senegal, in West Africa. Among the naval forces allocated to support this operation, code-named 'Menace', were the battleships *Barham* and *Resolution*. The details of the events that led to the eventual abandonment of the operation, read like the libretto of a comic opera, and are too involved to detail here. We must concentrate upon the movements of the two battleships.

At 09.37 hours on 24th September, *Barham* and *Resolution*, together with the cruisers *Australia* and *Devonshire*, opened fire on the French warships, including the battleship *Richelieu*, in Dakar harbour, at a range of approximately 16,000 yards. Visibility was poor, and conditions were far from ideal for a long-range bombardment, and the fire of the shore batteries prevented the British battleships from closing. The situation worsened when a French destroyer laid a smoke-screen across the harbour, and the battleships withdrew at 10.10 hours, having achieved little. During the bombardment, *Barham* was struck by two shells, probably from the shore batteries and judged to have been of 6.1-inch and 9.4-inch calibre. The 6.1-inch shell hit and exploded in the upper bulge abreast 'B' turret, on the starboard side, making a hole four feet in diameter in the bulge plating. The upper and lower bulge compartments in the vicinity were opened to the sea, but otherwise, no major damage was caused. The 9.4-inch shell hit the starboard side of the forward shelter-deck, passed through the superstructure and finally detonated on impact with the port paravane-davit. Minor splinter damage was caused to the superstructure.

The battleships began their second bombardment shortly before midday, and this was equally ineffective. *Richelieu* received minor splinter damage, and *Resolution* received four minor hits. The British fleet withdrew at 14.00 hours, but returned on the following morning with the object of renewing the bombardment, and landing British troops. At 09.02 hours on 25th September, as the two battleships approached their bombarding positions, *Resolution* was torpedoed by the French submarine *Beveziers.* The ship was manoeuvring at a speed of nineteen knots when the torpedo exploded on her port side, abreast the forward boiler room. The full depth of the bulge structure was wrecked for a length of fifty feet, and the double bottom was destroyed for a length of thirty feet. The forward boiler room flooded slowly through leaks in the protective bulkhead, and the bulge compartments, fore and aft of the damaged area also flooded slowly. The port 6-inch battery was damaged by the heavy column of solid water thrown up by the explosion, and two small fires were caused by electrical failures, but these were quickly extinguished. One hour after the explosion, another fire, caused by leaking oil fuel, was discovered in the forward boiler room but this was extinguished as the

Below: *Resolution*, after repair and refit, in mid-1942.

Bottom of page: *Nelson* on 20th June 1942.

boiler room flooded. *Resolution* heeled to an angle of twelve degrees, which made it impossible to train the main armament, and she withdrew from the scene. The initial list was corrected by transferring oil fuel and shifting portable equipment. Four and a half hours after having been torpedoed, the ship was temporarily immobilised as the result of a failure in the main machinery forced-lubrication system.

Barham continued with the operation and opened fire shortly after 09.00 hours. At 19.19 hours, one of her 15-inch shells hit *Richelieu* but caused no serious damage, and this bombardment was generally as ineffectual as those of the previous day. *Richelieu* returned the compliment by achieving a near miss with one of her 15-inch shells, which exploded underwater on *Barham*'s starboard side, amidships. The bulge structure in the immediate area was forced inboard, and was sufficiently strained to allow slow flooding of the lower bulge compartments. Later that morning, it was decided to abandon the attack on Dakar, and all the forces involved, withdrew to Freetown. During the withdrawal, *Barham* took the damaged *Resolution* in tow, and both ships arrived safely at their destination. *Resolution* subsequently received permanent damage repairs at Philadelphia, between April and September 1941.

North Africa, 1942

In November 1942, Allied forces landed in North Africa, in the areas of Oran, Algiers and Casablanca. Code-named 'Operation Torch', it was one of the first of several successful large-scale amphibious assaults that were carried out during the war. The British capital ships, *Duke of York*, *Renown*, *Rodney* and *Nelson*, were largely concerned with protecting the invasion force from interference by enemy surface ships, but no such threat developed. Only *Rodney* was employed in a fire-support role. On three occasions, she bombarded Fort-du-Santon, which was situated on a hill overlooking Oran. The last occasion was in support of US troops operating in the area. *Rodney* used her Walrus air-

Left: *Howe* in November 1942.

craft for spotting purposes during these bombardments, but the machine was so badly damaged by enemy anti-aircraft fire that it was considered beyond repair, and was deliberately jettisonned and sunk by gunfire.

Sicily, 1943

Among the forces covering the invasion of Sicily ('Operation Husky'), from July to September 1943, were the battleships, *Nelson*, *Rodney*, *Valiant*, *Warspite*, *Howe* and *King George V*. Again, their prime purpose was to protect the invasion force from the possible intervention of the Italian fleet, and only two bombardments were undertaken. The first was carried out by *King George V* and *Howe* during the night of 11/12th July, against Trapani and Marsala, at the western end of the island. This was intended to mislead the enemy and draw troops away from the main assault in the south-eastern sector of the island. The second was carried out by *Warspite* on 17th July, against enemy artillery positions around the town of Catania. The ship fired fifty-seven 15-inch shells, without seriously weakening the enemy position, and the army eventually by-passed the town. While steaming to carry out this bombardment, *Warspite* was estimated to have achieved a speed of 23.5 knots.

Salerno, 1943

The British capital ships that had covered the landings in Sicily, were also assigned to protect the assault force that was to invade the Italian mainland at Salerno ('Operation Avalanche'). The operation was due to take place on the 9th September, and as a preliminary to the main assault, it was decided to bombard the enemy defences at Reggio in the Straits of Messina. The area was first bombarded by *Rodney* and *Nelson* on 31st August, and *Rodney* scored a direct hit on an ammunition dump, thereby adding a spectacular explosion to an otherwise straightforward operation. The second bombardment was carried out by *Warspite* and *Valiant* on 2nd September. One of *Warspite*'s targets was a 6-inch gun-battery,

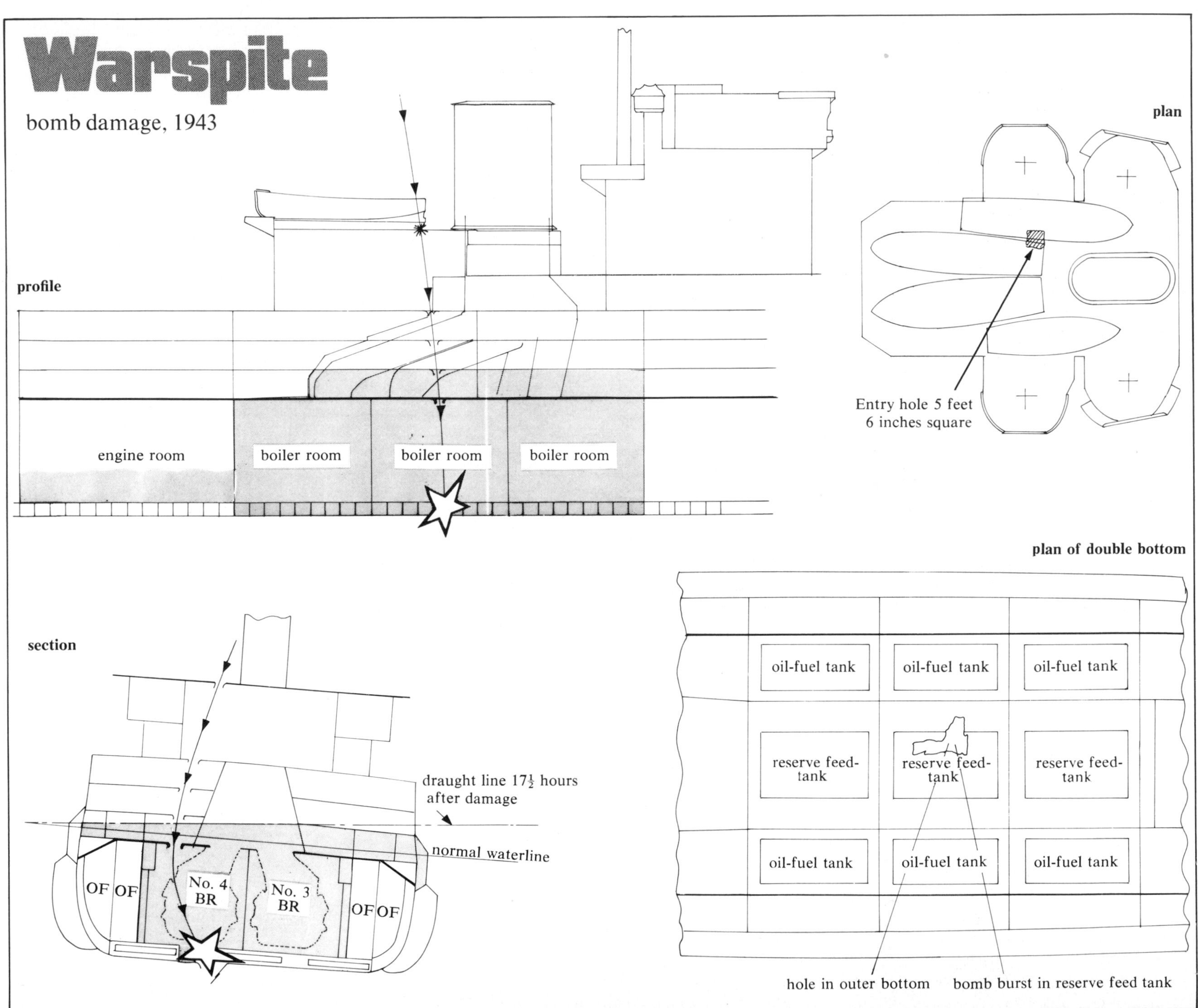
Warspite
bomb damage, 1943
plan
profile
Entry hole 5 feet
6 inches square
engine room
boiler room
boiler room
boiler room
plan of double bottom
section
oil-fuel tank
oil-fuel tank
oil-fuel tank
reserve feed-tank
reserve feed-tank
reserve feed-tank
draught line 17½ hours after damage
normal waterline
oil-fuel tank
oil-fuel tank
oil-fuel tank
OF
OF
No. 4 BR
No. 3 BR
OF
OF
hole in outer bottom
bomb burst in reserve feed tank

and this was inspected when the area had been taken by Allied troops. The battery had received no direct hits, but was surrounded by shell craters and apparently the bombardment had so disturbed the battery's personnel that they had abandoned their post.

On 8th September 1943, Italy surrendered and the British capital ships were released from their role of protecting the assault force from the Italian fleet. *Warspite* and *Valiant* were detailed to meet the surrendering Italian fleet and escort it into Malta, and *King George V* and *Howe* were sent to Taranto. After these operations had been carried out, the battleships were held in reserve in case their guns were needed to support the Salerno beachhead. Only one such demand was made; on 14th September, *Warspite* and *Valiant* had just sailed from Malta for the UK, when they were ordered to return to Salerno for bombardment duties. Arriving off the beachhead on the afternoon of 15th September, *Valiant* took up a position in the northern sector and *Warspite* occupied the southern sector. The battleships bombarded various enemy positions between 17.00 hours and nightfall, when they withdrew until the following day. The bombardments continued throughout the morning of the 16th, and during the afternoon, *Valiant* retired from action. *Warspite*, in the meantime, had suffered during an air attack.

Shortly after completing her third bombardment at 14.00 hours, *Warspite* was attacked by twelve FW 190 fighter-bombers. This attack was successfully repulsed, but drew attention away from another threat in the shape of three radio-controlled bombs that had been launched by their parent aircraft from a height of 20,000 feet. These armour-piercing bombs, known as FX 1400, could be guided on to their target as they descended. They weighed about 3,000 pounds, and when launched from the correct height, had a terminal velocity of about 800 feet per second. When the three bombs were first sighted by *Warspite*, they were at a height of about 7,000 feet and almost directly overhead. The first scored a direct hit amidships and penetrated all the ship's decks, including the armoured deck, passed through No. 4 boiler room and exploded in the double bottom. The detonation opened up the outer bottom over an area twenty feet long and seven to fourteen feet wide, and the inner bottom was holed and blown upwards over this area. No. 4 boiler room was completely wrecked, and all the bulkheads in the vicinity were buckled and damaged by splinters. It seemed as if the second bomb would miss the ship completely, but its line of descent suddenly changed, and, narrowly missing the ship on the starboard side, it exploded underwater, abreast No. 5 boiler room. The inner and outer bottom plating below this boiler room became corrugated, and the bulge plating was holed and distorted. The third bomb exploded in the sea off the starboard quarter, but it was too far away to do any damage. The immediate result of the direct hit and near miss was the flooding of five of the ship's six boiler rooms, together with the double-bottom compartments, oil-fuel compartments, lower bulge and cable passages in the vicinity of the boiler rooms. Slow flooding occurred in No. 1 boiler room, the engine rooms, two of the dynamo rooms, shaft passages and various wing compartments abreast the machinery spaces. All the boilers were damaged by shock, and the boiler-feed water was contaminated by sea water and oil, but No. 1 boiler managed to supply sufficient steam to the turbines, which were undamaged, and the ship was able to steam slowly away from the beachhead. This boiler eventually succumbed to the damage at 15.00 hours, leaving the ship without motive power. Most of the electric power failed, as a result of the loss of steam, but the diesel-generators supplied sufficient electrical power for the essential services. Loss of steam, shock damage, and flooding also put the radar and wireless equipment and the hydraulic-power supply for the main armament out of action.

The ship was eventually taken in tow and reached Malta at 08.00 hours on 19th September, more than two and half days after being damaged. She had taken in about 5,000 tons of water, and had a heavy trim by the bow and a four degree list to starboard. At Malta, she was patched up sufficiently to make her seaworthy, and on 1st November, she made for Gibraltar, towed by four tugs and escorted by four destroyers. She arrived seven days later and was dry docked on 12th November, but only partial repairs were carried out because the ship was required as part of the covering force for the invasion of Normandy. She sailed from Gibraltar for the UK on 9th March 1944, with two of her 15-inch turrets and No. 4 boiler room inoperative. Further repairs were carried out by Rosyth Dockyard during the latter half of March, during which time one of the turrets was repaired, leaving only 'X' turret inoperative. No attempt was ever made to repair the damage to No. 4 boiler room, but the bulkheads were made watertight, and a caisson was fitted over the hole in the ship's bottom. It is not understood why the 15-inch turrets should have been out of action; as far as is known, the main armament was not damaged by the bombs, which detonated some considerable distance from both the forward and after turrets.

Normandy, 1944

By comparison with earlier landings, those made at Normandy in June 1944 received a substantial amount of fire support from battleships. Moreover, this support continued for several months, as the ships moved eastwards along the coast, following the advancing Allied armies, and providing mobile bombardment facilities when required. In most cases, the results obtained by the heavy guns justified their employment, particularly those of *Rodney* and *Nelson*, whose guns could fire effectively at a considerable range. The gunfire was generally very accurate, and the majority of the targets which the battleships engaged were neutralised. This success was largely the result of an extensive programme of bombardment exercises and training that had been carried out before the landings, and of the use of air-spotting by naval fighter-pilots and land-based spotting-officers to

Below: *Malaya* in 1944. Her 6-inch guns have been removed and she carries the aerials for Type '650' jamming-gear on the after superstructure.

correct the gunfire. Few direct hits were scored on heavily-protected gun positions, and the most successful firings were against open gun-batteries, troop concentrations, armoured and unarmoured vehicle columns, and other unprotected targets occupying large areas.

Four battleships were assigned to the Bombardment Force, and two of these, *Warspite* and *Ramillies*, were present during the initial landings on the morning of 6th June 1944, while the second pair, *Rodney* and *Nelson*, were kept in reserve at Portsmouth. *Warspite* and *Ramillies*, together with the monitor *Roberts* and the cruisers *Mauritius*, *Arethusa*, *Frobisher* and *Dragon*, were assigned to protect the eastern flank of the assault area, and to bombard the shore batteries between Ouistreham and Le Havre. The two battleships and the monitor concentrated their fire on the heavily-fortified gun-batteries at Villerville, Benerville and Houlgate and had succeeded in silencing them by 09.30 hours. These batteries, however, were very heavily protected by reinforced concrete, and throughout this and the following day they required constant attention to keep them quiet. For example, on 6th June, *Warspite* engaged the battery at Villerville on six separate occasions, firing a total of seventy-three shells at this one target, and scoring nine direct hits, three of which were obtained in the first bombardment.

The two-gun battery at Benerville, which was the principal target of *Ramillies*, was similarly stubborn, and, although silenced several times, received no direct hits. During the afternoon, the Bombardment Force was reinforced by *Rodney*, but, between this time and her return to Portsmouth that evening, she fired only two 16-inch shells. These projectiles were aimed at gun-positions in the area of Le Havre, that had fired on a large convoy of landing-craft. They ceased fire when the convoy was hidden by a smoke-screen.

On 7th June, *Warspite* bombarded a variety of targets including the Benerville battery. Since the beginning of the landings, she had fired 314 15-inch shells (133 armour-piercing and 181 high explosive) and on the evening of 7th June, she returned to Portsmouth to replenish her ammunition.

Rodney rejoined the Bombardment Force on 7th June, and remained off the beaches for the next three days. Her first bombardment began at 18.30 hours on 7th June, and during the next two hours, she fired 200 rounds of 16-inch and 100 rounds of 6-inch at three targets in the area of Caen. During the next two days, she continued to bombard targets in and about this area, but on 8th June, she fired her 6-inch guns only. On 9th June, she also engaged the batteries at Benerville and Houlgate, before returning to Portsmouth to re-ammunition. Her place was taken by *Nelson* which, between 10th and 18th June, carried out twenty bombardments, firing 225 rounds of 16-inch and 687 rounds of 6-inch at targets that included the Houlgate battery, troop concentrations and enemy vehicles.

Warspite also returned on 10th June, but was diverted to support the American beachhead to the west, because the bombardment force in that area was short of ammunition. She fired ninety-six 15-inch shells at four targets and, despite the lack of air-spotting facilities achieved sufficient success to earn the gratitude of the US Army Commander. On 11th June, she returned to the British sector in the area of Arromanches, where she used her guns to break up a threatened counter-attack against the British 50th Division.

During the evening of 11th June, *Warspite* returned to Portsmouth, but on the following day was ordered to Rosyth to have her badly worn guns replaced. On 13th June, when about twenty-eight miles east of Harwich, she detonated an accoustic or pressure-operated mine, which was lying in the swept channel at a depth of seventeen fathoms. The mine, containing a charge of approximately 1,500 pounds, exploded on her port side, abreast 'Y' turret, and jammed the ship's rudder to starboard. Steaming at sixteen knots, *Warspite* made a sharp turn to starboard and eventually came to a halt with her main engines out of action, and a list to port of four and a half degrees. Damage to the ship's structure was extensive. Abreast the engine rooms and after magazines, the port bulge plating, and the outer bottom plating below this bulge, became

corrugated for a length of 150 feet. Between the two after turrets, the bulge structure was forced inboard to a maximum depth of two feet. Minor structural damage was also sustained by the inner bottom and the starboard bulge plating. Extensive flooding occurred in the port bulge, and minor flooding in the double-bottom compartments.

The main and auxiliary machinery was extensively damaged by shock, together with the electrical equipment, wireless and radar sets. The port outer propeller shaft seized and the port inner shaft was out of action with several plummer-blocks fractured. The gearing and thrust-block of the port inner high-pressure turbine were damaged and put out of action, and the fixed and sliding feet (mountings) of both this and the starboard inner high-pressure turbines were fractured.

The list was corrected by counter-flooding, and the transfer of oil fuel, and she was eventually able to proceed on her starboard engines, at ten knots, and arrived at Rosyth Dockyard on 14th June. Here, she was repaired sufficiently to allow her to continue operations as a bombardment ship. Her hull was patched up, and the two inner shafts that, in normal circumstances, would have been removed, were repaired 'in-situ'. No attempt was made to repair the port outer shaft which remained seized for the rest of the ship's life. In August, she ran trials on three shafts, two of which were running out of true, and achieved a maximum speed of 15.5 knots.

The Bombardment Force was again reduced on 18th June when *Nelson*, while returning to Portsmouth at 16 knots to re-ammunition, ran over and detonated two ground mines which were judged to contain charges of 1,500 pounds and to have been accoustically operated. They exploded almost simultaneously, one under the forward part of the ship and the other about 150 feet to starboard, abreast the bridge. The outer bottom plating became corrugated, and the double-bottom compartments were damaged from 'A' turret to the forward bulkhead of the engine rooms. Forward of 'A' turret, the double-bottom compartments below the store-rooms were also damaged. Flooding occurred in one of the wing spaces, and in several of the double-bottom oil-fuel tanks, and slow but controlled flooding occurred in the majority of the wing compartments, abreast the damage. The ship listed three degrees to starboard, but this was reduced to one degree by pumping out some of the buoyancy spaces on the starboard side. Shock damage was extensive, but generally of a minor nature, and affected the secondary armament-directors, ADO sights, radar, gyro-compass and 16-inch fire-control equipment. The ship was made "operationally fit" at Portsmouth in twenty-four hours, but permanent repairs were necessary, and eventually she proceeded to the USA, for refit and damage repairs.

Below: *Rodney* showing her appearance just two weeks prior to the Normandy landing. Note the aerials for Type '650' jamming-equipment fitted to outriggers on either side of the bridge.

Left: *Rodney* supporting the Normandy landings.

The temporary loss of *Warspite* and *Nelson*, and later, the withdrawal of *Ramillies*, which was needed for the invasion of the South of France, left only *Rodney*, and the monitors *Erebus* and *Roberts* to provide heavy gun support. *Malaya*, which had been placed in reserve at Gareloch, Dumbartonshire in October 1943, and used as an accommodation for army personnel, was hurriedly recommissioned for service with the bombardment squadron. She worked-up at Scapa Flow, and then sailed south for Portsmouth, but, in the event, she was not really required. She carried out only one operation, the bombardment of the island of Cezanne, in St. Malo Bay.

Rodney had taken over from *Nelson* on 18th June, but on the following day, bad weather almost brought the offensive activities of the naval forces to a standstill. Gales and heavy seas continued for almost a week, but eventually abated, allowing normal operations to be resumed. On 30th June, *Rodney* bombarded a concentration of armoured vehicles, seventeen miles inland, to the south of Arromanches. The enemy force, which had been preparing a counter-attack, was completely scattered.

During the afternoon of 8th July, *Rodney*, *Roberts* and the cruisers *Belfast* and *Emerald* began a long-range bombardment of Caen, in support of the assault on that town. The bombardments continued throughout 9th July, and during this second day, *Rodney* fired ninety rounds of 16-inch armour-piercing and high explosive shell.

The effect of *Rodney*'s shelling is described by Kenneth Thompson in *HMS Rodney at War*: "Quite by chance I afterwards heard what this bombardment was like from the receiving end. The story comes from an Englishman who was hiding from the Germans in Caen. He was fed and sheltered by a French family and he survived most of the raids on Caen, including the one made by over four hundred heavy bombers. Nothing, he said, was quite so demoralising as the *Rodney*'s shelling. It was uncannily accurate and the only consolation he had was watching the shells apparently remorselessly pursuing the fleeing Germans."

The town was captured on 9th July, and on 18th July, the same bombardment force was called in to provide fire support for the Second Army's assault to the south-east of Caen. *Rodney* continued to support the army's advance until the end of July, when she sailed for Devonport. From here, she made a brief excursion to bombard the island of Alderney, and then returned to Devonport, before sailing to Scapa Flow, early in September.

On 25th August, the partially-crippled *Warspite* rejoined the bombardment force. Her first targets were the coastal-defence guns at Brest, which were interfering with the advance of the American Army. (During that day she fired 213 15-inch shells.) She then moved back to the old bombardment areas in the west, and early in September bombarded the defences of Le Havre, in support of the advance of the British 49th and 51st Divisions. On 1st November, she carried out her last bombardments, in support of the assault on the island of Walcheren, in the mouth of the river Scheldt. During their shore-support operations in Northern Europe between 6th June and 10th September, the British battleships and monitors fired a total of 3,371 16-inch and 15-inch shells, and 1,034 6-inch projectiles.

The South of France, 1944

Only one British battleship, *Ramillies*, was attached to the bombardment force for the invasion of the South of France, which took place in the area between Toulon and Cannes on 15th August 1944. On the first day of the landings, *Ramillies* was called upon to bombard the fortifications on the island of Port Cros, which was captured two days later. She also fired a few rounds at one of the coast batteries to the south of St. Tropez. On 25th August she joined the forces bombarding the coastal defences of Toulon and Marseilles, and carried out several shoots before the towns were captured by the Allies on 28th August.

Below: *King George V* in Pacific waters during 1945.

Right: *Duke of York* arriving in Sydney on 1st July 1945.

Bombardments in the Far East and Pacific Ocean, 1945

The battleships of the Eastern Fleet and the British Pacific Fleet, were employed on few bombardment operations and, particularly in the case of the Pacific Fleet, they served mainly as floating AA batteries. The main bombardment operations of 1945 are summarised below:

21st January 1945. *Queen Elizabeth* formed part of the fire-support squadron provided for the invasion of the island of Ramree off the west coast of Burma.

4th May 1945. *King George V* and *Howe* bombarded Hirara airfield, on the island of Miyako Shima, part of the Sakishima Gunto group, east of Formosa. In four and a half hours, the battleships fired 195 rounds of 14-inch and 378 rounds of 5.25-inch. Very effective bombardment, suppressing Japanese AA defence.

6th May 1945. *Queen Elizabeth* bombarded enemy gun-positions covering Stewart Sound in the Andaman Islands, to the north-west of Malaya.

17th July 1945. *King George V* joined a US force in the bombardment of the industrial areas around Hitachi, north of Tokyo. The attack was made at night, and in three hours, *King George V* fired 267 rounds of 14-inch shell against three separate enemy engineering works.

29th July 1945. *King George V* again joined a US force, to bombard an industrial area, by night. This time, the targets were in the area of Hammamatsu, south of Tokyo. The battleship fired 265 14-inch shells at her target in about forty minutes, but although the area was saturated, she achieved only seven direct hits. This was the last occasion on which a British battleship fired her heavy guns in wartime.

17. Cause and Effect

As might be expected, the development and improvement of naval material during the period 1939 to 1945, was rapid and extensive. Some of these developments, such as radar, were merely accelerated by the war, but others, such as the improvement of AA defence, became necessary because of pre-war over- or under-estimation of the performance to be expected of various weapons and equipment. The Second World War – unlike the First – revealed few fundamental weaknesses in the design of British capital ships. The one major exception was the damage-control system, together with its equipment, which in many cases proved inadequate for its task. This difficulty was compounded by weak points in the distribution of electrical power, watertight integrity and pumping systems. Most of these problems, however, were solved during the war, and by 1945, the British battle fleet was at the peak of its efficiency. The following sections describe these developments and improvements and, where necessary, cover the work carried out immediately before the war.

Heavy ordnance

The development of the modern 14-inch and 16-inch 'all-steel' guns has been described earlier, and it is not proposed to repeat this here. The improvements made to the 15-inch Mk I, however, are worth detailing. This weapon, by the mid-Thirties, was lacking in performance when compared to modern guns. As a large part of the fleet was armed with the 15-inch twin mounting, it was decided to try and improve its performance, and this was achieved by increasing the elevation of the guns from twenty degrees to thirty degrees, thereby increasing the range from 23,400 yards to 29,000 yards. It was also decided to modify the 15-inch projectiles, by providing them with a more streamlined ballistic cap, 6 crh instead of 4 crh, which increased the range still farther to 32,200 yards. Old shells were converted to take the new cap, but both 4 crh and 6 crh shells were manufactured until 1943, after which only the new type was produced.

The rate at which the 15-inch turrets could be converted to Mk I (N), with thirty degrees elevation and loading arrangements capable of accepting the new shell, was limited. *Malaya*, *Barham*, *Repulse* and the five ships of the *Royal Sovereign* class retained the twenty degree elevation, but the latter ships were not considered worthy of the expense involved. It was decided, however, to increase the range of these guns by increasing the weight of the charge from 428 pounds to 490 pounds. This was calculated as the maximum safe charge that the existing gun would accept, and at an elevation of twenty degrees, using the 6 crh shell and the 'Supercharge', the range of the 15-inch Mk I was increased to 28,700 yards. Supercharges were not used in the thirty degree mountings, presumably because the increased barrel wear was not considered acceptable in guns whose range had already been increased.

Long-range anti-aircraft defence

All the long-range AA guns carried by British capital ships during the war, were designed before 1939. Wartime development was therefore confined to improving their fire-control equipment which included the provision of remote power-control gear and radar. Experience early in the war, demonstrated that long-range AA fire was comparatively ineffectual, particularly against high-level bombing formations. It did have a considerable harassing effect on aircraft during the final approach, but even this was not sufficient to break up a determined enemy attack. This lack of success resulted largely from the inadequacies of the HACS which calculated the required 'aim off' on the assumption that the target's height and course were constant, and that the target's speed had been correctly estimated. The system, moreover, was too slow to deal effectively with modern high-speed aircraft. However, it was improved during the war, principally, by the fitting of remote power-control, by which the guns automatically followed the director; by the fitting of '285' radar, from which accurate ranges, and therefore, rate of change of range, could be obtained, and by the stabilisation of the directors for pitch and roll (level and cross-level). (This last was only possible when remote power-control was fitted. Before this, stabilisation was only provided for the information fed into the HACP and not for the director itself), and the fitting of a small predictor. The design of this last item, known as the GRU (Gyro Rate Unit) was begun in 1937, and was intended for use in the high-angle control-system, although it was also fitted in pom-pom- and barrage-directors. By means of a gyroscope, it could automatically measure the vertical and lateral movements of a target which, when combined with radar-ranging, provided a fast and accurate system of fire-control.

A more ambitious project was the new tachymetric fire-control system, TS1, mentioned in Chapter 15. The design was started in about 1937 or 1938, but the production of this extremely complex equipment was beyond the capabilities of British wartime manufacturers, and was abandoned. This system would have been fully stabilised and capable of automatic target-prediction, and with the addition of radar, it would, no doubt, have been a considerable improvement on the high-angle control-system. The nearest equivalent was the US Mk 37 system, fitted in *Vanguard*. (The authors have found that it is very easy to become confused by the jargon and abbreviations used in relation to World War Two gunnery systems. Descriptions and explanations of these terms and systems can be found in Appendix 2.)

Because of these limitations, the use of HACS for predicted firing was only used against high-level bombing attacks, in which the aircraft were likely to maintain a reasonably stable course, speed and height. When dealing with aircraft that dived to attack, i.e., dive-bombers and torpedo-bombers, the long-range AA armament was used to set up a barrage at a fixed range. This produced a curtain of exploding shells through which the aircraft would have to fly in order to reach its target. Much was expected of this form of

Below left: the forward turrets of Renown in 1945. (Note also the aerials for Type '285' radar on the main and HACS directors.)

Below right: *Nelson*'s 'X' turret at full elevation.

Below: a close-up view of a Mk. IV HACS director.

defence, but the war demonstrated that a determined group of aircraft could penetrate such a barrage with few losses.

During the war, an improved system of barrage-fire was introduced using the high-angle control-system in combination with an Auto Barrage Unit (ABU) situated in the HACP. In this system, a pre-determined barrage range was set on the shell fuses and on the ABU. The radar measured the rate of change of range, and the predictor measured the vertical and horizontal movements of the target, which were fed into the Auto Barrage Unit. When the predicted position of the aircraft corresponded with the barrage range, the guns automatically opened fire. This system possessed the advantage of firing to hit the target rather than putting up a screen through which an aircraft had to pass.

In 1942, a small barrage-director was introduced to enable the main and secondary armaments (where applicable) of capital ships and cruisers to be employed for long-range AA fire. The first ten barrage-directors Mk I were converted from pom-pom directors Mk I and fitted in the cruiser *Shropshire* (two for 'X' and 'Y' turrets), *Nelson* and *Rodney* (four in each, to control the 6-inch turrets). Later, two pom-pom directors Mk II were specially converted to barrage-directors and fitted in *Rodney* to control her 4.7-inch AA guns, on the blind side. (*Rodney* had only one HACS (*Nelson* had two) and, therefore, could only control her 4.7-inch guns on one side, until the barrage-directors were fitted.) Barrage-directors were subsequently fitted in *Queen Elizabeth*, *Valiant*, *Warspite*, *Renown* and *Duke of York*. The system provided controlled barrage-fire on the same lines as that described in the previous paragraph.

Close-range anti-aircraft defence

By the end of the 1930s, the eight-barrel pom-pom mounting and the four-barrel 0.5-inch machine-gun-mounting had become the standard close-range anti-aircraft weapons of the fleet. Great confidence was felt in the ability of the multiple pom-pom to deal with close-range air attacks. The one major fault in the original weapon was it low muzzle velocity, but in the late Thirties, this was increased from 1,920 feet per second to 2,400 feet per second, and this was considered sufficient to satisfy the demands of war.

The same confidence was not felt for the 0.5-inch machine-gun which fired solid bullets only and had little chance of achieving the destruction of a modern aircraft. By 1937, it was clear that what was required was a new high-velocity small-calibre weapon, firing an explosive shell and capable of being easily aimed by one man, for tracking high-speed targets at close range. These requirements were almost met by the Swiss 20-mm Oerlikon cannon, which fired 550 rounds per minute at a muzzle velocity of 1,968 feet per second. The Admiralty asked the Oerlikon Company to produce a new version of this gun, with a higher muzzle velocity and the first of these was delivered in 1939. The Royal Navy's 20-mm Oerlikon Mk I fired 450 rounds of high explosive shell per minute at a muzzle velocity of 2,725 feet per second. Few guns had been delivered, however, before supplies were cut off by the German occupation of France. A set of production drawings for the gun were obtained before the Swiss border was closed, and were brought back to the Admiralty by a Royal Navy officer, Stewart Mitchell. This officer, with Commander S. W. Roskill (later Captain S. W. Roskill, author of the official British Naval History, *The War at Sea*), of the Admiralty Staff Division, set up a factory at Ruislip to manufacture the 20-mm

Below left: 5.25-inch turret P2 on *Prince of Wales* in May 1941. (The turret is facing aft.)

Below right: Mk. VI eight-barrelled pom-pom mounting on the port side of the fore-funnel of *Prince of Wales,* in May 1941.

Below: one of the UP mountings on *King George V*.

Oerlikon. Considerable difficulties were encountered in this project, but production was eventually started in 1941. The British version was known as the 20-mm Oerlikon Mk II. Initially, it was mounted in a single hand-operated mounting and, being of simple design, proved reliable and easy to maintain and handle. Within its maximum effective range of 1,000 yards, it also proved a very accurate and deadly weapon in skilled hands.

Early war experience confirmed that the 0.5-inch machine-gun was of little use against aircraft and also revealed the deficiencies of the 2-pounder pom-pom mounting. The former weapon was gradually replaced by the Oerlikon, but the latter problem was not so simple to solve. The ineffectiveness of the pom-pom must have come as a great disappointment, particularly as such a weapon was not easy to replace. Its main faults were its inadequate system of fire-control, and insufficient range, even when firing the high-velocity 2-pounder shell. Nothing could be done to improve the muzzle velocity, but as the war progressed, the system of control was greatly improved. The final model of the pom-pom director, the Mk IV, was equipped with a Gyro Rate Unit (GRU), to give automatic target-prediction, and Type '282' radar to provide accurate ranging. This, together with remote power-control, gave the weapon a reasonable level of accuracy within its limited range. Whatever its faults, the multiple pom-pom had a strong deterrent effect against dive-bomber and Kamikaze attacks.

The development and production of new guns, mountings and equipment takes time, and early in the war, the Admiralty found a 'stop-gap' weapon to increase the anti-aircraft fire-power of the fleet. This was the Parachute and Cable rocket (PAC), which was originally developed by the Air Ministry and was adapted for shipboard use by the Department of Miscellaneous Weapon Development, at the Admiralty. In June 1940, the first of these weapons came into service in ships of the Royal Navy, and in DEMS (defensively-equipped merchant ships), and was subsequently produced in a variety of configurations. So far as is known, the only type fitted in capital ships was the twenty-barrelled UP (Unrotated-projectile) mounting, which was carried by *Hood*, *Nelson*, *King George V*, *Prince of Wales* and *Barham*.

The Parachute and Cable rocket had a solid-fuel propellant, and on reaching a fixed height, a time-fuse separated the rear (propellant) section from the forward section by means of a small explosive charge. The forward section contained three parachutes and four hundred feet of wire cable, on the end of which was a small bomb. After separation, the parachutes opened and, with the bomb dangling at its end, the wire would descend slowly across the path of an attacking aircraft. It was hoped that the aircraft would then fly into the wire, allowing the bomb, which was fused to detonate on impact, to be dragged towards the aircraft by the action of the parachute trailing behind. Very little success was achieved with this weapon because the rockets tended to follow an irregular trajectory (which varied from round to round) and the parachute descent of the wire and bomb was subject to the effects of the wind. After it had been concluded that the ready-use unrotated-projectiles in *Hood*, contributed to the fire that occurred on her shelter-deck during the action against *Bismarck*, all such equipment was removed from the capital ships of the fleet.

As the war progressed, the improvements in the design and performance of aircraft, and the techniques of their use led to an equivalent demand for increased hitting power and performance from close-range anti-aircraft weapons. This need was met by (a) increasing the number of anti-aircraft weapons as they became available; (b) the development of new mountings; (c) the improvement of fire-control arrangements and (d) the introduction of the 40-mm Bofors. During the mid-war period, the needs of the capital ships were largely met by (a), but in smaller vessels, particularly destroyers, considerations of top-weight and complement precluded any large increases in the close-range anti-aircraft armaments. In May 1940, an ideal destroyer weapon arrived in Britain on board the Netherlands mine-layer, *Willem Van Der Zaan*. This ship carried four 40-mm Bofors guns, mounted in two 3-axis twin mountings. The weapons were manufactured by the Dutch firm of Hazemeyer. The mountings, together with their power units (in a compartment below), formed self-contained AA weapon systems, and only required to be fed with a main power supply and the ship's course. All the necessary fire-control equipment and stabilising gear was carried on the mounting. The design of this equipment had begun in 1936, and its general concept was years ahead of its contemporaries. It had the disadvantage of being insufficiently robust to withstand the rigours of sea service. The design was copied by the British, who made some improvements, including the fitting of Type '282' radar, and eventually, it was fitted in many destroyers and other small ships. No capital ships were fitted with the Hazemeyer Bofors mounting, but *Vanguard* was fitted with a British-designed equivalent, the stabilised tachymetric-anti-aircraft-gun (STAAG) Mk II, which was carried on the roof of 'B' turret. The reason why these weapons were not carried by capital ships is probably that the majority of the available mountings were required for small ships, where the need of a well-stabilised and compact AA mounting was much greater. Battleships were much steadier gun-platforms and had more space in which separate director-positions could be accommodated. The STAAG mounting on *Vanguard* can be explained by the fact that, the roof of 'B' turret was not an ideal place for a mounting controlled from a distant position, or with an off-mounting power unit.

Another weapon developed for small ships was the power-operated Oerlikon twin mounting Mk V, which was introduced in 1942. Unlike the Hazemeyer, this weapon was simple and easy to mass-produce, and it was fitted generally in the ships of the fleet. It was first fitted in capital ships in 1943. A 20-mm Oerlikon quadruple mounting, the Mk XIV, was under development during the latter years of the war, but its production was abandoned in favour of the 40-mm Bofors single mounting. By 1944, it was clear that the 20-mm Oerlikon was rapidly being outclassed by modern aircraft, able to attack from outside its effective range. The 20-mm shell, moreover, lacked stopping power and, like the pre-war 0.5-inch machine-gun, was unlikely to deter or destroy an attacking aircraft, unless the pilot, or a particularly vulnerable part of the aircraft were hit. It was essential that the close-range armament be capable of destroying or seriously damaging an aircraft with one hit, and the smallest guns capable of achieving this were the 2-pounder pom-pom and the 40-mm Bofors. This was particularly evident during the latter part of the war in the Pacific, where the Kamikaze suicide attacks by the Japanese made it essential that the aircraft be literally shot out of the sky, before it reached its target. Many ships of the British Pacific Fleet had their 40-mm armament augmented to meet this threat, and *Howe* serves as a good example of the importance attached to the provision of heavier calibre weapons. During her refit at Durban, in 1945, she had her entire 20-mm armament replaced by twenty-four 2-pounder pom-poms (6 x 4) and eighteen 40-mm Bofors (18 x 1).

Although possessing a rate of fire of 120 rounds per minute and a muzzle velocity of 2,700 feet per second, the introduction of the 40-mm Bofors gun was slow and, initially, hampered by a distrust of its method of operation. Like the Oerlikon, the Bofors firing-mechanism allowed the breech to open during recoil, a feature that for many years had been considered undesirable and dangerous, but, at the same time, it was this that gave them their high rate of fire. The first Bofors mounting fitted in a British capital ship, was the single Mk III, fitted in *Prince of Wales* in 1941. This was an Army model, adapted for naval service, and this, and the Hazemeyer, were the only 40-mm Bofors mountings in service with the Royal Navy until late 1942, when the US Bofors Mk II quadruple mounting was introduced into British service. Unlike the Hazemeyer and the STAAG, this weapon had a separate director, with remote power-control transmission. It had no stabilising system, but possessed the twin advantages of simplicity and reliability. Its Mk 51 director carried the US Mk 14 gyro gun-sight, which provided automatic target-prediction and was capable of great accuracy in reasonable weather. As no stabilisation was provided, it was necessary for the director operator to compensate the ship's movements by keeping his sight on the target, which, if the ship were rolling, introduced the likelihood of substantial inaccuracy. The system, though not perfect, was by far the best that could be produced quickly and in quantity, and in addition to equipping their own navy with large numbers of these mountings, the USA supplied a considerable number to Britain, under 'Lend-Lease'. Between 1943 and 1945, they were fitted in five British battleships, *Nelson*, and the four ships of the *King George V* class. The Americans also produced a twin version of this mounting, on which the British based the design of their own Mk V Bofors utility twin mounting. Neither of these, however, were fitted in British capital ships.

The performance of the 40-mm American, and the Hazemeyer mountings, convinced the British of the superiority of the 40-mm Bofors to the 2-pounder pom-pom and by 1945, a single Bofors was considered the equal of two pom-pom barrels. The Admiralty, therefore, designed a multi-barrelled 40-mm mounting to replace the existing Mk VI pom-pom mounting in capital ships. The result was the Mk VI six-barrelled 40-mm mounting with its own close-range barrage-fire director, remote power-control and Type '262' radar. The latter was a replacement for Type '282' and was the first radar set in the Royal Navy capable of 'locking-on' to a target and following it automatically. (Type '262' was also fitted on a number of other fire-control systems including that for the pom-pom and the STAAG.) The Bofors Mk VI mounting and its director system were fully automatic, and only required to be put on to a target and fed with ammunition. In service, it was very successful, but it came into production too late for the war and was mounted only in *Vanguard* and the aircraft carriers *Eagle, Ark Royal, Albion, Bulwark, Centaur* and *Victorious*.

As mentioned earlier, the single hand-worked Bofors Mk III mounting was originally a land-service mounting, adapted for use at sea, and later manufactured as a sea-service mounting designated Mk III.* It was widely employed in the ships of the Royal Navy, but with the exception of *Prince of Wales*, no capital ships were fitted with the weapon until 1945, when several were fitted in the remaining four ships of the *King George V* class. In May 1945, the trials of a prototype power-operated single Bofors mounting, designed for sea service, were carried out. This was the Mk VII mounting, based on the 20-mm Mk V twin mounting and specially developed for use against Kamakaze suicide attacks. It came into service shortly before the end of the war, and was fitted in *Vanguard* and the *King George V* class.

The shortage of 40-mm mountings during the last year of the war, led to a number of Oerlikon Mk V twin mountings being modified to carry a single 40-mm Bofors or a 2-pounder pom-pom. The former were known as Boffins, whereas the latter were given Mark numbers in the normal pom-pom range. It is unlikely that either of these conversions was fitted in capital ships, although it is known that it had been intended to fit six Boffins in *Valiant*.

Many of the smaller weapons in service during 1944 to 1945 were fitted with gyro gun-sights. Two types were available, the US Mk 14, which was the same as that fitted on the quadruple Bofors director, and later, the British Mk 6, an adaptation of an aircraft gun-sight. In principal of operation, these sights belong to the same family as the gyro rate unit of the pom-pom and HACS directors, and were also referred to as tachymetric sights and predictors. They were fitted to all types of close-range anti-aircraft weapons including the single and twin 20-mm, the Boffin, the single Mk III and Mk VII Bofors and the single 2-pounder mounting.

By the end of the war, the capital ships of the fleet carried a variety of close-range weapons and control-systems which, although representing a remarkable improvement over the situation in 1939, could not be regarded as fully incorporating the lessons learned during the war. The ideal system for 1945, was only to be found in *Vanguard* with a uniform armament of seventy-three 40-mm Bofors, and an adequate system of fire-control. It is doubtful, however, if even this armament could be considered adequate in the post-war world, with its extremely fast and manoeuvrable jet-propelled aircraft. Like the 0.5-inch machine-gun and the Oerlikon, the 40-mm steadily lost ground to modern aircraft, and again the need was felt of a gun with greater hitting power and range. This is, however, a matter of small consequence in the history of the battleship, which was, by this time, fading from the naval scene, but it is interesting to note that one of the developments of the late-war period was an automatic anti-aircraft twin mounting carrying two 3-inch guns, the same calibre as the first anti-aircraft guns to be fitted in capital ships before the First World War.

Radar

There are few items of wartime weaponry or equipment that can be said to have played a really decisive part in the Second World War. One could mention the aircraft carrier, the Spitfire, the Mustang, the Sherman tank and the Flower class corvettes, but along with these one would have to include the development and use of radar. There is no doubt at all that it played a truly vital part in the history of the war, and without it the long-drawn battle of the Atlantic would not have been won, and probably, the course of history would have been changed.

The theory of radar is simple. The theory of bouncing an electromagnetic pulse off an object and measuring the time delay of the echo had been advanced soon after the turn of the century, but it was not until the early 1930s that research began in earnest in France, Germany, Great Britain and the USA.

As might be expected, the first sea-going sets were fairly large, crude, underpowered pieces of equipment with aerials to match, and many of the early production types were not much better than the prototypes. They required constant care and attention and breakdowns were not infrequent. Some types commonly registered echoes from flocks of birds (and still do), and ships frequently went to action stations because of a radar echo from a cloud. Other problems included damage and breakdowns caused by vibration from the ship's own gunfire. This remained a problem throughout the Second World War, and was never solved. The advantages, however, far outweighed these nuisances. Developments and techniques were shared between Britain and the USA and by the last year of the war, radar had become indispensable, and was fitted, not only in the larger vessels, but in ships down to the size of motor torpedo-boats.

In the UK, serious research was begun early in 1935, under Robert Watson-Watt, who was instructed to look into the possibilities of producing a death-ray for use against aircraft pilots. He produced instead, an experimental electronic detection device. It was known, at first, as Radio Direction Finding, and later became known as radar. The first experimental set underwent sea-going trials in the minesweeper *Saltburn*, towards the end of 1936. The results of these trials were disappointing because of a lack of power at the shorter wavelengths and this was a problem with surface-warning sets, that was not solved until the war was well advanced.

Shortly after the trials in *Saltburn*, it was decided to concentrate on the development of a type of radar that would give long-range warning against aircraft. There were two reasons for this. The development of radio-detection equipment was under the control of the Royal Air Force, and also the problems of aerial array and obtaining sufficient power for aircraft-detection were less acute than for surface-detection. At that time, any naval set was governed by the frequency of the set, which, in turn, dictated the size of its aerial. The size and weight of an aerial were strictly limited, if it were to be fitted to a masthead, and this was the only possible position for an air-warning type, if maximum results were to be achieved. Consequently, a wavelength of seven metres was chosen. This would give the longest wavelength coupled with the maximum size aerial permissible on cruisers and battleships.

An experimental set for sea-going trials, was fitted in the cruiser *Sheffield*, in August 1938. As the equipment was purely for detection and not connected with gunnery, it was given a number in the ordinary wireless-transmission series; it was known as Type '79Y' and had an output of fifteen to twenty kilowatts. At this time, Britain had not developed the co-axial cable leads capable of carrying simultaneous transmitting and receiving loads, and this meant that separate transmit and receive aerials had to be carried. The size of the aerials for Type '79Y' and subsequent air-warning sets, were such that both the mainmast and a fore-topmast, had to be used to carry the two separate aerial arrays. (Where necessary, a foretopmast was fitted.)

Shortly afterwards, a second Type '79Y' set was fitted in *Rodney*, and she became the first battleship in the world to be fitted with air-warning radar. The second was the American battleship *New York*, which was fitted with an American set in December 1938. Trials of Type '79Y' in *Sheffield* and *Rodney* were successful, and aircraft were detected at heights of 10,000 feet at a range of 53 miles.

Development of '79Y' continued, and in mid-1939, Type '79Z', a set with increased power of up to 90 kilowatts, was fitted in the anti-aircraft cruiser *Curlew*. This, more powerful, set enabled *Curlew*, in 1940, to detect enemy aircraft approaching Scapa Flow from more than sixty miles away. The results of the 1939 trials of '79Z' in *Curlew*, were good enough to persuade the Admiralty to place an order for forty sets of this type. This 1939 order was placed only just in time for deliveries to commence in 1940, and the outbreak of war in September 1939, saw only the cruisers *Curlew* and *Sheffield*, and the battleship *Rodney*, fitted with radar.

Although the order for forty sets was for Type '79Z', a refinement was added to this type, in the form of a barrage-predictor for long-range AA fire within a seven-mile radius. This made the set a piece of gunnery equipment as distinct from wireless equipment, and to avoid confusion with the various wireless-transmitting types of which there were many, Type '79Z' with the predictor fitted, became known as Type '279' and production of Types '79Y' and '79Z' ceased. The three ships with Type '79' had Type '279' installed during 1940, thus bringing them into line with other cruisers and battleships that were being fitted with air-warning radar during that year.

Quite soon after the war had started, the need was felt for a set that gave surface-warning and ranging, as well as air-warning capability, a set that could be used with the main armament. As experience had already been gained with the earlier Type '279', the new type was ready for sea-going trials late in 1940, and was fitted in the cruiser *Dido*, in December 1940. Trials with the new set, which was given the Type number '281' ('280' had already been allocated for another type), showed a marked superiority over the performance of '279', and aircraft flying at heights of 25,000 feet were detected up to 120 miles away. Surface performance was only moderate. Large vessels were detected at ranges of eleven to twelve miles. However, as '281' was markedly superior to '279', many orders were placed for this type, and it became the most common air-warning set in the Royal Navy, during the war.

With the introduction of '279', and later, the more advanced '281', the air-warning (and to a limited extent the surface-warning) needs of the large ships were taken care of. It is not surprising, therefore, that the very influential gunnery department of the Royal Navy started lobbying for a set to be used solely with the main armament. In fact, development of a gunnery outfit had been in progress since 1938, and in the later part of 1939, an experimental set was fitted in the destroyer, *Sardonyx*. Successful trials of the set (which had no Type number) led to the first full-blown gunnery set for the main armament of large ships, and in June 1940, *Nelson* was the first ship to be fitted with the new set. The aerials were of the broadside type, twenty-six feet across, and were fitted on the top of and across the front of the main gun-director. The set was designated Type '284'. Trials of Type '284' in *Nelson* in mid-1940, gave good results. Large vessels were accurately ranged at up to 18,000 yards, and destroyers at up to 12,000 yards.

Type '284', though suitable for vessels of cruiser size and above, could not be fitted on to smaller ships because of the sheer size and weight of the aerial arrays. To overcome this problem, while retaining essentially the same set, the aerials were radically changed and the yagi array was introduced. This, considerably smaller and lighter array, meant that the set could now be carried in destroyers, and could be fitted to the HACS directors of larger ships, for use with long-range AA fire. This type was known as '285', and it was fitted in the *Hunt* class destroyer *Southdown* for trials in September 1940. Although having the same power output as that of Type '284' – twenty-five kilowatts – its range was only eight and a half nautical miles. A variation of Type '285' was produced for use with close-range AA weapons, including the multiple pom-pom, using only two yagi arrays, instead of the six as on the '285'. This variation was known as Type '282', and four sets were first fitted in the battleship *Prince of Wales* early in 1941. As each set was to serve a multiple pom-pom, the aerial arrays were positioned on the top of each of the pom-pom directors. Range was nowhere near so good as Type '285', being only three and a half nautical

Below: the two port-side pom-pom directors on *Prince of Wales*. This photograph also provides an excellent view of the aerials for Type '282' radar, which are mounted on the top of the directors.

miles, but as the maximum effective range of the pom-pom was 1,700 yards, this was not a drawback.

With the air-warning and gunnery needs taken care of, the one gap left to be filled was that of surface-warning, and this was most needed in the anti-submarine sector. Although development was in hand to produce a shortwave set suitable for surface-detection, something was needed immediately to help the escorts to counter the submarine menace. To this end, a stopgap set was introduced into service towards the end of 1940, and although primarily for destroyers and smaller ships of the escort type, it was fitted in several cruisers as a temporary measure. The set was given the Type number '286' and was an adaptation of air-to-surface warning equipment that the Royal Air Force was using.

Performance of '286' was poor, but as it was the only available outfit for small ships at that time, large numbers were produced and fitted to fleet and escort destroyers in 1941. Although quickly replaced in cruisers, Type '286' was still being carried by some destroyers – notably by ships of the *Hunt* class – until the end of 1942. The initial replacement for '286' was Type '290', a similar set but using a much smaller tier aerial and capable of rotation, unlike the earliest marks of '286'.

One of the problems associated with producing an efficient surface-warning set, was the amount of power required at the shorter wavelengths, and in February 1940, a breakthrough was made in this direction. A prototype was assembled and tested with good results. This set, working at a wavelength of 10 cm with a power output of fifty kilowatts, was fitted in the corvette *Orchis* for sea-going trials in March 1941. Tests with the new set, known as Type '271', gave very good results. A fully surfaced submarine could be detected at 5,000 yards; trimmed down, it could be detected at 2,800 yards and with eight feet of periscope above water, at 1,300 yards. These results convinced the Admiralty, who immediately placed orders for 350 sets.

Variations of Type '271', with increased power and definition, were developed for bigger ships, and given the Type numbers '272' and '273'. The latter was fitted in all battleships as it became available, but it is known that at least five ships, *Rodney*, *Duke of York*, *King George V*, *Warspite* and *Prince of Wales*, were fitted with '271' in 1941, as a temporary measure until they could be refitted with Type '273' in 1942. When *Prince of Wales* was lost in December 1941, she had not been refitted with '273' and was still carrying Type '271'.

By mid-1942, all the major vessels in the Navy had been equipped with a comprehensive outfit of radar, and the battleships were fitted as shown in Table 97.

Table 97: Radar equipment in British battleships, mid-1942

Queen Elizabeth	281	284	273	282	285
Valiant	279	284	273	282	285
Malaya	281	284	273	282	285
Warspite	281	284	273	282	285
Revenge	279	284	285	273	
Resolution	279	284	285	273	
Ramillies	279	284	285	273	282
Royal Sovereign	279	284	285	273	
Renown	281	284	273	282	285
Rodney	281	284	273	282	285
Nelson	281	284	273	282	285
King George V	279	284	273	282	285
Duke of York	281	284	273	282	285
Anson	281	284	273	282	285
Howe	281	284	273	282	285

Radar developments, from 1942

Although ships were now equipped with comprehensive outfits of high-performance and reasonably reliable equipment, the use of radar as a technical weapon, especially in an action involving many ships, was inhibited by its inability to distinguish friend from foe. This problem was illustrated by the night action

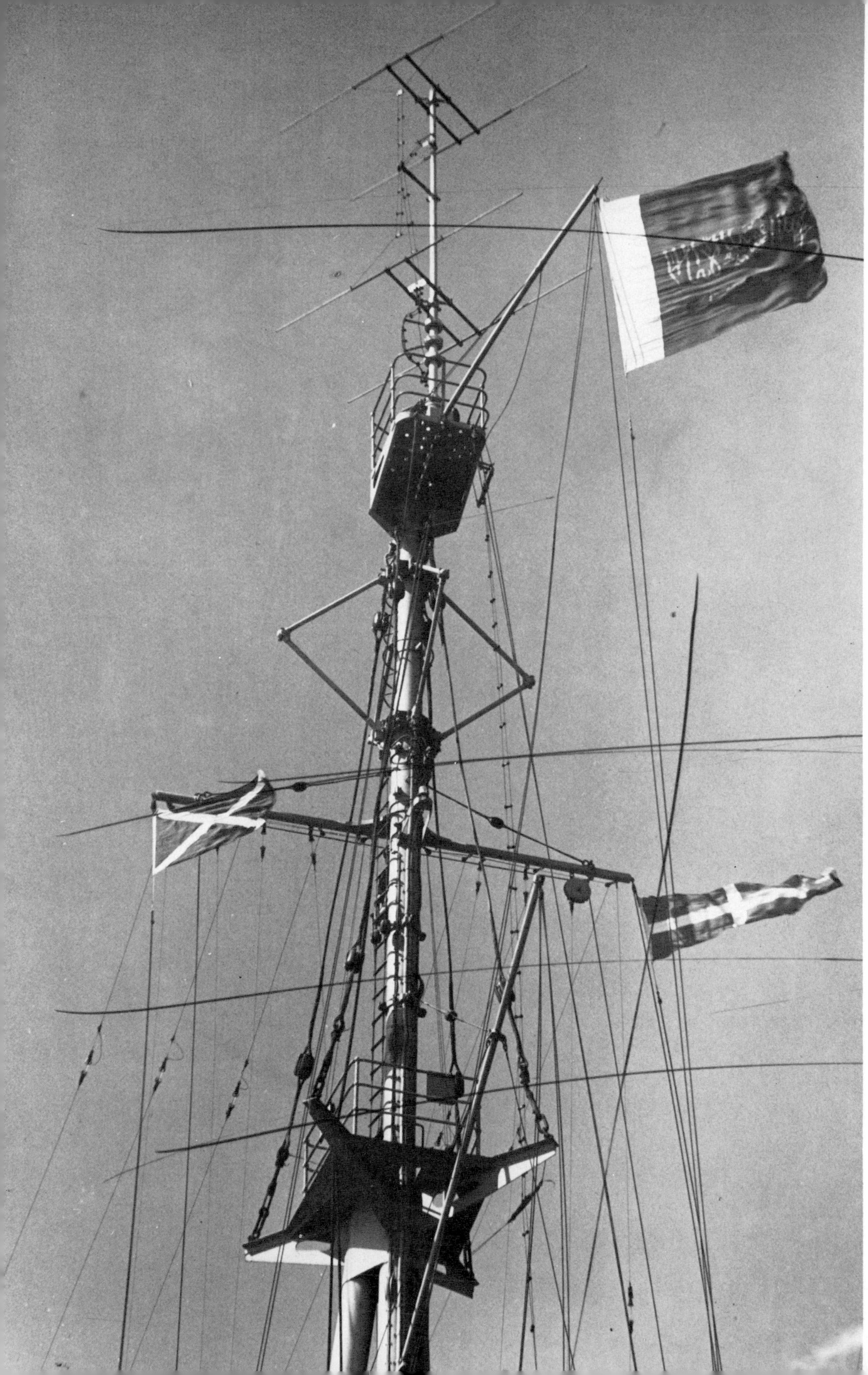

Left: the mainmast of *Queen Elizabeth* in 1941. (The thick horizontal streaks are scratches on the original negative.)

Radar Aerials

Foremast, 1944/45 period

1 Type '243' IFF for Type '279'
2 Type '279' Air Warning
3 Type '86' TBS
4 Type '91' TBS
5 Type 'FIV' Radar Direction Finding
6 Type '86M' Fighter Direction
7 Type '293' Air and Surface Target Indicating
8 Type '242M' IFF for Type '277'
9 Type '242M' Interrogator for Type '277'
10 Type '87' TBS
11 'Headache'
12 Type '277' Height-finder
13 Type '252' IFF for Type '293'

Mainmast, 1944/45 period

14 Type '251' Surface Radar Beacon
15 Type '240' IFF for Type '281'
16 Type '281' Air Warning

Type '281' aerial with Type '240' Interrogator fitted on top

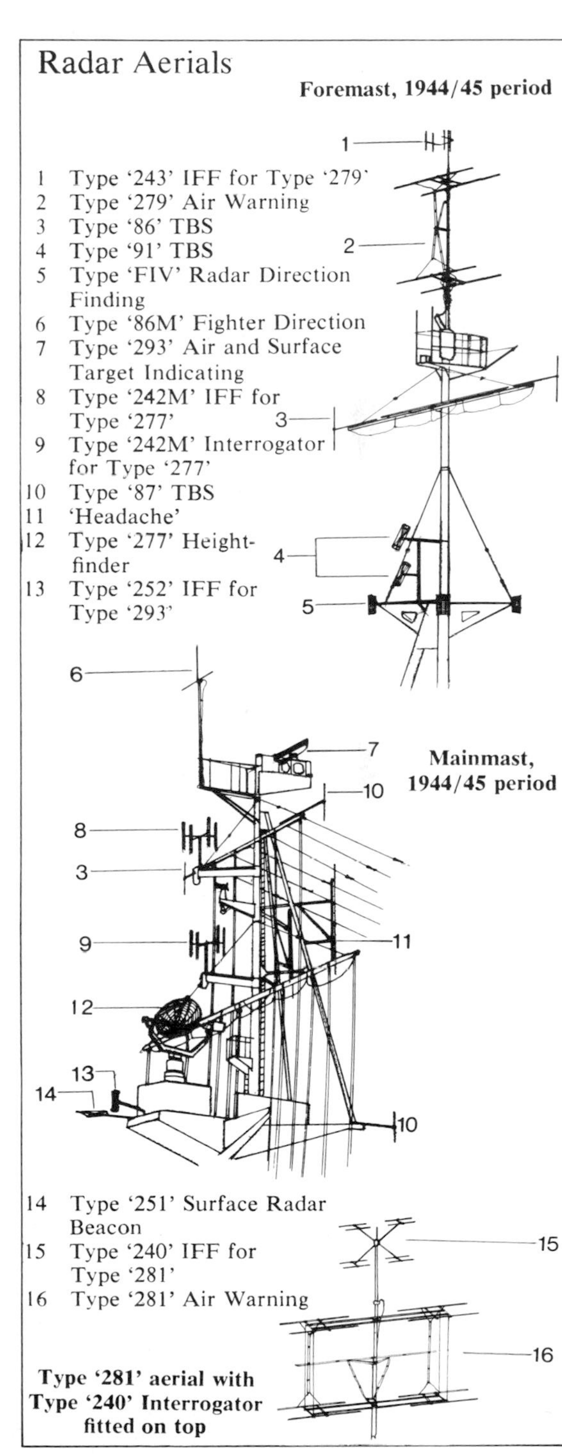

that took place off Guadalcanal on 14th to 15th November 1942, between Japanese and American surface forces. During this battle, the battleship *Washington* had been plotting enemy heavy units on her radar screen for some time, but had to withhold fire, in case one of the echoes was from her sister ship, *South Dakota*, and it was only after *South Dakota* had been badly damaged by heavy gunfire and eventually illuminated by Japanese searchlights, that *Washington* could open fire, confident that she was not firing on a friendly ship.

The problem was solved by the fitting of an aerial, working on the same line of bearing as the radar aerial. If the contact was friendly it would return a second echo or pulse, in addition to the main return echo, sent through its IFF aerial. The interrogator aerial would pick up this second pulse, and would show it on the radar screen as a double echo.

The fitting of IFF and interrogators began in early 1942, and by 1943, all battleships had been so fitted. Interrogator Type numbers were:

'240', used with '281' and '279'.
'252', used with '273', '272' and '271'.
'242', used with '291', '273', '272', '271', '277', '293' and '276'.
'243', used with '279' and '281'.

IFFs and interrogators were not required to be fitted to any of the gunnery sets, and were only used with the air- and surface-warning sets.

During the latter half of 1943, transceiver sets began to come into use on the air-warning Types '281' and '279'. This was an important step, as it meant that only one aerial frame was required for both transmitting and receiving. Several advantages were gained by this. First, the need of the two aerials having to rotate together was eliminated. Second, the radar set itself could now be contained in one office, whereas, hitherto, the transmitting and receiving equipment had had to be widely separated. Last, and most important, it freed one masthead of the very large aerial array

Below: the bridge of *Rodney* in 1942, showing an interesting array of aerials. At the mainmast-head are transmitting aerials for Type '281' radar. On the mainmast-starfish is the office and lantern housing equipment and aerials for Type '273'. The foremast head carries the receiving aerial for Type '281', with its associated interrogator aerial for Type '240' above it. On the roof of the HACS director are aerials for Type '285', and on the top, and across the front, of the main director control-tower are Type '284' aerials. The extension arms projecting from the air-defence platform bear aerials for Type '86' TBS, and projecting from the front of the bridge is the aerial frame for the MFDF outfit.

and made way for other types and equipment. Transceiver types were given the letter 'B' after the Type number, so that '281' and '279' were gradually replaced in many battleships and cruisers during 1943 and 1944, by Types '281B' and '279B'. The aerial array for '281B' and '279B' was always carried on the main-mast. In some of the battleships, an additional radar set, Type '293', now began to be fitted. This was a target-indicating set for both aircraft and ships, and it could range between 200 and 20,000 feet, up to a distance of twenty-five nautical miles. '293' worked on a wavelength of 10 cm with a peak power output of 500 kilowatts, and its small cheese aerial was fitted on a platform, positioned at the very top of the foremast. At the same time that '293' came into use, a radically new type appeared on the scene, Type '277'. This was a combined surface- and air-warning type, that also gave height indication. To obtain height indication, a different radiated-beam pattern was required, and to achieve this, a different design of aerial had to be used. Although '277' was a 10 cm 500-kilowatt set, similar to the '293', the aerial was completely different, as the drawings show. As well as having continuous rotation, '277' was the first British type to be fitted with a plan position-indicator display screen in place of the previous line-scan display. It gave as good a surface performance as Type '273' which it replaced in some ships, and was fitted in the same position on the foremast.

Table 98: Radar equipment in British battleships, mid-1944

Queen Elizabeth	279	273R	285(4)	282(4)	283(4)	284
Valiant	281	273R	285(4)	282(4)	283(4)	
Malaya	281	284	273	285(2)		
Warspite	281	284	273R	285(2)	282(2)	283(2)
Revenge	279	284	285	273		
Resolution	279	284	285	273		
Ramillies	279B	284	273R	285(2)	282(2)	
Royal Sovereign	279	284	273	285(2)	282(2)	
Renown	281	273R	285(4)	282(2)	284	283(3)
Rodney	281	273R	284	285	282(3)	283(6)
Nelson	281	273R	284	285(2)	282(9)	283(4)
King George V	279B	293	274	277	285(4)	282(7)
Duke of York	281B	293	274 277	285(4)	283(2)	282(4)
Anson	281B	293	274(2)	277	275(4)	262(7)
Howe	281B	293	274	277SQ	285	262(7)

Note. Numbers in parentheses indicate the number of sets fitted.

Table 99: British Naval Radar 1938 to 1945

Type	Wavelength	Power output	Range (n miles)	Main function	Remarks
271	10 cm	5–90 kw	10–25	Surface-warning	First microwave radar set. First fitted in corvette *Orchis* in May 1941. Very successful and fitted to hundreds of ships
272	10 cm	5–90 kw	10–25	Surface-warning	Variant of 271, used in destroyers and cruisers
273	10 cm	5–90 kw	10–25	Surface-warning	Variant of 271, used in cruisers and battleships
274	10 cm			Main gunnery for large ships	Replacement set for 284
275	10 cm		16	Long-range AA gunnery	Replacement set for 285, first fitted in 1945
276	3 cm			Surface-warning	Used in a few destroyers between 1943 and 1945 as 272 replacement
277	10 cm	500 kw	25–35	Combined air- and surface-warning height-finder	The first shipboard set with PPI height-finder, performance not very good, first fitted in late 1943
79	7 metres	70 kw	60	Air-warning	First British air-warning set, first used in August 1938 in *Sheffield*
279	7 metres	70 kw	100	Air-warning with barrage-predictor	First widely used air-warning type, gradually supplanted by 281
280	3½ metres			Air-warning/AA ranging	Adaptation of Army Type GL Mk I set, used for a short time in 1940 to 1941 on a few old AA cruisers, including *Carlisle*
281	3½–4 metres	350 kw	120	Air-warning	Most widely used air-warning set in use during the Second World War on large ships. First fitted in December 1940, to cruiser *Dido*
282	50 cm	25 kw	3½	Close-range AA gunnery	First fitted early 1941, to battleship *Prince of Wales*
283	50 cm	25 kw	8½	Blind-fire AA barrage for main armament of large ships	Came into use in late 1942, gradually fitted in all cruisers and battleships
284	50 cm	25 kw	10	Main gunnery for large ships	Very successful gunnery set for main armament of large ships. First fitted in June 1940 to battleship *Nelson*
285	50 cm	25 kw	8½	Long-range AA gunnery	Variant of 284, successful surface- and air-warning type for small ships as well as serving as long-range AA outfit
286	1½ metres			Air- and surface-warning	Naval version of RAF ASV set. First fitted in the autumn of 1940. Poor performance. First Mark of 286 had non-rotating aerial
290	1½ metres			Air-warning	First fitted in early 1941, was intended as a replacement for 286 but was supplanted by the introduction of Types 271 and 272
291	1½ metres		35	Air-warning	Widely used successful set for small ships throughout the Second World War. In use by the end of 1941
293	10 cm	500 kw	12½	Air and surface target indicating	First fitted in late 1943
294	10 cm	500 kw		Combined air- and surface-warning height-finder	Replacement set for 277
295	10 cm	500 kw		Combined air- and surface-warning height-finder	271–3 replacement introduced in 1945
298	3 cm			Surface-warning	

Below: *Anson* in the Captain Cook Graving Dock, Sydney, in January 1945. Note the office and aerial for the VHF/DF outfit and the four-barrelled pom-poms on the quarter-deck.

Right: *Ramillies* in mid-1944. At the rear of 'X' turret, and rising to just below the HACS on the mainmast, are the two transmitting aerials for Type '650' jamming-equipment.

Below right: *Anson* on 29th July 1946. On the legs of the mainmast are aerials for Type '651' missile-jamming equipment. (Note also the pom-pom mounting abreast 'B' turret.)

Improvements to standard sets continued throughout the war, especially to Type '271', where initially, the power output had been 5 kilowatts, but eventually rose to a maximum of 100 kilowatts, and this high power required the wave-guide feed.

With high-power short-wave sets, the problem of feeding the signal from the set to the aerial was overcome by the fitting of metal tubes, containing reflectors to guide the signal around any bends that the tube had. This then was the wave-guide. It was only practical to use the wave-guide on sets with a wavelength of below 10 cm.

Other improvements to all warning sets included continuous rotation of aerials, and the installation of the plan position-indicator.

Electronic equipment, other than radar

Direction-finding equipment. Direction-finder (DF) equipment was used on ships during the First World War, and gradually improved between the wars, so that by 1939, the direction-finder gear carried on a battleship could detect wireless transmissions over the full range from longwave to shortwave.

Aerials for high-frequency and medium-frequency direction-finders were carried either at the masthead and/or at the rear of the spotting-top. The aerial for the high-frequency direction-finder set was a fairly large double diamond-shaped frame, positioned on the manmast, some way above the starfish. The aerial for the medium-frequency direction-finder was either the large triangular-stay arrangement (fitted between the funnels as in *Hood*, or positioned around the mainmast) or the much smaller, double diamond frame, fitted on the fore-masthead.

As the war progressed, the need of more accurate information from DF became vital, with the result that the Type 'FH3' high-frequency direction-finder was supplemented by Type 'FH4' during 1941 and 1942, and the aerial was changed from the diamond-frame type, to a complicated basket affair of about the same size. The aerial arrays for MFDF also changed, and the diamond-frame and the stay arrangement type were replaced by a very small double-loop aerial. In battleships, this was always fitted on a bracket projecting from the front of the bridge.

By 1945, enemy wireless transmissions were being sent on very short wavelengths, with the result that very high-frequency direction-finding equipment was fitted in British ships from 1945 onwards. Also, direction-finding equipment that could cover a wide range of wavelengths had been fitted in almost all vessels from 1941 onwards. It was known as the variable-frequency direction-finder and the aerials consisted of three sets of frames placed at widely-spaced intervals on the fore-mast. Variable-frequency direction-finding was not so efficient as direction-finding sets that operated on specific wavelengths, but it was useful in that it could supply additional information to the main outfits.

As the enemy gradually began to use radar on board ships, a DF set was introduced, to intercept their transmissions and emissions. This equipment first appeared in late 1942, and had been fitted in almost all battleships and cruisers by late 1943. The aerials consisted of four small grid arrays, covering 360 degrees and were usually fitted on arms attached to the arms of the mainmast starfish.

Talk between ships (TBS) listening-gear. In 1940, the practice started, of listening-in to enemy talk between ships transmission using standard wireless equipment, but by 1942, a specially designed set was introduced into general service. The first ships to be fitted were the small escort destroyer types, protecting East Coast convoys. Ships on this duty were chosen because E-boat attacks were common, and there was often a great deal of chatter between the enemy vessels, thus, the equipment, which was given the name 'Headache', was particularly useful and by 1943, was being carried by several battleships and cruisers. The aerial for 'Headache' consisted of a single dipole, and was attached to a rectangular frame fitted on the upper foremast.

Jamming equipment. 1943 saw the introduction of the remote-controlled air-to-surface weapon. The Germans introduced two types into service at the same time. One was the 'HS293', which was a radio-controlled bomb with small wings, and the other was the 'FX 1400', again, a radio-controlled bomb, but with only a set of steering-vanes at the rear. The use of these weapons against ships in the later part of 1943, caused great concern to the Royal Navy and the US Navy, and considerable thought was given to the problem. Only after examples of the weapons, together with their guidance gear had been captured intact, in October 1943, could an effective counter-measure be devised. Examination of the weapons and their control-gear, revealed the wavelengths on which the guidance signals were transmitted.

The Royal Navy immediately searched for a suitable wireless set to transmit jamming

signals. Unfortunately, the only outfit suitable for shipboard use and transmission on the correct wavelengths, was an army set that had been phased out of service in 1942.

A certain amount of wrangling took place between the Army and the Navy during October and November 1943, about the purchase of the required number of sets, but finally, the army handed over 200 sets. As it was necessary to transmit jamming signals on more than one wavelength simultaneously, two sets had to be fitted in each ship, and this reduced the number of ships that could be fitted with Type '650' (as it became known) from 200 to 100. Fifty ships operating in the Mediterranean, and fifty operating in Home Waters were fitted with Type '650'. The first vessel to receive Type '650', was the frigate *Woodpecker*, in December 1943. Other ships were soon fitted out, and by the time the Normandy landings took place, jamming sets were fitted to several vessels supporting the landings. Of the battleships operating in European Waters, it is known that *Rodney*, *Nelson*, *Ramillies* and *Warspite* were fitted with Type '650'. By the end of 1945, the Royal Navy had produced its own improved version of Type '650', known as Type '651', and this set was used for a while during the late Forties.

Camouflage

The effectiveness of painted camouflage on warships of the Royal Navy during the Second World War has never really been determined, in spite of in-depth wartime and post-war studies, and in this section, the authors intend to remain neutral, and give only a brief outline of camouflage development during this period.

During the latter part of the First World War, dazzle camouflage had been used fairly widely on certain types of warships, including three battleships of the 'R' class, *Royal Sovereign*, *Ramillies* and *Revenge*. There was widespread belief in the 'dazzle' schemes, at the time they were in use, but an official verdict, rendered in the early Thirties, most definitely gave the thumbs down to the value of camouflage, in spite of a large amount of solid evidence to the contrary.

This official view held sway during the first six months of the Second World War when, aside from a handful of fleet destroyers, all ships in the navy were overall light or dark grey, depending on their role. It was not until the spring of 1940, that any of the large vessels started to use any sort of camouflage.

As was to be expected, the early designs were very amateurish – simple patterns, usually employing only two colours. So far as the battleships were concerned, two types were favoured. The first was an adaptation of the First World War dazzle pattern, but using only two or three colours; the alternative was a very drab dark brown and medium green. The dark brown type came into use during April to May 1940, but by August, it had almost completely disappeared, whereas, the dazzle types were retained into 1941 by several ships; at least one battleship retained it until 1942.

Sea experience during the spring and summer of 1940, persuaded the Admiralty to form a special Camouflage Section in the late autumn of that year. Some little time elapsed before official designs began to appear, and the first battleship to use an official pattern was *Queen Elizabeth*, in the first months of 1941. Other designs followed, and by 1942, most of the battleships were wearing an official camouflage, of one type or another. The battleships (unlike other types such as the cruisers) changed their paintwork only occasionally, and *Rodney* carried only one camouflage design during the whole of her wartime career.

By mid-1944, the Camouflage Section had introduced a series of standard schemes, of very simple design, to be used throughout the navy, and almost all the battleships in service at this time began to discard their disruptive designs, for one of the standard types. A notable exception, however, was *Rodney*, which retained the 1942 disruptive pattern, virtually unchanged, until she was scrapped.

Queen Elizabeth
Early 1941: Admiralty first disruptive type. Worn until damaged in late 1941 at Alexandria.
Mid-1943: Admiralty intermediate disruptive type.
August, 1943: Changed to a simpler intermediate disruptive type.
Late 1944: Changed to Admiralty standard type.

Valiant
Late 1939: Overall medium grey with white aircraft recognition circles carried on the roofs of 'A' and 'Y' turrets.
1940 to 1941: No information available.
1942: Unofficial type worn until 1943 refit.
Mid-1943: Admiralty intermediate disruptive type, worn until return to UK in 1945.

Barham
Late 1939: Overall dark grey.
Mid-1940: Unofficial design of large grey disruptions on white field.
Late 1940: Overall medium grey.
Early 1941: Modified Peter Scott scheme.

Warspite
Late 1939: Overall dark grey.
1940: No information available.
Late 1941: Unofficial design of medium grey and light grey disruption. This design was carried, with only slight variations, until she was scrapped.

Malaya
Late 1939: Overall dark grey.
Mid-1940: Unofficial type of dazzle design.
Mid-1941: Overall medium grey.
Late 1942: Admiralty light disruptive type, worn until the end of the war.

Revenge
Late 1939: Overall dark grey.
Mid-1940: Unofficial dazzle design.
1941: Variation of 1940 dazzle type, and worn until 1942.
1942 to 1943: No information available.

Resolution
Late 1939: Overall dark grey.

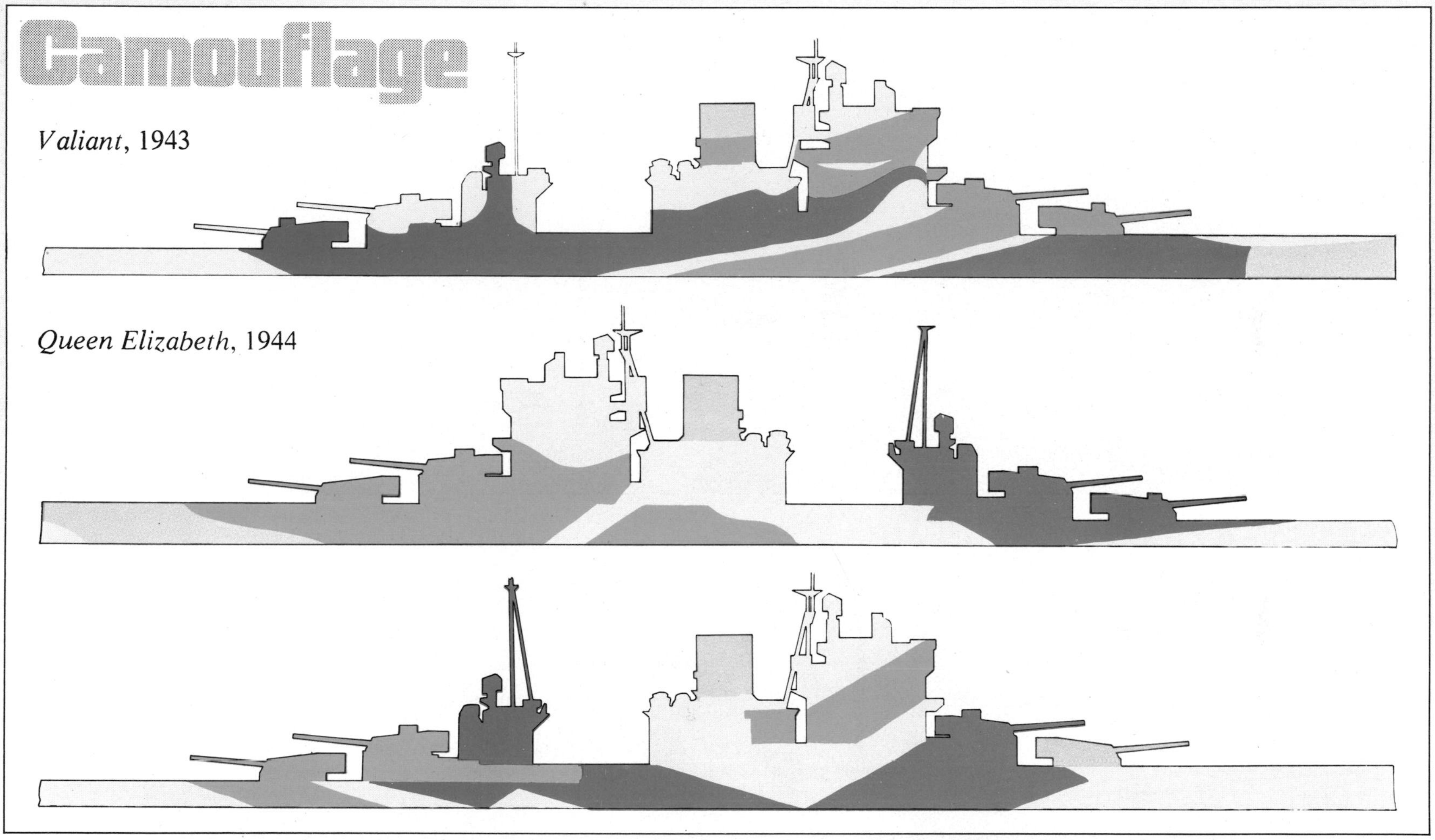

Camouflage

Valiant, 1943

Queen Elizabeth, 1944

Queen Elizabeth in 1941, after the completion of her reconstruction, wearing one of the first examples of official camouflage.

Camouflage

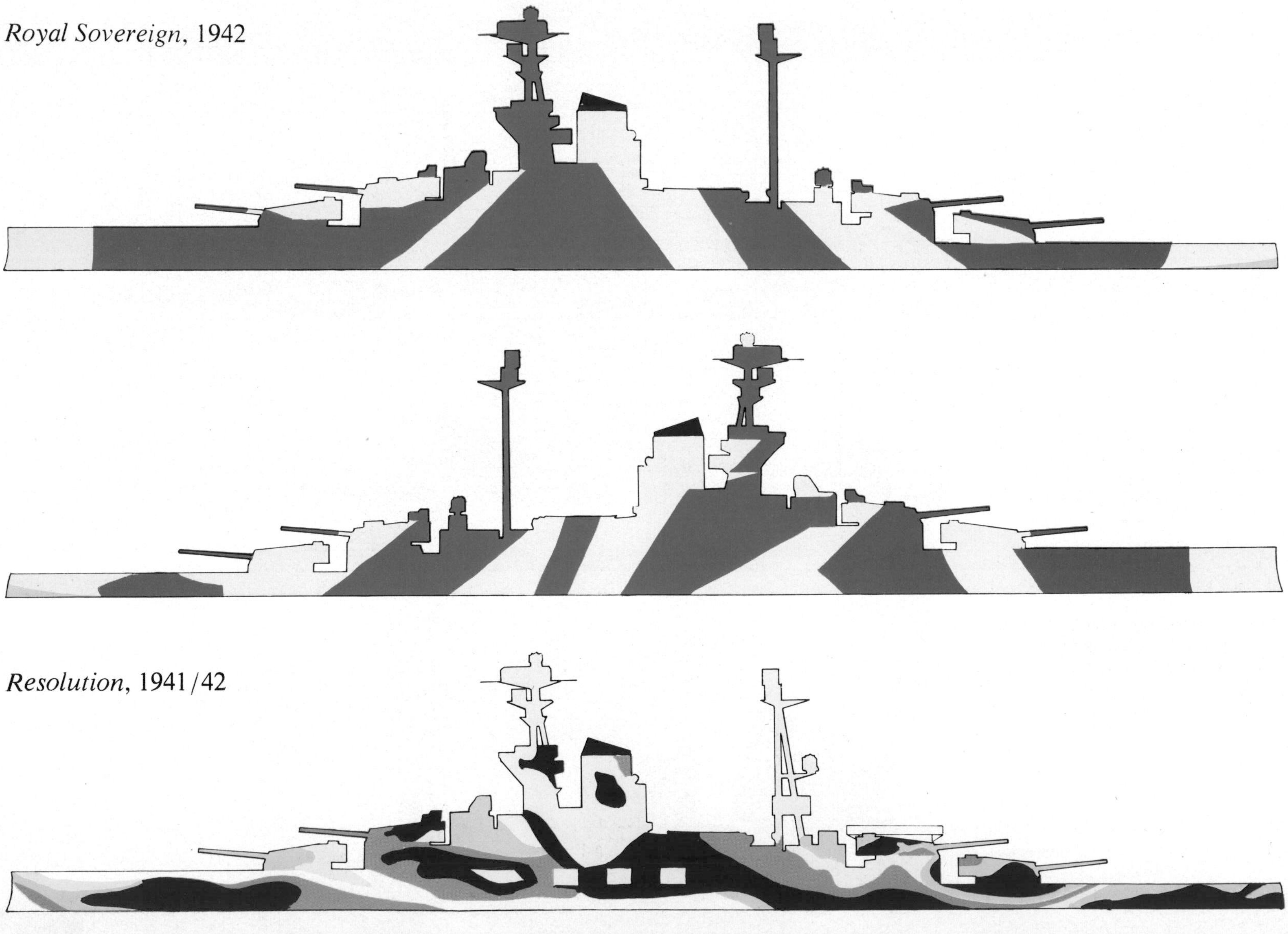

Royal Sovereign, 1942

Resolution, 1941/42

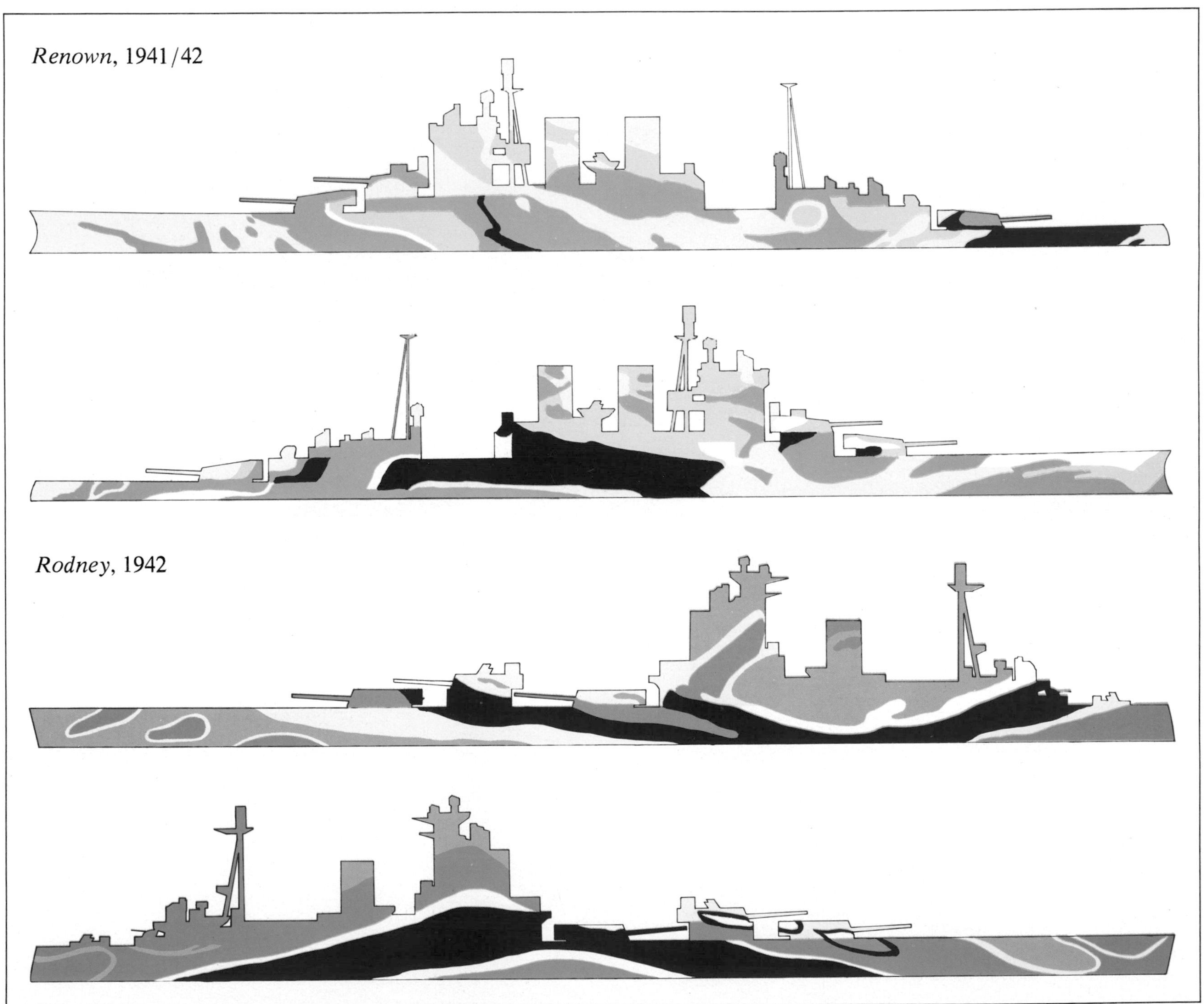
Renown, 1941/42
Rodney, 1942

Right: *Royal Sovereign* in 1941, wearing a dazzle-pattern camouflage.

Below right: *King George V* fitting out in the autumn of 1940, and wearing an unusual two-colour dazzle pattern.

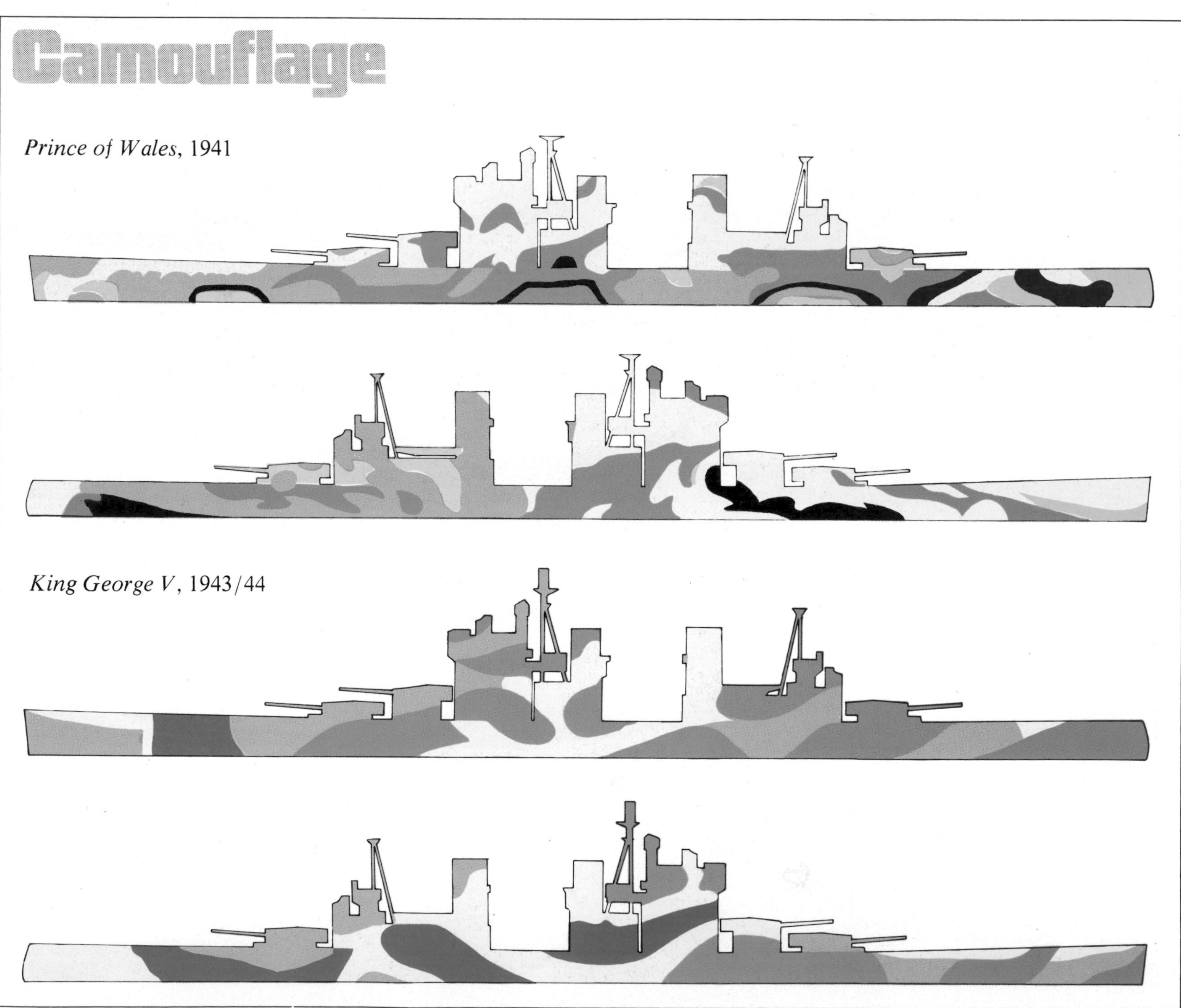

1667

Left: *Rodney* on the 29th June 1943. Note the camouflage pattern is carried on to the decks.

Below: a broadside view of *Anson* soon after completion, on 18th June 1942, wearing Admiralty intermediate disruptive type camouflage.

1940: No information available.
1941: Brown and green type.
Late 1941: Overall medium grey.
1942: Admiralty first disruptive type.
1943 to 1944: No information available.

Ramillies
Late 1939: Overall medium grey.
1940: Disruptive type worn, but insufficient photographic evidence available to determine colours and pattern accurately.
1941: Unofficial dazzle type of large dark and light grey disruption.
1942: No information available.
June, 1943: Admiralty intermediate disruptive type.
Mid-1944: Admiralty standard scheme.

Royal Sovereign
Late 1939: Overall medium grey.
Mid-1940: Unofficial dazzle type.
1941: Variation of 1940 dazzle pattern.
1942: Further slight variation of 1940 dazzle pattern.
September, 1943: Admiralty intermediate disruptive type, worn until end of war.

Royal Oak
Late 1939: Overall dark grey.

Hood
Late 1939: Overall dark grey.
Early 1940: Overall light grey.
Late 1940: Overall medium grey, remained this colour until she was sunk.

Nelson
Late 1939: Overall dark grey.
Mid-1940: Reported to have been painted overall dark brown.
Mid-1941: Overall medium grey.
1942 to 1944: Admiralty disruptive type.
1945: Admiralty standard scheme.

Rodney
Late 1939: Overall dark grey.
August, 1940: Appeared to be overall medium grey, but it is possible that the colour was Mountbatten pink.
Early 1941: Overall medium grey.
Early 1942: Admiralty first disruptive type, worn without any significant change until she was scrapped.

Renown
Late 1939: Believed to have been overall light grey.
1940: Overall light grey.
Late 1941: Admiralty first disruptive type.
Early 1943: Admiralty intermediate disruptive type.
March, 1945: Admiralty standard scheme.

Repulse
Late 1939: No information available.
1940: Overall light grey.
Mid-1941: Semi-official type of large dark grey and light grey panels, worn until sunk.

King George V
1940: Semi-official dazzle, two colour design.
1941 to 1942: Overall light medium grey or Mountbatten pink.
June, 1942: Admiralty intermediate disruptive type.
Mid-1944: Admiralty standard type.
Mid-1945: Dark hull and light upperwork type.

Prince of Wales
May, 1941: Overall medium grey.
August, 1941 until sunk: Admiralty first disruptive type.

Duke of York
September, 1941: Experimental Admiralty disruptive type.
November, 1941: Overall medium grey.
March, 1943: Dark hull and light upperwork type.
1944: Admiralty standard type.
April, 1945: Dark hull and light upperwork type.

Anson
Mid-1942 until late 1944: Admiralty intermediate disruptive type.
April, 1945: Admiralty standard type.

Howe
Mid-1942 until December, 1944: Admiralty intermediate disruptive type.
January, 1945: Admiralty standard type.
Mid-1945: Dark hull and light upperwork type.
September, 1945: Admiralty standard type.

Aircraft

During the latter half of the Thirties, the provision of aircraft in capital ships was seen as something of a liability, in space and weight, but, because of the restrictions placed on the building of aircraft carriers by Treaty and financial considerations, it was regarded as essential in order to provide the fleet with a reasonable number of torpedo-spotter-reconnaissance aircraft. The carrying of fighters had been abandoned some years before the war, and with the introduction of the Walrus spotter-reconnaissance amphibian, the torpedo-strike capability was also dropped. Early in 1939, consideration was given to fitting aircraft catapults on the quarter-decks of new capital ships, instead of amidships. This system, which was normal practice in foreign navies, had the advantage of leaving the midships structure clear for additional anti-aircraft weapons, galleys and workshops, and simplified the arrangement of the funnel and ventilators for the after boiler room. Unfortunately, it also had several disadvantages:

1. The catapult, crane and lift-opening would be subject to severe blast effects from the after turrets, and would restrict the arc of fire of 'Y' turret.
2. Previous experience, with *Hood* and other ships with quarter-deck catapult installations, had shown that the efficiency of the arrangement would be seriously affected by vibration at high speeds and by wetness in heavy weather, but this last consideration was not so serious in the *Lion* class, because of their greater freeboard aft.
3. The hangar cover could not be guaranteed to be watertight.
4. Any sort of motion of the ship, particularly pitching, would make aircraft handling very difficult.
5. The lift-opening and large hangar space in the after part of the ship, would affect the strength of the hull, increase the tendency to vibration and seriously reduce the watertight integrity.

All these objections were raised by the DNC who pointed out that (5) was his strongest reason for disliking the arrangement as the "loss of *Audacious* pressed home the need that efficient water-tight sub-division aft was of the utmost importance. It has recently been approved to fit additional bulkheads in *Hood* aft for this reason." (The battleship *Audacious* sank after striking a mine in 1914 and her loss was largely due to bad damage-control. The steady flooding of the after part of the ship led to an excessive trim aft, and eventually, capsizing.) With regard to the quarter-deck aircraft arrangements of the battleships of the US Navy, it was concluded that the Americans had accepted the above-mentioned difficulties, for the sake of convenience amidships, but it was also pointed out that British aircraft requirements were more severe:

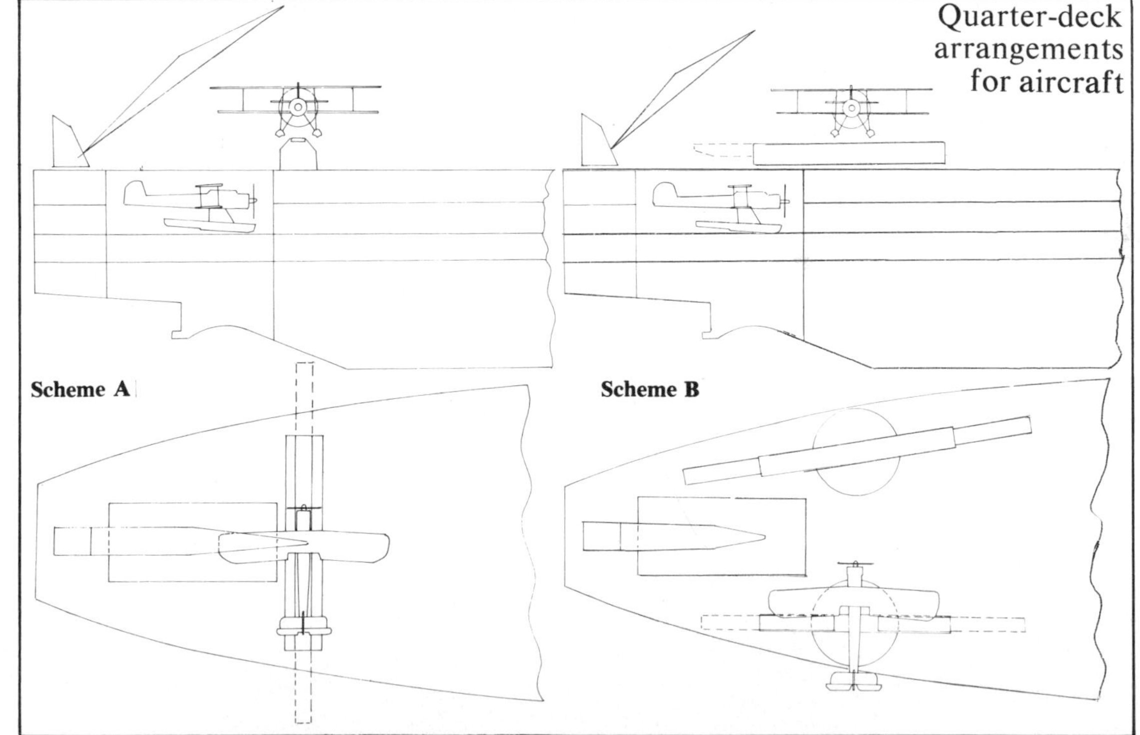

Quarter-deck arrangements for aircraft

Table 100: Comparison of British and American requirements for quarter-deck aircraft arrangements

	Size of lift opening	Length of catapult
Brooklyn class	35 × 20 feet	55 feet
Washington class	35 × 24 feet	65 feet
British requirements	45 × 22 feet	90 feet (extended)

Although never adopted, the question of providing quarter-deck aircraft arrangements was raised several times, before the carrying of aircraft was abandoned completely. Early in 1940, two aircraft arrangement plans for the after section of Design '15C' – one of the early designs for *Vanguard* – were drawn up for examination. The details are shown in the accompanying drawings. One has a fixed cross-deck 'D1VH' extending catapult; the second has two rotating 'E1VH' extending catapults.

Twice during 1940, the Admiralty received suggestions from the Home Fleet, that fighter-aircraft should again be carried by battleships and cruisers, to provide air-defence for the fleet, but on both occasions, an examination of the implications led to the idea being rejected. In October 1940, the Director of Air

Below: *Rodney*'s 'Walrus' aircraft in 1940.

Material, M. S. Slattery, took up this question and suggested that if the fighter-protection needs of the fleet were not being met by carrier or shore-based aircraft, then a battleship/carrier or cruiser/carrier might bear consideration. He prepared a sketch to illustrate his point, and hoped "that the departments better qualified will forgive him for inviting attention to the sketch plan which appears to show that, without inquiring into topweight, structural feasibility, etc., it will be possible to superimpose on a *King George V* or similar heavy ship, without it would seem, impairing the efficiency of the heavy armament, a short landing on deck of similar character to the *Illustrious* class, an assisted take off gear and a hangar for eighteen fleet fighters of our latest projected design". This last-mentioned aircraft was the Blackburn Firebrand, which was due for delivery in January 1942. It was to have been forty feet long, less than fourteen feet high and thirteen and a half feet wide, with folded wings, armed with four cannon and capable of a top speed of 300 knots. The prototype flew in February 1942, but after several more prototypes and alterations, delivery of the production model did not begin until 1945. (The Firebrand was a failure as a fleet fighter, lacking the performance and handling qualities required in 1943 and after, and was finally put into production as a torpedo-bomber, in which role it was scarcely more successful.) However, if eighteen of these aircraft, were not available, the DAM's battleship/carrier could carry twelve Seafires instead.

The idea was examined and rejected, which must have disappointed Slattery, who commented on 3rd January 1941 "It appears to DAM that in an attempt to satisfy Staff requirements the signatories of the minute have made the scheme impractical". The idea was soon revived, however, and in mid-1941, the Director of Naval Construction investigated the possibility of converting a *Lion* class battleship to a battleship/carrier. Drawings were prepared, and the idea was discussed, but was thought to be impracticable because the flight-deck was too short. The Controller then asked the DNC to prepare a design for a ship of the same type, in which the aircraft arrangements were not subordinated to the main armament requirements. This resulted in a design with the following particulars:

Table 101: Particulars of battleship/carrier, July 1940

Dimensions	800 feet (wl) × 112 feet (maximum hull) × 29 feet 10 inches (mean)
Displacement	44,750 tons standard, 51,000 tons deep
SHP	130,000
Speed	28/29 knots
Oil fuel capacity	4,650 tons
Endurance	14,750 miles at 10 knots
Armament	Six 16-inch guns (2 × 3) Sixteen 5·25-inch guns (8 × 2) Six Mk VI pom-pom mountings.
Armour	(as in *Lion* class)
Aircraft	Twelve fighters, two T.S.R.
Flight-deck	500 feet × 73 feet
Lifts	One 45 feet × 33 feet, one 45 feet × 22 feet
Petrol stowage	35,000 gallons
Catapult	One
Safety barrier	One
Arrester wires	Six
Hangar stowage for all aircraft	

The design, together with a number of others (for auxiliary aircraft carriers, cruiser/carriers, etc.) was submitted to the Naval Staff for examination. In his covering remarks, the DNC stated that the "Hangar is unprotected and the superstructure above the upper deck is vulnerable to shell fire and bombs. Funnel uptakes are difficult. As a battleship the vessel is very inferior to the battleship proper". The Naval Staff endorsed these views and raised several objections of their own. Briefly these can be summarised as follows: A dual-purpose ship, being neither carrier nor battleship, would be capable of doing two jobs rather badly, rather than one job well. The Director of the Gunnery Division was particularly vehement, and having spelled out his objections in a long report, concluded "that these abortions are the result of a psychological maladjustment. The necessary re-adjustments should result from a proper re-analysis of the whole question, what would be a balanced fleet in 1945, 1950 or 1955?" The Staff were less violent in stating that, "with the exception of the late D of P," they were of the unanimous opinion that the dual-purpose vessel was not a practical proposition.

As the war progressed, it became increasingly clear that the aircraft carrier was the only really effective method of providing air cover for ships at sea. The main problem of the early war years, was the shortage of these ships that led to the above proposals and to the suggestions to convert one of the *Lion* class, *Vanguard*, and even the old cruisers *Emerald* and *Enterprise* to aircraft carriers. As more carriers came into service, the need for capital ships to carry aircraft gradually diminished, and between 1942 and 1944, the rest of the battleships of the fleet had their aircraft installations removed.

Machinery

The main and auxiliary machinery of British capital ships, and indeed all classes of warship, stood up well to the test of war, despite the fact that they were regularly expected to steam great distances at high power, and operate for prolonged periods without refits or adequate dockyard maintenance facilities. Naturally, under these conditions, weaknesses were revealed, but the majority of these were related to action damage rather than to prolonged steaming. 'Condenseritis' which, during the First World War, had often made it necessary for important warships to be taken into dockyard hands when they could least be spared, was virtually non-existent. As might be expected, the older, unmodernised, capital ships, were more prone to problems than the new and reconstructed vessels. Even in these however, major breakdowns were rare, but long periods without adequate dockyard maintenance usually resulted in loss of speed, and an excessive increase in fuel consumption, with consequent reduction in endurance. The main lessons and problems of the war are briefly as follows:

Boilers. A certain amount of trouble was experienced with excessive corrosion of boiler tubes caused by salt-water contamination of

Left: the funnel of *Barham*, 1937.

boiler-feed water combined with prolonged periods of steaming. In some cases it was necessary to replace tubes after only two years' service. The problem was finally solved by the chemical treatment of boiler-feed water.

Oil fuel. The Admiralty specifications for the types of oil fuel that could be employed in HM ships are very strict, in normal circumstances, but in 1942, they were relaxed in order to expand the available sources of supply. Unlike the regular fuel oils, some of the new types would readily emulsify with sea water, which caused a number of problems, particularly in ships with water-displaced oil-fuel tanks, e.g., as in the underwater-protection compartments of the *King George V* class. This caused the following problems:
1. Emulsified oil fuel in oil-fuel tanks was difficult, and in some cases, impossible to pump.
2. Salt-water contamination of the oil fuel burnt in boilers, caused the formation of hard deposits on super-heater tubes which resulted in reduced boiler efficiency and the need of more frequent boiler cleaning.
3. Contaminated oil fuel in boilers, caused damage to furnace brickwork.

Furnace brickwork. During the war, it was found that the bricks, and their bolts, that formed the refractory walls of naval boilers were not of sufficiently good quality to withstand the high forcing rates and temperatures involved in prolonged periods of steaming at high power. The bricks tended to erode, crack and break, and the bolts were often burnt. Although these faults did not seriously affect the performance of the machinery, they increased the amount of maintenance required. As a result of these experiences, research was begun into improved designs of bricks and brick-bolts.

Shock damage. The use of magnetic-, acoustic- and pressure-operated ground mines and the effect of near-miss bombs, produced a form of damage that had received little attention before 1939. The shock wave produced by a distant underwater explosion was capable of causing severe damage to a ship's hull structure and machinery. The latter usually suffered most particularly from the fracturing of iron castings. Various steps were taken to reduce the likelihood of shock damage, by adding to, and modifying, machinery supports and fixings; by substituting fabricated or cast steel for iron castings, and by designing resilient mountings for machinery. In their final form, these were hard rubber pads, fitted between the machines and their mountings. Non-contact explosions also tended to trip the governors on auxiliary machinery, which, in the case of turbo- and diesel-generators, could cause partial or, in some cases, total loss of electrical power. To overcome this problem, governors were at first gagged but, towards the end of the war, trip-gear which could withstand the sudden shock of a distant explosion was being fitted in the ships of the fleet.

Propeller shafts. As has been related in the previous chapter, one of the causes of the excessive flooding that resulted in the loss of *Prince of Wales*, in December 1941, was the distortion of the port outer propeller shaft. It is believed that there was at least one other instance of this type of damage – although not in a capital ship – where a propeller shaft was distorted by a torpedo explosion, but continued to turn for a short period, thereby opening up the watertight glands in the bulkheads through which the shaft passed. A new design of bulkhead gland was developed, that would accept some degree of shaft distortion without losing its watertightness. A certain amount of difficulty was experienced at first, but a suitable type was eventually evolved and was fitted in all large ships. Consideration was also given to the fitting of a collar to the propeller shaft, at the aftermost plummer-block, to prevent it moving aft, if the shaft were fractured. This occurred in the US cruiser *Houston*, when she was torpedoed in October 1944, but, as far as is known, did not occur in any British ship. The war also showed the need of shaft-holding gear that could lock a damaged shaft if it could not be trailed, i.e., left to rotate freely as the ship moved through the water. Shaft brakes had been fitted before the war, but these were incapable of holding a shaft at speeds in excess of eight knots. Improved locking-gear, capable of holding shafts at higher speeds, had been introduced and fitted in ships, before the end of the war.

Ventilation of machinery compartments. In 1939, the supply and exhaust ventilation fans of the engine rooms in all major British warships, were driven by electric motors. Consequently, action damage resulting in the loss of electric power (as in *Prince of Wales* when she was sunk in December 1941) also caused the failure of the ventilation system in one or more of the engine rooms. These compartments soon became untenable and had to be abandoned prematurely. To prevent a recurrence of this situation, at least one steam-driven exhaust fan was subsequently fitted in engine rooms and important auxiliary machinery compartments. In the generator compartments, the electrically-driven fans were retained, but they were re-wired to run directly from the generator. If the generator were damaged (or – in the case of turbo-generators – the steam power failed) and unable to supply power, there would be little point in manning the compartment, which could be abandoned without further decreasing the available power.

Lubrication systems. Early in the war, it was found that the lubrication system for turbine machinery could not operate satisfactorily in a ship that was listing heavily, following underwater damage. This tended to cause damage to or failure of, the machinery and the forced-lubrication systems, therefore, were so modified as to operate in a ship that was listing up to fifteen degrees.

Electrical supply and fittings

Generally speaking, too much reliance was placed on electrically-driven auxiliaries before the war. The generators supplied power for ventilation fans, hydraulic machinery (for secondary and anti-aircraft armaments and steering gear) and for most of the pumps. It would have been equally bad if the auxiliaries had depended too much on steam power, and one of the main lessons of the war was that power for equipment should be divided as equally as possible between steam and electricity. The generation of electricity was itself too dependent on steam power, because the majority of the generators were turbo-driven, and for this reason, *Vanguard*'s proportion of turbo- to diesel-generators was changed from 6/2 to 4/4. The point can be illustrated by taking two extremes. When *Prince of Wales* was sunk, the loss of a high percentage of her electric power resulted in a situation where, although she still had steam power, high-angle /low-angle armament, pumping system, steering gear and ventilation were either partially or completely inoperable. At the other end of the scale, *Warspite* lost all her steam when she was hit and near-missed by radio-controlled bombs, off Salerno in 1943. Power supplies, therefore, depended entirely on the diesel-driven generators, which could just manage to supply the pumps, and it was fortunate that one or both of these generators was not put out of action by the bombs. On a more minor scale, three important lessons were learned:

1. Important services, such as the fire- and bilge-pumps, needed secondary electrical supplies, in case the main supply failed.
2. Electricity supply to essential services, needed to be watertight throughout.
3. Electrical fittings in areas that could be flooded from leaking oil-fuel tanks needed to be oiltight as well as watertight.

Damage-control

The war revealed many serious defects in the damage-control organisation, pumping systems, fire-fighting arrangements and watertight integrity, and as the war progressed these were gradually improved, so that by 1945, practically all weak points had been eliminated. The weaknesses revealed and the improvements made during the war are noted, briefly, as follows:

1. General:
1. Additional damage-control stores (cement, shores, steel boxes, etc.) were provided, and stowed in well-situated and widely separated positions.
2. The war revealed the need of keeping the corners and edges of compartments as clear of pipes and fittings as possible, in order to provide access for emergency repairs.
3. Communications with the damage-control head-quarters were improved, telephone communications were sound-powered, independent of the main exchange, duplicated, extended and made watertight.
4. It was shown that the damage-control head-quarters needed to be easily accessible.
5. Emergency oil-lamps were replaced by emergency battery-lamps.
6. It was found that access-trunks were, in some cases, too small to allow men and portable pumps to pass through with reasonable ease.

2. Watertight sub-division:
1. Trunked-access and escape was provided for important compartments, both inside and outside the citadel. These trunks were vertical shafts, extending upwards from a compartment through one or more decks. Thus, if the compartment itself were flooded and its entry hatch were not made watertight, any extension of the flooding would be restricted to the trunk. If the compartment(s) above were flooded, the trunk provided an escape route for the personnel in the lower compartment, and again, prevented the extension of the flooding via a non-watertight or open hatch.
2. To generally restrict the spread of secondary flooding (i.e., flooding not directly a result of fractured hull structures), side scuttles, hatches, skylights and watertight doors were reduced to a minimum.
3. It was found that certain watertight doors in longitudinal bulkheads, such as those to oil-fuel working spaces, needed to be so arranged as to open outboard, so that any flooding from outboard would tend to force them shut rather than open.
4. Ventilator-trunks were stiffened, and fitted with additional valves, where they passed through decks.

3. Fire-fighting and fire prevention:
1. The water-pressure in fire mains was increased, as was the number of hose-connections and isolating-valves in fire mains.
2. Branch-pipes and hose-nozzles were re-designed so that they could produce either a jet of water or a spray.
3. The number of portable fire-extinguishers was increased, and their design was improved.
4. The steam-smothering system fitted in boiler rooms to extinguish oil-fuel fires, was extended to the main engine rooms and, eventually, to almost all machinery compartments.
5. The design of portable foam-generating equipment was improved.
6. Diesel-driven fire-pumps were provided in case electrical power should fail.
7. To reduce first risks diesel-driven boats were substituted for petrol-driven, oil-fired ranges were replaced by electrical ranges in galleys and, although not entirely for this reason, aircraft-fuel was removed.

4. Pumping arrangements:
1. The pumping systems for the 350-ton pumps were extended.
2. Additional portable pumps were provided, and the number of electrical-power connections for them was increased.
3. During the later years of the war, diesel-driven portable pumps were provided, in case the loss of electrical power rendered the electrically-driven portable pumps inoperable.
4. Rapid-pumping facilities were provided for compartments inboard of the protective bulkheads.
5. The provision of turbine-driven pumps in machinery spaces was increased, and the number of electrically-driven pumps was reduced.

Weather damage

A ship encountering heavy weather in peacetime, would reduce speed and, if necessary, modify her course to that most suitable for keeping the ship dry and free of excessive strains or superficial damage. In very severe conditions, it might even be considered desirable for the ship to 'heave-to' until such time as the weather abated. In wartime, these precautionary measures were often overridden by pressing operational requirements, that might necessitate a speed or course which invited damage. It cannot be said that a large ship will suffer less than a small one under such conditions; in fact, under certain conditions, the reverse will be the case, but obviously the effect of such damage will not be so keenly felt in a battleship, as in a destroyer. The war, therefore, revealed weaknesses that would not normally have been apparent in peacetime. One of the more obvious lessons of the war was the need of a high freeboard, and a substantial sheer, forward, as in *Vanguard*. Others, included the following:
1. The breakwaters on forecastle-decks, in some cases, were found to be insufficiently supported to withstand the force of solid water coming over the forecastle, and a certain amount of stiffening was necessary.
2. The watertightness of gun-ports, particularly those in the 14-inch and 5.25-inch turrets, was insufficient to prevent water gaining entry in bad weather. The sealing of such ports was improved during the war.
3. The movements of upper-decks and forecastle-decks in heavy seas, tended to cause the rivets in the angle-connections between decks and barbettes to shear, allowing water to find its way below, into mess spaces, which caused considerable inconvenience. This problem was overcome by fitting flexible sheet steel parapets between the barbette and its angle-connection. Post-war research resulted in improved structural arrangements in the way of barbettes.
4. A considerable amount of water tended to find its way below, via mushroom-top ventilators, particularly those in forecastle-decks. Weather-deck ventilators were modified and valves were fitted in the trunks immediately below the deck, so that the ventilators could, if necessary, be shut off in heavy weather.

18. What Price?

What was the value of the British battleship during the Second World War? Was the construction and reconstruction of such ships necessary? Could the expenditure of time, money and lives have been put to better use elsewhere? These questions are often answered in hindsight, with little thought to the conditions and equipment of the period in question. It is hoped that, the following opinions of the authors will provide food for thought, and a clearer picture of the position occupied by the capital ship during the Second World War.

The chapter is divided under two headings: general considerations, and comparison with foreign ships.

General considerations

Before the war, it was thought that the main function of the battleship was to engage similar vessels of other navies in a fleet action. For the British, few actions of this type occurred during the war, and of these, only two – the *Bismarck* action and the sinking of *Scharnhorst* – resembled preconceptions that held sway, before the war. The Mediterranean provided the setting and circumstances required to bring battleships into direct conflict, but the extremely cautious handling of the Italian fleet usually resulted in short and indecisive battles which ended with the enemy making for base, at high speed. It was in circumstances such as these that pre-war strategists envisaged the aircraft carrier as providing the necessary long-range strike capability required to slow the enemy down sufficiently to allow the battleships to bring

Malaya on 28th January 1943. The aircraft arrangements have been removed, two twin 4-inch mountings added and two eight-barrel pom-poms fitted on the after superstructure.

him to action. Thus, even in the early years of the war, the Fleet Air Arm was seen as playing a supporting role to the battleship.

Supposing – as the air enthusiasts would have wished – that the aircraft carrier had been considered the prime unit of the fleet before the war. Assuming that it had been available in similar numbers to the battleship, and with adequate numbers of aircraft, there can be little doubt that it would have been equally as successful as the battleship, and in some cases, more so. Against *Bismarck*, a large force of carriers could have been equally as successful, but not more so. Against *Scharnhorst*, sunk during a night of darkness and storm, it would have been impossible for one carrier to have achieved the success of *Duke of York*. In the Mediterranean, a large force of carriers would, without doubt, have achieved much, particularly against the reluctant Italian fleet, and the heavy losses caused by enemy dominance of the air could have been minimised. There are, however, two many assumptions in these arguments, and they are achieved with the considerable advantage of hindsight. If the Admiralty had been able to visualise such events in the 1930s, then so would the other naval powers of the world. The building of aircraft carriers would have been, and was in many ways, equally as competitive as battleship construction, and the balance of power between the nations would not have materially altered. In any case, it did not take long for the Admiralty to change its priorities; of the pre-war programmes, five battleships and six fleet carriers were completed. During the war, one battleship was laid down, and more than thirty fleet, and light fleet carriers were ordered. (Large numbers of these ships were still building or not yet laid down, at the end of the war, and these were cancelled.)

It was not until after 1945, that the battleship was finally regarded as obsolete, and, bearing in mind that such important decisions require some factor of safety, it was not an over-cautious conclusion. The end of the era of the battleship had often been prophesied. The torpedo-boat and, later, the submarine, had been hailed as weapons that ultimately would cause the battleship to lose its command of the sea. Adequate counter-measures were developed, however, and when the supporters of aviation (mainly the RAF and USAAC) again proclaimed the end of the battleship, in the years following the First World War, the Admiralty, understandably, considered that adequate counter-measures would again be found. The air enthusiasts, moreover, did not show much understanding of naval construction and tended to overstate their case. Remarks regarding the dropping of bombs down the funnels of warships were not uncommon, and, although ridiculous, they could seem quite plausible to an uneducated public. There were of course men with a clear vision of the future of air warfare, but even they tended to confuse what was possible at the time, with what would be possible in the future. It must be remembered, that the Admiralty was responsible for maintaining a navy, adequate for the defence of Britain in existing and reasonably foreseeable circumstances, and not for the theoretical circumstances that might exist at some vague future period. Strangely, it was the bomb that was most quoted as the weapon that would ultimately destroy the battleship, and yet it was the aerial-torpedo that posed the greatest threat. It was not until the radio-controlled bomb, the rocket-assisted bomb, and, later, the guided-missile had been introduced, that the non-subsurface weapon achieved the power required to cause fatal damage to a modern battleship. (There were of course some very large bombs produced during the war, of which the most obvious examples are those used to sink *Tirpitz*. It must be remembered, however, that an extremely high degree of skill is required to hit a moving ship in a high-level bombing attack. When *Tirpitz* was sunk, she was at her moorings and not under way.)

The vulnerability of battleships to aircraft attack has often been given as the reason for its becoming obsolete. To support this view, the Fleet Air Arm attack on Taranto, the Japanese attack on Pearl Harbor, the sinking of *Bismarck*, *Prince of Wales* and *Repulse*, are the most frequently quoted examples of the superiority of aircraft over the battleship. These events, however, did not demonstrate the obsolescence of the battleship, but they showed very forcibly that they could not operate efficiently (or be considered safe from attack when in harbour) without adequate air cover. Thus, a battleship needed aircraft to defend it from enemy aircraft, in the same way that it required a destroyer screen as defence against enemy destroyers, torpedo-boats and submarines. The parallel goes further, in that the battleship itself, had to be armed with anti-aircraft guns, just as it was armed with anti-torpedo-boat guns, and its destroyer and aircraft escort could be used for offensive as well as defensive purposes. The Admiralty was correct, therefore, in assuming that adequate counter-measures could be provided to defend the fleet against air attacks. The presence of aircraft carriers in sufficient numbers (or shore-based aircraft when operating close enough to an airfield) could provide the air defence necessary to ensure a reasonable level of safety for the battle fleet. Why then, did the battleship become obsolete?

The answer to this question can be found in a simple illustration of the effect of the aircraft carrier on fleet operations. The prime purpose of the battle fleet was to bring to action and defeat in a gun duel, the battleships of the enemy fleet. To ensure this end, the subsidiary vessels of the fleet were intended to carry out the necessary supporting roles. The aircraft carrier was originally seen as another subsidiary vessel, that could provide reconnaissance, air-defence and air-strike capabilities, in support of the operations of the battle fleet. The aircraft carrier could, however, deliver an attack, well beyond the range of the largest gun afloat, and it is this that ultimately ensured the obsolesence of the battleship.

In a battle between aircraft carriers of opposing forces, the outcome could be decided without the battleships ever sighting each other, let alone engaging in a gun duel. The guns of the battleship were its *raison d'être*, and if they could not be used in battle, the battleship had no place in the fleet. The aircraft carrier, in achieving a position where it provided the main striking-power of the fleet, had become the new capital ship of the fleet, around which, the organisation of naval strategy and tactics was evolved.

Although the aircraft carrier was quick to establish its superiority in the Pacific Ocean, the events in the European theatre of war were less dramatic. Neither Germany nor Italy possessed an aircraft carrier (although both nations had begun building them) and the air threat to British ships came entirely from land-based aircraft. During the early years of the war, the Royal Navy had too few carriers, equipped with insufficient and obsolescent aircraft, so the rise of the Fleet Air Arm to its position of superiority was not achieved overnight. It can be said, therefore, that the construction and reconstruction of British battleships was justified for the following reasons:

1. Before 1939, the effectiveness of the aircraft carrier had not been proved.

2. British carrier aircraft and their methods of operation were insufficiently advanced in the early war years, to take the place of the battleships.

3. So long as other naval powers continued to build battleships, Britain was obliged to do the same.

4. If, by some chance, a battleship came within gun-range of a fleet that had no battleship protection, it could, theoretically, destroy that force or certainly disrupt any operation in which it was involved. Such an occurrence was possible if, say, the aircraft carrier escort had been neutralised by action damage, or bad weather had made it necessary to cease flying operations.

These arguments are weakened considerably, if one considers what might have been. If the ships of the *King George V* class had been aircraft carriers; if more finance had been available, if the Royal Navy had retained control of the Fleet Air Arm in 1917, but there are altogether too many 'ifs' in such assumptions. The best that can be said is, that via a rather untidy and involved process between 1939 and 1945, the emphasis of naval warfare shifted from the battleship to the aircraft carrier. Even then the battleship was seen as a valuable part of the fleet, and it is believed that the Admiralty was considering battleship designs, as late as 1946.

Comparison with foreign ships

Tables 102–4 give the basic details of the main battleship classes, constructed or designed by the major naval powers, between 1934 and 1940. *Scharnhorst*, *Dunkerque*, *Alaska* and the Japanese *B65* (cancelled) are not included, because they have no direct British equivalent. *Yamato* is similarly placed, but as this was the only class of modern Japanese capital ship to be built, it was considered necessary to include the details in order to illustrate Japanese practice. The cancelled *Montana* class are included to give a contrast to the Japanese ships. *King George V*, *North Carolina*, *Richelieu*, *Littorio* and *Bismarck*, all fall into the group of ships that should have been designed to the international 35,000-ton displacement limit. The British, American and French ships were designed to this limit, but the Italian and German ships were not. The increased displacements of the former vessels were the results of additions made to the ships, after the limit was raised to 45,000 tons. The *Iowa* class were designed to this 45,000-ton limit, but the *Lion* class were designed to the voluntary British limit of 40,000 tons.

Armament. Britain was alone in taking up the 14-inch gun as a main armament weapon, following the decision, at the London Naval Conference of 1936, to accept this as the maximum gun calibre. The only other signatory to this agreement was the USA, and the original design for *North Carolina* followed very closely that of *King George V* viz.: 35,000 tons, twelve 14-inch guns in three quadruple turrets, speed twenty-seven knots. The Americans, however, specified that provision be made to replace the three 14-inch turrets, should Japan fail to agree to the 14-inch gun. Moreover, they delayed the laying down of their new ships, until the Japanese failure to sign, raised the gun calibre to 16-inch. Among the other navies, with the exception of the Japanese, the most popular gun calibre was 15-inch. The British 14-inch gun and mounting, with its low velocity/heavy shell combination, appears to have been successful (after a few teething troubles) and it must be remembered, when comparing this gun to heavier foreign guns, that the relatively thicker armour on British capital ships tended to equalise differences in penetrating power.

The American 16-inch guns of the First World War, fired a 2,100-pound shell, at a muzzle velocity of 2,600 feet per second. The shell weight was later increased to 2,240 pounds with a muzzle velocity of 2,520, which indicates that the US Navy had problems similar to those experienced by the Royal Navy with high velocity/light shell guns. The US 16-inch Mk VI and VII guns were provided with an even heavier armour-piercing shell weighing 2,700 pounds, but these guns also employed the earlier 2,240-pound armour-piercing shell as an alternative. In the US 16-inch Mk VII gun, the muzzle velocity was raised by increasing the length of the bore. As far is is known, the American 16-inch guns and mountings were successful, but the triple mounting had problems with the loading-cycle similar to those experienced with *Nelson* and *Rodney*, mainly because of the odd number of guns. Both the British and the Americans retained the light shells (2,048 pounds for the British 16-inch Mk XII and 2,100 pounds for the US Mk VI and VII) as high explosive projectiles.

The German 15-inch guns were high-velocity weapons with a substantial range, and good accuracy. The twin mounting was successful, although it could not, in practice, maintain its designed rate of fire of two rounds per gun per minute. The flash-tightness of the turrets was good, but there were

Table 102: Comparison of the main battleship classes constituted or designed by the major naval powers between 1934 and 1940

Class:	*King George V*	*North Carolina*	*Richelieu*	*Littorio*	*Bismarck*	*Lion*	*Vanguard*	*Iowa*	*Yamato*	*Montana*
Nationality	British	American	French	Italian	German	British	British	American	Japanese	American
Programme year	1936	1936	1935	1934	1935	1938	1940	1940	1937	1940
Completed	1940 to 42	1941	1940	1940 to 42	1941	cancelled	1946	1943 to 44	1941 to 42	cancelled
Length (oa) feet	745	729	813¼	777	820	785	814	888	863	921
Length (pp) feet	700		794			740	760		800	
Beam (maximum) feet	103	108¼	108¼	108	118	104	108	108	128	121
Draught (deep) feet	34	35	35	34.5	35	33½	35	38	36	36
Standard displacement (tons)	36,700 (1940)	36,600 (1941)	40,000	41,377	41,700	40,550	44,500	50,000 (1945)	64,000	60,500
Deep displacement (tons)	42,000 (1940)	44,800 (1941)	47,548	45,963	50,900	46,000	51,420	59,300 (1945)	72,800	70,500
Main armament:	10 14-inch	9 16-inch	8 15-inch	9 15-inch	8 15-inch	9 16-inch	8 15-inch	9 16-inch	9 18-inch	12 16-inch
Armour (inches thickness):										
Main belt (maximum)	15 and 14	12	13.5	13.8	12.6	15	14 and 13	12.2	16	16 (+8 internal)
Barbettes (maximum)	13	16	16	13.8	13	15	13	17	20	
Turret (face)	12.75	16	17		14	15	13	17	20	
Turret (roof)	6	7	6.8–7.8		5 and 7	6	6	7.25	9	
Upper-deck	1.5	1.45		1.4 and 2.7 (+0.4) (*)	2	1.5	1.5	1.5		2.2
Main-deck	6 and 5	3.6 and 4.1	6 and 6.8	3.9 and 5.9		6 and 5	6 and 5	5	7.5	6 and 5
Middle-deck			2 and 1.6		3.2, 4 and 4.7			0.75 (splinter-deck)		0.75 (splinter-deck)
SHP	110,000	121,000	150,000	130,000	150,000	130,000	130,000	212,000	150,000	172,000
Shafts	4	4	4	4	3	4	4	4	4	4
Speed (knots)	28	28	30	30	30	30	30	33	27	28
Oil fuel capacity (tons)	3,700	7,150	6,800	4,450	6,500	3,700	4,400	7,000	6,300	
Endurance (nautical miles)	6,000 at 16 knots	15,000 at 15 knots	11,000 at 18 knots	4,580 at 16 knots	9,300 at 16 knots	6,000 at 16 knots	8,000 at 15 knots	15,000 at 12 knots	7,200 at 16 knots	
Boilers	8	8	6	8	12	8	8	8	12	8

* Forecastle-deck.

Table 103: Comparative weights of *King George V*, *North Carolina* and *Bismarck* (tons)

	King George V	*North Carolina*	*Bismarck*
General equipment	1,150	1,130	1,300
Machinery	2,770	3,120	4,200
Armament	6,570	4,450	7,400
Armour	12,410	8,150	17,300
Hull	13,830	19,600	11,500
Standard displacement:	36,730	36,450	41,700

Notes. Figures for *King George V* and *Bismarck* as completed in 1940, those for *North Carolina* are approximated from a 1939 estimate of weights. Reason for large differences in Armament/Armour/Hull for *North Carolina* and other ships is that USN included deck armour in hull weight and turret armour in armour weight. The RN included deck armour in armour weight and turret armour in armament weight. There were also a few other variations. As a very rough guide, the figures for *North Carolina* on the British system would be about 5,700 tons for armament, 11,000 tons for armour and 15,500 tons for the hull, give or take 1,000 tons.

Table 104: Comparison of battleship main armament in use by the major naval powers during the Second World War

Nation	Calibre (inches)	Year and Mark	Length (calibres)	Weights (tons)	AP Shell weight (tons)	MV fps	Range at maximum elevation (yards)
Britain	14	1936 Mk VII	45	90	1,590	2,475	36,000 at 40°
Britain	15*	1912 Mk I (N)	42	97	1,938	2,450	32,200 at 30°
Britain	16	1938 Mk II	45	??	2,375	2,450	43,800 at 40°
USA**	16	1937 Mk VI	45	96	2,700	2,300	36,900 at 45°
USA***	16	1940 Mk VII	50	119.6	2,700	2,500	42,345 at 45°
Germany	15	1934	47	109.2	1,758	2,690	39,590 at 35°
France	15	1935	45	110	1,936	2,725	43,600 at 35°
Italy	15	1931	50	102.4	1,950	2,800	46,800 at 35°
Japan	18·1	1939	45	181.5	3,220	2,556	45,960 at 45°

* With modified projectile.
** Mounted in *South Dakota* and *North Carolina* classes.
*** Mounted in *Iowa* class.

Below: *Howe,* arriving in Auckland, New Zealand, in 1945.

two weaknesses in the system. (a) The loading arrangements were such as to allow a dangerous build-up of ready-use charges in the loading-chamber. (b) The turrets were provided with no explosion-vents, and this is probably why the back of *Bismarck*'s 'B' turret was blown out during her action with *Rodney* and *King George V*. The French and Italian 15-inch guns fired shells of similar weight to those in the British Mk I, but with a higher velocity. In the Italian gun, this was achieved by increasing the length to 50 calibres, but it is not clear how the French achieved such a high figure unless they used more powerful charges, or unless the figure quoted in the Tables is incorrect. No details are known of the performance of Italian and French turrets, but it is interesting to note the use by the French of two quadruple turrets in *Richelieu*. This gave a substantial weight-saving over four twins or three triples, but at the same time, it did not tend to place critical importance on the protection and reliability of the mountings. Moreover, with both turrets forward, there was a risk of losing the entire main armament through the flooding of the main magazine group which was all in one block. (The last ship of the *Richelieu* class, which was never completed, was re-designed with one turret forward and one aft.)

The Japanese 18-inch guns stood alone, and little can be achieved by comparing them to smaller weapons. It is very unlikely that these guns and their triple mountings were very efficient, mainly because of the great weights and blast effects involved. Little detail is known about the success or failure of the design, but they were certainly slow in training; it took forty-five seconds to train a turret through ninety degrees – two degrees per second.

According to an American report produced after the war, the most reliable and accurate main-armament weapon of the war was the British twin 15-inch Mk I. Of course, there were guns and mountings with better individual characteristics, but none had the all-round efficiency of this mounting, which resulted from its simplicity, ease of maintenance, and from the fact that the 15-inch Mk I was an excellent gun. The German twin 15-inch probably ran a close second, but it is worth remembering that the British ships had been carrying the twin 15-inch continuously since 1915, which gave more than sufficient time to iron out any faults that may have existed in the original design, and to bring the mounting to its peak of efficiency.

Armour.* With the exception of Germany, all the naval powers employed the 'all-or-nothing' protection scheme in their modern capital ships. As has been stated earlier, there was probably very little to choose between the quality of the armour used by the various naval powers. Any differences would have been of a very minor nature, and would not have materially affected their powers of resistance to armour-piercing shells. The production of steel alloys is a commercial rather than a military industry, and the development of improved qualities of steel was in no way a secret affair. The type of steel used for armour could, therefore, be found in use in many other fields, although the percentages of the additives (nickel, chrome, etc.) would be varied to meet the use to which the steel was to be put. Armour-plate production is, nevertheless, a specialised industry, in that the armour has to be produced in very large and thick sections, and its heat-treatment process entails problems not encountered in other areas. The quality of armour, therefore, depended largely on the careful control of the production process, and it was in this field that the majority of improvements were made between the wars.

In *Bismarck*, the distribution of armour was generally similar to that employed in the last of Germany's First World War battleships, *Baden* and *Bayern*. This is not altogether surprising, for Germany had little reason to doubt the efficiency of the protection of their earlier ships, and having been deprived of sea experience and a large corps of naval constructors for so long, they naturally looked to their last successful design for a base from which to design their new ships. Thus, while all other nations gave their ships a comparatively uniform belt armour thickness, *Bismarck*'s belt reduced in thickness to ten inches above the armoured-deck, and to six inches between the main-deck and the upper-deck. The main armoured-deck was at middle-deck level. Over the machinery, it was 3.2 inches thick on the flat and 4 inches thick on the slope. Over the magazines, it was 4 inches thick on the flat and 4.7 inches thick on the slope. Lack of adequate protection above the middle-deck led to the rapid loss of internal communications in *Bismarck*, not long after the commencement of her action with *Rodney* and *King George V*. All other nations fitted their ships with a main armoured-deck, one level higher, at main-deck level, to restrict the volume of vulnerable structure above the citadel, but the Italian *Littorio* and the Japanese *Yamato* had an additional (forecastle) deck above the upper-deck. The thickness of the upper-deck is usually included in the armour thickness, but being the strength-deck, it is thick for structural reasons, and its protective qualities are of a purely secondary nature. Probably the best that could be expected of these decks is that they would decap an armour-piercing shell and slightly reduce its velocity. The only exception was the Italian *Littorio* class, which had protective plating on the forecastle-deck. It is not unusual to find the total thickness of all decks quoted as the horizontal protection for a ship. It is worth remembering, in these cases, that two or more thin decks are not so good as one of the same total thickness, and that protective plating does not have so high a resistance to penetration as armour. It is assumed here that, like the British, all the nations employed deck armour for the main protective-deck and not built-up protective plating as in the First World War.

Another factor, not always considered when comparing schemes of protection, is the depth of the armour belt. Approximate

*For clarity, the designation of decks used in this section follows British Second World War practice.

Below: the French battleship *Richelieu* at Trincomalee in 1944.

Opposite page: *Nelson* in March 1946.

NELSON

Below: the United States battleship *North Carolina*, shortly after completion.

figures for these depths, and their relationship to the deep waterline (dwl) established from the deep draughts given in Table 102, are shown on Table 105.

From these figures, it can be seen that the British and German ships have the deepest belt armour, but that for *Bismarck* is mainly above the waterline. This had its advantages in protecting the upper hull structure (although in the case of the 6-inch thick upper belt this is a debatable point) but it gave very poor protection against diving shell. The British ships, therefore, have the better side protection in terms of the depth covered and protection against diving shell, while the Italian ships have the worst. (The Japanese *Yamato* did in fact have better protection against diving shell, because her belt armour was continued vertically downwards to the bottom of the ship, in the form of a very thick torpedo bulkhead, gradually reducing in thickness.) The American ships of the *South Dakota* and *Iowa* classes, which are not shown in the Table, had protection against diving shell which, in the case of the former ship, was worse than that of the Italian ships, and in the latter, better than that of the British ships. This point serves to illustrate a lack of consistency in the schemes of side protection adopted in the battleships of the US Navy. Each of the four classes, built or ordered, were provided with a different form of side protection:

Table 105: Depth of armour belt

Class	Depth of armour belt (feet)	Below dwl (feet)	Above dwl (feet)
King George V	24	15	9
Vanguard	24	14	10
Bismarck	24	8	16
Richelieu	20	13	7
Montana	20	10	10
Yamato	18½	12	6½
North Carolina	16	11	5
Littorio	13	7	6

North Carolina:
This class had an external belt, set at an angle of fifteen degrees to the vertical, at the bottom of which was a small external bulge, which allowed partial outboard venting of underwater explosions. The main underwater-protection compartments were internal, being below and behind the belt.

South Dakota:
This class had a belt, 12.2 inches thick, set at an angle of nineteen degrees and fitted at the top of a 1-inch protective bulkhead. Thus, the belt was about sixteen feet inboard of the skin plating, with the underwater-protection compartments outside it. The armoured-deck – increased to 5-inch thickness in this class – was extended out over the belt to the ship's side. With the side armour so far inboard, there must have been a very real danger that a shell could penetrate the ship's vitals under the belt, and it would not necessarily have to dive, to do so. At a suitable angle of descent, a shell striking at the waterline, could have reached the machinery or magazines by passing through only the thin structure of the bulge protection and the torpedo bulkhead.

Iowa:
The 12.2-inch thick side armour of *Iowa* was arranged in a similar manner to that of *South Dakota*. The main belt was about fourteen feet deep, but it was extended to approximately thirty feet below the deep waterline, in reduced thickness tapering to one inch at the lower edge. This side-protection system thus gave better protection against diving shell.

Montana:
The 19° sloping main belt of this class was arranged on similar lines to that of *North Carolina*, with an underwater-protection system partly inboard and partly outboard of the citadel. They did, however, have an additional internal belt in the form of a very thick protective bulkhead, which extended from the middle-deck to the ship's bottom. It tapered in thickness from eight inches at its top edge, to one inch at its bottom edge.

Strangely enough, the British, who had instigated the sloping belt during the First World War, and the internal sloping belt in the *Nelson* class, abandoned both schemes in their new battleships while, with the exception of Germany, all the other naval powers adopted a sloping belt. Only the USA and France adopted an internal sloping belt, which, in the latter case (the *Richelieu* class), closely resembled that of *Nelson.*

It is interesting to note the high level of protection provided for turrets and barbettes in the American and French ships, relative to their side armour. In theory, the thicknesses of the belt abreast the magazines, barbettes and turret faces, should have been reasonably uniform – each is equally important, and, if anything, the belt is more so, for given adequate proof against flash, a penetrated turret or barbette will only be put out of action, whereas a penetrated magazine might cause the total loss of the ship. Another feature of interest, is the retention of the heavily-armoured conning-tower in the American, German and French navies. These structures were of little use, and added considerably to the top-weight and weight of armour. That of *Bismarck* certainly seems to have done little to protect her officers, communications and fire-control arrangements, all of which suffered heavily in the early stages of her action with *Rodney* and *King George V*.

The following theoretical conclusions can be drawn from a study of the schemes of protection and the armaments of British ships versus those of other navies:

King George V class:
In general, the battleships of the other navies could penetrate the armour of *King George V*, slightly beyond the range at which she could penetrate theirs.

Lion class:
In general, *Lion* could have penetrated the armour of all the battleships of the other navies (with the exception of *Yamato*) before they could get close enough to penetrate hers.

Vanguard:
The protection of *Vanguard*, relative to her gun power, gives her approximate equality in power to the battleships of the other navies.

These, of course, are very simple generalisations which cannot take account of the many variables that may result from tactics, inclination and so on. Insufficient evidence is available to prove the point, but it seems likely that, whatever the theoretical penetrating power of armour-piercing shells, the thick armour used during the Second World War was almost inpenetrable under normal battle conditions. If this were so, it would be the power of guns to destroy the control-positions and unarmoured portions of a ship, that would control the outcome of a gun duel.

Underwater protection. Very little is known of the value of the underwater-protection systems used by the various navies, and in order to make an accurate comparison, the results of the scientific tests carried out on the arrangements would be required. Nevertheless, some rough conclusions can be drawn from the information given in Table 106. The

Table 106: Underwater protection systems

	Depth of bulge compartments (feet)	Height of bulge compartments (feet)	Thickness of protective bulkheads (inches)	Remarks
King George V	13	25	$1\frac{3}{4}$–$1\frac{1}{2}$	Sandwich (air-liquid-air); internal venting
Vanguard	15	36	$1\frac{3}{4}$–$1\frac{1}{2}$	
North Carolina	20	30		Sandwich (air-liquid-air); external and internal venting
Bismarck	19	34	$1\frac{3}{4}$	Air space and oil fuel tanks; internal venting
Littorio	25	40	$1\frac{1}{2}$	Internal air drum surrounded by water; internal and external venting
Richelieu	20	32	$\frac{3}{4}$	Internal and external venting

height of the system is generally more important than its width, because an underwater explosion tends to vent itself upwards. For the same reason, external venting is preferable to systems that allow explosions to vent into the citadel. The attention of the British was very forcibly drawn to these points by the loss of *Prince of Wales*, and the resulting improvement can be seen in the increased height of the bulge-compartments for *Vanguard*. With this in mind, it can be seen that most countries seem to have provided better underwater protection for their ships than did Britain. The Italians appear to have produced the best system, about which, unfortunately, the authors know little, but it was certainly unusual and very extensive. No system of underwater protection was provided in *Bismarck* apart from that afforded by an outside air space (between the skin plating and the wing oil-fuel tanks) and her protective bulkhead. Abreast the forward engine rooms and boiler rooms, there were no wing compartments, so that any leak in the protective bulkhead in these areas would have resulted in the flooding of a major machinery compartment. This is a serious deficiency when one considers that *Bismarck* had ten feet more beam than the majority of other battleships, and fifteen feet more than the *King George V* class.

Machinery. All nations, except Germany and Japan, used some form of unit machinery arrangement to reduce the risk of their ships losing motive power if extensive flooding of the machinery compartments occurred. In *Bismarck*, the machinery compartments were very large, occupying an area 254 feet long and 78 feet wide compared to 174 feet x 72 feet in *Vanguard*, a ship of approximately equal speed and size. The individual engine rooms and boiler rooms of *Bismarck*, however, were of approximately equal size to those in British ships, the additional space being occupied by four extra boilers, and a vast amount of auxiliary machinery. This explains the apparently excessive 4,200 tons for *Bismarck*'s machinery. Of this weight, only 2,800 tons was for the main machinery, the remaining 1,400 tons being for auxiliary machinery, compared to 2,300 tons for the main, and 400 tons for the auxiliary machinery of *King George V*. An even stranger state of affairs existed with the machinery for the US battleships, which had very light machinery that nevertheless, occupied a comparatively large space. The main machinery for *North Carolina*, for example, weighed 1,900 tons and occupied an area 220 feet long and 72 feet wide. The combined engine and boiler rooms were forty-five feet long, seventy-two feet wide and twenty-four feet high. The largest machinery compartments in *King George V* were the boiler rooms; these were forty-five feet long, twenty-five feet wide and thirty-two feet high. The US ships were also given a parallel beam over the midship section – an expedient to keep the width of the ships within the limits of the Panama Canal, but the resulting hull form was not the most efficient for propulsion through the water – hence the much higher powers developed in the American ships when compared to other vessels of equal size and speed. The high speed of the *Iowa* class, thirty-three knots (designed) was the result of a requirement that they should operate with, and protect a fast carrier force. It is unlikely, however, that they could have maintained such a speed under normal action conditions, and any margin of speed they possessed over the ships of other nations, would have been of small tactical value – a lesson that the British had learnt with the *Queen Elizabeth* class during the First World War. Generally, the ships of the *Iowa* class seem to be under-gunned for their size; the additional space and weight having been put into the machinery and improved protection, compared to the earlier ships. By contrast, the earlier 35,000-ton (designed) American battleships appear to have been over-gunned, resulting in some sacrifice in protection. The British certainly regarded 35,000-ton ships armed with 16-inch guns as a poorly-balanced design.

A serious deficiency of British capital ships in the early years of the war, was that their electricity-generating capacity was insufficient for the demands made upon it. *King George V* had a generating capacity of 2,800 kilowatts, *North Carolina* could produce 8,800 kilowatts, *Bismarck* 7,910 kilowatts and nearly all other capital ships could produce more electrical power than their British counterparts. The very high capacity of the American and German ships, however, is partly explained by their use of electro-hydraulic pumps for the main armament. The British used turbo-hydraulic pumps. *Vanguard*'s generating capacity was 3,720 kilowatts, which war experience had shown would be sufficient for the requirements of this particular ship.

Another failing in British battleships was their lack of endurance when compared to the vessels of other nations. Only Italy had lower endurance figures for their capital ships, but this was because their vessels were designed to operate almost entirely in the comparatively restricted waters of the Mediterranean.

General conclusions. The successful design of warships depends to a very great extent on the amount of previous experience that has been accumulated by the designers. It follows, therefore, that the nation with the greatest amount of sea and battle experience will be the one most likely to produce a successful design. There can be little doubt that this was true of the battleships, in that the nations with the least experience produced the least satisfactory designs. The Japanese, for example, although possessing a large navy, lacked detailed design and modern battle experience. This is not apparent from the bare figures shown in tabular form, but it is true. In the words of an American report of 1946, on Japanese design methods: "The lack of attention to fundamental details of design, or rather the lack of search for the proper manner of accomplishing seemingly small details left 'holidays' that may have invited trouble from war damage and undoubtedly contributed to the sinking of some of the major Japanese ships".

Below: *Revenge* at Inverkeithing in September 1948.

For this reason, the authors believe that the USA and Britain produced the most efficient designs, and that the Royal Navy almost certainly had the edge because, before 1942, the American dreadnought fleet had acquired little battle experience. It is true, that there were many faults in the British designs, but most of these could be corrected without involving fundamental changes in the basic design of the ships. *Vanguard* incorporated a large part of the Royal Navy's war experience, which eliminated most of the faults that existed in 1939, but she retained the same basic system of protection, machinery and hull structure as the earlier ships. Her protection was good, her machinery was reliable, her speed was sufficient, she had an excellent armament and her sea-keeping qualities were unmatched. It is doubtful if any other nation could claim all these things for one of their ships.

Ultimate fates of British battleships

Barham: sunk by U331, 25th November 1941.
Malaya: sold for scrap, 20th February 1948.
Queen Elizabeth: sold for scrap, 19th March 1948.
Valiant: sold for scrap, 19th March 1948.
Warspite: sold for scrap, 12th July 1946, wrecked, 23rd April 1947.
Ramillies: sold for scrap, 20th March 1948.
Resolution: sold for scrap, 5th May 1948.
Revenge: sold for scrap, 1948.
Royal Oak: sunk by U47, 14th October 1939.
Royal Sovereign: sold for scrap, 5th April 1949.
Repulse: sunk by Japanese aircraft, 10th December 1941.
Renown: sold for scrap, 19th March 1948.
Hood: sunk by Bismarck, 24th May 1941.
Rodney and *Nelson*: sold for scrap, 1948.
King George V: sold for scrap, 1957.
Prince of Wales: sunk by Japanese aircraft, 10th December 1941.
Duke of York: sold for scrap, 1957.
Anson: sold for scrap, 1957.
Howe: sold for scrap, 1957.
Vanguard: sold for scrap, 1960.

PROJECTILES

AP shell

Armour-piercing shells were required to be of substantial strength in order to penetrate armour without breaking up. They were, therefore, made of special steel with thick heads and walls and a comparatively small bursting charge. The bursting charges of the APC shells for the 16-inch Mk II, 15-inch Mk I and 14-inch Mk VII guns were 59.5 pounds, 48.5 pounds and 40 pounds, respectively. To assist penetration, a cap was normally fitted over the nose of the shell. Briefly, this cap was intended to exert a high initial pressure on the face of the armour. The shell would then pierce its cap and strike the armour which, having been pre-stressed by the cap, would be easier to penetrate. In addition to the penetrative cap, a ballistic cap was often fitted to the nose of the shell. These caps were of light steel construction and were intended to provide the best streamlined shape for flight through the air. They did not assist perforation. The following types of piercing shell were employed in the capital ships of the Royal Navy during the Second World War:

1. APC (armour-piercing capped):
Supplied for 14-inch, 15-inch and 16-inch guns only, for use against heavily armoured targets.

2. CPBC (common pointed ballistic cap):
Supplied for 6-inch guns for use against medium thicknesses of armour.

3. SAP (semi-armour-piercing):
Supplied for guns of 5.25-inch calibre and less, for use against medium to light armour.

4. CPC (common pointed capped):
Supplied for guns of 6-inch calibre and above for use against lightly armoured and un-armoured targets. Low penetration, large bursting charge.

HE shell

High explosive shells were intended for use against unarmoured targets and had little or no penetrating power. They contained the largest possible charge consistent with the case of the shell retaining sufficient strength to withstand the shock of being fired from a gun. They could be used against ship targets but were primarily anti-aircraft and bombardment projectiles.

Star shell

Star shell were intended to illuminate targets during night action. They had thin walls and contained a small bursting charge, a parachute and a flare. The charge, detonated by a time nose fuze, ignited the illuminating star and blew it and the parachute through the base of the shell. Suspended by the parachute the star would then drop slowly emitting a brilliant white light until extinguished by the sea.

Smoke shell

Two types of smoke shell were used: (a) to provide smoke screens for amphibious assaults; and (b) an anti-aircraft gun projectile which on detonation produced a small grey smoke cloud which could be used as an AA target, or to indicate wind direction.

Shell fuzes

1. Base percussion fuzes. The fuzes for AP shell, were fitted in the base in order to avoid weakening the nose of the shell and damaging the fuze as the projectile passed through the armour. The fuze was activated when the shell struck its target but provided a very short time delay before detonation, in order to allow the shell to get well inside its target.

2. Percussion direct-action fuzes. These were provided for HE shells and were fitted in the nose of the projectile. They provided no time delay, and detonated the bursting charge on impact. There were two main types: (a) DA (direct action), which were very sensitive and were used in the 2-pounder shell and for bombardment projectiles; and (b) DAI (direct action impact) less sensitive than the DA fuze for use against ships.

3. Time fuzes. These were provided for HE anti-aircraft shell, star shell, target smoke shell and anti-aircraft practice shell. They were activated on being fired from the gun, and could be set to burst at any desired interval after leaving the gun. Some of these fuzes were also designed to operate on impact, should they hit a target before the time delay had functioned.

Bursting charges

The bursting charges of shell were high-explosives or "disruptives" which detonated instantly and with great violence. The high explosives employed as fillings for British shells during the War were RDX, TNT, Shellite and Lyddite.

Exploders

To assist the detonation of shells, an explosive composition, more sensitive than the bursting charge was usually interposed between the shell's fuze and the filling, to act as a booster. The explosives used for these exploders were TNT, Picric acid, CE (composition exploding), fulminate of mercury, lead arzide and picric powder. (The same types of explosives were used in the fuzes themselves). In addition to these, gunpowder was still employed for some applications, including star shell, fuzes, shrapnel shells and gun firing-charges (tubes, igniters and primers).

Propellant charges

The explosive charges used to fire projectiles from guns are known as propellant charges. Unlike bursting charges, they burn comparatively slowly and regularly in order to provide a continuous and even pressure behind the shell until it leaves the gun. The main explosive used for this purpose in British guns was Cordite, which consisted of a mixture of nitro-glycerine, nitro-cellulose and a stabilising agent. During the Second World War, a flashless cordite was introduced, which eliminated the problem of cordite flash revealing the position of the firing ship to the enemy during a night action.

The cordite, usually in the form of sticks, was made up into cartridges in one of two ways: (a) in silk cloth bags for breech-loading guns; and (b) in brass cartridge cases for quick-firing guns. The ammunition for quick-firing guns could be either "fixed" or "separate". In the former, the shell and cartridge were secured together; in the latter they were separate. In some quick-firing cartridges, a NH (non-hygroscopic) propellant was employed. This was a nitro-cellulose explosive containing no nitro-glycerine.

Breech-loading cartridges were fired by a tube placed in the breech of the gun. These tubes were small brass cases containing an explosive (usually gunpowder) which was ignited electrically or by percussion, sending a flash into the base of the cartridge. To assist the explosion of the cartridge, a gunpowder igniter was sewn into the end of the silk bag. The later types of breech-loading gun employed a 'one-inch tube' and the cartridges used in these guns were not fitted with an igniter.

Quick-firing cartridges were fired by a primer fitted into the base of the cartridge case, and were operated by percussion, or electrically.

The transom stern of *Vanguard*, last of the British battleships.

Appendix 1. Ordnance

MAIN AND SECONDARY ARMAMENT

15-inch Mk I wire-wound breech-loading gun
Date of entering service: 1915.
Calibre: 15 inches.
Length of bore: 42 calibres (630 inches).
Length of gun: 650.4 inches.
Weight of gun (excluding breech mechanism): 97 tons 3 cwt.
Weight of breech mechanism: 2 tons 17 cwt.
Rifling: polygroove, 76 grooves, uniform right-hand twist of one turn in 30 calibres.
Length of rifling: 516.33 inches.
Weight of shell: 1,920 pounds (4 crh AP shell); 1,938 pounds (6 crh AP shell, 1937).
Length of shell (1,938 pounds): 65.01 inches (APC) 67.4 inches (HE).
Weight of charge: 428 pounds cordite.
Weight of supercharge (Second World War): 490 pounds cordite.
Muzzle velocity: 2,450 fps (4 crh shell) 2,640 fps (6 crh shell with supercharge).
Muzzle energy: 79,890 f-t (4 crh shell); 93,630 f-t (6 crh shell with supercharge).
Barrel life: 350 efc.

Mountings:
1. Twin 15-inch Mk I (*Queen Elizabeth* class, *Royal Sovereign* class, *Renown* and *Repulse*):
Revolving weight: 750 tons (1915), 785 tons (1935).
Rate of fire: 2 rounds per gun per minute.
Maximum elevation: 20°.
Maximum range: 23,734 yards with 4 crh shell; 28,700 yards with 6 crh shell and supercharge.
2. Twin 15-inch Mk II (*Hood*):
Revolving weight: 860 tons.
Rate of fire: 2 rounds per gun per minute.
Maximum elevation: 30°.
Maximum range: 29,000 yards with 4 crh shell.
3. Twin 15-inch Mk I (N) (modified Mk I mountings in *Queen Elizabeth*, *Valiant*, *Warspite*, *Renown* and *Vanguard*):
Revolving weight: 855 tons (*Vanguard*) 815 tons (*Warspite*).
Rate of fire: 2 rounds per gun per minute.
Maximum elevation: 30°.
Maximum range: 32,200 yards with 6 crh shell.
RPC: RP 12 for training in *Vanguard* only.

16-inch Mk I wire-wound breech-loading gun
Date of entering service: 1927.
Calibre: 16 inches.
Length of bore: 45 calibres (720 inches).
Length of gun: 740 inches.
Weight of gun (excluding breech mechanism): 103 tons 10 cwt.
Weight of shell: 2,048 pounds (HE) 2,053 pounds (APC).
Length of shell: 66.57 inches (APC); 75.94 inches (HE with ballistic cap).
Weight of charge: 510 pounds SC cordite.
Muzzle velocity: 2,700 fps.
Muzzle energy: 103,600 f-t.
Barrel life: 200 efc (approx).

Mounting: Triple 16-inch Mk I (*Rodney* and *Nelson*):
Revolving weight: 1,480 tons.
Rate of fire: 1.5 rounds per gun per minute.
Maximum elevation: 40°.
Maximum range: 41,983 yards.
Note: problems were experienced with the original 16-inch Mk I guns which resulted in an improved system of rifling known as Mk II rifling

16-inch Mk II all-steel breech-loading gun
Date of entering service: cancelled.
Calibre: 16 inches.
Length of bore: 45 calibres (720 inches).
Length of shell: 72.92 inches (APC) 68.71 inches (HE).
Weight of shell: 2,375 pounds (APC) 2,048 pounds (HE).
Muzzle velocity: 2,450 fps.
Muzzle energy: 98,880 f-t.
Range: 43,800 yards at 40°.

14-inch Mk VII all-steel breech-loading gun
Date of entering service: 1940.
Calibre: 14 inches.
Length of bore: 45 calibres (630 inches).
Length of gun: not known.
Weight of gun (bare): 77 tons 14 cwt 84 lb.
Weight of gun (including counter-balance weight): 89 tons 2 cwt 84 lb.
Weight of breech mechanism: 1 ton 17 cwt.
Rifling: polygroove, 72 grooves plain section, uniform right-hand twist of one turn in 30 calibres.
Weight of shell: 1,590 pounds.
Weight of charge: 338 pounds.
Muzzle velocity: 2,475 fps.
Muzzle energy: 67,520 f-t.
Barrel life: 340 efc (designed).

Mountings: Quadruple Mk III Twin Mk II.
Revolving weight (excluding guns):
Quadruple Mk III: 1,582 tons
Twin Mk II: 915 tons.
Rate of fire: 2 rounds per gun per minute.
Maximum elevation: 40°.

6-inch Mk XII wire-wound breech-loading gun
Date of entering service: 1915.
Calibre: 6 inches.
Length of bore: 45 calibres (270 inches).
Length of gun: 280 inches (approx).
Weight of gun: 6 tons 14 cwt 56 lb.
Weight of shell: 100 pounds.
Weight of charge: 27 pounds 2 ounces.
Muzzle velocity: 2,825 fps.
Muzzle energy: 5,532 f-t.

Mounting: Single P IX (pedestal) casemate mounting (*Queen Elizabeth* and *Royal Sovereign* classes):
Rate of fire: 7 rounds per minute.
Maximum elevation: 15°.
Maximum range: 13,500 yards.

6-inch wire-wound Mk XXII and XXII* breech-loading gun
Date of entering service: 1927.
Calibre: 6 inches.
Length of bore: 50 calibres (300 inches).
Length of gun: 309.728 inches.
Weight of gun (excluding breech mechanism): 8 tons 17 cwt.
Weight of breech mechanism: 3 cwt 28 lb.
Rifling: polygroove system, 36 grooves, uniform right-hand twist of one turn in 30 calibres.
Length of rifling: 255.555 inches.
Weight of shell: 100 pounds.
Weight of charge: 30 pounds S.C. cordite.
Muzzle velocity: 2,945 fps.
Muzzle energy: 6,012 f-t.
Barrel life: 600 efc.

Mounting: Twin Mk XVIII turret (*Rodney* and *Nelson*):
Weight of mounting (including guns): 75 tons.
Rate of fire: 8 rounds per gun per minute.
Maximum elevation: 60°
Maximum range: 25,600 yards at 45° elevation.

5.5-inch Mk I wire-wound breech-loading gun
Date of entering service: 1916.
Calibre: 5.5 inches.
Length of bore: 50 calibres (275 inches).
Length of gun: 284.748 inches.
Weight of gun: 6 tons 1 cwt.

Rifling: polygroove, 40 grooves, uniform right-hand twist of one turn in 30 calibres.
Length of rifling: 235.92 inches.
Weight of shell: 82 pounds.
Weight of charge: 22 pounds 4 ounces MD cordite.
Muzzle velocity: 2,725 fps.
Muzzle energy: 4,222 f-t.
Mounting: Single CP II (centre pivot) open shield (*Hood*):
Rate of fire: 12 rounds per minute (maximum).
Maximum elevation: 30°.
Maximum range: 18,500 yards.

4-inch wire-wound Mk IX and IX* breech-loading gun
Date of entering service: 1916.
Calibre: 4 inches.
Length of bore: 45 calibres (177.4 inches).
Weight of gun (without breech mechanism): 2 tons 1 cwt 28 lb.
Weight of shell: 31 pounds.
Weight of charge: 5 pounds 14 ounces.
Muzzle velocity: 2,625 fps.
Muzzle energy: 1,480 f-t.
Mounting: Triple T.I. Mk I open shield (*Renown* and *Repulse*):
Weight of mounting (excluding guns): 8 tons 19 cwt.
Maximum elevation: 30°.
Maximum depression: 10°.

LONG-RANGE AA AND HA/LA WEAPONS

3-inch wire-wound Mk I quick-firing gun
Date of entering service (as an AA weapon): 1913.
Calibre: 3 inches.
Length of bore: 45 calibres (135 inches).
Length of gun: 143 inches.
Weight of gun (including breech mechanism): 1 ton.
Rifling: polygroove, 20 grooves, plain section, uniform twist and one turn in 30 calibres.
Length of rifling: 117.5 inches.
Weight of shell: 12.5 pounds.
Weight of charge: 2.5 pounds.
Muzzle velocity: 2,500 fps.

Mounting: Single open HA Mk II (*Queen Elizabeth* class, *Royal Sovereign* class, *Renown* and *Repulse*):
Weight of mounting (excluding guns): 1 ton 16 cwt 38 lb.
Rate of fire: 29 rounds per minute.
Maximum elevation: 90°.
Maximum depression: 10°.

4-inch Mk V quick-firing gun
Date of entering service (as an AA weapon): 1916.
Calibre: 4 inches.
Length of bore: 45 calibres (180 inches).
Weight of gun (complete): 2 tons 3 cwt.
Weight of shell: 31 pounds.
Weight of charge: 7 pounds 11 ounces.
Muzzle velocity: 3,000 fps.
Muzzle energy: 1,930 f-t.

Mountings:
1. Single 4-inch Mk III and Mk IV open HA (*Queen Elizabeth* class, *Royal Sovereign* class, *Renown*, *Repulse* and *Hood*).
2. Twin BD Mk XVII HA/LA turret (*Repulse*).
Weight of mounting (Mk III): 4 tons 11 cwt.
Rate of fire: 14 rounds per minute (maximum).
Maximum elevation (Mk III): 85°.
Maximum surface range (Mk III): 13,700 yards.

4.724-inch wire-wound Mk VIII* quick-firing gun
Date of entering service: 1927.
Calibre: 4.724 inches (120 mm).
Length of bore: 43 calibres (202 inches).
Weight of gun (complete): 2 tons 19 cwt 28 lb.
Total weight of fixed ammunition: 112 pounds.
Weight of shell: 50 pounds.

Mounting: Single 4.7-inch open HA Mk XII (*Nelson* and *Rodney*) fitted with shields during Second World War:
Weight of mounting (excluding gun): 9 tons 8 cwt.
Rate of fire: 8 rounds per minute.
Maximum elevation: 90°.
Maximum depression 5°.

4-inch all-steel Mk XVI quick-firing gun
Date of entering service: 1936.
Calibre: 4 inches.
Length of bore: 45 calibres (180 inches).
Weight of gun (including breech mechanism, counter-balance): 2 tons 1 cwt 11 lb.
Rifling: 32 grooves, uniform twist of one turn in 30 calibres.
Total weight of fixed ammunition: 63 pounds 8 ounces.
Weight of shell: 35 pounds 14 ounces.
Weight of charge: 9 pounds (SC cordite).
Muzzle velocity: 2,650 fps.
Muzzle energy: 1,934 f-t.
Barrel life: 600 efc.

Mounting: Twin 4-inch HA/LA Mk XIX (*Barham*, *Malaya*, *Warspite*, *Royal Sovereign* class and *Hood*). Originally hand-operated, later adapted for **RP** 50, 51 or 52 **RPC**:
Weight of mounting (including guns): 16 tons 11 cwt to 17 tons 4 cwt with RPC.
Rate of fire: 20 rounds per gun per minute (maximum).
Maximum elevation: 80°.
Maximum depression: 10°.
Training limit: 340°.
Maximum surface range: 21,300 yards.
Maximum effective surface range: 18,000 yards.
Maximum speed of operation with RPC: 20° per second.

4.5-inch all-steel Mk III quick-firing gun
Date of entering service: 1939.
Calibre: 4.5 inches.
Length of bore: 45 calibres (202 inches).
Weight of gun (including breech mechanism): 2 tons 16 cwt 32 lb.
Total weight of fixed ammunition: 87 pounds.
Weight of shell: 55 pounds.
Muzzle velocity: 2,350 fps (mean).
Barrel life: 650 efc.

Mountings: Twin BD Mk I (*Renown*) and Mk II (*Queen Elizabeth* and *Valiant*) HA/LA turrets:
Rate of fire: 12 rounds per minute.
Maximum elevation: 70°.
Maximum altitude range: 29,908 feet at 70° elevation.
Maximum effective surface range: 19,900 yards at 43° elevation.
Note: Mounting cramped and difficult to maintain. Loading heavy work due to high weight of fixed ammunition.

5.25-inch all steel Mk I quick-firing gun
Date of entering service: 1940.
Calibre: 5.25 inches.
Length of bore: 50 calibres (262 inches).
Weight of shell: 80 pounds.
Weight of charge: 18.6 pounds.
Muzzle velocity: 2,600 fps (mean).
Muzzle energy: 3,750 f-t.

Mountings: Twin 5.25-inch HA/LA Mk I (*King George V* and *Lion* classes) and Mk I* (*Vanguard*) turrets:
Weight of mounting: 854 tons (Mk I*).
Rate of fire: 7-8 rounds per minute.

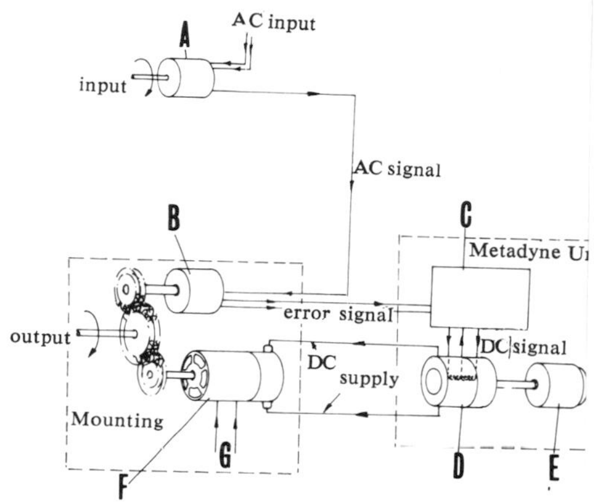

Appendix 2. Fire-cont

THE DIRECTOR SYSTEM

The director system consisted of a director, positioned high on the superstructure, a fire-control calculator, positioned in the transmitting-station, and the electrical transmitting arrangements necessary to pass information from director to calculator and from calculator to the guns.

The director-sight

This instrument positioned in the director-control tower was basically a sophisticated gun-sight and provided the target bearing. The telescopic sights were generally stabilised by a gyroscope which maintained a prism inside the telescope in the upright position so that even while the ship was rolling, the director layer and trainer could see the target continuously. The gyro also controlled the electrical gun-firing circuit so that when the director layer pressed his trigger, the circuit was not closed unless the ship was on an even keel, which eliminated any errors due to rolling (or pitching if the director was trained fore and aft). Cross-level i.e. longitudinal level with the director trained on the beam, or athwartships level when trained fore and aft, was measured by a cross-level unit which was basically a telescope mounted at right angles to the director line of sight and kept laid on the horizon by the cross-levelling operator. In cases where remote power-control was fitted, the director-sight could be gyro-stabilised for level and cross-level in a more efficient manner which not only stabilised the director-sight but the guns as well. The effect of cross-level gets progressively worse as elevation increases, and for high-angle fire it was vital that it be correct. In capital ships during the Second World War, this was only provided in HA/LA and HA systems; the LA system retained the arrangement described previously.

Range-finders

The British used coincidence range-finders which showed two images of the target, one above the other. When the upper and lower images were in line, the correct range had been obtained. High-angle range-finders also gave a 'height of target' figure. Stereoscopic range-finders, which were employed by the German Navy, were more accurate but were also delicate and more difficult to operate in battle conditions. They showed two overlapping images which provided the range when brought together to form one image.

Maximum elevation: 80°.
Maximum altitude range: 29,544 feet at 80° elevation.
Maximum effective surface range: 23,400 yards at 45° elevation.
RPC: RP10 in Mk I* only.
Note: mounting very cramped and difficult to maintain. Very difficult to train by hand mechanism.

CLOSE-RANGE AA WEAPONS

Vickers 2-pounder pom-pom Mk VIII gun
Calibre: 40 mm (1.575 inches).
Length of bore: 40 calibres (62 inches).
Length of gun: 102.6 inches.
Weight of gun: 600 pounds (approx).
Weight of shell: 2 pounds.
Rifling: 54.84 inches long, 12 grooves, uniform right-hand twist of one turn in 30 calibres.
Muzzle velocity: 1,920 fps. 2,400 fps with high-velocity shell (1938).
Maximum surface range: 3,800 yards.
Maximum effective range: 1,700 yards.
Rate of fire: 90 rounds per minute (115 rpm max.).

Mountings
1. Eight barrelled Mk V and VI mountings (all ships):
Date of entering service: 1930.
Weight of mounting: (Mk V) 11 tons 16 cwt 44 lb. Mk VI (including guns, RPC and 1,200 rounds of ammunition) 17 tons 7 cwt.
Maximum elevation: 80°.
Maximum depression: 10°.
RPC: RP 50 or RP 10.
Speed of operation: 15° per second (25° per second with RPC).
2. Four barrelled 2-pounder Mk VII mounting:
Date of entering service: 1938.
Orginally hand-operated but later modified for RPC being designated Mk VII* (P).
Weight of mounting (including guns and RPC gear): 11 tons (approx).
Maximum elevation: 80°.
Maximum depression: 10°.
Maximum speed of operation with RPC: 25° per second.
Training limit: 710°.
RPC: RP 50.

Vickers 0.5-inch Mk III machine-gun
Calibre: 0.5 inches.
Length of bore: 52 calibres (31.11 inches).
Weight of gun: 56 pounds (62 pounds with water jacket full).
Length of gun: 52 inches.
Weight of bullet and cartridge: 2.9 ounces.
Weight of bullet: 1.32 ounces.
Muzzle velocity: 2,520 fps.
Rate of fire: 600 rounds per minute; 700 rounds per minute (maximum).
Maximum effective range: 800 yards.

Mountings: Quadruple, Mk I, Mk I**, Mk II, Mk II*, Mk III hand-operated.

Weight of mountings:	Excluding guns	Including guns
Mk I	12 cwt	14 cwt 37 lb.
Mk I**	17 cwt 35 lb	19 cwt 72 lb.
Mk II*	1 ton 3 cwt 51 lb	1 ton 5 cwt 88 lb.
Mk III	1 ton 1 cwt 79 lb	1 ton 3 cwt 4 lb.

The Mk I** and Mk II* were Mk I and Mk II mountings modified as far as possible to Mk III standard.
Maximum elevation: 80°.
Maximum depression: 10°.
Training limits: none.

20-mm Mk II Oerlikon cannon
Date of entering service: 1941.
Calibre: 20 mm.
Length of bore: 65 calibres.
Weight of gun and mechanism: 150 pounds (approx).
Weight of shell: 0.27 pounds.
Weight of cartridge: 0.18 pounds.
Weight of charge: 27.7 grammes.
Muzzle velocity: 2,725 fps.
Rate of fire: 450 rounds per minute.
Maximum altitude range: 10,000 feet at 87° elevation.
Maximum effective range: 1,000 yards.
Maximum surface range: 4,800 yards at 35° elevation; 6,250 yards at 45°.

Mountings: Single hand-operated various marks with no significant differences:
Weight of gun and mounting complete: 1,695 pounds (approx).
Weight of shield: 250 pounds (approx).
Thickness of shield: 0.5 inches.
Maximum elevation: 87°.
Maximum depression: 5°.
Training limits: none except when fitted with US Mk XIV gyro gunsight which required the connection of a power cable to the mounting.

20-mm twin Mk V power-operated mounting
Total weight (including guns): 1 ton 1 cwt 70 lb.
Weight of power unit: 4 cwt.
Maximum elevation: 70°.
Maximum depression: 10°.
Training limit: none.
Crew: 2.

40-mm Bofors Mk NI, Mk NI/I, Mk IX and X quick-firing guns
Date of entering service: 1941.
Calibre: 40 mm (1.595 inches).
Length of bore: 60 calibres (96 inches).
Length of gun: 130 inches.
Weight of gun: 616 pounds.
Weight of shell: 2 pounds.
Muzzle velocity: 2,720 fps.
Rifling: 16 grooves.
Rate of fire: 120 rounds per minute.
Maximum surface range: 12,500 yards.
Maximum effective range: 2,500 yards.
Maximum altitude range: 18,000 feet.

Mountings:
1. Single Mk III* hand-operated RN version of Army Mk III, fitted with Mk NI gun:
Crew: 2.
2. Single Mk VII power-operated (*Vanguard*), fitted with Mk NI/I gun:
Weight of mounting (complete): 1 ton 12 cwt (approx).
Maximum elevation: 90°.
Maximum depression: 5°.
Training limit: none.
Crew: 3.
3. 40-mm Twin Mk II STAAG (*Vanguard*), fitted with Mk X guns:
Total weight (including guns): 17 tons (approx).
Maximum elevation: 90°.
Maximum depression: 10°.
Training limit: none.
4. US 40-mm Quadruple Mk II (*King George V* class and *Nelson*):
Total weight (with guns): 10 tons 10 cwt (approx).
RPC: US hydraulic or electric power drive.
5. Six-barrel Mk VI (*Vanguard*), fitted with Mk IX guns:
Weight (complete): 21½ tons (approx).
Maximum elevation: 90°.
Maximum depression: 15°.
RPC: RP50.
6. Boffin: 40-mm Bofors gun fitted on twin Mk V Oerlikon mounting.

PROJECTILES

AP shell

Armour-piercing shells were required to be of substantial strength in order to penetrate armour without breaking up. They were, therefore, made of special steel with thick heads and walls and a comparatively small bursting charge. The bursting charges of the APC shells for the 16-inch Mk II, 15-inch Mk I and 14-inch Mk VII guns were 59.5 pounds, 48.5 pounds and 40 pounds, respectively. To assist penetration, a cap was normally fitted over the nose of the shell. Briefly, this cap was intended to exert a high initial pressure on the face of the armour. The shell would then pierce its cap and strike the armour which, having been pre-stressed by the cap, would be easier to penetrate. In addition to the penetrative cap, a ballistic cap was often fitted to the nose of the shell. These caps were of light steel construction and were intended to provide the best streamlined shape for flight through the air. They did not assist perforation. The following types of piercing shell were employed in the capital ships of the Royal Navy during the Second World War:

1. APC (armour-piercing capped):
Supplied for 14-inch, 15-inch and 16-inch guns only, for use against heavily armoured targets.

2. CPBC (common pointed ballistic cap):
Supplied for 6-inch guns for use against medium thicknesses of armour.

3. SAP (semi-armour-piercing):
Supplied for guns of 5.25-inch calibre and less, for use against medium to light armour.

4. CPC (common pointed capped):
Supplied for guns of 6-inch calibre and above for use against lightly armoured and un-armoured targets. Low penetration, large bursting charge.

HE shell

High explosive shells were intended for use against unarmoured targets and had little or no penetrating power. They contained the largest possible charge consistent with the case of the shell retaining sufficient strength to withstand the shock of being fired from a gun. They could be used against ship targets but were primarily anti-aircraft and bombardment projectiles.

Star shell

Star shell were intended to illuminate targets during night action. They had thin walls and

contain
and a
nose fu
it and
shell. S
then d
until ex

Smoke
Two ty
vide sm
(b) an
nation
could b
wind di

Shell fu
1. Base
were fit
ing the
as the p
fuze wa
but pro
nation,
inside it
2. Percu
vided fo
of the
and det
There w
which w
pounder
and (b)
than the
3. Time
anti-airc
and anti
vated on
set to bu
the gun.
to opera
before th

Bursting
The burs
or "disr
with gre
ed as fill
were RD

Exploder
To assist
composit

Transmission systems

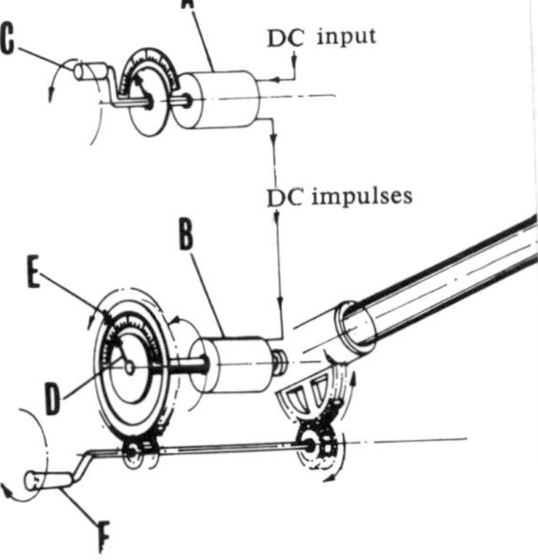

Illustrated in simple diagrammatic form is the step-by-step transmission system for communicating elevation information to the elevation receiver at the gun. The arrangements for training were basically similar.

An M-type transmitter (A) was connected electrically to an M-type receiver (B) in such a way as to achieve an electrical balance. Rotation of the input handle (C) moved the rotor of the transmitter (A) and disturbed this balance, causing a series of direct-current impulses to be transmitted to the receiver (B) which would rotate in small steps (two or six minutes of arc) in the same direction and by the same amount as the transmitter. The receiver, which was contained in the gun-elevation receiver, moved a dial (D) which indicated the elevation required. The gunlayer kept his pointer (E) in line with the pointer in the dial (D) by rotating the gun-elevating handle (F) and so long as these two pointers were in line, the gun was in the required position. This was known as the 'follow-the-pointer' system. The step-by-step transmitter could drive more than one receiver.

Counter-drum, as well as 'follow-the-pointer' receivers were employed with the system, but, though accurate, they had an inherent disadvantage in that the operator had to shift his eye from the receiver to the gun-dials and which involved dela possibility of error i transfer of informat the receiver to the 'Follow-the-pointer' eliminated this prob largely, though not replaced the counter

The main disadva step-by-step were:
1. If the transmitte moved too fast, the would lag behind an of step.
2. The number of that could be connec transmitter was limit
3. When changing one control-position the transmitters had lined-up before the t could be effected.
4. A fault in one re could put the whole of gear.

Auto-Synchronous T
The auto-synchronou mission system was a of the step-by-step sy was first tested in the cruiser *Tiger* during and was fitted in *Nel* *Rodney*, and in earlie ships when they were nised.

Rotation of the inp (A) turned a hunter (B) via a differential Movement of the hun an electric contact wh a direct-current suppl relay (D) which in tu supplied current to an motor (E). The directi

G.3 (NMM)
Nelson and Rodney (NMM)

The Technical History (Adm
Fire Control in H.M. Ship
Guns and gun mountings
Ammunition for naval guns

PUBLISHED SOURCES

ADMIRALTY: *Naval Marine*
1959).
BACON, Admiral Reginald
London, 1940)
BRASSEY'S *Naval and Shipp*
1920 and 1928).
BREYER, Siegfried: *Schlac*
Lehmanns Verlag, Munich,
1905–1970, Macdonald, Lo
CHATFIELD, Admiral Alfred
(Heinemann, London and T
—*It Might Happen Again* (
CHIHAYA, M: Yamato and
tions, Windsor, 1973).
CUNNINGHAM, Admiral of
Sailor's Odyssey (Hutchinso
INSTITUTE OF NAVAL ARCH

Maximum elevation: 80°.
Maximum altitude range: 29,544 feet at 80° elevation.
Maximum effective surface range: 23,400 yards at 45° elevation.
RPC: RP10 in Mk I* only.
Note: mounting very cramped and difficult to maintain. Very difficult to train by hand mechanism.

CLOSE-RANGE AA WEAPONS

Vickers 2-pounder pom-pom Mk VIII gun
Calibre: 40 mm (1.575 inches).
Length of bore: 40 calibres (62 inches).
Length of gun: 102.6 inches.
Weight of gun: 600 pounds (approx).
Weight of shell: 2 pounds.
Rifling: 54.84 inches long, 12 grooves, uniform right-hand twist of one turn in 30 calibres.
Muzzle velocity: 1,920 fps. 2,400 fps with high-velocity shell (1938).
Maximum surface range: 3,800 yards.
Maximum effective range: 1,700 yards.
Rate of fire: 90 rounds per minute (115 rpm max.).

Mountings
1. Eight barrelled Mk V and VI mountings (all ships):
Date of entering service: 1930.
Weight of mounting: (Mk V) 11 tons 16 cwt 44 lb. Mk VI (including guns, RPC and 1,200 rounds of ammunition) 17 tons 7 cwt.
Maximum elevation: 80°.
Maximum depression: 10°.
RPC: RP 50 or RP 10.
Speed of operation: 15° per second (25° per second with RPC).
2. Four barrelled 2-pounder Mk VII mounting:
Date of entering service: 1938.
Orginally hand-operated but later modified for RPC being designated Mk VII* (P).
Weight of mounting (including guns and RPC gear): 11 tons (approx).
Maximum elevation: 80°.
Maximum depression: 10°.
Maximum speed of operation with RPC: 25° per second.
Training limit: 710°.
RPC: RP 50.

Vickers 0.5-inch Mk III machine-gun
Calibre: 0.5 inches.
Length of bore: 52 calibres (31.11 inches).
Weight of gun: 56 pounds (62 pounds with water jacket full).
Length of gun: 52 inches.
Weight of bullet and cartridge: 2.9 ounces.
Weight of bullet: 1.32 ounces.
Muzzle velocity: 2,520 fps.
Rate of fire: 600 rounds per minute; 700 rounds per minute (maximum).
Maximum effective range: 800 yards.

Mountings: Quadruple, Mk I, Mk I**, Mk II, Mk II*, Mk III hand-operated.

Weight of mountings:	Excluding guns	Including guns
Mk I	12 cwt	14 cwt 37 lb.
Mk I**	17 cwt 35 lb	19 cwt 72 lb.
Mk II*	1 ton 3 cwt 51 lb	1 ton 5 cwt 88 lb.
Mk III	1 ton 1 cwt 79 lb	1 ton 3 cwt 4 lb.

The Mk I** and Mk II* were Mk I and Mk II mountings modified as far as possible to Mk III standard.
Maximum elevation: 80°.
Maximum depression: 10°.
Training limits: none.

20-mm Mk II Oerlikon cannon
Date of entering service: 1941.
Calibre: 20 mm.
Length of bore: 65 calibres.
Weight of gun and mechanism: 150 pounds (approx).
Weight of shell: 0.27 pounds.
Weight of cartridge: 0.18 pounds.
Weight of charge: 27.7 grammes.
Muzzle velocity: 2,725 fps.
Rate of fire: 450 rounds per minute.
Maximum altitude range: 10,000 feet at 87° elevation.
Maximum effective range: 1,000 yards.
Maximum surface range: 4,800 yards at 35° elevation; 6,250 yards at 45°.

Mountings: Single hand-operated various marks with no significant differences:
Weight of gun and mounting complete: 1,695 pounds (approx).
Weight of shield: 250 pounds (approx).
Thickness of shield: 0.5 inches.
Maximum elevation: 87°.
Maximum depression: 5°.
Training limits: none except when fitted with US Mk XIV gyro gunsight which required the connection of a power cable to the mounting.

20-mm twin Mk V power-operated mounting
Total weight (including guns): 1 ton 1 cwt 70 lb.
Weight of power unit: 4 cwt.
Maximum elevation: 70°.
Maximum depression: 10°.
Training limit: none.
Crew: 2.

40-mm Bofors Mk NI, Mk NI/I, Mk IX and X quick-firing guns
Date of entering service: 1941.
Calibre: 40 mm (1.595 inches).
Length of bore: 60 calibres (96 inches).
Length of gun: 130 inches.
Weight of gun: 616 pounds.
Weight of shell: 2 pounds.
Muzzle velocity: 2,720 fps.
Rifling: 16 grooves.
Rate of fire: 120 rounds per minute.
Maximum surface range: 12,500 yards.
Maximum effective range: 2,500 yards.
Maximum altitude range: 18,000 feet.

Mountings:
1. Single Mk III* hand-operated RN version of Army Mk III, fitted with Mk NI gun:
Crew: 2.
2. Single Mk VII power-operated (*Vanguard*), fitted with Mk NI/I gun:
Weight of mounting (complete): 1 ton 12 cwt (approx).
Maximum elevation: 90°.
Maximum depression: 5°.
Training limit: none.
Crew: 3.
3. 40-mm Twin Mk II STAAG (*Vanguard*), fitted with Mk X guns:
Total weight (including guns): 17 tons (approx).
Maximum elevation: 90°.
Maximum depression: 10°.
Training limit: none.
4. US 40-mm Quadruple Mk II (*King George V* class and *Nelson*):
Total weight (with guns): 10 tons 10 cwt (approx).
RPC: US hydraulic or electric power drive.
5. Six-barrel Mk VI (*Vanguard*), fitted with Mk IX guns:
Weight (complete): 21½ tons (approx).
Maximum elevation: 90°.
Maximum depression: 15°.
RPC: RP50.
6. Boffin: 40-mm Bofors gun fitted on twin Mk V Oerlikon mounting.

PROJECTILES

AP shell

Armour-piercing shells were required to be of substantial strength in order to penetrate armour without breaking up. They were, therefore, made of special steel with thick heads and walls and a comparatively small bursting charge. The bursting charges of the APC shells for the 16-inch Mk II, 15-inch Mk I and 14-inch Mk VII guns were 59.5 pounds, 48.5 pounds and 40 pounds, respectively. To assist penetration, a cap was normally fitted over the nose of the shell. Briefly, this cap was intended to exert a high initial pressure on the face of the armour. The shell would then pierce its cap and strike the armour which, having been pre-stressed by the cap, would be easier to penetrate. In addition to the penetrative cap, a ballistic cap was often fitted to the nose of the shell. These caps were of light steel construction and were intended to provide the best streamlined shape for flight through the air. They did not assist perforation. The following types of piercing shell were employed in the capital ships of the Royal Navy during the Second World War:

1. APC (armour-piercing capped):
Supplied for 14-inch, 15-inch and 16-inch guns only, for use against heavily armoured targets.

2. CPBC (common pointed ballistic cap):
Supplied for 6-inch guns for use against medium thicknesses of armour.

3. SAP (semi-armour-piercing):
Supplied for guns of 5.25-inch calibre and less, for use against medium to light armour.

4. CPC (common pointed capped):
Supplied for guns of 6-inch calibre and above for use against lightly armoured and un-armoured targets. Low penetration, large bursting charge.

HE shell

High explosive shells were intended for use against unarmoured targets and had little or no penetrating power. They contained the largest possible charge consistent with the case of the shell retaining sufficient strength to withstand the shock of being fired from a gun. They could be used against ship targets but were primarily anti-aircraft and bombardment projectiles.

Star shell

Star shell were intended to illuminate targets during night action. They had thin walls and contained a small bursting charge, a parachute and a flare. The charge, detonated by a time nose fuze, ignited the illuminating star and blew it and the parachute through the base of the shell. Suspended by the parachute the star would then drop slowly emitting a brilliant white light until extinguished by the sea.

Smoke shell

Two types of smoke shell were used: (a) to provide smoke screens for amphibious assaults; and (b) an anti-aircraft gun projectile which on detonation produced a small grey smoke cloud which could be used as an AA target, or to indicate wind direction.

Shell fuzes

1. Base percussion fuzes. The fuzes for AP shell, were fitted in the base in order to avoid weakening the nose of the shell and damaging the fuze as the projectile passed through the armour. The fuze was activated when the shell struck its target but provided a very short time delay before detonation, in order to allow the shell to get well inside its target.

2. Percussion direct-action fuzes. These were provided for HE shells and were fitted in the nose of the projectile. They provided no time delay, and detonated the bursting charge on impact. There were two main types: (a) DA (direct action), which were very sensitive and were used in the 2-pounder shell and for bombardment projectiles; and (b) DAI (direct action impact) less sensitive than the DA fuze for use against ships.

3. Time fuzes. These were provided for HE anti-aircraft shell, star shell, target smoke shell and anti-aircraft practice shell. They were activated on being fired from the gun, and could be set to burst at any desired interval after leaving the gun. Some of these fuzes were also designed to operate on impact, should they hit a target before the time delay had functioned.

Bursting charges

The bursting charges of shell were high-explosives or "disruptives" which detonated instantly and with great violence. The high explosives employed as fillings for British shells during the War were RDX, TNT, Shellite and Lyddite.

Exploders

To assist the detonation of shells, an explosive composition, more sensitive than the bursting charge was usually interposed between the shell's fuze and the filling, to act as a booster. The explosives used for these exploders were TNT, Picric acid, CE (composition exploding), fulminate of mercury, lead arzide and picric powder. (The same types of explosives were used in the fuzes themselves). In addition to these, gunpowder was still employed for some applications, including star shell, fuzes, shrapnel shells and gun firing-charges (tubes, igniters and primers).

Propellant charges

The explosive charges used to fire projectiles from guns are known as propellant charges. Unlike bursting charges, they burn comparatively slowly and regularly in order to provide a continuous and even pressure behind the shell until it leaves the gun. The main explosive used for this purpose in British guns was Cordite, which consisted of a mixture of nitro-glycerine, nitro-cellulose and a stabilising agent. During the Second World War, a flashless cordite was introduced, which eliminated the problem of cordite flash revealing the position of the firing ship to the enemy during a night action.

The cordite, usually in the form of sticks, was made up into cartridges in one of two ways: (a) in silk cloth bags for breech-loading guns; and (b) in brass cartridge cases for quick-firing guns. The ammunition for quick-firing guns could be either "fixed" or "separate". In the former, the shell and cartridge were secured together; in the latter they were separate. In some quick-firing cartridges, a NH (non-hygroscopic) propellant was employed. This was a nitro-cellulose explosive containing no nitro-glycerine.

Breech-loading cartridges were fired by a tube placed in the breech of the gun. These tubes were small brass cases containing an explosive (usually gunpowder) which was ignited electrically or by percussion, sending a flash into the base of the cartridge. To assist the explosion of the cartridge, a gunpowder igniter was sewn into the end of the silk bag. The later types of breech-loading gun employed a 'one-inch tube' and the cartridges used in these guns were not fitted with an igniter.

Quick-firing cartridges were fired by a primer fitted into the base of the cartridge case, and were operated by percussion, or electrically.

Appendix 2. Fire-control

THE DIRECTOR SYSTEM

The director system consisted of a director, positioned high on the superstructure, a fire-control calculator, positioned in the transmitting-station, and the electrical transmitting arrangements necessary to pass information from director to calculator and from calculator to the guns.

The director-sight

This instrument positioned in the director-control tower was basically a sophisticated gun-sight and provided the target bearing. The telescopic sights were normally stabilised by a gyroscope which maintained a prism inside the telescope in the upright position so that even while the ship was rolling, the director layer and trainer could see the target continuously. The gyro also controlled the electrical gun-firing circuit so that when the director layer pressed his trigger, the circuit was not closed unless the ship was on an even keel, which eliminated any errors due to rolling (or pitching if the director was trained fore and aft). Cross-level i.e. longitudinal level with the director trained on the beam, or athwartships level when trained fore and aft, was measured by a cross-level unit which was basically a telescope mounted at right angles to the director line of sight and kept laid on the horizon by the cross-levelling operator. In cases where remote power-control was fitted, the director-sight could be gyro-stabilised for level and cross-level in a more efficient manner which not only stabilised the director-sight but the guns as well. The effect of cross-level gets progressively worse as elevation increases, and for high-angle fire it was vital that it be correct. In capital ships during the Second World War, this was only provided in HA/LA and HA systems; the LA system retained the arrangement described previously.

Range-finders

The British used coincidence range-finders which showed two images of the target, one above the other. When the upper and lower images were in line, the correct range had been obtained. High-angle range-finders also gave a 'height of target' figure. Stereoscopic range-finders, which were employed by the German Navy, were more accurate but were also delicate and more difficult to operate in battle conditions. They showed two overlapping images which provided the range when brought together to form one image.

Radar largely superseded the range-finder during the Second World War and could provide not only accurate ranges, but accurate bearings.

Target Indication

Target indication is the method by which the commanding officer indicates to the director the target at which he wishes the armament to fire. This was achieved by training an instrument known as a bearing-sight (positioned on the bridge) on to the target. The bearing was automatically transmitted to an indicator in the director by a transmission system known as the Evershed System. Similar bearing-sights were used to control searchlights, star shell and torpedo direction. During the Second World War, target indicating radar was introduced.

Corrections

A considerable number of corrections was necessary for accurate firing with the director system and these can be briefly summarised as follows:

Correction	Where made
1. Dip: Correction to elevation to allow for differences in height of director-sight and guns.	Calculator
2. Differences in MV: The muzzle velocity of guns varies according to the temperature of the cordite charge and the condition of the gun, which necessitate a correction to elevation.	Elevation receiver at gun
3. Tilt: Elevation has to be corrected to allow for variations in the horizontal level of turret and director roller-paths.	Elevation receiver at gun
4. Displacement: Elevation correction to allow for any differences between the distance of individual mountings and the target.	Elevation receiver at gun
5. Convergence: Training correction to allow for distance between mountings.	Calculator
6. Drift: Training correction to allow for shell drifting in the direction of its spin due to gyroscopic effect.	Calculator
7. Aim off or deflection made up of corrections for enemy, speed and course, own speed and course, wind speed and direction, temperature and density of the air, rotation of the earth during time of flight.	Calculator
8. Spotting corrections: From observation of fall of shot.	Calculator

As can be seen, the majority of the corrections are made in the Calculator which would be an AFCC or AFCT, the former being a simplified form of the latter. These were complex mechanical computers which corrected the information from the director and converted it to gun range and elevation.

Transmission systems

Three main types of electrical transmission system were employed in the ships of the Royal Navy during the Second World War. They are shown in diagrammatic form in the drawings overleaf. Basically, they consisted of a transmitter and a receiver connected electrically. The transmitter was moved by a hand wheel to indicate angle of bearing or elevation. This movement was automatically reproduced by a pointer in the receiver.

Remote power-control

Remote power-control was similar in principle to the transmission systems except that it not only indicated the movement required but also carried it out, thus providing a fully automatic system. The principle of operation is shown in the accompanying diagram. Electric RPC systems were given numbers in the '50' series and hydraulic RPC systems were given numbers in the '10' series.

Electric RPC (Metadyne system):
RP50. Operating speed 15° per second, metadyne generator off-mounting, fine Magslip control.
RP51. Operating speed 20° per second, joystick control, metadyne generator on-mounting, fine and coarse Magslip control (40° and 360° arcs) not fitted in battleships.
RP52. Similar to RP51, but with off-mounting generator.
RP50 systems were eventually modified to RP51 or 52.

Transmission systems

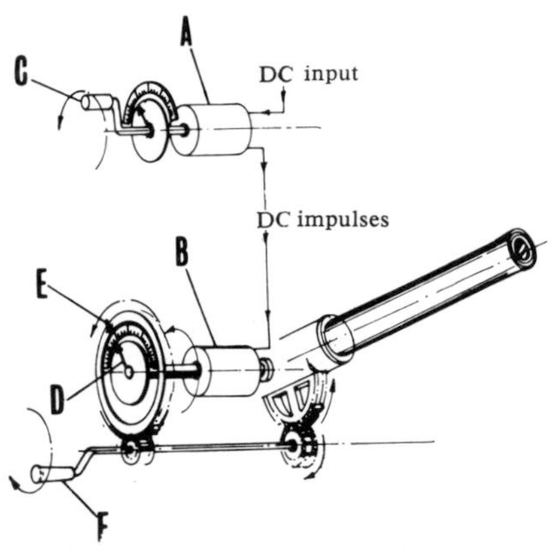

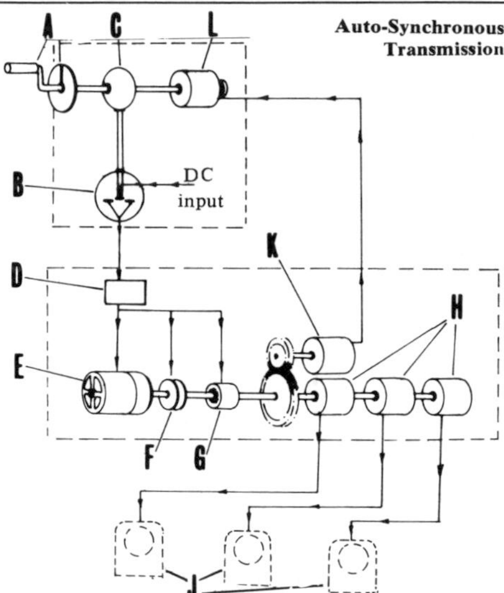

Indicator Magslip

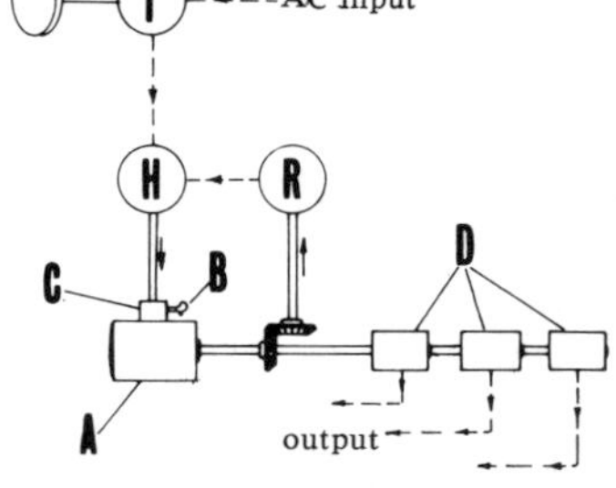

Illustrated in simple diagrammatic form is the step-by-step transmission system for communicating elevation information to the elevation receiver at the gun. The arrangements for training were basically similar.

An M-type transmitter (A) was connected electrically to an M-type receiver (B) in such a way as to achieve an electrical balance. Rotation of the input handle (C) moved the rotor of the transmitter (A) and disturbed this balance, causing a series of direct-current impulses to be transmitted to the receiver (B) which would rotate in small steps (two or six minutes of arc) in the same direction and by the same amount as the transmitter. The receiver, which was contained in the gun-elevation receiver, moved a dial (D) which indicated the elevation required. The gunlayer kept his pointer (E) in line with the pointer in the dial (D) by rotating the gun-elevating handle (F) and so long as these two pointers were in line, the gun was in the required position. This was known as the 'follow-the-pointer' system. The step-by-step transmitter could drive more than one receiver.

Counter-drum, as well as 'follow-the-pointer' receivers were employed with the system, but, though accurate, they had an inherent disadvantage in that the operator had to shift his eye from the receiver to the gun-dials and back again, which involved delay and the possibility of error in the transfer of information from the receiver to the gun. 'Follow-the-pointer' receivers eliminated this problem and largely, though not completely, replaced the counter-drum type.

The main disadvantages of step-by-step were:

1. If the transmitter were moved too fast, the receivers would lag behind and get out of step.
2. The number of receivers that could be connected to one transmitter was limited.
3. When changing over from one control-position to another, the transmitters had to be lined-up before the transfer could be effected.
4. A fault in one receiver could put the whole system out of gear.

Auto-Synchronous Transmission
The auto-synchronous transmission system was an extension of the step-by-step system. It was first tested in the battle-cruiser *Tiger* during the 1920s, and was fitted in *Nelson* and *Rodney*, and in earlier battleships when they were modernised.

Rotation of the input handle (A) turned a hunter mechanism (B) via a differential gear (C). Movement of the hunter, closed an electric contact which sent a direct-current supply to a relay (D) which in turn supplied current to an electric motor (E). The direction of rotation of the motor was determined by the way the hunter (which contained two sets of contacts) had been turned. The relay also operated a magnetic clutch (F) and a magnetic brake (G); the former prevented the motor driving the mechanism on over-run and the latter prevented over-run and the latter prevented over-run of the shaft. The electric motor drove several M-type transmitters (H) which supplied several receivers (J) on the step-by-step system. Geared to the motor drive shaft was an additional M-type transmitter (K) which transmitted the movement of the motor back to an M-type receiver (L). This receiver rotated the hunter, via the differential gear, until it was re-centred, causing the electric contacts to break and the system to stop, having transmitting the exact movement initially imparted by the input handle (A). The relay, motor, clutch, brake and transmitters were all contained in a "Synchronous Unit" below armour, usually in the transmitting-station. The hunter unit was fitted aloft in the director.

Unlike the step-by-step system, the input handle could be moved fast without the system getting out of step. The motor was designed to run just below the critical speed of the transmitters, and any movement that the motor could not impart instantly, was stored in the hunter. Moreover, it did not need to be lined-up when changing from one control-position to another, and if the electric current failed, it would re-align itself, provided that the transmitters were not moved. It was also capable of operating a large number of transmitters. However, it was not so accurate, nor so smooth at high speeds, and was more expensive than the step-by-step system. The initial lining-up process for the synchronous system was, moreover, a time-consuming process. The hunters and the training and elevating receivers were lined-up to a fixed lining-up position by hand knobs, and when the system was switched on, all positions had to read back their pointer-reading to the transmitting station, to ensure that the lining-up process had been carried out correctly.

Magslip Transmission
In 1935, one of *Barham*'s 6-inch gun-batteries was fitted with a Magslip (trade-name) transmission system, and it was tested against the synchronous equipment of the second battery. The results demonstrated the superiority of the new equipment, which came into general service in 1938 and was fitted in new and reconstructed battleships. There were two types of Magslip transmission, Indicator Magslip and Power Magslip. Unlike the earlier systems, they both operated on 50 volt, 50 cycle alternating electric current.

Indicator Magslip consisted of a pair of transmitters, any movement of which, was automatically followed by a similar pair of receivers. The slow transmitters (S.T.) sent a coarse signal, covering a 360 degree arc and accurate to within one degree, to a coarse receiver (C.R.) The fast transmitter (F.T.) sent a fine signal, accurate to within one minute of arc, to a fine receiver (F.R.) which, in reference to the coarse receiver, covered a smaller arc. This latter was necessary, because the accuracy of the coarse receiver was insufficient for gunnery purposes. The system needed no lining-up, ran smoothly and not in steps, and however fast the transmitters moved, the receivers could not become mis-aligned, even if power failed. It did have one disadvantage, however, its mechanism was delicate and difficult to repair.

Power Magslip. Indicator Magslip had only sufficient power to drive the very light pointers of the receivers. Power Magslip was provided with the necessary power to drive directly into fire-control instruments. Movements of the Magslip transmitter (T) were followed exactly by a hunter (H) which opened the control-valve (C) of an oil- or air-motor (A) which drove the output transmitters (D) or directly into the fire-control table. Geared to the motor shaft was a transmitter or re-setter (R) which re-centred the hunter (which acted as a differential), closed the control valve and stopped the motor when it had moved the same amount as the input-drive. Power Magslip was accurate to within one quarter of a degree which was insufficient for gunnery purposes. The input-drive, therefore, was geared down so that the system only covered on arc of twenty degrees, giving an accuracy of one minute of arc. An Indicator Magslip system was incorporated in the Power Magslip system, to provide the reference from which to select the correct sector.

The Indicator and Power Magslip transmissions were incorporated in the same dial, so that the operator could keep the Power Magslip pointer in line with the Indicator Magslip pointer, by moving the sector-control knob (B) which moved the control-valve of the motor and drove the system into the correct sector.

Metadyne Remote Power-Control
Introduced during the Second World War, remote power-control was designed to automatically synchronise the movements of a gun-mounting with its director. The system described here, is the electric version; the hydraulic system

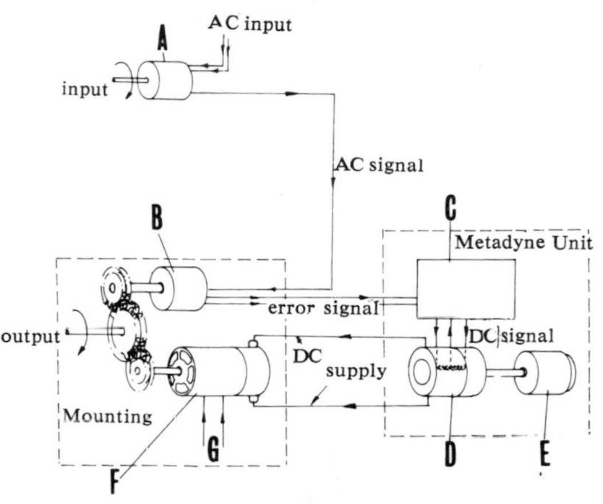

was similar in principle, but differed in detail.

A Magslip transmitter (A) contained in the fire-control table, was connected electrically to a similar Magslip re-setter (B) geared to the elevation or training mechanism of the gun-mounting. When revolved, the rotor of the transmitter became mis-aligned from that of the re-setter, causing an "electric error signal" to be induced in the rotor of the re-setter. This signal, which varied in strength according to the degree of mis-alignment, was led to an electronic amplifier (C) where the signal was converted from alternating to direct, electric current, and then led to a Metadyne direct-current electricity generator (D). The generator was turned constantly by a constant-speed, direct-current electric motor (E), but only delivered an electric current when it received an error signal from the amplifier the strength of which determined the power output of the generator. The electric supply from the generator was connected to the armature of a variable-speed, direct-current electric-drive motor (F) on the gun-mounting which had a fixed-field, direct-current electric supply (G) from the mains. The drive motor only ran when its armature received an output current from the generator. The generator also controlled the direction of rotation of the motor and its speed of operation, which were dictated by the direction and strength of the error signal that the amplifier had processed. Thus, if the error were great, the motor would run fast to bring the mounting quickly into its required position, but would decelerate as the error became smaller, allowing the guns to creep at low speed on to the target without over-running, or to follow a slow target smoothly. The system could run at speeds from four degrees per minute up to fifteen to twenty degrees per second.

The drive motor moved the elevation or training mechanism of the gun into alignment with the input signal, and, at the same time, drove the rotor of the re-setter back into alignment with the transmitter, thereby cancelling the error signal and stopping the gun in the required position. A magnetic brake was fitted to the training and elevating motors to prevent over-run. Between the transmitter and drive motor the system was accurate to within six minutes of arc. Separate systems were provided for training and elevating, but in 'RP50', the two Metadyne generators for these functions were driven by a single motor. The system was provided with 40-degree sector control to obtain the required accuracy. The sector-control arrangements were similar in principle to those described for the Magslip transmission system.

The '50' series were fitted in the twin 4-inch Mk XIX mountings, the Mk VI Bofors mountings, the Mk VI director and the Mk V, VI and VII pom-pom mountings.

Hydraulic RPC systems:
These were similar in operation to the electric systems except that the electric signal was used to operate a hydraulic valve.
RP10. Fitted in 5.25-inch Mk I* mounting and Mk V and VI pom-pom mountings.
RP12: Fitted to *Vanguard*'s 15-inch mountings for training only.
RP40. This was a special hydraulic system for remote training of 14-inch and 15-inch DCT's in *King George V* class and *Vanguard.*

Two-power-drive:
An American RPC system, either electric or hydraulic, used with US Quadruple Bofors Mk II.

No other battleships mountings had RPC fitted.

HIGH-ANGLE FIRE-CONTROL

The HA fire-control system is similar in principle to the director system as already described, but is complicated by the fact that the target can move faster and three dimensionally, and by the need of providing a fuze setting to the shells so that they detonate in the proximity of the aircraft. The HACS calculating-table, therefore, supplied not only elevation and training to the guns but also a fuze number. HACS types were as follows:

HACS Table	*Associate Director*
Mk I, I*, I**, I***	HA Mk I
Mk II	HA Mk II
Mk III	HA Mk III
Mk IIIc	HA Mk III* (*Warspite* only)
Mk IV	HA Mk IV (*Renown*, *Queen Elizabeth* and *Valiant*) stablised for roll
Mk IV*	HA Mk IV GB (*King George V*, *Prince of Wales* (fully stabilised)
	HA Mk V (*Duke of York*, *Anson* and *Howe*).

Note. The suffix 'M' after the HACS Mark means Magslip transmission and 'S' means Synchronous transmission.

Close-range AA fire

Eyeshooting: This simply means aiming the gun and estimating the necessary deflection by eye, without the assistance of a calculating instrument. This method was aided by open gun-sights in which the forward sight consisted of a number of concentric rings, forming a cobweb-like object.

Pom-pom directors

1. Mk I (series) and Mk IIA:
Simple hand-operated director with integral range-finder to give gun elevation and training, corrected for wind speed, convergence, etc., aim-off by eyeshooting.

2. Mk III:
Similar to Mk I, but modified for use with 2-pounder high-velocity ammunition.
3. Mk III*:
Similar to Mk III, but with Magslip instead of step-by-step transmission.
4. Mk IV and IV*:
Eyeshooting replaced by Gyro Rate Unit. Later fitted with Radar Type '282',

Tachymetric systems

Basically, tachymetric means speed measurement, but in fire-control it is used to describe a system that will automatically predict the future position of an aircraft target. This is achieved by measuring the rate of change of the vertical and lateral movements of the target with a gyro sight, and the rate of change of range with a range-finder or by radar. By this method, a target's future position could be predicted regardless of its speed or alterations in its height.

Appendix 3. Rodney's gunnery action with Bismarck

Wind NW, Force 6, heavy swell from NW, sea rough, sky overcast, visibility good.
Bismarck sighted at 08.43 hours at range of about 14 miles.
Fire opened from 'A' and 'B' turrets at 08.47 hours at a range of 25,000 yards.
First salvo fell far right of target.
Two salvoes fired at 08.48 hours, and hits obtained.
Altered course to port at 08.53 hours to open the 'A' arcs.
Salvo 18 fired at about 08.58 hours and hits observed.
Full salvoes fired from 'A' and 'B' turrets at 09.00 hours, both straddled.
At 09.02½ hours, *Rodney* altered course to 182°. On this course, ranging made difficult by cordite and funnel smoke, and firing interval became longer.
Salvo 24 observed as a straddle.
Salvo 25 fired without correction.
Hits observed with salvo 31 or 32.
Salvoes 37 and 38 fired at 09.14 hours.
Salvo 40 observed as a straddle.
Rodney altered course 180° to starboard.
Fire re-opened at 09.18 hours with salvo 41 – range about 10,000 yards.
Rodney altered course at 09.21 hours to 021° and at 09.26 hours to 0.37°.
Increased roll made ranging difficult, and between 09.22 hours and 09.27 hours no ranges were obtained.
Range down to 6,000 yards by 09.30 hours when salvoes 61 and 62 were fired.
Hits observed from salvoes 63 and 64.
From salvoes 65 until 73, no hits obtained due to over corrections for error in ranging.
Hits observed from salvoes 74 and 75.
Rodney altered course at 09.36 hours 180° to port.
After the firing of salvo 90 at about 09.47 hours the fire-control table broke down. As equipment could not be put right immediately, the Vickers clock was brought into use and ranges transmitted by hand. There was no accurate record of ranges employed subsequently.
Fire re-opened at 09.52 hours with broadsides.
Hits observed from broadside salvo 94, and subsequent salvoes.
Down 200 was ordered after salvo 98, to concentrate the fire along the waterline and in one subsequent full broadside as many as 5 or 6 hits were observed.
Rodney altered course at 09.59 hours, 190° to starboard to open 'A' arcs again.
Fire re-opened at 10.03 hours at a range of 4,000 yards. One broadside was fired and then salvoes reverted to, to avoid waste of ammunition.
Between 10.08 hours and 10.14 hours the last 12 salvoes were fired at a mean range of 3,800 yards.
Hits were observed from salvoes 102 through to salvo 113, which was the last.
At 10.14 hours, *Rodney* altered course to the northward to rejoin the C in C.
Bismarck was still afloat, but extremely low in the water and on fire.

General

A certain amount of difficulty was experienced in differentiating between *Rodney* and *King George V*'s salvoes, although close attention to the fall of shot hooter usually enabled *Rodney*'s salvoes to be picked out.
During the southward run from 09.02 hours to 09.17 hours, spotting and ranging made difficult by cordite and funnel smoke.

Performance of 16-inch turrets

The overall rate of fire during the action, allowing for the periods when no guns were in action, was 1.6 salvoes per minute, and performance was generally satisfactory, but a number of minor breakdowns occurred in the turrets due to mechanical failure or drill errors.

Performance of 16-inch shells

Shells used were 16-inch Mk I APC.
Exact number of hits unknown but estimated to be at least 40.
Ranges from 25,000 yards down to 3,000 yards.
All shells which were seen to burst on or immediately after hitting, produced black smoke, indicating detonation.
A number of shells passed through the upperworks without exploding.*

*To activate shell requires a 1-inch mild steel plate to be struck at the normal (90°).

The German battleship *Bismarck*.

Sources consulted

1. UNPUBLISHED SOURCES

Key to locations: AL, Admiralty Library, London; NMM, National Maritime Museum, Greenwich; PRO, Public Records Office, London. The numbers opposite the name of each document indicates the chapter in this book to which the document is immediately relevant.

Admiralty Books

Handbook of Naval Ordnance, 1916 (PRO)
Summary of progress in naval gunnery, 1914 to 1936 (PRO)
Handbook for 5.5-inch B.L. Mk I, 1917 (PRO)
Handbook for 15-inch Mk II mounting, 1920 (PRO)
Handbook for 6-inch B.L. Mk XXII (PRO)
Handbook for 6-inch Mk XVIII mounting (PRO)
Handbook for 16-inch Mk I, 1928 (PRO)
Notes on guns, 1933 (PRO)
Progress in Naval gunnery, 1937 to 1938 (PRO)
Armaments of HM ships, April 1938 (PRO)
Handbook for 16-inch Mk I, 1938 (PRO)
Handbook for 0.5-inch MG Mk III 1938 (PRO)
Handbook for 2-pdr Mk VIII H.V., Mk XIII* mounting, 1941 (AL)
Handbook for 4-inch QF Mk XVI* twin Mk XIX and single Mk XX mountings, 1944 (AL)
The Gunnery Pocket Book, 1945

Admiralty Papers (PRO)

Document	Chapter
Battlecruisers: design, 1916	4
Hood class: armour and deck protection, 1919	4
Warship design in the light of wartime experience, 1919	5
Capital ship designs 1920/21	5
Relative gunpower of British and German dreadnoughts, 1914–1918	5
Progress in Gun Material, 1920	5
Interim report of the Naval AA gunnery Committee, 1920	5
Protection of Magazines, 1920	5
Armaments of H.M. Ships, improvements, 1920	5, 6, 7
Tests on *Baden* and *Monarch*, 1923	5
Reconstruction versus U.S. and Japanese programmes, 1920	5, 6
16-inch Mk I gun mountings in *Nelson* and *Rodney*, 1927	7
Royal Oak: reconstruction, 1923	8
Renown: reconstruction, 1923	8
Queen Elizabeth: revised legend, 1926	8
Warspite: revised legend, 1926	8
Battleship; legends, 1927	9
Future battleships; design and arrangement of armament, 1928	9
25,000 ton battleship: legend and design, 1929	9
Future battleships: design, 1928–1929	9
Summary of the report of the Naval AA gunnery Committee, 1931	10
Capital ships replacement: requirements, 1933	9, 12
Future battleship replacement: requirements, 1934	12
Battlecruisers: legend and design, 1935	12
Capital ships: protection, 1935	12
Battlecruisers: legend and drawings, 1936	12
Capital ships, endurance, 1936	12
Capital ships: anti-aircraft defence, 1936 to 1937	12, 17
Capital ships: vulnerability to air attack, 1937	12, 17, 18
Capital ships: effect on British designs of Japanese infringement of regulations, 1937 to 1938	13, 14, 15
Battleships: sketch designs, 1937 to 1938	13, 14
Battleships: legend, 1938	14
Lion class battleships, legend and drawings, 1938	14
Construction of 15-inch gun battleship, 1939	15
King George V class; history of construction, 1940	13, 15, 17
HMS *Nelson*: report of damage and passage to Portsmouth, 1940	16
RDF research and development, 1940	17
Adaptation of battleships, cruisers and destroyers to carry fighter aircraft: consideration, 1941	17
HMS *Duke of York*: suggested exchange for American warships, 1941	13
Camouflage of capital ships: proposals, 1941	17
Aircraft in capital ships, discussions on projected design of battle-carrier, 1940–41	17
Refits of the *Royal Sovereign* class in the USA, 1942/43	11, 16
HMS *Rodney's* action with German battleship *Bismarck*: gunnery report, 1941 to 1942	16
Proposals by Rear-Admiral Mediterranean aircraft carriers, for aircraft-carrying capital ships, 1942	17
Capital ship construction; extracts from records, 1936 to 1942	12, 13, 14, 15
Correspondence on completion date for *Vanguard* 1942 to 1943	15
Loss of H.M. ships *Prince of Wales* and *Repulse,* 1941 to 1942	13, 15, 16, 17
Use of British and French capital ships, 1940 to 1943	11, 16
V.C.S. Committee – battleship enquiry, 1936 to 1944	12, 13, 14, 15, 16
Old battleships: discussion on possible uses, 1943 to 1945	11, 16
First Sea Lords' dockets: battleships versus aircraft, etc., 1944 to 1945	16, 17
Camouflage, 1940 to 1945	17
Radar reflectors, 1940 to 1945	17
Vanguard, improvements in AA armament	15
Guided missiles Types 'FX' and 'HS' (counter-measures), 1944	16, 17

Records of Warship Construction During the War, 1914–1918, (DNC Department, Admiralty 1919)

Document	Chapter
Battleships, *Queen Elizabeth* class, 1912–1919 (AL)	1
Battleships, *Royal Sovereign* class, 1913–1919 (AL)	2
Battlecruiser *Hood*, 1916–1919 (AL)	4
Aircraft Carriers, Part IV, Aeroplanes carried in fighting ships (AL)	3, 5

Ships' Books

Document	Chapter
Hood (PRO)	4, 8, 11
Howe (PRO)	13

Ships' Covers (DNC Department, Admiralty)

Document	Chapter
Queen Elizabeth class (NMM)	1, 2, 8, 11
Royal Sovereign class (NMM)	2, 8, 11
Renown and *Repulse* (NMM)	3, 8, 11
Hood (NMM)	4, 8, 11, 16

G.3 (NMM) 5, 6, 7
Nelson and Rodney (NMM) 7, 11

The Technical History (Admiralty, 1919)
Fire Control in H.M. Ships 1, 2, 3, 5
Guns and gun mountings 1, 2, 3, 5
Ammunition for naval guns 5

PUBLISHED SOURCES

ADMIRALTY: *Naval Marine Engineering Practice* volume I (HMSO, London, 1959).

BACON, Admiral Reginald H. S.: *From 1900 Onward . . .* (Hutchinson, London, 1940)

BRASSEY'S *Naval and Shipping Annual* 1920/1 and 1928/9 (Clowes, London, 1920 and 1928).

BREYER, Siegfried: *Schlachtschiffe und Schlachtkreuzer, 1905–1970* (J. F. Lehmanns Verlag, Munich, 1970: translated as *Battleships and Battlecruisers, 1905–1970,* Macdonald, London, 1973; Doubleday, New York, 1973).

CHATFIELD, Admiral Alfred E. M., Baron Chatfield: *The Navy and Defence* (Heinemann, London and Toronto, 1942)

—*It Might Happen Again* (Heinemann, London and Toronto, 1947).

CHIHAYA, M: Yamato and Musashi Warship Profile No. 30 (Profile Publications, Windsor, 1973).

CUNNINGHAM, Admiral of the Fleet Andrew B., Viscount Cunningham: *A Sailor's Odyssey* (Hutchinson, London, 1951).

INSTITUTE OF NAVAL ARCHITECTS: *Transactions* volume 91, 1949.

LE MASSON, Henri: *The French Navy* volume I (Macdonald, London, 1969).

LOTT, A. S. and SUMRALL, R. F.: *USS North Carolina* (BB55) Ship's Data Series No. I (Leeward, Pompton Lakes, N.J., 1973).

MACINTYRE, Captain Donald: *Narvik*, Evans, London, 1959; Pan, London, 1962).

MARDER, Arthur J. *From the Dreadnought to Scapa Flow: The Royal Navy in the Fisher Era, 1904–1919* 5 volumes (Oxford, 1961–1970).

NAVAL RECORDS CLUB: *Warship International* Toledo, Ohio; quarterly publication 1964–).

PACK, Stanley W. C.: *Night Action off Cape Matapan* (Ian Allan, Shepperton, 1972; Naval Institute Press, Annapolis, 1972).

PARKES, Oscar: *British Battleships.* (Seeley Service, London, 1957).

ROSKILL, Captain Stephen W: *The War at Sea* 3 volumes (HMSO, London, London, 1954–1960).

—*HMS Warspite: The Story of a Famous Battleship* (Collins, London, 1957).

—*Naval Policy between the Wars* volume I, 1919–1929 (Collins, London, 1968).

SCHMALENBACH, Paul: *Bismarck* Warship Profile No. 18 (Profile Publications, Windsor, 1972).

SCHOFIELD, Vice-Admiral Brian B: *The Loss of the Bismarck* (Ian Allan, Shepperton, 1972; Naval Institute Press, Annapolis, 1972).

'TAFFRAIL' (pseud. Captain Henry T. Dorling): *Western Mediterranean, 1942–1945* (Hodder & Stoughton, London, 1947).

THETFORD, Owen: *British Naval Aircraft since 1912* (Putnam, London, 1962.)

THOMPSON, Kenneth: *HMS Rodney at War* (Hollis & Carter, London, 1946).

WATTS, A. J.: *The Loss of the Scharnhorst* (Ian Allan, Shepperton, 1970).

WINTON, John: *The Forgotten Fleet* (Michael Joseph, London, 1969).

Index